Marketing Communications

SIXTH EDITION

Marketing Communications

Offline and online integration, engagement and analytics

PR Smith and Ze Zook

KoganPage

LONDON   PHILADELPHIA   NEW DELHI

Publisher's note

Every possible effort has been made to ensure that the information contained in this book is accurate at the time of going to press, and the publisher and authors cannot accept responsibility for any errors or omissions, however caused. No responsibility for loss or damage occasioned to any person acting, or refraining from action, as a result of the material in this publication can be accepted by the editor, the publisher or either of the authors.

First published by Kogan Page Limited in 1993
Second edition published in 1998
Third edition published in 2002
Fourth edition published in 2004
Fifth edition published in 2011
Sixth edition published in Great Britain and the United States in 2016 by Kogan Page Limited

2nd Floor, 45 Gee Street	1518 Walnut Street, Suite 1100	4737/23 Ansari Road
London EC1V 3RS	Philadelphia PA 19102	Daryaganj
United Kingdom	USA	New Delhi 110002
www.koganpage.com		India

© PR Smith 1993, 1998, 2002, 2004, 2011, 2016

The right of PR Smith and Z Zook to be identified as the authors of this work has been asserted by them in accordance with the Copyright, Designs and Patents Act 1988.

ISBN   978 0 7494 7340 2
E-ISBN   978 0 7494 7341 9

British Library Cataloguing-in-Publication Data

A CIP record for this book is available from the British Library

Library of Congress Cataloging-in-Publication Data

Names: Smith, P. R. (Paul Russell), 1957- author. | Zook, Ze, author.
Title: Marketing communications : offline and online integration, engagement
  and analytics / PR Smith, Ze Zook.
Description: Sixth edition. | London ; Philadelphia : Kogan Page, 2016.
Identifiers: LCCN 2015040201| ISBN 9780749473402 | ISBN 9780749473419 (ebk)
Subjects: LCSH: Communication in marketing.
Classification: LCC HF5415.123 .S65 2016 | DDC 658.8/02–dc23 LC record available at
http://lccn.loc.gov/2015040201

Typeset by Graphicraft Limited, Hong Kong
Printed and bound in Great Britain by Henry Ling Limited, at the Dorset Press, Dorchester, DT1 1HD

Dedicated to the memory of Chris Berry

Chris had the courage of his convictions
and was champion of the underdog.
He was generous in every conceivable way
– the kindest man I ever knew.
A genius in writing, teaching and marketing,
a gentleman and a true friend.
There'll never again be anyone quite like
Christopher Granville Berry.

PAUL R SMITH

CONTENTS

About the authors **xv**
Preface **xvi**
How to use this book **xvii**
Key features of this book **xx**
Acknowledgements **xxi**

PART ONE Communications background and theories 1

01 New marketing communications 3

Learning objectives 3
Introduction to new integrated marketing communications 4
The revolution has started 7
Marketing utopia is here 12
Climb the ladder (of engagement) 17
Analyse, create, integrate and be relevant 21
The race is on 27
Top 10 Tips for world-class marketing 29
Key points from Chapter 1 30
References and further reading 30
Further information 31

02 Branding 33

Learning objectives 33
Introduction to branding 34
Brand components 45
The branding process 48
Brand summary and the challenges ahead 62
Conclusion 66
Key points from Chapter 2 66
References and further reading 67

03   Customer relationship management 69

Learning objectives   69
Introduction to CRM   70
The power of CRM   71
What causes CRM failure?   73
What causes CRM success?   76
CRM components required   77
CRM creation and maintenance   91
Costs and timescales   95
CRM summary and challenges   97
Key points from Chapter 3   97
References and further reading   98
Further information   99

04   Buyer behaviour 101

Learning objectives   101
Introduction to understanding customer buying behaviour   102
Models of buyer behaviour   113
Psychological variables   122
Summary and conclusion   135
Key points from Chapter 4   136
Appendix 4.1: Hofacker's online information processing   137
Appendix 4.2: The post-PC customer   138
Appendix 4.3: Unilever's five steps to change behaviour   139
References and further reading   139
Further information   142

05   Communications theory 143

Learning objectives   143
Introduction to communications theory   144
Communications models   150
Future communications models   157
Key points from Chapter 5   160
References and further reading   161
Further information   162

06   Marketing communications research 163

Learning objectives 163
Introduction to market research and decision making 164
Information and competitive advantage 166
The market research process 170
Types and costs of research 173
In conclusion 188
Key points from Chapter 6 189
References and further reading 189
Further information 190

07   Media buying and planning 191

Learning objectives 191
Introduction to the media mix 192
Which media is most popular? 204
Summary 214
Key points from Chapter 7 214
References and further reading 214
Further information 215

08   Marketing communications agencies 217

Learning objectives 217
Agency types 218
Agency structure 220
Agency remuneration 224
Agency relationships – selection and retention 226
Key points from Chapter 8 240
References and further reading 240
Further information 241

09   International marketing communications 243

Learning objectives 243
The globalization of markets 244
International difficulties 248
International mistakes 255
Strategic global options 257

Agencies in the international arena   262
In conclusion   264
Key points from Chapter 9   264
References and further reading   265

10   The marketing communications plan   267

Learning objectives   267
Introduction to the SOSTAC® marketing communications plan   268
Situation analysis   271
Objectives   276
Strategy   278
Tactics   282
Action   284
Control   285
Key points from Chapter 10   290
References and further reading   290
Further information   291

11   The changing communications environment   293

Learning objectives   293
Introduction   294
Politics (regulations and laws)   295
Do consumers need more protection?   296
Self-regulation: codes of practice   301
Code of Advertising Practice   302
Economics   304
Social change   305
Technology   309
Summary   314
Key points from Chapter 11   314
References and further reading   314
Further information   316

PART TWO   Communications tools   317

12   Selling, social selling, sales management and key account management   319

Learning objectives   319
Introduction   320

Managing the sales force   325
Extending the sales force   329
Advantages and disadvantages   333
Summary   334
Key points from Chapter 12   334
References and further reading   334
Further information   334

13   Advertising   335

Learning objectives   335
From Mad Men to Maths Men – the changing nature of advertising   336
Data-driven ad campaigns   340
New data-driven targeting tools for advertising   342
New forms of advertising   348
Managing a 'traditional' TV ad campaign   352
Managing a location-based ad campaign   362
Case study 13.1: Pay-per-click ads boost sales: Halfords Autocentres   367
Case study 13.2: Pay-per-click ads boost ROI by optimizing: Cover my Cab   370
Case study 13.3: Shock tactics: viral TV ad reduces road deaths   372
Advantages and disadvantages   373
Key points from Chapter 13   374
References and further reading   374
Further information   375

14   Publicity and public relations   377

Learning objectives   377
Introduction   378
New and old PR tools   382
Advantages and disadvantages of PR   392
Case study 14.1: The gnome story that went viral   398
Case study 14.2: The Snack Dash viral game   401
Case study 14.3: Virgin Mobile's new tariff   402
Advantages and disadvantages summary   404
Key points from Chapter 14   404
References and further reading   404
Further information   405

15   Sponsorship   407

Learning objectives   407
Introduction   408

New and old sponsorship tools   410
Managing a sponsorship programme   412
Advantages and disadvantages of sponsorship   417
Case study 15.1: Liberty Insurance and GAA   419
Case Study 15.2: Citroën and beauty   422
Key points from Chapter 15   424
References and further reading   425
Further information   425

16   Sales promotions, gaming and content marketing   427

Learning objectives   427
Introduction   428
Gamification   433
Virtual promotions   435
Managing sales promotions   437
Content marketing   442
Case study 16.1: Content marketing delivers competitive advantage –
    Kelly HR   444
Case study 16.2: Topline's advertising boosts Christmas promotion   448
Case study 16.3: V&A activate young tech-savvys in collaborative
    digital art   453
Case study 16.4: Muzu.TV film soundtrack adds value and boosts
    engagement   454
Advantages and disadvantages   456
Key points from Chapter 16   456
References and further reading   456
Further information   457

17   Direct mail (including e-mail)   459

Learning objectives   459
Introduction to direct mail (and e-mail)   460
Opt-in e-mail and mobile messaging   463
Managing a direct mail campaign   467
Case study 17.1: PayPal – helping Britain's online retailers to go mobile   471
Case study 17.2: Acronis automated marketing campaign   473
Advantages and disadvantages   479
Key points from Chapter 17   479
References and further reading   480
Further information   480

18   Exhibitions, conferences and events 481

Learning objectives 481
Introduction 482
Managing exhibitions 483
12 reasons for poor performance 492
Case study 18.1: Sedgwick at RIMS Monte Carlo 493
Advantages and disadvantages 494
Key points from Chapter 18 495
References and further reading 495
Further information 495

19   Merchandising and point of sale 497

Learning objectives 497
Introduction 498
New digital challenges and opportunities 498
Case study 19.1: Useful shopping apps can help 500
Retailer empathy 501
Retail strategy 502
Merchandising tactical tools 504
Measuring merchandising effectiveness 506
Case study 19.2 Campbell's Soup: where packaging and point-of-sale form
      a foundation for an integrated campaign 507
Case study 19.3: Thomson Tours 509
Advantages and disadvantages 510
Key points from Chapter 19 510
References and further reading 510
Further information 511

20   Packaging 513

Learning objectives 513
Introduction 514
The designer's tools 518
The packaging design process 524
Case study 20.1: Brand range development in India 527
Advantages and disadvantages 530
Key points from Chapter 20 530
References and further reading 530
Further information 531

21   **Owned media – websites and social media**   533

Learning objectives   533
Owned media   534
Successful websites   534
Successful social media   547
Case study 21.1: Brazilian football club creates immortal fans via social media   553
Case study 21.2: *The Damned United*, Brian Clough microsite   555
Case study 21.3: American Greetings e-cards optimized landing pages   557
Case study 21.4: Social media helps stop smoking   559
Advantages and disadvantages of permanent media   562
Conclusion   562
Key points from Chapter 21   563
References and further reading   563
Further information   564

Index   565

All lecturers who use this sixth edition can obtain
instructor support materials from Kogan Page – visit
www.koganpage.com/marketingcommunications

ABOUT THE AUTHORS

PR Smith

PR Smith created the SOSTAC® Plan (which can be learned in four minutes and mastered in an hour) and also SOSTAC® Certified Planners. Voted in the Top 3 Planning Models worldwide by the Chartered Institute of Marketing's Centenary Poll, it can be applied to business, marketing, digital marketing or any kind of plan. It is applied throughout this book. From Dubai to Dublin and Cairo to London Paul's talks and workshops are inspirational. He is a best-selling author (his six books are translated into seven languages). Paul also advises innovative companies from renewables to disruptive start-ups on behalf of the UK government's Growth Accelerator programme. Paul has also worked with an intriguing variety of companies from blue chips like IBM to highly innovative global renewable energy companies to marketing automation specialists to marketing Christmas crackers in the United States to short-game golf in China. Paul publishes regular updates and insights into cutting-edge marketing on his blog and other social platforms:

w: **PRSmith.org/blog** f: **PRSmithMarketing**
t: **@PR_Smith** l: **PRSmithMarketing**

Paul is also the founder of the not-for-profit innovative online edutainment programme The Great Sportsmanship programme, which inspires a new generation of global citizens through true two-minute stories about sportsmanship. w: **www.GreatSportsmanship.org**.

Ze Zook

Ze Zook is an integrated marketing author, lecturer and consultant specializing in the creative industries. He has worked with ballet, film and music, working with sponsors such as Sainsbury's and The Prince's Trust. He has also worked with PR Smith for over 20 years on projects ranging from an award-winning, innovative, three-screen PR Training video to the Chartered Institute of Marketing's online eLearning programmes. Having started as a video/ media producer and photographer, Ze developed a unique creative perspective on integrated marketing. He helps put creativity into businesses, to help them achieve both their missions and their business goals. He writes about media and digital marketing for public and private sector clients. Ze is a visiting academic at Regent's University London and he consults on digital marketing for private sector disruptive start-ups. l: **www.Linkedin.com/in/zzook**

PREFACE

When we wrote the fifth edition we said that Marketing, and Marketing Communications in particular, had changed forever with the emergence of social media. Now, with this sixth edition, the pace of change is accelerating, particularly with the availability of more analytical tools, the emergence of more marketing automation, the importance of content marketing and the challenge of the single user experience (UX) across multiple platforms as customers engage across platforms both offline and online.

Marketers still face the challenge of maintaining high standards of marketing execution. Have we slipped backwards? Has customer service got sloppier, whether due to arduous automated telephone queuing systems, sloppy websites or de-motivated staff suffering incessant corporate culls?

The good news is that marketers are now effectively presented with a major opportunity to be outstanding by just doing the basics right. In fact, they can become world-class players if they layer on top some creativity, disciplined processes and a craving for constant improvement.

Marketers still have the opportunity of getting back into the boardroom as social media, analytics and marketing automation can position marketing at the centre of the business; listening to customers, extending the brand experience and reaching out and collaborating with stakeholders in previously unimaginable ways.

This sixth edition also draws upon the subtle theme of creative integration. Right-brain thinking (creativity) is required alongside left-brain thinking (structured processes, workflows, automation and analytics).

Please do alert us about any examples of creative marketing that delivers results offline or online at **www.PRSmith.org** or **www.Facebook.com/ PRSmithMarketing**.

What's new in this sixth edition?

This new edition incorporates a range of engaging new insights into relevant marketing communication theories and practices. In particular, see the segments on Location Marketing, Mobile Marketing, Mobile-Friendly Websites, Marketing Automation, Programmatic Advertising, Analytics and Big Data, and Augmented Reality. These are in addition to the fifth edition changes which included new chapters on Branding, Relationship Marketing, and Social Media integrating with Content Marketing.

HOW TO USE THIS BOOK

This book should not be read from cover to cover but rather it should be used as a reference when addressing a particular aspect of marketing communications. The integrated nature of the subject does, however, refer the reader to other chapters and sections that are relevant to the particular area of interest. The anecdotal style, examples, case studies, questions, key points and sections have been carefully structured so that the reader can dip into an area of interest, absorb the information and cross-refer if required. This allows the reader to extract specific answers quickly and easily. This book is designed to entertain as well as inform and so it is hoped that when dipping into a particular area, the reader will be lured into reading more.

Part 1 (see Figure 0.1), Chapter 1 introduces the new thinking and new tools (largely driven by marketing automation, social media, virtual worlds and new analytics tools) alongside 100-year-old business principles that are, surprisingly, much required today. Part 1 continues to build a background to marketing communications by exploring branding, customer relationship management, buyer behaviour and communications theory and how information reduces risk (what information market research can and cannot provide), how to work with agencies and consultancies of all types, understanding the media, moving with the changing business environment, international marketing and ultimately shows how to write a marketing communications plan using the simple SOSTAC® Planning System.

Part 2 covers specific marketing communication tools that marketing professionals have to manage at some time or other. These include selling and sales management (and Key Account Management), advertising, PR, sponsorship, sales promotion (particularly free 'content marketing'), direct mail, exhibitions (all online and offline), packaging, and finally, websites that work and social media that wins.

The case studies at the end of each chapter in Part 2 have been carefully selected to show a range of different types and sizes of organizations using various communications tools across a range of different industries and markets. Materials are drawn from both small organizations with small budgets and larger businesses with multi-billion-dollar budgets.

This book should prove useful to anyone interested, or working, in marketing. The reader will discover that all of the communication tools can and should integrate with each other, as shown in Figure 0.2 and explained at the end of Chapter 1. Equally we need to be able to think creatively (right brain) and analytically (left brain) to make better-quality marketing decisions to ensure we satisfy exactly what our stakeholders need, at the right time in the right place amidst the white heat of competition.

It is sometimes difficult to separate and categorize an activity as being one type of tool or another. For example, direct marketing and sales promotions should probably be called 'direct promotions' since they both more than likely involve each other. The chapters are not listed in order of importance. Selling and sales management is not always included in a marketing communications budget but the sales force is a potent form of communication and generally they (or the sales manager) report to the marketing manager. In fact it has been put to the top of the list because all the other chapters thereafter tend to lead into each other.

The successful application of the marketing communications mix is helped by an understanding of communication theory and buyer behaviour theory. Marketing research can provide some practical and specific answers to the questions that the theories generate. This provides the building blocks for the marketing communications plan, which draws upon an understanding of how agencies operate and how different media work. The details of the plan are worked out within the sometimes complex, but always integrated, web of the marketing communications mix (see Figure 0.2). The changing marketing communications environment and international opportunities/threats constantly affect the whole marketing communications mix. The world has moved on since the fourth and fifth editions.

Different organizations allocate the same communication tools to different departments/budgets,

FIGURE 0.1   Part One: Background to the communications process

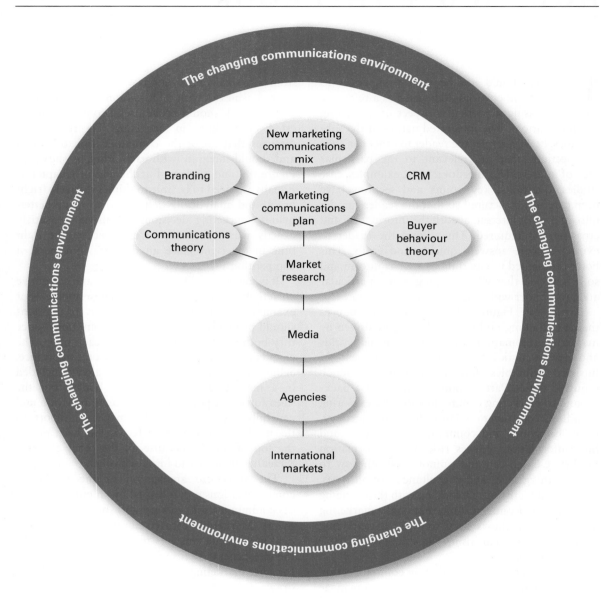

eg exhibitions may be seen to be part of public relations, although the sales team will man the stand and benefit from extra sales. Sponsorship is considered by some to be an extension of advertising, while others consider it to be part of PR. And no one is too sure about whose budget covers the website. Regardless of classifications, ownership and responsibilities, each tool must integrate with many others.

We are always looking to update the material within the book and our readers are invited to contact us with any ideas, suggestions and contributions to the next edition. As our subject of marketing communications is ever changing, we are keen to keep the content fresh and lively. Please post your examples of excellent marketing communications to us at **www.Facebook.com/PRSmithMarketing** or **@PR_Smith**

FIGURE 0.2   Part Two: The marketing communications mix

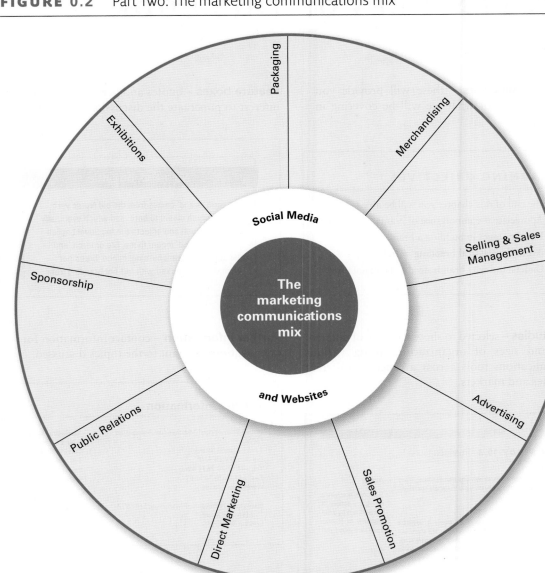

KEY FEATURES OF THIS BOOK

Learning objectives – these will provide you with an outline of what we will be covering in each chapter.

Feature boxes – quotes and pertinent points of interest to punctuate the discussion.

Case studies – selected to show a variety of different types and sizes of organizations using various communications tools across a range of different industries and markets.

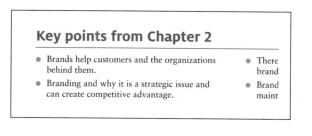

Further information – contact information for organizations relevant to the topics discussed.

Key points – a checklist of all the issues covered within the chapter.

ACKNOWLEDGEMENTS

Kristina Allen, ion interactive

Warren Allot, Photographer

Zaid Al-Zaidy, McCann, London

Jeremy Baker

Riccardo Benzo, Managing Expectations

Tanya Binks, Wild Card

Michael Bland, Author

Sarah Botterill, European Interactive Advertising Association

Adrian Brady, Eulogy

JoAnna Brandi, The Customer Care Coach®

Alan Briefel, StratCom

Scott Brinker, ion international

Juan Pablo Castro, LanderApp.com

Ged Carroll, Racepoint Global

Dr Dave Chaffey, Smart Insights

Mary Pat Clark, Pew Research Center

Alistair Clay, Plan UK

John Coffey, Liberty Insurance

Amelia Collins, Photographer

Keith Curley, Muzu.TV

Allan Edwards, Ogilvy PR

Jenny Ellery, Saatchi & Saatchi

Annie Fong, Mischief PR

Stuart Fowkes, Oxfam

Rob Gotlieb, Muzu.TV

Jonathan Grant, Grenadier Advertising

Mark Grey, Grey Corporate

Gavin Grimes, McBoom

Paul Hague, B2B International

Dr Hansen, Hansen

Chloe Haynes, Cadbury

Neil Hegarty, BMP Optimum

John Horsley, Digital Doughnut

Martin Hutchins, Cambridge Professional Academy

Peter 'Magic' Johnston, MediaZoo Studios

Nigel Jones, Herdman Jones Associates Ltd

Jeff Kirk, Corporate Magic

Isobel Kerr-Newell, Saatchi & Saatchi

Helen Lamb European Sponsorship Association

Mike Langford, BT

Basil Long, Kroner Consultants

Jez Lysaght, Green Tomato Cars

Toby Marsden, Survival International

Ian Maynard, Murphy Cobb Associates

Davy McDonald, davymac.com

Paul McFarland, Goldhawk

Gerry McGovern, Gerry McGovern

Sharon McLaughlin, McLaughlin Gibson Communications

Blair Metcalfe, Ogilvy PR

Claire Mitchell, Natural History Museum

Ian Morton, Happy Tuesdays

Jorian Murray, DDB London

Jasmin Naim, Kogan Page

Orson Nava, Director/Content Producer

Julia O'Brien, Moonshine Media

Brian O'Neill, Freshideas.ie Ltd

Paul O'Sullivan, Dublin Institute of Technology

Marie Page, Musicademy.com

Hina Patel, Creating Results From Vision Ltd

Alexandra Phelan, Paddy Power

Ben Queenborough, Photographer

Suresh Raj, Borkowski

Charles Randall, SAS Solutions

Mark Read, Photographer

Josh Rex, This Is Open

Kevin Roberts, Saatchi & Saatchi

Phil Robinson, ClickThrough

Danielle Sammeroff, Fuse

Dennis Sandler, PACE University

Richard Sedley, Seren

Heather Sewell, ICE

Adam Sharp, CleverTouch

Joel Simon, Flickerpix Animations Ltd

Graeme Slattery, PSG Communications

Dr Meixian Song, University of Exeter, School of Law

Tery Spataro, CCG Catalyst Consulting Group

Merlin Stone, The Customer Framework

Dr Peter Tan, World Financial Group

Jonathan Taylor, former co-author

Jamie Tosh, Kick4change

Jon Twomey, Student Support Group

Neil Verlander, Friends of the Earth

Gian Walker, Network Co-op Ltd

Steve Wellington, Havavision Records

Todd Wheatland, King Content

James Whelan, James Whelan Butchers

Ze's particular thanks: I dedicate this work to my wife, Revital and daughter, Nessa, for their patience and understanding and to my mother and father for their acceptance and nourishment of my being.

Paul's particular thanks to Aran, Cian and Lily and the ever-patient, lovely, Beverley. And lastly, a very special thanks to Owen Palmer (RIP) who gave me my first break in UK Academia and never ceased to inspire and encourage me even long after he had retired.

PART ONE
Communications background and theories

01
New marketing communications

LEARNING OBJECTIVES

By the end of this chapter you will be able to:

- Understand why this a new opportunity for marketers
- Grasp the importance of customer-driven marketing communications
- Explore the long-term ladder of engagement
- Appreciate that analytics and creativity are required

Introduction to new integrated marketing
    communications 4
Why do you have a website? 4
100-year-old principles win 4
Customer-centric mission 5
Customer empathy essential 5
Single well-defined customer experience 5
Use left brain and right brain 6
SOSTAC® Plan – marketing mix and communications mix 6

The revolution has started 7
Death of the colouring department 8
Customer service time bomb 8
Hyper-competition 9
Creative destruction 11
Social media revolution 11

Marketing utopia is here 12
Why social media works 13
Social media maths 14
Networks, herds or individuals 14
Social media cultural shift 15
Engaging in virtual reality 16

Climb the ladder (of engagement) 17
Customer engagement creates stronger brands and
    more advocates 17

Identifying engaged customers 17
The ladder of engagement 17
Collaborative co-creation 18
Offline's different type of engagement? 21

Analyse, create, integrate and
    be relevant 21
Analysis builds foundation for success 21
Nurture creativity 22
Create added value and relevant content
    marketing 24
Communications, customer experience and
    product morphing 26
Integrate data, staff and communications 27

The race is on 27
Cut through the clutter 27
Enter the boardroom 28
The opportunity knocks twice 28

Top 10 Tips for world-class
    marketing 29

Key points from Chapter 1 30

References and further reading 30

Further information 31

Introduction to new integrated marketing communications

Why do you have a website?

This is a great question to ask. What is the single most important reason why you have a website? Ask your colleagues. You'll typically get answers like 'to make money' (wrong), 'to sell more' (wrong), 'to be online along with everyone else' (wrong), 'to demonstrate our products' (wrong), 'to compete' (wrong), 'to be available' (getting a little closer), 'to give information' (closer), 'to be accessible' (closer) but still not giving a real marketer's answer. Many of these answers indicate a product-orientated approach to business – all about you and or your products. It's not. The single most important reason why you have a website is: 'To help customers (or stakeholders)'. In fact, Peter Drucker, known as 'the father of business' and arguably America's greatest business author, once said 'the purpose of business is to create and keep a customer'. We go further and say, 'There is only one reason that you are in business: to help customers.' The moment you stop helping customers better than your competitors is the moment you start sliding down the subtle, slippery slope to lost sales and spiralling towards extinction.

> 'There is only one reason why you are in business. It is, simply, to help customers. The moment you stop helping customers (better than your competitors do) is the moment your business starts to die.'
>
> PR Smith

100-year-old principles win

Despite the emergence of digital body language, marketing automation, programmatic advertising, retargeting, content marketing, multichannel funnels, hyper competition (we'll explore these later) the same old marketing principle remains intact: be customer-centric. It's interesting to see that although customers are changing, technology leaps are rampaging through markets and wonderful new tools are becoming available to marketers, the same basic business principles survive from over 100 years ago. Interpreted by Mark Zwilling (2014), here are Carnegie's Top Tips which still work today.

Andrew Carnegie's Top 10 Tips For Success:

1 Definiteness of purpose (a real and passionate mission).
2 Master-mind alliance (marketing marriages and strategic alliances).
3 Going the extra mile (help customers).
4 Applied faith (believe in the opportunity you see).
5 Personal initiative (be proactive).
6 Imagination (ability to see opportunities/ vision).
7 Enthusiasm (a contagious quality).
8 Accurate thinking (analyse carefully before deciding).
9 Concentration of effort (on key success factors).
10 Profiting by adversity (learn and improve from failure).

Zwilling's (2014) interpretation of Carnegie's Tips is worth a read. In fact, arguably the best marketing book ever written is a 2,000-year-old book by the Chinese military strategist, Sun Tzu, who always believed that battles can be won without confrontation. Proper application of intelligence wins wars, often peacefully. A few thousand years later, we (in the West) are getting excited about the power of analytics.

> **Stop, look at who you are and what your business is for**
>
> 'If you believe your business is a machine for making you rich, you are going down the wrong road. If you believe your purpose is to make the world a better place, then do so, and wealth will come to you.'
>
> Witzel (2015)

Customer-centric mission

Now consider the world's largest eCommerce company, relatively unknown (to many westerners); they're called Alibaba. Bigger than Amazon and eBay combined, they focus on helping customers. Their **customer-centric mission** reads: 'making it easier to do business across the world', and is followed by their motto: 'Customer first, employee second, shareholder third.' Their founder Jack Ma says, 'We know well we haven't survived because our strategies are farsighted and brilliant, or because our execution is perfect, but because for 15 years we have persevered in our mission. In 2013 they handled $240 billion worth of merchandise with 7 million merchants, $8 billion revenues, $3.5 billion profits and the largest IPO ever ($160 billion+).

Gerry McGovern (2014) also points out that Amazon's motto is very similar: 'We seek to be Earth's most customer-centric company for four primary customer sets: consumers, sellers, enterprises, and content creators.' These businesses are customer centric. They can empathize with customer needs both now and in the future. Top American digital marketing blogger, Brian Solis (2015) insists that businesses must empathize with customers and develop strong missions.

Temper profit with customer empathy

'Learn to temper (balance) their profit goals with empathy and look at the bottom line as part of a larger mission, doctrine or ethos.'

Solis (2015)

Customer empathy essential

Success 'requires true empathy for what your customers are thinking and an ability to identify what they want or need even before they do' (Solis, 2015). Apple consistently did it with the Mac, iPhone and iPad. You 'have to see your customers for who they are becoming, not just who they are today', Solis continues, 'This all starts by defining the experience you want your customers to have. How do you

want them to feel? What should they share? Define it. Build it.' Building it includes integrating marketing systems, logistics systems, CRM systems. Being customer-centric goes beyond the marketing team, it has to be in customer-centric operations also. It also requires a different perspective. Campaigns cannot reach buyers if say, an ad campaign is shorter than a buyer's journey.

Long-term success – think about customers differently

'To succeed means thinking about customers differently as groups of connected people and not simply demographics. It requires a level of leadership that can see something others don't or find inspiration in what others feel or hope to feel. These traits – not the technology itself – are what will define the most resilient companies in the years to come.'

Solis (2015)

Single well-defined customer experience

Although customers are on a multichannel journey (from websites to offline stores to social media etc.), they want a single customer experience. Whether they touch (have contact) with your brand via your mobile site, your website, your app, your in-store display, your staff, your social media, your customer care, telesales, direct mail – it is all one journey for the customer. They want a nice consistent experience regardless of channel. This requires systems that integrate data and multichannel marketing. 'Information and data is going to be a critical source of advantage' says McKinsey's David Edelman (2014). Integrated data helps to deliver highly relevant and attractive offers for shoppers as they enter specific stores. These offers and vouchers can be served via mobile (location marketing) if customer data is integrated (eg integrating historical purchasing data and/or previous use of promotions data combined with location data). The importance of delivering an integrated and consistent customer experience is demonstrated by the acknowledged shift in the role of mobile marketing 'from outbound communications to managing the total customer experience'. (Stoke, 2014).

> 'Strive not to be a success, but rather to be of value.'
> Albert Einstein

Use left brain and right brain

Both left brain (analytics) and right brain (creative) skills are required in marketing today. Good use of analytics helps marketers to make much better

FIGURE 1.1   Campbell's Soup's creative point of sale grabbed attention and much more, as it integrated with many tactical tools

decisions – informed decisions – which reduce risk and deliver better results. Today, we have a plethora of new analytical digital tools that can be combined with the more traditional analytics (eg surveys and in-depth interviews). But we also need to be more creative to help break through the clutter and noise created by both competitors and the busy, multi-tasking lives we all lead today. Creativity can grab attention and generate engagement if what is created is somehow relevant or challenging or entertaining or enticing or shocking for the target audience. Creativity ideas naturally integrate. A creative concept (such as Campbell's Soup Point of Sale) can, and should be, leveraged or stretched across all ten marcomms tools, and both offline and online (including social). Marketing tins of soup may not appear to be exciting but Campbell's made it exciting by creating an attention-grabbing, photo opportunity, branded selfie generator point of sale which integrated offline with online and social. In fact they integrated and leveraged this across many different tactical tools. For the full story see Chapter 19.

You will find many more creative themes exploited across all tactical tools both online and offline throughout this book. A cocktail of relevant creativity and analytics-driven decision-making help to deliver great marketing results.

SOSTAC® Plan – marketing mix and communications mix

There are many approaches to writing marketing plans, some far more complicated than others. The SOSTAC® approach (see **www.PRSmith.org/ SOSTAC**) simplifies marketing plans (PR Smith, 2014) and it was voted in the Top 3 Marketing Models in the Chartered Institute of Marketing's Centenary Poll. We will explore it in detail elsewhere.

- Situation analysis (where are we now?).
- Objectives (where do we want to be?).
- Strategy (how do we get there?).
- Tactics (the details of strategy eg the marketing mix and communications mix).
- Action (execution – checklists, guidelines, processes including internal marketing).
- Control (are we getting there? – metrics and measurement – daily, monthly).

- + 3Ms – the key resources: Men and women (human resources), Money (budgets) and Minutes (timescales).

The old marketing mix (McCarthy, 1960) comprises product, price, place, promotion (4Ps) and the 'service mix' comprises people, processes and physical evidence (bringing it up to 7Ps). However, digital blurs the lines and morphs the mix (eg social media is part of the product experience, promotional reach, physical evidence, and place/distribution) – see next section. Meanwhile here is the communications mix which lists the 10 Tactical Tools (communications tools) both offline and the online equivalent.

TABLE 1.1 The communications mix: 10 tactical tools, offline and online

Advertising	Interactive ads, pay per click keyword, display ads, remarketing/retargeting
Public relations	Online editorial, newsletters, ezines, discussion groups, viral marketing, Vine
Sponsorship	Sponsoring online events/sites service
Sales force/agents/tele-marketing	Virtual sales staff, affiliate marketing, web rings, links/chat
Exhibitions, events and conferences	Virtual exhibitions, virtual events, webinars
Direct mail	Opt-in e-mail and eNewsletter
Retail store or office HQ	Website (SEO and marketing automation opportunity)
Word of mouth	Social media platforms, review platform (eg reevoo.com), forums
Sales promotion	Content marketing, incentives, rewards, online loyalty schemes, competitions
Merchandising and packaging	e-tailing, QR codes, augmented reality, virtual reality (real packaging can be displayed online)

The revolution has started

A **new marketing era** was ushered in when **social media** put customers back at the centre of the organization and also gave marketers a new set of tools to reach out, engage and listen to customers. **Paid, Owned and Earned Media** (ads, social media platforms and word of mouth, respectively) was the new marketing jargon. However, the free ride soon ended (2014) when some social media platforms (initially Facebook) reduced the reach (or reduced number of followers that would have an opportunity to see a particular post). They encouraged brands to promote their posts (paid media) to reach large audiences. Read 'The Rise and Fall of Owned and Earned' (Smith 2014) for further details on this.

MySpace and LinkedIn were launched around 2003 with Facebook launched privately (Harvard only) in 2004 and rolled out publicly in 2007. Other platforms will continue to emerge.

Since the 2010s some marketers have joined another, quieter revolution, called **Marketing Automation**. Almost every aspect of business can be standardized and automated. So too a lot of marketing can be automated so that highly relevant, personalized, useful information is shared just at the right time, on the right platform with the right customer. This may be a tailored web page, a pop-up panel, an e-mail, real letter, text message, telephone call or even a personal visit from a sales rep.

Some organizations are revolutionizing their approach via **Social CRM** (Customer Relationship

Management), engaging in high-impact, cost-efficient communications (see Chapter 3 for more details). Others are integrating customer data from many new sources (including **Big Data**), while other organizations are using the ladder of engagement to revolutionize their complete business model. And some are using new tools such as remarketing and retargeting advertising to target potential customers as they move around the internet.

Finally, customer **analytics** can change the nature of how marketing operates, and how to make better decisions that boost business, ultimately delivering competitive advantage to those that do avail themselves of these new tools and techniques. More on all of these later.

Death of the colouring department

A lot of 'old' marketing has had too much emphasis on just marketing communications. This is a weakness. Once upon a time this worked, as customers had far fewer communication channels and therefore it was easier to get a customer's attention if marketers had the budget. And the big budget brands often announced 'as seen on TV' on their packaging, at point of sale and in their press advertisements. Being on TV gave the brand a level of credibility, perhaps because customers unconsciously assumed that being on TV meant that the company was a big company and big companies were trustworthy. Or perhaps customers trusted TV and the authorities that regulate the advertisements that are allowed on TV.

This may have led to communications strategies that told customers about product benefits. Today, marketing strategies ask 'How will customers engage with us and each other?' This leads to the bigger question: 'What kind of customer experience are marketers creating?' This in turn brings marketers back to the quintessential marketing question: 'How do we help customers?' This is, for example, the ultimate reason why any company has a website. Yet many, if not most, marketers answer this question incorrectly. Ask around and see. In fact, helping customers is the only reason a company exists, as American guru Peter Drucker used to say.

These kinds of questions move marketers beyond communications, into customer experiences, customer relations, new product development processes, service processes and, of course, brand evaluation, which affects market capitalization. This, ultimately, invites marketers back into the boardroom, hopefully speaking the language of the board. Social media and the ladder of engagement, in particular, have opened the door to the boardroom for marketers.

> ### Stop calling marketers 'The Colouring Department'
>
> 'Not so long ago I was invited into a major global bank and given the brief: "To stop the board from referring to the marketing department as the colouring department."'
>
> PR Smith

Customer service time bomb

Continual culling of employees and general cost cutting combined with sloppy marketing execution has put marketers on the cusp of a customer revolution. Many organizations' efforts to continuously cut costs and cull employees have finally delivered a threshold of inefficiency, leaving in their wake an overburdened, over-anxious and, frankly, less caring staff. Customer surveys reveal that many customers are angry, irritated, impatient and ready to switch to another brand as soon as something better becomes available. In a word, they are dissatisfied. This is a real marketing problem, or opportunity, depending which way the CEO and CMO see it.

We have gone backwards in marketing. Look around. You will see falling satisfaction scores, sloppy websites, telephone queues, customer service people who can't answer questions and others who simply don't really care. Have salespeople lost their vocation, their passion and their deep product knowledge? How many bad experiences do customers suffer whilst seeking service from a utility, a phone company or a bank either on the phone or on a website? Why are there so many sloppy websites?

Look at the stats. Look at the surveys – even the UK National Customer Satisfaction Index shows falling satisfaction scores amongst the top-performing brands.

One recent customer service conference speaker showed falling customer satisfaction scores across a range of industries. When asked if this meant that we were getting worse at marketing, the speaker said, 'No, it's the customers' rising expectations combined with lower tolerance levels that have changed.' So is it the customers' fault?

Lower tolerance levels: perhaps customers have simply become angrier. And, if so, why so? Perhaps anxiety is on the rise. Don't customers like endless automated telephone queuing systems, robotic rerouting or, if they are lucky, after queuing and rerouting getting to speak to someone whom they cannot understand, or to someone who cannot solve the problem, who then puts them back into a queuing system? We have gone backwards in marketing.

How many people have had bad experiences online with websites that are confusing, have dead ends or just don't work, sites that waste precious time and cause irritation? And all the time advertising budgets are wasted driving customers to these sites. Why are there so many sloppy websites? They forget the basics – regular usability testing. This is basic stuff, which many brands are ignoring to their detriment. Check the website to see it works all right on-screen and across different browsers also.

Harvard's Ram Charan and business CEO Larry Bossidy wrote a book called *Execution: The discipline of getting things done* (2002), where they claimed that the ability to execute better than the competition was the last source of real sustainable competitive advantage. Even though it was written in 2002, it is now more appropriate than ever before as major organizations damage their brands day after day with dead-end websites and atrocious, systemized but sloppy customer care. It is relatively easy to be better than most if the basics are executed professionally.

So have companies got worse at marketing? If yes, this creates a huge opportunity for those organizations that have a process for listening to their customers, and can continually improve and stay relevant.

Hyper-competition

We are experiencing **accelerated change**. Consider **accelerated brand creation**. Once upon a time it took two generations to build a major brand; now it takes just a year or two if you get it right. Look at Amazon, Uber and Twitter. Once upon a time it took several generations to acquire 50 million users. Facebook did it in less than one (in fact Facebook acquired 100 million in one year). This simply could never have happened 10 years ago. Radio took almost 40 years to reach 50 million users, while TV took 13 years, the internet four years, the iPod three years, Facebook one year and the iPhone less than a year to get 100 million users.

Global boundaries are falling; the Iron Curtain has been swept aside, the Berlin Wall torn down and the Chinese gates flung open partly by political movement, partly by aggressive businesses seeking growth overseas and partly by the internet giving instant global access driven by customers who are ready to buy from anywhere in the world whenever they want. And, all the time, **category-less competitors** quietly step across old borders. Once upon a time, supermarkets sold groceries and petrol stations sold petrol. Now petrol stations sell DVDs, fresh coffee, groceries, gambling and a lot more, while grocery stores sell petrol, garden furniture, car insurance and soon legal advice (including DIY divorce kits), as well as groceries. Powerful category-less brands take more 'share of wallet'. Customers trust some brands sufficiently to try other products from the same brand name. Despite some bad publicity for the company in 2014 and 2015, the Tesco brand is so strong it could probably sell customers anything (as long as it meets reasonable quality standards). This is 'share of wallet'. Growth for most US companies was forecast to come from share of wallet rather than growth from finding new customers. Enlightened boardrooms understand the power of the brand, its access to 'share of wallet' and its impact on the balance sheet. Combine category-less, fast-moving competitors with borderless markets and you get hyper-competition. No market or business can sit back and relax.

Competitors targeting your visitors, your fans, your employees

Both Facebook and LinkedIn enable competitors to target their ads by age, interests, location or company. They can even target their ads at your employees (LinkedIn), your fans (Facebook) and even your website visitors (may soon become accessible).

The need to wholeheartedly adapt to and embrace change is akin to the need for frogs to stay out of the kitchen. If you take a frog and put it into a

---

Competition in your pocket

'Amazon and eBay mobile apps invite customers, while in another store, to scan in a product to see how much cheaper they can get it via the app (plus they deliver it to your door). So retailers have to have even better apps to compete inside your hypercompetitive pocket. Meanwhile Amazon can target ads at customers within a radius of one mile of a competing store.'

PR Smith (2014)

'If a retailer is not motivating people to use its app in store, their customers may use a competitor's instead.'

Gray (2013)

---

boiling pot of water, it will jump out somewhat blistered, but it will survive. If, on the other hand, you put a frog in a cold pan of water and slowly raise the temperature it will boil to death. Business is similar. No one will change your environment so rapidly that you have to change your behaviour immediately. It just changes continually.

Amidst this hyper-competition some CEOs wake up in the middle of the night in a cold sweat worried about their value chain and wondering who is unpicking the lock on it. Teams of analysts and MBAs from Boston to Beijing analyse industry after industry, sector by sector, to find businesses with a weak link in their value chain that would benefit from a third-party supplier fulfilling a piece of the chain. Most CEOs know some parts of their value chain, whether production, logistics or after-sales, are more profitable than other parts. When they get an offer to replace the weakest link with a higher-quality link (or service) at lower cost and seamlessly linked by web technology, many CEOs find this a very attractive proposition.

'We have only two sources of competitive advantage: the ability to learn more about our customers faster than the competition; the ability to turn that learning into action faster than the competition.'

Former GE CEO Jack Welch

Chaffey and Smith (2013)

As the company moves from a value chain to a seamlessly connected value network, CEOs are forced to consider the most basic of questions: 'What business are we in?' This can only be answered by asking another very basic question: 'What do customers want now and in the future and what is our sustainable competitive advantage (SCA)?'

30,000 illegal competitors

'Some competition is legal and some not so legal and vast! The Premier League is targeting 30,000 illegal, competing, streaming sites. This can require a lot of resources.'

iSport Connect (2012)

When I ask CEOs what is their SCA, I usually get answers that include patents, product differentiation, cost efficiencies, and sometimes distribution channels. Most of these can be, and are being, attacked. Two major sources of SCA, if managed carefully, are the brand and customer relationships – inseparable, you may say.

However, many companies damage these two critical assets. Sloppy customer service and negative customer relationship management (CRM) destroy brands. (See Chapters 2, 3 and 21 for more on this.) Despite the importance of CRM, many companies are still sitting on a customer service time bomb. And it's ticking. Those who ignore it will be left behind, in the same way that those who ignore the golden opportunity presented by social media will also be left behind. Those who embrace it, seize the opportunity, develop rigorous processes around the new technologies and continually strive to find and satisfy customer needs will survive and thrive.

Who are the survivors?

'It is not the strongest of the species that survives, nor the most intelligent that survives. It is the one that is the most adaptable to change.'

Charles Darwin

Creative destruction

Sony's famous president and co-founder, the late Akio Morito, once said: 'My job is to make our products obsolete before competition does.' These sentiments were recently echoed by an interesting American author, Brian Solis, who said that 'resilient companies intentionally break their business models in anticipation of what customers want and need. For example, the "sharing economy" – companies like Uber, Airbnb, TaskRabbit and other services that allow people to rent or share their cars, homes or skills' (Solis, 2015). These resilient companies recognize evolving consumer values and aspirations.

Anyone with vision and empathy can upend entire industries

'Anyone today has the power to disrupt entire industries with a single, smart idea. Most companies are built to keep things from going wrong, not to try to break things apart. Creative disruption becomes a business strategy to either invest in or acquire the very things you feared, rather than simply protecting what it is you have.

Companies identify and develop products, processes and philosophies that allow them to flourish at first but later cause stagnation… paralyzed by their success.'

Solis (2015)

Social media revolution

'Social Media is the biggest change since the industrial revolution' reported *Business Week* approximately a decade ago (2005). A month later the *Economist* magazine went further and simply said: 'companies that don't understand digital communities will die'. Social media became the centre of many marketing strategies. Despite the reduced reach of some social media platforms, the free ride is over, social media has changed the buyers' journey and put customers at the centre of enlightened businesses that want to listen to their customers, engage them and encourage them to shape the future of the business (see 'The ladder of engagement' p. 17).

Customers have discovered a whole new way to find out about products and services. Product review sites, ratings, discussion groups, Facebook petitions, blogs, mobile price comparison applications (apps), YouTube demonstrations (positive and negative videos), Instagram, Pinterest and Flickr photos: these are social media tools. And customers, not companies, are controlling the flow of marketing information as they shut out interruption marketing and use, instead, social media to find products, ratings and reviews.

Outbound marketing (the old interruption marketing model of advertising, direct mail and telesales) has suffered as audiences switch channels or fast-forward through TV ads, turn on ad blockers on their browsers, stop e-mails with aggressive spam blockers and use caller ID to bar unwanted phone calls. Some outbound marketing does get through but not as much as a few years ago.

Channels fragment (eg TV has approximately 500 channels, while 20 years ago it had five) and the sources of trust shift. Which of these has the biggest influence on your customers: *The Times*, BBC, Sky or Google?

Social media has arrived and customers love it. Social media gives customers control. Marketing has been democratized courtesy of the internet and social media. And within the mass of customers lie the new opinion formers and opinion leaders: bloggers and tweeters. Marketers have a choice: join the conversation or fail to communicate.

Old mass communications interruption models like TV advertising have simply got to be a lot more creative to cut through the clutter and grab the eye of the busy consumer. They must also integrate with social media to spread the message (if the content is good enough). Any social media content has not only to be more creative but also highly relevant to the target audience. Suddenly the marketing of a vacuum cleaner has become so creative that it becomes compulsive viewing (see further discussion of this on p. 27).

Social media is not just a marketing tool. It is, effectively, a new way of running a business – social business. It requires a new company culture: 'engaged, transparent (gives direct access to subject matter experts) and nimble (react really quickly)' (Mell, 2013). This, in turn, requires company-wide support, systems and incentives. It requires a new mindset: more listening, less shouting. Think relationships and not just sales or transactional marketing. Hasn't this been said before? Yes, it has. It is basic old-school marketing, except that social media allows marketers to listen to customers more easily and more cost-effectively. Social media also relies on a 'sharing' culture, which means sharing information and being helpful. This, in turn, nurtures relationships, which again is the essence of good marketing – developing and strengthening relationships.

Social media is **not about making short-term sales.** It is about sharing and listening and channelling information into systems that alert certain staff to negative discussions, positive discussions, suggestions, complaints, and ideas for new products, new ads, new promotions and new discussions. Harnessing all these conversations requires new skill sets and new organizational structures. In turn this helps marketers to create a marketing utopia where customers drive the business while marketers lend a helping hand.

There is a **new opportunity** to use social media to improve marketing in a radically different way – in fact, one so profound that social media has delivered a new marketing utopia.

Marketing utopia is here

Social media, and in particular, discussions which suggest new product ideas or improvements can be harnessed and fed into a systematic process to collect, assess, select and develop new products. The systems must also communicate to those that are engaging and making suggestions.

The more enlightened companies build information architecture and business processes around social media: processes that pick up comments about the brand wherever they occur; systems that respond (sometimes auto-responses and sometimes individual human responses); and systems that categorize the discussions. The dialogue generates valuable feedback that is often quicker and cheaper than focus groups. This research needs to be fed to the right people in marketing. Social media allows us to learn a lot more about customers very quickly – if the systems and processes are in place. The key is to use this information to make better decisions.

Other levels of engagement invite customers as stakeholders to engage at a higher level by creating user-generated content or fully blown collaborative co-creation to deliver new products and solutions. See page 17 for more.

Social media is more than just communications; it is a new way of working that requires new information flows. They affect more than just communications, but feed into new product development, distribution channels and even pricing.

Marketing is being forced out of the communications silo and back into full-blown marketing courtesy of social media.

The X Factor – Utopian marketing system

'Customers queue for hours with their new product ideas. They eventually get to present their ideas. They make a TV show out of the customer presentations which generates significant revenues. They then pick the best product ideas (customers) and invite them to come back and present the product concept again. They make another TV show during these product concept presentations. Then the mass heaving market is allowed to select/vote for their favourite product (and they pay for the privilege of supplying this free market research). After several rounds of refining the product concepts, recording new TV programmes and more free market research, the market (voting viewers) selects the best product and then Simon Cowell sells this product back to the heaving mass that researched it in the first place. IRD (Identify needs, Reflect them with what the crowd want and Deliver the music the next day). Cowell's customers are happy. Cowell is in Utopia.'

PR Smith

Why social media works

Social media fulfils a fundamental **human need**: to communicate. We are social animals. We like to communicate with each other. Social media facilitates this by helping us to communicate more easily, to more people, whenever we want. That is why social networks like Instagram, Twitter, Facebook, YouTube and blogs are so successful. Social media is huge because it simply helps

customers to communicate with each other and organizations to communicate with customers (this includes listening).

This new business environment **allows marketers to listen** to customers and opinion formers (and other stakeholders), channel their feedback into suggestions and new product ideas, and even test out new concepts and brand names, while all the time engaging customers, developing higher levels of customer loyalty and nurturing brand ambassadors. It's a marketer's utopia.

Social media is participatory. Organizations that tap into that willingness to participate can do very well. Think beyond the old one-way communications and even beyond a basic dialogue between customer and brand and instead consider a **trialogue** amongst customers, opinion formers and the brand. Brands can reinterpret themselves as facilitators.

Think **engagement**. Marketers are searching not only for ways to connect brands to customers, but also for ways to connect those customers to each other – with the brand simply facilitating the discussion. The brand can be a place where the community can congregate and discuss and collaborate.

From customer feedback, to product ratings, recommendations and discussions, through to prosumers (customers who help to create, or produce, the next product): this is collaborative co-creation (see 'The ladder of engagement' on p. 17 for more). Customers are encouraged to be part of an organization's product/service design system and production system. Many customers feel their favourite brand is engaging with them, and they feel some reciprocity as the organization demonstrates that it is listening and consequently taking action. This inherently deepens brand loyalty, purchasing and advocacy.

Many customers like to have a meaningful input into the products and services they consume. Some don't, but many influential ones do. Getting private previews or input into shaping what is yet to come creates a sense of being an insider as opposed to being just another external customer sitting on a 'customer service time bomb'.

'If you're paying attention, you get the answers to questions you didn't even think to ask.'

Schlack (2008)

Social media makes it easy for both customers and organizations to communicate with each other. They allow everyone to get to know each other better, understand each other's needs and issues, nurture relationships and collaborate, sometimes in highly destructive ways and sometimes in highly creative ways.

To summarize, it is not surprising that social media has grown so quickly (the **Facebook population now equals that of the fourth-largest country** in the world), because social media taps into something deep inside us all – the need to communicate, talk, share and be part of a community. This is fundamental to us as social animals, and satisfies a deep need that is profoundly embedded into our genetic structure. The **old push marketing model** (of interrupting audiences and pushing ads at them) with 'sell, sell, sell' is being replaced by 'listen and respond' to the conversations (conversation also includes digital body language, observing click behaviour and seeing what it tells us so that we can help visitors even more).

It is easy to see why social media is now so powerful. The next section reveals why and also proves the power of social media by explaining the maths behind it.

Social media maths

Consider a target audience of 20 people. Here's how Lilley (2007) calculates how many messages can spread around depending on what media is being used.

Broadcast network is based on a 'one to many' model (eg old TV advertising). It is called a Sarnoff network (after David Sarnoff, the broadcasting legend). A hypothetical Sarnoff network with 20 viewers has a score of 20. The network score is simply the number of nodes (audience members) = 20.

Telephone and e-mail network is based on a 'many to each other' model. It is called a Metcalf network (after Bob Metcalf, one of the inventors of the Ethernet). This communications model allows everyone to contact each other. Because everyone can call each other, the total possible number of calls or e-mails is 20 squared, or 400. This is potentially much more powerful for communicating messages among people than a Sarnoff network. The network score is node to the power of 2 or $20^2 = 400$.

Social network is an 'immensely more powerful category of network' based on a 'many belong to numerous networks' model. It is called a Reed network (after David Reed, who observed that people in social situations belong to more than just one network). The possible value of a Reed network is 2 to the power of the number of nodes on the network. Take the same group of 20 people in a social situation, whether virtual or real. A Reed network generates a score of 2 the power of the node. This generates a network score of 2^{20} = more than 1,000,000.

Moving from a broadcast network to a telephone/e-mail network, even if only 10 per cent of the people pass the message (maybe a special offer, or perhaps a criticism), it still means that 40 messages will be sent around. This is twice as powerful as the TV network, which only had a possible total of 20 messages being received. Moving on to the Reed network (social media network), if 10 per cent spread the message, that generates 100,000 possible messages that can be received. Or, even if only one-tenth of 1 per cent pass the message on, it would still generate 1,000 messages, which is 50 times more powerful than the old TV model with just 20 messages.

Admittedly, the reach is reducing as some social media platforms now will only allow a few per cent of a brand's fans to see posts. So social media (owned media) and word of mouth (earned media) needs to be supported by 'promoted posts' (paid media).

Networks, herds or individuals

Group behaviour is well documented in social studies. Marketers understand the natural impulse to follow the crowd. Some sociologists believe humans are just copying machines, basically. Because humans are social animals, a large percentage of an individual's brainpower is devoted to interacting with others, watching their behaviour and wondering what they think of us. We carry this legacy with us every time we buy a particular brand of washing powder or choose what movie to watch in the cinema. We have learnt or evolved to be animals that are good at copying.

The Mexican wave – why? Because everyone in the crowd at a sports game can see everyone else and is aware of the group behaviour. The Mexican wave cannot be re-created in a shopping centre, because people can't see each other, nor can they see the group behaviour.

Facebook, on the other hand, is like a digital version of the Mexican wave, because people can see what all their friends are doing. They can not only see if their friends are online but also what they are currently doing and what they have been up to in the past. If someone gets an invite to Facebook and joins, that person in turn sends invites to his or her friends. Wherever the herd moves next, people follow. The internet just manifests or provides the mechanics for what we are naturally programmed to do.

If someone stands staring at the sky and pointing, that person is bound to get strange looks from passers-by, but get six or seven people standing together staring and pointing at the invisible spaceship and the crowd will swell.

Harnessing the knowledge of the herd has greater potential when it comes to building brand loyalty.

Social media cultural shift

Organizations that are not listening to online conversations about their brand are missing a major opportunity. If someone attacks a brand there is an opportunity to address any criticisms and rectify the issues before rumours spread out of control. If someone applauds a brand there is an opportunity to leverage this comment. Conversations cannot be controlled like advertising messages, but organizations can feed accurate information as well as being seen to listen and care. In addition to collecting crucial feedback, ideas and public comments from the marketplace, marketers are provided with a welcome platform to get their message across if it is relevant. This also grows a brand's presence

wherever the market congregates online. Ignoring these conversations leaves an organization on the outside, soon to be replaced by another brand that does want to be a part of the conversation.

Social media provides a platform to:

- reach out to increasingly difficult-to-contact customers;
- help customers by sharing expertise (and the brand) with audiences;
- listen and engage in conversations about your brand.

This **requires a cultural and organizational shift** and more of a listening and sharing culture than a selling culture. It requires a real customer orientation, which drives the marketing utopia. After the listening and sharing, relationships can blossom. After this warm awareness and affection, all things being equal, sales will eventually follow when the customer is ready (as opposed to when the organization wants to sell).

Develop a systematic listening team and a system to use the information.

Who monitors what? Who compiles the analysis and the reports? Who responds to comments on blogs and in group discussions on LinkedIn? Who analyses the comments, complaints, suggestions, worries, issues and opportunities? What happens to all this highly useful information? What systems channel which information to whom? If embarking on the highest level of customer engagement, collaborative co-creation (see page xx), who manages the channelling of new ideas into new product development processes? Who handles the responses back to the original contributor? These are some of the questions that need to be addressed. More and more organizations are using third-party organizations or their software to scan for any online comments, discussions or tweets regarding their brand, their company, their customers or their competitors.

Engaging in virtual reality

As the online experience may become more 3D and more virtual world-orientated, marketers require inquisitive minds and some experimentation to find what works and what doesn't.

Although somewhat criticized, virtual worlds are worth exploring. One of the most popular virtual worlds, Second Life, was reported to be having a 'second life' as its population starts to grow again. Separate to this, some 20 million+ immerse themselves in virtual worlds, engaging in massively multiplayer online games (MMOGs) with 23 million subscribers to MMO gaming in 2014, generating a $15 billion market (Statista 2014).

However, virtual reality may come to us rather than us going to it. So, instead of logging into the above environments VR may come to us as avatars on websites, augmented reality images on a car window screen, hovering holograms or shopping bots or even static, attractive bots that stand beside us as we queue and offer helpful advice – as did this talking, moving bot who kindly helped me in Dubai airport two years ago by reminding me to put my liquid containers in a plastic bag.

FIGURE 1.2   Virtual reality can come to us in the form of helpful bots reminding us of security procedures in airports

More and more customer service avatars (interactive cartoon characters) are appearing on websites, particularly in the customer care sectors, where they offer themselves as 'your assistant'.

Virtual immersion in a non-real world has been around for many decades and has crept into people's living rooms in the form of Wii games. These popular virtual games convert a living room instantaneously into a gymnasium, a tennis court, a boxing ring, a dance studio, a keep-fit studio or even a golf course, and players play happily in their virtual worlds. It will become a lot more sophisticated.

It may become more blurred as virtual reality and 'real' reality morph. Back in 2007, I held a parallel product launch of Northern Ireland's creative digital hub, CRE8IVITY.COM in Second Life. The Minister for Enterprise's avatar spoke to an international virtual audience (of avatars) who were overseas bloggers who could not physically attend the main 'real' event in Belfast. The virtual world presentation was simultaneously beamed into the 'real-world' audience in Belfast.

FIGURE 1.3   PR Smith speaks to a real audience

The University of Tokyo perfected virtual rain that looks and probably feels like water dropping on to a surface approximately five years ago. It may well be that the next wave, combining virtual worlds with intelligent systems, will create whole new opportunities for those who embrace the technology.

Augmented reality allows users to see additional information, eg text or photographs, by pointing a mobile phone and reading any hyper-data posted; for example a building site might show AR information on the site and what it will look like when finished. Through use of AR software like Layar or other apps from the iStore, the horizon expands as augmented reality emerges.

FIGURE 1.4 PR Smith's avatar speaks to a virtual audience

Climb the ladder (of engagement)

The ladder of engagement makes it easy to nurture customers up to higher levels of involvement.

Customer engagement creates stronger brands and more advocates

Marketers who understand and influence customer engagement better than their competitors are more likely to develop stronger brands and more loyal customers. Engaged customers are more likely to become brand zealots. Therefore it is important to identify engaged customers and start a brand ambassador programme to further strengthen the relationship and energize their word of mouth.

The ideal customer, or most valuable customer, does not have to be someone who buys a lot. The ideal customer could be an influencer who is a small irregular buyer but who posts ratings and reviews, which could influence another 100 people.

Identifying engaged customers

Monitoring the quantity and frequency of blog posts, comments, forum discussions, reviews and profile updates helps to identify opportunities and also acts as an early warning system to any future problems. Consider targeting brand evangelists rather than just purchasers. Some companies ask customers to give a product rating or even post a product review as a standard part of their after-sales contact strategy. This way the more engaged customers identify themselves by their own self-selection.

A customer who doesn't care about the product is likely to be less committed or less emotionally attached to the brand. On the other hand, a customer who is engaging is likely to be more emotionally connected to the brand. Marketers need to know about the sentiment, opinion and affinity a person has towards a brand. This is often expressed through repeat visits, purchases, product ratings, reviews, blogs, discussion forums and, ultimately, their likelihood to recommend a friend.

Is customer engagement measured? Does this identify the engaged customers and use their feedback to improve your promotion and products? It is possible to increase some customers' level of engagement by moving them up from giving a product rating, to writing a product review, to joining a discussion, to suggesting ideas, to screening ideas, to testing ideas and eventually to buying the ideas when they become products or services. Many of these will become brand champions, evangelists or brand ambassadors. This is why moving some customers up the 'ladder of engagement' is valuable.

Product reviewers want to engage more

'Seventy per cent of customers who left reviews for products wanted to help improve those products, and they purchased more products, more often than non-reviewers did.'

Aarons, Edwards and Lanier (2009)

The ladder of engagement

Moving customers up the ladder of engagement creates brand loyalty, unleashes brand zealots, and can help improve an organization's processes, products and services. This can also create sustainable competitive advantage for an organization as customers become more engaged and more loyal to the brand that they feel a part of.

The lower half of the ladder encourages customers to engage via product ratings, reviews and discussions. The upper half of the ladder is user-generated content (UGC), which encourages customers to become co-creators of content for the organization. This is sometimes referred to as crowd-sourcing. The highest level of co-creation occurs when customers co-create the products that they subsequently buy (see examples in 'Collaborative co-creation' below).

Not everyone will rise to the top of the ladder. In fact, Nielsen suggest only 1 per cent of website visitors will; 90 per cent lurk, 9 per cent occasionally contribute and 1 per cent regularly contribute. They call it the 90–9–1 rule. But those 1 per cent are important: hence the need to identify engaged customers.

While moving customers and other stakeholders up the ladder of engagement strengthens brand loyalty and boosts sales, it does require careful planning, systems and resources. This is a long-term strategic decision.

FIGURE 1.5   The Ladder of Engagement

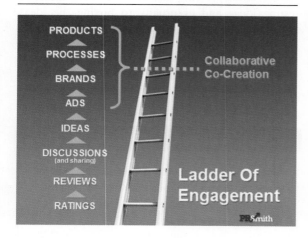

Beginning of a beautiful relationship

Remember the second visit to a website is the beginning of a relationship. Therefore it is always worth asking the question: what is a brand doing to bring relevant visitors back to the site?

At the highest end of the ladder, the virtual circle completes itself. It is a self-fulfilling system. As the customers create the product, they create their own demand. However cutting-edge this is, it does require basic business skills of systems of communications, registration, processing, feedback, rewarding and putting into action. So back to basics – developing systems that work requires careful planning and rigorous testing. Here are some examples of how companies use the different steps on the ladder of engagement.

Ratings and reviews: Amazon

Amazon will try to engage customers by asking for a product rating, which takes just a few seconds. They then invite you to write a product review, which takes a few minutes. As mentioned, some companies make ratings and reviewing a standard part of their after-sales contact strategy. Customers value reviews from their peers. This shows that consumers are able to apply their own filters and, effectively, rate the ratings. There is a hierarchy of trust online, which starts with personal friends.

Discussions – ask and answer: The Home Depot

One level of discussions is 'ask and answer', where customers throw out questions and other customers answer them. US DIY chain The Home Depot invites customers to ask DIY questions and eventually get other customers to answer the questions. Issues of liability for any careless advice obviously need to be addressed, and real experts may be preferred to casual customer experts.

Discussions – passionate stories: great sporting moments

Another level of discussion is where customers talk about the product or, in the case of the sporting book, passionately discuss sporting stories. They also reveal themselves as potential brand ambassadors. Those who do engage in discussions are usually passionate about the brand or product.

Collaborative co-creation

Ideas

Dell's Ideastorm (**www.ideastorm.com**) generates ideas on how to improve the business and uses systemized suggestion boxes. Customers, and even non-customers, can suggest new products and features, as well as better ways of running the business, eg improvements in their processes. Dell have earned $10 million from the early stages of Ideastorm. This may seem tiny to a company of Dell's size but, remember, this is brand engagement, a form of brand promotion to the brand zealots, and it also contributes something to the bottom line.

TV advertisement

Co-creating ads is more common in the United States, where customers are asked to help generate them. In 2008, Chrysler's Tahoe supplied graphics, music, photos and video clips and asked its audience to make an ad. The best one would be shown during the Super Bowl, the most sought-after TV spot in the world. It generated a huge response. It also discovered some user-generated discontent (UGD), with several negative ads posted on YouTube. It took the brave decision to allow both positive and negative ads to be created – a classic double-sided argument, which generated more discussions and a lot of press coverage. By the time the Super Bowl came, the PR surrounding the user-generated ad campaign had boosted anticipation of the ads, and an enthralled audience watched with great intrigue.

Kraft Foods in Greece scored a hit with a user-generated 27-minute long-form ad for its Lacta chocolate bar. The crowd sourced the story and the casting, and some even appeared as extras. The Love in Action campaign started using traditional TV advertisements to invite people to send in their love stories. Thirteen hundred love stories and one month later (it took a month to sift through the stories), the winning story was selected. Online polls voted for and selected the cast (full screen tests were put up online), the characters' names and even their costumes. Updates were posted on Facebook and Kraft's blog, which was followed by over 11,000 registered voters and 20,000 fans and eventually watched over 150,000 times. It created such a buzz that Greece's leading TV station, MEGA Channel, offered to screen it free of charge on 14 February as part of its Valentine's Day programming, which attracted a 12 per cent share of viewers and was seen by more than 335,000 people. Lacta sales are also up in a declining market (Hall, 2010).

Brand names

Co-creation can go way beyond ads and promotions; it can even generate brand names, if the basic systems are in place. Boeing created a buzz around the launch of the new 787, the Dreamliner, by inviting input from potential customers and passengers online. Indeed it was the community that named the aircraft the Dreamliner, with some 500,000 votes cast online from 160 countries (O'Dea, 2008).

Products and services

Some say that UGC has been used offline for many years now. MTV has been getting users to screen or research products through user text votes, and reality TV has been using the UGC formula and enjoying great success. The X Factor attracts UGC to create new product concepts, new product screening and new product testing.

Back to the online world, Peugeot invited their online audience to submit new product concepts, ie submit car designs. This attracted 4 million page views. Peugeot built a demonstration model of the winning design to exhibit at marketing events. It also partnered with software developers to put it into a video game.

Take product variations and product components. *Great Moments of Sportsmanship* is a book about sportsmanship. Customers send in their sportsmanship stories for further discussion in the blog and possible inclusion in the next edition. The goal is to have future editions totally user generated. In addition, more UGC is added as YouTube videos that match the stories in the book are added to the site.

Occasionally B2B is mixed with B2C, as in the case of the InnoCentive site, which allows 180,000 freelance scientists, engineers, entrepreneurs, students and academics to work on problems posed by industry, creating and selling solutions in return for cash rewards. Major players, including Procter & Gamble, are involved.

One outstanding UGC website is called threadless.com, whose loyal community of graphic designers, artists and generally creative people send in designs for new T-shirts. The community votes for the best one, which is then produced and sold back to the community. The retail trade has spotted these high-quality, unusual and limited edition T-shirts and now orders significant quantities of them.

Remember, **UGC is not always B2C**, as almost always many of the best online examples are actually B2B. Consider MMOGs, where dozens, hundreds and even thousands of players around the world participate in an online game. Now imagine dozens, hundreds and even thousands of scientists collaborating on and creating new products. The Atlas particle detector, which measures subatomic particles in high-energy physics, involved 2,000 scientists disaggregated across 165 working groups who then found a successful solution online. IBM has adopted Linux for some of its computer products and systems. Linux is continually improved by a huge global community of software developers, mostly non-IBM-ers. Sun Microsystems developed the Solaris operating system with a global community of software developers. Some call it 'crowdsourcing'; others call it 'open innovation'. It is interesting to note that Apple netted some $1 billion in app sales in the first year, and shares 70 per cent of revenues with the 125,000-strong developer community in the iPhone developer programme (Kennedy, 2009). IBM also uses open innovation for its Big Green Innovations unit. Likewise, P&G revamped its innovation model by adopting open innovation a few years ago.

From Intel to Xerox, NASA to Novell and Vodafone to Virgin, more and more organizations are unleashing the collective brainpower of people outside their organization. Offline, LEGO have been collaborating with customers for years, asking children to suggest, create and screen new product ideas. They then financially reward 'those whose ideas go to market'.

Successful UGC and even the lower levels of engagement are **dependent on a vibrant, responsive audience** and one of marketing's often forgotten fundamentals – systems and processes that work, and basic marketing principles of testing interfaces and back-office systems. Usability testing is a prerequisite. Remember, websites are fun, but back office means business.

All of these UGC systems draw from the basics of perfect marketing processes and the passionate attention to detail required if user-generated systems are to work successfully.

Ask: 'How well are we measuring the engagement of our different online audiences and then closing the loop by using the data to identify the advocates and deliver more relevant communications?'

Collaborative co-creation has been extended into management. Results to date are inconclusive as to how successful this can be. Consider MyFootballClub.co.uk, which is a group of approximately 50,000 football-obsessed internet users who pooled resources and bought a minor English football club. Members paid £35 and acquired a majority stake in Ebbsfleet United, which plays five divisions below the premiership. Members vote on transfers,

player selection and all major decisions affecting the club. Since then it has won the FA Trophy at Wembley – the club's greatest achievement since it was founded in 1890. Now it is aiming for promotion to the football league proper. This has been done before.

BBC Radio Northern Ireland take UGC to a new level

Co-creation and user-generated content have been around for a long time, as is the case with radio show phone-ins, whereby the audience's input and opinions are a key part of the programme. However, BBC Radio Northern Ireland took it to a new level a few years ago when they felt that the audience input was so funny that they should make an animated TV show from it. They even kept, with permission, the callers' actual voices and dubbed them into the animation. Called On the Air by FlickrPix, some of the series is still on YouTube.

FIGURE 1.6   On the air

'We've moved from "The Attention Economy (push)" to "The Attraction Economy (pull)" to "The Participation Economy (share)".'

Roberts (2010)

Offline's different type of engagement?

Engagement offline is not always the same as engagement online – say with banner ads or TV ads, engagement means something different. Here, it means catching attention, being allowed to pass through the customer's perceptual bias and perceptual selection. This requires a different kind of engagement. Digital is physical: a click, a like, a share, a comment, while offline has a different type of engagement, perhaps purer mental engagement – simply allowing yourself to see an ad and becoming aware of it or even thinking about the ad, or better still, talking about it.

Analyse, create, integrate and be relevant

Analytics and relevant creativity in marketing are both necessary to break through the clutter of noise and hyper-competition. 'Relevant Creativity' means that somehow whatever is created will be of interest to the target market.

Analysis builds foundation for success

As previously mentioned, arguably the greatest marketing book ever is *The Art of War*, written over 2,000 years ago by the Chinese military strategist Sun Tzu (translated version Wing, 1989). Most senior marketers have a copy of it on their shelves. It has become a classic read, particularly for some enlightened marketing managers. Interestingly confrontation, or war, is seen as a last resort and the best military strategies win the war without any bloodshed. They win wars through intelligence.

'Much computation' or much analysis is required. The better the analysis, the easier the decisions will be later. Decisions about strategy and tactics become a lot easier when you know your customers, your competitors, your competencies and resources as well as market trends. Knowing your customers and prospects better than they know themselves is possible. Old tools (in-depth discussions) and more contemporary tools like digital body language (analysing click behaviour on your website) both give marketers vital information which helps deliver better messages, better websites, apps, ads, presentations, sales pitches – you name it.

That's why half of your marketing communications plan should be devoted to the situation analysis. It doesn't have to be at the front of the plan (you can dump a lot of it in the appendices) but the detailed analysis must be carried out if you are to succeed.

The first year you do this analysis it will be particularly challenging, but as you find better (and often free) sources for highly relevant information, the analysis gets easier, the intelligent information gets stronger and consequently, you make more informed decisions. This ultimately boosts your results.

More good news – there is a plethora of new listening tools available to marketers. Although traditional market research is still useful, there are faster ways of monitoring online discussions and analysing customers, competitors and spotting trends.

> 'All markets are conversations' declared the influential Cluetrain Manifesto (Levine *et al*, 2000).
> The subsequent rampant growth of social media since that time confirms the classic Cluetrain vision.

'The old marketing ship is sinking.' All marketers need to monitor, analyse and engage in these conversations because the old 'shouting' model, consisting only of advertising and PR, no longer works as well as it used to.

FIGURE 1.7
The marketing ship is sinking

Photo courtesy of DavyMac.com

> ### Most marketers don't fully know who their customers are
>
> 'Only 45 per cent of marketers are capturing and consolidating customer behavioural data from multiple channels in a single database.'
>
> Forrester (2013)

Nurture creativity

> ### Creativity – in the mushy word category?
>
> 'For many, the word "creativity" is as soft as "nice". Such people had better revise their lexicons.'
>
> John Kao, Harvard Business School professor (1997)

Look at the more successful companies out there; they nurture creativity. It is not accidental. The importance of creativity is recognized, encouraged and nurtured. Listen to what some of these organizations say:

- 'Either you'll learn to acquire and cultivate [creative people] or you'll be eaten alive' (Leon Royer, Executive Director, 3M).

- 'My job is to listen to, search for, think of, and spread ideas, to expose people to good ideas and role models' (Jack Welch, former CEO, GE).

- 'The first step in the creative process is "hiring the best of the best". This is how HP maintains an environment that "crackles with creativity and intellectual spirit"' (Mary Patterson, former Director of Corporate Engineering, Hewlett-Packard).

- 'To make money in a disinflationary period takes real innovation and creativity at all levels of the corporation' (Michael Fradette, Manufacturing Consultant, Deloitte & Touche).

> ### Creativity is a blood sport
>
> The reality is that creativity is hard work. And managing creativity is, as Harvard's professor John Kao says, 'if anything, even harder work. It has nothing to do with finding a nice safe place for people to goof off. Managing creativity is much more difficult. It means finding an appropriate place for people to contend and collaborate – even if they don't particularly want to. It means scrounging from always-limited resources. It means controlling the uncontrollable, or at least unpredictable, process. Creativity, for many, is a blood sport.
>
> Kao (1977)

Nurturing creativity and channelling it in the right way is hard work. As Ed Catmull said in the *HBR*, 'If you want to be original, you have to accept the uncertainty, even when it's uncomfortable, and have the capability to recover when your organization takes a big risk and fails. What's the key to being able to recover? Talented people!' Such people are not so easy to find (Catmull, 2008).

The *Forbes* columnist, Greg Satell (2013) agrees and emphasizes that creative collaboration is absolutely essential: 'Creativity is no longer a "solo act." Today, collaboration is not just important, it's absolutely essential and that's why digital marketing is so hard.'

Customers do not always understand their needs – particularly innovations

However valuable market research is, significant creative leaps can sometimes be too difficult for customers to grasp. Therefore negative customer feedback for discontinuous innovations (significant innovations) can sometimes be misleading. In some cases, 'Listening too much to customer input is a recipe for a disaster' (Christensen, 2003). 'If I'd listened to my customers, I would have invented a faster horse', said Henry Ford.

Whoever could have imagined that a device created for engineers to communicate with each other would one day become a global necessity for all young people – text messaging? Whoever could have imagined that one day people would walk around with record players or DVD players on their heads (headphones)? Whoever could have imagined a nation seemingly talking loudly to themselves (hands-free mobile phones)?

Here are some classic quotations that demonstrate how not just customers but even experts in their field could not see the benefit of a significant innovation that subsequently went on to become a massive global success:

- **Telephone:** 'This "telephone" has too many shortcomings to be seriously considered as a means of communication. The device is inherently of no value to us' (Western Union, internal memo, 1876).

- **Radio:** 'The wireless music box has no imaginable commercial value. Who would pay for a message sent to nobody in particular?' (David Sarnoff's associates in response to his urgings for investment in the radio in the 1920s).

- **Movies (with sound):** 'Who the hell wants to hear actors talk?' (Harry M. Warner, Warner Bros, 1927).

- **TV:** 'TV will never be a serious competitor to radio because people must sit and keep their eyes glued on a screen. The average American family doesn't have time for it' (*New York Times*, 1939).

- **PCs:** 'I think there is a world market for maybe five computers' (Thomas Watson, Chairman of IBM, 1943).

- **Home PCs:** 'There is no reason for any individuals to have a computer in their home' (Ken Olsen, President, Chairman and Founder of Digital Equipment Corp, 1977).

- **The Beatles:** 'There is no demand for guitar bands' (Decca Records turning down The Beatles, 1962).

Looking back on it, there are many innovations in common use now, the need for which simply did not exist 5 or 10 years ago. This applies to both B2C and B2B markets. As organizations, and marketers in particular, embrace creative thinking, new solutions will emerge and contribute to continued success once we learn to think 'outside the box'.

> ## 'Seeing what everyone else can see but thinking what no one else has thought'
>
> 'It's seeing one thing in terms of something else. That eureka moment. You don't have to be a brilliant novelist or painter or musician… it can be about some private matter. It can be about economics. It can be while you are reading a novel, you suddenly make a connection that suddenly gives you an insight that no one else has had. Someone defined science as "seeing what everyone else can see but thinking what no one else has thought".'
>
> Greenfield (2007)

Market research: a fundamental part of Edison's creative process

Despite the lack of vision by many CEOs and the challenge of researching innovations (since customers often don't know what they want, particularly with innovations), the United States' greatest inventor, Thomas Edison, used market research creatively in the 19th century. He literally went to homes and places of work and analysed what people did in order to gain insight to invent products that could help them do it better and faster. He looked first for unmet needs and then applied science and creativity to fill them. The first example of Edison's success using a 'needs-first' approach to invention is one we seldom associate with him: document duplication. Post-Civil War newspaper accounts of the re-building of the South and the tremendous demand it created for insurance policies led him to think that the insurance business could use some efficiencies. Edison got permission from insurance agents to watch their clerks at work. He saw that most of their day was spent hand-copying documents for each party to the insurance sale instead of selling insurance. Edison realized that if he could invent something that would save both the insurance clerks' and agents' time writing, they could all make more money (Caldicott, 2010). Interestingly today's top CEOs spend time with customers. In fact Martin Sorrell, CEO of the world's largest communications services group ($66 billion turnover) spends one third of his time with clients (Rogers, 2014).

Edison combined creativity with customer needs

Thomas Edison was indeed a creative genius, but it was not until he discovered some of the principles of marketing that he found increased success. One of his first inventions was, although much needed, a flop. In 1869, he created and patented an electronic vote recorder, which tallied the votes in the Massachusetts state legislature faster than the chamber's old hand-tab system. 'To Edison's astonishment, it flopped. Edison had not taken into account legislators' habits. They don't like to vote quickly and efficiently. They do like to lobby their fellow legislators as voting takes place. Edison had a great idea, but he completely misunderstood the needs of his customers' (Caldicott, 2010). He learnt from his failure the relationship between invention and marketing. Edison learnt that **marketing and invention must be integrated**. 'Anything that won't sell, I don't want to invent', he said. 'Its sale is proof of utility, and utility is success.' He realized he needed to put the customers' needs first and tailor his thinking accordingly, despite any temptation to invent for invention's sake. His change of mindset led to tremendous success (Caldicott, 2010).

Anything that won't sell, I don't want to invent

'This was said by Thomas Edison, best known for the light bulb. He was a prolific inventor, registering an extraordinary 1,093 US patents and 1,293 international patents. The six industries he pioneered between 1873 and 1905 – and their offshoots – are estimated to be worth more than $1 trillion today. He was one of the world's first market researchers.'
(Caldicott, 2010)

Create added value and relevant content marketing

Digital can create so much added value for the customer. Arguably this digital experience is better than the real-world product experience. Arguably this is the best website in the world (well it's my favourite and it's only got two buttons). The Sistine Chapel website allows visitors to look at Michelangelo's paintings for as long as they want; climb up the walls and examine the stunning art. Go right up to the ceiling and even see where Michelangelo painted donkey ears on some of the bishops that he didn't like. All of these things you cannot do if you visit the chapel. Many people tell me that the digital experience is better than the real-world visit – since you have to keep moving, cannot take photos and it's busy. The digital version has beautiful choral music playing, you can do a 360-degree pivot, climb the walls, explore the ceiling – it is simply amazing.

Biggest marketing trend

'Customer experience is the stand-out imperative for 2015.'

eConsultancy (2015)

FIGURE 1.8   Some would say the Sistine Chapel digital experience beats the real thing

Photo courtesy of The Sistine Chapel Digital Experience, http://www.vatican.va/various/cappelle/sistina_vr/index.html

A brand needs to be wherever its customers are and when they have a need. Find out what they really want and then help them. People searching for information about the Vatican or Rome might welcome a virtual tour of where customers go (offline and online). Be creative with messages and media/channels.

Find creative partnerships that take the brand's message and products to its target audience in a completely different environment (wherever the target market is) and just when they need help. Be where customers go online and offline. There may be ways of reaching them through collaborative partnerships both offline and online. Field marketing or the slightly more elaborate experiential marketing partnerships may occur, eg a rugby book sold at the grounds of a rugby stadium, or new iPods being sold at a concert. And help customers tell their friends about you.

Be relevant to customer needs – if a brand gives customers useful, relevant information at just the right time, it strengthens the brand relationship. Being creative always helps. But being relevant is even more important, as customers only want and listen to whatever is relevant (or interesting). Constant monitoring of their changing needs is critical. Whether it is at the lowest levels of interaction, ie product ratings, reviewing products or creating user-generated content, engagement helps to keep customer attention and to nurture stronger relationships.

> 'Anyone who has never made a mistake has never tried anything new.'
>
> Albert Einstein

Create relevant content

Most organizations already have a lot of marketing content (market research, white papers, presentations, speeches, articles, videos, photos, graphics, as well as social media content). Some potential content is less obvious but nevertheless easy, such as book reviews (if written by the CEO). FAQs (frequently asked questions) collected by customer service teams can be a rich source of content recreated into '10 most popular questions', '10 questions you've got to answer', '10 reasons why' or '10 things you've got to know'. These can be converted into quizzes with multiple answers, or self-assessment widgets. Speeches – record them and then edit them into shorter clips. Slide shows – share them on SlideShare.

Re-use the graphics. Work out what customers need first, then create a content plan and calendar and deliver it. Being creative is great but it has to be relevant/interesting to the customer. One problem remains. Most customers do not fully know what they want nor what they might like in the future (as they cannot imagine it).

> ### Creativity will fuel growth in the future
>
> 'The search for value has led companies to seek efficiency through: downsizing; rationalizing; right-sizing approaches that eventually result in a diminishing level of return. But what will fuel growth in the future? Growth will come through mastering the skills of creativity and making creativity actionable.'
>
> Professor John Kao, Harvard Business School

Nurture the inquisitive mind – it can create competitive advantage

I asked the former President of McKinsey's Japan and highly respected author Kenichi Ohmae, if he could sense whether a company was going to be successful. Was there something he could smell or sense when he was in an organization that suggested this company was going to be a winner? He said 'yes' and went on to explain that 'if a company is not afraid to ask questions, if everyone asks questions from the CEO down to the office boy, if they ask questions like "Why do we do it this way?" then this company will succeed' (Ohmae, 1996). So the inquisitive mind is an essential ingredient for future success.

This is echoed by Susan Greenfield of the University of Oxford when speaking at the Third European Futurists Convention in Lucerne in 2007. She confirmed the need for creativity and the need to challenge old dogma: 'So creativity, this eureka connection (neuronal connection) that triggers a new insight in yourself and others, is all about forging connections and so providing environments that will foster a challenging of dogma, of old stale connections, a forging of new ones that trigger even more connections that give a meaning and an insight to both yourself and others' (Greenfield, 2007).

Kenichi Ohmae spends hours visiting shopping malls to observe human behaviour. People are fascinating; the way they behave, move, talk, walk, shop, browse. Shopping malls can provide 360-degree wide screen interactive entertainment (observing customers), or to many real marketers, malls provide real consumer behaviour insights.

Communications, customer experience and product morphing

Marketing communications is more than just communicating and promoting. Marcomms is now merging with customer experiences and product development and distribution as digital marketing (and particularly social media) 'morph' or merge and social media banter and special offers become part of the brand relationship, ie part of the UX (user experience). This has not gone unnoticed by the world's best marketers. Almost a decade ago Unilever moved its digital marketing out of the media mix and into the marketing mix (WARC, 2007). It realized that its digital budget was part of the overall marketing mix, rather than part of its media spend/marketing communications mix 'in recognition that successful digital campaigns are based more on producing engaging content than paying for media time and space'. Engaging digital communications and content enhances the customer experience. Creative marketing content can reach new audiences and extend product purchase opportunities to them.

The search for added value is now relentless, whether through new features or more likely through enhanced online experiences, social media sharing or simply the addition of features to a product or service never dreamt possible before the arrival of the iPhone apps. For example, Gibson Guitar's app includes a guitar tuner, a metronome and a chord chart, all of which are extremely useful for any guitarist. Kraft's iFood Assistant delivers recipes and a feature that creates a shopping list that automatically includes the ingredients for the chosen recipes. It even identifies the locations of nearby grocery stores and which aisles stock the items.

Nike's search to help customers led it to the Nike+ – a joint venture with Apple's iPod that enables runners to access a running community website, log their runs and connect with and compare to other runners by using their iPods (or their iPhones) and a Nike+ branded transmitter that can be fitted into some specially designed Nike shoes or attached to other running shoes. This is a far cry from just marketing communications, but it is all about helping customers and strengthening the brand and growing revenues. Word-of-mouth marketing has become an 'overriding industry preoccupation for marketers as it provides a good measure of success (if customers endorse brands to their peers). Nike's initiative has generated impressive results with Nike's director of digital and content claiming "97 per cent of Nike+ users said they would recommend the service to a friend. That figure is unheard of' (Grande, 2007).

Think of '4Es instead of 4Ps' (Rothery, 2008) from the old marketing mix. A product is an experience (including online), place becomes 'everyplace', price becomes 'exchange' and promotion becomes 'evangelism' or advocates. Alternatively, promotion is just morphing with product as communications seek to engage customers with relevant added-value experiences.

Previously marketing would basically create messages for a passive audience with little choice and less empowerment, where the most active element was the decision whether to notice or ignore an advertisement. The once-passive audience has been unshackled and empowered by social media and technology. Marketers face a brave new world, one that has changed forever, and one that offers new opportunities to those who choose to seize them.

'Location Marketing'. It identifies customers with mobile phones in specific places and then offers special prices and promotions. So here again, the old marketing mix is morphing since a single digital decision impacts several elements of the marketing mix.'

PR Smith 2014 SOSTAC® Plan

Integrate data, staff and communications

Inbound and outbound with online and offline communications delivers higher impact and more cost-effective 'joined-up marketing'. **Customer data needs to be integrated** since customers are touched by many contact points or 'touch points' such as social media, point of sale, ads, e-mail etc. Customers need a consistent (integrated) message. Equally companies are collecting information from many different customer touch points (website registration, website body language, customer service, social media and much more). It's a gold mine if they collect and store it safely in a data warehouse and then use it all to build better profiles of customers. Customer data needs to be integrated. This a major challenge for many organizations.

Staff need to be integrated. What does this mean? Well every customer-facing member of staff is a brand ambassador. They have to feel part of it. They have to integrate with the brand values (sometimes they are selected in accordance with the brand values). This requires internal marketing (investing in internal communications and motivation). If you get this right, staff can become your most potent communications tool. Have a look at this member of staff who made his own YouTube product demonstration video – eating his dinner off the subway floor (after he cleaned it with his hard floor cleaner that both vacuums and steams).

FIGURE 1.9 This employee is sufficiently motivated that he made his own 'Shockvertising' video for his company. Will this start a surge of employee product demo ads?

SOURCE: https://www.youtube.com/watch?v=NHznDFD3V3k

Marketing communications have to be integrated for two reasons. Firstly, unintegrated databases cause many problems and complications, as there is no single picture of the customer and therefore customers receive many different types of experiences and messages from the brand. This confuses customers and dilutes the brand's presence in the marketplace. Secondly, as communications morph into customer experiences, all communications need to be integrated to deliver a consistent experience.

The race is on

Amidst hyper-competition, a carefully structured ladder of engagement can help to build a ring fence of protection around the precious customer, if you capture these customers before your competition does and then continue to be relevant in their lives or their jobs. There is a golden opportunity for marketers to create stronger brands and sustainable competitive advantage. The race is on to capture those customers who will engage and collaborate and help to create anything from better promotions to better products.

This utopian marketing model encourages customers to engage and drive the business (albeit with some checks). It is a new era of collaborative co-creation, which moves marketing into a strategic position and earns its seat at the board. There has never been a better time to be involved in marketing.

> **Grab your offline browser online – before competition does**
>
> 'Now advertisers can use beacons to make the shoes you were looking at inside a physical store follow you around the internet.'
>
> O'Reilly (2015)

Cut through the clutter

The challenge of cutting through the clutter and grabbing a customer's attention grows greater as attention spans shrink and hyper-competition grows. After getting attention, brands then have to repeatedly cut through the clutter and give attention to their customers, delivering relevant added value continuously.

Amidst the hyper-competition is a heaving mass of communications, whether outbound, inbound, online or offline, and the race is on to somehow break through the clutter, engage with customers (and other stakeholders) and ultimately nurture lifetime loyalty.

Once a real dialogue is established and is used to continually improve and service the customers' continually changing needs, a platform of loyalty begins to emerge. This can build a wall around your customer, protecting them from the prying eyes of hyper-competitors.

In many ways, the first organizations that get it right are likely to prevail and win in the longer term as they strengthen customer relationships and secure loyalty.

The social media revolution started quietly 10 years ago. The race is now on to win and keep customers before the competition does. Marketers have to find new ways to engage customers and move a percentage of them up the ladder of engagement.

If the brand can build a **network of engaged customers** around it, this is potentially very powerful as the brand facilitates the network and the network uses and engages with the brand at the appropriate level, at the right time.

Enter the boardroom

The missed opportunity

Marketers can and should demonstrate to any board of directors how marketing can create two sources of sustainable competitive advantage by creating two assets – one on the balance sheet, the other off the balance sheet. Brands appear as an asset on the balance sheet, and a well-maintained, integrated customer database does not.

A well-integrated website helps to grow a database of customers and prospects, as well as boosting a brand's value as more and more relevant 'services' and 'sizzle' are added to the customer experience. Well-managed databases create a mini-monopoly of customers and prospects, and can be used with a variety of channels to communicate intimately with customers (e-mail, snail mail, telephone calls and personal visits). Although the value of a database can be quantified by estimating lifetime values, it still does not appear on the balance sheet.

Marketers missed their chance to enter the boardroom when the web first emerged in the early 1990s.

The internet, and websites in particular, presented a whole new way for businesses to exploit the 5S's (sell more, serve better, save money, speak with customers, and sizzle or create some magic around the brand by doing things that simply could not be done offline). Three of these S's will attract the ears of the financial director and the CEO: sell, save and sizzle.

'Sell' means revenue, and any promise to boost revenues is taken seriously. 'Save' is of interest, and any proposal that offers to make 99 per cent savings will demand attention, as there is no other aspect of business that can attain such massive savings as that of well-designed, self-service websites. Some financial directors and CEOs will appreciate the importance of brands on the balance sheet, in fact the necessity to have them on the balance sheet if in an acquisition or merger situation. Hence brands, and 'sizzle' that enhances a brand's value, will be of renewed interest to the CEO and CFO.

However, the moment was missed by marketers, and it seems that websites became the responsibility of other departments such as IT, corporate PR and sales. The benefits were diluted and the cohesive marketing argument lost. One other opportunity was missed also. As businesses move from the linear value chain to the web-linked value network, boards have to ask themselves, 'What business are we in?' Whilst the web created a golden opportunity to re-evaluate brands (what added value they could give and ultimately what they represent), it also created a golden opportunity to re-evaluate 'What business are we in?' As businesses outsourced chunks of the value chain, the business effectively became a 'box of contracts'.

The opportunity knocks twice

The emergence of social media almost 10 years ago presented the opportunity for marketers to get back in the boardroom with the social business model (and the ladder of engagement). This swept aside the old boardroom thinking that marketing was just a 'colouring department' that 'shouts' at customers.

A McKinsey survey (2009) reported that marketing and sales and IT will derive the most **benefits from social media** (as opposed to procurement, production and finance). In their words, 'Social media engages customers, deepens relations, generates extra sales, faster time to market, better NPD [new product development] and lowers the cost of doing business.'

Now we have marketing automation combined with relevant content marketing presenting an additional opportunity to get back into the boardroom. In addition, nurturing a constant beta culture allows marketers to talk about optimization, sweating their assets, lifetime value, cost per acquisition, ROI, sentiment scores and net promoter score. An analytics-driven business makes it a lot easier for board directors to understand marketing and the requests for budgets.

Social media and the opportunity it gives organizations to create sustainable competitive advantages cannot be left to IT or production departments, as these by definition are production-orientated. Social media is driven by the marketplace and is therefore the centre of a marketing-driven business.

So social media, the ladder of engagement, integrated marketing and creativity offer marketers another golden opportunity to get back into the boardroom and influence the strategic directions of a business in such a way that it becomes truly market-orientated, primed and ready to satisfy customers and enjoy continued success.

Why marketing was marginalized

'Seeing marketing as a series of distinct activities has been the reason that marketing has become more marginalized over the last 15 years, because it has been positioned as managing communications rather than managing the whole business orientation.'

Jenkinson (2004)

'Joined-up marketing' brings the old 'outbound marketing' (eg advertising, direct mail, telemarketing, news releases etc, sending out messages) together with inbound marketing (quality content that pulls people toward your organization).

'Sizzle'

Through the organization, real competitive advantage emerges. Consider National Semiconductor in the United States. They make chips for mobiles and DVD players. Their target market was design engineers and purchasing agents. Their enlightened CEO asked that quintessential marketing question:

'How can the website help engineers more?' A truly inquisitive mind forced them to understand how design engineers work and whether any online tools could help. They explored customer scenarios and discovered that the design process of choosing a part was to create a design, analyse the design, build a prototype, test, etc.

Now the engineer logs on and is prompted to specify the overall parameters and key components. The system auto-generates possible designs and technical specs, parts list, prices and cost-benefit analysis. Engineers share it with colleagues. They test and refine it. The result is that engineers can do in two hours what previously took two months. By the end of the first year they had 31,000 visitors generating 3,000 orders or referrals every day. One integrated socket with Nokia was worth 40 million units. This site helps customers so well that it creates sustainable competitive advantage whilst delivering a highly engaging brand experience. The change was made in 2000.

Top 10 Tips for world-class marketing

- Develop credibility before raising visibility.
- Continually ask 'does my website/ platforms help visitors (better than competition)?'
- Continually ask 'what am I doing to bring visitors back?'
- Stop thinking about campaigns and think about customer life cycle and continued engagement.
- Develop a process of listening and responding to customers.
- Reward customers who are socially positive with your brand.
- Build a culture that worships customer knowledge.
- Build a constant beta culture (constant optimization, analysis and ROI analysis where possible).
- Ask great questions.
- Embrace change and be creative – plus invest in internal marketing.

Key points from Chapter 1

- Is this business going places?
- What's your process of listening and responding to your customers?
- Why do you have a website?
- Do people ask good questions?
- Do they embrace change?

- This is the beginning of a new era in marketing amidst hyper-competition.
- Social media is here to stay.
- The ladder of engagement can create competitive advantage.
- There is an opportunity for marketers to take a seat on the board and drive a marketing culture.

References and further reading

Aarons, C, Edwards, A and Lanier, X (2009) Turning blogs and user-generated content into search engine results, Marketing Vox and Nielsen BuzzMetrics, *SES Magazine*, 8 June

Beck, S (2010) Make your product work for your brand: Why what you're selling has become your primary advertising channel, *Financial Times*, 4 May

Bird, Drayton (2008) *Commonsense Direct and Digital Marketing*, 5th ed, Kogan Page, London

Brogan, C (2009) The serendipity engine, www.delicious.com/chrisbrogan/casestudy

Caldicott, S (2010) Invention and marketing: Joined at the hip, *Media Week*, 28 April

Catmull, E (2008) How pixar fosters collective creativity, *Harvard Business Review* – The Magazine, Sep

Chaffey, D and Smith, PR (2013) *Emarketing Excellence*, 4th edn, Routledge

Charan, R and Bossidy, L (2002) *Execution: The discipline of getting things done*, Crown Business, New York

Christensen, C (2003) *The Innovator's Dilemma*, Harper Business Essentials, New York

Earls, M (2002) *Welcome to the Creative Age: Bananas, business and the death of marketing*, Wiley, Chichester

eConsultancy 2015 Quarterly digital intelligence briefing: digital trends [online] https://econsultancy.com/reports/quarterly-digital-intelligence-briefing-2015-digital-trends/

Edelman, D (2014) Mastering digital marketing, *McKinseys Insights & Publications* [online] http://www.mckinsey.com/insights/marketing_sales/mastering_digital_marketing?cid=other-eml-nsl-mip-mck-oth-1407

Fletcher, W (2010) author, lecturer and former chairman of the Royal Institution in conversation with PR Smith

Forrester (2013) www.forrester.com

Garvey, D (2002) BT Ignite, *Marketing Business*, March

Goldberg, C (2013) Marketing on Mobile: Why is this Platform Different? *High Tech Communicator*, 3 June

Grande, C (2007) Cannes diary: Six of the best by Carlos Grande, *Financial Times*, 24 June

Gray, R (2013) Retail Revolution, *The Marketer*, March/April

Greenfield, S (2007) The future of brain – the brain of the future, Third European Futurists Convention, Lucerne

Hall, E (2010) In Greece, Kraft scores a hit for Lacta chocolate with crowdsourced film, *Advertising Age*, 24 March

Hoffman, D (2009) Managing beyond Web 2.0, *McKinsey Quarterly*, July

iSport Connect (2012) Premier League to clamp down on illegal streams after 30,000 sites taken down last Year [online] http://www.isportconnect.com/index.php?option=com_content&view=article&id=13758:premier-league-to-clamp-down-on-illegal-sreams-after-30000-sites-taken-down-last-year&catid=36:football–soccer&Itemid=42

Jenkinson, A (2004) The bigger picture, *Marketing Business*, March

Kao, J (1997) *Jamming: The art and discipline of business creativity*, HarperCollins, New York

Kennedy, J (2009) App-fab, *Marketing Age*, November

Levine, R *et al* (2000) The Cluetrain Manifesto [online] http://www.cluetrain.com/

Lilley, A (2007) Why Web 2.0 adds up to a revolution for our industry, *Media Guardian*, 1 October

Manyika, J (2008) Google's view on the future of business: An interview with CEO Eric Schmidt, *The McKinsey Quarterly*, September

McCarthy, Jerome E (1960) *Basic Marketing. A Managerial Approach*, Irwin, Homewood, IL

McGovern, G (2010) Time is (still) money: Increasing employee productivity (Part 1) [online] www.gerrymcgovern.com

McGovern, G (2014) Customer-centric and easy-to-use is the new business model (The Alibaba story) *Gerry McGovern//New Thinking* [online] http://www.gerrymcgovern.com/new-thinking/customer-centric-and-easy-use-new-business-model-alibaba-story

McKinsey (2009) How companies are benefiting from Web 2.0: McKinsey Global Survey Results, National Customer Satisfaction Scores, Technology Office, *McKinsey Quarterly*, September

Mell, J (2013) IBM What does social business mean? *Bright Talk*, 10 April

O'Dea, A (2008) Innovation, *Marketing Age*, September/October

Ohmae, K (1996) Video interview with PR Smith, The Marketing CDs [online] PRSmith.org

O'Reilly, L (2015) Now advertisers can use beacons to make the shoes you were looking at inside a physical store follow you around the internet, *Business Insider* [online] http://uk.businessinsider.com/total-communicator-solutions-unacast-beacon-retargeting-2015-1?r=US#ixzz3QIfHL8sj

Qualman, E (2009) Statistics show social media is bigger than you think, *Socialnomics* [Online] http://socialnomics.net/2009/08/11/statistics-show-social-media-is-bigger-than-you-think/

Roberts, K (2009) in conversation with PR Smith, The Worshipful Company of Marketors, The Great Hall at Barts, St Bartholomew's Great Hall, 17 November

Roberts, K (2010) Video interview with PR Smith [online] www.PRSmith.org

Rogers, D (2014) Praise for the underdog, *PR Week*, Oct

Rothery, G (2008) The matchmaker, *Marketing Age*, November/December

Ryan, D and Jones, C (2009) *Understanding Digital Marketing*, Kogan Page, London

Safco, L and Brake, D (2009) *The Social Media Bible*, Wiley, Hoboken, NJ

Satell, G (2013) How to build an effective social marketing strategy, *Forbes*, 6 Oct

Schlack, W (2008) Open for innovation, Business and Leadership, [Online] http://www.businessandleadership.com/marketing/item/11417-open-for-innovation

Scott, D (2009) *The New Rules of Marketing and PR*, Wiley, Hoboken, NJ

Smith, PR (2014) Social Listening Skills, PR *Smith Marketing* [online] www.PRSmith.org/blog

Smith, PR (2014) The rise and fall of owned and earned but not paid media – world cup marketing wars? PR Smith Marketing Blog [online] http://PRSmith.org/the-decline-of-owned-but-not-earned-nor-paid-media-world-cup-marketing-wars/

Smith, PR (2014) The SOSTAC® guide to your perfect digital marketing plan [online] www.PRSmith.org

Solis, B (2015) Crossing the Experience Divide: Creating positive, lasting experiences is a crucial mandate for any brand, *Technology of us* [online] http://technologyofus.com/

Statista (2014) Statistics and facts about MMO gaming, July [online] http://www.statista.com/topics/2290/mmo-gaming/

Stoke (2014) A consistent customer experience builds a trusted brand, 7 May, *Tracy Stokes' Blog/Forrester* [online] http://blogs.forrester.com/tracy_stokes/14-05-07-a_consistent_customer_experience_builds_a_trusted_brand?cm_mmc=RSS-_-MS-_-73-_-blog_2701

WARC (2007) Unilever changes online focus, 25 June

Wing (1989) *The Art of Strategy: A new translation of Sun Tzu's 'The Art of War'*, Broadway Books

Witzel, M (2015) Philip Kotler turns gaze from marketing to capitalism's flaws, *Financial Times*, 2 April (regarding Kotler's new (2015) book: *Confronting Capitalism*, Amacom)

Zwilling, M (2014) Ten rules for business success survive a century, *Start-Up Professionals Musings*, 17 Oct [online] http://blog.startupprofessionals.com/2014/10/ten-rules-for-business-success-survive.html

Further information

Advertising Association
7th Floor North
Artillery House
11–19 Artillery Row
London SW1P 1RT
Tel: +44 (0)20 7340 1100
www.adassoc.org.uk

Chartered Institute of Marketing
Moor Hall
Cookham
Maidenhead
Berkshire SL6 9QH
Tel: +44 (0)1628 427120
Fax: +44 (0)1628 427499
www.cim.co.uk

CIPR
52–53 Russell Square
London WC1B 4HP
Tel: +44 (0)20 7631 6900
www.cipr.co.uk

Communications Advertising and Marketing
Education Foundation Limited (CAM Foundation)
Moor Hall
Cookham
Maidenhead
Berkshire SL6 9QH
Tel: +44 (0)1628 427120
Fax: +44 (0)1628 427158
www.camfoundation.com

Incorporated Society of British Advertisers
ISBA
12 Henrietta Street
London WC2E 8LH
Tel: +44(0)20 7291 9020
Fax: 020 7291 903
www.isba.org.uk

Institute of Promotional Marketing Ltd
70 Margaret Street
London W1W 8SS
Tel: +44 (0)20 7291 7730
Fax: +44 (0)20 7291 7731
www.ipm.org.uk

International Organization for Standardization
(ISO)
ISO Central Secretariat
BIBC II
Chemin de Blandonnet 8
CP 401
1214 Vernier, Geneva
Switzerland
Tel: +41 22 749 01 11
www.iso.org

Marketing Society
1 Park Road
Teddington
Middlesex TW11 0AR
Tel: +44 (0)20 8973 1700
Fax: +44 (0)20 8973 1701
www.marketing-society.org.uk

Public Relations Consultants Association
Willow House
Willow Place
London SW1P 1JH
Tel: +44 (0)20 7233 6026
Fax: +44 (0)20 7828 4797
www.prca.org.uk

02
Branding

LEARNING OBJECTIVES

By the end of this chapter you will be able to:

- Appreciate the importance of branding and why it is a strategic issue
- List the stages in building a brand process
- Avoid the classical branding mistakes
- Understand why brands need to be maintained

Introduction to branding   34

What is a brand?   34

The power of branding   34

Customers benefit from brands   34

Company benefits from branding   35

Business disadvantages of weak
     brands   41

Brand self-destruction   41

Brand components   45

What exactly is a brand?   45

A brand's rational and emotional
     appeals   46

The emotional connection   46

The brand components   46

The branding process   48

Research   49

The brief   52

Concept generation and
     development   53

Roll-out/delivery   56

Brand maintenance   57

Brand expansion/strategy   61

Brand summary and the challenges
     ahead   62

Sloppy brand self-destruction   63

The rise of the anti-brand   63

The rise of the own brand   64

Short-term sales versus long-term
     brand building   64

Brands – the bridge between
     marketing, finance and the
     boardroom   65

Marketers and the language of
     finance   65

Conclusion   66

Key points from Chapter 2   66

References and further reading   67

Introduction to branding

What is a brand?

A brand is an intangible, legally protectable, valuable asset. It is how a company or product is perceived by customers (or the target audience). It is the image, associations and inherent value customers put on your product and services. Brands include intangible attributes and values. For a brand to be successful, its components have to be coherent, appropriate, and appealing to consumers. A brand is a promise to the customer. A brand also embraces vision, values and personality (see 'Brand components' later in this chapter). A brand is far more than just a logo or a name (this is just brand identity). It is the complete customer experience; the integrated sum of all the marketing mix and the communications mix from products to customer service, from packaging to advertising, from rumour to discussion. The last two components are less controllable, from a brand management perspective, but they can nevertheless be influenced, as good brand management participates wholeheartedly in social media too. So a brand is everything a customer (or stakeholder) sees, feels and experiences about a product or service (or organization). A brand is the 'magical' difference between many competing products and services.

A (favourable) consensus of subjectivity

'Because brand reputations exist only in the minds of their observers – and all observers are different… the strongest brands are those that enjoy what's been called "a (favourable) consensus of subjectivity". And that's when their brand managers, in the widest sense of that phrase, should be most warmly congratulated. They didn't build those brands themselves; but they fed such enticing titbits to their audience that their audience gratefully did the rest.'

Millward Brown Optimor BrandZ survey (2010)

The power of branding

How do brands become so powerful that they control economies, determine corporate takeovers, or make customers pay almost 1,000 per cent price premiums? How do brands become the most valuable asset in a company, determining the whole financial value of a company and driving corporate takeovers? How do brands create sustainable competitive advantage? What makes people all around the world hand over their hard-earned cash for the same brand whether in Taiwan or Tokyo, Kashmir or Carlisle? Today, the power of branding is such that brands defend organizations from competitors, nurture customer relationships, and boost sales, profits and balance sheet assets.

Customers benefit from brands

So we know how brands help businesses, but how do they help customers? What do they do for customers? Brands save customers time, reduce their perceived risk and fulfil their aspirations. Now consider each benefit.

Brands save customers time

Brands help customers' busy lives by saving them time, helping them to find goods and services more quickly. Imagine trying to buy books or DVDs on the internet if you couldn't remember the name of Amazon or CD WOW. Or it could be beans in the supermarket or mortgages on the high street. Unilever's chairman, Niall FitzGerald, calls a brand 'a storehouse of trust which matters more and more as choices multiply' and we face what David Ogilvy once called 'the misery of choice'. People want to simplify their lives and simplify their decision making.

Brands reduce perceived risk

A strong brand is an implicit guarantee or promise of consistent quality, image and style. A brand is built on trust. Customers trust the promise made in the advertisement and on the pack. Customers form relationships with brands. Brands, in turn, provide a reassuring sense of order. Brands provide a safe and trusted option. Would you buy from someone you didn't know? Customers would prefer to reduce the amount of time and energy involved in decision making. That's one of the reasons why brand extensions are valuable. The brand is an implicit guarantee or promise. Customers trust the promise made in the advertisement and on the pack.

Brands satisfy aspirations

Brands give status and recognition. Brands reflect aspirations, images and associations that are carefully gleaned from in-depth customer motivation research. This is compounded by our search for identity and beliefs. 'In an irreligious world, brands provide us with beliefs', says Wally Olins of Wolff Olins. Some brands unconsciously create a sense of belonging from their cultish quality. In a way, buying and consuming brands actually defines who we are. Brands signal our affiliations. 'You are what you shop.' Brands reflect aspirations and act as a badge of self-image or desired self-image.

> ### Do brands fill the vacuum left by the decline of organized religion?
>
> 'In the developed world, they [brands] are seen by some to have expanded into the vacuum left by the decline of organized religion.'
>
> *Economist* (2001)

Consider the magic marketing formula: identify needs; reflect them; deliver/satisfy them. Remember, brands need to continually do this. Think about what needs Coca-Cola advertising reflects. It reflects people's own aspirations, so that when they buy a can or a case of Coca-Cola they actually buy a slice of their own aspirations (and a product whose promise of refreshing cola is consistently delivered anywhere in the world).

Company benefits from branding

Brands create sustainable competitive advantage from hyper-competition, boost relationships, boost sales, boost profits and boost balance sheets. Why would any managers not nurture their brand very carefully? The truth is that many do not (see 'The customer service time bomb' in Chapter 1). However, consider these individual benefits of nurturing strong brands.

Brands create sustainable competitive advantage

Brands will be, for many organizations, the critical success factor in the hyper-competitive 21st-century marketplace. Strong brands create sustainable competitive advantage. For the first time in the history of business, the most powerful barriers to competition are no longer controlled by companies but by customers. The old barriers are falling. Factories and even access to finance are not as powerful barriers as those erected inside customers' minds. Only a few chosen winners are allowed inside. These are the successful brands with which customers have relationships. Successful brands build differentiators.

The CEO of one of the world's greatest brands, Coca-Cola, reputedly once said: 'They can take everything we have, our machinery, our plants, our distribution – as long as they don't take our brand – and we will be able to rebuild our organization in six months.'

For many years now more people in Britain have trusted top brands than trust the church. In fact Heinz and Nescafé are trusted more than the church, the police and Members of Parliament (Croft (1998), in Reynolds, Cuthbertson and Bell, 2004). How come British people give their credit card details over the internet to an unknown, invisible American on the other side of the Atlantic? How come Americans pour down their throats water from an unknown source in France? Brand trust in Amazon and Evian is strong.

> ### Brands control people and brands control economies
>
> 'What gives brands their power to influence – if not quite control – people's purchasing decisions and thus their power to influence – if not quite control – modern economies?'
>
> Fletcher (2010)

Brands differentiate a company's products or services and help them to stand out from a crowd. Brands are often the primary source of competitive advantage and a company's most valuable strategic asset. All markets tend towards commodities (as patents run out and the competition catches up and copies others). Brands protect and defend a business from competition, as they differentiate the product by adding perceived value. This creates barriers to entry for potential new competitors that are constantly tempted to enter the new borderless and category-less market space.

> ### Chinese president visits a brand before visiting the president
>
> 'When visiting the United States, President Hu Jintao of China chose Microsoft's Bill Gates as his first visit, followed the next day by a visit to President Bush. The *International Herald Tribune* headline read "Chinese president's itinerary for US visit: Gates first, Bush later".'
>
> Yeong and Yu (2006)

Some years ago it was suggested that two-thirds of the stock market capitalization of US companies was attributable to intellectual assets (brands, patents and know-how). That's a massive $4.5 trillion. One-third of global wealth is accounted for by brands (Clifton, 2004).

Brands boost relationships

Brands create (mostly unconscious) relationships between the user and the brand. Brands add a subtle meaning to the act of consumption. We allow these brands into our homes and offices and into our lives because they generally mean something to us all. They represent something. At the heart of any successful brand proposition there is a human dimension. That's why brands have personality, values and associations. Brands used to be just a seal of quality. Today brands have emotional connections that differentiate them. Brands provide reassurance to customers and differentiation from competitors. Brands save customers time by being easily recognizable and providing a reassuring sense of order in an increasingly destabilized and chaotic world. Brands inspire loyalty, trust and continuity. Brands are built upon a platform of reliable quality. As in any relationship, a brand's promise must never be broken.

Brands are even used to pigeonhole people: 'He drives a Porsche and drinks Pimm's.' A person's entire life can be effectively categorized by his or her use of brands. Some brands are even definitive, eg 'He is the Rolls-Royce of hosts.'

> 'Coca-Cola sells more because our love of a particular brand is as important as our love of a flavour.'
>
> Ronay (2004)

Brands boost sales

Brands help customers by making their purchasing process easier. Brands are easier to recognize and to associate with quality; it is easier to understand their benefits, and they are less risky than unknown commodities. Brands encourage repeat purchases and brand relationships, which in turn boost sales. Strong brands are easily recognizable and build single-minded awareness, ensuring they have a greater chance of being included in the customer's 'considered set' of possible purchases or, better still, 'preferred purchases'. Brands inspire loyalty, trust and most importantly continuity, providing a re-assuring sense of order in an increasingly chaotic, insecure and fast-changing world. Established brands also provide a platform from which to launch other products under the same brand names, thereby increasing share of wallet.

Brands boost profits

Brands, rightly or wrongly, can command premium prices, which results in increased profits, which consequently allows more money to be spent on better (relevant and tested) communications with clearer messages – which continually strengthens the brand. For example, in the same store, Coca-Cola charges a price premium of almost 1,000 per cent with its 1.75-litre bottle priced at £1.85 (compared to Asda's two-litre bottle at £0.15). Incidentally, Coca-Cola knows the long-term power of its brand and invests in it accordingly (eg investing $65 million in 12 years' Olympic sponsorship until 2012). Profits are also boosted by repeat purchase customers, who generate on average five times more profits than sales to new customers. In online sales, this figure rises to 10 times more profitability (Eltvedt and Flores, 2005). Strong brands also boost margins, as they increase bargaining power within the trade.

Brands boost balance sheets

As well as affecting politics and economics, brands affect company valuations. Brands can indicate future profit trends and assist decisions and investor relations. Today, brands are recognized as assets, and more companies are putting brand values on to their balance sheets. Opposite is a list of brand values taken from the Millward Brown BrandZ survey (2014). The 2010 survey revealed the world's first $100 billion brand – Google. Now there are three brands worth over $100 billion: Google, Apple and IBM.

FIGURE 2.1   BrandZ™ Top 100 Most Valuable Global Brands 2014

BRANDZ™ Top 100 Most Valuable Global Brands 2014

	Brand	Category	Brand value 2014 $M	Brand contribution	Brand value % change 2014 vs 2013	Rank change
1	Google	Technology	158,843	3	40%	1
2	Apple	Technology	147,880	4	-20%	-1
3	IBM	Technology	107,541	4	-4%	0
4	Microsoft	Technology	90,185	4	29%	3
5	McDonald's	Fast Food	85,706	4	-5%	-1
6	Coca-Cola	Soft Drinks	80,683	4	3%	-1
7	VISA	Credit Card	79,197	4	41%	2
8	at&t	Telecoms	77,883	3	3%	-2
9	Marlboro	Tobacco	67,341	3	-3%	-1
10	amazon.com	Retail	64,255	3	41%	4
11	verizon	Telecoms	63,460	3	20%	1
12	GE	Conglomerate	56,685	2	2%	-1
13	Wells Fargo	Regional Banks	54,262	3	14%	0
14	Tencent 腾讯	Technology	53,615	4	97%	7
15	China Mobile	Telecoms	49,899	3	-10%	-5
16	UPS	Logistics	47,738	4	12%	-1
17	ICBC 中国工商银行	Regional Banks	42,101	2	2%	-1
18	MasterCard	Credit Card	39,497	3	42%	2
19	SAP	Technology	36,390	2	6%	0
20	vodafone	Telecoms	36,277	3	-9%	-3
21	facebook	Technology	35,740	4	68%	10
22	Walmart	Retail	35,325	2	-2%	-4
23	Disney	Entertainment	34,538	4	44%	3
24	American Express	Credit Card	34,430	4	46%	4
25	Baidu 百度	Technology	29,768	4	46%	8

Source: Valuations include data from BrandZ™, Kantar Retail and Bloomberg.
Brand contribution measures the influence of brand alone on earnings, on a scale of 1 to 5, 5 highest.

Reproduced with the kind permission of Millward Brown

FIGURE 2.1   *Cont'd*

BRANDZ™ Top 100 Most Valuable Global Brands 2014

	Brand	Category	Brand value 2014 $M	Brand contribution	Brand value % change 2014 vs 2013	Rank change
26	TOYOTA	Cars	29,598	3	21%	-3
27	T	Telecoms	28,756	2	20%	0
28	HSBC	Global Banks	27,051	3	13%	-3
29	SAMSUNG	Technology	25,892	3	21%	1
30	LV	Luxury	25,873	4	14%	-1
31	Starbucks	Fast Food	25,779	3	44%	13
32		Cars	25,730	4	7%	-8
33	China Construction Bank	Regional Banks	25,008	2	-7%	-11
34	Nike	Apparel	24,579	4	55%	22
35	Budweiser	Beer	24,414	4	20%	-1
36	L'ORÉAL	Personal Care	23,356	4	30%	6
37	ZARA	Apparel	23,140	3	15%	-2
38	RBC	Regional Banks	22,620	4	13%	0
39	Pampers	Baby Care	22,598	5	10%	-7
40	Home Depot	Retail	22,165	2	20%	1
41	HERMÈS PARIS	Luxury	21,844	5	14%	-1
42	Mercedes-Benz	Cars	21,535	4	20%	1
43	SUBWAY	Fast Food	21,020	4	26%	8
44	Commonwealth Bank	Regional Banks	21,001	3	18%	4
45	ORACLE	Technology	20,913	2	4%	-9
46	movistar	Telecoms	20,809	2	56%	20
47	TD	Regional Banks	19,950	3	12%	-1
48	ExxonMobil	Oil & Gas	19,745	1	3%	-9
49	hp	Technology	19,469	2	19%	5
50	IKEA	Retail	19,367	3	61%	24

The Brand Value of Coca-Cola includes Lights, Diets and Zero
The Brand Value of Budweiser includes Bud Light

MillwardBrown
Optimor

FIGURE 2.1   *Cont'd*

BRANDZ™ Top 100 Most Valuable Global Brands 2014

	Brand	Category	Brand value 2014 $M	Brand contribution	Brand value % change 2014 vs 2013	Rank change
51	ANZ	**Regional Banks**	19,072	3	15%	1
52	**Gillette**	**Personal Care**	19,025	4	7%	-7
53	(Shell)	**Oil & Gas**	19,005	1	8%	-4
54	中国农业银行 AGRICULTURAL BANK OF CHINA	**Regional Banks**	18,235	2	-9%	-17
55	accenture	**Technology**	18,105	3	10%	-2
56	*Colgate*	**Personal Care**	17,668	4	2%	-6
57	citi	**Global Banks**	17,341	2	30%	7
58	FedEx.	**Logistics**	17,002	4	24%	4
59	SIEMENS	**Technology**	16,800	2	36%	13
60	G U C C I	**Luxury**	16,131	5	27%	8
61	ebay	**Retail**	15,587	2	-12%	-14
62	orange	**Telecoms**	15,580	3	13%	-2
63	H&M	**Apparel**	15,557	2	22%	6
64	BT	**Telecoms**	15,367	2	61%	30
65	usbank.	**Regional Banks**	14,926	3	9%	-2
66	TESCO	**Retail**	14,842	4	-9%	-11
67	Sinopec	**Oil & Gas**	14,269	1	9%	0
68	中国银行 BANK OF CHINA	**Regional Banks**	14,177	2	0%	-10
69	YAHOO!	**Technology**	14,174	3	44%	23
70	HONDA	**Cars**	14,085	3	14%	1
71	(Twitter)	**Technology**	13,837	4	New	New
72	CISCO.	**Technology**	13,710	2	16%	5
73	DHL	**Logistics**	13,687	4	53%	25
74	bp	**Oil & Gas**	12,871	1	12%	4
75	SBERBANK	**Regional Banks**	12,637	3	0%	-5

Source: Valuations include data from BrandZ™, Kantar Retail and Bloomberg.
Brand contribution measures the influence of brand alone on earnings, on a scale of 1 to 5, 5 highest.

FIGURE 2.1   *Cont'd*

BRANDZ™ Top 100 Most Valuable Global Brands 2014

	Brand	Category	Brand value 2014 $M	Brand contribution	Brand value % change 2014 vs 2013	Rank change
76	PetroChina	Oil & Gas	12,413	1	-7%	-11
77	中国平安 PING AN	Insurance	12,409	2	18%	7
78	Linked in	Technology	12,407	4	New	New
79	J.P.Morgan	Global Banks	12,356	2	28%	14
80	MTS	Telecoms	12,175	3	14%	2
81	中国人寿 China Life	Insurance	12,026	2	-21%	-24
82	Woolworths the fresh food people	Retail	11,953	3	8%	-2
83	KFC	Fast Food	11,910	3	20%	8
84	Ford	Cars	11,812	3	56%	New
85	Westpac	Regional Banks	11,743	3	17%	3
86	intel	Technology	11,667	2	-15%	-25
87	CHASE	Regional Banks	11,663	3	8%	-6
88	pepsi	Soft Drinks	11,476	3	-5%	-13
89	Scotiabank	Regional Banks	11,351	2	9%	-4
90	NISSAN	Cars	11,104	3	9%	-4
91	Santander	Global Banks	11,060	3	20%	5
92	Red Bull	Soft Drinks	10,873	4	3%	-9
93	MTN	Telecoms	10,221	3	-11%	-14
94	Bank of America	Regional Banks	10,149	2	New	New
95	NTT docomo	Telecoms	10,041	2	0%	-5
96	PRADA	Luxury	9,985	4	6%	-1
97	PayPal	Payments	9,833	4	New	New
98	ING	Global Banks	9,771	3	29%	New
99	UBS	Global Banks	9,683	2	30%	New
100	ALDI	Retail	9,584	2	8%	-1

The Brand Value of Pepsi includes Diets
The Brand Value of Red Bull includes sugar-free and Cola

MillwardBrown Optimor

There are now 10 Chinese brands in the world's top 100 list. The best known in the West is probably Baidu, the Chinese search engine (coming in at number 25). But don't forget about Alibaba, whom we mentioned in Chapter 1. Although most westerners haven't heard of them, they had the biggest IPO (initial public offering to sell their shares) at a value of $160 billion.

New accounting rules worldwide require companies to value their intangible assets – such as brands – on their balance sheets when they are acquired (IAS 38). When these assets are judged to have an indefinite life, which is often the case with a brand, they will be subject to annual review for impairment. This means that the difference between the price paid and the current value will be calculated. Any resulting write-downs can often have major implications, as seen in 2002 when AOL Time Warner (as it was then known) had to write off $54 billion for the value lost when AOL acquired Time Warner at the end of the dotcom boom in 2000.

> 'Financial analysts are already using next-gen social analytics to predict future brand performance. Credit Suisse have partnered with NetBase to compile sentiment data on handbag designers.'
>
> Brun-Jensen (2014)

There is no doubt that brands can add value to the balance sheet, grow the value of the business (market capitalization) and therefore boost the sale price of a business. They also, as mentioned, save customers time, satisfy their aspirations and reduce perceived risk.

You have the factory and staff; I'll have the brand

> 'If we split the business tomorrow, you kept all the factories and staff and I kept the brand name, within two years I would be a multimillionaire and you would be bankrupt.'
>
> CEO, Quaker Foods

Business disadvantages of weak brands

If a product or service does not have a single strong unifying brand, its presence becomes diluted, seen differently by different people. A diluted brand is less recognizable, therefore less known, therefore less trusted and ultimately a more risky purchase. Without a strong unified brand, products and services become buried in a busy world of other, stronger brands. If a product or service has no real strong brand, it may be symptomatic that the management team are themselves not sure of what the brand really is, what it is really good at, what distinguishes it, what needs it meets and what emotions it connects with. Without a strong brand most of the marketing efforts fragment, splinter and disappear.

No brand, no cattle

The term 'brand' comes from the old Norse verb *brandr*, which meant to burn, and which eventually became a noun and adjective in medieval English. The noun 'brand' meant flame, fire or torch, and the adjective meant burning, hence 'brand hot'. Animals were marked with red-hot branding irons as a sign of ownership and an easy way to identify particular cattle.

So strong brands beat weak brands. But, despite creating protection against competition and boosting relationships, sales, profits and balance sheets, brands are continually damaged and weakened. Why do so many marketers allow so many brands to press their own self-destruct button? Read on.

Brand self-destruction

The brand relationship is always fragile. Constant sloppy service or a single moment of disaster, such as contamination or a misplaced word (eg Ratners; see 'Uncontrollable publicity – any publicity is good publicity?' on p. 393 of Chapter 14), can destroy the customer's trust. And customers are changing. They're becoming more demanding.

FIGURE 2.2   The most valuable global brands

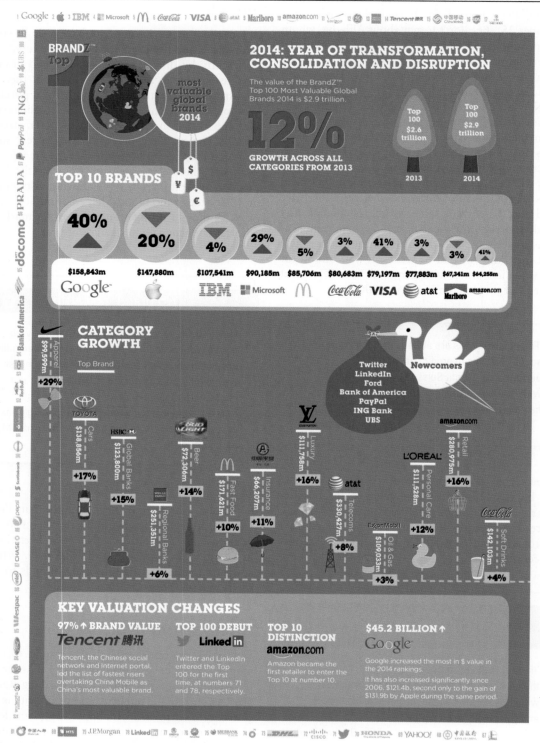

Reproduced with the kind permission of Millward Brown

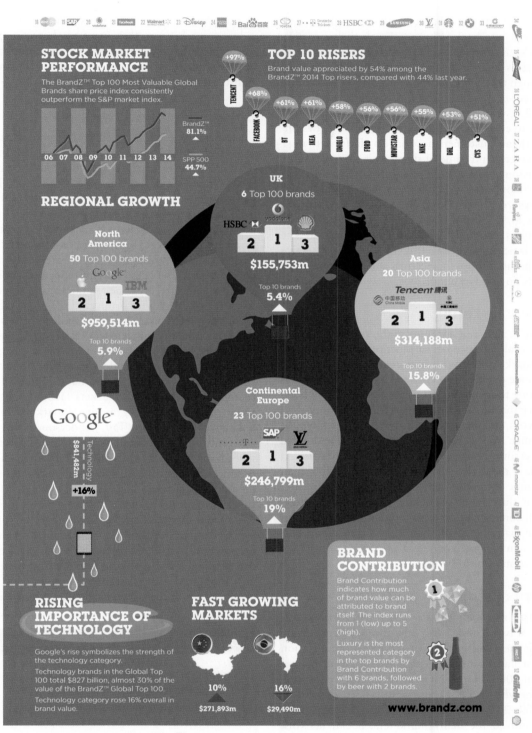

STOCK MARKET PERFORMANCE

The BrandZ™ Top 100 Most Valuable Global Brands share price index consistently outperform the S&P market index.

BrandZ™ **81.1%**

SPP 500 **44.7%**

06 07 08 09 10 11 12 13 14

TOP 10 RISERS

Brand value appreciated by 54% among the BrandZ™ 2014 Top risers, compared with 44% last year.

+97% TENCENT
+68% FACEBOOK
+61% BT
+61% IKEA
+58% UNIQLO
+56% FORD
+56% MOVISTAR
+55% NIKE
+53% DHL
+51% CVS

REGIONAL GROWTH

UK
6 Top 100 brands
HSBC · Vodafone · Shell
2 · 1 · 3
$155,753m
Top 10 brands **5.4%**

North America
50 Top 100 brands
Google · Apple · IBM
2 · 1 · 3
$959,514m
Top 10 brands **5.9%**

Asia
20 Top 100 brands
Tencent 腾讯 · 中国移动 China Mobile · HSBC 中国工商银行
2 · 1 · 3
$314,188m
Top 10 brands **15.8%**

Continental Europe
23 Top 100 brands
SAP · T · LV
2 · 1 · 3
$246,799m
Top 10 brands **19%**

Google
Technology $841,482m
+16%

RISING IMPORTANCE OF TECHNOLOGY

Google's rise symbolizes the strength of the technology category.

Technology brands in the Global Top 100 total $827 billion, almost 30% of the value of the BrandZ™ Global Top 100.

Technology category rose 16% overall in brand value.

FAST GROWING MARKETS

10%
$271,893m

16%
$29,490m

BRAND CONTRIBUTION

Brand Contribution indicates how much of brand value can be attributed to brand itself. The index runs from 1 (low) up to 5 (high).

Luxury is the most represented category in the top brands by Brand Contribution with 6 brands, followed by beer with 2 brands.

www.brandz.com

Not only do they talk back, but they now shout back and even bite back if brands break their promise. Today's customers have unlocked 'brand control' from marketers and set up their own brand discussions. Although they are still time pressed and information fatigued, they have found a new energy, fuelled by Web 2.0, which allows them to fulfil their age-old desire to communicate about what interests or concerns them. Customers now have a platform to raise their voices, and some of them can't stop shouting!

Customers have been abused by businesses that dump sloppy service on them, again and again. Surveys reveal that marketers have, in fact, got worse at marketing over the last 10 years. And customers are angry. They are also impatient. The clock is ticking. We are sitting on a customer service time bomb. Sloppy marketing and self-destructing brands go hand in hand.

Lousy marketing

We are in an era of declining marketing skills, measured by falling customer satisfaction scores in market after market. Meanwhile automated customer service telephone queuing systems and unworkable websites continue to insult and frustrate customers. Robotic answer machines with self-service menus dump all the work on the information-fatigued, time-poor customer. Add websites that don't work, with dead ends, error messages, complicated navigation and, if you have the patience to struggle through all of that, electronic shopping carts that crash. The customer service time bomb is ticking (see Chapter 1 for more). Some angry customers publicize their feelings on the many blogs and hate sites attacking brands. These can fuel an exponential spreading of negative word of mouth (or 'word of mouse').

Angry customers

Research shows that today's customers are less tolerant of bad service, with 80 per cent of consumers saying they will never go back to an organization after a bad customer experience, up from 68 per cent in 2006 (Harris Interactive, 2006). Add in customers who talk back and who talk to each other via Web 2.0 social media facilities. The goal posts have moved for many marketers. Social network sites facilitate customer discussions about all sorts of brand-related content. Coca-Cola never asked for rockets, but it just happened that customers discovered that mixing Coke and Mentos mints caused an explosive reaction and they started posting videos

of this phenomenon. Customers talk with text and video, some because they want to share opinions, others because they are hungry for fame and others because they want to meet new friends or, simply, transcend their everyday lives.

Unlocking control with Web 2.0

Customers have unlocked 'control' from companies, with Web 2.0 facilitating user-generated content (UGC). Not surprisingly, UGC is not totally controllable. Online social networks are here to stay. They will continue to grow in line with the very human need for social contact. Customers have been mobilized by blogs, social network sites and invitations to create their own UGC, whether comments and feedback or conversations, joint research or creating advertisements, services or even products. Customers are no longer slovenly couch potatoes, and some are active co-creators who produce discussions, advertisements or even products: hence the term 'prosumer' (see 'The ladder of engagement', Chapter 1).

We are possibly on the cusp of a customer revolution bringing an end to accepting sloppy service and, also, an end to the mass dumbed-down customer. Online digital markets facilitate obscure niche markets as easily as mass markets. In the online world, the 'Long Tail' (Anderson, 2006) suggests it can be as profitable to serve 100 customers spread across the world with 100 different digital products as it is to serve 100 local customers with one standardized product. This opens a gate to discrete consumer taste, which effectively moves markets away from the mass market and its tyranny of the lowest common denominator. Instead of a handful of powerful marketers recommending, and often determining, what is in and what is out, there are now mobilized niche customers, alerting their own networks about their own particular preferences.

Death of the dumbed-down customer?

'For too long we've been suffering the tyranny of lowest-common-denominator fare, subjected to brain-dead summer blockbusters and manufactured pop. Many of our assumptions about popular taste are actually artefacts of poor supply-and-demand matching – a market response to inefficient distribution.'

Anderson (2006)

Global niches

Although spread across the world, customers with similar interests can communicate and share thoughts through images, audio, video and text anywhere they want. This means that clusters of customers with similar tastes and interests are connecting with each other to form new global niches and segments. Global markets are here. For example, Manchester United Football Club has an estimated 70 million fans around the world, and Al Jazeera's English-language TV news service has 100 million people in its audience worldwide. As media follow markets, media consumption may go global; therefore marketers must remember that brands with international ambitions must have a consistent global image – production should be international in mind, and content rights should be global. True brand masters also 'think global and act local' by paying attention to local market needs and having the nous to express this in local terms.

Creating content that users can pass on via their social networks is an increasingly important channel of communication. But, as Universal McCann (2007) suggests, 'when using these channels it is fundamental that brands and media organizations think global'. Multiple local and conflicting brand identities fragment the brand. In addition, localized brand names can often exclude brands from international sales.

Some brand names restrict international sales or global brand ambitions. See Chapter 9, page 255 for a list of names that damage the brand when used in some international markets.

The internet's new business dynamics

The internet, and broadband in particular, has changed business dynamics. It has created a level playing field for the smaller niche brands to compete with the established global players. Small brands have access to bigger, global markets and can communicate directly with customers across the world in new and more meaningful ways – ways never dreamt of 10 years ago.

Power will be prised away from those major brands that are not prepared to change. Maybe it will be the database holders that take control. Imagine consumers opening a fridge and as they take the last can of Guinness the fridge asks 'Would you like a new delivery of beer, but this time at a special price from a different brand?' Here, it is the database holder that knows who drinks what beer, when and where, as it records the last beer's bar code when the beer is taken out of the fridge. The key to accessing the customers' databases embedded in fridges, microwaves, cars, phones and PDAs is not the hardware but the intelligence (or software system) to know exactly when customers might like to replace something. The invasion of the infomediary starts here.

So marketers who ignore new trends and real customer needs and, worse still, deliver sloppy service are simply pressing a self-destruct button that damages and ultimately destroys a very valuable brand.

Before exploring the right way to nurture a brand (ie the branding process), consider exactly what a brand is and what its component parts are.

Brand components

What exactly is a brand?

A brand is far more than just a name, term, design or symbol that identifies and distinguishes a product or service from that of other competitors. A brand is still a badge of origin, a promise of performance and a point of differentiation. Today, a brand is a holistic experience that stretches beyond the physical and into the psychological. It is the sum of the real product or service experience and the perceived values, images, associations and promises made through marketing communications.

'Brand' is both a verb and a noun. It is a verb, as it is a continual process, and a set of skills is required to create and nurture brands. Branding is a core competency for serious marketers. 'Brand' is also a noun, as it is an asset on the balance sheet and something people buy. Some commentators define brands as simply the difference between a bottle of sugared, flavoured, fizzy water and a bottle of Coca-Cola.

'Harley-Davidson does not sell motorcycles. Starbucks do not sell coffee. Club Med does not sell vacations. And Guinness does not sell beer. Think about it.'

Peters (2003)

A brand's rational and emotional appeals

A brand is a cluster of rational or functional and emotional aspects that match customers' rational and emotional needs. Strong brands are designed to trigger specific emotional responses in the minds of customers. Nike promises 'personal achievement', while Coca-Cola promises 'carefree fun'. What we buy says more about us than we might want to admit. It reveals our inner, often unconscious desires and aspirations. If the brand gets it right (understands a customer's deep needs and reflects these through a range of communications) then customers are simply buying some of their own aspirations. They are, in fact, buying a slice of their ideal self.

Brands, therefore, have both rational and emotional benefits. For example, Red Bull's physical (rational) benefit is that it keeps you awake (physical stimulation), and its emotional benefit is that you feel you can do more (feel stimulated). Natural food drinks' functional benefit is 'pure fruit juice', and their emotional benefit is 'feel healthy/feel good'. Kellogg's Corn Flakes' physical benefit is 'breakfast nutrition', and the emotional benefit is 'a great start to the day'. As a brand develops, it should elicit an emotional connection from customers.

Some authors, like Kapferer (2008), see strong brands as a deeply held belief or 'an attitude knitted into consumers' hearts. This attitude goes from emotional resonance to liking, to belonging to the evoked set (or consideration set), to preference, attachment, advocacy, to fanaticism.' Some customers are really attached to their brands and simply will not buy anything else.

The emotional connection

Once upon a time brands used to be all about trust and a seal of quality. Today quality is taken for granted. Now brands fight for an emotional connection as a way of differentiation. Another platform for brands to slug it out on is corporate values. Who is the brand, or the corporation behind the brand? Is it socially responsible, environmentally friendly, an animal tester, politically neutral, charitable, or good for its community? The founders of some of the world's strongest brands, like Guinness,

Cadbury and Boots, had huge commitments to their employees' and communities' lives, ranging from building spacious towns, to better schools, hospitals, libraries and parks. Today's brands also need a platform of social responsibility.

> ### There's never been so much emotion in business
>
> 'What will happen is based on emotional drives. That's why you can't predict the future. If people worked on pure economic logic, I could predict the future, but I can't.'
>
> Sir John Browne, BP (in Jones, 2001)

The brand components include brand equity, brand essence, brand experience, brand identity, brand personality, brand positioning, brand promise, brand role, brand values and brand vision. They must all integrate with each other. Here is an explanation of each component.

The brand components

Brand equity

Brand equity is the total awareness and perceived value of the brand in the mind of customers. Badly managed brands can result in negative brand equity. Brand equity components include the brand identity (brand name, symbols, jingles, colours, associations and any sensory features such as unique smells or tactile experiences), awareness, customer loyalty, perceived qualities and reputation. Brand awareness, brand preferences and brand loyalty are also part of the brand equity. Above all, actual brand experiences contribute to brand equity.

Brand essence

Brand essence is the brand's soul and spiritual centre, which draws on its core value(s). It is the brand's mission statement (how it will help the world) that motivates customers (and employees). The brand essence is the primary functional and emotional benefits. For example, Apple Computers' essence might be 'artful technology', while Amazon's might be 'unparalleled breadth of selection' and Hallmark's might be 'helping people define and express themselves'. The brand essence must have 100 per cent recall amongst the whole business team and influence every decision they make. It starts with what the brand excels at and then connects to an important cultural truth or trend, eg Apple: the world would be a better place if people had the technology to unleash their potential.

Brand experience

Brand experience is what the customers feel or experience when actually consuming a product or service. This includes all touchpoints of the brand (see below). Somehow this seems to be forgotten by many companies. The actual experience customers enjoy, or suffer, directly affects the brand image. Brand moments are all those moments of contact between the brand and the customer. This includes the website, e-mail responses, telephone responses, handling enquiries, the actual consumption of the product or service, and handling complaints and after-sales, as well as all the marketing communications contacts with the customer. These are critical brand moments.

Brand identity

Brand identity is part of brand equity. Identity is how the brand looks and is sometimes called the 'visual narrative', ie logo, colours and graphics. Brand image, on the other hand, is perception, ie how consumers see the brand based on identity plus all other communications, discussions and experiences. Identity is reality. Image is perception. Identity precedes image. Identity helps customers to remember a brand, recognize it and eventually build associations with the brand values, personality and promise promoted through all communications tools.

Brand personality

People have relationships with brands just as they do with people. That's why marketers define the brand personality carefully. Some brands have subtle, and often unconscious, relationships with customers. A brand's personality has those human personality traits. What kind of person would the brand be if it were human? Think of brands as actual people. How would the brand talk and walk? What kind of clothes would it wear? What kind of car would it drive? What kind of parties would it go

to? For example, the Marlboro Cowboy and the Singapore Airlines Girl have very different but well-defined personalities.

'Hello Gorgeous'

Virgin's website greets you with 'Hello Gorgeous'. This is part of the whole brand experience and is consistent with the brand values and slightly naughty brand personality.

Brand positioning

Brand positioning is all about perception – how the brand is to be seen, or perceived, by customers using just one or two (or sometimes a maximum of three) key variables. For example, a certain drink could be positioned as a young sick person's drink or a healthy adult's drink. A positioning statement identifies the best space for a brand to be positioned in the minds of customers. As markets change (customers' attitudes and needs change) so too brands change to meet customer needs. Positioning studies identify what is important to customers, where competitors are positioned (or what they are seen as by customers) and if there are any gaps for a brand to fill or take over. This is brand strategy and is absolutely critical to success.

Ask these questions when choosing a positioning:

1 Is it important to our target customers (will it drive their buying behaviour)?
2 Is it distinctive and specific?
3 Is it sustainable or can the competition copy it?
4 Can the brand deliver it?

Brand promise

Brand promise or proposition is what the brand offers the customer. For example, Perrier is a premium-priced carbonated mineral water with unique packaging, etc. It is quite product related as opposed to consumer benefit related. Another brand of water might be the healthiest water for your body. The actual proposition flows from the positioning.

Brand role

What role does this brand play in target customers' lives? The brand role is an extension of brand personality or lifestyle, or as a social facilitator. Where does it fit in the life of the customer? Is the brand a champion, a chum, a comforter, a confessor, a conscience, an enabler, an expert, an entertainer, a friend, a servant, a patron, a ringleader, a guide, a guru, etc? For example, Red Bull might be a 'portable comforter for tired people' or Ryanair possibly enables people to access Europe.

Brand values

Brand values are not necessarily seen, as they are declared internally. Imagine again the brand as a person. What does your brand believe in? What does it stand for? What standards does it attain? How should it behave? Brand values are a belief system or a way of working and communicating. Mose (2003) asks:

> Which values are so inherent in your company that, if they disappeared, your company would cease to exist as it is? Thousands of companies disappear every year. So why has your company survived? Why are investors still investing in your company? Why do your customers still buy your product? Why do people come to work for your company? Why do you still work for your company? These questions can help determine your company's true core values.

Brand vision

Brand vision is what the brand should be. In Virgin's case it might be to provide a service that is 'the people's champion and which shakes up the status quo'. In Nike's case the vision is one of achievement, of personal best, of being part of a community of athletes. The brand allows people to reconnect with an Olympic ethos that sits somewhere deep inside the psyche.

> 'Do not relax until you have identified the irreducible core of a brand – what drives its connection with consumers. This will mean getting inside consumers' heads, and understanding deep-seated motivations and thought processes.'
>
> Braun (2004)

Sensory branding may become more of the brand experience, as trademark regulations in almost all countries are accepting applications for registering components of the brand that incorporate all five senses. Lindstrom (2005) reported that:

> Decades ago, Texas developed the Texas touch, albeit on their calculators. Texas was one of the first companies to actually trademark the specific 'clicks' – the feel of the number pad on their calculators. The interesting fact is that users of the product may not recognize Texas's logo, but they still recognize the 'touch'. Singapore Airlines currently has nine patents including a patent on the Stephan Florida Smell – the characteristic 'Singapore Airline smell' of the hot towels served onboard. Kellogg's invested in the power of auditory stimulus, testing the crunching of cereals in a Danish sound lab to upgrade their product's 'sound quality'. We all recognize Intel's jingle even in other brands' advertisements.

Brand touchpoints are sometimes called 'brand moments' or 'customer touchpoints'. Touchpoints are anywhere the brand touches the customer, eg packaging, advertisements, websites, telephonists, sponsorship, events, etc. While customers are waiting on the phone, what brand experience do they have? While they are receiving a bill, letter, fax or e-mail, what experience do they have? These are part of the brand experience. Marketers need to pinpoint the relevant attributes that distinguish the brand and the touchpoints that can deliver these (in order of importance). This requires input from everyone – from CEO, MD, marketing, operations and sales teams to advertising people and webmasters.

One of the ultimate touchpoints for a brand is experiential marketing – traditionally live events offline where customers get to interact with the brand in a new and immersive environment.

> 'Great marketers do not sell products. They evoke emotion.'
>
> Farrell (2008)

The branding process

A big prize awaits brands that can develop deeper and longer-lasting connections with their customers.

Marketers should treat the word 'brand' as a verb and not a noun, as branding is a continual process. Brand building and brand maintenance are, in fact, a core competency. Outstanding marketers use a development process when creating an advertising campaign, an exhibition, a website or an actual brand. They also use it when reviewing and updating a brand, since brands have to be redefined for a new era (otherwise markets can move away from old, outdated brands). The best brand stewards or guardians have an inbuilt review process to ensure the brand is kept fresh. They ensure it does not allow obsolescence to creep in, and tweak it if necessary. So, whether you are creating a new brand or maintaining an existing one, here are the four main steps in the process: brief, concept generation, concept development and roll-out/delivery. Figure 2.3 shows the process required to create and maintain strong brands.

FIGURE 2.3
The brand development process

A clear brief covers details of the target market, required brand role, personality, values, positioning, etc. Concepts or ideas are generated. One or two are selected and developed, and finally one is rolled out as the new brand. What's missing in this process? Research. Research is required before and after each stage. So now the brand development process reads:

FIGURE 2.4 The brand development process including research

Research

In order to explore the brand opportunity, research is used at the early stage of a brand's development (way before any brand names, logos and colours). Target markets are analysed, buyer behaviour drivers explored, brand personalities defined and the most cost-effective brand moments identified.

Successful brands use a platform of information to help to nurture the brand. Initial exploratory research is used to:

FIGURE 2.5   The complete brand development process

Research	Identify long-term customers, their needs (including aspects of a brand that drive behaviour) and key brand moments or touchpoints. Identify brand personality, values, associations and promise. Identify competitors and trends.
BRIEF	Take all the preceding research and summarize it into a one-page brief highlighting target markets, brand personality, positioning, values, etc.
Research	More market research to identify ideal brand personality, values and promise – sometimes carried out by the agency or design team.
CONCEPT GENERATION	Generate several creative ideas or concepts.
Research	Concept research, eg focus groups to discuss initial concepts, identify the best concepts and identify other questions or issues for further research.
CONCEPT DEVELOPMENT	Take the chosen concept and develop it into finished artwork.
Research	Final concept testing, eg hall tests and test market – often easier to do with advertising concepts than brand concepts.
ROLL OUT/ DELIVERY	The biggest cost of any brand development is its establishment on all stationery, buildings, cars, etc. Staff buy-in, training and motivation.
Research	Measure and improve: tracking studies (eg independent brand popularity rankings or studies). Measure staff performance and customer satisfaction.

- identify long-term profitable customers;
- develop a deep understanding of the customer;
- identify aspects of a brand that drive behaviour;
- identify the emotions that drive brand behaviour;
- identify personality, values, associations and the promise;
- identify critical brand moments – or critical touchpoints;
- identify the most cost-effective, high-impact brand moments.

Let's consider each of these in more detail.

Identify long-term profitable customers

Do not invest branding efforts in unprofitable segments (particularly those with weak long-term potential). The profit potential of each segment needs to be measured. Also watch out for trends that may affect the relevance of the traditional segmentation approach (eg size, income, age, ethnicity, consumption patterns, loyalty, locations, lifestyles, needs and attitudes). For example, the business traveller hotel segments may be changing from service-orientated business travelling to value-driven business travelling and luxury-driven business travelling. The latter may split into 'fashion seeker' segments (who see their hotels as a way of expressing who they are) and 'escape seeker' segments (who want to feel pampered and far from the pressures of business).

Identified trends are a marketer's friend.

Develop a deep understanding of the customer

Rudyard Kipling's six honest serving men were the questions who, what, why, where, when and how. Outstanding marketers can answer all of these questions about their customer segments. The most difficult is 'why' – why do customers buy? (We'll look at this further in Chapter 4.) Excellent marketers know their customers better than they know themselves. A deep understanding of the customers is required; for example a hotel might uncover that the core need underlying the desire for comfort is to 'feel as though I'm at home while I'm away'. As desires change, trends must be watched continuously to ensure the right offers are made; some retail sectors have discovered that speed is now far more important to customers than credit card facilities and accordingly offer cash-only transactions. An airline may have to prioritize between easier upgrades, more onboard services, faster check-in, a bigger baggage allowance and more frequent-flyer miles. Getting the proposition right is critical when building brands.

Invite a brand into your life

'Marketers need a deeper understanding of what makes people invite certain brands and propositions into their lives and what makes them reject others.'

Fauconnier (2006)

Identify aspects of the brand that drive behaviour

A brand's specific features may clearly distinguish it from its competitors but not be important to customers. This is what McKinsey refer to as the 'fool's gold of branding'. Different but non-important features are irrelevant if they do not drive customer behaviour. Without knowing which features really do affect customer behaviour, an organization can squander limited resources promoting unwanted aspects of the brand. It's a little bit like getting high satisfaction scores but wondering why customers are leaving in droves. You're probably measuring features that were important in previous years but are no longer so. Customer desires change, and so trend spotting and brand adjusting are required to keep brands up to date and out of the great brand graveyard in the sky.

Identify the emotions that drive brand behaviour

A brand is much more than a product. It is a lifestyle or a personality that appeals to the emotions as well as the rational, thinking side of the brain. Emotions are very important. Branding is about creating and maintaining emotional ties. Marketers must probe and discover their customers' emotions, since they often drive behaviour.

Le Pla, Davis and Parker (2003) identified three triggers to create an emotional tie that ultimately strengthens brand loyalty: 1) congruence with deeply rooted life themes (values); 2) helping the accomplishment of life projects; 3) resolution of current concerns. 'If all three triggers can occur through the customer's personal relationship with the brand then it is likely that the customer will see the brand as a friend or partner, or as the heart of a community of users – where the community becomes a significant part of the customer's life.'

In the US car market, Mini created huge sales and high brand loyalty when it appealed to the emotions of drivers. The advertisements declared 'opposition to bigness' and promised to 'wage war on SUVs'. The Mini 'celebrated the joy of motoring' as opposed to 'the lobotomized, cruise control movement of most car transport on America's highways and streets'. GM's Saturn also used emotion in car advertisements that said very little about the car but lots about the company's ideology. The car wasn't even shown in the advertisements, but the ordinary people who made it were. The ad explained GM's beliefs and values. The car became the top-selling small car two years after launch, with a community built around the brand (some 45,000 customers and families turned up at a factory to meet each other and the company at its open day, which had barbecues, bands and a factory tour).

> 'We don't know how to sell on performance. Everything we sell, we sell on image.'
> Robert Gouezeta, ex-CEO, Coca-Cola

Identify personality, values, associations and promise

Identify the kind of brand personality that reflects the ideal personality that the target market aspires to or admires. Build in the values and associations that matter to the target market. Make a very clear simple promise and stick to it – never break it.

Identify critical brand moments – or touchpoints

These are the places, often beyond the consumption of the actual product or service, where a large part of the total brand experience is really delivered. This is where the customer has a large emotional investment, for example a phone call to the customer service line to make a complaint. It includes anywhere that customers interact with the brand (phone, store and web, as well as ads and events, etc).

Identify the most cost-effective, high-impact brand moments

Channel creativity and resources into these high-impact areas. This is where the brand will be enhanced or destroyed. Remember, a beautifully designed logo and clever brand name mean nothing if the website doesn't work or the customer service person cannot solve the problem. Equally, a wonderful product can be destroyed if it is delivered uncaringly.

Service training or website redesign?

Which is the priority? Creating a new customer service training programme or redesigning a website? Answer: find the high-impact touchpoints and allocate resources that have the biggest effect on them.

Equipped with answers to all of the research questions, we now know what we want and what is the priority. Having completed the research, we can now write the brief.

> 'Secure the .com version of your new brand name's URL.
>   Secure the Twitter handle you want for the new brand.'
> PR Smith

Run focus groups with customers in your target markets to uncover any hidden issues with your proposed rebranding.

> 'When Netflix first announced its ill-fated rebranding to split the Netflix and Qwikster services, it quickly became apparent that one vital element of the due-diligence process had been glossed over. Because the company had failed to secure the "@Qwikster" username on Twitter, the handle was snatched up by a user who flooded his feed with images of a beloved children's character making use of illicit substances.
>   Netflix quickly scrapped the launch of the DVD-only service Qwikster in the face of negative publicity.'
> Kumar (2012)

The brief

The starting point for any branding initiative is to ask what its objectives are: what is it trying to achieve in the customers' minds? The brief should include the brand promise, personality, values, associations and positioning (as well as the 3Ms: men/women, money and minutes – who is responsible for what, how much budget is allocated to creating this brand, and how much time there is before the launch, testing and concept development stages). Brand logos and clever names come later. A good brief should be written and agreed or signed off by all the key decision makers.

As well as defining the target market, the brief includes the brand's promise to customers. What makes it different? What needs is it fulfilling? In addition to target markets, distribution channels and regulatory guidelines, the brief should include brand vision, role, and essence.

An example of promise is Volkswagen promising the most reliable car. Volvo promise the safest. The brand's personality (the tone, manner and style of how you speak to customers, what you look like and how your staff behave) gives guidelines both for marketing communications and for staff behaviour. Virgin's personality is consistently irreverent; their airport luggage-size signs state 'The size of your bag has a limit – but the size of your ego can't be too large!' Brand values are included, as they influence how you work, your beliefs and your standards of behaviour. The brand's positioning must be crystal clear. This summarizes all the other questions and is key to marketing strategy. Positioning defines how your brand's distinctive benefits should be perceived by customers alongside competitive offers.

Two important aspects for any brand brief are relevance and differentiation. The proposition must make customers an offer, firstly, that fits their needs and, secondly, that the competition cannot (easily) offer. Relevance and difference increase the likelihood of success. But remember, relevant product differentiators may change over time.

A useful aide-mémoire for any brief is SOS + 3Ms, which is taken from the marketing planning system called SOSTAC®. The SOS brief provides a useful framework, as it includes situation analysis (where are we now?), objectives (where are we going?) and strategy (how do we get there?); the 3Ms are men/women (the brand manager and team who decide), money (budget) and minutes (timescale). For more on SOSTAC®, see Chapter 10.

> A brand that does not stand for something stands for nothing.

Concept generation and development

The answers to questions about the brand's promise, personality, values, associations, and positioning give clear guidance to any creative ideas. A good brief saves a lot of time, as it steers creative thinking in the right direction and avoids generating time-consuming concepts that do not fulfil the brand prerequisites.

However, once the brief has been signed off, some additional research may be carried out into customers, distributors and even competitors. On the basis of a clear brief and any additional research required, brand names and brand logos can be generated and then researched, with the best one(s) being selected for refinement or development. The finished brand name and logo are then tested once more. Early-stage research should include global use, ie whether the name or the logo has any strange meaning in other key languages, and whether it is protectable. Let us look at brand name development and brand logo development.

Brand name development

Developing brand names is a specialized business in itself. A brand name should be distinctive and easy to say, spell and remember. It should also be relevant, brief (maximum four syllables) and legally protectable (ie not generic) and lend itself to advertising and promotion. Lastly, a really good name can be used almost globally.

Three different approaches to brand name development are: product function; classic names (Latin or Greek); and benefit based. Product function, eg International Business Machines (now IBM), is difficult to protect. The classic approach is more protectable; Nike is a Greek name, which relates to the specific cultural values of the Olympic Games and the glorification of the human body. Thirdly, benefit-based names are less directly associated with a product or service's functions and closer to a name that evokes product benefit or even a certain state of mind, eg Nectar for a 'reward points' programme.

And there are always exceptions to the rule. Richard Branson claims to have named his brand Virgin because he was a virgin when it came to business. Tech giant Cisco's name comes from the last five letters of San Francisco, reportedly chosen when the founders were inspired by a drive past the

Golden Gate Bridge en route to register the company. Aldi supermarket's founder, Theo Albrecht, supposedly combined his name with 'discount'.

Names need to be distinctive and protectable (to register them as trademarks). Functional or descriptive names are difficult to register, as they may be deemed to be generic words commonly used by others (and therefore owned by everyone).

Once a short list of names has been generated, a name search is carried out in the target market (and potential target markets) to check to see if anyone has registered these names already in the same business sector. After that, some simple concept testing in each target market reveals whether the brand name has any negative meanings in different languages, as Coca-Cola discovered in China (see Chapter 9). Without these checks, subsequent opportunities for global expansion are curtailed without an expensive and time-consuming rebranding exercise.

Brand logos

The crucifix, the hammer and sickle, the swastika, the red cross or a national flag immediately arouse emotions, feelings, images or interpretations of some kind. Logos are a language (sometimes international) of emotional response. Symbols, shapes and colour all have conscious and unconscious meanings. Visual symbols or devices can also be powerful as a means of increasing awareness by facilitating easy recognition. A logo can act as a focal point to summarize or encapsulate an organization, although it should not be too complex. If an identity needs too much explaining, then it isn't working. The acid test for a logo is: distinctive, easily recognizable, memorable and reducible (can work when reduced on to a business card or postage stamp). It should work in black and white as well as colour, since many corporate images appear in black and white in the press. Ideally, the logo should also be symbolic, or relevant to the business, but this is rarely the case. With the growth of the internet it is increasingly important that it works well on-screen, as well as in its more traditional applications.

'When you develop a brand the primary audience for it is the employees.'

Ken Morris, Siehel+Gale

Logos are an important part of the brand identity and often are described as a key component of brand equity; Nike's swoosh and McDonald's Golden Arches help audiences and customers to recognize the brand instantly and also help to differentiate the brand. A logo also acts as a stamp or guarantee. It should, ideally, reflect the values of the brand. Logos can protect a trademark when combined with generic words (as generic words themselves are usually not protectable on their own, but the combination of the words with the logo may be). Good logos (unique, easily recognizable, relevant and well maintained) become icons, and not only are they recognizable but even parts of them are recognizable, such as the Heinz chevron or the 'M' in Marlboro.

Don King's hair

World boxing promoter Don King's elevated hairstyle (brushed up six inches or more into the air) makes him stand out in a crowded post-fight boxing ring. His unique visual symbol helps to ensure that he is easily recognized and seen to be involved with the big fights.

Colour also plays an important part. Colours instantly access our emotions (think of what the colour red does to a bull). Colour also affects our physiological state and propensity to make a decision.

Logo development

The process of developing a logo is similar to the process of developing any aspect of marketing communications: brief, concept generation (and selection), concept development and finally launch or roll-out. In between each stage, research gives crucial feedback. This helps to select the best concept, which when guided by feedback (research) is developed into the final logo design. It does get one last check with more research before roll-out.

One UK design consultancy developed a new logo for Saudi Arabian Airlines that looked, to the uninitiated, distinctive, unique and easily recognizable. The logo contained golden palm trees, crossed Arabian swords and a crescent moon and appeared to be suitably upmarket and regal. In fact, it contained four major errors:

1 the wrong type of palm tree – Saudi Arabia is the number two producer of dates, but the palm tree shown was not a date palm tree;

2 the wrong type of sword – the traditional Saudi sword is a fighting sword, but the sword shown in the logo looked weak, old and ceremonial;

3 the wrong moon – the crescent of the new moon used by Saudi Arabia represents a new beginning, but the proposed crescent was that of an old moon, suggesting 'the end';

4 the wrong colour – the old green colour was replaced by cream, which represents hot, barren sand in the desert when Saudi Arabia was trying to irrigate the kingdom and make it green.

This confirms the need for designers to invest in detailed research before attempting to develop any design concepts. Designers who neither budget nor plan for research (or several stages of research) vastly increase the likelihood of problems. Worse still, if problems occur after implementation of a new design, the costs immediately spin out of control, and there is a highly embarrassed management team.

Research is also carried out into logo trends. In the 1970s, corporate images hardened. The 1980s saw them becoming soft and decorative. Some cynics say that, if you wanted to make an abstract organization look purposeful in the late 1980s, you gave it a face – preferably a neoclassical one. The Woolworths group, on the other hand, changed its name, logo and total identity to Kingfisher, which was certainly distinctive, easily recognizable, memorable, and symbolic of its progressive leadership expansion and growth potential (although some argued that the bird had a life expectancy of only one year and that robins and blue tits were more popular anyway). Bovis construction company chose a hummingbird, which again fitted the above criteria. Others suggest that there was a trend towards humanizing logos, since organizations are all about people.

More recently, there has been a trend towards purely graphic devices (in other words, away from figurative symbols). This has been driven by a number of factors. On the one hand, it is part of a general

FIGURE 2.6   The Prudential logo

FIGURE 2.7   The Shanks logo

shanks. waste solutions.

trend towards more direct communications, which has resulted in a stripping out of superfluous elements. On the other, the internet has become a more important channel of communication for many organizations. As Mark Wilson of identity specialists Bamber Forsyth says, 'The lower resolution of the internet and digital television has driven us towards simpler, highly graphic identity elements that are seen smaller, and in more places, than ever before'; see for example Google and Amazon.

Shanks & McEwan, a British waste management business, updated its identity at the turn of the millennium, simplifying its name and adopting a straightforward graphic logo. When introducing the new identity to staff, the company said:

We're linking the phrase 'waste solutions' to our name in order to emphasize that we are a problem-solving company. We're also using the 's' as our symbol to make the new identity more distinctive and memorable. The full stops within the logotype and after the 's' symbol are important. This is our way of saying that we're the last word in waste management.

The logo can be literal (eg Shell), a logotype (a stylized treatment of the company name with no additional symbol, eg Kellogg's), wordmarks that integrate a graphic element into the name (eg BHS), company initials (eg IBM) or purely abstract. Whichever type of logo is chosen, it is essential to research the choice carefully, particularly in global markets where symbols, colours and words can have very different meanings.

> ### End of logos?
>
> 'A logo today has turned out to be a warning sign of a commercial message. The trend is that it will disappear and be replaced by other non-conscious signals – everything from iPod's white ear plugs, to Tiffany's blue packaging, to the United Colors of Benetton photos or whatever you are imaging.
>
> If you look at Formula 1 today, you'll see that most of the Ferrari cars have these funny red-coloured bar codes. That is the secret logo from Marlboro. There's no logo, there's no name on it.'
>
> Martin Lindstrom, in Rothery (2009)

Roll-out/delivery

The roll-out of a brand requires far more than just press launches and lavish branding events. It starts internally; the whole organization needs to be mobilized. They must live and breathe the brand, starting with the CEO acting as brand champion and cascading down through the organization by:

- living the brand;
- linking operational targets to brand ratings;
- linking rewards to customer satisfaction and brands ratings;
- putting brand values in job specifications.

Living the brand means internalizing it and living its values. What a business does reveals its personality and values far more than any amount of advertising. Any significant disconnection between what an organization says about itself and what it actually does will seriously undermine people's relationship with the brand.

Living the brand occurs when employees actively and enthusiastically deliver the brand promise day in, day out. It helps if the brand and brand responsibilities are written into the job description of every member of the team. This is where marketing and HR work closely together. The brand effectively becomes everybody's business.

Do all employees know (and memorize) what the brand promise and brand values are? Do they know what the business stands for? Are they able to tell the brand story in a compelling way to different stakeholder audiences including shareholders, employees, customers and vendors? To ensure that a brand comes to life throughout the organization, ask whether you need structural or departmental changes. It is that important. Consider every aspect of the organization from employee behaviour to premises. Inject the brand DNA into your organization structure.

Motivate and train staff

Develop operational targets to build the brand. Try linking customer satisfaction scores and brand ratings to operational targets. (You should measure criteria that are important to customers, not those you think are important.) All staff are brand ambassadors.

Brand consistency stops a brand from splintering, diluting and ebbing away. Crystal-clear brand guidelines can include templates for all marketing collateral so that brochures, websites and signage are all consistently produced anywhere in the world. The brand guidelines also include the Pantone colours, size and layout of logos and straplines for a range of different uses, online and offline, as well as above and below the line.

> 'Nike bought its iconic "swoosh" logo for a mere $35 while Twitter paid iStockphoto less than $15 for its now famous bird logo.'
>
> Stampler (2013)

At first a new logo has little or no value because it has no franchise. First it must be associated with the right kind of images, and then its recognition levels can be developed (eg Lloyds Bank's black horse). This takes time, since initial reaction to change or anything new is often quite negative. Sometimes the initial reaction is one of upset, dislike or disgust, as the new logo does not fit in with the previous set of cognitions (and thereby creates 'cognitive dissonance' and possibly tension). The value of the logo eventually starts to increase as the years roll by and it becomes better understood. However, it helps enormously if internal marketing carefully brings staff on board throughout the development and ultimately before the launch.

Whether the logo trend is towards simplicity, swooshes or sharp-edged internationally understood symbols, the corporate identity demands careful management across all the points of public contact.

Brand maintenance

Creating a brand is relatively easy. The difficult part is maintaining it. Great brand managers constantly develop or reinvigorate the brand so that it is seen as relevant (not 'hip' or necessarily modern, but definitely always relevant to the target market). Remember, target markets move and change. The classic Lucozade drink once upon a time was positioned as a drink for sick children. As the market demographics moved from a disproportionately large number of children in the 1960s to a disproportionately large number of young adults in the 1980s, Lucozade repositioned itself as a healthy adult's drink. Today it has moved on again, twisting and tweaking itself to stay relevant to its key target market. Maintaining a brand requires vision, system, determination and people.

Mobilize staff and channel partners

The brand requires a system that mobilizes the entire organization. Bringing a brand to life requires a completely integrated approach beyond marketing. Operations and HR must develop a system that inspires and motivates all staff to support the brand. Ideally, job descriptions should explain the responsibilities that staff have to 'live the brand'. Operational targets can be linked to building and maintaining the brand (such as measuring relevant customer satisfaction). The brand needs to be embedded into the DNA of the business.

This, in turn, helps the company to live the brand, ensuring that all those crucial 'brand moments' (when the business interacts with the customer) actually reflect the brand. The primary audience for a brand is the employees – as they need to be mobilized to support it; then come the channel partners (distributors). Brand managers need to ensure that the brand is never compromised or tarnished on its journey to the end customer.

A fatal mistake some marketers make is to focus too heavily on external marketing communications (developing advertising campaigns, direct mail campaigns, websites and opt-in SMS campaigns to boost cross-selling and up-selling), rather than ensuring all customer touchpoints are consistently executed.

> ### Subconscious air travel worries?
>
> Attention to detailed design management can subconsciously influence air travellers. The same logo, typeface, primary and secondary colours and trim on all visual points of contact help to reassure the traveller, while reinforcing the airline's identity. The check-in desk logo, signs, colours and trims should be coordinated with the uniform (and badge), ticket holder, baggage tag and departure lounge carpets, right through to the plane's exterior graphics, interior carpet and even the trim on the china and linen. Without this coordinated corporate identity, cognitive dissonance can set in. There is a subconscious unease or discomfort created by the inconsistent messages. A coordinated identity reduces this often unconscious tension, which in turn creates a more satisfied passenger. The cohesive identity does not make the traveller leap off the plane and scream for joy on arrival, but it might make the subconscious difference next time around when choosing between two airlines if one offers a reassuring sense of order.

Instigate brand policing

Brand managers are guardians who need to ensure the brand is consistently used in all touchpoints. Brand policing is important. If an organization's identity is not coordinated or managed precisely, confusing signals go out to different audiences around the world. A splintered identity fragments the corporate image, which in turn dilutes the corporate presence among key audiences. The potential asset (corporate brand) depreciates to the point where it becomes a liability. The organization dilutes its presence and has an uncoordinated image. This sends out disorganized messages that weaken the initial or final impression left by the organization.

A logo displayed prominently in an office or on a letterhead makes a good strong statement, but it is the consistent 'echoing' of the logo, its exact primary and secondary colours, the specific typeface and the overall design style on the 'secondary format' of products, packages, business forms and employee uniforms, that provides the all-important, if subtle, consistent reinforcement.

There is a need to think it through in detail and then to police the usage of all visual points of contact. This is where a design manual guides managers in different buildings and in different countries to specify, in a consistent manner, the exact graphic requirement for every point of visual contact.

Sweaty identity

In corporate identity terms, attention to detail needs to spread beyond just graphics. The classic 1990 US Hall of Shame reported the following:
'To upgrade its image in 1982 AT&T told its repair people to wear dress shirts and ties, gave them attaché cases for their tools, and renamed them "system technicians". But Ma Bell didn't install air conditioning in its cars. So during the summer the technicians arrived on the job looking like they had just stepped out of a sauna. Said a union official, "It's hard to have corporate appeal if your shirt is wringing wet."'

Nash and Zull Products (1989)

The importance of consistency applies right across the communications spectrum. In John Murphy's book *Branding* (1991), Klaus Morwind Henkel points to consumer research that 'has indicated that a lack of consistency between the brand name, the packaging and the advertising is subconsciously recognized by the consumer and leads to a feeling of detachment, ultimately resulting in brandswitching'. So it is important to be consistent and to reinforce identity through all the appropriate points of public contact. This should include advertising and all elements of the communications mix, which includes permanent media like corporate headquarters.

The logo is just the tip of the iceberg. It is often the most visible part of an organization. A corporate identity scheme may have a logo at its heart, but it will generally include a whole array of other elements, often referred to as 'visual language'. This may include typefaces, a colour palette, the use of photography and illustrations, a layout style for using these items and even a particular style of written language, as well as briefs for interior design and exteriors of buildings (plus, today, eco-friendly building requirements).

A good corporate brand can help sales and boost employee relationships, financial relationships and media relationships during a crisis. Corporate branding, however, requires a lot more than just a corporate identity. The impact of a corporate identity programme goes far beyond a logo or a lick of paint. It influences almost every manifestation of an organization, its corporate headquarters, its staff and even the way they work. All of the components need to be in place. A new logo raises stakeholder expectations.

Boards, doors, logos and skunks

'A new letterhead and a new logo is no substitute for a new board of directors.'

Rodney Fitch (2003)

'Painting the lavatory door won't cure the plumbing.'

Bernstein (1984)

'If you take a lousy low-profile company and give it a major corporate revamp, you end up with a lousy high-profile company.'

Wally Olins (1989)

'Even if you paint out a skunk's stripes it will still smell extremely nasty.'

Source unknown

Corporate brands and sub-brands

An umbrella brand, such as the Virgin brand, can have various sub-brands, such as Virgin Atlantic and Virgin Trains. A corporate brand, such as GlaxoSmithKline (GSK), Unilever or Procter & Gamble (P&G), on the other hand, remains in the background and offers an endorsement, while a mainstream brand like Persil can have sub-brands such as Persil washing-up liquid and Persil powder.

Invest in the brand asset

Constant investment is also required to maintain a brand's profile and avoid it getting buried in the communications clutter. Some companies take the long-term, brand investment view; Coke is investing $65 million in sponsoring the Olympics from 2009 to 2020.

Constant reviews of brands, and in particular large portfolios of brands, can result in a major strategic consolidation of the brand portfolio, as in the case of Unilever when it cut its portfolio of 1,600 brands down to 400. Brands are under increased challenges today.

Brands fade as tastes change, unless of course they are maintained and nurtured carefully to meet the new market conditions. Even in steady-state markets where there are no great trends pulling the market away from the brand, marketers still need to ensure that it is policed carefully, particularly as a brand grows globally. Rigorous use of brand guidelines is required here to ensure that exactly the same features appear correctly anytime and anywhere.

Review the brand

Brands require constant reviews and investment of energies and money. They often need to be reinvented or reinvigorated to avoid being left behind by a fast-changing marketplace. A constant flow of market research should ensure the brand really addresses customers' deep needs, which change over time. Otherwise brands fade as tastes change. Constant market research also reveals how the brand is positioned against existing competition and new competitors. As Olins (1989) says, 'In a complex and changing company the corporate identity [for an overall company] bears a great

strain, twisting and turning to fit every new requirement. But a good corporate identity should last a generation.'

When does a brand identity become out of date? Can the business environment change and move away from the organization and its values, leaving behind the obsolete, irrelevant and even damaging corporate identity? When do the staff and other audiences get tired of it? Mergers and acquisitions sometimes necessitate a new corporate identity. Occasionally, legal reasons force a change. Sometimes overseas ambitions are restricted by the use of a home-grown logo (eg BT's old logo clashed with that of overseas companies).

Shell reviews and updates its corporate identity. The shell device has served it well, despite its being a petrol company with a 'high explosive' name. Global markets are constantly moving and changing, so much so that some organizations fear they are being left behind. A review and redesign can help an organization to keep abreast of trends and avoid being left isolated by a redundant identity.

Sometimes new brand identities are developed simply because old management wants to say something new or a new CEO wants to announce he or she has arrived. This is a dangerous game, as a new brand identity or a new corporate identity raises expectations that the organization has new ways of working, new customer benefits or new customer experiences.

FIGURE 2.8   The Shell logo and its redesigns

Aggressive hand-held torch of learning gets the chop

The National Union of Teachers' 25-year-old 'hand-held torch of learning' was considered to have become 'too strident, aggressive and uncaring, with none-too-desirable connotations of the Conservative party and the Greek fascist party. Although it was designed in the 1960s, it had a 1930s look. It appeared that the time was right to move the logo on but keep it relevant and maintain the link with the union's heritage. The updated design shows an outstretched hand embraced by the spelt-out words of the NUT, tying the symbol together as one cohesive form, either male or female, adult or child, to avoid alienation.

FIGURE 2.9

Hand-held torch of learning

Constant watch: the customer experience

Brand maintenance also requires careful attention to the customer experience (which as we've seen is often very poor). Poor product quality and sloppy service destroy brands more quickly than any large advertising budget can build them. Unacceptable product or service quality, complicated order forms, late delivery, incomprehensible customer service agents and error-laden websites all destroy a brand. Slow e-mail responses damage the brand. Non-responses can kill it.

Attention to the customer experience both offline and online is important. Online brands still deliver offline (eg Amazon books), hence marketers monitor the offline aspects carefully also. And all brands (online and offline) have opportunities to extend the brand experience online by layering in new and exciting value-adding benefits. They add some 'sizzle'. Embellishing and extending the brand experience online can be achieved with 'sizzle', which cannot be found offline.

Nurturing brands can include lavishing wonderful brand experiences on customers, otherwise known as experiential marketing. It also includes engaging customers and moving them up into higher levels of brand engagement (see Chapter 1, 'The ladder of engagement').

Finally there is the experience – the quality of the experience, both online and offline, directly affects the brand and its image. Remember, sloppy websites, unanswered e-mails and comments, unpleasant receptionists and any other touchpoints can damage the brand. Many marketers now see the online opportunity to build both the brand image and the overall company value.

> In just a few seconds sloppy websites destroy brands that took years to build.

Social media now engages the customer in new ways (as discussed in Chapter 1). A brand's own website can add deeper, richer brand experiences by adding some 'sizzle' (Chaffey and Smith, 2012).

> Ask 'What experience could a website deliver that would really wow customers?'

What experience could a website deliver that would really add value for customers, be truly unique and be representative of the brand? Ultimately ask 'How can my website help my customers (or other stakeholders)?' Here are a few examples:

- A camera company can help customers to take better photographs by simulating taking photographs with different settings and allowing customers to compare and contrast the results (and can also give tips on how to maintain cameras and protect films and photos, and invite customers to send their best photos in for a competition).

- A travel company can give you a 'virtual friend'. After you tell the company what your interests are (via an online questionnaire), the 'friend' can suggest ideas for things you would like to do in the cities you choose to explore.
- Cosmetic companies offer online games, screensavers, viral e-mails, video clips and soundtracks to help customers use the products.
- Food companies offer printable recipes, video demonstrations and discussion forums, as well 'ask the expert' sessions.
- Chocolate companies generate ideas for desserts (using the chocolates), dinner party games and designs for table layouts.

Create customer engagement

If marketers understand customer engagement better than their competitors, then this helps them develop brand loyalty. How else can the ideal customer engage with the brand? As discussed in Chapter 1, the ideal customer, or most valuable customer, does not have to be someone who buys a lot. They could be an influencer who may be a small irregular buyer who posts ratings and reviews. The reviews can influence another 100 people. 'Engaged customers' are probably going to become brand zealots if they are kept engaged.

Marketers can easily monitor the type, quantity and frequency of blog posts, forum discussions, reviews, profile updates, etc. This identifies opportunities and also acts as an early warning system to any possible future problems. Consider targeting brand evangelists rather than just purchasers.

A customer who doesn't care about the product or service is likely to be less committed or less emotionally attached to the firm supplying the product or service. On the other hand, a customer who is engaging is likely to be more emotionally connected to the brand. Marketers need to know about the sentiment, opinion and affinity a person has towards a brand. This is often expressed through repeat visits, purchases, product ratings, reviews, blogs and discussion forums and, ultimately, the person's likelihood to recommend a friend.

Ask 'How well are we measuring engagement amongst different online audiences?' and then close the loop by using the data to identify the advocates and deliver more relevant communications.

> Engaged customers = customer engagement = stronger brands.

Brand expansion/strategy

Brand extensions and the brand portfolio

There are few single-product companies. Many companies start up that way, but they soon develop other products as they grow and markets fragment. A product line is a string of products grouped together for marketing or technical reasons. Guinness started as a single-product company. Since then it has extended the product line to fill market needs as they emerged. It has also expanded beyond the basic product line of beers to offer whiskeys, soft drinks and more: different lines of product.

Add all the product lines together and you get the product mix. Finding the right product mix is a subtle balancing act. How far should a product line be extended? How many different lines should be in the product group?

Advantages

'Brand (or line) extension is attractive but dangerous' (Smith 2003). There are advantages and disadvantages lurking behind this apparently easy option. Extending an existing brand name on to a new product is one of many different ways of increasing sales. Some feel that it reduces the risk of launching an unknown brand. Using a recognized brand name on a new product can give the new product immediate presence in the marketplace – customers will recognize, trust and try the new product more easily. This also creates savings in advertising and other promotions, so as the original product matures the extended brand ensures some continuity and survival of the brand in the longer run. Generally, brand extensions work if the new product actually satisfies a real relevant need amongst customers and they like the idea. Ultimately the new product should enhance the promise of the original brand as opposed to cannibalizing it. Careful consideration must be given to what happens if the extension fails.

Brand extension is a tempting option, as it uses the same sales team with the same distribution channels and often the same customers. It can also fill any unoccupied positions in the market, which might otherwise invite unwanted competitors. Finally, a full product line builds the image of the complete player, a big player, which in turn suggests reliability.

Disadvantages

But there are disadvantages lurking behind brand and line extensions. A low-quality product will damage the original brand's reputation. A really good new product can also cannibalize the original product if the new product merely takes sales away from the old one. When contemplating brand extension, ask how much of the 'extra sales' actually replace existing sales of the original product. Constant brand extensions may dilute the brand's strength and its unique positioning, particularly if the extensions are not appropriate to the central brand. When easyJet extended into easyInternetcafes it was reported to have lost £75 million (Taylor, 2004), whereas easyJet Holidays appears to be a better fit. Although Virgin is another successful company and has enjoyed a variety of brand extensions, some of them have failed, including Virgin Vodka, Virgin Jeans, Virgin Brides, Virgin Balloons and Virgin Cosmetics.

Failed extensions

'Unfortunately, the hard truth is that many brand extensions don't work. Each brand has its own special positioning. The extension won't succeed if it works against that. Any time a brand is extended, its focus gets blurred in the minds of consumers. When the image is unclear, the original promise is broken. When the promise is broken, the brand loses value and me.'

Jacobson and Knapp (2008)

In a sense, product deletion should be a standard activity, as companies constantly replace old products with improved ones. Some corporations like to balance the product portfolio by ensuring they have a minimum of 30 per cent of 'new products' (products developed in the last five years). Phasing out and deleting products that have had their day is a delicate task. They have to be withdrawn carefully and gracefully without damaging employee morale or upsetting small groups of customers who may still

want spare parts or simply to continue consuming the product. Interestingly, one of the world's best-marketed companies, Unilever, chopped its product portfolio from 1,600 to 400 in 2004.

Although criticized by some, the Boston Matrix can help to balance the product portfolio, as it helps managers identify which products generate surplus cash, which need extra marketing resources to support them and which need a lot of resources. 'Cash cows' (high market share in a low-growth market) generate the surplus cash that in turn funds other products, such as the high-growth 'star' products. Low-growth (and low-market-share) 'dogs' often absorb a disproportionate amount of management resources. This analysis is from a cash-flow perspective as opposed to that of the customers.

Riezebos (2003) on the other hand analyses a brand portfolio from a competitor perspective. Different types of brands have different roles to play within the brand portfolio. Bastion brands are the key brands, usually the most profitable, with a large market share. Their success attracts competitors. Some companies expand their portfolios to protect their brands by introducing 'flanker brands' and 'fighter brands'. The flanker brand may be priced differently or have a different set of attributes and tends to fend off any new competitors that are considering occupying that space. Fighter brands are lower priced and compete with existing or potential competitors trying to occupy lower price points (the quality perceptions need to be shifted downwards so as not to dilute the bastion brand). Many organizations prefer to lose some premium-priced brand sales to an internal less profitable brand than to lose the sales to competitors. However, today many companies of a certain size reject brands that will not become star performers, as they prefer to direct their limited resources to major winners. The tasks of product extinction and extension require rigorous analysis of customers, competitors and overall trends. The marketer's task of being the guardian of the brand is a challenging one.

Brand summary and the challenges ahead

Twenty-first-century brands face new challenges, including hyper-competitive markets, unknown competitors (category-less and borderless), short-ened product life cycles, more demanding, time-pressed and information-fatigued customers, media fragmentation and message clutter, anti-brand pressure groups, own brands and two other internal challenges – short-termism and fear of the boardroom.

Sloppy brand self-destruction

Some brands deliver inconsistent experiences across many channels as well as the real product experi-ence not matching the promoted brand experience. Winning, regaining or even retaining brand loyalty is a major challenge for all marketers. The challenge grows 'when the consumers that brands are trying to influence are often so inconsistent about their own sense of purpose. The secret to creating an in-fluential brand? Be honest. Deliver a great product or service' (Gabay, 2012).

> 'Any brand that believes it has decisively "got" it right is the one that never will.'
>
> Gabay (2012)

The rise of the anti-brand

A direct challenge to brands are the 'ethical anti-branders', who attack premium-priced branded training shoes (allegedly made in sweatshops in the Far East).

Various anti-brand feelings have been aroused by many publications, ranging from Vance Packard's 1957 classic *The Hidden Persuaders* to Eric Schlosser's *Fast Food Nation* (2002) to Robert Frank's *Luxury Fever* (2000) to *The World Is Not for Sale* (2001) by José Bové (a French farmer who is best known for vandalizing a McDonald's restaurant) and François Dufour. Brands are vulnerable to a rising tide of antipathy to branding and marketing.

The demise of major corporations like Enron has further fuelled a cynicism towards big business. However, Naomi Klein's *No Logo: Taking aim at the brand bullies* (2000) articulated a certain kind of brand frustration where global brands represent, in her words, 'a fascist state where we all salute the logo and have little opportunity for criticism be-cause our newspapers, TV stations, internet servers, street and retail spaces are all controlled by multi-national corporate interests'. The ubiquitous global brand bullies effectively reduce the colourful variety of choice and force a grey cultural homogeneity on customers instead of an array of interesting local alternatives. Even the *Economist* magazine back in 2001 pointed the finger at today's global businesses: 'So companies are switching from producing prod-ucts to marketing aspirations, images and lifestyles. They are trying to become weightless, shedding physical assets by shifting production from their own factories in the first world to other people's in the third.'

This provides all the more reasons for brands and the businesses behind them to behave ethically and to demonstrate publicly their social responsibil-ity. This includes environmental policies (and actions), supporting charitable endeavours and local communities, racial integration, not supplying or contributing to military regimes, and political dona-tions (see Chapter 11).

And of course there are the brand haters who create anti-brand websites dedicated to venting their frustrations and anger about certain brands, usually resulting from alleged poor customer service, eg **www.aolsucks.com**, sometimes even without consuming the brand, simply because they don't like it, eg **www.ihatemanunited.com**. As Dell has demonstrated by listening to these criticisms, addressing the reasonable issues and fixing them can strengthen a brand and grow its relations and sales.

Do brands reflect our own instability?

'Everyone needs a sense of purpose. To have a cause, to feel that we belong and are admired. Brands promise to fill the voids between who we are and what we could become. But by putting so much belief on which brand is in today but out tomorrow, we reflect our own instability. People increasingly judge others by what they have, rather than who they are. How much a person is esteemed is measured by the boots they wear, rather than the individual they are.'

Gabay (2012)

The rise of the own brand

As major retailers flex their muscles and demand that suppliers also create and deliver the retailers' own brand in almost every category, it is easy to understand why brand owners are concerned, particularly when they have to deliver a constantly high-quality own brand also. Many retailers' brands are so strong that customers are happy to give them more and more share of their wallets. Look at Tesco: what can't they sell to customers now those customers trust the brand to deliver a consistent quality at reasonable prices?

The brands do, however, have a source of continual competitive advantage, and that is continuous innovation. Although own brands are getting smarter and smarter, Saatchi & Saatchi CEO Kevin Roberts (2009) says:

> The game has changed. Own labels deliver quality. They are as strong in many categories as traditional consumer brands. But will they deliver innovation? No. This is where real marketing comes into play. A big retailer cannot possibly develop the innovation in a category that a P&G, Unilever or a Nestlé can. So as long as those companies continue to keep their core, their focus on innovation, they will continue to develop new value in this reclaimed world.

The rise of people brands, humanity and product switching

'"People are now brands and brands are now people" said Brian Solis (2015). Some see this a good thing since it is all about human to human. This evolution has been guiding our society back into one that requires a more personal approach. It is time for a reminder about our humanity.

Product switching happens faster than ever. Customers are ready to move on unless they have one thing – an undying relationship with a person or people at your brand who made them feel uniquely special.'

Kramer (2014)

Social media

Each tweet you send is either building or destroying your brand. The tone, content and timing of a tweet impacts how an audience perceives you. The same applies to Facebook, Instagram, Pinterest and so on. Brands that do not have crystal clear social media guidelines will find that social media can destroy the very essence of their own business – the brand and how it helps its customers.

The experience divide and leveraging advocacy

What you say your brand is and what others may share are different. This is what Brian Solis calls the 'experience divide'. This, if ignored, can destroy a brand. We need to create customer experiences that firstly they want and secondly want to share. As Solis says, 'If we're not creating the types of experiences we want people to have and share, we're simply reacting to them.' And this is missing the social media opportunity.

Solis continues: 'Positive experiences feel good to express outwardly, too, though we're not innately inclined to share them. NB it's in the business's best interest for consumers to share these positive experiences, because we know that they define the ultimate moment of truth – the moment when the consumer enters into a partnership with the brand.'

Solis suggests that your strategy for loyalty and advocacy determines the future of the brand. So do you have a system to reward advocates?

> 'Do you have a system to reward advocates?… particularly when they define the "ultimate moment of truth" – the moment when the consumer enters into a partnership with the brand.'
>
> Solis (2015)

Short-term sales versus long-term brand building

Brands are not for the short term. Think of them like people. They are strategic assets that need to be nurtured and grown over the long term. After that, relationships can last a lifetime and beyond, as some brands are handed down from generation to generation (if the brands manage to stay relevant to the needs of the next generation). There is a constant tension between sales and marketing and, for that matter, finance and marketing. Quarterly results-driven businesses require quarterly results, which usually means seeing quarterly growth in sales and profits. Brands do not deliver quick returns, particularly new and repositioned brands. They take time to research and develop. They take time to build relationships. Although some brands have developed in one or two years, these are exceptional. Certainly brands emerging within a quarter is, even today, highly unlikely.

The impatience of the CFO or the board or the shareholders may jeopardize the long-term work of the brand builder. This also manifests itself in the advertising debate: whether a campaign is sales or brand building. Ad campaigns can of course do either, but rarely can do both really well. One usually takes priority. Yes, campaigns can deliver sales and grow a brand, but each objective has different priorities. Brands are for the long term and can secure higher sales, higher prices and higher profits. These are some of the factors that can bring the marketer back into the boardroom.

Brands – the bridge between marketing, finance and the boardroom

Marketers may have slipped from being the potential heroes of the boardroom back in the 1980s when brands were suddenly touted as a 'surefire means of differentiation in the face of increased competitive pressures and rampant product proliferation activities. They were secret weapons of sorts: legally-protectable assets that brought unrivalled powers to the firms that developed them' (Madden, Fehle and Fournier, 2002).

A study revealed that shareholders should insist on systematic performance feedback on branding. It actually suggested systematic performance feedback on all key items in the balance sheet including branding. However, it suggested that very few companies had this optimal balance between financial performance and branding (Ohnemus, 2009). The report went on to say that 'the board of directors should systematically assess and monitor the strategic branding position of their company and how their branding investments are performing against

key competitors'. Board directors acknowledge the value of brands but do not understand how they are built and sustained or, in particular, how marketing makes this happen.

What has marketing got to do with brand building?

'To quote David Bell, Chairman of the *Financial Times*: "The value of brands as shareholder assets has been widely recognized, but the crucial role of marketing and advertising in building this brand equity and so enhancing these assets now on the balance sheet is still not fully recognized."'

Beenstock (1998)

Has it improved since?

The irony of it all is that, now that brands appear on the balance sheet, they are recognized as a financial asset of the business, yet budgets required to grow them are considered to be 'expenses rather than investments' (Ohnemus, 2009).

When Harvard's Madden, Fehle and Fournier (2002) suggested that 'the demonstration of brand value to stockholders would prove most useful in reconceptualizing marketing from expense to investment', an opportunity knocked for marketers. But the lingering, unanswered question remains to this day: 'Do brand-building investments really pay off? Lacking conclusive evidence concerning branding and the bottom line, brand "investments" remain "expenses" and the promise of the brand remains unfulfilled.'

Marketers must learn the language of finance and apply it to marketing. Marketing language and jargon have been charged as 'inaccessible and disconnected from the financial metrics by which firms are ultimately steered' (Davis, 2001). If there is no common language, there is no communication and with that comes no understanding of marketing's crucial role in brand building.

Marketers and the language of finance

So here it is. ISO 10668 (International Organization for Standardization) standard on monetary brand valuation requires legal, market research and financial analysis must be completed in determining a brand's value. Since 2004, International Financial Reporting Standard (IFRS) 3 has required that on acquisition of a brand, the purchase price paid must be allocated to the individual assets acquired for inclusion in the balance sheet of the acquirer at their fair values. 'The requirement to conduct brand valuations for financial compliance purposes has forced CFOs and financial regulators to take brand valuation seriously' (Haigh, 2011).

Prior to 1988, brand values were never shown in balance sheets. In fact in 1988 Hovis chose to put a financial value on its brand and then add it in the balance sheet as part of a takeover defence. This triggered a major debate that has been running ever since. Today, there are several approaches to valuing a brand including the market approach, the cost approach and the income approach (Roberts 2011).

Gone are the days when brand managers were logo cops making ads and briefing PR firms. Nowadays they are more likely to be rubbing shoulders with tax advisers and investment bankers. Brands have become big business and managing them has become a branch of high finance (Haigh 2011).

The words of the late great Peter Doyle (2000) still ring true for many marketers today:

Marketing managers rarely see the necessity of linking marketing spending to the financial value of the business. Given today's enormous pressure on top managers to generate higher returns to shareholders, it is hardly surprising that the voice of marketing gets disregarded. The situation will never be resolved until marketing professionals learn to justify marketing strategies in relevant financial terms.

If managers can show that marketing will increase returns to shareholders, marketing will obtain a much more pre-eminent role in the

boardrooms of industry. The discipline itself will also obtain more respect for its rigor and direction.

Marketers have much to do. But, with some work, the doors of the boardroom will be flung wide open so they can secure funds to develop great brands and, in return, deliver dividends back to shareholders.

Conclusion

Brands are being challenged. However, they are powerful assets that generate many benefits to both an organization and its customers. Surprisingly, many brands allow themselves to self-destruct with sloppy service and inconsistent brand applications. Brand components include name, logo, colours, positioning, promise, personality, values, association and experience. Brand creation is a process that starts with a brief and goes through concept generation, concept development and roll-out. Copious research is carried out before and after each step. Brand maintenance focuses on the customer experience, extending it online and considering customer engagement as a way to move customers up the ladder of engagement towards becoming brand zealots. Experiential marketing is also considered. Finally, brand expansion/strategy has both advantages and disadvantages. The strategic corporate brand is also explored.

> ### Strong brands survive through careful management
> It is no accident that these brands have been around for over 100 years: Bass, Coke, Kellogg's Corn Flakes, Guinness, Pears Soap.

Key points from Chapter 2

- Brands help customers and the organizations behind them.
- Branding and why it is a strategic issue and can create competitive advantage.
- There is a disciplined approach to the brand-building process.
- Brands, like any other asset, need to be maintained and require resources.

References and further reading

Anderson, C (2006) *The Long Tail: Why the future of business is selling less of more*, Hyperion Books, New York

Atkin, D (2004) New priests for the new religion, *Marketer*, September

Aufreiter, N, Elzinga, D and Gordon, J (2003) Better brands, *McKinsey Quarterly*, 4

Banham, Russ (1998) Making your mark: Time for finance to play a role in brand management, *CFO: The magazine for senior financial executives*, **14** (3), 1 March

Bayley, S and Mavity, R (2008) *Life's a Pitch*, Corgi Books, London

Beenstock, S (1998) Raising brands' stock in the City, *Marketing*, 26 November

Bernstein, D (1984) *Company Image and Reality: A critique of corporate communications*, Holt, Rinehart and Winston, London

Bové, J and Dufour, F (2001) *The World Is Not for Sale*, Verso Books, London

Braun, T (2004) *The Philosophy of Branding*, Kogan Page, London

Brun-Jensen, P (2014) Next-gen social analytics are transforming digital marketing, *Adweek*, 22 September

Chaffey, D and Smith, PR (2013) *Emarketing Excellence*, 4th edn, Routledge, London

Clifton, R (2004) The big debate, *Marketer*, July/August

Davis, S (2001) Taking control of your brand's destiny, *Brandweek*, 15 October

Doyle, P (2000) *Value-Based Marketing*, Wiley, Chichester

Economist (1998) The rebirth of IBM – blue is the colour, 6 June

Economist (2001) Who's wearing the trousers? 6 September

Eltvedt, H and Flores, L (2005) Beyond online advertising – lessons about the power of brand websites to build and expand brands, ESOMAR Online Conference, Montreal, June

Farrell, S (2008) A million dollar branding secret, How-to Internet Marketing Network

Fauconnier, C (2006) Humanising the marketplace: A manifesto for brand growth, *Admap*, **471**, April

Fitch, R (2003) in Balmer, J and Greyser, S (2003) *Revealing the Corporation: Perspectives on identity image reputation*, Routledge, London

Fletcher, W (2010) Author, lecturer and former chairman of the Royal Institution in conversation with PR Smith

Frank, R H (2000) *Luxury Fever: Money and happiness in an era of excess*, Princeton University Press, Princeton, NJ

Gabay, J (2012) Q&A: Jonathan Gabay, The Marketer, p 50, 29 June, available in hard copy from the CIM library

Haigh, D (2011) A brand new approach, *The Marketer*, February, available in hard copy from the CIM library

Harris Interactive (2006) Second annual *Customer Experience Impact Report*

Hooker, S (1991) Applying psychology to market research: The theory of raised expectations, *Market Research Society Newsletter*, January

Jacobson, T and Knapp, K (2008) Brand extensions, Vistage chief executive organization online papers [online] www.vistage.com

Jenkins, N (1991) *The Business of Image*, Kogan Page, London

Jones, B (2001) *The Big Idea*, HarperCollins, London

Kanter, R (2009) The downsides of branding, 23 July [online] http://blogs.hbr.org/kanter/2009/07/the-downsides-of-branding.html

Kapferer, J (2008) *The New Strategic Brand Management*, 4th edn, Kogan Page, London

Kramer, B (2014) A return to simplicity, empathy and imperfection in communication: human to human #H2H, *BrianSolis*, 25 February [online] http://www.briansolis.com/2014/02/return-simplicity-empathy-imperfection-communication-human-human-h2h/

Klein, N (2000) *No Logo: Taking aim at the brand bullies*, Flamingo, London

Kumar, A J (2012) How to effectively rebrand your social media profiles, *Social Media Examiner*, 5 November

Le Pla, F J, Davis, S and Parker, L (2003) *Brand Driven: The route to integrated branding through great leadership*, Kogan Page, London

Lindstrom, M (2005) *Brand Sense*, Kogan Page, London

Madden, T, Fehle, F and Fournier, S (2002) Brands matter: An empirical investigation of brand-building activities and the creation of shareholder value, Working paper, Harvard Business School, Boston, MA

Millward Brown Optimor (2010) *BrandZ Top 100 Most Valuable Global Brands*, Millward Brown Optimor, New York

Mose, M (2003) *United We Brand: How to create a cohesive brand that's seen, heard, and remembered*, Harvard Business School Publishing, Boston, MA

Murphy, J (ed) (1991) *Branding: A key marketing tool*, Macmillan, London

Nash and Zull Products (1989) *1990 US Hall of Shame*, Universal Press Syndicate, Kansas City

Neumeier, M (2007) *Zag*, New Riders, Berkeley, CA

Ohmae, K (1994) Interview with PR Smith, *Marketing CDs*, PRSmith.org

Ohnemus, L (2009) B2B Branding: A financial burden for shareholders? *Business Horizons*, 52 (2), pp 159–66

Olins, W (1989) *Corporate Identity: Making business strategy visible through design*, Thames & Hudson, London

Olins, W (1996) *The New Guide to Identity*, Gower, Aldershot

Olins, W (2003) *On Brand*, Thames & Hudson, London

Packard, V ([1957] 1960) *The Hidden Persuaders*, Penguin Books, Harmondsworth

Peters, T (2003) *Re-imagine*, Dorling Kindersley, London

PRTV (1993) *Corporate Image Video*, PRTV, London

Reynolds, J, Cuthbertson, C and Bell, R (2004) *Retail Strategy: The view from the bridge*, Elsevier Butterworth-Heinemann, Oxford

Riezebos, R (2003) *Brand Management: A theoretical and practical approach*, Pearson, Harlow

Roberts, K (2009) Short cuts (part 2), 6 July, formerly at www.saatchikevin.com; see hard copy journal kept in Chartered Institute of Marketing library (www.cim.co.uk)

Roberts, S (2011) Brand valuation: methodologies, *Intellectual Property Magazine*, Feb [online] http://shop.bsigroup.com/upload/Standards%20&%20Publications/IPM_Brand_Valuation_article.pdf

Ronay, A (2004) Emotional brands, *Marketer*, 5, September

Rothery, G (2009) All in the mind, *Marketing Age*, 3 (6), November

Schlosser, E (2002) *Fast Food Nation*, Penguin Books, Harmondsworth

Smilansky, S (2008) *Experiential Marketing*, Kogan Page, London

Smith, PR (2003) *Great Answers to Tough Marketing Questions*, Kogan Page, London

Solis, B (2015) Crossing the experience divide: Creating positive, lasting experiences is a crucial mandate for any brand [online] www.Brian Solis.com, 12 Jan

Stampler, L (2013) How much the world's most iconic logos cost to design, *Yahoo Finance*, 27 Mar [online] https://ca.finance.yahoo.com/news/how-much-the-world-s-most-iconic-logos-cost-companies-to-design-them-151333867.html

Taylor, D (2004) More bangers for your bucks, *Marketer*, 5, September

Universal McCann (2007) Power to the people: Tracking the impact of social media wave, 2.0, May

Valentine, V (1988) *Signs and Symbols*, Survey, Market Research Society, London

Yeong, C L and Yu, H-y (2006) Chinese president's itinerary for U.S. visit: Gates first, Bush later, *International Herald Tribune*, 13 April

03
Customer relationship management

LEARNING OBJECTIVES

By the end of this chapter you will be able to:

- Discuss the importance of relationship marketing and how CRM creates competitive advantage
- See how social and CRM are a natural fit
- Outline the CRM planning process
- Understand the benefits and resources required by CRM
- Identify and avoid the classic CRM errors
- Present the case of long-term brand building vs short-term sales growth

Introduction to CRM   70
What is CRM?   70
What is Social CRM?   70

The power of CRM   71
Company benefits   72

What causes CRM failure?   73
Poor CRM process skills   74
Poor project management skills   74
Lack of motivation and training   74
Forgetting customer needs   74
IT and other hijackers   75
Other hijackers create a fragmented
   approach   75
Angry impatient customers   75

What causes CRM success?   76
The CRM philosophy   76
The ladder of loyalty   76
Permission-based marketing   76

CRM components required   77
Processes   79
Database   82
Personalization and tailored offers   88
Human architecture   90
Credibility and trust   91

CRM creation and maintenance   91
Writing a CRM brief   91
CRM system creation, development, testing
   and roll-out   94
CRM maintenance   94

Costs and timescales   95
Control issues   95
Measuring customer satisfaction   96

CRM summary and challenges   97

Key points from Chapter 3   97

References and further reading   98

Further information   99

Introduction to CRM

Your marketing strategy should, amongst other things, highlight which has priority: Customer Acquisition, or Customer Retention (and therefore influences what resources will be allocated to each) in various markets.

> A customer's LTV (Life Time Value) might be worth sales of, say, 20 cars or 20 mobile phones (during the customer's life). Obviously this is worth a lot more than selling one car or one mobile and hence why customer retention is deemed to be, on average, at least six times more profitable than customer acquisition. It is therefore, generally speaking, worth investing in customer retention.
>
> Smith (2014)

So deciding how to split resources between customer acquisition and customer retention is a strategic decision which comes from your overall marketing strategy. Once a company embraces customer retention (or LTV) the culture becomes more customer-centric, and part of this is carefully anticipating and planning when a customer is due to move back into the repeat buying cycle; marketers can help them with exactly the right information at exactly the right time on exactly the right platform. Marketers can optimize their offers, block out competition with timely/relevant service and keep nurturing the customer relationship in between times. Customer retention depends on customer relationship management.

What is CRM?

Some call it customer relationship management (CRM); others call it customer experience management (CEM); others call it customer managed relationships (CMR). Regardless of its name, it is a strategic decision to invest in and develop your customer relationship process. Customer retention is different to customer acquisition as it requires different messages, incentives, and channels... in fact a different communications mix. Given that it has been suggested that it is six times more profitable to sell to an existing customer than to a new customer, it follows that the decision to invest in CRM is a relatively easy strategic choice. What may be more challenging is choosing and executing a

suitable CRM system that connects to all customer touchpoints, both online and offline. Contacting customers pre, during and post sales with relevant, tempting and timely offers, as well as responding to customers' direct and indirect (on social platforms) comments requires carefully planned systems. Some of this may be automated; we'll look at this later.

There is a direct overlap between nurturing customer relationships and nurturing a brand (see Chapter 2), and growing the longer-term profitability of the business. Carefully managed brands help customers develop good relationships with those brands. CRM is a set of processes, usually linked to a database, that help an organization keep in contact with customers and deal with their queries, complaints, purchases, suggestions and post-purchase issues as well as seeking to nurture loyal customers and advocates. Today, this involves multiple channels, particularly social media. Hence the term: Social CRM.

What is Social CRM?

Firstly Social CRM is a strategic decision, similar to the strategic decision to engage customers (and visitors) at different levels via the ladder of engagement (for more on this, see Chapter 1, p. 17). Essentially Social CRM integrates social media conversations into your CRM systems. Ideally, it links all of these conversations with telephone calls, e-mails and online chats into information to understand and service customers better. Probably the simplest form is training (and motivating) some of the customer service telephone team to help customers online.

Customer relationships – same as any relationship

Think about how personal relationships grow stronger and stronger: listening, understanding, responding and communicating. Understanding what is important and what makes a difference; delivering it regularly; never breaking the promise; occasionally surprising or even delighting the other person; caring about the person; helping the person when things go wrong; always being there for them. The same applies to customer relationships. It is not rocket science.

Even remembering someone's name makes a difference. People generally like it when their names are remembered, particularly when their preferences and needs are also remembered. How nice is it when a waiter or receptionist remembers your name? 'Your name is the most important sound in the world' say the classic sales training programmes. Remembering names and needs (and satisfying them) helps to build relationships. This applies to a small business with 50 customers or a website with millions of customers.

Remembering names and needs

Remembering a customer's particular needs and providing the right response is rarely the result of guesswork. In the case of a company with a small number of customers, it requires a good memory, good interpretive skills and attention to detail. In the case of an organization with many customers on a database, it is largely dependent on accurate analysis and building up valuable insights. As customers are more demanding and have more channels of communication, organizations simply have to be able to respond to them continuously – wherever, whenever and however required. A system is required, whether automated or manual.

Business is entering the post-'ad loyalty' era, where the power of advertising is waning as other communication tools, particularly social media, can generate attitudinal shifts. The old loyalty model used advertising primarily to build brand awareness and, ultimately, to build a lasting bond with customers. Securing loyalty today is a never-ending process requiring outstanding CRM and ongoing customer engagement.

> 'Do you have a system for rewarding your advocates?
>   If not, why not?'
>
>   PR Smith

Rewarding customers

A lot of CRM is about serving customers properly and occasionally rewarding them, identifying advocates and regularly rewarding them in a carefully planned process, and finally, identifying potential defectors and stopping them (that is, if they are worth keeping). Not all customers are equal. Some

are ideal and some you lose money on. Those ideal customers who buy a lot, recommend you a lot and give useful feedback, deserve to be rewarded. After all they generate six times more profit than new customers and they spread awareness and positive attitudes, so why wouldn't you identify them, contact them and surprise them just like when Canadian bank, TD, decided to 'wow' their customers. Watch the video on **www.PRSmith.org/blog** called 'Customer retention isn't boring – here's wow'.

FIGURE 3.1   'Customer retention isn't boring – here's wow'! Watch the video on PR Smith's blog at **http://PRSmith.org/ customer-retention-isnt-boring-heres-wow/**

SOURCE: TD Bank, Canada

TD Bank turned ATMs into Automated Thanking Machines™ to create some very special moments for a selection of their loyal customers across Canada. A simple thank you can change someone's day. A simple thank you with a highly relevant and valuable gift can help to create advocates. Warning: the video captures some very emotional customer reactions which make many viewers feel quite emotional too.

The power of CRM

CRM builds a protective wall around customers, in the same way as a brand does. CRM enhances the customers' relationship with the brand. In fact CRM is part of the brand experience, therefore it is part of the brand. As the relationship strengthens, loyalty builds and gives you some protection from losing customers to the constant onslaught of competitive promotions. Relationships built on excellent service and occasional rewards are more enduring (see TD bank example) than relationships built on price discounts which can dilute the perceived value of your brand.

Regardless of what it is called, managing customer relationships is critical to an organization's future. Nurturing excellent customer relationships builds this defensive wall around a business that most competitors struggle to break down. Customer relationships add value to the brand, boost repeat sales, boost profits and, ultimately boost the balance sheet assets (as brand financial values can be included on the balance sheet).

Your best defence

'Customer relationships are the only thing that cannot be replicated by a competitor.'

Hochman (2008)

Company benefits

Boost sales

Good customer relations boost sales, as they simply help customers to repeat-buy during their 'customer lifetime', as well as buying other products and services as they increase their share-of-wallet spend with the same trusted brand (customers still buy almost any product or service from Tesco). Good relations also help to recruit new customers, as happy customers spread the word.

Excellent CRM systems can predict customer preferences and prompt customers with tempting offers when they are ready to buy or sometimes just before they are ready to buy. Some of this is purchase triggered, time triggered, event triggered or digital body language triggered (particular click behaviour can trigger an automated response in the form of a tailored web page, an e-mail, a pop-up or an offline phone call).

Equally good CRM systems can identify potential defectors (customers who are about to leave), pre-empt them and trigger win-back programmes for those who might otherwise have slipped through the net.

Database opens up £billions of new sales

Rothmans cigarettes' sales promotion built a powerful database by offering their customers a free pack of cigarettes when they collected 10 coupons and returned them with a completed form. They generated 750,000 names within 18 months; 500,000 of this new customer database were subsequently offered an FGF promotion (friend get a friend). The database members were entered into a free competition after sending in their own name and the address of any friends who were over 18 years old and who smoked a competitor's brand. There were 250,000 smokers of competitors' brands named. Follow-up market research showed that 90 per cent were genuine. This database would be offered a stream of tempting offers to switch brands. Say the lifetime value of a smoker is £130,000 (for an average 20-a-day smoker over a 40 year smoking life). If only 10 per cent convert, that's 22,500 new customers who generate £2.9 billion in sales revenues.

Reduce costs

Good CRM systems save money as the systems monitor customer feedback or issues before they grow into a major problem. Take Federal Express's 1–10–100 rule. They believe that for every pound your company might spend on preventing a quality problem, it will spend 10 to inspect and correct the mistake after it occurs. In the worst case, the quality failure goes unanswered or unnoticed until after your customer has taken delivery. To fix the problem at this stage, you probably pay about 100 times what you could have paid to prevent it from happening at all.

Boost profits

Marketing to both existing and referred customers costs a lot less than marketing to new ones. As mentioned, estimates suggest that it is six times more profitable to sell to existing customers, hence the importance of customer retention versus customer acquisition. Keeping existing customers happy and keeping in contact with them boosts sales in a more cost-efficient way. This boosts profits.

1% customer satisfaction = $500 million

'Some years ago IBM calculated that each percentage point improvement in customer satisfaction translates into $500 million more revenue over five years.'

Kirkpatrick (1992)

Creates and strengthens assets

A well run CRM programme strengthens assets such as brand assets and also creates another 'asset' called a customer database.

Strengthen brand assets

Stronger relations create stronger brands. This builds brand loyalty, which effectively builds a defensive wall around the customer, protecting them from the inevitable onslaught of hyper-competition as it advances across this 'borderless and category-less' marketplace (see Chapter 1). Good relations also boost the brand image and consequently the brand value, which is eventually reflected on the balance sheet.

Create a 'database asset'

CRM systems can create and maintain a good-quality database. This is significant and, although not shown on the balance sheet, a very real asset to a company. It gives you, if used correctly, a monopoly of your own market share. It gives you access (assuming the database includes fields for various contact channels from e-mail to phone to Twitter). Some companies quantify the value of their databases by calculating lifetime values of different customer profiles and discounting back to today's net present value. This is similar to one of the approaches to evaluating a brand.

What causes CRM failure?

Many organizations appear to have steadily got worse at CRM because of the lack of a customer-driven culture (failed leadership), poor CRM project management skills (in particular scope creep, lack of training and lack of motivation

programmes), constant cost cutting and forgetting customer needs.

Organizations are sitting on a customer service time bomb. Customers are more demanding, and marketers are not delivering. Yes, many products have got better (eg rustproof cars and hybrid cars), but service and CRM are generally going backward, as witnessed by declining customer satisfaction scores and customer defections (even when they do give a 'satisfactory' score). Customers are not happy. They are ready to swap suppliers. They are bombarded with competitive offers. They have less time but more demands. And marketers are not delivering, perhaps because they are not in control of their own CRM (IT may hijack the process). Regardless of the reasons, the stats do not seem to get any better over time.

Here are the reported CRM failure rates identified by Michael Krigsman (2009):

- 2001 Gartner Group: 50 per cent;
- 2002 Butler Group: 70 per cent;
- 2002 Selling Power, CSO Forum: 69.3 per cent;
- 2005 AMR Research: 18 per cent;
- 2006 AMR Research: 31 per cent;
- 2007 AMR Research: 29 per cent;
- 2007 Economist Intelligence Unit: 56 per cent;
- 2009 Forrester Research: 47 per cent;
- 2014 NetProspex: 84 per cent of databases are barely functional.

'Avon cancelled a $125 million investment in an enterprise system that had taken four years of effort to install. Basically, Avon salespeople refused to use it because it was a usability nightmare. This should not be remotely surprising. Many of the systems organizations give to their employees are usability monstrosities.'

McGovern (2014)

Although different measurement criteria from different research companies make these figures less comparable, there is no denying a serious shortage of the skills required for managing CRM. This trend started more than 15 years ago, but even then

Gartner's Trip Report (2009) alerted management that more than 55 per cent of CRM projects deliver unacceptable results. Another Forrester report followed and confirmed that 'More than 50 per cent of CRM projects fail to fully meet expectations.'

The Gartner report (2009) continues to paint a picture of sloppy CRM:

> CRM success continues to elude most companies. Eighty-six per cent of survey respondents say that CRM will be important to their companies over the next three years. Despite this, more than 40 per cent of respondents do not have a formal CRM strategy in place. Of those who do, 44 per cent say that they have seen only 'acceptable' results from their efforts.

Working the maths here suggests that of the 60 per cent of companies that do have a formal CRM strategy, only 44 per cent have seen acceptable results – that is, 26 per cent of companies (44 per cent of 60 per cent) have seen acceptable results. This means that 74 per cent of companies have either no CRM strategy or have unacceptable results. Then the NetProspex Annual Marketing Data Benchmark Report 2014 revealed that 84 per cent of databases are barely functional.

> '80% of companies believe they deliver a superior customer experience, but only 8% of their customers agree.'
> Allen, Reichheld and Hamilton (2005)

Poor CRM process skills

Many CEOs and CMOs fail because they lack an understanding about the development and implementation of customer-driven marketing.

Many marketers have previously failed because they have not mastered CRM systems, or managed to integrate the culture across the organization, nor helped the CEO to understand the importance of CRM. Assuming marketers do address these issues, they have an opportunity to integrate the potential of marketing automation and content marketing (more about these later) to create powerful new CRM systems that will nurture lifetime customers (many of whom may become advocates).

Poor project management skills

Poor project management skills stop CRM systems from being implemented on time and within budget. CRM projects are relatively large to any organization. Failings like scope creep (constantly adding extra and late requirements into the brief), unnecessary and often poor system design, and an over-dominant IT department also wreck potential CRM programmes. One possible reason why 74 per cent of IT projects fail is because they are called IT projects (IT is a service that supports business functions, not an end in itself). IT simply uses information technology processes to help run a business.

Lack of motivation and training

As with any changes introduced to an organization, they need to be supported by training and motivation programmes. Many CRM projects lack buy-in from staff who both fear and resist change. Motivation and training programmes are required to bring people on board. Marketers became aware that this was a serious problem in 2004 when a BusinessEurope.com survey revealed that 25 per cent of marketing professionals record customer details incorrectly and 40 per cent do not share customer contacts with colleagues. Training and motivation are critical components in any CRM programme.

Last but not least, constant cost cutting and operational failings have shifted the emphasis of many CRM programmes from value creation to value restoration. Overburdened and demotivated staff may also be struggling with a work overload. Sometimes competitors see this as a service gap in the market and develop an improved customer service programme, until years later new management cuts costs, reduces service and some other competitor seizes the opportunity.

Forgetting customer needs

It may seem ironic to have a CRM system that forgets about the customer's continuously changing needs. As highlighted in *Emarketing Excellence* (Chaffey and Smith, 2013):

> Old CRM systems were effectively automated selling systems that took little or no account of what customers actually want. Danger bells should start ringing when an IT consultant offers a front-end automated solution that cuts costs and streamlines operations and processes because this does not necessarily make marketing more effective.

IT and other hijackers

Harvard's Allen, Reichheld and Hamilton (2005) think the CRM problems have something to do with growth. They call it 'the dominance trap' and explain it as follows:

> The larger a company's market share, the greater the risk it will take its customers for granted. As the money flows in, management begins confusing customer profitability with customer loyalty, never realizing that the most lucrative buyers may also be the angriest and most alienated. Worse, traditional market research may lead the firm to view customers as statistics. Managers can become so focused on the data that they stop hearing the real voices of their customers.

Some years earlier, another Harvard Business School professor, Susan Fournier (in an interview with Manda Mahoney, 2002), suggested that IT was hijacking CRM projects:

> Most customer relationship management technology (CRM) programs are failing. Why? CRM programs are expensive and take a long time to install. One consequence is that IT has 'hijacked' the process. In emphasizing technology decisions over marketing decisions, we've lost the opportunity to build better relationships with customers. To get back in balance, marketers have to help design CRM systems from the get-go.

Given that 74 per cent of IT projects fail (Tranfield and Braganza, 2007), there is a natural concern over IT driving CRM. Incidentally, this 74 per cent failure rate is surprisingly the same percentage as found in the survey by Standish Group and Gartner Group back in 1980 (IBM, 2001).

Given that we've moved from 47 per cent CRM failure in 2009 (Forrester Research) to 84 per cent CRM failure defined by barely functional databases in 2014 (NetProspex), one wonders if senior management appreciates the importance and value of CRM.

84 per cent CRM failures

'84 per cent CRM failure defined by barely functional databases in 2014.'
NetProspex (2014)

Other hijackers create a fragmented approach

Effectively, marketers need to take control of CRM to ensure a cohesive, integrated system is embraced by all departments. A fragmented approach, with different departments running different CRM systems or, as mentioned earlier, IT hijacking CRM, loses the critical usefulness that CRM should provide to customers. They don't want to be passed from department to department. They want a consistently caring seamless 'single experience' whether engaging online or offline. Two classic findings from a few years ago pose real tough questions for businesses today:

1 Failure to know customers. Fifty per cent of the FTSE 1000 did not know who their customers were. They could not profile their own customers, even though they had the customer data collected and safely stored (MORI, 2003). We thought this was crazy but has it improved since?

2 Failure to satisfy customers. Of all calls to Fujitsu call centres, 50–70 per cent were for value restoration (fixing a problem, such as late delivery, wrong delivery or poor product quality) rather than value creation, eg adding value with helpful advice over the phone (Mitchell, 2004).

How many organizations today can say:

1 They know exactly who their ideal customers are?

2 How many inbound or outbound calls, today, are for value creation rather than value restoration?

Angry impatient customers

Customers know how to use social media and how to generate publicity if required. Meanwhile, remember that even though customers are tired, have no time, are angrier, and are often simply wrong, we need to manage, now more than ever before, our customer care to nurture lifetime relationships.

Angry customers become militant complainers and smash Mercedes

'The chairman of a Chinese wildlife park destroyed his $60,000 SLK230 Mercedes sports car as a protest because he was unhappy about the warranty. With an astute understanding of the media, he "intended to cause maximum embarrassment" to Mercedes-Benz by inviting hundreds of spectators and journalists to watch five workers with sticks smash the car. After that he attached ropes to the wreck and got several bulls to tow it through the city. Compensation negotiations resumed immediately but progressed too slowly, so Mr Wang (who wanted a full refund) asked a friend to also destroy his Mercedes. The friend obliged and drove his white S320 1,000 miles from Beijing to Wuhan. In another public event, six men armed with batons smashed the windows and doors. Mercedes-Benz claimed that Mr Wang had "used the wrong fuel and had subsequently refused a complimentary cleaning of the engine".'

August (2002)

What causes CRM success?

The good news is that poor CRM presents a golden opportunity to create competitive advantage by developing an integrated CRM system that creates value or adds value to customers' experiences, brings them closer to the organization, listens to them, collects data and serves their needs better than ever before. This grows sales from both repeat sales (lifetime customers) and share of wallet (what else does the customer need that the company can supply?). Organizations like McKinsey forecast the after-sales market (after-sales service, consultancy and training) to be where many companies will find new growth. This emphasizes the critical importance of CRM systems that actually work.

The CRM philosophy

Building a customer-driven business requires a specific corporate culture where the organization, at all levels, recognizes the need for customer service and

FIGURE 3.2   The ladder of loyalty

customer focus. A real CRM philosophy sees customers at the centre of the business (or organization). This customer focus requires a longer-term, strategic view of the business as opposed to a short-term 'transactional marketing' approach that focuses on quarterly sales results.

In the CRM philosophy, the organization continually seeks to learn about customer needs and preferences in order to deliver excellent relevant services, and satisfy customer needs in better ways. The organization must also continually measure the right criteria. Ultimately, a CRM philosophy seeks to move customers up the ladder of loyalty from suspect to advocate (remember this is different to the ladder of engagement – which is about engaging visitors and customers).

The ladder of loyalty

This ladder was devised by Considine and Raphel (1981) and is now widely used. Organizations seek to move prospects up the ladder of loyalty from suspects to devoted loyal customers who advocate an organization's product or service. There is some overlap with the ladder of engagement (discussed in Chapter 1), where customers engage more and more with the brand and ultimately become advocates. In fact, some relationship marketing works so well that the seller is not seen as a vendor but as a friendly helper who knows the customers and helps them with their lives.

Permission-based marketing

This customer-sensitive culture is based on permission-based marketing as originally defined by Seth Godin

Never sell to a stranger

'Think of the old corner shop. If the shopkeeper ordered a new type of pickle, he wouldn't expect strangers to flock in and buy it. He'd recommend it to his regular pickle buyers and to people buying cheese and pork. You wouldn't call that hard sell. You'd call it personal service, based on the shopkeeper remembering the preferences of individual customers and using this knowledge to anticipate their needs. No matter what the size and character of your marketplace, direct marketing now lets you offer that personal service to every customer.'

Young (nd)

in 1999. Marketers first gain permission to speak to customers; then they develop trust and, ultimately, loyalty. The first step is to get customers' permission for future communications, whether by mail, e-mail, RSS feed, etc. Although incentives are often used when gaining permission, relevance is key. The next step is collaborative, where marketers help customers to buy and customers help marketers to sell (customer forums and testimonials). The third step is dialogue between the organization and the customers and trialogue between the organization and customers, and customers amongst themselves. A trialogue can flow via blogs, discussion forums, focus groups, feedback forms or even real meetings between customers and sales reps, as well as amongst customers themselves.

When customers 'opt in' for further e-mail, they give their permission to be contacted. This is a first step in using their permission to develop the relationship. Do not abuse this by passing customers' data on (which is illegal unless you have explicit permissions to do so). Do not contact customers too frequently. In fact permission can and ideally should be extended to be quite specific by asking customers exactly what they prefer:

- content – news, products, offers, events;
- frequency – weekly, monthly, quarterly or alerts;
- channel – e-mail, direct mail, phone or SMS;
- format – text vs HTML.

Ensure future contact with customers always adds value. It is a moral and legal requirement (in B2C markets) to offer the customer the option to 'opt out' every time you contact them. The number of existing customers who opt out from further contact is the 'churn rate'. Marketers watch the churn rate closely and try to understand why it varies.

All of these approaches are dependent on an overall customer philosophy that is more strategic than tactical, with customers being nurtured over the medium to long term rather than by a one-off transactional sale approach. This strategic approach requires several components to be in place, including an IT architecture and a human architecture, which depends on a customer culture (see 'CRM components required' below). These take time and require an investment of the three key resources, the 3Ms: men/women, money (budgets) and minutes (time).

CRM components required

CRM is a strategic decision and has a long-term impact on how a business is run. However, CRM programmes need resources, the 3Ms: men/women (commitment, including the CEO's support, an expert project director and teams of trained people to carry out the service); money (to pay for the software, outside consultants, installation, testing, training and motivation programmes); and minutes (the time required to develop a major CRM project can be several years, and even the training can take months). An excellent CRM system often requires a cultural change, which may be a challenge for many organizations.

CRM fails without senior management support cascading right down throughout the organization. CRM implementation is disruptive, expensive and time-consuming and requires extra resources, training and motivation programmes. Return on investment (ROI) can also be difficult for some companies to measure.

'How much will you pay to retain an average customer?'

PR Smith

Overambitious CRM system suppliers sometimes recommend a 'rip and replace implementation'. This can be expensive. Here, CRM suppliers convince the client company to dump their existing systems and start again from scratch.

Integrating customer interactions and data across a range of channels from website to mobile to telephone to sales rep to e-mail is a key requirement.

Blame storming

'Companies who do not appreciate the importance of an effective complaint handling system risk internal friction (passing on the blame). This may lead to a vicious circle, as internal friction generates poor motivation and cynicism, staff disloyalty and worse service. This is why customer loyalty and staff loyalty are closely linked.'

Merlin Stone, Neil Woodcock (source unknown)

There are several components required for CRM success. Without all of these, the CRM system will fail:

- CRM architecture (IT architecture);
- processes including contact strategies and marketing automation, as well as **'universal customer record'** to integrate customer data from every channel;
- database and database management (including profiling and data analytics);
- personalization and tailored offers and rewards;
- human resources;
- content (marketing);
- credibility.

CRM (IT) architecture

CRM needs an integrated enterprise architecture. Not all of the software that will enable better CRM delivery in future goes under the CRM banner. Here are some of the applications sometimes associated with CRM:

- collaboration tools (eg instant messaging, community support on websites);
- portals and self-service;
- customer feedback;
- knowledge management;
- content management;
- call centres becoming interactive contact centres;
- business information and analysis;
- enterprise process management;
- marketing automation;
- gamification.

Samsung's gamification boosts results

'Samsung uses game mechanics to offer incentives and rewards to users who review products, advocate on social networks, participate in Q&As and register products. After deploying game mechanics in conjunction with social login, Samsung has experienced increases in time on site, reviews written, comments published and shop clicks to its ecommerce site.'

Janrain (2012)

'Read "The good, the bad and the ugly of gamification" for broader use of gamification.'
PR Smith (2014a) **www.PRSmith.org/blog**

IT can be supplied as hosted, outsourced and web-service solutions becoming increasingly available from service suppliers. Organizations should make the most of these.

In hyper-competitive markets – ie markets with no categories, no boundaries and no borders – differentiation is important. What difference is perceived between Visa and MasterCard, or L'Oréal and Clairol? Brands should be distinct from the competition. They need a 'personality' that can be promoted and brought to life through all the CRM touchpoints. Brand promotion offers a promise; CRM, or CX (the customer experience) is the physical delivery of that promise. This can be achieved by having the right systems and, most importantly, the right people, or human architecture (we'll explore this later). For now let's consider 'processes' or systems.

Processes

How does an organization manage complaints, money-back requests, queries, compliments, suggestions, and requests for additional services? How does it handle a sale, a cancellation, a complaint or a customer defection? Are there processes or systems in place? After an order, do you send out an order acknowledgement? And after a sale, do you send out a delivery alert, followed by a post-sales service satisfaction questionnaire, or score sheet or feedback request? What happens with this information? Who decides to act on a particular customer suggestion? Who tells the staff? Who tells the customer what's happening with their complaint, query or suggestion? How many times should a customer be contacted after a sale? If customers have outstanding issues, it is not the time to cross-sell them something else. Should different types of customers get different types of offers? Who decides? Who implements this? Processes are important.

Does everyone know how to process an order or a complaint? What happens if someone phones with an unusual enquiry? Who deals with it? How many times are customers left hanging on the phone, being passed around from department to department?

Marketing automation

Many processes can now be automated in very sophisticated ways. Marketing automation (MA) can improve campaign results, as it generates automatic tailored communications triggered by profiles and events (such as purchases). It is all rules based, using variables including transaction history and cost history (call centre returns, order volumes and order frequency). It delivers a single customer view and identifies which media (including social media tools) work best using propensity models (propensity or likelihood to open, propensity to buy, etc).

Marketing optimization analyses all contact history to identify what communications mix generates the best return on investment. It identifies which channels (or tactical tools) generate the best results, whether e-mail, direct mail (snail mail), call centre, search engine traffic (resulting from SEO campaigns), social media or any other sources of customer acquisition (or retention).

3M complaints system generates innovative ideas

'3M claim that over two-thirds of its innovation ideas come from listening to customer complaints. Some organizations have systems and processes that stop complaints before they happen. Compared to fixing a complaint, telemarketing (or even an e-mail) can provide a low-cost method of ensuring customer satisfaction. For example, some customers may have a question that does not merit them making a telephone call, but nevertheless they would like it answered. If left unanswered, the question can fester into a source of dissatisfaction, so regular outbound telephone contact (the company calls the customer) picks up any issues or problems before they become major ones. This is usually more cost-effective than fixing problems. Inbound (0800 and freephone) customer service lines can also reassure customers if they are made aware of the facility. Some technology companies, like ICL, have a team of telephone diagnosticians who handle fault reports from customers. Linked to a sophisticated computerized diagnostic kit, they can identify whether the fault really exists or not. Many problems arise from the user's lack of knowledge, which means many potential problems or frustrations can be sorted out over the phone. If a fault is identified, the diagnosis informs the engineer in advance so that he or she arrives with the right spare part.'

Smith and Zook (2011)

Customer feedback process

Some organizations value customer feedback. They encourage it with 0800 numbers, feedback buttons on websites, questionnaires, rating cards and even outbound telemarketing to collect feedback. Others employ the services of third-party feedback specialists like reevoo.com, who aim to gather feedback from 30 per cent of your customers. There are so many new listening tools and many of them are free (read 'The old marketing ship is sinking', **www.PRSmith.org/blog**). Listening is just the beginning. It is vital to have a system that enables a listening process as well as a constructive response, or sometimes a series of responses (see the Tesco auto contact example that comes later).

Contact strategy process

Too much contact can wear out a relationship. As in personal relationships, you can become a bore, a nuisance or irrelevant. On the other hand, too little may close the relationship-building opportunity. The key to building the best relationship is to have the right number of contacts of the right type at the right time for specific types of customers. This is a contact strategy. It specifies which kinds of customers and enquirers get which sequence of contacts and incentives and from what method (e-mail, mail, telephone, personal call, etc). Some organizations ask their customers how they prefer to be updated about special offers, reminders and announcements (including, if e-mail, whether text or HTML is preferred). The database stores their preferred media and ensures that they are contacted in the preferred manner. So organizations vary their contact strategy depending on how customers (and prospects) react.

Some garages maintain contact with their customers via e-mail or SMS, sending them reminders

Maximize the customer's opportunity to complain

Companies can set up suggestion boxes and other feedback systems to maximize the customer's opportunity to complain, compliment, create or engage with the brand. Feedback (even negative) is food and drink to marketers. However, only one in every 24 dissatisfied customers bothers to complain, according to E-Satisfy Ltd (formerly TARP). Rather than facing an unknown enemy of bitter, disappointed and dissatisfied customers, an organization, through its complaints process, can offer a chance to sort out previously unknown problems. It also gives the organization the opportunity to find the enemy within (internal problems such as quality control or demotivated staff). One company chairman takes time to listen to taped telephone complaints while driving home in his car. Many services companies actually ask their customers to fill in a form about levels of satisfaction or dissatisfaction. Solutions are relatively easy. Identifying the problem is the difficult part. Complaints are generally helpful. Welcome them.

Morton's Klout steak story

Companies are reportedly incorporating Klout scores into their customer service operations – for example, as a basis for expediting tickets or processing upgrades. In a recent case, Morton's Steakhouse even arranged for the surprise delivery of a deluxe meal at Newark airport, after noticing that Peter Shankman (an influential entrepreneur and investor with 100,000 followers on Twitter) had tweeted the following message mid-flight:

Hey @Mortons – can you meet me at Newark airport with a porterhouse when I land in two hours? K, thanks :)

The effort won Morton's considerable publicity, via traditional and social media, and demonstrated their ability to engage creatively with loyal customers. As one technologist noted, 'few companies would be agile enough to pull off a stunt like that in under three hours – it says a lot about the freedom that Mortons have chosen to give their social media team'.

Curragh (2012)

Stew Leonard's: US retail chain's listening process

At Stew Leonard's grocery stores there are monthly focus groups and a daily suggestion box. Suggestions are typed up by 10 am the next day, and store managers either act or call the customers about the complaints or suggestions. The chain averages approximately 100 comments per day – they are the pulse of the store. By actively listening to customers (and their complaints), companies can save, rather than spend, money.

when their car is due for a service. If no response is generated then this triggers a prompt for staff to make a phone call to see whether the customer still wants to receive reminders (maintaining permission). A contact strategy defines an initial welcome strategy when the prospect is first added to the database, based on the best interval and sequence of messages. The contact strategy should then be extended for later stages in the customer life cycle, with messages designed to convert customers to purchase, encourage repeat purchases, encourage customers to try new products or reactivate customers when their interest wanes. Here are three steps to a contact strategy from Chaffey and Smith (2012):

Step 1: Welcome programme process

Develop a welcome programme where over the first three to six months targeted auto-triggered e-mails are sent to educate subscribers about the brand and its benefits and deliver targeted offers. For example, the Renault B2C welcome strategy has a container or content pod within its e-newsletter to deliver personalized information about the brand and model of car in which a prospect is interested. This is updated each month as the customer gets to know the brand better and the brand gets to know the customer better!

Segment list members by activity (responsiveness) and age on the list. Assess the level of e-mail list activity (ask what percentage of list members haven't clicked within the last three to six months – if they haven't, they are inactive and should be treated differently, either by reducing frequency or by using more offline media). Some customers become less responsive. A specific contact strategy is required to reactivate waning customers.

Step 2: 'Contact strategy' process

Here is how Tesco, arguably the world's most sophisticated relationship marketer, develops different contact strategies relevant to four different customer types and relationship stages:

1 new website visitor registers;
2 first-time customer;
3 repeat customer;
4 lapsed customer.

BA puts VIP faces to a welcome name via Google

'Three years ago British Airways were reported to be watching out for its most important customers with its then-new "Know Me" programme which involved a thorough Googling of their passengers, so that check-in staff can "put a face to the name before the customer sets foot in the airport". Staff searched Google images for specific VIP passengers, and those with high Klout scores. "Results of the searches will be forwarded to front-line staff equipped with iPads, making for more personal interactions with check-in staff or cabin crew." BA were hoping to send out about 4,500 daily "personal recognition messages" in 2012.'
Huffington Post (2012)

Tesco monitors customer actions during the customer life cycle. Different customer actions trigger different automatic responses (ARs) by e-mail:

- *Trigger event 1*. The customer first registers on the site (but does not buy).
  - AR1: Two days after registration, an e-mail is sent offering phone assistance and a £5 discount off the first purchase to encourage a trial.
- *Trigger event 2*. The customer first purchases online.
  - AR1: An immediate order confirmation is sent.
  - AR2: Five days after purchase, an e-mail is sent with a link to an online customer satisfaction survey asking about the quality of service from the driver and picker (eg item quality and substitutions).
  - AR3: Two weeks after the first purchase, a direct mail approach offers tips on how to use the service and a £5 discount on the next purchase intended to encourage reuse of online services.
  - AR4: A generic monthly e-newsletter with online exclusive offers.
  - AR5: A bi-weekly alert with personalized offers for the customer.

- AR6: After two months, a £5 discount for the next shop.
- AR7: A quarterly mailing of coupons.
- *Trigger event 3.* The customer does not purchase for an extended period.
  - AR1: The dormancy is detected, and a reactivation e-mail is sent with a survey of how the customer is finding the service (to identify any problems) and a £5 incentive.
  - AR2: A further discount incentive is used in order to encourage continued usage after a break.

Remember, markets are conversations. Listen to what customers say or watch what they click on and use this information to tailor relevant added value with every contact you make. Then ask customers how often they want contact and what type of information or offers they would like. This increases relevancy – a key success factor.

> ## The higher the relevance, the greater the value – it's a continuum
>
> 'If you want to protect and enhance the value of your brand, your offer must be valuable.'
>
> 'Customers get what they want; your margins are protected; everyone's a winner.'
>
> Dunnhumby (2006)

Step 3: Customer defector reduction process

All organizations lose customers. It's called 'churn'. Some customers change job, leave the country, grow old or die, and some switch to a competitor. Organizations need a process for following up any lost customers. Essentially the organization needs to listen carefully, find out why customers have defected, clarify what can be done to win back the business, and ask for the business (sometimes with an added incentive). All of this has to be recorded on to the database for review (particularly why customers are leaving).

Patience is required, as the defecting customer may have just bought a competitor's product or service and the organization has to wait for the next purchase cycle to start again. So be patient. Keep in touch. Make it easy to come back to the organization. When defectors actually do return, the organization has to go out and win their business every day.

Marketers must know what aspect of the organization's procedures, customer care and customer experience causes customers to leave. They must also know which types of customers are defecting. If it is a disproportionate number of high-value customers, then alarm bells should start ringing.

Catch the at-risk customer defectors

It is surprising how many major brands do not have any alarm systems to highlight customers who are about to switch to a competitor. They can be easily identified or profiled by their behaviour (or lack of behaviour/spending). At-risk (of defecting) customers or even recently 'churned' customers need to be followed up with a 'contact strategy' which might comprise a sequence of calls, e-mails, gifts/incentives (if they fit the ideal long-term customer profile).

Profiling is a continuous activity, which includes continually collecting customer information, mining it and using it to profile and target more successfully. For example, Grattan's ladies' fashion mail-order company decided to experiment with a new product, a grandfather clock. They guessed the likely target profile would be something like middle-aged, well-off ABs living in ACORN types J35 (villages with wealthy older commuters) and J36 (detached houses, exclusive suburbs). They then asked for a print-out of names and addresses that fitted this profile. The subsequent mailing generated 60 orders at £1,000 each. They then analysed those 60 orders with a view to identifying any hidden characteristic that could be added to the profile and fed into the database again to produce a different, more accurate target list. When they mailed this list they sold every one of the 1,000 limited-edition clocks.

Database

The database is at the heart of CRM. A database can contain a lot of information about customers depending on how many 'fields' or variables an organization wants to capture. It contains customer names and addresses, enquiries, purchasing patterns, preferences, areas of interest, incentives and a lot

Do you measure self-service CX?

'A survey of 637 contact centres in 72 countries across Asia, Australia, Europe, the Americas and the Middle East and Africa found that "few businesses have implemented systems (or processes) to gauge their customers' experience of non-agent, self-help channels." In other words, few organizations measure the true potential of the Web.'

Dimension Data's Contact Centre
Benchmarking Report (2012)

more depending on how many 'fields' are kept and what kind of analytics are used. It can even be progressively improved with each interaction (or even each click). The database can be enriched with data from publicly available social media information if required. A database gives an organization access to its own private marketplace. As mentioned earlier, it can create a monopoly of your own customers.

A good database contains highly relevant and up-to-date customer data. It is a valuable repository of information on prospects and customers from all sources and channels, including websites, interactive TV, sales reps and customer service staff. Organizations with properly managed databases enjoy a competitive advantage over competitors without databases. A good database is a powerful asset.

Historical data and predictive data

There are two types of information kept: historical data and predictive data. Historical data ('transactional data' or 'back data') includes name, address, recency and frequency of purchases, responses to offers and value of purchases. Predictive data can identify which groups or subgroups are more likely to respond to a specific offer. This is done through statistical scoring: customer attributes (eg lifestyle, house type, past behaviour, etc) are given scores that help to indicate the customers' future behaviour. The database can identify best ('ideal') customers and worst customers. The worst customers have 'negative value': these are customers who are bad debtors or who buy only when special offers are available.

Data analytics

Data analytics improves customer intelligence, which in turn improves targeted marketing, which in turn improves campaign management and, most importantly, customer relationship management. Forget how this boosts profitability for a moment, and just consider how more relevant benefits make customers happier, and how happy customers generate more business and more word-of-mouth referrals. It's a virtuous circle that starts with a bunch of processes: identifying customer needs, reflecting those needs through marcomms and then delivering more relevant products, services and incentives in a timely and cost-efficient manner which ultimately boosts customer sales and satisfaction. ROI improves. The deep analytic tools can now also be applied to online social media as well as the more traditional scenarios. First, consider how data mining works to build better customer profiles and contact strategies while exploiting purchasing cycles with automated marketing.

Data mining

Data mining and segmentation can identify potential long-term, loyal customers as opposed to those who are promiscuous 'bonus seekers' (short-term shoppers who grab sales promotions and then switch when another brand offers a new sales promotion). The latter are costly and increase the 'churn rate' (customers who leave). Since the long-term loyal customers are far more profitable and the promiscuous customers are loss making, every business needs to know where each of these segments comes from, ie which channels and incentives work best. Within channels, businesses need to know which offline advertising, online advertising, direct mail (online or offline) and social media (specifically which ones) are generating the right or wrong traffic or conversions.

Databases have to be stored securely. Large databases require large warehouses. Data mining drills down into these data warehouses and applies advanced statistical analysis and modelling techniques to the data to find useful patterns and relationships. It can, for example, explore each and every transaction of millions of customers and how they relate to each other. Data mining can find correlations that are beyond human conceptual capability (see the seafood bikers and cellist DIYers

Intelligent miner saves Safeway's top customer

'Before Safeway delisted a particular cheese product, ranked 209th in sales, an intelligent miner discovered that this cheese was frequently purchased by its ideal customer profile – the top-spending 25 per cent of customers, the last clientele Safeway would want to disappoint. Under conventional analytical principles, the product would have been delisted; in actual fact, the item was quite important.'

DB2 (1997)

in the 'Unexpected relationships' box below). A range of statistical tools is used, including regression analysis, time-series forecasting, clustering, associations, logistic regression, discriminant analysis, neural nets and decision trees. A sequence-discovery function detects frequently occurring purchasing patterns over time. This information can then be layered with demographic data (from the main database) so that a company can tailor its mailings on each household's vulnerability or propensity to buy certain items at certain times.

Unexpected relationships

'Data mining can reveal unexpected database connections. For example 82 per cent of motorcycle owners buy frozen seafood and 62 per cent of amateur cellists buy power tools. It can be mathematically interesting to see these techniques in action. However, it is also important that a manager knows roughly what the purpose and possible benefits are of any such data-mining analysis.

The ability to ask a good question or write a good data-mining brief is a relatively new skill for today's marketing manager.'

PR Smith

Profiling

Fifty per cent of FTSE 1000 companies do not know who their customers are. They cannot describe how their ideal customers are different to their negative-value customers (ones that cost the organization money). They cannot profile them. They may have their names and addresses etc, but they cannot build useful profiles describing them. If an organization doesn't know its customer profiles (identities, needs and preferences), how can it firstly, give them relevant offers that satisfy them better and secondly, find other customers like them? It is like searching for a needle in a haystack if customers are not profiled.

Chaffey and Smith (2013) explain how profiling can combine explicit data (customer information collected from registrations and surveys) and implicit data (behavioural information gleaned from the back end, ie through the recorded actions of customers on a website). Valuable profiles combine both implicit and explicit data continually. This provides a real picture (or profile) of the target markets, the characteristics that define each segment and how to serve each segment. For example, certain car buyers might have different demographic profiles, show an interest in particular features (pages) of a car and request a test drive. If this group of visitors (or segment) fits the ideal customer profile then they may get an immediate incentive to buy now, whereas another group, or segment, of visitors with a less likely profile may only get an e-newsletter once a month.

Website visitors are observed as they leave an audit trail of what they did, what they looked at and for how long. Cookies enable marketers to track which pages they access, what they are interested in (pages visited, times, duration spent there) and what they buy, which then helps to build their profile. Drill down deeper to see how well different segments respond to different offers or features in a newsletter. Profiling helps to identify who the most profitable customers are and whether they have any similar characteristics (eg whether they respond to certain mailshots, came from a certain type of site or search engine, searched using a particular key phrase, or spent a certain amount of time on particular pages).

Profile customers, visitors and enquirers

Build profiles of both customers and enquirers and then segment them according to their different interests, enquiries, requirements or purchases.

Marketers can build sophisticated consumer profiles based on previous purchasing decisions and even identify the consumer hierarchy of criteria, whether quality, speed of delivery, level of service, etc. This enables tightly targeted tailored offers that match the specific needs of each segment or profile type.

The better the profiling, the better the results, because the more accurate the targeting, the less resources are wasted. Different customers have different needs. It is actually easier to satisfy them by dividing them into groups sharing similar needs (segments) and then treating each segment differently (different contact strategies for each).

Progressive profiling

'Incorporate progressive profiling to build a richer understanding of your audience. Hopefully you wouldn't put someone through the wringer on your first date by asking 50 questions… right? Dating advice is surprisingly relevant when it comes to learning more about your online users. Don't ask your users to share their life story on your first date. Build progressive profiling workflows that invite users to share more information about themselves at the right moments. The points at which people post comments, share content, purchase products or write reviews all present an opportunity to inquire and build a deeper, more comprehensive customer profile.'

Janrain (2012)

Building a profile with fields of data

So what kind of data, or 'fields', should be captured? In addition to a customer's name and address, there are obviously other fields of data worth capturing for either a B2C or a B2B business.

There is an ever-expanding stream of data that can be collected about customers.

Today marketers can collect a plethora of customer data. There are many fields of data, and many ways to collect it. A single universal customer record can be used to link all the data together.

FRAC

Another useful approach to building immediately useable profiles relates to their likelihood to buy based on four common sense factors collectively known as FRAC. It stands for: frequency (of purchase/visit), recency (of purchase/visit), amount (of money spent on purchases) and category of purchase. These were in use a long time before the internet emerged.

Chaffey and Smith (2012) show how some CRM systems use RFM (recency, frequency, monetary value) analysis for targeting e-mails according to how a customer interacts with a website. Values could be assigned to each customer as shown in Table 3.1.

Customers can be combined in different categories and then appropriate message treatments sent to encourage purchase. There are many approaches here; for example, a theatre group uses nine categories to tailor its direct marketing for customers who have attended once, twice or more over the last year, previous year, etc. Other companies will have hundreds of segments with very tailored offerings.

TABLE 3.1 Using RFM analysis

Recency	Frequency	Monetary value
1 Over 12 months	1 More than once every 6 months	1 Less than £10
2 Within last 12 months	2 Every 6 months	2 £10–£50
3 Within last 6 months	3 Every 3 months	3 £50–£100
4 Within last 3 months	4 Every 2 months	4 £100–£200
5 Within last 1 month	5 Monthly	5 More than £200

FIGURE 3.3   Types of data that can be collected from customers

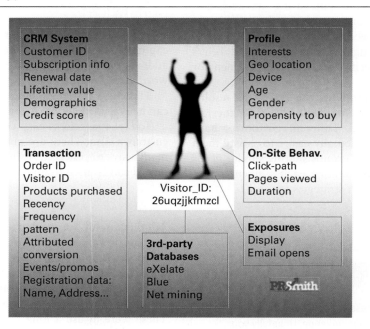

First published on PR Smith's SOSTAC® Guide to The Perfect Digital Marketing Plan (2014c)

FIGURE 3.4   Digital body language and marketing automation

First published on PR Smith's SOSTAC® Guide to The Perfect Digital Marketing Plan (2014c)

There are a lot of other useful data worth collecting also, such as promotions history or responses to specific promotions, share of wallet or customer share (potential spend), timing of spend and more. In B2B, we are interested in business type (standard industrial classification (SIC) codes), size of business, holding companies and subsidiaries, competitive products bought, etc. Customers can be segmented by their activity or responsiveness levels, and then strategies to engage them can be developed. For example, Novo (2004) recommends the use of hurdle rates, which are the percentage of customers in a group (or segment) who have completed an action. Hurdle rates can then be used to compare the engagement of different groups or to set targets to increase engagement with online channels, as the examples of hurdle rates below show:

- 60 per cent of registrants have logged on to the system in the past year;
- 30 per cent have clicked through on e-mail in the past year;
- 20 per cent of customers have visited in the past six months;
- 5 per cent of customers have made three or more purchases in the past year.

When marketers identify their customers' purchasing cycles, they can increase sales significantly, by targeting customers with attractive offers just before they start their next search. Delaying this by a month or a week reduces the probability of purchase because, once they start searching, customers explore competitive offers. Data mining reveals the average purchasing cycle and subsequently identifies those customer segments that are about to start their buying process again. The database can then automatically trigger an e-mail or direct mail or telephone call to a customer (once certain sets of rules are applied). For example, a computer company mined its database to identify individual purchasing cycles and see how frequently different types of customers replaced their PCs. Once the frequency was identified, the company started sending catalogues and discount offers inside the buying frame, with a 95 per cent confidence level, ie 95 per cent of the prospects were just about to start searching for a new PC. Sales jumped up.

Predictive analytics

Data mining can also be used to analyse buying behaviour to identify clues for cross-selling and up-selling. For example, a bank that monitors its customers' spending may identify a segment of customers buying products from Mothercare, which suggests they have young children. This can be combined with typical profile information such as age and marital status to further identify a cluster, or segment, of the bank's customers who might be likely to consider buying a bigger car (as their family is growing). The bank's subsequent offers of a car loan might receive a 30 per cent conversion rate (request more information, call the bank, register an interest or take out an actual loan).

Data analytics treble conversion ratios

Wolters Kluwer UK provides publications such as Croner's information and consulting services that help businesses and professionals comply with constantly changing laws in key areas including tax and accountancy, health and safety, and human resources. The company has annual revenues of around €3.7 billion and employs over 19,000 people. After they installed and employed SAS Analytics, ROI on marketing spend increased threefold; customer retention rates increased from 75 to 83 per cent; improved efficiency and targeting meant reduced marketing headcount and costs; and in customer acquisition, sales conversion rates improved from 1 in 33 (3 per cent conversion) to 1 in 11 (9 per cent conversion). The overall project ROI ratio was 2.25:1.

Non-scientific profiling

Deleting older home dwellers – a less scientific profile building. In the absence of completely reliable data, a less scientific analysis is sometimes used to separate or take out names that do not fit the target profile. For example, Rediffusion cable services felt that older home dwellers did not fit their ideal prospects' profile, so they did not target prospects with older-generation Christian names such as Albert, Alfred, Alice, Amelia, Arthur, Bertram, Constance, Grace, Harold, May, Mildred, Rose, Sabena, Samuel, Victor, Violet and Winifred.

Gaming company profiles big gamblers vs loss-making bonus seekers

Internet gaming company Victor Chandler uses SAS to do a behavioural analysis to predict lifetime values of new customers. For example, if a new customer comes in and bets on casinos (instead of poker tables), the company can predict whether that customer is more likely to become a long-term customer or a short-term, expensive, loss-making customer. The predictive analysis suggests which customers are worth investing in (with regular contact and regular incentives) and which are not – those loss-making 'bonus seeker' customers, whose profile is: young male, tight betting (as opposed to betting all of their stash), declining betting frequency, infrequent betting, and middle-aged female. If visitors display these characteristics, they'll stay three weeks and leave and therefore do not warrant any relationship-building efforts (ie no regular contact or incentives). The other customers are worth investing in, and it is worth developing 'retention activity' (a regular attractive incentivized contact strategy) for them. Predictive analytics use historical data to highlight and optimize marketing messages that work better for certain social networks.

London Fire Brigade data analytics predict fires

Database mining can even be used for non-marketing purposes, such as fire prevention. Take the London Fire Brigade. It carries out 65,000 home safety visits each year, but with over 3 million homes in London it would take over 50 years to cover everyone. More than 60 different data elements are fed into the model, including census data and population demographics, broken down into 649 geographical areas (ward level), plus type of land use, data on deprivation, Mosaic lifestyle data, historical incidents and past prevention activity. The model predicts where fires are most likely to occur. London Fire Brigade use the information to predict where there is a high risk of fire, eg in a small estate of houses or industrial buildings, so they can then send in an assessor to investigate and perhaps circulate information, set up some advisory services and ultimately reduce the number of fires.

Data integration, analytics and direct mail campaign costs

Costs can vary from company to company and project prices can range from several hundred thousand customer records to several million (or in some cases 40 million records). A data integration, data-mining campaign optimization and a full direct marketing suite from companies like SAS range from £500,000 to £5 million, with social media customer link analysis starting at around £250,000.

Personalization and tailored offers

The most important sound in the world is… your own name! It's personal. It's a compliment – an expression of respect. Marketers depend on a good

database to remember customer names, needs, interests and preferences. Specialized software combined with an up-to-date and well-cleaned database allows marketers to personalize communications such as e-mails, voicemails (voice-activated e-mails), snail mails (traditional direct mail), SMS text messages (for mobiles) and, most interestingly, websites – personalized websites.

Personalization can help to build relationships. When someone remembers your name and, even more importantly, your interests, it demonstrates that the person cares about you. Similarly, an organization that remembers your name and your interests is, at least, trying to do a good job.

There are three distinct approaches to personalization as explained by Chaffey and Smith (2012):

- customization;
- individualization;
- group characterization.

Customization is the easiest to see in action: it allows visitors to select and set up their specific preferences. Individualization goes beyond this

fixed setting and uses patterns of a visitor's own behaviour (and not any other user's – it is known that
it's a particular customer because of the log-in and
password choices) to deliver specific content to the
visitor that follows his or her patterns of contact.

In group characterization, visitors receive recommendations based on the preferences of people
like them, using approaches based on collaborative
filtering and case-based reasoning. Mass customization is where a different product, service or content
is produced for different segments – sometimes
hundreds of them. Personalization is different. It is
truly one to one, particularly when not only the
website and communications are personalized but
also the product or service.

Another way of thinking about the many options
for online personalization is suggested by the
Gartner Group (range from simple to complex):

- Addressing customers personally:
  - address customers or prospects by name
    in print communication;
  - address customers or prospects by name
    in electronic communication.
- Real-time personalization:
  - keyword query to change content;
  - clickstream data to dynamically change
    website content;
  - collaborative filtering to classify visitors
    and serve content.
- Customer profile personalization:
  - geographic personalization to tailor
    messages in traditional media;
  - demographic personalization to tailor
    messages in traditional media;
  - geographic personalization to tailor online
    messages;
  - demographic personalization to tailor
    online messages;
  - give website visitors control over content
    from set preferences;
  - registration data to change website content.

There are other interesting options for tailored
offers and ads, including 'content interested in'
(pages visited) combined with other live data such
as a bank account balance. For example, when HSBC
Bank International wanted to move customers into
more valuable segments, it tested personalized
banner ads on its own website. *New Media Age*
reported that this was a challenge: since 60 per cent
of total weekly visitors to offshore.hsbc.com log on
to the internet banking service, HSBC wanted to
market to them effectively while they were engaged
in this task, disrupting their banking experience
without infuriating them' (Rubach, 2007). HSBC
developed some rules to serve different offers
dependent on the type of content accessed and the
level of balance in the customer's account. The
personalized approach worked, with new banners
having an 87.5 per cent higher click-through rate
than non-personalized banners (6.88 per cent versus
3.67 per cent); savings accounts opened via internet
banking increased by 30 per cent (based on the six
months pre- and post-launch); and non-premier
customers upgrading to premier accounts (requiring
a balance of £60,000 or more) increased by 86 per
cent (based on the four weeks pre- and post-launch
of the targeted banners).

Personalization enhances relationships. Personalized web pages help to give customers a sense of
ownership – not the marketer owning the customer,
but the customer owning (or controlling) the site.
When you make customers feel that their home
page is truly theirs, then the offers you make available
belong to them, the information they access is put
together just for them, and you allow the customers
to own you.

Personalization challenges

Many personalized sites require users to log in with
a password, which can be frustrating when customers
forget. Many visitors give up and leave the site. The
use of cookies here can avoid the need for passwords
and log-ins. However, privacy laws now require
e-marketers to ask permission before placing a
cookie on a user's device (and also explain the use
of cookies within the privacy policy). Here are some
other personalization problems.

Although personalization is important, it is
possible to over-personalize. American Express
once tried too hard to be too personal and upset
customers. UK Online for Business reported that
American Express call centres discovered that
customers resented being greeted in person before
they had actually declared who they were, even
although a powerful database can recognize an
incoming phone number and reveal the caller's

name, address, purchases, issues, etc. The practice of immediate personalized greeting was swiftly discontinued.

Dear Rich Fat Bastard

Security becomes even more important when personalized information is collected. A credit card company once had a direct mailshot to 30,000 of its best customers (its gold card holders) intercepted by a disenchanted employee. He changed the salutation in each of the personalized letters to 'Dear Rich Fat Bastard'.

Nike's website once offered customers the opportunity to personalize their own shoes by stitching on their own personal logo. One customer filled out the online form, sent the $50 and chose 'sweatshop' as a personal logo. Nike refused. The publicity soared.

Automated personalized systems can present challenges. However, listening to feedback, ensuring security measures are in place and motivating staff to spot issues (eg Nike) are all simply best practice.

Now just before we look at human architecture, let's just mention the importance of having desirable marketing content if a CRM is going to work successfully.

Marketing content

Content marketing is content that will be of value to your customers. This can be a book, ebook, white paper, post, photograph, graphic or video. Some include games, responses and even direct mail and text messages (a sequence of e-mails needs simple yet carefully crafted messages). A newsletter requires interesting and relevant content. A social media feed requires great content with lots of visuals. A public talk requires an interesting speech and visuals. A sales promotion whether offered on TV, via e-mail, at a conference or on social media needs to be interesting and desirable. Suffice to say that before developing any content suitable for your customers on, say, your social media platforms, it is worth carrying out a social media audit. This will help you decide what information/marketing content and interactions customers will actually engage with, and what they won't.

There is a process to ensure your marketing content is relevant and desirable plus a sequence or continual stream throughout the year. We will look at this process in more detail in Chapter 16 on sales promotions.

Now let's look at the importance of the human touch, such as real staff in CRM systems – have you got the right people fully trained and capable? Have you got the human architecture?!

Human architecture

Systems and processes are just part of the equation. Even though a significant proportion of repetitive CRM tasks can be automated (if very careful analyses and planning is carried out many months in advance), the human factor is still deemed critical to most CRM systems. Here are a few tips to ensure you get the best from your CRM team who are on the frontline, dealing with customers:

- Benchmark current culture with staff via story techniques about customers, their work and CRM. Establish the problem areas and use the information for internal brand alignment through change programmes.
- Spread customer insight among staff and ensure they can use it in their work. Link knowledge of management processes to customer interaction processes for greater collaboration and learning. The big mistake of previous process re-engineering was not doing this. Good customer experience depends on the learning and support that staff give each other as a natural part of everyday life.
- Establish the new skills required and 'cast' staff into the new roles. Develop skills through continuous coaching in delivering the brand values.
- Redesign organizational structures to support new ways of working. Put flexible delivery teams together, pulled from 'communities of practice' (ie similar skill pools) as and when required. CRM and CEM challenge old structures because of the need for:
  - a segmented approach to customers;
  - non-siloed thinking and working;
  - new and scarce skills.

- Link key performance indicators through performance management to staff incentives; banish incentives that misdirect activity. The right incentives are vital. Do not focus just on 'what' is being delivered in terms of financial targets. Focus also on the 'how' of good performance delivery. Gamification can and is used here – see how Target retail stores motivate their checkout teams (Smith 2014).
- Link the brand values to the team and the CX (Customer Experience):
  - basing brand values on what customers want;
  - involving employees in developing the values;
  - linking the values to the main brand promise;
  - recruiting employees with appropriate brand values;
  - encouraging staff to align their behaviour with the values;
  - rewarding employees for delivering the brand values.

The CEO needs to develop a real customer culture where staff really care about customers. This is no easy task. It's a mindset. It is more an attitude than simply a set of processes. It affects the whole organization, as everyone is responsible – not just the customer services, marketing or sales departments. It's everyone's job, from the delivery driver to the receptionist to accounts and finance. Everyone can use every customer experience to create a strategic advantage over the competition.

Credibility and trust

Develop credibility before raising visibility. If you don't do this you will waste an awful lot of money annoying customers. Many organizations spend a lot of money on advertising and generating traffic to their websites (raising visibility) before they have established their credibility. Effectively, all they have done is to take a poor low-profile company and make it a poor high-profile company. What is the point of that? Yet how often do you see this?

Do the basics right. Give your business a chance of getting customers to return a second time. Ensure that your product or service has sufficient quality to

---

> ### 150 rules are not as good as one simple value statement
>
> 'I know an organization whose number one value is "to conduct our business with integrity and professionalism". The MD just keeps asking the question, "Do you think that sale/meeting/task was completed in a professional way?"'
>
> Butler (2004)
>
> Remember Alibaba's CEO talking about their **customer-centric mission** in Chapter 1: 'Making it easier to do business across the world', followed by their motto, 'Customer first, employee second, shareholder third'.

match the promises made via all of your marcomms. Use customer feedback regularly and rigorously. Then check the basics such as whether your website works all right (usability testing).

Use the 20 credibility factors listed in Table 3.2 to ensure you do not damage your credibility, get the basics right and give your business a chance to woo customers back again and again.

CRM creation and maintenance

Writing a CRM brief

Careful thought and considerable advice are needed when setting up a CRM system. It requires vision, strong leadership, CRM experience, integrated skills and an integrated team. When choosing a CRM system, you need to consider the current and future requirements. This involves:

- objective;
- scenarios;
- contact strategies;
- communications tools.

Objective means purpose. What are you trying to achieve with a new CRM system (customer retention, customer win-back, customer acquisition, complaint

TABLE 3.2   20 ways to develop credibility, boost online trust and drive repeat visits

	Yes/No
1 Privacy statement	
2 Security icons	
3 Guarantees	
4 Memberships of professional bodies	
5 Credible third-party endorsements	
6 Customer endorsements	
7 Customer lists	
8 Awards won	
9 Demonstrate expertise	
10 Real people in the About us/Contact us section	
11 Community links	
12 Ethical policies (corporate citizenship)	
13 Text-only version	
14 Full address and contact information	
15 Proof everything – typo free?	
16 Reliable systems	
Four factors that drive repeat visits:	
17 High-quality content	
18 Ease of use	
19 Quick download	
20 Updated frequently	
Score out of 20	

processing or customer feedback)? How can it help customers? Then how can it help you and your team? What kind of scenarios does this involve (customer feedback, suggestions, complaints, enquiries, sales – all of these can be online and offline, or on a telephone line)? Is the system designed to facilitate 'welcome cycles' (welcome letters and new member offers), up-selling (moving the customer on to higher quality levels), cross-selling (other products or services) and reactivation (of previous customers),

all of which help to nurture the relationship? What kind of contact strategies might this involve? What kind of marketing tools will generate the data, eg e-mail, snail mail, outbound telemarketing, inbound telemarketing, sales teams and website dialogue?

Sources of data

Customer data is collected from website registration, guarantee forms, sales promotions, telemarketing, customer service teams on the phone, and salespeople either face to face or over the phone. Often the best source of data lies dormant, thrown in the bottom of a drawer or a customer file somewhere in an organization. Every customer and his or her purchasing pattern, every enquiry and every complaint, comment or item of feedback can be stored in a database. The database can build up a detailed customer profile, identifying issues, preferences, incentives that work and the buying cycle. This facilitates sequence selling, where interest is aroused and relevant tempting offers are made through a series of communications (contact strategy) rather than going for an immediate straight sale.

Dialogue

The system should accommodate and develop a dialogue or a two-way flow of information between the customer and the organization. Does it prompt three-way communication ('trialogue') by sharing engaged customers' opinions, scores, ratings and reviews with other prospects? Every time customers respond, they can be encouraged to give information about their needs and situation (eg whether they want to opt out or stay on the database).

Data retrieval

Remember, input is one thing, but retrieving it in a sensible format is another. The art lies in the retrieval of the data in an appropriate format, for example a list of 'all enquirers for product x from the south-west in the past six months', a list of a particular category of business customer (SIC code), a list of 'customers who have bought all product x but not product y', and so on.

Scale is important too. Will the database grow? How many sources of data might there be? How many scenarios might exist?

Project leader

A strong CRM project leader is also required to nurture an interdisciplinary team. The project team comprises different users of the system, analysts to understand their requirements, technical staff to create the system and a project manager with sufficient time to devote to the job. You've got to involve all departments that may use the CRM system, from customer services, sales and marketing to finance (invoicing), admin, production and

quality control. Don't forget IT, but I strongly recommend that marketers must take control, not IT – IT simply supplies the service expertise. It rarely has a customer focus. Remember, the primary reason is to help customers to do business with you. This is not a technology-driven project. It has to be a customer-driven project with measurable customer criteria, such as increased sales, satisfaction, referrals, etc.

Using SOS + 3Ms in a brief

Taken from the SOSTAC® marketing planning (see Chapter 10), SOS + 3Ms helps briefings. SOS stands for situation (what kind of CRM do we have now and why does it need improving?), objectives (what are we trying to achieve with the new CRM system?) and strategy (how does CRM integrate with all the company's operations?):

- Situation (where are we now with CRM?).
- Objectives (what do we want to achieve?).
- Strategy (how will we get there?) This is why the brief is critical, as it should be clear about contact strategies and scenarios (including how it can, now and in the future, integrate with other systems, such as invoicing and debt collection).

The 3Ms are money (the budgets required for software licences plus training and motivation schemes to ensure staff buy into the new system), minutes (the timescales required to specify the brief, source it, test it, modify it, train the team and roll out the system), and men/women (who will champion the project, do the work and be involved in data capture, analysis and use). Every brief must have these. When should the new system be tested, staff training take place and the system eventually go live?

Beware of scope creep

Scope creep destroys projects. Finally, when you've done your research, discussed everything, written up a detailed brief, got it signed off by the key people and issued it to a supplier or several suppliers, some member of staff thinks of something really quite helpful and asks for it to be included in the brief. This is scope creep. It delays projects, allows suppliers to be late with delivery ('you changed the brief') and to charge a lot more money. Although it's tempting to keep adding extra ideas, a CRM project manager has got to be strong and comprehensive in the initial exploratory discussions and ensure everyone knows that this is the last chance to discuss the brief before it goes out to tender, because once it goes out it stays out.

Clearly defined development stages

Any systems development should follow a structured process and go through clearly defined development stages. Note though that, just as for website development, prototyping is the most effective approach, since it enables the system to be tailored through users' experience of early versions of the system.

Ultimately, CRM is an attitude as much as a system. Success depends on a customer culture where all staff always ask 'How can we help the customer?'

CRM system creation, development, testing and roll-out

Systems development should follow a structured approach, going through several stages (see Figure 3.5).

Prior to each stage there is research or testing. Prior to drawing up a brief, a lot of research goes into reviewing what each department requires and how it all integrates. After the brief is issued several supplier tenders are reviewed and researched.

FIGURE 3.5   CRM development process

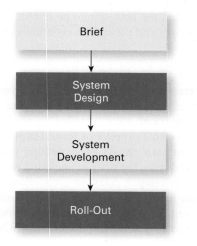

These solutions may be off-the-shelf, tailor-made or a mixture, ie an off-the-shelf system tweaked to suit the organization's specific requirements. When a system is selected and developed it is then tested before being rolled out.

System development involves prototyping and refining the prototype. This enables the system to be tailored through users' experience of early versions of the system. However, beware of 'scope creep'. **Marketers need to improve their IT skill sets.** They need to get better at speaking the language of IT and develop a greater understanding of how technology can translate into improved customer knowledge and ultimately an improved customer experience. IT people can sometimes use 'scary language' that can intimidate other staff. Marketers need to constantly bring conversations back to the benefits for the customer, which would help build a common language around the customer and put technology back in its place.

Front end is fun, back end is business

Marketers are reasonably good at developing websites (front end) but we have to become experts with the database and the e-CRM systems (back end) required to build continual success.

Roll-out requires an investment of the 3Ms into training and motivation. Training ensures all staff are fully familiar with the system, how it works, how it can make their lives easier, how it will help the customer and how it will help the business.

CRM maintenance

Although it does not appear on the balance sheet, the database is an asset. Like any asset it deteriorates or depreciates over time if it is not properly maintained. In the same way that a physical asset, like a building, needs to be maintained to avoid it becoming run down and eventually a liability (if tiles fall off the roof or a wall collapses), a database asset needs to be cleaned and maintained to stop it deteriorating and eventually becoming a liability. For example, sending out direct mail to people who have died naturally upsets their relatives. Careful management of the database is required.

Managing the database

The database is at the heart of the CRM system. The database manager has many responsibilities in addition to the database design (which allows relevant customer data to be accessed rapidly and queries performed):

- Data quality – ensuring data are accurate, relevant and kept up to date.
- Data security – ensuring data cannot be compromised by attacks from inside or outside the organization.
- Data coordination or user coordination – specifying exactly who has access to data retrieval and who has access to data input. Too many uncontrolled inputs may result in files being deleted or changed by too many different people. The database spins out of control.
- Data back-up and recovery – ensuring that data can be restored when there are the almost inevitable system failures or attacks.

The manager also monitors performance, particularly checking the system is coping as either the database or the number of interactions grows (driven by the contact strategies).

Costs and timescales

When it comes to the crunch question of 'How much does it all cost?' there are many variables to consider:

- the set-up costs of the system;
- the type of system;
- the scope of the system;
- the size of the system;
- the choice made about the database management system;
- the maintenance programme;
- where the physical database management system is geographically located.

It is a complex job but, once all these variables are taken into consideration, a task breakdown can be performed, and analysis, design, set-up, maintenance and running costs can be calculated.

What's missing is customer service staff, who are a key component, particularly when they are handling wide-ranging, non-standard requests or complaints. Here's a crucial question: how many customer service staff are required?

A strong project manager

An effective CRM programme needs a strong project manager who can unite the business and technical team members. A defined database administrator is also required who will champion the system and own it to ensure appropriate data quality, security and performance. Planning using the systems development life cycle provides a framework for costing, scheduling and monitoring the project. Remember also that CRM programmes never end; they evolve.

The other key question is: how long does it take to set up a CRM system? The variables are similar to those for cost:

- time allowed for the investigative stage;
- time allowed for design;
- time for writing programmes;
- time for data capture, reassessment and input;
- time for trials, piloting, testing and debugging.

Control issues

One of the toughest jobs is to know which data matter most – especially where they are conflicting. Some customers will give incorrect information, consciously or unconsciously. Some staff input data incorrectly. Other staff leave data fields empty. Marketers and data managers have to come up with ways to acquire the correct and relevant information in the first place and then make it useful to the organization.

The issue of the invasion of privacy is a difficult one. Laws, ethics and codes of practice come into play. Ethics have a role, but the main arbiters of 'How much contact is too much contact?' are the customers themselves. They reveal how ready they are to be communicated with by their response (or lack of response). Permission to contact customers is only temporary. Organizations have to continually win it by delivering relevant added-value communications continuously.

Asking for information is a delicate affair. Marketers can be too greedy. This can create 'form friction' by presenting a customer with 20 questions to answer. Beyond the basic information, you may need to offer incentives for more information or simply wait for the relationship to develop and gain permission to ask for more. Progressive profiling means asking for a little bit of extra information with each visit or purchase. But remember that customers value their privacy. All organizations' privacy policies should be clearly posted on the website and any other access points customers may have with you.

aim of many companies. Many marketing managers view call centres as a means of gathering customer data rather than as a highly influential brand-building 'brand moment'.

Those marketers who do measure customer care also need to tread cautiously, as it can be misleading. For example, an increasingly high customer care score (say up from 84 per cent to 92 per cent) may seem good, but it ignores two critical elements. Firstly, which service components are very important to customers? The ultimate goal is to score 5 out of 5 ratings for all those customer service components given an importance rating of 5 by the customer. Secondly, how do customers rate the experience in comparison to that from competitors?

The Net Promoter Score

Some authors are even suspicious of three-dimensional customer satisfaction scores, as they believe conventional customer satisfaction scores 'typically only draw responses from the bored, the lonely and the seriously aggrieved' (Reichheld and Allen, 2006). The key, they suggest, is to ask customers one simple question: 'How likely is it that you would recommend us to a friend or a colleague?'

The customer cube

One-dimensional customer surveys usually rate product quality, after-sales service, maybe price, etc with 1 being extremely dissatisfied, 2 dissatisfied, 3 neutral, 4 satisfied, and 5 completely satisfied. This ignores how the customer ranks the importance of each variable.

Two-dimensional customer surveys weight these satisfaction factors according to how important they are to the customer: 1 is not important, 2 of minor importance, 3 fairly important, 4 very important, and 5 essential. However, this ignores how customers compare the brand to those of competitors.

Three-dimensional customer surveys also ask customers to rate the organization versus the competition for each customer service component: 1 is significantly worse, 2 somewhat worse, 3 about the same, 4 somewhat better, and 5 significantly better. The Net Promoter Score is an excellent example of this (see opposite).

Accountants cannot distinguish between good and bad profits

'Business measures success based on profits but accountants cannot distinguish between a dollar of bad, customer abusive, growth-stifling profits and a dollar of good, loyalty-enhancing, growth-accelerating profits.'

Reichheld and Allen (2006)

Measuring customer satisfaction

Call centre agents' performance is often measured by number of calls taken. This ignores customer satisfaction, although customer service is a stated

Companies like GE focus on one statistic that nets the percentage of unhappy customers (scoring 0–6) from the percentage who are very happy customers known as 'loyal promoters' (scoring 9 or 10). This net promoter score provides a crystal-clear single number that is as actionable as net profit or net worth.

04
Buyer behaviour

LEARNING OBJECTIVES

By the end of this chapter you will be able to:

- Appreciate the complexity of buying behaviour
- Understand the critical nature of a continual feed of information on customer behaviour
- Appreciate the emotional influences in decision making
- Compare and contrast various approaches to buying models
- Apply the psychology of marketing by exploring different intervening variables

Introduction to understanding customer buying behaviour   102
Who is the customer?   103
Decision-making units   104
Why do they buy?   105
The rational–emotional dichotomy   106
Brain science   109
How do they buy?   111

Models of buyer behaviour   113
The buying process   114
Response hierarchy models   118
Black-box models   119
Personal-variable models   120
Complex models   121

Psychological variables   122
Perception   122
Learning   127

Motivation   129
Attitudes   132
Group influence   133

Summary and conclusion   135

Key points from Chapter 4   136

Appendix 4.1: Hofacker's online information processing   137

Appendix 4.2: The post-PC customer   138

Appendix 4.3: Unilever's five steps to change behaviour   139

References and further reading   139

Further information   142

Introduction to understanding customer buying behaviour

The first step in formulating a marketing communications strategy is to identify, analyse and ultimately understand the target market and its buying behaviour. This chapter considers some of the theories and models that the marketing professional can use to help to communicate with and influence the buyer at various stages before, during and after purchasing. Buying behaviour is often more complex than it appears. Individuals are generally not very predictable, but, in the aggregate, groups of customers (or percentages of markets) can be more predictable.

Whether in the industrial or consumer market, or whether they are buying products or services, buyers respond in different ways to the barrage of marketing communications that are constantly aimed at them. Theoretical frameworks borrowed from psychology, sociology, social psychology, cultural anthropology and economics are now added to by both commercial and academic market research into consumer and business-to-business buyer behaviour. All of this contributes to a better understanding of customers. It is this understanding that helps to reveal what kind of marketing communications work best.

This chapter can provide only an outline of the vast amount of work written in this area. The complex burger buyer example is used to open up some of the types of question that need to be considered. The chapter then looks at types of purchases and the buying process (including some buying models) and then considers how the 'intervening variables' of perception, motivation, learning, memory, attitudes, beliefs, personality and group influence can influence the communication process and, ultimately, buying behaviour.

Three key questions

There are three key groups of questions that have to be answered before any marketing communications can be carried out:

1 Who is the buyer (target market profiles and decision-making units)?

2 Why do they buy (or not buy) a particular brand or product?

3 How do they buy (how, when and where do they buy)?

The second question, 'Why do they buy?', is the most difficult to answer. It requires qualitative rather than quantitative data (which often answers the other questions also). Products and services are bought for a range of different reasons or benefits, some conscious, others unconscious, some rational, others emotional. Many buyers buy for a mixture of reasons. Consider a simple hamburger.

The complex burger buyer

Why buy a burger? The answer might be as simple as 'Because I was hungry – so I bought a Big Mac.' The real reason, however, may be quite different. Perhaps the buyer was in a receptive state for food because of the time of day. In the same way that a stimulus such as a bell for Pavlov's dog (see 'Learning', p. 127) can cause a dog to salivate, the highly visible yellow McDonald's logo can act as a stimulus to customers to remind them of food and arouse feelings of hunger – even salivation. Perhaps the yellow logo also acts as a cue, by triggering memories of the happy advertising images that are learned and stored in memory banks.

Choice is influenced by motivations. Consider that a teenage burger buyer may prefer McDonald's because friends hang out there and it feels nice to be in with the in-crowd (Maslow's need to be accepted or loved; see 'Motivation' on pp. 129 and 131). Maybe the friendly image and the quick service simultaneously satisfy two basic needs – love and hunger. Many convenience purchases today are, in fact, about purchasing time, ie buying a time-saving product or service releases free time to do something else, to satisfy another need. It is likely that buyers have many different reasons with different orders of importance. Different segments can seek many different reasons with different orders of importance. But why don't they go into a Burger King restaurant or a fish and chip shop instead of a McDonald's?

Choice is often influenced by familiarity with the brand, or sometimes the level of trust in a brand name. Familiarity can be generated by actual experience and/or increased awareness boosted by advertising, sponsorship and PR. If one brand can get into the front of an individual's mind ('front-of-mind awareness') through advertising etc, then it will stand a better chance of being chosen in a simple buying situation like this, unless of course the buyer has a preferred set of fast-food restaurants that specifically exclude a particular brand. In this case the buyer is usually prepared to search a little harder (even cross the road) before satisfying the aroused need.

Choice can be influenced by location – offering the right goods or services in the right place at the right time at the right prices. Assuming this is all supported by the right image (eg clean and friendly, nutritious, fast service, socially responsible), then the marketing mix has succeeded in capturing this segment of non-loyal burger buyers who have no strong 'preferred set' of fast-food outlets.

More health-conscious buyers may prefer a nice warm cup of soup. Why? What motivates them? Health? A desire to live longer? A fear of death? A desire to be fit, stay slim, look good (esteem) or just feel healthy and feel good? Or perhaps it's cheaper than a burger? Or is it because everyone else in the office recommends the local delicatessen's soup (pressure to conform to group norms, desire to be accepted by a group – again, the need to be loved)?

We like soup because of prenatal sensations of being surrounded by amniotic fluid

There are other possibilities that lie in the dark depths of our vast information storage chambers otherwise known as our unconscious. For example, in 1957 Vance Packard suggested that 'the deepest roots of our liking for warm, nutritious and plentiful soup may lie in the comfortable and secure unconscious prenatal sensations of being surrounded by the amniotic fluid in our mother's womb'.

Packard (1957)

Impulse buying and repeat purchasing of low-cost fast food obviously differs from the buying behaviour involved in the purchase of, say, a new audio system, a house, a holiday or a fleet of new cars for the company. It is likely that more 'information search' will occur than in the simple stimulus–response buying model (McDonald's yellow logo stimulates the senses and arouses hunger, which generates the response – buy a Big Mac). Regular low-cost purchases are known as 'routinized response behaviour' and therefore have a different buying process than a high-cost, high-risk, irregular purchase, which is known as a 'high-involvement purchase'. Some basic buying models help to explain the different types of purchases and the types of buying process involved. These will be considered later in this chapter.

Get customers to form new habits with their mobile phone

If a brand can become part of someone's life it can become a habitual behaviour. Getting customers to develop a new 'mobile habit' of using your brand's app will nurture stronger brand relationships and deliver a new form of competitive advantage. So think mobile. As Meri Rosich (2015) says: 'Being mobile does not just mean being able to access information – it also means a lot of new habits. Habits that are only possible with an ever-present mobile device.'

Who is the customer?

So many organizations do not know who their customers are. This means they have no real idea who they are trying to target. This is high-risk marketing, something akin to trying to find a needle in a haystack. In fact there is more chance of finding the needle, because at least we can describe what a needle looks like. But in marketing if we cannot describe (or profile) who the ideal customer is then the organization is almost totally dependent on luck. The few outstanding marketing companies out there really do spend a lot of time and effort constantly researching and analysing exactly who is their target market (in great detail), the needs of the target market (why they buy) and how they buy. It can be more difficult online. Some people behave differently online than offline. They assume different pseudonyms and personalities. Sometimes it's hard to know who's who online. As they say, 'Who knows you're a dog online?'

Different personalities below the surface

'A 25-year-old New York stockbroker had an online fling with a 21-year-old blue-eyed blonde Miami beauty. They arranged to meet at JFK airport with red roses. The young New Yorker was horrified to see a 70-year-old man sitting in a wheelchair, wearing a red rose and roaring with laughter at him.'

PR Smith

Who are Generation 'C' or the 'perpetuals' (perpetually connected customer)?

- mostly young (18–34 year olds);
- well educated;
- average income $110,000+;
- spend most money online;
- 4/5 tablet + smartphone/phone;
- use lots of apps;
- connect everywhere, frequently;
- multitask and have fast-paced lives;
- first adopters of new technology;
- Generation C (for connectedness).

Pun (2013)

Knowing who the customer is, is not as easy as it seems. As discussed in Chapter 3, many businesses do not know who their customers are. Despite having large databases, they do not know how to put profiles on their customers. Without this information, companies are shooting blind and just hoping for the best. This is high-risk marketing. For example, a European battery supplier noticed that its highest-margin, high-tech batteries were frequently sold out in one of its most powerful retailers. As it wanted to boost sales at this retailer, it invested in a new point-of-sale. It assumed the high-tech batteries were bought by high-tech users. It designed a prominent new display rack describing the batteries' benefits for digital services. Sales fell. Research revealed that ordinary (non-high-tech) users were buying the batteries, as they perceived the hi-tech batteries would simply last longer (a fact not emphasized in the displays). The company returned to the original displays, and sales went up by 20 per cent (Forsyth, Galante and Guild, 2006).

If you are targeting 'perpetuals', those people who are 24/7 connected, what age are they? What income levels, education, spending habits do they have? You need information to build their profile to tell you who they are. Once you know this (in great detail), suddenly marketing to them gets a lot easier.

Who are your visitors to your website? What is their profile? You can collect information via forms and monitoring click behaviour (digital body language). Google analytics (and other packages) can give you aggregate profile data (geographic, preferred content, conversion rates etc.). There are services today that will profile approximately at least 20 per cent of your visitors on B2B sites delivering company name, telephone number, address, number of employees, location, key words used and a lot more for individual visitors. See PR Smith's SOSTAC® Guide to Your Perfect Digital Marketing Plan (2014) for these and many more services and free tools that answer the 'who, why and how?' customer questions.

Decision-making units

As mentioned previously, there are often several individuals involved in any one person's decision to purchase either consumer or industrial products and services. The choice of a family car may be influenced by parents, children, aunts, uncles, neighbours, friends, the Automobile Association and so on. Each may play a different role in the buying process. Similarly, the purchase of a new factory machine may have been instigated by a safety inspector, selected by a team of engineers, supervisors, the shop steward and production manager, agreed by the board, bought or ordered by the purchasing director and paid for by the financial director or company secretary.

PAGES is a simple acronym that helps to build a marketing communications decision-making unit (DMU) checklist:

Purchaser	The person who orders the goods or services
Adviser	Someone who is knowledgeable in the field
Gatekeeper	A secretary, receptionist or assistant who wants to protect his or her boss from being besieged by marketing messages
End user	Sometimes called 'the customer'
Starter	The instigator or initiator

The actual decision maker is sometimes separate from the purchaser and/or the user. The payer (cheque authorizer) may be different to the purchaser in the B2B environment.

One other, non-human, influencer that needs to be added to the DMU is the intelligent shopping bot. Some are here already. They can take many different forms. One form is the futuristic 3D floating holograms that appear beside the customer when the customer is in buying mode, giving advice, or even haggling with the salesperson (if buying offline). Another form is the intelligent fridge (referred to in Chapter 2), which can offer the customer a tempting online voucher to replace the last can of Guinness with an alternative brand. Another form is the mobile phone. My iPhone has various apps: one identifies the prices at all petrol stations near my location, and another scans in bar codes and compares prices locally. As mobile phones become smarter, with predictive devices delivering real-time contextualized and personalized services and information, the device knows, through the aggregated filters of our location, our timeline and our social graph, what we did just before and what we are expected to want or do later on (courtesy of our online calendar, contacts database, web search history and geo-location information). Very soon, context-based technology will predict our needs and desires. It is 'aware' because it holds a complete record of our past actions and habits and of our future intentions – where we are heading and who we will meet via calendar entries, contacts, web/search history, etc (Frank, 2010).

> ### It's only a matter of time before your mobile device knows your every want and need
>
> 'I am on a business trip to Madrid, have just finished my meetings and have three hours until my flight back to New York. My device "senses" I started moving and "knows" my schedule, therefore it asks me if I prefer to get a taxi to the airport, or if I prefer to stay in the city since the drive to the airport takes about 15 minutes. I choose the second option, slide the "ambient media streams" all the way from "privacy please" to "hit me with everything you've got", and the device offers me all the tourist attractions around me, even a nearby coffee shop that has received exceptionally high ratings (I love coffee). I choose the coffee shop, and as I am drinking my second cup, the device alerts me that my flight has been delayed by an hour and will board through gate E32. I drink another cup of coffee and read from my device the history of Madrid until the next alert updates me that I should call a taxi – immediately providing me with an application that directly books one.'
>
> Frank (2010)

Why do they buy?

Marketing people really do need to know the reasons why buyers buy. More often than not, customers do not even know the real reasons they buy (they like to think that they are rational decision makers). There is a range of conscious and unconscious reasons underlying why people buy what they buy. Some reasons are more important than others to a particular segment. Some reasons are rational, and some are emotional. The split between the two is called the 'emotional–rational dichotomy'. The late Robert Gouezeta, former CEO of Coca-Cola, once said, 'We sell on image. We don't know how to sell on performance. Everything we sell, we sell on image.' So their customers are persuaded emotionally. However, ask anyone why they buy Coca Cola and they'll give you rational reasons like 'it tastes better'. This not always true. Often customers don't know why they buy what they buy. But marketers must know. Marketers may know why customers buy (or don't buy), why they visit your website for a second time (or why they never come back). Marketers need to know what is motivating these customers and new prospect customers. Marketers need to know their customers better than customers know themselves. Marketers need to get deep insights into the minds of their market. These deep insights can create competitive advantage.

So it's not surprising to see the CEO of the world's largest communications group, WPP, sign a strategic global partnership with Twitter. Why? Unique Customer Insights from Twitter. 'The global strategic partnership between WPP and Twitter allows the communications giant to integrate Twitter data into its media and analytics platforms' (Ibrahim 2013). The CEO, Martin Sorrell, says two thirds of the benefits of Twitter are brand insights and customer research. So take note; WPP see Twitter as a listening tool and as an analytics tool more than an advertising tool with tremendous reach.

Rational shoppers?

'Typically, shoppers give the correct price of only 50 per cent of what they have just put in their trolley. Consumers remain loyal to brands even when better products are available. Is this a time-efficient way of dealing with repetitive purchases, or emotional madness?'

East *et al* (2008)

Useful insights can be gleaned just from the words, or phrases, people use to find firstly, your website and secondly, things on your site. These words and phrases describe the benefits or features they want. Consequently, it can also tell you what is missing on your site. Any analytics package reveals these key phrases that give you insights into your visitors' needs and wants.

Why do people share things on social media?

'We share things to look good online and build our own brand.'

PR Smith

By using a next-gen tool to analyse social media chatter across many social channels, one consumer packaged-goods company discovered that one of its beverages was routinely perceived as 'a reward for a good workout'. This led to the product being placed near the exit of health clubs (Brun-Jensen, 2014).

The rational–emotional dichotomy

This rational and emotional quagmire is not restricted to consumer purchasing but applies also to supposedly hard-nosed rational professional buying behaviour. Take small businesses selling to other businesses: they don't have the option of scale, price or bulk orders to gain an edge over the competition; they have to have a story or relationship, and need to cultivate that 'unreasonable loyalty' (Roberts, 2010b). And B2B buyers do buy into relationships built on reliability, trust and personality, as B2C buyers also buy on emotion. In fact, as noted in Chapter 2, Harley-Davidson does not sell motorcycles, Starbucks do not sell coffee, Club Med does not sell vacations, and Guinness does not sell beer. Coke doesn't sell cola. Porsche buyers (many of them) don't buy a transport vehicle; they buy it because they 'simply want to prove to themselves that they have the ability to buy such a car' (Kapferer, 2004).

Perhaps Professor East was conservative when, in fact, many UK customers are prepared to pay 800 per cent more for the 'the real thing' than for an own-brand cola from Asda. A 1.75-litre bottle of Coca-Cola may sell at £1.85 while on the same shelf an Asda own-label 2-litre cola was selling for £0.15. John Roberts (in Egan, 2007) believes that Coca-Cola's 'core concept is product engagement, how warm customers feel towards the brand, how engaged and intimate their relationship has become through the events. You'll never see a Coke ad with just one person.' And, for this intimate privilege that reflects our deep desires (the magic formula), we are prepared to pay an 800 per cent price premium.

As one of the masters of the magic marketing formula, Kevin Roberts, CEO of Saatchi & Saatchi Worldwide, acknowledges, 80 per cent of decisions are emotional. Yet 80 per cent of marketing communications (marcomms) are rational. Rational decision making equals conclusion, whereas emotional decision making equals action. Hence master marketers search for emotional benefits as well. For example, the back pain medication rational approach is 'This medication solves the problem', whereas the emotional approach shows the joy of movement. That's why Roberts says: 'Let emotion rip!'

The difference between emotion and reason

'You spend three seconds. You do not think about every benefit, every attribute, every demonstration. There's an emotional connection through the packaging, through the advertising and through your memory that you make. And then you decide. Neurologist Donald Khan says the difference between emotion and reason is: "Reason leads to conclusions – emotion leads to action."

Most of the research asks: "Do you remember it? Do you get the brand benefits?", whereas the only question you need to ask in research is: "Do you want to see it again? Does this connect with you?"'

Roberts (2006a)

The toothpaste test

'Why do you buy toothpaste? 'To keep teeth clean.' 'To stop cavities and visits to dentist.' 'To keep a full set of beautiful shining teeth.' Some people will admit that 'it is habit' or that 'my parents taught me always to clean my teeth'. All of these answers suggest different benefits that different groups or segments want from their toothpaste, and so the toothpaste suppliers oblige by positioning certain brands as those that deliver a particular benefit. But when do you brush your teeth? First thing in the morning? If people were serious about seeking the benefits they would carry a small portable brush and use it after each meal. Why do most people brush first thing in the morning? To avoid bad breath (which destroys one's confidence). Yet many people do not like admitting it. The real reason is often hidden beneath the surface.'

PR Smith

The bottom line is that marketing managers have constantly to ask the question: 'Why are they buying or not buying our products or services?' Customers need to be probed deeply to find the answers to questions like: 'How do you feel about the brand? Does the brand connect with you? How? How much emotional connection have you got with the brand?' The answers are not static, one-off pieces of research findings but a constant flow of information. Rational reasons need to be understood also. And remember: reasons change; people change; markets change; competition and technology change. A valid reason for buying a particular product yesterday may become obsolete tomorrow. Likewise, an apparently irrelevant feature yesterday may become a key reason for buying tomorrow.

A company executive might buy a well-known brand of laptop rather than another simply because of an unconscious fear of being fired for buying a bad laptop. This is further complicated by the fact that some customers buy the same product for different reasons. For example, Americans may buy iPods because they enable them to listen to their favourite music without being disturbed by others, while Japanese buy them to listen to their favourite music without disturbing others. Even an apparently simple product like toothpaste presents a complex web of reasons for buying. The toothpaste manufacturers respond by supplying different images of different benefits of different types of toothpaste to different segments who have different reasons (needs or motives) for brushing their teeth. The following toothpaste test explains.

The now classic Colgate 'ring of confidence' was one of the UK's best-known toothpaste advertisements. It was basically selling a tube of social confidence. This need to be accepted is relatively obvious although not always admitted initially. There are, however, deeper feelings, emotions, memories, moods, thoughts, beliefs and attitudes locked up inside the dark depths of our unconscious. Sigmund Freud suggested that the mind was like an iceberg in so far as the tip represents the conscious part of the mind while the greater submerged part is the unconscious. Even long-forgotten childhood experiences can affect buying behaviour, including that of hard-nosed US industrial buyers (see 'Mommy's never coming back', p. 182). Some theories of motivation are discussed further in this chapter (see the 'Motivation' section on p. 129).

In the UK many organizations use in-depth research; Guinness for example carries out in-depth research to tap into drinkers' deeply ingrained feelings about the product. Individuals are asked to express their (often unconscious) feelings through clay modelling, picture completion and cartoon completion techniques. This kind of research has revealed that people associate natural goodness and quasi-mystical qualities with the brand. The section 'Motivation' (p. 129) looks at in-depth feelings in more detail.

In B2B markets studies reveal that emotion plays a significant part when making buying decisions, 'B2B buyers are people too, and just because they work in a corporate environment, it doesn't mean they want to digest staid, dry and "typical" content. It also means that business marketers need to connect with their audience in a way that empathizes with their pains and offers workable solutions to them in a language that is human and that they can understand' (Langton, 2013).

Bloatware – emotional wins over rational

Forty-five per cent of software features are never used, 19 per cent are rarely used, and 16 per cent are sometimes used, so some software suppliers launched 'liteware' with fewer functions and lower prices. It flopped. Why? Because people didn't want to be without features that other people had – so bloatware prevails.

FIGURE 4.1   How emotion influences B2B buying

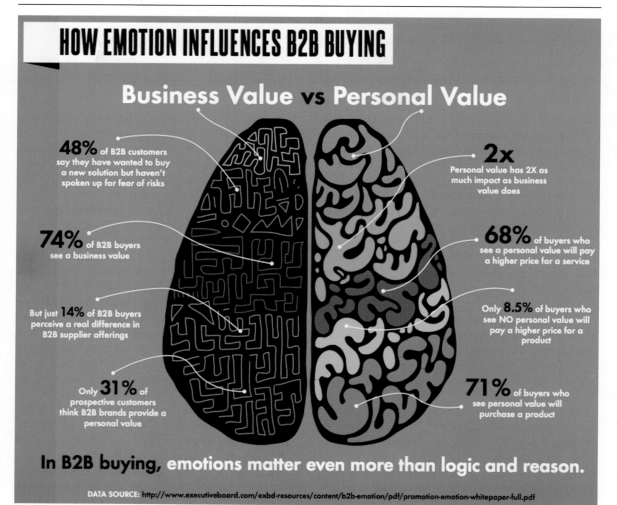

HOW EMOTION INFLUENCES B2B BUYING

Business Value vs Personal Value

48% of B2B customers say they have wanted to buy a new solution but haven't spoken up for fear of risks

74% of B2B buyers see a business value

But just **14%** of B2B buyers perceive a real difference in B2B supplier offerings

Only **31%** of prospective customers think B2B brands provide a personal value

2x Personal value has 2X as much impact as business value does

68% of buyers who see a personal value will pay a higher price for a service

Only **8.5%** of buyers who see NO personal value will pay a higher price for a product

71% of buyers who see personal value will purchase a product

In B2B buying, emotions matter even more than logic and reason.

DATA SOURCE: http://www.executiveboard.com/exbd-resources/content/b2b-emotion/pdf/promotion-emotion-whitepaper-full.pdf

Brain science

There is no doubt that conscious reasoning accounts for only a small part of our thinking. David Penn (2005) talks about how brain science helps to throw some light on the dark depths of emotion and consciousness:

> By reuniting psychology with philosophy and biology, it shifts the scientific focus back onto the mysteries of consciousness and emotion. Increasingly, we've come to understand that unlocking the mystery of consciousness actually depends on figuring out the unconscious functions of the brain. Not Freud's unconscious – a repository for repressed memories – but rather the many things the brain does that are not available to consciousness. Unconscious processes include most of what the brain does – we can often be aware of what we're doing when these things happen, but much of the time consciousness is informed after the fact through the cognitive unconscious. The area that's generating hottest debate is emotion, and its operation through the so-called emotional unconscious, and it's here that the fusion of biology and psychology is changing the whole way we understand human behaviour. The unconscious explains most of what we feel, think and do. Conscious reasoning accounts for only a small part of our 'thinking'.

Penn warns of the dangers of overemphasizing the importance of brand awareness when he says: 'It is clear that if we only base an assessment of effectiveness [advertising effectiveness] on conscious recall, we potentially miss out on those [customers] who are positively affected yet have no conscious recall of having seen it [an ad or a product].'

Penn highlights the four big ideas in brain science:

1 Unconscious processes (either cognitive or emotional) account for most of what we think, feel and do.

2 Conscious reasoning may account for only a small part of our 'thinking', with most taking place in the cognitive unconscious.

3 Emotion precedes our conscious feelings and works in tandem with rational thinking to help us make (better) decisions.

4 The interconnectedness of the thinking and feeling parts of the brain facilitates the interaction of rationality and emotion in decision making.

Each one of these has fundamental implications for marketing and research. Marketers must tread with caution and measure the emotional aspects – some of which are often unconscious emotional connections. Now consider the types of buying situations in which customers have different approaches to choosing products and services.

Nudge theory

'Nudging is about orchestrating persuasion on a subconscious level by sidestepping arguments and leading people down the road' says Ogilvy analyst Daniel Stauber. Nudge theory is a way of appealing to people's logic or emotions.

The UK government has its own Nudge Division (or behavioural insights team – or 'nudge unit') which was set up by UK Prime Minister, David Cameron in 2010 and privatized in 2014. Using insights from behavioural economics it finds canny, cost-effective ways of encouraging people to make choices 'that are beneficial to them and society'.

It has used these techniques successfully with the HMRC to increase tax payments by tapping into peer group pressure (and sending out reminder letters stating that most people in the area have paid their tax). These services are now being sold to other countries like Guatemala who have seen income tax declaration increase by 52 per cent (Benady, 2014).

Communications agency Ogilvy has recently invested six years collecting 800 studies using behavioural economics, neuroscience and narrative theory to create a body of knowledge and customer insights that can be used by clients.

Ogilvy has worked with the Royal Borough of Greenwich to reduce street violence by putting pictures of the faces of local babies on shop shutters (18 per cent reduction) and also *The Times* to design new 'choice architecture that nudges people into buying higher-priced subscriptions'.

Unilever brands (including Magnum and Comfort) use nudge theory to boost participation in branded competitions by simply asking people to opt-out rather than opt-in. 'Orchestrating the choice architecture' like this resulted in a 65 per cent increase in social sharing, saving Unilever chunks of budget because of a reduced need for paid advertising.

Place cues on website landing pages to trigger concepts unconsciously

Robert Cialdini, author of the classic book *Influence: The psychology of persuasion* (1984) recently suggested that marketers should place certain cues on the landing pages of websites so that a particular concept is triggered in the unconscious mind. He continues: 'What many marketers forget to do is to establish the brand's trustworthiness before expecting the target market to adopt the product... once the brand's trustworthiness is established, they can – ironically enough – mention its drawback, which can then be overcome. By failing to do that they miss the opportunity to differentiate the brand from competitors.'

Cialdini (2014)

We are what we shop

Effectively, marketers have to know their customers better than the customers know themselves. This involves deep customer insights, sometimes generated by intense psychoanalysis, sometimes by employing anthropologists and sometimes by cleverly looking at customers through several lenses to get a deeper insight. What people buy reflects their motivations and even their perceptions about themselves.

We are what we 'like'

Researchers at Cambridge University in the UK and Microsoft Research claim that they were able to use 'easily accessible digital records of behaviour, Facebook likes', to accurately predict a wide range of attributes that included: sexual orientation, ethnicity, religious and political views, personality traits, intelligence, happiness, use of addictive substances, parental separation, age, and gender (Kosinski *et al*, 2013).

Goethe and the magic marketing formula

'Behaviour is a mirror in which everyone displays his own image.'

Goethe, *Elective Affinities* (1809)
(quoted in Schifman and Kaunk, 1991)

We are where we are and where we have been

Basically, location-based marketing (explored in the Chapter 13) uses our physical location data (determined by our mobile phone if location settings are turned on) and our previous locations to build a profile of who we are, what we do, what we like. They can now layer on top actual browsing behaviour also.

Top UK retailers vary their research techniques to generate customer insights that they then apply to their marketing immediately. Many combine loyalty card data on what customers were buying with survey research on what customers were not buying. This revealed for example in Tesco that 'young mothers bought fewer baby products in its stores because they trusted pharmacies more. Tesco launched a Baby Club to provide expert advice and targeted coupons. Its share of baby product sales in the UK grew from 16 per cent to 24 per cent over three years' (Forsyth, Galante and Guild, 2006). The better marketers look at customers through a variety of lenses. Tesco have found the hyper-competitive marketplace to be increasingly challenging since then.

Tesco varies the individual store's format to reflect the needs of its local customers (the magic marketing formula). For example, 'stores located near large concentrations of affluent male professionals offer more high-end home theatre equipment, specialized financing and same-day delivery while stores closer to soccer moms feature softer colours, personal shopping assistants, and kids-orientated technology sections. Sales surged by 7 per cent and gross profit by 50 basis points' (Forsyth, Galante and Guild, 2006). So knowing your customers really does pay dividends.

Know your customers intimately – their hopes, dreams, fears and aspirations

'The job now is to be so intimate with consumers, so empathetic with their hopes and their dreams, their aspirations and their fears that we can develop revelations which we then put into creative departments and from great revelations awesome ideas will come, eg T-Mobile UK – revelation – life is for sharing, the power of tribes, the power of communities, and the power of all this social stuff.'

Roberts (2009b)

How do they buy?

Types of buying situation

The amount of time and effort that a buyer is prepared to put into any particular purchase depends on the level of expenditure, the frequency of purchase and the perceived risk involved. Relatively larger expenditure usually warrants greater deliberation during the search and evaluation phases. In consumer markets this buying process is classified as 'extensive problem solving' (EPS) if the buyer has no previous product experience and the purchase is infrequent, expensive and/or risky. The situation is different where the buyer has some knowledge and experience of, and familiarity with, a particular product or service. This is called 'limited problem solving' (LPS). In the case of strong brand loyalty for a habitually purchased product, routinized response behaviour (RRB) can be identified by the repeat brand purchasing of convenience products like baked beans. The buyer chooses quickly and has a low involvement with the purchase. EPS requires high involvement from the buyer, which means that the buyer spends time and effort before actually deciding to buy a particular product or brand. This can be complicated by further advisers and influencers who form part of the decision-making unit. LPS requires lower levels of involvement than EPS but more than RRB.

Industrial buying is even more clearly influenced by decision-making units, particularly when the purchase is considered large, infrequent or risky. As in consumer buying, types of purchase situation also vary in industrial markets. A 'new task' buying situation means what it says – the organization has no experience of the product or service and is buying it for the first time. A 'modified rebuy' situation is where the industrial buyer has some experience of the product or service, while a 'straight rebuy' is where the buyer, or purchasing department, buys on a regular basis.

Analytics – reveals how customers buy

Whatever the type of buying decision, marketers need to know: how do customers make their decisions? What was their journey or route? How do they discover your site or your store? Channels include advertising (PPC and banner ads), social media, direct mail, referral links (using your web url).

Here are 10 questions which we can now answer using analytics:

1 How do customers buy (what is their online journey/what route did they travel – eg from Facebook to website or e-mail to website)?

2 How many channels do your visitors use and how long do they stay?

3 Did customers move between online and offline?

4 What stage are your visitors at in the buying process?

5 How many pages are ideal during a visit?

6 Which routes or channels bring you the most traffic?

7 Which ones bring you the best traffic (that converts to say repeat sales)?

8 When is the best time to post content and engage customers?

9 What percentage of your visitors view your site on a mobile?

10 Do customers see things differently on their mobile?

These questions are taken from SOSTAC® Guide to Your Perfect Digital Marketing Plan (Smith, 2014). There are many more questions answered here including how to use many of the new free tools available to marketers.

Google Analytics and multichannel funnel reports provide an intriguing insight into how customers buy. Just like sport, where an assist is very valuable, so too some channels, whether ads, e-mail or social media, bring traffic that converts to sales or registrations. These 'assisting' channels can be measured via an Assisted Conversions report. While the Top Path Reports reveals the different routes customers take before the conversion, the Time Lag Report reveals the amount of time customers take from the first channel interaction to conversion and Path Length Report shows the number of interactions customers had with your channels. The Overview Report summarizes it all.

The buying process even differs between Google and Facebook users. On Google, potential customers go through a discovery phase during which they gather detailed and rich information, while on Facebook, potential customers may post a message saying that they are looking for a 'new family people carrier', and soon recommendations will flow in from their friends, brands and third parties (Pun, 2013). These forms of information gathering affect the models of buyer behaviour which we are about to explore.

Customers process information from different social media platforms differently

'People use social networks like Facebook and Twitter in many different ways for different reasons. Twitter is mostly known as a place to find real-time information in a compact format, but Pinterest is used in a completely different way. Most users on Pinterest are either looking for ideas or browsing images related to topics they like. If you try to lump all the social networks together and send one update to all of them you will likely have information that is not suited for any social network.'

Hagy (2013)

Marketers also need to know how customers process information, eg how do they read their e-mails? Surprisingly, approximately one third of marketers surveyed did not know their e-mail open rates, ie what percentage actually open the e-mails (Burstein, 2013). This information, or basic analytics is available for free from most e-mail systems. Equally important is to know what devices your customers use to read e-mails, your posts and peruse your website. How many use a mobile instead of a laptop? Professional marketers make it their business to know which words/images/colours/offers work better in e-mails, websites, apps as well as offline in direct mail, ads and exhibitions. It is even easier online as A/B testing is used constantly to learn what works best, then roll it out and ultimately optimize the responses.

Think mobile: how will customers use your information on their mobile

'Don't deliver same "vanilla" experience to your mobile customers. Personalize the experience. Use information that is unique to smartphones and tablets (device type, operating system, connection speed, location, and sensors etc) to combine with information in the consumer's profile (preferences, time, behaviour, social graph and offline data). This is the end of the era of "one size fits all".'

Pun (2013)

Think mobile

Can customers process your information on their mobiles? Big clunky thumbs do not work well on tiny icons or links. So be 'mobile optimized', or as some say, 'optimize conversion paths for mobile' (make it easy for your visitors, followers, customers to use all of your marketing and your services on a mobile). We all know mobile is one of the biggest trends right now. So a lot of marketers are having their websites delivered in responsive and mobile-friendly design. Many stop there, assuming that because the website looks great on a mobile that customers can easily interact with the brand. Not true; there is much work still to be done. This is just the start of optimizing for mobiles.

Here are five tips from Hubspot's Ginny Soskey (2015):

1 That blog post you wrote? The image file shouldn't be so large that it slows down your load time.
2 That CTA (Call To Action) at the end of a blog post to download an ebook? It'd better be large enough for real fingers to tap.
3 That landing page form people have to fill out to receive that ebook? It should be easy to fill out on mobile.
4 That ebook you put behind that landing page form? It's gotta be easy to read – and you'll also want to send the person a follow-up e-mail with that ebook so they can access it on another device later on.
5 That e-mail? It should be easy to read on a device – no pinching or scrolling required. And after someone clicks on that e-mail to eventually buy something from you, your site better make it easy to get in touch with your sales department and/or make a direct purchase.

New currencies required: privacy, trust and time

Privacy, trust and time are new currencies that have a very high value in customers' minds. Customers are cautious about giving up private information. They are also busy and don't like wasting time (if you can save your customers time, they will like you even more). They expect their privacy to be protected (hence privacy statements are *de rigueur* for every website). Equally, customers resent being asked for too much information or being asked for information when they haven't yet established any relationship – so much so that many customers just lie when filling in online forms.

Trust is increasingly important, as online customers live in a dangerous environment of privacy invasion and identity theft. Surprisingly many customers trust a website more than a person. People trust well-known and well-respected brands. Why else would they give an unknown American their credit card details, home address and money? Trust. In the UK, several major brands score higher in trust than the church and the police. Well-managed brands are trusted as long as their promise is never broken. How does it feel when a website remembers your name? And when it remembers your preferences? It seems customers are happy to have unconscious relationships with brands, robots and machines as well as people. Enlightened companies remember information for customers, not just about them. This builds trust in the relationship. Ask: what is a website that might attract a visitor to come back a second time and, ultimately, regularly revisit the site and develop a relationship? Remember, the second visit is the start of the relationship.

The perpetuals, who we mentioned earlier, are (they think) immune to traditional marketing. Their default stance toward marketers is: I don't trust you. They resent banner ads but may put up with them if it offers a reward to watch the ad. They expect user-friendly personalized experiences across all devices and channels. As Pun (2013) says, obstacles are unacceptable (eg tiny, impossible to navigate websites on mobile) and so marketers should think like a digital disrupter and think 'about ways to increase the frequency of interactions' with perpetuals. 'Pleasantly disrupt customers with digitalized products that add value.'

Models of buyer behaviour

There are many different models that attempt to model the buyer's behaviour. Figure 4.2 shows how a buyer in either an EPS or an LPS situation moves through the purchasing cycle or continuum. The basic model can be borrowed and used in industrial markets also. It highlights some of the stages through which a potential buyer passes. Sources and channels of information plus buying criteria can also be identified, which in turn provide a checklist for the marketing plan, whether online, offline or integrated.

The buying process

The buying process can be complicated or simple depending on the type of purchase. High-involvement purchase is where a customer spends a lot of time researching and evaluating the choice of brand. Low involvement, on the other hand, is almost impulsive or habitual repeat buying of low-price items. Let's explore both.

High-involvement purchase model

We can demonstrate this simple buying model (Figure 4.2) by considering, say, the purchase of a new car, which is a high-involvement buying process (or extensive problem solving). Somewhere, somebody or something makes the customer aware that he or she needs a new car.

This is known as problem recognition, which is followed by 'information search'. This may include ads and editorial in magazines, visits to stores, discussion among friends, etc. Today, a flow of reviews and recommendations can come to the buyer.

Next comes evaluation. Leaflets, catalogues, ads and discussions are amassed, and a set of criteria is further refined. This may include engine size, eco-friendliness, space, in-car facilities, number of doors, shape, colour, delivery, guarantee, etc. Evaluation is relatively easy with plenty of reviews and feedback available. Customer comments and reviews are becoming increasingly influential in helping buyers make decisions. Many businesses now build gathering customer reviews into their standard post-sales service. And since reviews are now pulled into Google search results, you can see why companies want more reviews.

Finally, a decision is made to choose a particular car. It isn't over yet. The chosen brand may be out of stock (in which case the communications mix has worked but the marketing mix has failed, since distribution has not got the product available).

Regardless of which particular brand of car is eventually purchased, a tiny sense of doubt often trickles into the customer's mind. This is called 'post-purchase dissonance' and it needs to be managed to avoid large-scale product returns, cancellations or complaints. It can be managed by reassuring the buyer (with a congratulatory note, additional advertising, after-sales service and, most of all, a product or service that lives up to the promise made in the advertising). And, if the product matches the promise,

FIGURE 4.2   A simple model of the buying process for a high-involvement purchase

then both repeat business and word-of-mouth referrals are more likely to occur in the longer run.

The simple buying model shown in Figure 4.2 serves as a useful checklist to see whether you are filling in all the communication gaps in the buying process. Interestingly, many websites now use this as a checklist to ensure that the site helps different customers to move through different stages of their buying process. The model should not be hierarchical, since in reality there are loops, eg between information and evaluation, as the buyer learns about new criteria not previously considered.

This model is more relevant for a high-involvement purchase, whether extensive problem solving (consumer) or new task (industrial).

A routinized response situation, like buying a Coca Cola, is low-involvement, and therefore it would not involve any lengthy decision-making process.

An alternative high-involvement purchase model is suggested by Dave Chaffey of Smart Insights (2014). It starts with something that 'triggers' awareness of the need or want. This is followed by the Initial Consideration Set (preferences and pre-conceived ideas), leading to the Zero Moment of Truth (ZMOT) when the customer gets some information including price, performance, reviews, social media… to the First Moment of Truth (a final shortlist of possible suppliers) to Purchase Decision (the moment of purchase) to the Second Moment of Truth.

Showrooming

Another high-involvement buying model is called 'Showrooming' and can cost retailers a lot of money as they lose customers who walk into their store, browse, find the right product, leave without buying, go online, price compare and buy from a competitor who perhaps doesn't have the overhead costs of bricks and mortar retail stores on high streets.

How John Lewis stop stores 'showrooming'

John Lewis has recognized the explosion in 'showrooming'. Instead of battling this phenomenon, the brand has installed wifi in its stores to allow price comparison and product research whilst in store. They have also endeavoured to make the shopping experience more convenient and stress-free. 'John Lewis not only provided an enhanced offering to customers but avoided conflict between its channels – a smart use of its data', says ICLP general manager Stuart Evans (Bolger 2012).

Low-involvement purchase model

Low involvement can sometimes appear to be thoughtless (impulsive) responses (purchases) to stimuli (point-of-sale displays or well-designed packs). If attention can be grabbed, then some brands can be bought, apparently, without much considered thought processing. Basically, if you see the brand, you try it, and if you like it you rebuy it. Some advertising aims to remind customers and reinforce the benefits of the brand. This is routinized response behaviour (RRB).

Advertising can also reassure existing customers that they have bought the right brand. This defensive advertising (defending market share) reduces any post-purchase dissonance (or worries) and also keeps the brand on the buyer's shopping list (or 'considered set' of brands).

In contrast with attitudes towards high-involvement purchases, attitudes towards low-involvement brands can be formed after the brand experience and not before. In the more considered, high-involvement purchases attitudes are formed after awareness but before any purchasing behaviour actually occurs. The attitude may subsequently be reinforced by first, the real experience of buying and using the brand and second, any subsequent advertising or word-of-mouth communications.

Ehrenberg's 1974 awareness trial reinforcement (ATR) model suggested that consumers become aware of a brand, try it (buy it) and then are exposed to reinforcement by advertising (or even the actual brand experience).

Trial can occur many months after an advertisement has created awareness. Advertising here is also seen as defensive, in so far as it reassures existing buyers that they have made the right choice, as opposed to advertising that might make them run out and buy the advertised brand immediately. Ehrenberg acknowledges that some advertising actually does prompt (or 'nudge') people to buy, as demonstrated with his more explicit 1997 awareness trial reinforcement plus occasional nudging (ATR + N) model. Ehrenberg's specific views differ from many other approaches highlighted in this chapter, yet his research findings are used by top blue-chip companies around the world.

Many other academics believe that different buying situations (high- and low-involvement) require different thought processes and timescales. Even within the same product sector, different processes can occur. Take grocery shopping. Australian academics Rossiter and Percy (1996) identified differences in thought processes within the grocery sector. They suggest that most grocery brands (65 per cent) need recognition at the point of purchase, since buyers tend to see the brand first and then realize they want it. Less than 10 seconds elapse between recognition and putting the product into the trolley. The other 35 per cent of groceries are chosen in advance, so brand awareness (before purchase) is important for these.

FIGURE 4.3   An alternative model

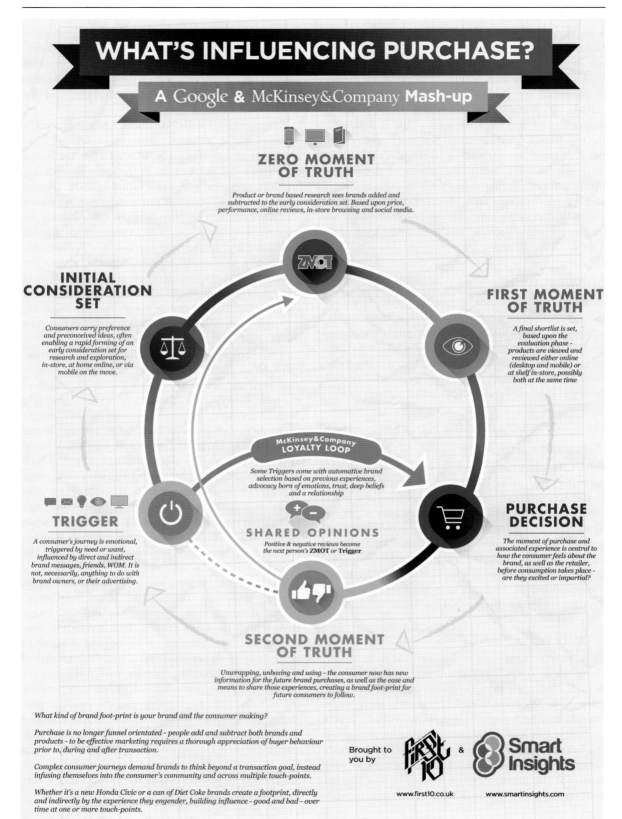

WHAT'S INFLUENCING PURCHASE?

A Google & McKinsey&Company Mash-up

ZERO MOMENT OF TRUTH

Product or brand based research sees brands added and subtracted to the early consideration set. Based upon price, performance, online reviews, in-store browsing and social media.

INITIAL CONSIDERATION SET

Consumers carry preference and preconceived ideas, often enabling a rapid forming of an early consideration set for research and exploration, in-store, at home online, or via mobile on the move.

FIRST MOMENT OF TRUTH

A final shortlist is set, based upon the evaluation phase - products are viewed and reviewed either online (desktop and mobile) or at shelf in-store, possibly both at the same time

McKinsey&Company LOYALTY LOOP

Some Triggers come with automative brand selection based on previous experiences, advocacy born of emotions, trust, deep beliefs and a relationship

SHARED OPINIONS

Positive & negative reviews become the next person's **ZMOT** or **Trigger**

TRIGGER

A consumer's journey is emotional, triggered by need or want, influenced by direct and indirect brand messages, friends, WOM. It is not, necessarily, anything to do with brand owners, or their advertising.

PURCHASE DECISION

The moment of purchase and associated experience is central to how the consumer feels about the brand, as well as the retailer, before consumption takes place - are they excited or impartial?

SECOND MOMENT OF TRUTH

Unwrapping, unboxing and using - the consumer now has new information for the future brand purchases, as well as the ease and means to share those experiences, creating a brand foot-print for future consumers to follow.

What kind of brand foot-print is your brand and the consumer making?

Purchase is no longer funnel orientated - people add and subtract both brands and products - to be effective marketing requires a thorough appreciation of buyer behaviour prior to, during and after transaction.

Complex consumer journeys demand brands to think beyond a transaction goal, instead infusing themselves into the consumer's community and across multiple touch-points.

Whether it's a new Honda Civic or a can of Diet Coke brands create a footprint, directly and indirectly by the experience they engender, building influence - good and bad - over time at one or more touch-points.

Brought to you by **first 10** & **Smart Insights**

www.first10.co.uk   www.smartinsights.com

SOURCE: Smart Insights

FIGURE 4.4   The showrooming buying process

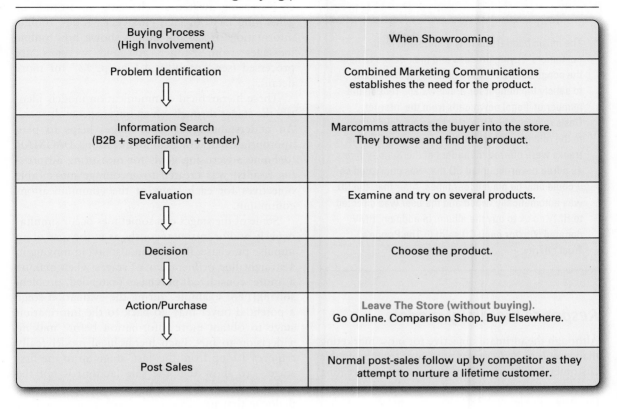

Buying Process (High Involvement)	When Showrooming
Problem Identification ⇩	Combined Marketing Communications establishes the need for the product.
Information Search (B2B + specification + tender) ⇩	Marcomms attracts the buyer into the store. They browse and find the product.
Evaluation ⇩	Examine and try on several products.
Decision ⇩	Choose the product.
Action/Purchase ⇩	Leave The Store (without buying). Go Online. Comparison Shop. Buy Elsewhere.
Post Sales	Normal post-sales follow up by competitor as they attempt to nurture a lifetime customer.

FIGURE 4.5   The ATR model

Awareness

Trial

Reinforcement

Relief purchases vs reward purchases

It does not stop there. There are more differences depending on whether the purchase is a relief purchase (to solve a problem such as dirty clothes) or a reward purchase (to provide gratification, like ice cream). The relief purchases require a more rational approach and the reward purchases a more emotional approach. So each market and each brand needs to be carefully analysed. Robert Shaw (1997/98) points out that 'many different measures such as brand knowledge, esteem, relevance or perceived quality may need to be monitored'. Any marketing manager, whether industrial or consumer, product or service, has constantly to watch the market, its segments and how it is fragmenting.

Marketers need to understand their customers' buying process, whether online, offline or a mixture of both. Dulux paints found that its brand share is 11 per cent higher when customers choose their paint colour at home rather than in-store. But 75 per cent of colour decisions are made in the store. It therefore tried to lock people into a Dulux purchase before they visit a shop by creating a value-added online experience whereby users can decorate a virtual room (with colour coordination suggestions) and receive swatches delivered free to their home with directions to their nearest Dulux retailer.

Now you have it, now you don't: Oasis CD

The music band Oasis fully understand their customers' buying process and their desire to hear the songs before they are officially released. So, to satisfy the hunger for previews and reduce the number of illegal downloads from the internet, Oasis released four trial tracks seven days prior to the release of their Heathen Chemistry CD. The tracks were offered to readers of the *Sunday Times* as a free cover-mounted CD that was encrypted so it could only be played four times. After that, the CD was automatically wiped and the user was directed to HMV.co.uk to buy the album. In addition, HMV donated 50p (for each CD sold) to The Prince's Trust charity.

Response hierarchy models

Although the ultimate objective for most marketing managers is to build repeat purchases from profitable customers, there are many stages between creating problem recognition or need arousal and purchase (as shown in Figure 4.3). The communication models in Figure 4.6 show what are thought to be the sequence of mental stages through which buyers pass on their journey towards a purchase.

These models are sometimes called 'message models' or 'response hierarchy models', since they help to prioritize the communication objectives by determining whether a cognitive, affective or behavioural response is required, ie whether the organization wants to create awareness in the target audience's mind, or to change an attitude, or to act in some way (buy, vote, participate, etc). (See 'Attitudes' on p. 132 for a more detailed explanation of the cognitive, affective and behavioural/conative elements of an attitude.) Message models are helpful but not conclusive, since 1) not all buyers go through all stages, 2) the stages do not necessarily occur in a hierarchical sequence, and 3) impulse purchases contract the process.

Although expanding repeat purchase (loyal behaviour) from profitable customers is the ultimate marketing goal, a PR campaign, advertisement or sales promotion may have a tactical objective focusing on a particular stage in the above models, eg increasing awareness, changing an attitude or generating trial. In fact, Hofacker's (2001) online information processing model shows how online messages from banner ads and websites are processed (see Appendix 4.1 on p. 137 for more detail).

These hierarchical communication models identify the stages through which buyers generally pass. An understanding of these stages helps to plan appropriate marketing communications. DAGMAR (defining advertising goals for measuring advertising results) was created to encourage measurable objectives for each stage of the communications continuum.

Some of the stages can sometimes occur simultaneously and/or instantaneously, as in the case of an impulse purchase. Buyers can also avoid moving in a straight line or hierarchy of stages when making a more considered purchase (extended problem solving). For example, during the evaluation stage a potential buyer may go back to the information stage to obtain more information before making a decision to buy. Each hierarchical model really requires a loop from the 'last' stage up to the first stage – to show that the sale (action) is not the end stage, but rather the beginning of an ongoing dialogue that nurtures a relationship and a report buying process.

Ideally, these models should allow for these and other loops caused by 'message decay' (or forgetting), changes in attitudes, competitive distractions, etc. The models also ignore the mind's 'intervening variables', some of which are identified in both the 'personal-variable models' of Fishbein (1975) and the 'complex models' of Howard and Sheth (1969) and Engel, Blackwell and Kollatt (1978). The complex models, do, in fact, allow for both loops and the complexities of the intervening variables (see p. 121).

Three types of model, 'black-box', 'personal-variable' and 'complex', will now be considered briefly. Black-box models consider external variables that act as stimuli (such as price, shops, merchandise, advertisements, promotions and the social environment, including families and friends) and responses such as sales. Personal-variable models focus on some of the internal psychological variables such as attitudes and beliefs. The complex models attempt to include both the internal and the external variables

FIGURE 4.6   Response hierarchy models

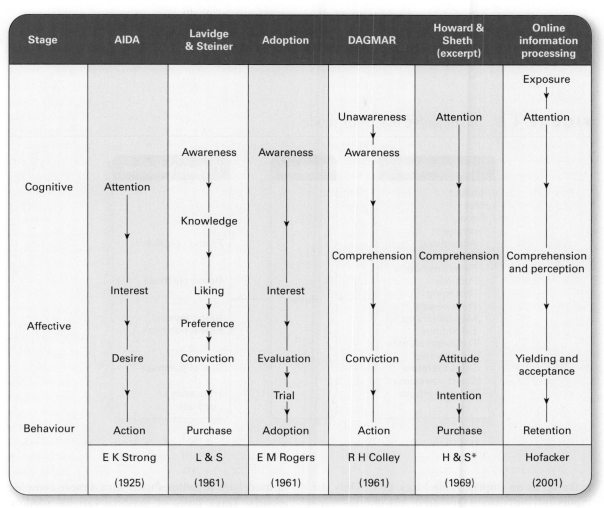

Stage	AIDA	Lavidge & Steiner	Adoption	DAGMAR	Howard & Sheth (excerpt)	Online information processing
						Exposure ↓
				Unawareness ↓	Attention	Attention
		Awareness ↓	Awareness ↓	Awareness ↓		
Cognitive	Attention ↓	Knowledge ↓	↓	Comprehension ↓	Comprehension ↓	Comprehension and perception ↓
Affective	Interest ↓	Liking ↓ Preference ↓	Interest ↓			
	Desire ↓	Conviction ↓	Evaluation ↓ Trial ↓	Conviction ↓	Attitude ↓ Intention ↓	Yielding and acceptance ↓
Behaviour	Action	Purchase	Adoption	Action	Purchase	Retention
	E K Strong (1925)	L & S (1961)	E M Rogers (1961)	R H Colley (1961)	H & S* (1969)	Hofacker (2001)

*The Howard and Sheth excerpt is taken from the full model shown on page 122

in one grand model. To some this proves impossible. As Gordon Foxall (1992) pointed out, 'No one model can capture human nature in its entirety; nor can a handful of theoretical perspectives embrace the scope of human interaction.'

Black-box models

The behaviourist school of psychology concentrates on how people respond to stimuli. It is not concerned with the complex range of internal and external factors that affect the behaviour. The complexities of the mind are left locked up in a 'black box'.

The resulting stimulus–response models ignore the complexities of the mind (including the intervening variables such as perception, motivation, attitudes, etc) and focus on the input or stimulus, eg advertising, and the output, eg purchase behaviour. A classical approach to stimulus–response models is considered in 'Learning' on page 127. Figure 4.7 shows a black-box model.

As Williams (1989) says: 'Black-box models treat the individual and his physiological and psychological

FIGURE 4.7   Black-box model

FIGURE 4.8   An enlarged black-box model

make-up as an impenetrable black box.' Only the inputs and outputs are measured. Any internal mental processes (the intervening processes) that cannot be measured are ignored. The model in Figure 4.8 shows some examples of 'input' and 'output'.

The black-box approach considers only the inputs and outputs. Careful analysis under controlled tests (using reasonably sophisticated computer models) can reveal the optimum price, the optimum level of advertising and so on.

Personal-variable models

These models take a glimpse inside the black box of the mind. They only involve a few personal variables such as beliefs, attitudes and intentions. These kinds

of model are sometimes used within more complex models. Three types of personal-variable models, 'linear additive', 'threshold' and 'trade-off', are briefly considered below.

Linear additive models

Linear additive models like that of Fishbein are based on the number of attributes a particular product or service has, multiplied by the score each attribute is perceived to have, multiplied by the weighting which each attribute is deemed to have. This model opens up attitudes by indicating which attributes are considered to be important to the customer and how each attribute is scored by the customer. Attitudes are not always translated into purchasing behaviour. Even intentions are not always translated into action. Nevertheless, marketing strategies can be built around changing beliefs about attributes, and altering their evaluation or scores.

Threshold models

Most purchases have cut-off points or thresholds beyond which the buyer will not venture. It may be price or some particular feature that a product or service must have (or must not have in the case of some environmentally damaging ingredients) if it is to be considered at all. Here, the buyer has a selection process that screens and accepts those products or services within the threshold for either further analysis or immediate purchase. Those beyond the threshold are rejected and will not be considered any further.

Trade-off models

Buyers generally have a wide array of choices, many with different types and amounts of attributes. A trade-off occurs when the buyer accepts a product that is lacking in one attribute but strong in another. A sort of compensatory mechanism emerges. When someone is buying a car, engine size and price can be traded off against each other, eg a bigger engine means a worse (higher) price. A number of combinations of price and engine size can be researched to find the value or 'utility' for different prices and engine sizes.

Complex models

The cognitive school attempts to open the lid and look inside the mind's black box. Here more complex buying models, like that of Howard and Sheth

(1969), try to incorporate into the hierarchical communication models the intervening variables of perception, motivation, learning, memory, attitudes, beliefs, group influence, etc – in fact, almost everything inside the mind.

Howard and Sheth

A simplified version of Howard and Sheth's complex model divides the black box into perceptual constructs and learning constructs, as shown in Figure 4.9. The exogenous variables are external to this model and include personality traits, social class, financial status, the social/organizational setting and even the importance of the purchase to the individual.

The complete complex model in Figure 4.10 includes perception, learning, attitudes and motivation. Stimulus ambiguity implies inadequate information to make a decision. Perceptual bias (see 'Perception' below) basically means that there is a certain amount of distortion in the way that an individual perceives a stimulus.

This complex model has been criticized for lacking a clear definition of the relationships between some of the variables and for a lack of distinction between the endogenous variables (within the model) and exogenous variables (external to the model). The model is, for many readers, difficult to understand and, for many practitioners, impossible to use. Nevertheless it does provide a useful insight into the possible workings of the mind.

The remainder of this chapter looks at some of the influencing variables such as perception, learning, motivation, values, attitudes and lifestyles, and considers how an understanding of them helps to make more effective marketing communications.

FIGURE 4.9   A simplified version of Howard and Sheth's model

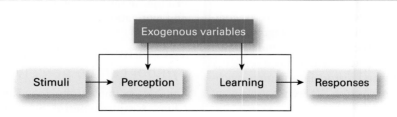

FIGURE 4.10   The complete Howard and Sheth model

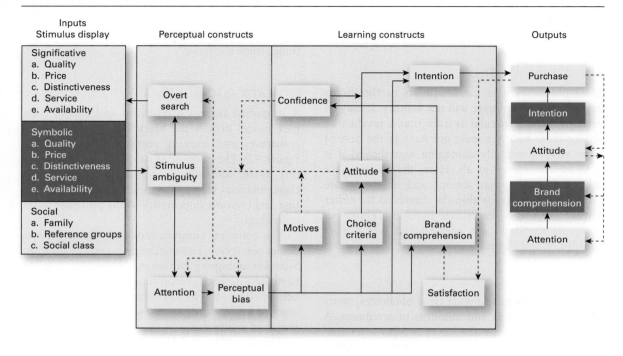

Psychological variables

These are the intervening psychological variables that include:

- perception;
- learning;
- motivation;
- attitudes;
- group influence;
- habit.

Perception

Perception means the way stimuli, such as commercial messages, advertisements, packaging, shops, uniforms, etc, are interpreted. Messages and Chisnall (1985) say: 'Our perceptual system has a tendency to organize, modify and distort information reaching it.' Perception is selective. We see what we want to see.

Here's a simple test. Ask smokers to recall exactly what the health warning says on the side of their packet of cigarettes. Few will be able to tell you the exact words. This is because we all selectively screen out messages or stimuli that may cause discomfort, tension or 'cognitive dissonance'. Imagine that smokers allow the message (warning) to be perceived. This will cause discomfort every time a cigarette is taken, since the box will give the smokers an unpleasant message. In order to reduce this tension, the smokers have two options: 1) change behaviour (stop smoking) or 2) screen out the message and continue the behaviour (smoking).

Many stimuli are screened out by the perceptual system, which, it is estimated, is hit by between 500 and 1,500 different advertisements a day. The example in the box opposite shows how preferences and motivations affect perception.

The same brand logo, icon or a symbol can be perceived differently

Take this example from Hong Kong, where in 1997 China regained control over this former British

Millions perceive same moment differently: the infamous Brian O'Driscoll incident

'The captain, and some say potential match winner, of the British and Irish Lions rugby team, Brian O'Driscoll, was spear-tackled by two players, off the ball, in the first minute of the first test match in New Zealand. O'Driscoll's shoulder was shattered and his test series over. He was lucky not to have broken his neck, as a spear tackle involves lifting and throwing a player head first to the ground. It can result in a broken neck. It is extremely dangerous and totally illegal. The Lions' manager, Sir Clive Woodward, called for a citing and disciplinary action. It never happened. Here's the interesting bit about perceptions. The author interviewed over 100 New Zealand fans, and every one of them saw no problem with the incident. Ask Lions fans, and every one will say it was an absolute disgrace. Everyone saw the same thing, but the two groups saw (perceived) something different. Perception is selective and hugely biased by our motivations.'

PR Smith

Note: This incident was the trigger that founded **www.GreatSportsmanship.org**, an edutainment programme designed to inspire global citizens through sportsmanship stories.

colony. The committee responsible for celebrating the resumption of Chinese sovereignty chose the white dolphin as its symbol. A British newspaper, the *Independent*, pointed out that this was a species threatened with extinction in Chinese waters. The committee also chose to place it alongside the new symbol for the future special administrative region of Hong Kong, the Bauhinia flower, which, reported the newspaper, was a sterile hybrid that produces no seed. The newspaper perceived Hong Kong to be marching into the future under the symbols of an endangered species and sterility. The Hong Kong committee saw the friendly dolphin as appealing to everybody, especially children: 'Its leaping movement symbolizes Hong Kong's vibrancy.' They differed vastly even over the same symbol or stimulus.

The same ad can be perceived differently

Perceptions can vary even within the same region. A UK TV advertisement for Unilever's Persil washing powder showed a Dalmatian dog shaking off its black spots, a white horse breaking away from black horses and a skater dressed in white beating other skaters dressed in black. The advertisement was perceived by some as being racist. Despite the advertisements having been tested with Afro-Caribbean women before going on air, the Independent Television Commission (ITC) received 32 complaints.

The same website can be perceived differently

You need to know how visitors see your website. Session maps and heat maps are used to try to understand how customers process information on a website. Session maps record an individual's eye movements across a web page (erratic/random eye movement suggests confusion). The larger the circle the more time spent looking.

The results of all the individual Session Maps are aggregated to generate a single Heat Map with warmer colours revealing areas most looked at and 'black' indicating no one looked at this part of the page (in this case no one noticed the 'Sale' sign).

That's probably why most organizations put their brand top left. Incidentally, the eye movement used to be an 'F', starting top left, scanning across, reverting to top left and then scanning down and across (to complete the top two rows of the 'F'). (Taken from the SOSTAC® Guide to Your Perfect Digital Marketing Plan (2014), PR Smith.)

Usability testing is different. Basically it asks customers (and other stakeholders) to use the website to carry out specific tasks with an observer watching to see how easy or difficult it is to complete the tasks. See the 'Control' section in Chapter 10 for more.

Regardless of what region your audience is in attention spans are shrinking and a shift towards visual is occurring.

FIGURE 4.11   Session map showing movement of eyes across a web page

Courtesy of **www.etre.com**

FIGURE 4.12   Heat Map showing which areas of a web page are looked at most

Courtesy of **www.etre.com**

The shift towards visual and social

A picture paints 1000 words:

- Blogs have 500–1000 (or more) words;
- Facebook has just a few words;*
- Twitter: 140 characters;**
- YouTube: no words;***
- Vine: 6s video – ditto;
- Pinterest: no words;
- Instagram: ditto.

 *Facebook posts with pictures and videos get more engagement.
 ** Tweets with pictures get more engagement.
*** well, very few words – just some in the title, caption, credits and description (and the full transcript plus annotations can also now be included).

Adapted from Joe Dalton (2012)

Attention before perception

Generally, before perception occurs, attention has to be gained by, say, the advertiser (there are exceptions – where subtle icons, colours or images don't grab attention but do affect perception, see Nudge Theory). As Williams (1989) says, interests, needs and motives determine 'not only what will arouse attention, but also what will hold it'. For example, advertisements for a new house are ignored by the mass population. But there is a sector of the population that is actively looking for a house. This sector has a need for a new house, and it is therefore receptive to any of these advertisements. Individuals from this sector positively select information relevant to their needs. This is known as 'selective attention'.

Shrinking attention spans

Attention spans are shrinking. Estimates from Harvard for the first televised live TV debate between Nixon and JFK in 1960 suggested the attention span of the audience was only 42 seconds. Kennedy delivered key points within 40 seconds.

He won the election. Fast forward to Obama in 2008 and 2012; some estimates suggested attention spans had fallen to just five seconds. Hence Obama's snappy one liners such as 'Yes We Can' were repeated across many platforms. Obama won. There was of course a lot more than just snappy one liners in the Obama campaign – see SOSTAC® Guide to Your Perfect Digital Marketing Plan for a PR Smith interview with Teddy Goff, Obama's Head Of Digital.

Goldfish a have greater attention span than some Americans

'Well, probably Europeans too. According to Harvard Business School historian Nancy Koehn, our average attention span today is eight seconds down from 12 seconds over a decade ago. Goldfish are believed to have attention spans lasting 9 seconds. We live in an "age of distraction". However, context is important as TV attention spans shrink, and smartphones, surprisingly "trump desktop computers for receptivity to ads, especially when the viewer is at school or work" (sorry, boss). Overall, a highly attentive audience was shown to boost purchase intent by 23 per cent and overall favourability by 14 per cent.'

Dishman (2014)

There are also certain physical properties that increase the likelihood of a message gaining attention: intensity and size; position; sound; colour; contrast; and movement (eyes are involuntarily attracted to movement because of the body's instinctive defence mechanism). Given that an individual's attention is constantly called upon by new stimuli, repetition can enhance the likelihood of a message getting through. Novelty can also be used to jar expectations and grab attention.

Perceived differences in brands are not necessarily dependent on real product differences (in either function or form). As Chisnall (1985) says, 'Consumers evaluate products against the background of their experiences, expectations and associations. Perception is seldom an objective, scientific assessment of the comparative values of competing brands.'

Colour affects our perception

'The colour red makes food smell better.'

Kanner (1989)

Perceptions are delicate and need to be managed carefully. Take Google: it is loved by everyone, but could easily be feared by all if it was perceived to be too powerful (as perhaps Microsoft experienced). Kennedy (2009) suggested: 'One of the main hurdles Google faces in its quest to manage the world's information, becoming a virtual library of books, movies, music, maps, tools, news, communication, even our very voices, is that it also becomes a figure of suspicion. How safe is that information, are they reading our every e-mail, do they know too much about us?' Google CEO Eric Schmidt admits these are real fears, and he says:

> Trust means there is a sacred line the company must never cross. In fact, its greatest strength is, in truth, its Achilles heel. If it crosses that line it can never go back. Privacy and trust are sacrosanct. There's a lot of things we could do that would upset our users so there's a line you can't cross. We try very hard to stay very much on the side of the consumer (Manyika, 2008).

Even if the company stays on the right side of the line, it still has to manage customer perceptions very carefully.

Certain words work better than others

Certain words must be perceived to have different meaning or inference. President Obama's digital director, Teddy Goff, told me that one of these statements had a much higher impact than the other:

- 'you should be a donor'
- 'you should donate'

Which one, do you think, worked best during the last Obama campaign? Stop and think for a moment before reading the answer. Teddy Goff discovered that people were more likely to be persuaded by the first statement as nouns were found to be more powerful than verbs (Lee, 2013). Sometimes we just don't fully know why this is, but testing and analysis will reveal which works best. Hence the importance of developing a constant beta culture. Do check out how changing one button on a website boosted revenues so much that they named it the $300 million button.

Spared Jool (2009) Excerpt from the SOSTAC® Guide to Your Perfect Digital Marketing Plan, PR Smith (2014)

Gestalt psychology

An understanding of the way our perceptual system organizes information has helped some brand advertisers to exploit perceptual systems through an understanding of gestalt psychology. Gestalt means 'total figuration'. One of the four basic perceptual organizing techniques from the gestalt school is 'closure'. Individuals strive to make sense of incomplete messages by filling in the gaps or shaping the image so that it can fit comfortably into their cognitive set (or set of knowledge). Marlboro's 'MARL' advertisements and Kit-Kat's 'Kit' adver-tisements play on the need to fill in these gaps. This may happen so fast that viewers are not aware of what is going on inside their heads. Effectively, the mind momentarily becomes the medium, since the complete image is visible only inside the head, while the external advertisement shows the incomplete image. In a sense, a giant billboard inside the forehead is switched on by an incomplete stimulus. The natural perceptual tendency towards 'closure' completes the advertisement's image inside the audience's mind. Perception is also inextricably linked with past experiences, motivation, beliefs, attitudes and the ability to learn.

Everybody is scared

'Everybody is scared; everybody is insecure; everybody is nervous. Nobody knows what's coming next. Nobody. So people are looking for intimacy. They're looking for brands that understand them. They're looking for services that deliver for them in their new environment. I think most brands and most companies are operating in a time lag and a time warp. Consumers are way ahead of us. Their insecurities are much more to the surface… The challenge is to get more intimate with her fears, her needs, her desires. Let's face it: she needs to enjoy her life today – because there's not a lot of it coming her way. So she will still use brands. She will still find some pleasure in shopping. What we've got to do is provide that pleasure, provide that joy, that delight so that we can delight her in her new environment through being very intimate in her current situation.'

Kevin Roberts, CEO, Saatchi & Saatchi
Worldwide (2009c)

Remembering people's names at a party

'When introduced to someone at a party, do you ever forget the person's name? An inability to learn and remember names can create embarrassment. Perhaps the host should increase the frequency of the branding process by repeating the individual's name three times during the introduction? Or would this be irritating? Perhaps it would be better if the individual's name was inserted in a "drip" strategy rather than a "burst" strategy, ie occasionally the host would pass by, casually drop the individual's name into the conversation and move on. Brands face similar challenges of embedding their names in our awareness (and ultimately into the considered set, followed by the referred set of brands).'

PR Smith

Connectionist learning theories

Simple connectionist theory suggests that associations can be made between messages, or stimuli, and responses, hence the term 'stimulus–response model'. Remind people they are hungry (stimulus) and they might just go to a particular takeaway (response), where they are quickly rewarded with nice tasty warm food.

Learning via classical conditioning

In the late 1890s the Russian physiologist Ivan Pavlov demonstrated how 'classical conditioning', or involuntary conditioning, worked on dogs. By regularly hearing the ringing of a bell before being presented with food, a dog learnt to associate (or connect) the bell with food. After a period of conditioning the dog would salivate (respond) upon hearing the bell (stimulus) without any food arriving. As Williams (1989) says, 'It is the idea of association that underlines the concept of branding in modern marketing.' Constant repetition can build associations between needs, products and brands, eg if you are thinking of beans, think Heinz: 'Beanz Meanz Heinz'. Can we be conditioned into buying brands? Can constant repetition build immediate associations between needs and brands, or needs and behaviour? Some people, if they are

Learning

Marketers obviously want customers to learn about first, the existence of their brand or company and second, its merits. A knowledge of the learning process is therefore useful in understanding how customers acquire, store and retrieve messages about products, brands and companies. How are attitudes about companies, products and brands developed (or learnt)? Advertising and sales promotions can help customers learn in different ways (see 'classical conditioning' and 'operant conditioning' in 'Connectionist learning theories' below). In addition, how many times (frequency) should an advertisement be shown before it is remembered or, alternatively, before it causes irritation? Should it be repeated regularly once a week for a year (a 'drip' strategy) or concentrated into 12 times a week for four weeks only (a 'burst' strategy)? Differing levels of intelligence, memory capacity, motivations, perceptual systems, associations and rewards (reinforcement) affect the learning process.

hungry, when they see a yellow McDonald's arch sign, they start salivating. Is this classical conditioning? What about the pub, when the bell rings (Pavlov) for last drinks, there is sometimes a surge towards the bar? Or the ice-cream van jingle (stimulus) which makes children and parents come out of their houses to buy an ice cream (response)?

Humans behaviour is influenced by music

'High-tempo music may be appropriate in fast food restaurants because it encourages faster knife and fork activity, leading to quicker table turnover. Customers buy more expensive wines in a retail environment playing classical music rather than pop music. French wine significantly outsold German wine in a store when stereotypical French accordion music was played. Marketers frequently match the volume of music in different time zones of their store to the age band of the target market… younger shoppers spend more in a retail environment playing loud music, while shoppers aged 50 and over spend more in an environment with quiet background music.'

Oakes (2008)

'London Underground started piping "uncool" classical music in the booking halls of tube stations in December 2005 to deter youths from loitering, resulting in a 33 per cent drop in abuse against staff.'

Marketer (2010)

Learning via operant conditioning

Whereas classical conditioning is non voluntary, ie we cannot control the situation fully as lights flash, bells ring or ads roll, operant conditioning is voluntary in so far as the participant actively searches for solutions. The Skinner box was devised by Dr Burrhus Frederic Skinner in the United States during the 1940s. By placing a hungry rat in a box where food only arrived once the rat pressed a lever, Skinner observed that the rat would search, investigate and, eventually, press the lever accidentally. Food then arrived. Over a period of time the rat, when aroused by the hunger motive, learned to press the lever for food. An association or connection was made between the lever pressing and the drive to satisfy the hunger need. This approach to building associations through voluntary participation suggests that sales promotions, discussions, competitions, and engagement at various levels effectively invites the buyer to participate, be rewarded, and eventually connect, or learn that a particular product or service is associated with a particular need.

Stimulus–response

Connectionist theories of learning highlight the importance of first, timing and second, frequency of marketing communications. The establishment of a connection or association between a stimulus and a response is fundamental to the conditioning process. Advertising jingles, pictures and even smells are some of the stimuli that can arouse emotional or behavioural responses. Some people still feel good when they hear the Coca-Cola jingle 'I'd like to teach the world to sing…'; others are aroused and excited when they hear the sound of a sports commentator's voice with crowd sound effects in the background. Ice-cream van jingles arouse children. McDonald's large, highly visible yellow 'M' logo can trigger a response, particularly if an individual is involved in goal-orientated behaviour (is hungry and is ready to consider eating food). Could this yellow logo be the equivalent of Pavlov's bell? Do some humans salivate just at the sight of the logo?

Cyber-logo makes customers salivate

'Seeing your logo on the net made me hungry' (feedback from a McDonald's website visitor, demonstrating classical conditioning).

Smith, Berry and Pulford (1999)

Certainly the release of certain aromas can stimulate immediate responses. For example, as customers leave a pub and walk down the street they are often greeted by the wafting smell of frying chips, which can stimulate or arouse the need for food, and lead to an immediate purchase.

Lunn Poly created a full sensory holiday environment in its stores using a coconut aroma, fresh coffee in the Parisian-style café area, holiday music, travel images and a variety of film footage.

Reinforcement and reward enhance the learning process. In other words, good-quality products and services reward the buyer every time. This consistent level of quality reinforces the brand's positive relationship with the buyer. On the other hand, if the quality is poor, there is no reward (the response does not satisfy the need), and the response (to buy a particular brand or visit a particular shop) will not be repeated.

Positive reinforcement helps the learning process (or helps the buyer to remember the brand or shop). It is possible to 'unlearn' or forget ('message decay'), so many advertisers seek to remind customers of their products, their names and their benefits. Some advertisements seek to remind buyers what a good choice they have already made by frequently repeating messages. The connectionist approach ignores all the other complex and influential variables involved in learning and, ultimately, buying. Arguably, it oversimplifies a complex process.

Packaging design can also act as a cue to arouse momentarily the happy images conveyed in the previously seen and unconsciously stored advertising images. This is where a 'pack shot' of the product and pack in the advertisement (usually at the end) aids recall of the brand, the advertisement and its image when the consumer is shopping or just browsing along shelves full of different brands.

All brand managers would like to have their brand chosen automatically every time. Some brands achieve this through an unconsciously learned response. How? By building a presence through frequency of advertising and maximum shelf facings (amount of units displayed on shelves – see

Chapter 19) and, most importantly, by supplying an appropriate level of reinforcement (an appropriate level of quality in the product or service itself). Chapter 3 emphasizes the importance of quality in the long-term repeat-buying success strategies of today and tomorrow.

Cognitive learning

Cognitive learning focuses on what happens in between the stimulus and the response. It embraces the intervening mental processes that lie within the black box.

Insight, meaning, perception, knowledge and problem solving are all considered relevant concepts. Cognitive learning is not dependent on trial and error. It depends on an ability to think, sometimes conceptually, and to perceive relationships and 'what if' scenarios. It is not dependent on an immediate reward to reinforce the learning process; in fact, 'latent learning' occurs in the absence of reward and without any immediate action. Of course, an individual has to be suitably motivated to achieve this kind of learning. The next intervening variable – motivation – will now be considered.

> ### China learns about Coca-Cola, Pepsi and Starbucks
>
> 'Just as they helped the Europeans to learn to eat with their hands (McDonald's) and drink ice-cold beer (Budweiser), mostly through classical advertising, Coca-Cola, Pepsi and Starbucks are conditioning a massive market to learn a new way of satisfying their needs, especially young Chinese. These brands are turning a tide in tastes. Tea houses in China already are being replaced by coffee houses and Starbucks.'
>
> PR Smith

> ### Adopt positive psychology to create shareable meaningful moments
>
> 'Positive conditioning: if the future of a brand is dependent on shared experiences, it is important to adopt positive reinforcement and positive psychology in order to create shareable, meaningful moments... invest in the consumer as well as in these positive moments... I ask you in return to share a great experience you've had with my brand, I should have a loyalty programme that rewards you for your advocacy.... a strategy for loyalty and advocacy determines the future of the brand... Do you have a system to reward advocates?
>
> Solis (2015)

Motivation

Motivation is defined as the drive to satisfy a need. Some motives are socially learnt (eg wanting to get married), and others are instinctive (eg wanting to eat when hungry). Sigmund Freud suggested that an individual is motivated by conscious and unconscious forces. Many motives are unconscious but active in that they influence everyday buying behaviour. Brands carry covert messages that are fleetingly understood at a subconscious level. As the Market Research Society said in its 1996 conference paper, 'It is often this deeper meaning which is what is exchanged for money. These deep underlying feelings are often the real reason why people buy products or services.'

Freud's psychoanalytical approach broke the personality into the id (instinctive drives and urges, eg to eat food or grab food), the ego (the social learning process that allows the individual to interact with the environment, eg to ask politely for food or pay for food) and the superego, which provides a conscience or ethical/moral referee between the id and the ego. Freud suggested that all actions are the results of antecedent conditions (see how childhood experiences might affect industrial buying behaviour some 30 or 40 years later in 'Mommy's never coming back', p. 182). Occasionally these unconscious stirrings manifest themselves in dreams, responses to ambiguous stimuli and slips of the tongue (Freudian slips).

Clinical psychology uses thematic apperception tests, Rorschach tests and word association tests to help it to analyse the underlying and sometimes unconscious personality traits and motivations of an individual. In-depth market researchers (qualitative researchers) use metaphors, picture completion and montages in an attempt to throw the interviewee's ego off guard and dip into the real underlying feelings that interviewees find difficult both to become aware of and to express in an articulate manner.

In the 1950s, Vance Packard was concerned about how in-depth researchers like Ernest Dichter were attempting to extract buyers' unconscious feelings, aspirations and motivations, which were then subtly reflected through advertising imagery, which in turn manipulated buyers unconsciously. Although discredited by some and criticized by others, Dichter's *Handbook of Consumer Motivations* (1964) is an extremely thought-provoking and entertaining read.

Here are some other well-known, in-depth research findings from the 1950s that were thought to reveal the deep underlying motivations that drive certain forms of behaviour, including buying behaviour:

- A woman is very serious when she bakes a cake, because unconsciously she is going through the act of birth.
- Soon after the trial period, housewives who used a new improved cake mix (no egg needed, just add water) stopped buying it.

The new improved cake mix provoked a sense of guilt, as the cooking role of the housewife was reduced.

- A man buys a convertible car as a substitute mistress.
- Smoking represents an infantile pleasure of sucking.
- Men want their cigars to be odoriferous in order to prove that they (the men) are masculine.
- Shaving for some men is the daily act of cutting off this symbol of manliness (stubble). It is therefore a kind of daily castration.

Of course, this is all outdated now. Humans are rational animals and are not concerned with such psychoanalytic interpretations of everyday, ordinary and, supposedly, common-sense behaviour. Consider 'A close shave?'.

A close shave?

There is a simple test that has been used in lectures with different groups. A question is posed, with a request for male respondents only. The question is 'How many of you find shaving a hassle?' Usually a unanimous show of hands emerges. 'How many of you would like to be able to dispense with the aggravation of shaving?' Slightly fewer hands emerge. 'Well, here is a cream that will solve your problem. This cream closes your hair follicles so that hair will never grow there again. It is medically approved and cleared for a market launch next year. Who would like to try some right now?' All the hands are gone. The question 'Why not?' is usually answered faintly with 'Freedom to choose to have a beard later in life' and so on. Or is there something deeper here? Dichter would have said 'Yes'.

Abraham Maslow's (1954) hierarchy of needs provides a simple but useful explanation of the way an individual's needs work. Essentially he showed that one is driven or motivated initially to satisfy the lower-level needs and then, when satisfied, move up to the next level of need. This theory also implies that motivation can be cyclical, in so far as buying a

FIGURE 4.13   Maslow's hierarchy of needs

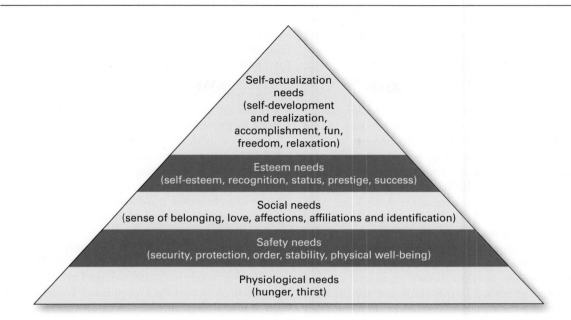

house may be motivated initially by the lower-level survival needs and subsequently by the higher-level need of esteem. Figure 4.13 shows Maslow's hierarchy of needs.

Cars transport people from A to B. Sometimes the need to buy a car is a basic survival need (eg to get to work, to earn money to buy food). Sometimes it can provide a cocoon (or shelter) from the mass of bodies scrambling for the public transport system. Sometimes it can provide freedom to explore the countryside, visit friends or do what you want (self-actualize). Cars can also act as status symbols (esteem). Some cars position their benefits (power, speed, safety, environmental, etc) so that they dominate the ad and appeal to the predominant need of a particular segment.

The invisible badge: motivation beyond conspicuous consumption

In 1899 Thorstein Veblen introduced 'conspicuous consumption', which suggested consumers buy products to impress other people, with his example of the man who parades down Main Street in 'stainless' linen, with a superfluous walking stick. These items told a story and provided 'evidence of leisure' – to an audience of strangers. Today's customers also wear badges (Guinness is a badge that tells everyone that the drinker is a discerning beer drinker). Even hybrid cars are said to be eco-status markers (or signals) that show 'conspicuous concern' about the environment. According to Walker (2008), conspicuous consumption is no longer valid:

There is a better idea – the invisible badge. What the Joneses might think is, really, beside the point. Because what you are really doing is telling that story to yourself. In other words, yes, a fancy 'product' really is a badge in the sense that it's a symbolic confirmation or expression of identity (an identity that we may wish for rather than actually embody – aspirational rather than authentic). But the fact that hardly anyone sees it, let alone accepts the meaning it supposedly projects, hardly matters. In fact, if the real audience is us, the badge may as well be invisible.

Sometimes customers simply do not understand the new benefits delivered by innovative products and services. For example, research originally rejected ATMs, with typical comments like, 'I wouldn't feel safe withdrawing money on the street'. Interestingly, the wheel is turning full circle, as customers are once again becoming nervous about cash withdrawals on crime-ridden streets.

Different people (or groups of people) extract different benefits from the same product. Some people want to drive a Porsche because it gives them power; others want to because they see it as a symbol of success (good for the ego and esteem); others just want the thrill of driving very fast (self-actualization, as in the case of the driver's last wish in Nevil Shute's *On the Beach*); others again may simply want a very fast, reliable car that allows them to get from A to B (around Europe) without delay (see the iPod example on page 107). Markets can be broken up into 'benefit segments' so that communications can be tailored to develop the ideal positioning for a particular segment. In some cases benefit segmentation demands different products for different segments, as in the case of the toothpaste market (see p. 107).

What motivates Sears' best customers?

Which of the following benefits motivates customers of the US department store Sears?

* priority repair service;
* special zero financing;
* free special catalogue;
* private sale events;
* money-saving certificates;
* personal recognition.

Answer: personal recognition – customers love it when staff call over the store manager to meet the VIP customer. You can see how this fits with Maslow's hierarchy of needs.

Attitudes

Attitudes affect buying behaviour. Attitudes are learnt, and they tend to stick; they can be changed,

but not very quickly. As Williams (1989) says: 'If a marketer is able to identify the attitudes held by different market segments towards his product, and also to measure changes in those attitudes, he will be well placed to plan his marketing strategy.' An attitude is a predisposition towards a person, a brand, a product, a company or a place.

An interesting question is 'Which came first, the attitude or the behaviour?' Are attitudes formed prior to purchase or post-purchase? Can attitudes be formed without any experience? The answer is 'yes' to both. Attitudes are sometimes formed without direct experience and, equally, products are often bought without any prior attitude. In the latter case, however, it is likely that an attitude will form as a result of word of mouth, or an engaging advertisement.

Attitudes can be broken down into three components, which are often explained as 'think', 'feel' and 'do' or 'cognitive', 'affective' and 'conative'. The cognitive element is the awareness or knowledge of, say, a brand. The affective element is the positive or negative feeling associated with the brand. The conative element is the intention to purchase. It can be important to measure all three components, since an isolated element can be misleading. For example, Rolls-Royce scores highly on the cognitive and affective elements of the attitude, but few of those who express awareness of and liking towards a Rolls-Royce will actually buy one. Identifying the levels of each attitudinal element helps to set tighter communication objectives. For example, the creative strategy for increasing brand awareness would be different from the strategy required to change the target market's feelings (or reposition the brand). A different communications strategy (perhaps an emphasis on sales promotions) would be required if the objective was to convert high awareness and positive feelings into trial purchases.

Attitudes can be changed, but it does take time. There are several options:

1 Change the beliefs held about the product or service (or its attributes and features).
2 Change the importance ratings (or weightings) of various attributes.
3 Introduce another attribute.
4 Change the association of a particular product or service with the others.
5 Change the perception of competitors' products or services.

Groups also influence attitudes: hence the importance of opinion formers and opinion leaders. Now consider group influence in the buying process.

> ### Attitudes and consumer values are changing
>
> 'Buying a house is no longer the American dream. Consumers may not even need a car.'
>
> Solis (2015)

Group influence

Much of human behaviour, and buyer behaviour in particular, is shaped by group influence. Whether cultural, religious, political, socio-economic, lifestyle, special interest groups or just family, social groups affect an individual's behaviour patterns. Watch explicit group influence occur as thousands of people perform a Mexican wave at football matches, the Olympics, etc.

> The effects of group influence are often seen in a queue or waiting area where charity collectors are attempting to collect money. Success or failure is often determined by the reaction of the first encounter, ie if the first person acknowledges the collector and makes a contribution, the next person is more likely to do so too. We have often seen a whole platform generously giving money after a successful start. Equally, we have seen almost total rejection by a whole queue once the initial contact has refused to donate. This is a bizarre or perverse form of charity giving and seems to be about peer group pressure. In a sense, a donation buys some relief from guilt or embarrassment.

Most individuals are members of some kind of group, whether formal (eg committees) or informal (eg friends), primary (where face-to-face com-munications can occur, eg family) or secondary (eg the Chartered Institute of Marketing). Groups develop their own norms or standards that become acceptable within a particular group. For example, normal dress among a group of yacht club members differs considerably from the norm or type of clothes worn by a group of clubbers. Yet both groups adhere to the rules (mostly unwritten) of their own group. Both groups also go through some sort of purchasing process.

Roles are played by different members within a group. An individual may also have to play different roles at different stages of the same day, eg a loving mother, tough manager, loyal employee, client entertainer, happy wife and, perhaps, sensuous lover. In the online world the same person can adopt different roles and even multiple personalities (see 'Different personalities below the surface', p. 104).

Activities, interests and opinions can form useful segmentation criteria. Roles within groups help to target decision makers and influencers in the decision-making units. Roles are also identifiable from the family life cycle, which shows how an individual moves from single to newly wed to full nest 1 (youngest child under six) to full nest 2 (youngest child six or over) to full nest 3 (dependent children) to empty nest 1 (children moved out) to empty nest 2 (retirement) or solitary survivor 1 (still working) to solitary survivor 2 (retired). The income levels, needs and spending patterns are often predictable as the income earner moves through various family life cycle roles. Spending patterns, influenced by changing roles, can be monitored and forecast before communicating any marketing messages. For example, direct mail companies often mail new mothers within a few days of the arrival of their baby.

Like everything else, roles are changing. Men aged 25–39 are experiencing a massive role change, and some find it hard to cope. 'Generation Y and X men expect to balance work and family, whereas their parents didn't' (Kimmel, 2008). Perhaps this is something women have been doing for some time. And perhaps this multitasking, multi-role life is more alien to young men, as Harold, a 39-year-old Swede, says in the Discovery Channel survey into the male species: 'Men of my age have to be successful in their jobs and take care of the house, kids, cook, fix the car and be a great lover' (Discovery Channel, 2008).

FIGURE 4.14   Which communications tools do what

	Unawareness	Awareness	Acceptance	Preference	Insistence/buy now	Reassurance
Advertising		→		→		→
PR		→				
Sponsorship		→				
Direct mail		→			→	
Selling					→	
Packaging		→			→	
Point of sale		→			→	
Exhibitions		→				→
Sales promo						→
Website		→				→
Social media						→
CRM/WOM						→

Absenteeism out, 'presentee-ism' in

'Men have to work harder than ever before to make themselves indispensable, to the point where we are now seeing "presentee-ism", which occurs when men feel that they have to get to work earlier and leave later to show their commitment. This is having a detrimental effect on their home lives.'

Coopere (2008)

Many young men today even see their home as having a different role to that of their parents' home. For many, home is a 'refuge from an uncertain world' and a 'haven from the stresses of life'. In addition to being a long-term financial investment, a home can also be a hub of technology that 'connects a guy with his sense of self through a variety of media experiences'.

Finally, the mix of communications tools helps move customers through the stages of a buying model from unawareness to reassurance. Each tool can affect different stages. Although there is always some vagueness about exactly where the effectiveness starts and stops, Figure 4.14 is arguably an oversimplified graphic that may help in understanding which tools do what.

Powerful analytics can help change customer buying habits, by Charles Duhigg

In the 1980s, a team of researchers led by a UCLA professor named Alan Andreasen undertook a study of peoples' most mundane purchases, like soap, toothpaste, trash bags and toilet paper. What they discovered was that few shoppers paid any real attention to how they purchased such articles – they were purchases that occurred routinely, without involving any deep thought or complex decision making. Naturally, this causes difficulties for marketers, who rely on displays, coupons and product promotions to persuade shoppers to deviate from ingrained habits. However, they also discovered that when consumers go through a major life event – for instance graduating from college, getting a new job, moving home, etc – shopping behaviour can become more flexible and predictable. This is therefore extremely valuable for retailers. The study revealed that when a person marries they are likely to begin buying a new brand of coffee. Similarly, if a couple moves house, there's a higher than usual chance that they'll opt for a new brand of breakfast cereal. Divorce, however, leads to new brands of beer.

As would be expected, no life events lead to more drastic changes in purchasing behaviour than the arrival of a baby. The new parents' habits are more changeable then than, arguably, any other point in their lives. Clearly, this represents huge opportunities for companies: if they can identify expectant mothers, they can earn millions.

To see this in action, consider a fictional shopper at Target. If a female shopper purchases cocoa butter lotion, a bag big enough to transport nappies and baby equipment, zinc and magnesium supplements, and a blanket, there's an excellent chance she's pregnant. If she makes her purchases using her customer loyalty card, the store will know how to reach her and trigger her shopping habits. They can logically assume that if she receives a coupon via e-mail, it will be a strong prompt for her to buy online. Alternatively, if she receives an ad in the mail on Friday, she's likely to use it on a weekend trip to the store (Duhigg, 2012).

Many customers dislike their privacy being invaded by third parties using 'clever' analytics – both in the United States, Europe and elsewhere. This will become a bigger issue as privacy is a new currency. People do not want to be spied upon as they live their lives and do their shopping. So retailers like Target need to be careful. Although they can sell baby products which customers didn't even know they needed yet, they have to be careful. They have discovered that some women react badly if they

Analytics may know more about your family than you do

Approximately 12 months after the Target team created their pregnancy-prediction model, a man clutching coupons for baby clothes that had been sent to his daughter walked into a Target store and demanded to see the manager. Enraged, he demanded to know whether Target was encouraging his school-girl daughter to get pregnant, as they were sending her incentives to buy baby clothes. The manager looked at the mailer promoting maternity clothing, nursery furniture and pictures of smiling infants and duly apologized. He followed up with a courtesy call to apologize again a few days letter. However, the father answered the phone and said 'I owe you an apology, my daughter is due to have a baby in August'.

receive incentives for baby products (imagine if the woman had not told her partner yet)? So they learned from this and now add random products that these customers would never buy such as lawnmowers and wine glasses, 'so the baby ads look random. Target stores learned that pregnant women will use the coupons as long she thinks she hasn't been spied on. "She just assumes that everyone else on her block got the same mailer for diapers and cribs. As long as we don't spook her, it works" said a staff member' (Duhigg, 2012).

This raises all sorts of delicate privacy and ethical issues about the use of personal shopping data (and other data). Chapter 11 on the Changing Communications Environment explores this ethical issue and more.

Summary and conclusion

Marketers must understand the target market's buying behaviour before, during and after the actual purchase. Even the apparently simple act of purchasing a hamburger can reveal a host of hidden motives. In-depth research reveals some deep and unconscious reasons that demonstrate some of the complexities of buying behaviour. The time and effort spent in

the buying process depend on the type of buying situation. Decision-making units affect the process.

Buying models highlight some of the stages through which the buyers pass, offering a kind of checklist for marketing communications to ensure that they carry the buyer through each stage successfully. The behaviourist school differs from the cognitive school of more complex buying models. Motivation, perception, learning, values, attitudes and lifestyles all interact and influence the buying process.

Once marketing professionals are equipped with a clearer understanding of both the motives for buying and the buying process itself, a marketing communications strategy can be developed to ensure that it covers as many avenues to the mind of the buyer as resources allow.

Reasons and motives range from the rational to the bizarre. Motives are, however, only one variable among many other intervening variables that integrate and influence buying behaviour. For example, beliefs and attitudes affect motives, which in turn affect the way an individual sees or perceives things (images, ads, products, shops, etc). We learn these opinions, attitudes and beliefs partly from groups (such as friends and colleagues), partly from commercial messages carefully aimed at us through advertising, sales promotion, etc, and partly from real experiences of products or services.

All these influences interact with commercial stimuli such as advertisements. The effects are ultimately reflected in our behaviour (or lack of behaviour in some circumstances).

In consumer markets, buying behaviour is affected by the complex web of mostly internal intervening variables (motivation, perception, attitudes, learning, memory, lifestyle, personality and groups). Sex, age, income and even an individual's face or body affect their behaviour. Other external variables such as laws and regulations, the weather, opening hours, an out-of-stock situation or an emergency can all change buying behaviour.

A B2B buyer is also influenced by internal variables, including the organization's objectives, policies, procedures, structure and systems, and

> Perhaps Oscar Wilde was too generous when he said that 'man is a rational animal except when asked to act within the dictates of reason'.

variables external to the organization such as the state of the economy, the level of demand and competition, the cost of money, etc. B2B buyers are not perfectly rational buyers. They too are affected by emotions.

Some argue that it is impossible, as Foxall (1992) says, to 'capture human nature in its entirety' because of the complexity of the decision-making process. This complexity is created by the web of rational and emotional factors that are generated from internal processes and guided by external influences.

Marketing communications can change a nation's behaviour. Marcomms do affect aggregate buying behaviour, as evidenced by changed behaviour patterns after the National Lottery integrated campaign, which stimulated some 65 per cent of the British adult population into shops to buy lottery tickets on a regular basis. The same changes in buyer behaviour are evident in China and across Europe, where marketers really do change customer behaviour patterns. It is no accident. It is never the result of guesswork. It is largely dependent on accurate analysis of customers and subsequently building up valuable customer insights. If you want to protect and enhance the value of your brand, your offer must be valuable. See how Unilever change behaviour in appendix 4.3. You will see that the higher the relevance, the greater the value – it's a continuum. It's the magic marketing formula delivering success.

Key points from Chapter 4

- Buying behaviour is complex.
- There are many different approaches to buying models.
- Marketers need a continual feed of information on customer behaviour.
- Emotional influences in decision making are still dominant in B2C and exist in B2B markets.
- Marketers must understand how the intervening psychological variables influence buyer behaviour.
- Marketers must know their customers better than the customers know themselves.

Appendix 4.1: Hofacker's online information processing

One approach to online information processing is Charles Hofacker's five stages of on-site information processing

1 Exposure.

2 Attention.

3 Comprehension and perception.

4 Yielding and acceptance.

5 Retention.

Each stage acts as a hurdle, since if the site design or content is too difficult to process, the customer cannot progress to the next stage. The e-marketer fails. The best website designs take into account how customers process information. Good e-marketers are aware of how the messages are processed by the customer and of corresponding steps we can take to ensure that the correct message is received.

The first stage is *exposure*. This is straight-forward. If the content is not present for long enough, customers will not be able to process it. Think of splash pages, banner ads or Shockwave animations: if these change too rapidly the message will not be received.

The second stage is *attention*. The human mind has limited capacity to pick out the main messages from a screen full of single-column format text without headings or graphics. Movement, text size and colour help to gain attention for key messages. Note though that studies show that the eye is immediately drawn to content, not the headings in the navigation systems. Of course, we need to be careful about using garish colours and animations, as these can look amateurish and distract from the main message.

Comprehension and *perception* are the third of Hofacker's stages. They refer to how the customer interprets the combination of graphics, text and multimedia on a website. If the design uses familiar standards or metaphors, it will be most effective, since the customer will interpret them based on previous experience and memory. Once relevant information is found, visitors sometimes want to dig deeper for more information.

Changing the layout of a website will be as popular with customers as a supermarket changing its store layout every six months! Metaphors are another approach to aid comprehension of e-commerce sites; a shopping basket metaphor is used to help comprehension.

Fourthly, *yielding* and *acceptance* refers to whether the information you present is accepted by the customer. Different tactics need to be used to convince different types of people. Classically a US audience is more convinced by features than benefits, while the reverse is true for a European audience. Some customers will respond to emotive appeals, perhaps reinforced by images, while others will make a more clinical evaluation based on the text. This gives us the difficult task of combining text, graphics and copy to convince each customer segment.

Finally, *retention* – how well the customer can recall their experience. A clear, distinctive site design will be retained in the customer's mind, perhaps prompting a repeat visit when the customer thinks, 'Where did I see that information?' and then recalls the layout of the site. A clear site design will also be implanted in the customer's memory as a mental map and they will be able to draw on it when returning to the site, increasing their flow experience.

To summarize, understanding how customers process information through the stages of exposure, attention, comprehension and perception, yielding and acceptance, and retention can help us design sites that really get our message across and deliver memorable messages and superior customer service.

Appendix 4.2: The post-PC customer

The post-PC customer may occasionally accept payment to view some ads. The rest are screened out by both sophisticated browser software and little 'TiVo-type' boxes attached to wall-to-wall screen TVs. Neither governments nor society permit old-style intrusive advertising any more. No more evening telephone calls from script-reading intelligent agents. It is also illegal to litter anyone's doorstep or house with mailshots and inserts. Heavy fines stopped all that a long time ago. The only ads that do get inside are carried by the many millions of private media owners who rent out their cars, bikes and bodies as billboards.

The tedious task of shopping for distress purchases like petrol, electricity or memory storage is delegated completely to embedded shopping bots.

Non-embedded bots spun out of control some years ago when they first appeared in three-dimensional hovering holograms – always at your side, always double-checking the best price for hire cars, hotels, even drinks at the bar. Some are programmed to be polite, aggressive or even abusive. All are programmed to be intrusive whenever anything is being bought. Delays on buses and traffic jams regularly occurred when argumentative bots engaged in lengthy negotiations. Frustration broke out. Bots attacked bots, people attacked bots and bot owners. Eventually bots were banned from buses, planes, trains and several 'peaceful supermarkets'.

Next came the great worm wars: programming bots so they only buy your brand – for life. But, unlike humans, bots can be reprogrammed by a competitor. The advertising agent worm was born. Agent eaters soon followed. Despite being information fatigued and time compressed, the post-PC customer lives a lot longer than many bots. And certainly longer than most of the new brands that seem to come and go. The 150-year-old person has already been born.

Meanwhile, back at the ranch, microwaves insist on offering suggestions of ideal wines to go with your meal, offering instant delivery from the neighbourhood's wired-up 24-hour roving delivery van. Your fridge offers special incentives to buy Pepsi when you run out of Coke (or whichever brand owns or hires the fridge-linked database). Children

Live longer

Humans may develop smaller ears (from constant use of headphones) and better body organs, replaced as a result of early-warning systems carried by miniature submarines constantly patrolling in the bloodstream. These wireless database-driven devices identify wearing parts and organs, check cloned stock availability, reserve beds and preferred surgeons and estimate time before breakdown replacement is required. Discounts for early bookings into leisure hospitals are also negotiated automatically.

happily play chess and interact with their opponents on the giant vertical screens, called refrigerators. Voice-operated computers are considered noisy and old fashioned as discreet, upmarket, thought-operated computers operate silently, but extremely effectively.

And all the time blue-tooth type technology facilitates ubiquitous communications, which allows constant interaction between machines. Man and machine integrate into a vast database. We have more IT power in today's average luxury car than the rocket that went to the moon. Yes, Moore's law suggests the tectonic shift will continue. Yes, marketing will continue in a new guise (probably not even called marketing but just common sense).

Time-compressed, information-fatigued and disloyal, the post-PC customer seeks relationships not from brands themselves but from databases that know, understand and seemingly care about them. Witness the virtual girlfriend relationships in Japan, relationships with shops and vending machines, oh, and relationships with people, real, quaint, touchy, feely, physical people.

And all the time the technology, if truly mastered, can free up time to do the important things in life, to give the post-PC customer a genuinely higher quality of life both at work and at home with family and friends.

Appendix 4.3: Unilever's five steps to change behaviour

Unilever publishes its marketing behaviour change principles 'Five Levers for Change' to inspire sustainable living

To coincide with a public debate on mainstreaming sustainable living, Unilever has today published the behaviour change model its marketers use to encourage sustainable changes in consumer living habits: 'Five Levers for Change'.

Based on Unilever's long history of research and insights into consumer behaviour, the tool is based on a set of key principles, which, if applied consistently to behaviour change interventions, increases the likelihood of having an effective and lasting impact. Unilever is sharing the model in the hope that others will find it helpful and use it to inspire people to turn their concerns about sustainability into positive actions.

The model outlines five techniques to apply when looking to encourage new behaviours, based on five key insights.

The 'Five Levers for Change' are:

1 Make it understood. Sometimes people don't know about a behaviour and why they should do it. This Lever raises awareness and encourages acceptance.

2 Make it easy. People are likely to take action if it's easy, but not if it requires extra effort. This Lever establishes convenience and confidence.

3 Make it desirable. The new behaviour needs to fit with how people like to think of themselves, and how they like others to think of them. This Lever is about self and society.

4 Make it rewarding. New behaviours need to articulate the tangible benefits that people care about. This Lever demonstrates the proof and payoff.

5 Make it a habit. Once consumers have changed, it is important to create a strategy to help hold the behaviour in place over time. This Lever is about reinforcing and reminding.

References and further reading

Benady, D (2014) A nudge in the right direction, *PR Week*, September

Bolger, M (2012) Brand loyalty, *The Marketer*, 17 Dec [online] http://www.alternatives.ie/knowledge_hub/article/brand_loyalty_5_top_tips_for_success

Brun-Jensen, P (2014) Next generation of social analytics are transforming digital marketing, *Adweek*, 22 September

Burstein, D (2013) Mobile marketing: 31% of marketers don't know their mobile email open rate, *Marketing Sherpa*, 1 February [online] http://sherpablog.marketingsherpa.com/email-marketing/moblile-marketing-email-open-rate/

Chisnall, P (1985) *Marketing: A behavioural analysis*, McGraw-Hill, Maidenhead

Cialdini, R (2007) *Influence: The psychology of persuasion*, Harper Business, New York

Cialdini, R (2014) An interview with Dr Robert Cialdini, *The Marketer,* 2 October

Colley, R H (1961) *Defining Advertising Goals and Measuring Advertising Results*, Association of National Advertisers, New York

Coopere, G (2008) Species – a user's guide to young men, Discovery Channel, Discovery Communications Europe

Dalton, J (2012) How brands can leverage the power of visual social media, Media Matters, 20 Dec.

Dichter, E (1964) *Handbook of Consumer Motivations: The psychology of the world of objects*, McGraw-Hill, New York

Dishman, L (2014) Study: people are not most attentive when watching TV at home, *Adweek,* 29 September [online] http://www.adweek.com/brandshare/study-people-are-not-most-attentive-when-watching-tv-home-160382

Duhigg, C (2012) How companies learn your secrets, *New York Times*, 16 February [online] http://www.nytimes.com/2012/02/19/magazine/shopping-habits.html?pagewanted=all&_r=0

East, R, Wright, M and Vanhuele, M (2008) *Consumer Behaviour: Applications in marketing*, Sage, London

Egan, J (2007) *Marketing Communications*, Case study 4.1, Thomson Learning, London

Ehrenberg, A (1974) Repetitive advertising and consumer awareness, *Journal of Advertising Research*, **14**, pp 25–34

Ehrenberg, A (1997) How can consumers buy a new brand? *Admap*, March, pp 20–27

Engel, J F, Blackwell, R D and Kollatt, D T (1978) *Consumer Behaviour*, 3rd edn, Dryden Press, Hinsdale, IL

Engel, J F, Kinnear, T C and Warshaw, M R (1994) *Promotional Strategy: Managing the marketing communications process*, 7th edn, Irwin Shaw, Homewood, IL

Fishbein, M (1975) Attitude, attitude change and behaviour: A theoretical overview, in P Levine (ed), *Attitude Research Bridges the Atlantic*, American Marketing Association, Chicago

Forsyth, J, Galante, N and Guild, T (2006) Capitalizing on customer insights, *McKinsey Quarterly*, **3**

Foxall, G (1992) *Consumer Psychology in Behavioural Perspective*, Routledge, London

Frank, O (2010) Goodbye, smartphone; hello, predictive context device, *Advertising Age*, 25 June

Hagy, D (2013) How to create the perfect post on social media, *Dashburst*, 20 June http://blog.dashburst.com/infographic/create-perfect-post-social-networks/

Hofacker, C (2001) *Internet Marketing*, 3rd edn, Wiley, New York

Howard, J A and Sheth, J N (1969) *The Theory of Buyer Behavior*, Wiley, New York

Humby, C (2008) *Brand is Dead, Long Live the Customer*, dunnhumby

Ibrahim, M (2013) Twitter and WPP in global partnership, *PR Week*, 14 June, p17

Jones, H (2008) How to tackle foreign markets, *Marketer*, 8 September

Kanner, B (1989) Colour scheme, *New York Magazine*, 3 April

Kapferer, J (2004) *The New Strategic Brand Management*, Kogan Page, London

Kennedy, J (2009) A wave of optimism, Interview with Eric Schmidt, *Marketing Age*, November

Kimmel, M (2008) Species – a user's guide to young men, Discovery Channel, Discovery Communications Europe

Kosinski, M, Stillwell D and Graepel, T (2013) Private traits and attributes are predictable from digital records of human behaviour, PNAS Proceedings of the National Academy of Sciences of the United States of America [Edited by Kenneth Wachter, University of California, Berkeley, CA] [online] http://www.pnas.org/content/early/2013/03/06/1218772110

Kotler, P (1998) *Practice of Marketing*, Prentice Hall, Englewood Cliffs, NJ

Langton, N (2013) Emotion influences B2B buying more than you might think, *The Laws Of Attraction*® [online] http://lawsofattraction.com/news/2014/5/emotion-influences-b2b-buying-more-than-you-might-think/2/

Lavidge, R and Steiner, G (1961) A model for predictive measurements of advertising effectiveness, *Journal of Marketing*, October, p 61

Lee, J (2013) Obama digital director praises social media, *Yale News*, 9 April

Luechtefeld, L (2012) Overcoming the challenges of branded video content, *Spotlight iMediaConnection*, 19 September http://www.imediaconnection.com/summits/coverage/32543.asp?imcid=spotlight

McGovern, G (2010) The rise of the anti brand – Ryanair, www.gerrymcgovern.com/search/node/ryanair

Manyika, J (2008) Google's view on the future of business: an interview with CEO Eric Schmidt, *The McKinsey Quarterly*, September

Marketer (2010) Facts and stats, *Marketer*, March

Market Research Society (MRS) (1996) Research is good for you: the contribution of research to Guinness advertising, Conference papers, MRS, London

Maslow, A (1954) *Motivation and Personality*, Harper & Row, New York

Oakes, S (2008) Mood maker – music to set your till ringing, *Marketer*, September

Packard, V (1957) *The Hidden Persuaders*, Penguin Books, Harmondsworth

Penn, D (2005) Brain science, that's interesting, but what do I do about it? Market Research Society Conference

Peters, T (2003) *Re-imagine*, Dorling Kindersley, London

Pun, R (2013) Why you must understand the perpetually connected customer: Part I, Adobe Digital Marketing Blog (Adobe) 25 June [online] http://blogs.adobe.com/digitalmarketing/mobile/why-you-must-understand-the-perpetually-connected-customer-part-i/

Roberts, K (2006a) Excerpt from a Saatchi & Saatchi presentation, Madrid, 8 June [online] http://www.saatchikevin.com/kevin-video/emotion-reason/

Roberts, K (2006b) Saatchi & Saatchi presentation, Madrid, 8 June

Roberts, K (2009a) Short cuts (part 1), 6 July; see hard copy journal kept in Chartered Institute of Marketing library (www.cim.co.uk)

Roberts, K (2009b) Short cuts (part 5), 6 July, see reference above for further details

Roberts, K (2009c) Annual City Lecture to the Worshipful Company of Marketors, 6 November

Roberts, K (2010a) Creativity, 21 January [online] KRconnecttoblogspot.ca

Roberts, K (2010b) Spreading the love, *Marketer*, February

Rogers, E M (1961) *Diffusion of Innovations*, 1st edn, Free Press, New York

Rosich, M (2015) Digital Outlook (Singapore conference) 2015, reported by Rajeck, J (2015) Five new mobile marketing strategies for 2015, eConsultancy blog, 21 Jan [online] https://econsultancy.com/blog/65928-five-new-mobile-marketing-strategies-for-2015/?utm_campaign=Twitter&utm_content=11477997&utm_medium=social&utm_source=twitter

Rossiter, J and Percy, L (1996) *Advertising Communications and Promotion Management*, 2nd edn, McGraw Hill, New York

Schifman, L G and Kaunk, L L (1991) *Consumer Behaviour*, 4th edn, Prentice Hall International, London

Shaw, R (1997/98) Appreciating assets, *Marketing Business*, December/January

Smart Insights (2014) The consumer decision journey (infographic) [online] http://www.smartinsights.com/marketplace-analysis/consumer-buying-behaviour/what-influences-purchase/

Smith, PR (1996) Video interview with Kenichi Ohmae

Smith, PR (2001) *Online eMarketing Course: eCustomers*, Multimedia Marketing.com, London

Smith, PR (2010) Video interview with Kevin Roberts, CEO, Saatchi & Saatchi Worldwide

Smith, PR (2014) SOSTAC® Guide to Your Perfect Digital Marketing Plan [online] www.PRSmith.org

Smith, PR (2014) The Rise & Fall Of Owned & Earned But Not Paid Media – World Cup Marketing Wars? 27 June [online] www.PRSmith.org/blog

Smith, P, Berry, C and Pulford, A (1999) *Strategic Marketing Communications*, Kogan Page, London

Solis, B (2015) Crossing the experience divide: creating positive, lasting experiences is a crucial mandate for any brand, *Technology of Us*, 12 January [online] http://technologyofus.com/

Soskey, G (2015) What to cut from your marketing, *Hubspot Blog* 7 Jan [online] http://linkis.com/blog.hubspot.com/mar/Yy9bk

Spool, J (2009) The $300 million button, *User Interface Engineering*, 14 January [online] http://www.uie.com/articles/three_hund_million_button/

Strong, E K (1925) *The Psychology of Selling*, McGraw-Hill, New York

Unilever (2011) Unilever Reveal 5 Steps To Change Consumer Behaviour, 23 November, Unilever Global

Veblen, T (1899) *The Theory of the Leisure Class*, Oxford University Press

Walker, R (2008) The invisible badge: Moving past conspicuous consumption, ChangeThis.com, **47** (1)

Williams, K C (1989) *Behavioural Aspects of Marketing*, Heinemann, Oxford

Williams, T G (1982) *Consumer Behavior*, West Publishing, St Paul, MN

Further information

Market Research Society (MRS)
15 Northburgh Street
London EC1V 0JR
Tel: +44 (0)20 7490 4911
www.mrs.org.uk

Ofcom
Riverside House
2a Southwark Bridge Road
London SE1 9HA
Tel: +44 (0)300 123 3000
www.ofcom.org.uk

Semiotic Solutions
1 Manor Cottages
Kenninghall Road
Garboldisham
Norfolk IP22 2SJ
Tel: +44 (0) 1953 681012
www.semioticsolutions.com

05
Communications theory

LEARNING OBJECTIVES

By the end of this chapter you will be able to:

- Understand that communication involves a two-way flow of information
- Appreciate the subtle variables involved in communications
- Apply communication theories to practical marketing situations
- Exploit contemporary models to ensure successful innovations
- Explain why new models are required to meet the changing communications landscape
- Understand why new skills are required to match new communications models

Introduction to communications theory   144

Non-verbal and non-symbolic communications   144

Symbolic and semiotic communications   145

Source credibility   145

Opinion formers, opinion leaders and connectors   146

Advocates   149

Communications models   150

A single-step communications model   150

A two-step linear communications model   151

Multi-step linear communications models   151

Multi-step non-linear communications models   154

Classic and contemporary communications models   155

Future communications models   157

The end of the traditional marcomms funnel model?   157

Make way for the Semantic Web – new models required   158

New marketing communications skills required   160

Key points from Chapter 5   160

References and further reading   161

Further information   162

Introduction to communications theory

A dictionary definition of 'communications' is as follows: 'communication n. 1. a transmitting 2. a) giving or exchange of information, etc by talk, writing b) the information so given 3. a means of communicating 4. the science of transmitting information'.

What is interesting is the exchange of information. Communication is not a one-way flow of information. Talking at or to someone does not imply successful communication. This only occurs when the receiver actually receives the message that the sender intended to send. Message rejection, misinterpretation and misunderstanding are the opposite of effective communication.

Millions die from ineffective communications

'There is evidence that a mistake in translating a message sent by the Japanese government near the end of World War II may have triggered the bombing of Hiroshima, and thus ushered in atomic warfare. The word "mokusatsu" used by Japan in response to the US surrender ultimatum was translated as "ignore", instead of its correct meaning, "withhold comment until a decision has been made".'

Cutlip, Center and Broom (2004)

This is an extreme and tragic example of communications gone wrong. Communication errors in marketing generally do not cost lives but can, if allowed to continue unchecked, cost market share, company survival and jobs. On the other hand, good marketing communications help an organization to thrive by getting its messages across in a focused and cost-effective way.

Good marketing communications is not as simple as it may appear. Even David Ogilvy, the advertising guru, was once reported to have used the word 'obsolete' in an advertisement only to discover that (at the time) 43 per cent of US women had no idea what it meant. The delicacy and difficulty of creating effective communications to target audiences can be explained by Douglas Smallbone's analogy of radio communication.

Perfect transmitting conditions might exist if there were no noise (extraneous factors that distract or distort the message, such as other advertisements, poor reception, a flashing light, a door bell or an ambulance). Without noise, perfect transmitting conditions would exist. In reality, there is almost always noise, so perfect transmitting conditions do not exist. Cinemas may be the exception, where a captive audience is in an attentive state and receptive to, say, a well-produced X-rated advertisement. But even when the target audience is seemingly tuned in (watching, listening to or looking at a particular organization's package, promotion, advertisement, etc) it may not be on the same wavelength because of the hidden internal psychological processes that may be reshaping or distorting the message to suit the audience's own method of interpretation.

The human receiver is in fact equipped with five distinct means of receiving messages or information or marketing communications – the five senses of hearing, sight, touch, taste and smell. Marketing communications tools can address many senses simultaneously (for example with packaging).

The human radio

'Given good transmitting conditions and receiver and transmitter tuned to the same wavelength, perfect reception can be effected.'

Smallbone (1969)

Non-verbal and non-symbolic communications

Although verbal and visual communications gain a lot of conscious attention, there are non-verbal and non-symbolic ways of communicating, such as space, time and kinetics. Crowded areas, or lack of space, send messages to the brain that, in turn, can stimulate a different set of thoughts and a different behavioural response. The opposite is also true: a spacious office or living room conveys different images. In fact spacious websites (minimalist design) can quickly communicate the purpose, or benefit, of a web page. Visitors are impatient and fast-moving. 'If within a couple of seconds a person does not understand what a page is about they tend to leave. Therefore, we need very minimalist design that clearly and rapidly communicates the purpose of any particular page' (McGovern, 2013). We also need minimal choices as Hick's Law (1952) states the greater the number of potential choices/decisions the longer it will take to make a choice.

Visitors also seek consistency across website pages as well as community and belonging (you can use language and imagery that helps visitors to feel included in your business). And of course, colour communicates; Google tests prove blue links receive more clicks (Golson 2009) than links using other colours. A visual hierarchy also helps since visitors are also drawn to objects that stand out. They jump along prominent items on a site which means you can guide them to information you want them to see. Audiences tend to look at faces more than other objects.

In Western cultures the use of time creates images; a busy but organized person gives an impression of authority. 'Thanks for your time' immediately conveys a respect for and an appreciation of a seemingly important person's time. A busy diary can project an image of importance. 'I can squeeze you in on Friday at...' implies seniority in the relationship. In the UK, the term 'window' is now used for free time or space in a busy diary. Some advertisements sell products and services primarily on time-saving and convenience benefits. In fact, banks are really time machines that allow an individual to move forward in time by buying, say, a house that would not normally be affordable for 30 years. Finally, kinetics communicate. Gestures and movements send messages. Even the simple, swift clicking of a briefcase, entering or leaving a room or closing or not closing a door can communicate (in China sitting opposite the door means you are paying for the meal). Most of all, body language and facial gestures are powerful communicators. An understanding of body language allows an individual to learn more about what another person is really feeling. A smile, for example, communicates immediately, effectively and directly. Today we also analyse digital body language (click behaviour) to determine what a visitor is interested in and what stage of the buying process they are at.

Symbolic and semiotic communications

The field of semiotics (or semiology) opens up a rich discussion of how symbols and signs are used in communications, particularly advertising. Audiences often unconsciously perceive images stimulated by certain symbols.

Engel, Warshaw and Kinnear (1994) demonstrated how Lever's fabric softener Snuggle used a cuddly teddy bear in its advertising. It has been suggested by some psychologists that 'the bear is an ancient symbol of aggression, but when you create a teddy bear, you provide a softer, nurturant side to that aggression. As a symbol of tamed aggression, the teddy bear is the perfect image for a fabric softener that tames the rough of clothing.'

Engel, Warshaw and Kinnear (1994) comment: 'The key point here is that if marketing communicators are not aware of the subtle meanings of symbols, then they are liable to communicate the wrong message.'

Carol Moog's advice to Pierre Cardin on its men's fragrance advertisement, which was designed to show men who are 'aggressive and in control' splashing on fragrance, was accepted but rejected! Moog saw 'cologne gushing out of a phallic-shaped bottle' creating a conflict of images, since it 'symbolized male ejaculation and lack of control'. Pierre Cardin acknowledged that she was probably right, but decided to keep the shot, as it was 'a beautiful product shot plus it encourages men to use our fragrance liberally'.

Source credibility

The success or failure of an advertisement, or any message, is partially determined by whether it is a credible message in the first place. This, in turn, is influenced by the credibility of the source of the message, the deliverer of the message and the chosen media vehicle.

The perceived credibility of the message source is influenced by trustworthiness and expertise. These are key factors that organizations must constantly prove so that they have a platform of credibility ('Develop credibility before raising visibility': see Chapter 3). Endorsements from customers and venerable bodies, published papers, conference speeches, awards won, memberships and of course the perceived quality of the brand itself all help to establish trustworthiness and expertise, ie source credibility. In addition to the credibility of the brand, the message credibility is also influenced by the individual delivering the message, such as the presenter in an advertisement. For example, some brands in the UK stopped using supermodel Kate Moss when her public behaviour was deemed to be 'unsuitable'. On the other hand, a highly credible presenter adds credibility to a brand.

Content design also affects credibility. Researchers asked subjects to look at two websites: one was professionally designed, and the other looked dated and ugly. When the researchers asked people why they mistrusted the information on either site, 94 per cent said it was because of design. And get this: the content on both websites was exactly the same (Sillence *et al*, 2014). Poor design is one of the main reasons why visitors distrust a site. Therefore your site should look up to date and display relevant content and images. State your business purpose/ OVP (online value proposition) clearly. Display 'trust badges', high profile customer logos, members of trade bodies, payment methods, security protection.

Positive and negative reviews = two-sided arguments create more trust.

'Reevoo research shows bad reviews actually reduce site abandonment, with time on a site leaping from just over three minutes to 18 minutes. The research revealed that consumers trust reviews more when they see both positive and negative comments. In fact, an absence of negative reviews can lead consumers to distrust a brand. "Shoppers are suspicious when reviews don't include any complaints", says Reevoo founder Richard Anson.'

Manning (2012)

The media vehicle affects the credibility, eg a message that 'using a laptop damages your fertility' would have less credibility if it came from the *Sun* newspaper than it would have if it came from the *FT*, or even more credibility if it came from a learned medical journal rather than a newspaper survey. The media vehicle's perceived expertise,

prestige and editorial tone (style, eg upmarket or mass-market, and other content, eg sex and violence) all affect the credibility of a message.

Kelman (1961) suggested that the message source has three variables: 1) perceived source expertise and neutrality (or objectivity); 2) perceived source attractiveness (if it is deemed attractive, the recipients may be more likely to develop a similar opinion or position); and 3) perceived power to reward or punish message receivers (eg a teacher or perhaps an owner of a social media group). In summary, a great message delivered from a source with low 'source credibility' will not be as effective as the same message coming from a source with high 'source credibility'.

Message likeability

'This is about how much an individual likes an advertisement. It is determined by how interesting, meaningful, relevant and enjoyable an advertisement is deemed to be. When researching advertisements, and in particular, how much customers like an advertisement, "likeability is deemed to have four elements: entertainment, relevance, clarity and pleasantness".'

Source unknown

Opinion formers, opinion leaders and connectors

Opinion formers and opinion leaders include journalists, judges, consultants, lecturers, religious leaders and group leaders. Today they also include bloggers, Facebook fan page owners, Facebook group owners, LinkedIn group owners and many more online group leaders. Officially, opinion formers such as journalists are formally paid to give their opinions, while opinion leaders such as bloggers are not. Identifying influencers is important, and high-profile bloggers can be easily identified, as can group leaders, whether on Facebook or LinkedIn. Indeed LinkedIn now has a feature that identifies the top influencers in a group and not just the group owners.

Malcolm Gladwell's fascinating book *The Tipping Point* (2000) explores how to create an epidemic of demand for a product or service or idea. He calls opinion leaders 'socially contagious connectors' and suggests that, instead of pandering to the mass-market herd, marketers should focus on satisfying the connectors' needs. Connectors are estimated to be 10 per cent of a target audience (Keller and Berry, 2002).

It is worth identifying and partnering with the 'infectious few' so that organizations can focus on the 'consumers that count, who have the power to unleash an epidemic of demand for products and services' (Marsden, 2004). Connectors, opinion leaders, style leaders, innovators, early adopters, influential individuals and opinion formers: call them what you want, they spread messages.

Connectors know a lot of people

'They are the kind of people who know everyone. All of us know someone like this. But I don't think we spend a lot of time thinking about the importance of these people. I'm not even sure that most of us really believe that the kind of person who knows everyone really knows everyone. But they do.'

Gladwell (2000)

Marketers recognize that in each market there are smaller target groups of opinion leaders who influence other members in the marketplace. Major brands can maintain their credibility by talking (advertising) specifically to these leaders, as well as talking to the mass through other media channels (sometimes with messages tailored for the two groups). Whether marketers are advertising hi-fis, fashion, tennis rackets or social issues, multi-step communications can be employed.

In the world of fashion, the leaders are called **'style leaders'**. Even cult fashion products can be mass-marketed by carefully splitting the messages between style leaders and the mass. While the leaders want to set themselves apart from the rest, the mass market consciously and/or unconsciously looks to the leaders for suggestions about what to buy. The difficulty lies with success – as the mass market buys more, the leaders lose interest unless they are reinforced with brand values that preserve the brand's credibility among the cognoscenti. This is important because, if the leaders move away today, the mass sales will eventually start falling away next year or

the year after. So, in addition to the mass advertising, some brands use small-audience, targeted, opinion-leader media to send the 'right' messages to reinforce the leaders' relationship with the brand.

Hi-fi trendsetters need a different kind of advertising than just colour supplements with glossy brand images. These innovators and early adopters read additional magazines and look for more detailed technical information in music magazines or specialist hi-fi magazines, buyers' guides, etc. Less knowledgeable buyers often refer to a friend who is a bit of a music buff (innovator or adopter) for an opinion on a brand of hi-fi before deciding to buy.

Just getting the product into the hands of the opinion leaders can help a brand competing in a large market. Special offers to opinion formers can work wonders: for example a new tennis racket is offered initially to the school tennis team stars at a special low price in the hope that these 'star school players' (or influential individuals) will influence others by talking about the new racket.

Microsoft calls on influencers to launch new windows phone

Molly O'Donnell, Director of Influencer Marketing, Microsoft says that before any influencer campaign, they identify (1) who they want to reach (2) where they are (3) what media they consume and (4) how do they behave? More than 70 per cent of its target consumers are influenced by their peers. Microsoft partners with Klout through its Perks programme and gave a free phone to individuals with a score of 55+ (and invited them to an event). Others with scores of 29–54 were invited but didn't get a phone. Microsoft placed ads on Facebook Marketplace and partnered with Flavorpill, a daily guide to cultural events, to reach 'tastemakers (massive following) and influencers'. Result: thousands of people vying to get into the events and conversations reaching tens of thousands before, during and after the event.

Solis (2012)

It is worth identifying and keeping a list of advocates, particularly those that are influential and innovators/early adopters if in the business of innovative products or services. When Twitter started, many of the early users were self-identified as opinionated innovators and early adopters. Users of new technology are, by definition, innovators and early adopters.

An understanding of multi-phase communication processes can contribute something to the development of social issue campaigns, such as that concerning AIDS. The initial stages of the campaign were temporarily restricted by inaccurate editorial coverage. Some tabloid journalists were feeding conflicting messages to the same mass that the advertising was addressing. The factual advertising was switched into the press so that opinion formers (journalists) could not write any more conflicting and inaccurate reports.

Influencers bite back

'United Airlines baggage handlers allegedly damaged musician Dave Carroll's expensive Taylor guitar but denied his claim for reimbursement. He took to YouTube and produced a series of three funny videos – watched over 11 million times by Dec 2011. *Times Online* estimated the negative PR cost UA shareholders $180 million in lost market capitalization.'

PR Smith

The power of influential individuals and organizations can also be seen in industrial markets. An entire industry may follow a well-respected and highly successful company that makes an early decision to buy. Expert sales teams focus on these kinds of companies initially. Marketers in consumer markets can also focus on the people who are the first to buy new ideas. Better information today can provide a focused approach through database marketing, while the imagery used can reflect the lifestyles, attitudes and aspirations of these innovators and early adopters of fresh ideas. We are also particularly interested in the influencers, opinion formers (informal often bloggers and tweeters) and opinion leaders (formal leaders like journalists, judges, consultants) who spread information. Communications agencies regularly use 'blogger outreach programmes' to identify and work with opinion formers.

FIGURE 5.1   You can watch digital guru, Zaid Al Zaidy, talking about how agencies use 'Blogger Outreach' programmes on the PRSmith1000 channel on YouTube

There are several different approaches including Campbell's Soup's Warhol campaign (see Chapter 20); they approached key media and opinion formers through an intensive sampling campaign, whilst also offering product for photo shoots.

Virtual influencer – the search engine

Instead of watching ads, building brand relationships over time and eventually buying a particular product or service, customers can now speak into their phone and ask it to get a certain product or service. It duly obliges, as this virtual influencer, Google Voice, searches carefully and delivers useful suggestions for purchase. A high Google ranking, for some, acts as an endorsement of quality (or at least relevance). Mobile apps compare prices by just swiping the phone screen over the bar code or just keying in the brand name.

Influence is a measure of social capital

'Social capital is a culmination of 3 pillars: Reach (popularity, proximity, goodwill); Relevance (authority, trust, affinity); and Resonance (culmination of reach and relevance: frequency, period, amplitude). Resonance is also how long something will stay alive in the stream before attention dissipates.'

Solis (2012)

Advocates

Brand advocates are invaluable as they promote your brand, usually to your target market. These are your precious 1 per cent of customers that demonstrate high levels of engagement, strong brand loyalty and tell others about your brand. Sometimes called the 1 per cent rule, they are the ones that write nice reviews about your brand and recommend your brand to other people. They are special. They need to be treated as special. The 1 per cent rule may be a derived from the 90-9-1 rule from Ben McConnell and Jackie Huba (2006), which describes activity on online forums. Ninety per cent lurked (or observed or read posts). Nine per cent commented. One per cent created new posts (McConnell and Huba, 2006). Although it is referred to as the 90-9-1 principle or rule (and occasionally the 1-9-90 rule) it is in fact the 89:10:1 ratio, but this is not very memorable, hence the 1 per cent rule is also used.

> Nokia has a community of advocates in each country who are managed through a specialist agency, with updates centred around a special blog for influencers, Nokia Connects, which has resources put into it reflecting its importance.
> **Nokia Connects for Nokia advocates**
> **(www.nokiaconnects.com)**

Brands need cross-channel CRM programmes to communicate with their connected customers, strengthen relationships, recruit into ambassador programmes, engage them with relevant events, and reward them for their advocacy and their social status. Virgin America takes influencers for test flights (and partners with Klout's Perk Performance programme to give rewards), while Starbucks targets coffee lovers with Klout (who have a large Twitter following).

The ladder of engagement discussed in Chapter 1 suggested that only about 1 per cent of your visitors will engage at collaborative co-creation (eg creating new products) while about 9 per cent (at best) would engage at lower levels such as reviews, ratings and discussions. About 90 per cent would nothing other than 'lurk' (read).

Interestingly, Wikipedia suggest that in a collaborative website such as a wiki, 90 per cent of the

> ### Starbucks targeted coffee lovers with Klout
>
> 'Klout influencers who were ranked as top influencers on the "topic of coffee" were offered a free sample. Starbucks measured the number of offers and click-throughs that led to redeemed samples, as well as "mentions" and conversations tied to each source. Mentions were translated into reach and sentiment to determine impressions and brand lift. Marketers can spark conversations, positive sentiment, and trigger desirable actions and outcomes that track towards ROI.'
>
> Solis (2012)

participants of a community only view content, 9 per cent of the participants edit content, and 1 per cent of the participants actively create new content. These numbers may reduce as people find themselves increasingly busy.

What percentage of your audience, your fans, your likers will engage with your site, blog, page or whatever platform/s you use? Some are more active than others. And some of the active audience are more active than others. You need to know (and reward) these active people as they are your advocates.

> ### Pareto's 80/20 rule
>
> 'The Pareto rule suggests that 80 per cent of your sales come from 20 per cent of your customers. Vilfredo Pareto originally revealed in the 1890s that 80 per cent of the land in Italy was owned by 20 per cent of the population. Many years later (in 1941), management consultant Joseph M Juran stumbled on Pareto's work and applied it, initially, to quality control (80 per cent of a problem comes from 20 per cent of the causes) and eventually to sales and customers; he called it Pareto's 80/20 rule. This ratio can, and does, vary from organization to organization; for example, in 2011, Paul Schneider (2011) found that his ratio was 70:20:10 while The Community Roundtable observed a 55:30:15 ratio.'
>
> Crystal (2013)

Communications models

No simple diagram can reflect all the nuances and complexities of the communication process. This section considers some basic theories and models.

A single-step communications model

There are three fundamental elements in communication: the sender (or source), the message and the receiver, as shown in Figure 5.2.

This basic model assumes that the sender is active, the receiver is inactive or passive and the message is comprehended properly. In reality this is rarely the case. Chapter 4 demonstrates how we see what we want to see and not necessarily what is sent. An understanding of the target receiver or audience helps to identify what is important to the audience and how symbols, signs and language are interpreted. The message is 'dressed up' or 'coded' in an appropriate way, sent through a media channel and, if it gets through all the other noise, finally 'decoded' by the receiver. Guinness advertisements basically ask their target audience to drink Guinness, but they are very carefully coded. For example, 'It's not easy being a dolphin' were the only words uttered in one of their television advertisements.

The audience decodes the message (correctly or incorrectly) and ultimately rejects, accepts, stores or decides whether to include Guinness in its 'considered set of brands' or not. Correct decoding does not always work, eg an anti-drink ad campaign backfired by inadvertently glamorizing the habit (see the box 'Decoding drunken messages' opposite). Amidst the careful coding and decoding there is noise; the extraneous factors that distract or distort the coded messages. Figure 5.3 demonstrates this.

The sender monitors feedback (eg whether the receivers change their behaviour, facial expression, beliefs or attitudes) so that the message (and/or the channel in which it is sent) can be modified or changed. With so many other advertisements out there it is easy to understand why so little communication actually gets through and works on the target market.

Despite the attractions of one-to-one marketing, mass communications such as television advertising are still considered attractive because they can reach a large audience quickly and cheaply (when comparing the cost per thousand individuals contacted – see page xxx). In fact, although TV channels are fragmenting, TV viewing is increasing year on year in most of Europe and the United States (see Chapter 7). Having said that, much of this kind of mass advertising is often ignored or distorted by an individual's information processing system. However, there is usually, within the mass audience, a percentage who are either actively looking for the particular product type or who are in a receptive state for this type of message (see the financial services example in the box 'Floating targets' on page xxx). Mass communication is therefore of interest to many marketing communicators. It is not the single-step process it was considered to be in the early mass communications model shown in Figure 5.4.

FIGURE 5.2

A simple communications model

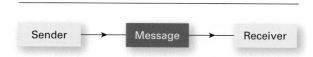

FIGURE 5.3   The communication process (based on Schramm's 1955 model)

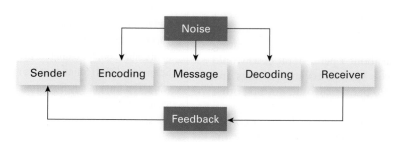

FIGURE 5.4

One-step communications model

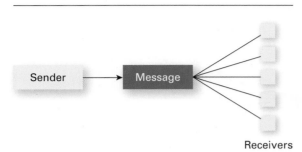

Receivers

Decoding drunken messages

'Drinks manufacturer Diageo's "The Choice Is Yours" campaign implied that being very drunk with friends carries a penalty of social disapproval. However, for many young people the opposite is often the case. University of Bath research team found adverts which show drunken incidents – such as being thrown out of a nightclub, or passing out in a doorway – are often seen by young people as being typical of a "fun" night out, rather than as a cautionary tale. Lead researcher Professor Christine Griffin said: "Extreme inebriation is often seen as a source of personal esteem and social affirmation amongst young people."'

BBC News Channel (2007)

This kind of inaccurate model of mass communication suggests that the sender has the potential to influence an unthinking and non-interacting crowd. Audiences (receivers) are active in that they process information selectively and often in a distorted manner ('We see what we want to see'). Receivers (the audience) talk to each other. Opinion formers and opinion leaders also influence the communications process. Today's communications models are more sophisticated.

A two-step linear communications model

Katz and Lazarsfeld's two-step hypothesis (1955) helped to reduce fears of mass indoctrination by the all-powerful media. It assumed that mass messages filtered through opinion leaders to the mass audience. Figure 5.5 shows how messages are filtered through opinion leaders, as well as going directly to some members of the target audience.

When **opinion formers** (**OF**) are added in, the communications model becomes a little bit more interesting. Opinion formers can be separated from opinion leaders, as shown in Figure 5.6. Opinion formers are formal experts whose opinion has influence, eg journalists, analysts, critics, judges or members of a governing body. People seek their opinions, and they provide advice. Opinion leaders, on the other hand, are harder to identify – they are not formal experts and do not necessarily provide advice, but other buyers are influenced by them. Other customers look toward them. Opinion leaders often enjoy higher social status (than their immediate peer group), are more gregarious and have more confidence to try new products and services. Endorsements from both opinion formers and opinion leaders are valuable.

The opinion formers are often quoted in promotional literature and advertisements, while the style leaders are often seen with the brand through clever editorial exposure engineered by public relations professionals. This can be generated by collecting third-party endorsements, creating events around celebrities and 'placing' products alongside celebrities (eg branded mineral water on the top table at press conferences or actual product placement in films). In **B2B markets**, blue-chip customers are opinion leaders and are much sought after, as their presence on a customer list influences other customers. Both opinion formers and opinion leaders can contribute towards credibility. 'Credibility before visibility' means that a solid platform of credibility should be developed before raising visibility with any high-profile activities.

Multi-step linear communications models

Communication is in fact a multifaceted, multi-step and multi-directional process. Opinion leaders talk to each other. Opinion leaders talk to their listeners. Listeners talk to each other (increasingly with discussion groups and internet groups) and subsequently feed back to opinion leaders, as shown in Figure 5.7. Some listeners or readers receive the message directly.

FIGURE 5.5   Two-step communications with opinion leaders

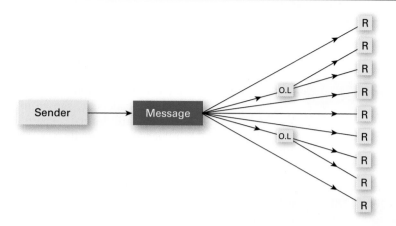

FIGURE 5.6   Two-step communications with opinion leaders and opinion formers

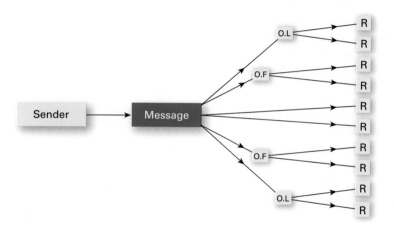

FIGURE 5.7   Multi-step communications model (a)

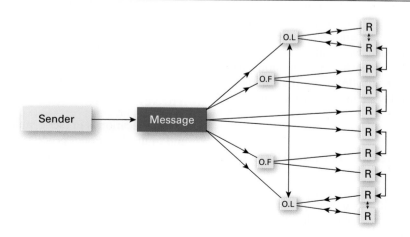

FIGURE 5.8   Multi-step communications model (b)

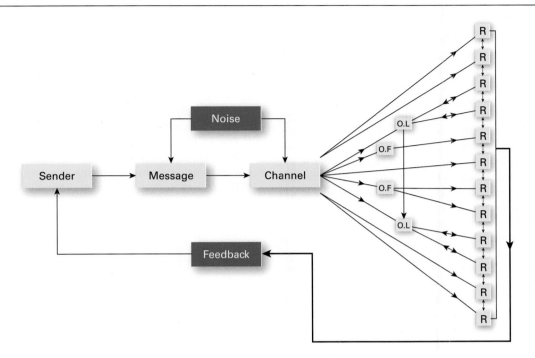

Noise, channels and feedback can be added to the multi-step model to make it more realistic, as shown in Figure 5.8.

The process of communicating with groups is fascinating. Group roles (leaders, opinion formers/leaders and followers), group norms and group attitudes are considered in 'Group influence' (page xxx). In fact, all the intervening psychological variables can be added into the communications models to show how perception, selection, motivation, learning, attitudes and group roles all affect the communication process. The intervening variables and some more complex models of buyer behaviour are considered in more detail in Chapter 4.

Winning over opinion leaders can be key to any marketing communications campaign, whether B2B or B2C. Take B2B: IBM linked up with the Marketing Society, as its 3,500 members represented key movers and shakers in the business world. Consider B2C: KangaROOS trainers targeted opinion-leading celebrities such as Cat Deeley, Edith Bowman and children's TV show presenters by giving them free shoes. P&G, Unilever and Microsoft trial products with hundreds of thousands (see page xxx).

James Bond: opinion leader

'Product placement does not always have to be expensive. In 1997 European Telecom touted their new piece of mobile technology (a car fax) to all the major product placement agencies that act on behalf of the film company giants. They had no budget for any deals or link-ups with any film, but they had a visually interesting piece of technology. To their surprise and delight, the placement agency handling the James Bond film *Tomorrow Never Dies* requested two working prototypes, which were duly delivered and demonstrated at Pinewood Studios. The product was shown as Moneypenny receives a fax from the clearly branded prototype, and hands it to Bond, who is sitting alongside M in the back of the Daimler. An additional car fax is also clearly seen alongside Bond in the back of the car. Now the PR team can really milk the opportunity. After all, "a portable fax that is approved by James Bond surely has more cachet than one that isn't".'

Lucas (1997)

Multi-step non-linear communications models

Let's take this a stage further and consider today's new web communications models, which revolve around the brand instead of simply being sent to the masses by the brand owner. Markets are conversations. The ladder of engagement in Chapter 1 is an example of this. Word of mouth works much more quickly online than offline. With the internet came the easier facilitation of customer communities, where customers can talk, **first to each other (C2C)** and **second, back to the company (C2B)**. The flow of communications eventually becomes like a web between customers and opinion leaders – all built around the brand (see Figure 5.9).

The company facilitates these conversations. In doing so, it keeps close to customers, as it can look and listen to what's being said. It can also communicate easily with the customers and ultimately develop strong relations with them. Newsgroups and discussion rooms hosted by the brand discuss the brand, its applications, problems, issues, ideas, improvements and a broader array of topics linked

with some of the brand values. In a sense, a web of conversations is spinning around the brand. Customers talk to each other. For example, more than half of eBay's customers come from referrals (Reichfield and Schafter, 2000).

The marketing team also monitors the blogosphere (including Twitter) and user group sites it does not host; some of the truths may be painful but extremely useful. C2C communications can be negative. Remember the Pentium chip problem? It spread like wildfire as the worry spread online. C2C communications can also be fuelled by some customer groups who set up fake sites and hate sites that are devoted to spreading negative messages about brands. One type of C2C that is positive – and in fact generates a lot of business – is referrals, where happy customers become advocates and recommend other customers. Another positive form of C2C and P2P is viral, where customers pass the message on. This is accelerated word of mouth. Clever, creative messages with interesting ideas, special offers, announcements and invitations are good for viral marketing, where messages are passed between customers and from opinion leaders to customers and from opinion leaders to opinion leaders and, of course, from the brand also (see Figure 5.10).

FIGURE 5.9

Simple web communications model

FIGURE 5.10

Advanced web communications model

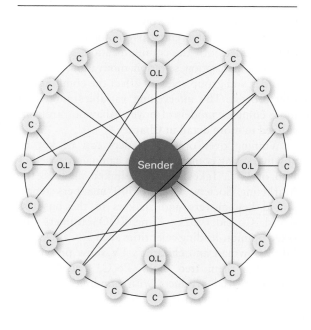

Affiliate marketing also spreads awareness of a brand among a community of relevant customers, who in turn talk to each other and can spread ordinary or clever viral messages among their own communities. Implicit in all of these communications models is permission-based marketing. In this time-compressed, information-cluttered world, customers resent unsolicited spam. Marketers must win permission to send future messages. If the customer agrees, a message is finally sent.

Individuals do talk to each other, particularly when sharing personal product experiences. In fact, dissatisfied customers tell up to another 11 people about their bad experience, whereas satisfied customers tell only three or four. As marketing guru Philip Kotler says, 'Bad news travels faster than good news'. Although this is not in the realm of mass communications, it does demonstrate how everything an organization does communicates something to someone somewhere. Chapters 2 and 3 looks at this whole process in a lot more detail. Suffice to say, at this stage, that many advertisers use teaser, surreal and puzzle advertising (by sending incomplete or obscure messages) to arouse involvement and discussion among target audiences.

Classic and contemporary communications models

Adoption model

Several different hierarchical message models are considered in Chapter 4. The adoption model (Rogers, 1962) is such a model. As shown in Figure 5.11, it attempts to map the mental process through which individuals pass on their journey towards purchasing, and ultimately adopting (or regularly purchasing), a new product or service. This somewhat simplistic hierarchical model is nevertheless useful for identifying first, communication objectives and second, the appropriate communications tools.

For example, television advertising may create awareness, while a well-trained salesperson, expertly designed brochure or product comparison website (or iPhone app) may help individuals in the evaluation stage. In reality, the process is not simply hierarchical. Some individuals move directly from awareness to trial, while others loop backwards from the later stages by never actually getting around

FIGURE 5.11   The adoption model

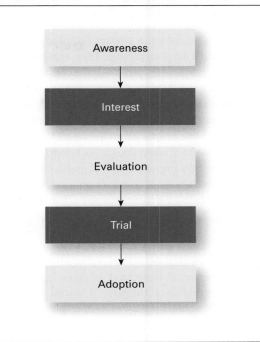

Chewing gum hysteria

Rumours spread in the Egyptian university town of Al-Mansura that after chewing certain brands of gum female students experienced uncontrollable passion for their male peers. *Time* magazine reported that 'in a society where girls are expected to remain virgins until marriage the news has generated considerable anxiety. Suspicion of who might be spiking the gum with aphrodisiacs fell on the usual suspect, Israel, frequently accused of supplying the Egyptian black market with pornography. However, laboratory analysis showed that some gum samples actually lowered the libido.' Scientific fact may not be relevant. For once a rumour gets going, 'the suggestibility factor can be so strong that it can greatly affect one's mind and actions without there being a scientific explanation', says sociologist Madiha El Safty.

Time magazine (1996)

to trying the new idea, subsequently forgetting it and then having to go through being made aware of it again.

Guinness: an individual's adoption process

Although it is not a new product, Guinness has adapted the adoption process. They researched the adoption process for a pint of Guinness because high increases in consumption among young session drinkers resulting from the previous ad campaign were not sustained. This prompted the questions: How does one adopt a pint of Guinness? How many pints, sessions or weeks does it take before becoming a regular, fully converted, loyal Guinness drinker? The answers to these questions were carefully collected before the commencement of the campaign.

FIGURE 5.12
The diffusion of innovations (Rogers, 1962)

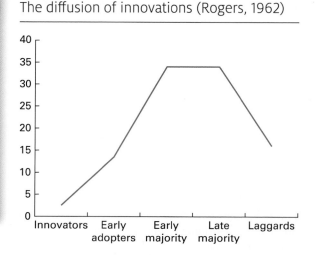

The diffusion of innovations

Rogers was also interested in how a new idea spreads or diffuses through a social system or market. He defined diffusion as 'the spread of a new idea from its source of invention or creation to its ultimate users or adopters'. Several groups who moved towards adoption – at different rates – were identified. The first group to try a new product were called 'innovators'. They represent approximately 2.5 per cent of all of the buyers who will eventually adopt the new product. Their profile was very different from those who were last to try a new idea (the 'laggards'). Opinion leader characteristics were part of the innovators. The key to successful marketing of innovations is to identify, isolate and target resources at the innovators rather than everyone (84 per cent will not buy the product until they see the innovators and early adopters with it first). The 'early adopters' are the second group to adopt a new idea (they represent 13.5 per cent of the total market), followed by the 'early majority' (34 per cent), the 'late majority' (34 per cent) and the 'laggards' (16 per cent) (see Figure 5.12).

Each group has a different profile, encompassing income, attitudes, social integration, etc in a B2C market. Innovators are venturesome and socially mobile, and they like to try things that are new. The early adopters tend to be opinion leaders who carefully adopt new ideas early. In the retail sector, Nielsen identified early adopters as multiple card holders (among other things), who are very different from single card holders in that they are significantly more promiscuous in their card usage. The early

majority adopt earlier than the majority of the market, and they are even more careful, almost deliberate, in their buying process. The late majority adopt only after they have seen the majority of people try it. They tend to be sceptical. The laggards are self-explanatory – tradition-bound and the last to adopt.

Crossing the diffusion chasms

Geoffrey Moore (1999) adopted the diffusion of innovations and applied it to the B2B sector and, in particular, technology innovation. Although he gave different names to the segments, the principle was the same: focus and find the innovators and early adopters first. When they have been penetrated and are happily using the product or service, the next segments can be approached. The key point is that there are gaps between the segments – vast gaps so big that they are like chasms into which many companies fall and never climb back out (see Figure 5.13). The gap between early adopters and the early majority is massive. Whereas the former seek innovative products, like exploring how they work and accept some teething problems, the latter group (the early majority) will accept only a tried-and-tested fully functional solution with zero risk. They will also seek a different package. In the e-learning market, whilst early adopters like IBM were happy to buy CDs and make them integrate with their training programmes, the early-majority customers like BT needed a different solution: CDs, workbooks, textbooks, workshops and accredited

FIGURE 5.13

Diffusion of innovations: the chasm between the segments (Moore, 1999)

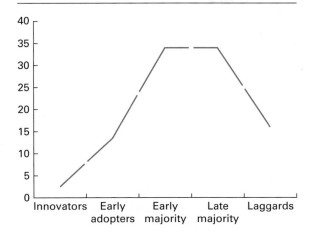

1 *The law of the few.* A relatively small group of adventurous influencers are powerful. Marketers need to identify these gregarious and socially active 'connectors' and then develop relationships with this small group of 'socially infectious early-adopters' or connectors (Gladwell, 2000).

2 *The stickiness factor.* The product, service, idea or message has to be intrinsically infectious. Marketers need to systematically 'tweak and test' or refine and improve against diffusion criteria. 'By tinkering with the presentation of information we can significantly increase stickiness' (Gladwell, 2000).

3 *The power of context.* Ideas and innovations spread quickly when they fit the context or are relevant to the group or its environment. You can exploit the bonds of memory and peer pressure in groups of 150 or less. 'In order to create one contagious movement, you often have to create many small movements first' (Gladwell, 2000). That's why many small, tightly targeted movements are better than one large movement.

training programmes. This was a completely different solution (to the same problem), albeit a much more lucrative sale. So many other e-learning companies did not understand the difference between the two types of customers and the subtle but deep chasm between them. Many threw millions of dollars at the e-learning market and it all fell into the chasm. Casualties followed.

The same principle applies: identifying and targeting the innovators and then moving on sequentially through the other segments. In addition, however, marketers must recognize that the different segments are different, ie they have different needs. Offering exactly the same solution to the total marketplace will fail. Matching the proposition (and the actual solution delivered) to the needs of each segment will generate success. It is the magic marketing formula once again (identify needs, reflect and deliver).

Accelerating diffusion – the tipping point

Malcolm Gladwell's *The Tipping Point* (2000) applies to both B2B and B2C. It explores that moment when ideas, products, trends and social behaviour cross a certain threshold and spread like wildfire. In his book, Gladwell suggests three key initiatives that release the viral potential of new ideas, products or services:

Many organizations, including giants like P&G, Unilever, Diageo and Microsoft, started their tipping point initiatives several years ago. P&G set up its 'connector panel' in 2002 in the United States with 200,000 infectious teen connectors used to research and seed new products. Prior to that, Microsoft recruited 450,000 early adopters to trial Windows 95 in 1995 ('ensuring that one in every 189 PC users had a pre-release copy'), enabling Microsoft to 'capture critical pre-launch feedback for the mass market launch whilst giving the consumers that count a unique preview of their product that would generate word of mouth' (Marsden, 2004).

Future communications models

The end of the traditional marcomms funnel model?

Marketers aim to reach customers at the moments that most influence their purchasing decisions. **The** old 'funnel' communications model started with creating awareness (the wide end of the funnel with many brands) and then familiarity, followed by consideration followed by purchasing a single brand (followed by repeat purchasing of the same brand, ie loyalty, where only one brand is chosen). The number of brands is reduced as customers move through the funnel and finally end up with a single brand.

McKinsey's David Court *et al* (2009) suggest the funnel is out of date: 'Today, the funnel concept fails to capture all the touch points and key buying factors resulting from the explosion of product choices and digital channels, coupled with the emergence of an increasingly discerning, well-informed consumer.'

> ### Is the old funnel dead? Should we change your model?
>
> 'Consumers are moving outside the purchasing funnel – changing the way they research and buy your products. If your marketing hasn't changed in response, it should.'
>
> Court *et al* (2009)

A more sophisticated model is required to help marketers plan their marketing communications. The old linear funnel model misses many of the new touchpoints, which can occur late in the buying process, eg a customer is looking at buying brand X, but just before clicking the 'buy' button checks for customer comments and ratings both on the same site and on other sites, effectively going back to the 'evaluation' stage of other buying models despite being apparently at the 'decision' stage.

Marketers need to be where these points of influence occur, whether at the offline point-of-sale or merchandising point or the online point-of-sale, or in the offline and online word-of-mouth discussion. For the latter, marketers monitor discussions about their brand (and their competitors' brands), whether on Twitter, forums or blogs, and automatically post their messages (some 'canned' or pre-prepared) into the conversation, with links to videos, demonstrations, testimonials or the brand itself. This can be done manually or as part of automated marketing (scanning, identifying and rules-based selection of responses).

> ### Late deciders wait until inside the store
>
> 'Consumers want to look at a product in action and are highly influenced by the visual dimension: up to 40 per cent of them change their minds because of something they see, learn, or do at this point – say, packaging, placement, or interactions with salespeople.'
>
> Court *et al* (2009)

Marketers need to increase relevancy, ie more tightly targeted ads (the magic marketing formula: identify needs, reflect them and deliver the product or service). Today, marketers can create dozens or hundreds of variations of an advertisement to reflect the context of the past browsing behaviour of customers (and also match what an organization wants to promote according to stock levels or trials of new product variations). 'Many airlines manage and relentlessly optimize thousands of combinations of offers, prices, creative content, and formats to ensure that potential travelers see the most relevant opportunities' (Court *et al*, 2009). Marketers now have the tools to do this.

Integrated marketing communications are more important than ever. CMOs now have a broader role, which realigns marketing communications with the new realities of customer decision making. Firstly, they have to manage the usual marcomms, product development, market research and now data management. Interestingly, McKinsey recognizes the importance of marketing: 'It's hard but necessary to unify these activities, and the CMO is the natural candidate to do so' (Court *et al*, 2009).

Make way for the Semantic Web – new models required

The **Semantic Web** enables any piece of data to communicate with other data. It will integrate web-based connectivity into any pieces of data (not just web pages) 'so that it can communicate with other information' (Richards, 2008). It will give access to structured collections of information as well as sets of inference rules that can be used to conduct automated reasoning, eg if the phone rings and music is playing in the same room, as soon as the phone is answered the phone automatically sends a message to all of the music audio devices to instantaneously lower the music volume while the phone conversation is taking place. The iPod already does this when taking a call: it automatically lowers the music volume. Customers will probably enjoy much more sophisticated applications than anything on the 'traditional' web. This Semantic Web may change communications models, as clever technology will serve up extremely relevant messages that will help satisfy needs even before they emerge into the customers' conscious stream of thoughts.

Berners-Lee (the inventor of the World Wide Web), Hendler and Lassila explained in 2001 that:

> The Semantic Web is not a separate Web but an extension of the current one, in which information is given well-defined meaning, better enabling computers and people to work in cooperation. The first steps in weaving the Semantic Web into the structure of the existing Web are already under way. In the near future, these developments will usher in significant new functionality as machines become much better able to process and 'understand' the data that they merely display at present.

By 2013 more than four million websites contained Semantic Web markup.

Web 3.0

John Markoff of the *New York Times* coined the phrase 'Web 3.0' when he referred to the next generation of internet-based services in 2006. Merlin Stone (2009) suggested that these new services constitute 'the intelligent Web', using Semantic Web, microformats, natural language search, data mining, machine learning, recommendation agents, and artificial intelligence technologies. These technologies emphasize machine-facilitated understanding of information to provide a more productive and intuitive user experience. Stone feels that the main characteristics of Web 3.0 seem to be an open, intelligent, seamless, interoperable, access-anywhere-by-any-channel, distributed system where software is a service. Perhaps customers' lives are about to get a little easier, with the Semantic Web communicating and helping to satisfy their needs. New communications models are required.

The Internet of Things

We also have the **Internet of Things (IoT)** – the network of physical objects (or things) connected together via embedded chips and sensors so that exchanging data can add value, or improve the customer's life. For example, if a patient does not break the seal to take a tablet an alert is sent to his or her doctor so that they can remind them. With it come all sorts of privacy issues. The IoT term was created by an MIT researcher when he was working for P&G in the 1990s.

> ### Information-smart marketers or just traditional marcomms marketers?
>
> 'Marketing is increasingly split between people who are information smart and those who are involved in more traditional marcomms functions... knowing where your competitors are moving in terms of the marketplace will have a far greater impact than doing a focus group or logo... New marketers are going to have to be much more IT savvy.'
>
> Regis McKenna, in Rothery (2008)

Dark Social

And then there is the 'Dark Social' which is not as bad as it sounds. The term is used to describe sharing content, or links, outside of social media, ie via e-mail or instant messaging. A 2012 study by the eAtlantic and Chartbeat (Madrigal, 2012) revealed that more than two thirds (69 per cent) of social referrals were from dark social – ie not Facebook, Twitter, Reddit, etc. This suggests that most traffic cannot be seen by most analytics programmes. Madrigal called it the 'Dark Social', acknowledging that it might show up as 'direct ' or 'typed/bookmarked' but the original reference, or referral, to some content or a page came via non-social media. This is not surprising as many marketers only achieve 30 per cent e-mail open rates which in terms of very basic engagement is quite high. If 30 per cent of those that open the e-mail actually click through to a link (ie 9 per cent of the total universe in the e-mail list), then we have a net engagement rate of 9 per cent.

Marketing automation

Next came marketing automation which needs a model to explain itself fully but essentially a visitor's click behaviour (on a website or opening or not opening); an e-mail is their digital body language. Rules can be created so that certain behaviour identifies visitors with certain interests moving in or out of certain stages of the buying process. This in turn triggers an automated marketing response whether as a pop-up on the website, a tailored web page, a subsequent e-mail etc.

New marketing communications skills required

Scott Brinker (2009) suggests marketers need five new skills:

1 *Analytical pattern skills.* Mastering the flow of data from social media feedback, web analytics, transaction histories, behavioural profiles and industry aggregates.

2 *Agile project management.* As tactical campaigns fragment into more granular, relevant, niche-like propositions, each one targeted at dozens, hundreds or even thousands of different contexts, fast-moving, multiple project management skills are required.

3 *Experimental curiosity and rigour.* As marketers seek constant improvement on their marketing ROI, marketers manage a constant flow of tests, testing new alternatives, exploring new creative executions and monitoring changes in response rates to identify immediate opportunities and threats.

4 *Systems thinking.* Marketing is a set of processes. This means connecting all the parts. Who gets customer comments, summaries and key issues arising from social media conversations? Which decisions does it influence? Who else needs this information (eg salespeople, PR people, the board of directors) and what decisions can it affect?

5 *Mashable software fluency.* Those marketers who understand the mashable web – a world of mash-ups, widgets and application programming interfaces (APIs) – will have competitive advantage. For example, it is possible to connect and integrate a website's content management system with site search, RSS feeds, e-mail alerts and e-newsletters, all serving very relevant content. Rose (2006) defines mashable in terms of a 'Web page or application that uses and combines data, presentation or functionality from two or more sources to create new services'.

Many of the previously discussed models offer some insight into the communication process but, almost invariably, they distort or oversimplify the process of communication. Chapter 4 draws on some of the communication models discussed here and looks at buying models, the buying process and the intervening psychological variables. How do we buy? Why do we buy? What influences our choices? Are there unconscious motives playing havoc with our day-to-day shopping behaviour? Chapter 6 attempts to look inside the customer's mind and answer some of these questions.

Key points from Chapter 5

- Communication involves a two-way flow of information.
- Communication theories can be applied to practical marketing situations.
- New models are required to meet the changing communications landscape.

References and further reading

BBC News Channel (2007) Warning on anti-drinking adverts, 10 December

Berners-Lee, T (2008) Google could be superseded, says web inventor, *Times Online*, 12 March

Berners-Lee, T, Hendler, J and Lassila, O (2001) The semantic web, *Scientific American*, May

Bernstein, M, Bakshy, E, Burke, M and Karrer, B (2013) Quantifying the invisible audience in social networks, CHI 2013, 27 April–2 May

Brinker, S (2009) 5 new skills for the future of marketing, *Chief Marketing Technologist* (blog), 23 February [online] http://chiefmartec.com/2009/02/5-new-skills-for-the-future-of-marketing/

Carroll, G (2010) CoJargon watch: Delinkification, *Renaissance Chambara* (blog), 5 June [online] http://renaissancechambara.jp/2010/06/05/jargon-watch-delinkification/

Court, D *et al* (2009) The consumer decision journey, *McKinsey Quarterly*, June

Crystal (2013) The 90-9-1 Rule: Dead, different, or a distraction? *Cultivating Community*, 8 July

Cutlip, S, Center, A and Broom, G (2004) *Effective Public Relations*, international edn, Prentice Hall International, Englewood Cliffs, NJ

Ehrenberg, A (1988) *Repeat Buying*, 2nd edn, Charles Griffin, London

Engel, J, Warshaw, M and Kinnear, T (1994) *Promotional Strategy: Managing the marketing communications process*, 8th edn, McGraw-Hill Education, Homewood, IL

Floch, J-M (2001) *Semiotics, Marketing and Communication*, Palgrave, Basingstoke

Gladwell, M (2000) *The Tipping Point*, Little, Brown, New York

Godin, S (1999) *Permission Marketing*, Simon & Schuster, Hemel Hempstead

Golson, J (2009) When It Comes to Links, Color Matters, *Gigaom* 9 July

Guirdham, M (1999) *Communicating across Cultures*, Palgrave, Basingstoke

Katz, E and Lazarsfeld, P (1955) *Personal Influence: The part played by people in the flow of mass communications*, Free Press, New York

Keller, E and Berry, J (2002) *The Influentials: One American in ten tells the other nine how to vote, where to eat, and what to buy*, Simon & Schuster, New York

Kelman, H (1961) Process of opinion change, *Public Opinion Quarterly*, **25**, Spring

Kotler, P (2000) *Marketing Management: Analysis, planning, implementation and control*, international edn, 11th edn, Prentice Hall, Englewood Cliffs, NJ

Lee, K (2015) Why your social media posts are more popular than you think: inside the invisible audience, *Buffer Social*

Lucas, J (1997) License to sell, *Marketing Director International*, October

Madrigal, A (2012) Dark Social: We have the whole history of the web wrong, *The Atlantic*, 12 October

Manning, J (2012) 5 trust-winning tactics, *The Marketer*, 26 October

Markoff, J (2006) Entrepreneurs see a web guided by common sense, *New York Times*, 12 November

Marsden, P (2004) Tipping point marketing, *Brand Strategy*, 1 April

McConnell, B and Huba, J (2006) The 1% Rule: Charting citizen participation, *Church of the Customer Blog*, 3 May http://web.archive.org/web/20100511081141/http://www.churchofthecustomer.com/blog/2006/05/charting_wiki_p.html

McGovern, G (2013) New thinking: The functional heart of web design, 21 April [online] http://gerrymcgovern.com/new-thinking/functional-heart-web-design

Moore, G (1999) *Crossing the Chasm*, 2nd edn, Capstone, Oxford

Reichfield, F and Schafter, P (2000) Eloyalty: Your secret weapon on the web, *Harvard Business Review*, July–August

Richards, J (2008) Google could be superseded, says web inventor, *Times Online*, 12 March

Rogers, E (1962) *Diffusions of Innovations*, Free Press, New York

Rose, B (2006) Marketing mashup tools, *iMedia Connection* (blog), 27 June [onine] http://www.imediaconnection.com/content/10217.asp

Rothery, G (2008) The real deal: Interview with R McKenna, *Marketing Age*, February

Schneider, P (2011) Is the 90-9-1 Rule for online community engagement dead? *BlogSocious.com*, Aug 11

Schramm, W (1955) *The Process and Effects of Mass Communications*, University of Illinois Press, Urbana

Sillence, E, Briggs, P, Fishwick, L and Harris P (2014) Trust and mistrust of online health sites, 2004 Conference on Human Factors in Computing Systems

Smallbone, D (1969) *The Practice of Marketing*, Staples Press, London

Smith, PR (2001) Online eMarketing Course: eCustomers, *Multimedia Marketing.com*, London

Smith, PR and Chaffey, D (2001) *eMarketing eXcellence*, Butterworth-Heinemann, Oxford

Solis, B (2012) The Rise of Digital Influence, *Altimeter*, 21 March

Stone, M (2009) Staying customer-focused and trusted: Web 2.0 and Customer 2.0 in financial services, *Journal of Database Marketing and Customer Strategy Management*, **16**, June

Time magazine (1996) Chewing gum hysteria, 22 July

Tuck, M (1976) *How Do We Choose? A study in consumer behaviour*, Methuen, London

Further information

The Nielsen Company B.V.
85 Broad Street
New York, NY 10004
Tel: +1.800.864.1224
www.nielsen.com

Ofcom
Riverside House
2a Southwark Bridge Road
London SE1 9HA
Tel: +44 (0)300 123 3000
www.ofcom.org.uk

The Semiotic Alliance (formerly Greg Rowland Semiotics)
172 Court Lane
London SE21 7ED
Tel: +44 (0)20 8693 1413
www.semiotic.co.uk

06
Marketing communications research

LEARNING OBJECTIVES

By the end of this chapter you will be able to:

- Understand how market research reduces risk and improves decision making
- List and explain the different types of research tools available
- Apply the marketing research process
- Appreciate the advantages and disadvantages between online and offline research
- Identify and avoid the potential problems

Introduction to market research and decision making 164

Relevant information reduces risk 164

Relevant information increases power 164

Relevant information improves decision making 165

How to make the perfect decision 166

Information and competitive advantage 166

Marketing intelligence and information systems 167

Information overload 168

Information prioritization 169

Common sense 169

The market research process 170

Problem definition and research objectives 170

Research plan (or strategy) 170

Problems and challenges 172

Types and costs of research 173

Quantitative research 174

Online vs offline research 180

Qualitative research 181

Test marketing 185

Think 'secondary' first 187

In conclusion 188

So, what is the best type of research? 188

Key points from Chapter 6 189

References and further reading 189

Further information 190

Introduction to market research and decision making

Relevant information reduces risk, increases power and creates competitive advantage if used correctly. Today's marketers have to be ruthless with their information needs and know exactly what it is they need to know. Then prioritize it, collect it, digest it and then, make better decisions equipped with this information.

The X Factor – market research makes the decisions

'Simon Cowell's TV phenomenon The X Factor uses research in a very structured and systematic manner. He researches various product concepts (singers) by testing them with customers (audiences at home and at the theatre). The customers provide free market research, revealing which product they prefer. The customers also pay for this privilege (as they vote by phone). He then refines the product concepts (trains them and adds some production effects) and repeats the market research exercise (all the time making money from the research). The final product testing is done with a chosen song, which has already been recorded by each finalist. This final layer of market research almost guarantees the success of the new product (a pop star). The finalists present their version of the song. The market research respondents (audience) complete the 'survey' via a text message (whilst paying for this privilege and simultaneously being highly engaged with the X Factor brand). The most popular product is identified (most votes). The product (star) is launched and usually becomes a chart-topping product.'

PR Smith

See Chapter 1 on the ladder of engagement which integrates customer input via social media platforms to sometimes create and distribute new products.

Relevant information reduces risk

As more and more relevant information becomes available, risk eventually reduces to zero and certainty emerges. The young woman in the card trick story (later in this chapter) could pick the ace as soon as she knew what the other three cards were. Market research (information) also reduces risk. So why not use research to reduce all risks? There are three reasons – the three key resources (the 3Ms, men and women, money and minutes). First, knowing exactly what information is required and how to gather it (whether commissioning a research agency or handling the research in-house) is a relatively rare management skill; secondly, research costs money; and thirdly, it takes time to define and write a brief, carry out the fieldwork, analyse the data, write and read a report and, ultimately, act upon the information. The fieldwork (asking the questions and collecting the answers) can also give competitors an early warning of intended activities. In a sense, it can, sometimes, alert them and give them time to respond.

Relevant information increases power

In both military and marketing strategies, information creates power. If an organization knows what its customers really want, and its competitors do not, then it has a powerful advantage. If the organization knows what a competitor's next move is before they make it, then the organization is in a stronger position to react or even pre-empt the move. In negotiations, if one party knows more about the other party's real needs, their resources and their options, then the information holder has a huge hidden advantage.

The classic salesperson versus buyer situation emphasizes how sales and profits can be increased as a direct result of information: the salesperson desperately wants an order and is prepared to cut prices to get the business. The buyer desperately needs to buy the salesperson's product because all the buying company's existing stocks were destroyed the night before in a fire in one of its factories and the salesperson's company is the only company that can supply the goods immediately. If the buyer knows how desperate the salesperson is, then a low price will be negotiated by the buyer. On the other hand, the salesperson seizes control over the negotiations (power) if he or she has the information about the buyer's desperate situation. In addition, the salesperson takes total control if the buyer does not know how desperate the salesperson is for the order. In this situation the salesperson will make the sale, probably at a higher price. Information is power. Information boosts profits.

Asking great questions increases success

Notice how senior managers always seem to ask questions that are potentially embarrassing (because sometimes you don't know the answers). When they ask the question, you might think, 'I wish I'd thought of that'. Questions are indicators of ability and seniority, or potential seniority. The ability to ask the right question is a precious skill that usually takes time and practice to develop. The ability to ask the right question is the precursor to providing the right answer. This is becoming increasingly important as too much information becomes available and the potential for information overload and information fatigue grows.

Information advantage: world chess championship

To avoid giving his competitor too much information, Bobby Fischer wore a green visor to stop Spassky, the challenger, from looking into his eyes during an alternative world chess championship.

Relevant information improves decision making

The best marketing managers always ask whether they have enough information. They define what information they need to make their decision making easier. They get this information, digest it and then, and only then do they make a decision. This is an informed decision. The alternative is guesswork, which relies on luck, and is usually an unnecessary, high-risk activity. On the other hand, proprietary relevant information (or knowledge) effectively creates competitive advantage, eg if an organization has unearthed some deep customer insights that no

one else has. Research is an aid to decision making and not a decision in itself.

What is Big Data?

Big Data refers to relatively large amounts of structured and unstructured data that require machine-based systems and technologies in order to be fully analysed. 'The much-hyped term has inspired a slew of definitions, many of which involve the concepts of massive volume, velocity and variety of information. In other words, what turns data into Big Data is the amount of information, and the speed at which it can be created, collected and analysed' (Kaye, 2013). Big Data is not scary nor Draconian nor Orwellian; here's 10 useful applications that help us all – from Lady Gaga to premature babies.

Big Data is everywhere

Here are 10 useful ways Big Data is used – that you probably didn't know – from Lady Gaga to premature babies:

1   The FBI is combining data from social media, CCTV cameras, phone calls and texts to track down criminals and predict the next terrorist attack.

2   Supermarkets are combining their loyalty card data with social media information to detect and leverage changing buying patterns. For example, it is easy for retailers to predict that a woman is pregnant simply based on the changing buying patterns. This allows them to target pregnant women with promotions for baby-related goods.

3   Facebook is using face recognition tools to compare the photos you have uploaded with those of others to find potential friends of yours.

4   Politicians are using social media analytics to determine where they have to campaign the hardest to win the next election.

5   Video analytics and sensor data of baseball or football games is used to improve performance of players and teams. For example, you can now buy a baseball with over 200 sensors in it that

will give you detailed feedback on how to improve your game.

6 Artists like Lady Gaga are using data of our listening preferences and sequences to determine the most popular playlists for their live gigs.

7 Google's self-driving car is analysing a gigantic amount of data from sensors and cameras in real time to stay on the road safely.

8 The GPS information on where our phone is and how fast it is moving is now used to provide live traffic updates.

9 Companies are using sentiment analysis of Facebook and Twitter posts to determine and predict sales volume and brand equity.

10 A hospital unit that looks after premature and sick babies is generating a live steam of every heartbeat. It then analyses the data to identify patterns. Based on the analysis the system can now detect infections 24 hours before the baby would show any visible symptoms, which allows early intervention and treatment.

Marr (2013)

See the CRM chapter for information on using some big data for profiling and prospecting, progressive profiling and integrating all contact points and layering on top third-party databases to deliver even more specific profile information defining exactly who our customer is and how to reach them. See also the advertising chapter on using location-based data combined with third-party databases to target prospects very precisely.

How to make the perfect decision

1 Define the issue, opportunity or problem clearly.
2 List what information you need to make a great decision.
3 Get the information.
4 Digest the information.
5 Decide.

Cloud wars

'The marketing cloud is marketing nirvana – a place, or a hub, where marketers automate and integrate all customer data, automatically analyse it then continuously and automatically serve highly relevant engaging content across multiple channels at just the right time on the right platform to the right customer. Fast-moving marketers will use the marketing cloud (multichannel marketing automation, content management tools, social media tools and analytics platforms – more later) to create a wall around their customers, which competitors will consequently find difficult to break down (particularly because of customers' changing behaviours). This is now a race towards an automated integrated digital marketing hub.'

PR Smith (2014)

Try this next time you have a big decision to make. You will find that you need some of the 3Ms (men/women, money and minutes); usually there is not enough minutes or time. However, if you plan ahead you will get more information to help you make better decisions. A lot of the information is free.

Information and competitive advantage

Can information be the principal source of competitive advantage? Certainly intellectual property such as patents, trademarks and designs and copyright can create competitive advantage. Brands and, more importantly, brand relationships can certainly deliver it. A large, comprehensive, well-maintained database creates a mini market belonging, at least in the short term, to the company that owns the database. And databases are essentially carefully structured customer information. This delivers an advantage over a poorly managed database. Equally, information about your competitors can create competitive advantage if they do not have access to this information.

The card trick

An Oxford Street card trick man places four cards face down on a portable table. As the crowd gathers, he shouts, '£10 to anyone who picks the ace.' Embarrassment, scepticism and even mistrust run through the crowd. No one responds to the offer of a simple £1 bet to win £10. As the card man leans forward to show the crowd a crisp £10 note, a grinning young man leans behind the card man and sneaks a look at the outside card. It's a jack of diamonds. Word quickly spreads through the crowd that the outside card is not the ace. Prompted by the fun (and the improving odds) someone shouts, 'That's not a real tenner.' The card man responds by stepping into the crowd to allow a closer inspection of the £10 note. A second stranger boldly leans across and briefly turns the other outside card over. It's a two of hearts. The card man returns. 'Come on now. Who wants to win £10?' A well-spoken young woman replies, 'If you show me one of the two middle cards, I will place a £2 bet against your £10.' The card man accepts. What has happened here?

Marketing intelligence and information systems

Every organization needs a marketing intelligence and information system (MIIS) that lists secondary information sources and also includes online information tools (many of which are free) that reveal instant information about your customers, competitors, channels and market trends. An MIIS should be structured and constantly refined as new sources become available and old ones become redundant.

Good marketing departments monitor competitors' prices, products, leaflets, advertisements, marketing content, social media platforms, satisfaction scores and customer comments if they can. This can be outsourced or done in-house. Estimating a competitor's marketing spend on, say, ads, social media and marketing content can also be done manually (by collecting all the competitor's press ads, social media content, seeing which content performs best on which platforms manually and then calcu-

lating the costs from experience and/or rate card costs less bulk discounts) or it can be done automatically online (by services like **www.spyfoo.com** for ads and **www.buzzsumo.com** for marketing content across different platforms).

The sales force can, if trained, provide the most up-to-date and relevant information from the MIIS. They are closest to the marketplace and in touch with what is happening. They need to be encouraged to collect relevant information.

The intelligent rep

In the United States one particular chain of stores that sold Christmas crackers held buying days when their buyers would see visiting sales representatives. Appointments were not accepted and, once they had registered with the receptionist for the appropriate buyer, reps proceeded to queue in a waiting room on a first-come, first-served basis. The room had rows of desks with telephones, where the reps sat down quietly filling in order forms, drafting letters, completing call sheets and making phone calls. Although it was only 7.30 am, a dozen registered reps were already busily working away. By 8.05 am the room was packed. The large chap beside me was on the phone at 8.00 am reporting some hot information he had come across during another breakfast appointment earlier that day. He told his boss how the competition had offered the other buyer a new buyer-incentive scheme which would commence next month, followed by a new consumer-incentive programme scheduled four months down the road. They had now four months to react or pre-empt the competition!

Good salespeople are also masters at collecting information about new product ideas, market trends, and competitors' strengths and weaknesses. Some reps also ask buyers what words and phrases they use to search for their products and services. The answers need to be regularly and systematically sent back to the marketing team to be added to the key phrase inventory for SEO and pay–per-click (PPC) purposes.

Staff members throughout an organization can be trained or briefed as to what type of information is considered important. Staff, if motivated, can scan their preferred trade journals, newspaper, online newsletters, blog, pinterest board etc, for items of interest to the company. Alternatively, a press clipping agency can do this work, or Google Alerts will do a lot of the online scanning for free.

Some of this information can then be fed into a SWOT analysis (strengths, weaknesses, opportunities and threats). This is particularly useful in monitoring uncontrollable external opportunities and threats (OT) variables such as political, economic, social and technical (PEST) factors. Many forecasting companies specialize in certain aspects such as social forecasting, and they will also carry out econometric forecasting, which correlates the likely sales effect resulting from a change in pricing or advertising expenditures (price elasticity or advertising elasticity).

As with all information, you must decide exactly what information and intelligence you need and when. Know which questions really need answers.

Today there are many online tools that can almost instantaneously deliver a stream of intelligence, answering questions about your competitors. Here are some questions that can be answered easily online by using some specific tools:

- How good are your competitors' websites?
- How good are your competitors' social media platforms?
- What social content works for your competitors?
- What Facebook content works for your competitors?
- What do customers say about your competitors?
- What keywords work best in your competitors' ppc ads?
- What inbound links are your competitors using?
- Do you have enough share of voice?
- How big are your competitor's marketing team and budget?

These and many more questions are explored in the SOSTAC® Guide to Writing Your Perfect Marketing Plan (PR Smith, 2014). Remember to choose carefully which questions you need to prioritize, to avoid drowning in a sea of information, otherwise known as 'information overload'.

Information overload

By the end of today, another 4,000 books and another 7 million new web pages will have been published around the world. As Google CEO, Eric Schmidt (2010) said, 'Every two days we create as much information as we did up to 2003'. That means every two days we create as much information as was produced in 2,000 years. That's why we've got what Gerry McGovern calls 'content wars'.

Way back in 2010, McGovern observed:

> Never before in history has the human being had such an ability to create information. Never before have we been faced with so much information. It's not faster computers. It's not bigger hard drives. It's information literacy we need. We need to create less information of a higher quality. We need to be able to manage information much, much better, getting rid of the junk and out-of-date stuff. We need skills that help us search better, and to be able to judge better and faster the quality of the stuff we find.

Way back at the turn of the millennium, University of California professors Varian and Lyman (2000) noted that our ability to create information had far outpaced our ability to search, organize and publish it: 'Information management – at the individual, organizational, and even societal level – may turn

---

Amidst the information overload and fatigue, remember to laugh

'There is a very simple way of dealing with stress that is not often considered, however – laughing. Laughter cures stress by pumping adrenalin and endorphins into the bloodstream. It reduces muscular tension, improves breathing and regulates the heartbeat.'

Nurden (1997)

This is very much required in today's hyper-competitive marketplace.

out to be one of the key challenges we face.' Marketing managers must learn to manage information pollution; otherwise they will make ill-informed decisions and may well end up suffering from 'information fatigue syndrome'. Reuters reported that information overload combined with analysis paralysis and poor quality of life reveals that 'one in four people admit to suffering ill health as a result of the amount of information they now handle' (Reuters, 2009). Out of 1,300 managers, two-thirds said that their social life was affected by having too much information to process at work.

Information prioritization

There is an unlimited amount of information available and obtainable to all marketing managers; more than any manager can absorb, let alone pay for, in any one period. So the key is to define what the problem is and outline the kind of information that might help. An experienced market researcher (whether in-house or from an agency) can guide the marketing manager towards defining specifically what kind of information is needed. Since the research budget is usually limited, the manager may then have to prioritize which kinds of information are more important than others. Ask for ambiguous information and a lot of ambiguous answers will be delivered. Ask for a dashboard and you will get a dashboard crammed with dials, charts and scores. It's worth thinking about what information you really need before accepting any information.

A certain amount of discipline is needed to focus on relevant issues and not become side-tracked by indulging in 'interesting' bits of information. When briefing a market researcher as to the kind of information that is required, it is often tempting to add extra, 'interesting' questions. Before adding extra information requests, think about your information priorities and check that the following questions are answered satisfactorily:

- What will I do with this information?
- How will it affect my strategy or tactics?
- What action or withdrawal may result from this information?
- How much is the information worth?
- How much will it cost?
- Can I afford it?
- When do I need it?
- Have I checked all secondary sources? (See Table 6.2 on p. 175.)

Are you an information junky?

It has been suggested in previous editions of this book that a growing proportion of internet users find themselves addicted to information online. Over 50 per cent of managers were accumulating information they didn't have the capacity to assimilate; in fact, they were overwhelmed by it. Over half the respondents pronounced themselves to be 'information junkies' who got 'cravings' for new information, especially online information. Do you find yourself constantly checking your e-mails, text messages and Facebook?

Do you allow yourself to interrupt your own conversations when you hear the ring of your phone or the ping of a new text message? Hoping, perhaps unconsciously, that this new information will be more interesting than the person you are talking to?

Common sense

For example, the highly successful ice cream manufacturer Ben & Jerry's observed an increase in complaints from buyers of Cherry Garcia ice cream. Many customers were upset because they felt that the product had too few cherries. What would you do? What extra information would you collect? This is what they did – they asked the following questions. First, was it only a regional problem? They checked by matching shipment records with complaints. Second, did the problem arise from the manufacturing process – was the quality not up to scratch? But the ingredients turned out to be normal. After questioning almost every aspect, they finally found the source of the problem. The photograph on the ice cream carton was not of ice cream but of frozen yogurt, which appeared laden with cherries in comparison with the paler pink ice cream. They simply changed the image on the carton and the complaints melted away.

> ## Correlation is not causation – using mugs with coffee increases job promotion
>
> 'The survey found that 37 per cent of people who have a coffee mug with their company logo on it have been promoted within the last 6 months, compared to just 8 per cent of those people who did not have a coffee mug with their company logo on it.'
>
> A merchandise company
>
> 'Statistically this is bordering on the ridiculous. Counting numbers is one thing but suggesting the correlation is predictive is another. We need proof that this hypothesis has been tested properly and can prove that there is a statistically significant association between owning a corporate branded mug and getting promoted. To begin with, samples (that is, the number of respondents being surveyed) need to be large enough and also randomly chosen to be statistically meaningful. The structure of the questions, selection of respondents, statistical analysis all need to examined before validating this "research".'
>
> PR Smith

The market research process

Using information efficiently starts with the ability to define exactly what information is required. This is a valuable management skill. Defining the problem or defining the research objectives is the first step in the market research process (see Table 6.1). Then you can decide whether you and your team can collect this information, or whether you need to use an external market research agency and/or a data analytics company that can analyse big data (such as historical location data combined with real-time location and demographic data).

Problem definition and research objectives

Before going through the steps of the market research process, it is worth emphasizing the importance of defining exactly what information you need and which decisions it will affect. Otherwise you get information creep, delays and confusion. Rushing into research will probably deliver sloppy results or maybe you might somehow get some well-structured research findings but miss some key information, because you did not have time to think carefully about what are the really important questions that need answering.

It is important to identify specific segments and what information is required from each segment. A one-size-fits-all survey will not yield the quality of market research findings that a carefully refined and tailored survey will. Although 'most companies lack the roles, processes, and integrated customer metrics needed to create unique customer experiences for select segments or to respond quickly to shifts in a segment's value' (Collins, Dahlstrom and Singer, 2006), the few that do really must ensure their research is tailored to different segments. This applies to any kind of research, online or offline. There has been an increase in the amount of research carried out online.

Research plan (or strategy)

The plan, or strategy, clarifies whether to do the research via your internal team or to go to an external market research agency and whether desk research (secondary research) is required before commissioning any primary research. Research methodology (eg observation, survey, experiment, focus group or survey) along with the tactical choice of fieldwork type (face-to-face, phone, online or post) and the required degree of confidence plus sample size, cost and timings, need to be clarified.

After the questionnaires have been agreed (and sometimes piloted), and the interviewers have been trained, the fieldwork commences. Once that is completed the data must be analysed carefully to identify any significant findings. Conclusions (and sometimes recommendations) are subsequently reported or presented to the management team. Equipped with this information, the marketers can make their decisions.

TABLE 6.1   The market research process

Step	Actions
1 Problem definition	Define what you need to know. Decide clearly what information is needed and why it is needed. Is it qualitative and/or quantitative? What will be done with it? What is the objective of this research?
2 Research plan	Internal or external (if using a market research agency a briefing must be prepared along with a carefully structured selection process). Data sources: secondary/primary. Research techniques: observation, survey, experiment, focus group. Sample: size and type. Degree of confidence. Fieldwork: face-to-face, phone or post. Questionnaire design. Cost and timing.
3 Fieldwork	Actual interviews/data collection and supervision.
4 Data analysis	Coding, editing, weighting, summing, consistency/check questions, extracting trends and correlations, if any.
5 Report presentation	The interpretation of the figures, summary, and sometimes conclusions.
6 Action taken/not taken	If the information is not used, then perhaps it wasn't worth collecting in the first place.

Research brief

Depending on the type of research, the brief can include SOS plus 3Ms from SOSTAC® (see p. 268):

- Situation analysis (including target and marketing mix).

- Objectives of the research (problem definition – what information is required and what decisions should be made as a result of the research finding?).

- Strategy (why the information is required and how the research findings may affect the communications strategies).

- Men/women (who will liaise with the agency?).

- Money (how much is the research budget?).

- Minutes (timing – when is the information needed?).

Note that some clients prefer not to divulge too much strategic or tactical information for security reasons. On the other hand, the more the research agency knows, the more useful the contribution to the success of the project will be.

Subcontract research but not understanding

'There are certain research functions, marketing research functions, that are sometimes provided by outside firms that are specialists in doing nothing but research. But the core aspect of marketing, which is understanding our customer and having a close bond with the customer, that should never be turned over to anybody else.'

Kanter (1996, 2000)

Agency selection

If the organization is not handling the research in-house, a market research agency will be chosen. Some of the usual agency selection procedures will apply (see 'Agency selection process overview', p. 226).

A shortlist of agencies can be developed from personal recommendations from colleagues and advertising agencies, and from the organization's own observation of research agencies and their advertisements or editorial coverage. Agency size, specialism or expertise, reputation, location and whether the agency works for any competitors can be used as shortlisting criteria. The agencies that 'pitch' or make a presentation will then be judged by the quality of their research proposal (Step 2 in Table 6.1), security of data, cost, credentials and spin-offs (like free training). Even small details can make an impression – for example, the number of bound reports that will be delivered when the research findings are eventually presented, or e-mailing presentations and providing client access to extranets, so that clients can monitor project progress. The personal chemistry or relationship between the client and the agency presenter is often the key variable that swings the choice of agency one way or another. It is also important to find out who will be handling the project and, if it is a junior member of staff, the degree of supervision that will be offered. The Interviewer Quality Control Scheme (IQCS) follows rigid procedures to supervise and check the quality of the information.

Some agencies demonstrate great care about the security of the data they hold. Computer hackers pose a problem to any computer-stored data. Product test samples need to be controlled carefully and securely. All samples, mock-ups and concept boards need to be returned by the interviewers, and logged as returned once they are received by the research agency. They can then be kept under lock and key.

Market researchers as drunks?

'Market research, to paraphrase a witty adage, is frequently used like a drunk uses a lamp post: for support rather than illumination.'

Gray (2010)

Problems and challenges

There are many challenges associated with getting good market research. These include researching new ideas, sloppy briefs, sloppy interviews and much more.

Researching new ideas

How can answers to questions about anything that is new, unseen or previously untried be valid? The first commercially produced electric car, the Sinclair C5, had the benefit of some product research, but how can research ask people about something they cannot experience? Driving a C5 in a hall is very different from driving one along a coast road or a busy, wet and windy dual carriageway with a 40-foot truck trying to overtake. Here lies one of the difficulties with researching a new idea: how can the reality of some markets and product usage be simulated? Another problem lies with the difficulty in taking the novelty factor out. When presented with something new, buyers may be prepared to give it a try, but can the marketing people sustain the marketing effort after the excitement of the initial launch?

No one asked for a burger – until they were invented

'Consumers can't be expected to embrace previously unseen solutions. Let us not forget that no one had asked for a hamburger until they were invented.'

Murray (1997)

The same applies to advertising. Most advertisements try to be new, different and refreshing. So how can research help produce something that is radically different to people's existing levels of expectancy? One of the UK's most successful advertising campaigns, 'Heineken refreshes the parts other beers cannot reach', had the normal focus groups and concept research carried out. It 'researched poorly', ie the results said, 'This is rubbish. We don't understand this type of ad. Don't do it.' Sir Frank Lowe (chairman of the advertising agency Lowe Group) tells the story of how he had to tell the client

(Heineken) about the negative concept research findings on their radically different advertising concept. 'He [the client] took a very brave decision and placed the research report document in the bin. He said, "We had best leave that alone and get on with the ad!"' Expensive and carefully prepared market research findings are sometimes ignored.

Expensive research also gets it wrong if it fails to ask the right question. Even world-class companies can ask the wrong question and make huge mistakes. Take Coca-Cola – although it researched the taste of the new Coke, its 1985 flop occurred because it failed to research how consumers felt about dropping the old Coke. It is classic marketing history now. Here is Philip Kotler (2000):

> Blind comparisons which took no account of the total product... name, history, packaging, cultural heritage, image – a rich mix of the tangible and the intangible. To many people Coke stands beside baseball, hotdogs and apple pie as an American institution. It represents the fabric of America. The company failed to measure these deep emotional ties, but Coke's symbolic meaning was more important to many consumers than its taste. More complete concept testing would have detected these strong emotions.

Real innovations are difficult to research because both customers and experts struggle to visualize their benefits. Henry Ford once said: 'If I'd listened to my customers, I would have invented a faster horse.' This is echoed by Clayton Christensen (2003) in *The Innovator's Dilemma*: 'Listening too much to customer input is a recipe for a disaster.' Listening to experts in the field can also be a recipe for disaster, as demonstrated by the now classic quotations regarding innovations from so-called industry experts (see Chapter 1, p. 23).

Errors to avoid

Here are some of the areas where problems can occur in market research:

1 ambiguous definition of the problem;
2 ambiguous questions;
3 misinterpretation of the written question by the interviewer;
4 misinterpretation of the question by the interviewee;
5 misinterpretation of the answer by the interviewer;

Flawed research: why New Coke flopped

'Sometimes research gets it wrong because it fails to understand that people can only buy a complete brand. People don't buy products; they don't buy packages; they don't buy brand names. They most certainly don't buy advertising. They buy the sum total of all those things. At one point the Coca-Cola company thought they could improve Coke and invented a new Coke. They had thousands of consumers in the US blind-test new Coke vs old Coke without telling them what it was. New Coke won. So the Coca-Cola Company launched new Coke. It failed miserably. When the company researched new Coke versus old Coke they missed the understanding that the brand Coca-Cola was far more than just a product. It's the sum total of all elements of the brand.'

Bradt (1996, 2000)

6 interviewer bias (street interviewers may select only attractive-looking respondents and exclude anyone else from the sample);
7 interviewee inaccuracies (trying to be rational, pleasant, offensive, disruptive, knowledgeable when ignorant, etc);
8 interviewer fraud (falsely filling in questionnaires);
9 non-response (a refusal to answer questions);
10 wrong sample frame, type or size;
11 incorrect analysis;
12 freak clustering or result (an inherent danger of sampling);
13 timing (researching seasonal products out of season).

Types and costs of research

There are basically two types of research sources: primary and secondary. Primary data are gathered specifically for and commissioned by an organization for a particular purpose (eg a research survey to find out about attitudes towards a company's brand).

Secondary data, on the other hand, already exist and have been gathered by someone else for some other reason (eg government statistics, newspaper features or published reports). Desk research can be carried out in a library or office, since it requires researching secondary sources. It is worth doing some desk research before embarking on the more expensive primary research. There are essentially two types of primary research: quantitative and qualitative. Analytics (like Google Analytics) are quantitative while neuromarketing/neuroscience (researching the effects of marketing stimuli on the brain) tends to be more qualitative (with smaller numbers of respondents than say a field survey).

Table 6.2 summarizes some of the many different types of research information that are readily available. The cost figures give only a very rough indication of the budget requirements. They have been included to give some idea of the costs involved.

Anything can be researched and tested, including sales promotion ideas (concepts), mailshots and even press releases and journalists' attitudes to particular companies and brands.

Quantitative research

Whereas qualitative research asks difficult 'Why?' questions like 'why do you buy or not buy something?' or 'why did you stay, or not stay, on this website?', quantitative research, on the other hand, asks numerical questions like 'Who?', 'What?', 'How?', 'Where?' and 'When?' – what percentage of buyers buy which type of product, or what percentage remember a particular advertisement, where do they buy (what percentage buy from different channels), when do they buy etc.

Quantitative research uses surveys based on a representative sample of the target market. Qualitative research involves an in-depth, unstructured exploration with either small groups of individuals (group discussions or focus groups) or individuals on a one-to-one basis ('in-depth interviews').

Research can provide the marketing professional with information on just about anything from markets to distributors, to customers, to competition, to new products, new packs, new promotions, new advertisements, new prices and so on. Different types of research can reveal information about customers, where they are located, what they buy, read and watch online and on TV, how they spend their holiday time, which competitors they prefer and so on.

Ideas on new, or modified, products, packs, brand names or advertisements can be discussed initially in focus groups (six to eight people), which generate information explaining how people feel about a concept. This kind of concept testing can be used to reduce a number of ideas to just one or two for further testing, or can be used to give feedback to the creative people so that they can refine a particular concept. These qualitative interviews open up and identify areas that may need further investigation on a larger scale (a quantitative survey) to find out how important certain aspects are among a statistically valid sample (minimum 400 in the sample). In the case of a new advertising concept, or a new pack or brand name concept, the refined concept can then be shown in a hall test (where respondents are invited into a hall to make comments). The packs and brand name concepts can be shown as mock-up artwork, and the advertisements might be shown as either a storyboard or an animatic (video cartoon). A new product (concept) can be tested by using in-home trials or hall tests. Some data sources, such as the Target Group Index (see 'The Target Group Index' on p. 177), are often used in the early research stages of consumer campaigns to identify buying behaviour, socio-economic groups, lifestyles, locations and appropriate media channels.

After all of this, a new pack or brand name (or product) can be test-marketed. This reduces the risk by holding back from national or international roll-out until the advertising campaign (or pack or name or product) can be tested within a representative test area. Owing to the high cost of test marketing, and the increasing difficulty in the UK of truly isolating the test market area (especially in terms of distribution, where the national retail chains do not want to limit stocks to certain parts of the country), companies often prefer to conduct a simulated market test instead of carrying out a test marketing exercise. Some of the main research companies in the field are Burke (BASES test), Nielsen (QUARTZ model) and Research International (MICROTEST). These models use information from the concept test or product test, simulate an expected level of distribution penetration (percentage of stores that will stock the product), assume a certain level of advertising spend required to generate certain levels of awareness, and then assume competitive activity, prices and other factors to predict the likely sales of a new product with an accuracy of +/–20 per cent.

TABLE 6.2   Types of research or information available

Information on	Type of research or information	Sources	Approximate costs
Markets	Market reports (analysing market size, structure, market shares and trends, prices, key players, etc)	Mintel Jordans Keynotes Syndicated *FT* and trade magazines	£750–£5,000 £1,000–£15,000 £1
Distributors	**Retail Audit** (analysing a brand's penetration into various retailer store categories, average stocks bought, held and sold per period, retail prices)	Nielsen	£15,000–£50,000*
Customers' attitudes and awareness	**Surveys** – recommended minimum of 200 interviews; preferably a minimum of 500 interviews	Quantitative market research agencies Omnibus surveys	£10,000–£60,000 £10–£100 per person interviewed** £200 entry fee + £300–£700 per question
Customers' motivations and perceptions	**In-depth research**, sometimes using projective techniques, children's groups, supergroups	Qualitative market research agencies	£650 per individual, £3,000–£5,000 per group of eight
Customers' future lifestyles	**Social forecasting, futurology**, etc	Future forecasting	£1,500–£5,000 annual subscription
Customers' buying behaviour and trends over time	Who's buying what, when and from where; how buyers respond over time to various marketing activities, eg special offers, new ads and competitor activities	Consumer panels, eg AGB's Super	£15,000–£40,000
Customers' penetration	**Market Penetration** of production into percentage of homes and frequency of usage	Omnibus survey	£500 per yes/no question; £1,500 per multiple answer/ranking

Continues over

TABLE 6.2 *Continued*

Information on	Type of research or information	Sources	Approximate costs
Competition	As for markets, distribution and customers, if the budgets are available. The sales force and marketing departments' 'ear to the market' can also provide much competitive information. There are now many digital tools that gather competitor information very quickly.	As for markets, distribution and customers	As for markets, distribution and customers
Simulated test market	Total mix test of product, brand name, price, positioning	Nielsen Research International; RSGB	£25,000–£100,000
Test market	Running a new product or variation of its mix in a test area	Sales analysis	–
Product	New product concepts can be researched ('concept research')	Focus groups	£3,000–£5,000 per group of eight
Packs	New pack design concepts can be discussed	Focus groups	£3,000–£5,000 per group of eight
		Hall tests	£5,000+
Advertisements	New advertisement concepts can be researched before going to expensive production. Pre- and post-advertising research measures levels of awareness before and after a campaign (tracking studies)	Focus groups	£3,000–£5,000 per group of eight
		Hall tests	£1,000+
		Quantitative survey	£20–£40 per person
		Online tests	£5,000–10,000
Exhibitions	Stand design, memorability, number of passers-by, number who stopped and looked, number who visited, percentage of total exhibition visitors	Exhibition surveys	£3,000

* Prices can vary enormously, eg a single brand retail price check might be carried out for as little as £750, while a full-blown retail audit for multiple products can run into hundreds of thousands of pounds.
** Depending on location and methodology plus set-up plus analysis costs.

Since television advertisements are so expensive, many companies prefer to do all the careful checking and testing through focus groups and hall tests instead of testing the advertisement in a specific test region. They can, and do, however, test the weight of advertising in different regions and measure the incremental sales to help them to find the most cost-effective levels (frequency and timing) of advertising expenditure.

If a product is launched nationally or regionally, its launch can be monitored in several ways. Its usage (user profiles, frequency of purchase, etc) can then be monitored through consumer panels. Retail audits provide information about distribution penetration and how the product is moving off which shop shelves. It is also likely that tracking studies will monitor the immediate reactions and effects of the launch advertising. Pre- and post-quantitative surveys can monitor the levels of branded awareness before and after a new campaign breaks, and can then be used again to measure the effect of the advertising and the product's development in the marketplace.

Omnibus surveys

Omnibus surveys allow marketers to add a few very specific questions (eg one standard question with up to 10 options or two statements against a scale) and get quick, statistically valid answers from over 2,000 respondents within 48 hours. A popular one is the UK government's own **www.yougov.com**.

Home audits

Instead of, or in addition to, retail store research, home audits research the customer directly. The retail audit data can be backed up with customer usage data. Representative families (sample size: 8,500) are recruited and asked to log all their purchases using a bar code recorder. The device asks for the name of the store and the price paid per brand, etc. Non-bar-coded items are recorded on paper. Analysis of this wealth of data over time shows consumers' repertoire of brands, the effects of sales promotions on purchases, frequency of purchase, etc. This is automatically cross-referenced with the household's demographic data already held. Diaries and dedicated dustbins were once used to collect this type of information. Today the automated online bar code system is preferred.

Retail audits

Retail audits monitor share of shelf space, prices and turnover of particular brands (including competitors') in a large and representative sample of retailers. It is worth noting that Boots, Sainsbury's and Marks & Spencer do not allow auditors to come into their stores. This means that the audit results have to be weighted and adjusted. Where auditors are allowed access, they check shelves, facings, prices and stock levels. Most FMCG companies buy these audits, since they provide a picture of what is happening at the retail level. Bar codes and laser scanning can provide much of this information online directly to the user. Sales out of shops do not necessarily reflect actual customer usage. Home audits (see below) can provide customer purchase information.

Personas bring market research to life

Internal figures, such as sales, percentage of sales expenditures (of say advertising), response levels, cost per order or enquiry, etc, can and should be compared with external industry averages or competitor activities. Not all the information is readily available immediately, but competitors' sales figures (of grocery products and some other large markets) are available from companies such as Nielsen Retail Audits. Information on levels of advertising is available from Nielsen Media Research.

The Target Group Index (TGI)

TGI global network of market research surveys provides comparable consumer insights for over 60 countries across six continents. TGI quarterly surveys identify who a brand's target customers are, why they behave and make choices the way they do and how best to reach them. They deliver the most comprehensive insight into the online and offline behaviour of consumers.

TGI studies explore the motivations of the individual, from the conscious to the subconscious, across different product sectors:

- lifestyle attitudes;
- social DNA: economic and cultural capital;

- values;
- motivating factors/criteria of choice;
- the purchasing process;
- consumer segmentations, including electronic, shopper, social media and holiday.

TGI surveys measure the relationship between and exposure to nearly 1,500 media sources for comparative and competitive analysis at a granular level:

- press (weighted to the NRS (National Readership Survey));
- radio;
- television;
- internet;
- mobile internet;
- out of home;
- cinema;
- direct mail.

The Target Group Index (TGI) collects and compiles information on consumer brands and the profiles of heavy, medium and light users, and non-users, in a vast range of product categories and subcategories. This is all cross-referenced to types of papers read, TV programmes viewed, and lifestyle or attitude statements. It can even classify 'light users' according to whether they buy a brand exclusively ('solus users'), whether they prefer it to another brand also used ('most often users') or whether they are more casual in their use ('minor users'), again cross-referenced to demographic data, lifestyles and media used. Advertisers use the TGI to find out who the users of a particular brand are and what they read, watch and listen to. The same information is available on competitors and their brands.

Elsewhere the index also gives lifestyle data, eg 'heavy drinkers of low-alcohol lager'. This gives an insight into what motivates them. The excerpt in Figure 6.1 shows that they are keen pub-goers and have a propensity to try new drinks. They are highly

FIGURE 6.1   An example of lifestyle data from the TGI

```
Base: NEW 18+
Pop: 20699
Private Eye Target: HEAVY DRINKERS OF LOW ALCOHOL BEER AND LAGER
Pop: 1155(000)     X of Base: 5.57
```

		INDEX	UNWTD RESP	PRJ (000)	VERT (%)	HORZ (%)
1	D8 DRINK LAGER RATHER THAN BEER THESE DAYS	176	183	366	31.68	9.83
2	PA9 I LIKE TO KEEP UP WITH LATEST FASHION	165	53	121	10.47	9.20
3	T7 HOLIDAY-ONLY WANT TO EAT, DRINK, SUNBATHE	165	75	158	13.67	9.18
4	PA15 MEN'S FASHION MORE EXCITING NOWADAYS	161	105	238	20.60	8.96
5	F7 I TEND TO SPEND MONEY WITHOUT THINKING	160	65	141	12.20	8.96
6	SP3 CO'S/PRESTIGE SPONSOR ART/SPORT	157	88	190	16.45	8.76
7	DH6 HEALTH FOODS ONLY BOUGHT BY FANATICS	155	78	179	15.49	8.65
8	D9 I LIKE TO TRY NEW DRINKS	155	70	143	12.38	8.65
9	D12 I REALLY ENJOY A NIGHT OUT AT THE PUB	146	164	345	29.87	8.12
10	P4 I WOULD LIKE TO BUY A HOME COMPUTER	142	58	148	12.81	7.92
11	F4 I AM NO GOOD AT SAVING MONEY	138	87	190	16.45	7.72
12	F15 USUALLY CONSULT FINANCIAL ADVISOR	138	62	114	9.87	7.68
13	PA2 IT'S IMPORTANT TO LOOK WELL DRESSED	137	104	247	21.38	7.65
14	T11 TRY TO TAKE ONE+ HOLIDAY ABROAD A YEAR	135	60	116	10.04	7.55
15	PA13 I REALLY ENJOY SHOPPING FOR CLOTHES	134	70	130	11.25	7.50

image conscious, aiming to keep abreast of new fashions. They appear to be fairly 'flash with the cash' and admit to being no good at saving money. In spite of, or maybe because of, this, they show a strong tendency to seek the advice of a financial consultant. They see their holidays as a way of achieving total relaxation, not wishing to do anything but eat, drink and lie in the sun.

Just about anything can be cross-referenced with any other variable. For example, the index can identify Heinz beans users and what kind of cars they drive. Another package, called 'trender', can be used to track product, brand, attitudinal, demographic or media trends. The index can also link into various online geodemographic packages.

Social media audits

Look before you leap. It is essential to carry out an audit before jumping into the blogosphere. As always, the brand and the organization need to check that it is credible and ready to become more transparent, as social media can probe into many previously protected areas of the business. **A social media audit explores how an organization (and/or its brands and high-profile staff) and its competitors are seen in relevant online communities:** what is being discussed, what is required, whether the organization has existing assets (contents, eg speeches) and how ready the organization is (includes training, systems and processes and generating content and partici-pating in discussions). The audit also looks at current presence, whether blog, Twitter, Flickr or YouTube, and the levels of engagement and traffic or followers. The audit explores the organization's social media goals (eg a direct channel with customers, to gather research, to improve customer service, to reach out to new audiences or markets, to add value to existing customers, etc), as well as its resources and restrictions (policy issues about content or trade secrets, any legal or political constraints or any internal issues about sensitive information).

Online analytics and behavioural insights

Analytics packages, like Google Analytics, can tell you who your visitors are (or at least give a general profile), what they are interested in (page views and key phrases used), where they are coming from

(how they found your site, via search engine or referral from another site etc), their journey (multichannel analytics), which types of journeys converted the best (got the most newsletter sign-ups or sold the most products). Many free packages like Twitter analytics or hootsuite can tell you where your followers are from, which of them are influencers, where they are from, who is talking about you, what they are saying, even who is attending a conference and what they are talking about before, during or after the event (if they add the conference hashtag to their tweets).

Behavioural Insights

Behavioural Insights can come from customer observations, click behaviour analytics or drawing upon a range of inter-related academic disciplines (behavioural economics, psychology, and social anthropology). 'These fields seek to understand how individuals take decisions in practice and how they are likely to respond to options'. Formal research can be requested from groups like The Behavioural Insights Team, data analysis companies (like Blismedia Mobile Location Analysis – see Chapter 13 on advertising) or managers can be simply tasked to present their key 'learnings' from their marketplace, when they present their KPIs (key performance indicators).

Potential behavioural insights are sitting on many people's desktops unused. Most analytics packages can be used to identify what works best by split testing single variables (such as price, image, words, or colours on website pages, ads or e-mails).

> ### Behavioural insights – the greatest untapped marketing asset
>
> 'Most marketers are not exploiting the value of behavioural insights (capturing and consolidating customer behavioural data from multiple channels in a single database). Despite newly automated processes (marketing automation), marketers are increasingly capturing this data, but not using it to build better marketing campaigns.'
>
> Forrester (2013)

President Obama's head of digital, Teddy Goff, believes that behavioural information is more important than demographics. Online click behaviour revealed what people were interested in. Two people with very dissimilar demographics may have a lot in common. 'Everything we did was informed by data.' They were determined to serve their supporters with the best experience possible, so they used 'the stuff people were telling us they wanted.' (Note this is the magic marketing formula mentioned in Chapter 2.) So they used these behavioural insights to 'Create platforms for niche interests to connect and develop relationships; they had up to 18 different versions of e-mails going out to different niche groups. (Source: Teddy Goff interview with PR Smith in Lansdowne Road, Dublin.)

FIGURE 6.2   Watch Teddy Goff discuss behavioural information at **www.PRSmith.org/blog**

Geodemographics and location-based mobile analytics

Geodemographics originally mixed geographical population data together with basic demographic data. It uses neighborhood types to predict the kind of people who live within them and thus their behaviour as consumers. If a brand is found to appeal to certain geodemographic groups, their locations can be mapped and the subsequent communications can be targeted at the geographical areas that offer the greatest potential.

ACORN (a classification of residential neighbourhoods) uses postcodes to identify different types of houses and generally gives useful indications about buying behaviour. Other UK online demographic analyses can be cross-referenced, eg PINPOINT, which uses 60 different neighbourhood classifications. MOSAIC has 58 neighbourhood categories linked with financial information. SUPER PROFILES uses 150 neighbourhood types.

Today we use location data to monitor behaviour and more. See Chapter 13 for more.

Location-based mobile analytics are all driven by deep analysis of behaviour (within milliseconds) including both where you've been visiting/browsing online and where you've physically been visiting/travelling in the real offline world. However, they can only monitor those who have opted in via using free wifi (terms and conditions) or via accepting cookies when visiting various websites.

New market research platforms, gamification and research

Research professionals have started to use games to gain consumer insight, which has resulted in more creative surveys. Sony Music wanted to understand the connections between fans and artists: a quiz, which was introduced into Jeff Wayne's The War of the Worlds forum, resulted in nearly 2,000 completed quizzes in less than 24 hours. Despite such encouraging results, the number of clients and agencies using gamification is still fairly low. Nevertheless, the Market Research Society reports that gamification is a growth area for training so we should be seeing more of it. A case study of parenting club Bounty is also included (Fisher, 2012).

Online vs offline research

Qualitative research such as in-depth interviews and focus group discussions give insights into the real reasons why customers buy or don't buy, or what they think about a new advertisement, a new pack design or an app. A lot of this can be done online, for example by observing online discussions (some say is akin to having access to a one-month focus group), or engaging in a one-to-one discussion in real time, or a simple pop-up exit survey. In addition, accessing real-time discussions, or even real-time behaviour and layering it with additional data can reveal valuable customer insights (see location-based mobile marketing layering digital body language with physical journeys in Chapter 13 on advertising). More traditional surveys can also be carried out online. However online research has its advantages and disadvantages.

Online advantages

- Access – it is easier (and cheaper) to get respondents online than to drag them out of the office.

- Researchers can observe consumers in their own community (without taking them somewhere else).

- Researchers can observe passively as people interact with each other very naturally online.

- It is quicker – online dialogue and feedback are immediate and in some cases within minutes of something happening, as opposed to face-to-face surveys, which might take days, weeks or months, giving people time to think, forget or get confused. Equally split-testing ads, e-mails and web pages give almost instantaneous results. Do remember if multivariate testing (testing many variables), you have to have a big enough audience and sufficient duration to gather to be able to extract significant results.

- Online also allows for more longitudinal studies – instead of an intense one-hour dialogue, online can encourage conversation over months or years, which can yield very different insights to traditional face-to-face.

- There is a wider spread of respondents, as online focus groups can recruit from across geographical and social boundaries.

Online disadvantages

- Too much information generated by too many social media conversations means marketers potentially face 'an overload of untargeted data that is costly to analyse and requires specific expertise and resource' (Gray, 2010).

- There is less control. As the discussions reside within their own online communities, the role of a focus group moderator has become more passive and observational, with less control over the direction of the discussion. This can open up new, previously unknown aspects, but can also make it harder to get feedback on specific questions.

Facebook research platform

Restaurant chain Nando's asked its Facebook fans for their thoughts on a possible new product. Overnight, more than 500 fans clicked their 'like' button, and there were 657 comments for the marketing team to analyse.

Websites and research

Websites can help identify customer needs in the following ways:

- Identify what customers are interested in (the most popular web pages).

- See what customers really want by looking at key phrases used to arrive at the site and within the site (seeing what phrases are keyed into the onsite search engines).

- Employ polling for brand names, straplines, packaging design concepts or any concepts.

Use questionnaires sparingly, as they can cause people to leave a site, particularly if the questionnaire is on the home page. Every click potentially captures data, building a better profile about visitors and their interest. Chat rooms offer a wonderful opportunity to listen, free of charge, to customers discussing your product or service. And more sophisticated data-mining software can drill down into data mines and build profiles that help companies to understand their customers better.

Qualitative research

An in-depth interview with an individual provides a lot of qualitative information. There is usually a series of individuals interviewed on a one-to-one basis. This type of research attempts to reveal what customers sometimes don't even know about themselves by delving deep into their unconscious motivations. In-depth interviews can reveal deep customer insights.

How young men retain their youth (unconsciously)

Amongst the most popular destinations from the stresses of life are the worlds of the computer game: 'One way that men retain their youthfulness is by spending large amounts of time playing video games.'

Kimmel (2008)

Mommy's never coming back

'In-depth research for a US manufacturer of security doors revealed deeply ingrained unconscious fears of being trapped inside, or abandoned, when doors are closed. The report suggested that a young child's first experience of a door is when its mother puts it to bed and closes the door behind her as she leaves. The child fears that it may never see its mother again. Many years later, the adult's unconscious mind can react to the sight of a closed door with an 'underlying feeling of discomfort and anxiety'. The Simpson Timber Company was reported as having gained a significant increase in its market share when they changed their advertisements to show partly open security doors rather than their traditional images of securely closed doors.'

Knave (1991)

As Gordon (1991) says, 'Consumers are often unaware as to why they do or don't use/buy/choose a particular brand. Asking for this kind of information in a direct way is like shouting at a foreigner in the belief that he will then understand English more easily.'

Work and family aren't the only important things in life

'As time pressures increase on young men, so does their value of "me time". There's more of an "I deserve it" attitude towards leisure activities. What's more, leisure can enrich and reconnect a young guy with his sense of self.'

Discovery Channel (2008)

In-depth researchers employ a variety of techniques (including psycho-drawings, word associations, metaphors, collages, picture completion, clay modelling and role playing) that throw the ego off guard and allow the subconscious feelings to be expressed. Chapter 4 considers the underlying motivations and complex information processes through which buyers pass on their journey towards a purchase.

Focus groups

Group discussions can be a more cost-effective way of collecting information that is perhaps less in-depth but nevertheless useful in understanding why and how people (in the target market) feel about certain brands, advertisements or just new ideas (concepts).

A variety of creative stimuli materials are used within these groups, including cartoons, pictures, words and brand maps. One of the most common types is the collage or mood board, which is made up from scrap art taken from a wide variety of magazines and newspapers. It is used to explore a variety of themes, such as user lifestyles, occasion usage and abstract concepts such as freshness or vitality. Two examples of collage boards are featured here and have been developed by The Collage Shop for use in focus groups. Figure 6.3 is a simple mood board showing different eating experiences or occasions. Figure 6.4 is more complex, exploring concept pack themes for a shower gel.

Some companies, like MTV, use online discussions and discussion groups as online focus groups – 'a year-long focus group'. But all of this is wasted if the right questions are not asked (see the box on p. 183).

Concept research

Concept testing helps every element of the communications mix. Whether it is an advertisement, new sales promotion, new piece of packaging, new direct mail leaflet or even a product or service, the concept should be researched and discussed at least among colleagues and customers and, ideally, among unattached, unbiased focus groups that are representative of the target audience or customer.

Advertising concept testing measures responses to advertisements before they are fully produced. Storyboards and key frames (see Chapter 13, the Hovis campaign concept) or animatics are made up and shown to focus groups. This kind of group discussion is used to identify the best idea from a range of different concepts, to iron out any glaring problems with a chosen concept or simply to help to refine the concept itself.

Qualitative research is also used to define parameters or types of questions that should be asked in future quantitative research. For example, focus group or qualitative research into newspapers may have revealed that some readers feel mentally uncomfortable if they don't read all of their

FIGURE 6.3   Eating experiences and occasions

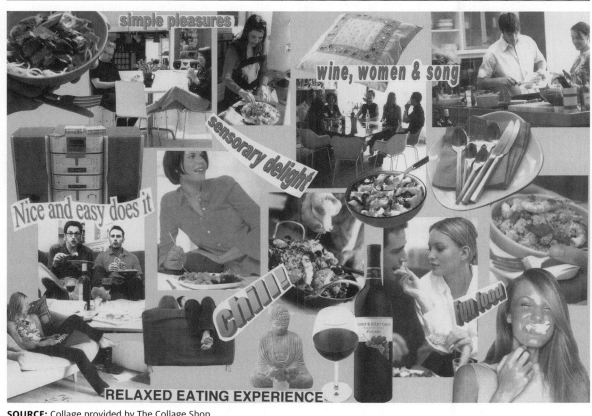

SOURCE: Collage provided by The Collage Shop

newspaper before throwing it out. This is obviously a problem if part of the paper's advertising proposition is 'the newspaper you can digest on the way to work'. So quantitative research will seek to substantiate the variables or issues revealed during the initial qualitative stage. The quantitative stage may be carried out by surveying several hundred or a thousand respondents. The interviewer's questionnaire might ask, 'Which papers on this list do you find a quick and easy read [or long, difficult, etc]?'

Eye tracking – monitoring customers' information processing

The best website designs research how customers process information. Some companies use eye tracking and heat maps to try to understand how customers actually process information presented on a web page (Chaffey and Smith, 2013). We explored these in Chapter 4 when looking at how the same website can be perceived differently by different people. Heat maps and session maps can be used to show where a customer looks, what they pay the most attention to, and most importantly, what they miss (see p. 123 in Chapter 4 for more).

Neuroscience

Neuromarketing and biometrics have received a lot of publicity as marketing research tools. Whether it is about mapping eye movement or measuring heart rate, sweat response or any neurological activity, many marketers are sceptical, yet companies like Google, Microsoft and Mercedes-Benz use neuromarketing to improve their marketing communications (Rothery, 2009).

Specialist companies such as Mindlab, Innerscope, Eyetracker, NeuroFocus and Neurosense all use slightly different approaches, and each one is more likely to be associated with hospitals or university laboratories rather than 'normal' marketing approaches.

Neuromarketing (and neurological techniques such as wearing a skull cap studded with electrodes to identify which parts of the brain are stimulated by ads or images) is an additional, albeit expensive, market research tool that helps marketers literally to 'get inside the heads' of their customers.

EEG (electroencephalograph) correlates physiological reactions (such as skin temperature or eye movement) with stimuli (like ads) being shown.

'I don't like it' really means 'I do like it' – neuroscience digs below the surface

TV show Quizmania invited viewers to call in and win money if they guessed the answer. Before the show was released in the United States, the concept testing (people watched it and filled out questionnaires) revealed that people clearly didn't like the programme. 'But when we scanned their brains, it showed they loved it. They didn't like the show because from a rational point of view it's ridiculous. However, the emotional part of the brain is so engaged that you keep watching it' (Martin Lindstrom, in Rothery, 2009). When the show was finally broadcast, the ratings matched the predictions from neuroscience research.

'Using EEG is like standing outside a stadium and listening to the crowd to figure out what happened.'

Brian Knutson, a professor of neuroscience and psychology at Stanford University
Kotler and Keller (2012)

Opinion-forming panels

Chapter 5 highlighted companies that use opinion-forming panels, including Microsoft (450,000 early adopters), and Procter & Gamble (nearly 200,000 recruited respondents in its 'connector panel'). 'Connector panels' are used to research and seed new products. Note: in the UK market, research cannot be blended with selling (it's called 'sugging' – selling under the guise of research). Not only are these testers giving very valuable feedback, but they are also taking ownership of the product and the brand as they become more and more engaged.

Use panel data to estimate your traffic, break it down by socio-demographic characteristics and compare it to competitors. A panel member is profiled in terms of socio-demographics and software is installed on their PC to monitor the sites they visit. Examples of online panel data providers are Nielsen NetRatings (**www.nielsen-online.com**)

FIGURE 6.4   Concepts for shower gel packs

SOURCE: Collage provided by The Collage

and comScore (**www.comscore.com**). Similar data are available from Hitwise (**www.hitwise.com**) which aggregates data from ISPs with which it has signed agreements to show the relative popularity of sites (online audience share) within a sector. Hitwise is particularly valuable since it gives information on competitors – eg which keyphrases they rank well for – and shows which traffic sources drive visitors and clickstreams showing sites their audience visit before and after the evaluation of the site. The Google DoubleClick Ad Planner is also recommended for this information (Smith and Chaffey, 2008, p. 515).

Test marketing

Test marketing refers to new packs, new brands and new products that are marketed only in a limited test region or geographical area, eg the Yorkshire TV area. A full marketing drive (distribution and

Post-it notes failed the test

'Post-it notes failed in concept testing, prototype testing and a test launch. Although a great product, consumers, when researched, simply did not like it. Just before pulling the plug on this potential new product, 3M focused on "highly connected CEO secretaries". These respondents were given boxes of the 3M Post-it notes, invited to share them with their colleagues and gather any feedback re possible uses. The goodwill, engagement and word of mouth generated pushed this product beyond the Tipping Point to become the fifth-largest office supply.'

Marsden (2004)

advertising, etc) is released in the test area only. This gives the company a chance to spot any last-minute problems that previous research has not identified. If the test market proves to be positive, then the marketing campaign can be extended nationally.

As mentioned, everything can be tested. A new advertising campaign, a new sales promotion or even a direct mail campaign can be tested among a few thousand names on a mailing list (in direct mail, some companies test right down to whether different-coloured signatures affect direct mail response levels). Some organizations do not, however, test-market because of the associated problems of security, timing, costs and seasonality.

Some tests are considered to create security problems since they can alert the competition with an early warning about, say, an intended new brand. Testing also costs time and money, which may not be available as launch deadlines loom closer. The limited time period of a test often restricts the accuracy of the measured results, since additional time may be required to monitor whether repeat purchases continue beyond the 'trial period'. That is, do customers keep buying, or still remember a particular advertisement, after the impact of the initial launch has died down? Seasonal products and services are further complicated, since they may need to be tested 12 months in advance. Testing, of course, costs money, which needs to be budgeted for at the beginning of the planning period. Both freak results and results manipulated by competitors can also invalidate certain tests. If this kind of inaccurate information is used to decide whether to launch or not, or to find out how much advertising spend is required nationally, etc, then the results could be disastrous. As mentioned in Chapter 5, Microsoft has 450,000 early adopters who trial its software, and P&G has 200,000 on its 'connector panel' who research (test) and seed new products.

Constant optimization: A/B testing and multivariate testing

Multivariate testing is a more sophisticated form of A/B testing which enables simultaneous testing of many variable (multi-variables) on, say, website pages. Multivariate testing involves setting up the server to display the different web page variations (or combinations) to equal proportions of incoming visitors. You need sufficient traffic and time so that you can split it up and have significant numbers of visitors land on the many variations. The goal is to find the combination of the various page elements that delivers the best results.

The kind of variables (or elements) which are tested simultaneously on a single web page include:

- page headline: message and typography;
- photo button (size, colour, placement and call-to-action text plus arrow);
- page copy;
- benefits (messages).

Multivariate testing can eliminate the need to run several sequential A/B tests. It can save a lot of time and find the optimum blend of variables that deliver the best results.

Tracking studies – advertising campaigns

Advertising tracking involves pre- and post-advertising research that aims to measure levels of awareness and brand recognition before and after an advertising campaign. It can also be used to measure the series of mental stages through which a customer moves: unawareness, awareness, comprehension, conviction and action. These are the stages identified in **DAGMAR** (defining advertising goals for measuring advertising results). It is worth remembering that some elements of the communications mix, such as sales promotions, packaging and point-of-sale, can be more effective than advertising when pushing the customer through the final stage of 'action' or buying.

An analysis of the sales figures can identify an advertising campaign's effect on overall sales. Home audit panel data like SuperPanel can reveal information on what is happening within the total sales figures, such as who is switching brands, who are the heavy users, etc. Quantitative techniques involving street surveys, in-home interviews or telephone surveys (obviously not used if prompting respondents with visual prompt material, eg storyboard, press or poster ad) can measure the other DAGMAR stages listed above.

The percentage of respondents with spontaneous awareness (which brands of beer can you remember seeing an advertisement for this week?) is always lower than those with prompted awareness (since the interviewer prompts the respondent by showing a list of brand names or a storyboard of the ad).

See *Marketing Magazine*'s weekly brand awareness results for an example of who is leading the awareness tables. Incidentally, telephone surveys cannot currently be used for measuring prompted awareness of a TV campaign (they can be used to research a radio campaign) since prompt materials such as storyboards, press advertisements or lists of brands can only be shown to a misrepresentative sample (homes with videophones). Verbal prompts can be made, but this is obviously not the ideal situation. This situation may change as more homes begin to use videophones (ie as penetration increases and 'the diffusion of innovations' occurs).

Although awareness is of interest, 'salience' is, as Gordon (1991) points out, 'a far more valuable tool for understanding what a brand means than brand awareness'.

Think 'secondary' first

All communications plans should be based on sound research. Expensive primary data should be used only when all possible secondary data sources have been checked. Why pay £25,000 for a market research report analysing your industry when it may be possible to subscribe for less to a syndicated survey carried out specifically for a group of companies in an industry sector (eg air travel or car manufacturers)? Alternatively, some markets are researched regularly by market report companies such as Mintel, Keynote and Jordans. These reports can be purchased by anyone for a few hundred pounds. Academic institutes often publish reports on various markets or aspects of the marketing process within a particular industry. Sometimes these are available at not much more than the cost of duplication and dispatch. A newspaper like the *Financial Times* may have done its own analysis or survey, which will cost you less than £3. Other research reports are available free of charge, as the commissioning companies see published surveys as a useful marketing tool to generate free media coverage. It also gives them something to talk to clients and prospective clients about. On the other hand, some free survey results may be biased in favour of the organization that commissioned the research in the first place, particularly if they have a vested interest in revealing certain positive results or trends. In addition, some surveys can be hijacked or manipulated.

FIGURE 6.5   Awareness questionnaire

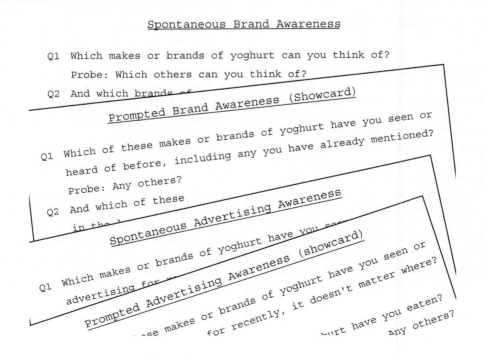

Do you believe everything you read in the papers? The same secondary source printed completely different 'factual' reports about David Beckham:

'Gaultier-saronged, posh-spiced, cool Britannia, look-at-me, what-a-lad, loadsamoney, sex and shopping, fame-schooled, day-time-TV, over-quaffed twerp.'
Daily Telegraph, June 1998, after Beckham was sent off in the World Cup.

'Elegantly-dressed, charmingly-espoused, golden-jubilees, self-effacing, paternally perfect, deservedly-rich, superbly tasteful, uniquely tele-visual, gloriously-maned hero.'
Daily Telegraph, June 2002, after Beckham captained England in the World Cup.

Even the *Telegraph* recognized the vagaries of newspaper reporting, as it reprinted both paragraphs side by side in June 2002.

In conclusion

So, what is the best type of research?

Many marketers, and market researchers in particular, have their own favourite research techniques. Some believe the only way to understand customers is to explore their minds through qualitative research carried out on small numbers of people (from psycho drawings to clay modelling to focus groups of say six people at a time, to in-depth 1-2-1 discussions and even neuroscience) while others say this information only gives some clues and is statistically insignificant and therefore the only way to draw real significant conclusions is from quantitative research (such as surveys of, say, a thousand people). The truth is that qualitative research identifies the issues that need to be researched quantitatively. For example a focus group may reveal that

price might be an issue for some people so a survey will, amongst other things, analyse whether this is true or not.

Today, online, we have free and automated analytics generating behavioural information about how customers and prospects react to prices, promotions, and special offers, whether in an ad, on a web page or in an app. Originally, metrics measured the effects of marketing decisions. Today's nimble marketers can use instant metrics (analytics) to help decide what is the best price, colour, ad, name or even phrase to use. Split-testing e-mails, ads and even web pages informs marketers what works best. So we can now use instantaneous measurement of the effects of our marketing decisions, to make even better marketing decisions. This is constant optimization. Constant improvement. Kaizen (Japanese original phrase).

'Data trumps intuition.'
Matt Round, former director of personalization at Amazon (speaking at emetrics Marketing Optimization Summit in 2004).
Chaffey and Smith (2008, p. 515)

Analytics are used in digital marketing. In the offline world of marcomms we tend to use the words 'market research' and 'testing' – there is no reason why we can't call all market research and digital analytics market research – a lot of the digital analytics is free and most of the traditional market research (focus groups, hall testing, ad tracking) are paid for. But can we call all market research 'analytics'? Perhaps yes – as market research does analyse an audience, their response to ads, offers, content. However, right now, analytics means digital analytics.

Research is valuable but, as can be seen, it does require experienced advice and strict control if the data are to be usefully applied. 'Dodgy data is worse than no data!' Having said that, good data can make the difference between winning and losing. Asking good questions is a great skill. It is important to know what you need to know.

Key points from Chapter 6

- Budgets allowing, research can reveal anything required.
- Consider carefully exactly what information is required, because there is too much information out there.

- Always check secondary sources before commissioning expensive primary research.
- Consider online as well as offline research.
- Set up a marketing intelligence and information system.

References and further reading

Birn, R (ed) (2003) *The Handbook of Market Research Techniques*, Kogan Page, London

Bradt, G (1996, 2000) *Online Marketing Course 5: Marketing research*, Multimedia Marketing.com, London

Cerha, J (1970) Inventing products to fit the future market, Paper given at ESOMAR, Neu-Isenburg, November

Chaffey, D and Smith, PR (2013) *Emarketing Excellence*, Routledge

Christensen, C (2003) *The Innovator's Dilemma*, Harper Business Essentials, New York

Collins, S, Dahlstrom, P and Singer, M (2006) Managing your business as if customer segments matter, *McKinsey Quarterly*, August

Crimp, M (2000) *The Marketing Research Process*, 5th edn, FT Prentice Hall, Englewood Cliffs, NJ

Crouch, S, Housden, M and Wright, L T (2003) *Marketing Research for Managers*, Butterworth-Heinemann, Oxford

Discovery Channel (2008) Species – a user's guide to young men, Discovery Communications Europe

Dunkley, C (2008) Gender psychology: differentiate to accumulate, *Marketer*, October

Fisher, L (2012) Game on to keep consumers engaged, *Marketing Week*, 8 November, pp 33–36

Forrestor Consulting (2013) Use behavioural marketing to top up the ante in the age of the customer, *Silverpop*, May

Gordon, W (1991) Accessing the brand through research, in *Understanding Brands*, ed D Cowley, Kogan Page, London, pp 31–56

Gordon, W (1999) *Goodthinking*, Admap, Oxford

Gray, R (2010) How to do 'qual' research, *Marketer*, June

Holder, S (1999) Talking to the right consumer, *Design Week*, May

Holder, S and Young, D (1995a) A journey beyond imagination, Paper given at ESOMAR, Berlin, February

Holder, S and Young, D (1995b) Managing change: Moving towards a leaner future, Paper given at Business Industry Group, May

Holder, S and Young, D (1997) Researching the future in the present, Paper given at ESOMAR, Edinburgh, September

Holder, S and Young, D (2000) Getting to the future first, Paper given at AEMRI, Paris, June

Kanter, R (1996, 2000) *Online Marketing Research Course 5: Marketing research*, Multimedia Marketing.com, London

Kaye, K (2013) Data defined: what is 'big data' anyway? *Ad Age*, 15 Jan

Kimmel, M (2008) Species – a user's guide to young men, Discovery Channel, Discovery Communications Europe

Knave, M (1991) Unlocking deepseated reactions makes ads more sympathetic, in *Marketing Breakthroughs*, ed Bruce Whitehall, p 9

Knave, M (1996) Rescuing Boris, *Time* magazine, 15 July

Kotler, P (2000) *Marketing Management: Analysis, planning, implementation and control*, millennium edn, Prentice Hall International, London

Kotler, P and Keller, K L (2012) *Marketing Management*, Pearson, Harlow

Lynch, M with Manchester, P (1999) How to uncover knowledge and make it available, *Financial Times*, 10 November

Marr, B (2013) Big Data: The mega-trend that will impact all our lives, Linkedin Update, 27 August

McGovern, G (2000) Information overload – the sequel, *New Thinking*, 23 October

McNally, F (2002) Wolfe Tones' rebel ballad beats off Bollywood classic to be top choice, *Irish Times*, 21 December

Marketing guide 6: Market research (1989) *Marketing Magazine*, Haymarket Publishing, 13 April

Market Research Society (1986) Research is good for you: The contribution of research to Guinness advertising, Conference papers, MRS, London

Marsden, P (2004) Tipping point marketing, *Brand Strategy*, 1 April

Moore, A (2004) Enterprise search: the Holy Grail of KM? *KM World*, 1 January

Murray, R (1997) Clone zone, *Creative Review*, November

Nurden, R (1997) Managers pay price for office pressures, *European*, 27 November

Reuters (2009) Information overload, 15 August

Rothery, G (2009) All in the mind, Interview with M Lindstrom, *Marketing Age*, **3** (6), November

Schmidt, E (2010) Every 2 days we create as much information as we did up to 2003, Techonomy conference, Lake Tahoe, CA, (Reported by Siegler, M G (2010) Eric Schmidt: Techcrunch, 4 Aug)

Smith, PR (2014) SOSTAC ® Guide to Writing Your Perfect Digital Marketing Plan, www.PRSmith.org/SOSTAC

Varian, H and Lyman, P (2000) *How Much Information?* UC Berkeley School of Information Management of Systems

Wurman, R (1996) Information anxiety, system overload, *Time*, 9 December

Further information

Businessmagnet
Businessmagnet Ltd
9 Meadway Court
Meadway Technology Park
Stevenage
Herts SG1 2EF
Tel: + 44 (0) 870 350 7767
www.businessmagnet.co.uk

European Society for Opinion and Market Research (ESOMAR)
Atlas Arena, Azië building – 5th floor
Hoogoorddreef 5
1101 BA Amsterdam
The Netherlands
Tel: +31 20 664 2141
Fax: +31 20 589 7885
www.esomar.org

Market Research Society
15 Northburgh Street
London EC1V 0JR
Tel: +44 (0)20 7490 4911
www.mrs.org.uk

Millward Brown (London)
24–28 Bloomsbury Way
London WC1A 2PX
Tel: +44 (0)20 7126 5000 (Dale Beaton)
Fax: +44 (0)20 7126 5001
www.millwardbrown.com

Nielsen Media Research (formerly known as Media Monitoring Services)
Atrium Court
The Ring
Bracknell
Berkshire RG12 1BZ
Tel: +44 (0)1865 742742
Fax: +44 (0)1865 732461
www.nielsen.com

07
Media buying and planning

LEARNING OBJECTIVES

By the end of this chapter you will be able to:

- Appreciate the importance of media planning and buying
- Discuss media choice
- Understand the advantages and disadvantages of various media
- Embrace media language
- Evaluate media options according to consistent criteria

Introduction to the media mix   192

Changing media consumption   192

Changing media platforms   198

New media categories: POEM (Paid, Owned and Earned Media)   201

Traditional media   201

Which media is most popular?   204

Media selection (overview)   204

Media selection (detail)   206

How much space, how often and when?   209

Media research   211

Media jargon and vocabulary   212

Summary   214

Key points from Chapter 7   214

References and further reading   214

Further information   215

Introduction to the media mix

In advertising terms, media is where the big money is traditionally spent. A £10 million TV ad campaign may only spend £1 million on producing the actual ad, but it may spend £9 million on media, ie nine times more on the media. It follows, in this case, that nine times more time and effort should be spent on choosing the right media mix. And the mix has got a lot bigger.

Some marketing managers and agency media people consider that media include communications tools such as sponsorship, direct mail and point-of-sale, as well as the mainstream media such as TV, cinema, radio and the press. Buildings, they would say, are permanent media, which, planning permission allowing, can be used to carry a message. For the purposes of this chapter, 'media' means the more traditional advertising media (press, TV, cinema, radio and posters), as well as new media such as web radio, interactive television, mobile, apps and websites. Although good media planners also consider media outside the traditional advertising realm, this chapter focuses on the mainstream advertising media, while other communications tools are addressed separately in their respective chapters in Part Two.

Deciding to include advertising in the communications mix is a relatively easy decision compared to deciding which media (say press) and which media vehicles (eg the specific magazine title) to use. Should the press, TV, radio, cinema and/or posters be used, online and offline? If so, how much of each? Should they be mixed together (the media mix)? If press advertising is chosen, which publications should be used – national dailies, Sunday newspapers, evening newspapers, daily or weekly regional papers, or magazines? How many times should the audience see or hear the ad (optimum frequency)? When should it happen? On which page? Even a great advertisement will not work if:

1 it is in the wrong place;
2 it is placed at the wrong time; or
3 it is in the right place at the right time but not seen enough times (insufficient frequency).

Today it gets even more complicated, as changing media consumption patterns (eg multitasking) show more and more online media consumption, yet TV viewing in most markets is still strong. What about when TV audiences watch programmes on their mobiles, iPads and plain old PCs? Media mashing means audiences are multitasking (watching TV and being on the internet). The media planners' and buyers' job has become even more complicated, with a plethora of channels, social media sites, apps and more. Remarketing and location-based marketing add an interesting layer. Promoted posts and tweets add yet another layer, or level of complexity (or new opportunity) to media planners and media buyers. And some of this buying of ad space is increasingly being automated (programmatic advertising). All of these are considered later in this chapter.

Since most of the advertising budget gets spent on the media, careful attention to detailed media planning and razor-sharp negotiating skills are important. Expert media planners and buyers get the best out of advertising by finding the right spaces or places for an ad campaign at the lowest cost. Media planning is both a science and an art. Traditionally it has been based on number-crunching media analysis and the application of complex computer models. Today media planners are also interested in the qualitative side, which tells them how audiences actually use (and feel about) different media. So let's start with the changing media consumption patterns.

Changing media consumption

Media consumption is continually changing. In the last edition of this book (2011) we talked about newspapers and radio being consumed less while online and TV were up. Now, newspapers and radio can be consumed online, and in particular, on mobile. A steadily growing percentage of your prospects and customers are now accessing your website and reading your e-mails via mobile. So much so, that Google now penalizes your rankings if your site is not mobile friendly. Why? Because non-mobile friendly sites deliver a bad UX (User Experience) as big thumbs and fingers try to click tiny links and read minuscule text. Check that your Calls to Action are clearly visible and easily clickable on a small screen (Smith, 2015). The mobile UX is unique as users process information differently when they are on their mobiles because they are often multitasking, more likely to be interrupted and the small screen size means that reading comprehension plummets (Smith, 2015).

Here are a few media consumption facts from Ofcom 2014 (Ofcom is the UK's independent regulator and competition authority for the communications industries):

- **The average adult in the UK spends over half of their waking hours engaged in media or communications activities.** On average, UK adults sleep for 8 hours 21 minutes in a 24-hour period, while they spend 8 hours 41 minutes engaged in media or communication activity.

- **UK adults squeeze over 11 hours' worth of communications and media activity into less than nine hours.** The total volume of media and communications activities undertaken by an individual each day equates to 11 hours 7 minutes. But as some media activities are conducted simultaneously, this is squeezed into 8 hours 41 minutes per day.

- **Our media and communications consumption is growing.** Comparisons with results from our 2010 study indicate an increase in total media consumption: from 8 hours 48 minutes of total media activity in 2010 to more than 11 hours in 2014. This is likely to be due to increased take-up and use of smartphones,

and generally more time spent on communication activities, especially among the 16–24 age group. Overall, 16–24s spend a substantially greater amount of time communicating, at 261 minutes per day as opposed to 146 minutes for UK adults as a whole.

- **Media multitasking is undertaken by almost every person.** Almost every adult (99 per cent) recorded conducting two or more media activities at the same time at some point during the week. This simultaneous activity amounted to an average time of two hours and three minutes a day. Watching live TV and making voice calls was the most popular multitasking combination, with 42 per cent of adults doing this throughout the week.

- **Children are advocates of technology.** Seven in ten claimed to tell their friends and family about new technology, compared to 47 per cent of adults. Almost nine in ten (88 per cent) claimed to do 'lots of different things' on the devices that they use.

Table 7.1 shows more summary statistics regarding the way UK citizens consume media currently.

TABLE 7.1   Media consumption in the UK

Digital TV	
Proportion of UK homes with digital TV Q1 2014	97%
Minutes spent watching TV per day (person aged 4+)	232
Proportion of homes with a DVR	60%
Radio	
Proportion of radio listeners with a DAB radio in their household	48%
Proportion of listener hours through a digital platform (DAB, online DTV)	37%
Minutes spent listening to radio per day (among radio listeners)	183 (3 hours 3 minutes) (Q2 2013–Q1 2014)
Number of local radio stations broadcasting on analogue (excluding community stations)	345 (May 2014)
Number of community radio stations currently on air	215 (May 2014)
Number of national radio stations (analogue and DAB)	25 (May 2014)

Continues over

TABLE 7.1   *Continued*

Internet

Total household internet take-up	82%
Number of fixed residential and SME broadband connections	22.6 million (Dec 2013)
Proportion of adults with broadband (fixed and mobile)	77%
Proportion of adults with mobile broadband (dongles/PC datacard)	8% (March 2014)
Superfast broadband take-up (proportion of non-corporate connections)	26.7%
Average actual broadband speed	17.8Mbit/s (Nov 2013)
Proportion of homes with a PC or Laptop	79%
Proportion of people who use their mobile to access the internet	57%
Number of mobile broadband subscriptions (dongles/PC datacard)	4.9 million (Dec 2013)

Fixed and mobile telephony

Number of residential fixed landlines	25.0 million (Dec 2013)
Number of fixed landlines in the UK, including ISDN channels	33.4 million (Dec 2013)
Proportion of adults who personally own/use a mobile phone	93%
Proportion of adults with a smartphone	61%
Proportion of adults who live in a mobile-only home	16%
Proportion of prepay mobile subscriptions	35%
Number of text messages sent per mobile subscriber per month	169 (2013)

Post

Addressed mail volume in 2013	14.8bn
Approximate no. items received by residential consumers per week	8.7 (Q2 2013–Q1 2014)
Approximate no. items sent by residential consumers per month	6.7 (Q2 2013–Q1 2014)

SOURCE: Fast facts 2014 © Ofcom Communications Market Report Aug 2014

Invisible kids

Time spent by the average child watching television: 1,491 minutes per week or almost 25 hours per week.
Nielsen Wire (2009)

Parents' time spent in meaningful conversation with their children: 3.5 minutes per week.
TV Free America (2010)

Several years ago some sad media consumption statistics were observed from the United States.

Children were becoming invisible as they watched 25 hours of TV per week while parents spent just 3.5 minutes per week having meaningful conversations with their children.

American post-millennial children (born after 2005) today consume 35 hours of television per week (Common Sense Media Research, 2013). Yet 80 per cent of American kids said they wanted to spend more time with their parents. Meanwhile The American Academy of Pediatrics recommends that children only spend an hour or two in front of a screen each day (Rayman 2013). *Time* magazine's Noah Rayman also reported that more than 33 per cent of kids under two use tablets.

From broadcasting to narrowcasting

With hundreds of channels, television has moved from broadcasting to narrowcasting, from broad or mass audiences to smaller and more distinct target audiences, often leveraging the TVX (TV experience) into social media such as Twitter (real-time chat), YouTube (clips, trailers and even episodes) and Facebook for ongoing discussions and exclusive materials (backstage/production shots, interviews and a lot more). The new, wider choice means that audiences are fragmenting into many smaller interest groups fed by sports channels, kitchen channels, children's channels, educational channels, religious channels, music channels, etc. Different channels attract (or 'deliver' to advertisers) different audience profiles or different psychographic and demographic segments. This gives marketers access to more distinct and tighter target audiences.

Audience migration towards new tools

However, audiences will continue to migrate online away from the traditional TV viewing model as TV is watched on other devices (eg mobiles, iPads and car TVs). Demand for measurable ROI will keep taking marketing budgets away from TV and direct channels and on to the internet. The marketers' dilemma of whether to use ads for brand building or making sales may be beginning to blur as 'engagement' becomes the burning issue (see ladder of engagement in Chapter 1). Interestingly, 'completion' is a KPI (how many that started watching a 30-second or 60-second ad, actually watched it to the end). How can advertisements or any marketing communications engage customers so that they are aware of the brand, embrace it and engage with it to ensure stronger brand relationships and, ultimately, better lifetime sales? And before the debate broadens to the new challenges and opportunities presented by social media, marketers already have a new arsenal of advertising tools, including:

- transactional banners (see p. 343);
- contextual ads (serving ads relevant to whatever a visitor is searching for);
- geolocation ads (serving ads relevant to your location);
- remarketing/retargeting (presenting ads to a website's visitors as they move around online);

- mobile ads (new mobile ad models emerging);
- gaming ads (ads placed in games);
- one-second ads (eg Miller Beer in the United States);
- long-form ads (a 27-minute ad which is really a mini feature film wrapped around a brand);
- intelligent media units (banner-sized panels with useful widgets and streams);
- PPC vs PPA (pay-per-click ads vs pay-per-customer acquisition);
- apps;
- virals (a natural extension of many TV ads);
- ...and much more is emerging every day.

Transactional ads let users purchase items by interacting with the banner instead of having to click through to another page or website, helping impulse buyers buy immediately (see Chapter 13).

Media consumption through the day

Overall use of the internet for UK adults stays steady all day from 9am to around 8.30pm while TV viewing starts at breakfast time and steadily grows all day, peaking at around 10pm. Multitasking is now the most popular way of watching TV (in the UK).

Weekly reach of devices during the day

In the UK, for most of the day, the television set is the most-used device, peaking between 8.30pm and 9pm, when over 90 per cent use it. However, smartphones maintain a steady reach of approximately 25 to 30 per cent throughout the day from 8am to 10pm, and from 4pm to 10pm they are the second-most-used device, after TV sets. Desktop PCs are popular during the daytime period, used by approximately 30 per cent of adults during 9am and 4pm (probably linked to the working day), whereas laptops/netbooks maintain a steady reach of between 20 and 25 per cent of adults until 10pm. (Source: Ofcom Communications Market report, 2014.)

Figure 7.2 shows a perspective from Ofcom on how we consume media during the day.

FIGURE 7.1   Media consumption during the day

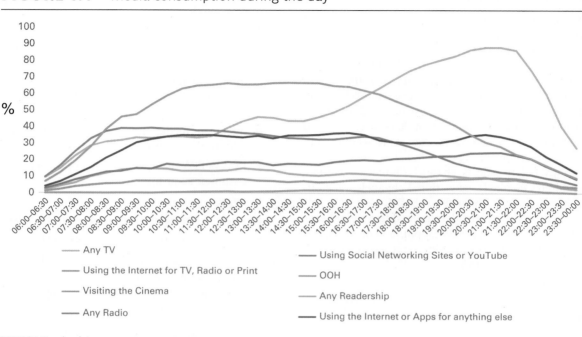

SOURCE: Touchpoints

FIGURE 7.2   Proportion of media and communication activities across the day, all adults

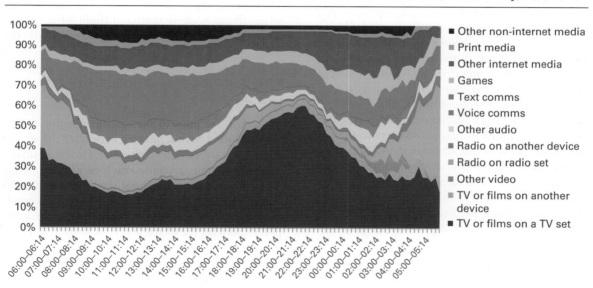

All activity records for adults aged 16+ (108782) – data aggregated to 15 min slots.
NOTE: The base of media activities changes every 15 min slot, so is much lower during sleeping hours
SOURCE: © Ofcom Communications, Market Report 2014, Ofcom Digital Day 7 day diary

FIGURE 7.3   Media mashing, media stacking and media multitasking

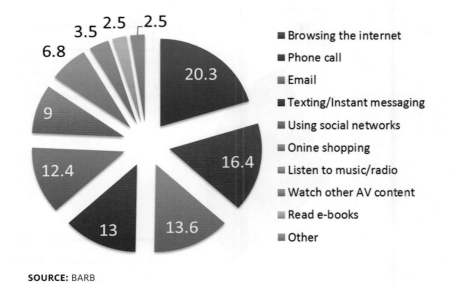

- ■ Browsing the internet
- ■ Phone call
- ■ Email
- ■ Texting/Instant messaging
- ■ Using social networks
- ■ Onine shopping
- ■ Listen to music/radio
- ■ Watch other AV content
- ■ Read e-books
- ■ Other

SOURCE: BARB

Multi-screening during the day

People are more distracted whilst they're watching TV and multi-screening has become the norm. In fact today we engage in media mashing, media stacking and media multitasking.

Media mashing, media stacking and media multitasking

In the UK, media mashing is conducting activities or communicating via other devices while watching television; these activities are related to the television programme being watched. Media stacking describes doing activities on, or communicating via, other devices on issues not related to the television programme currently being watched. Combined, they make up media multitasking. More than half UK adults are regular media multitaskers (with TV on and using other devices).

In fact 53 per cent are regular media multitaskers, ie they 'stack' or 'mesh' while watching TV weekly or more often. One-quarter (25 per cent) of all UK adults regularly engage in media meshing (interacting or communicating about the TV content they are viewing) and around half (49 per cent) are regularly media stacking (conducting unrelated media tasks while watching TV). Twenty per cent of UK adults claim to do both at least weekly.

Over half of all UK adults are regular media multitaskers.

Tablet owners are significantly more likely than average to multitask with other media while watching TV (81 per cent); this compares to 74 per cent among smartphone owners. Tablet owners are 'meshing' significantly more than the UK population, specifically looking online for programme and advertising information. Tablets also lend themselves to 'stacking' and play a significant role in these activities; particularly for e-mail, internet browsing, general social networking, watching AV content and online shopping.

Paying customers to watch your ad

'Apex, a Japanese vending machine company, developed a dispenser that gives free coffee in return for watching a 30-second video advertisement while it prepares and pours the coffee.'

Marketer (2008)

A few years ago, we suggested that Silicon Valley companies could be incentivized less on ad sales and more on creating bigger and better programmes.

FIGURE 7.4   Media multitaskers

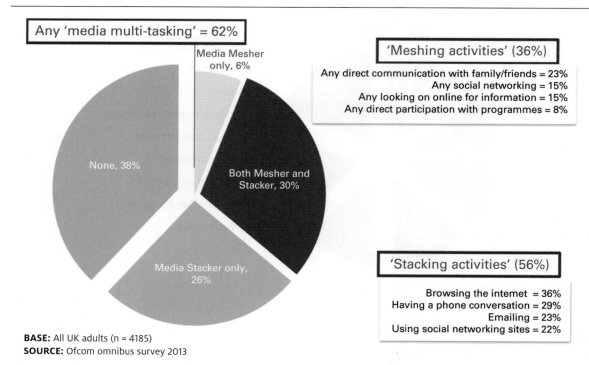

BASE: All UK adults (n = 4185)
SOURCE: Ofcom omnibus survey 2013

The days of just selling ad space are over. Marketers need media owners to think creatively about using the media for reaching out, engaging, sharing experiences and building stronger relationships, as well as selling more products, since it is all part of the UX (User Experience).

Online marketing potential is for interactive relationships and not just ads

'But marketers have realized the internet isn't just a place for ads but a means to create bigger interactive relationships with consumers. For savvy digital players such as Unilever, the digital tour (of major social media owners) wasn't about CPMs or page views; rather, it's about learning how to interact with consumers who spend more and more of their time online, and to discover new social tools to participate in what's going on there.'

Learmonth (2010)

Changing media platforms

A 2015 Google sponsored survey found that over 66 per cent of US adults report using their devices while in-store for shopping support, including looking for offers and coupons, comparing prices, and contacting friends for advice on purchases (Signal, 2015). So as customers consume media differently, marketers shuffle their pack (of media options) accordingly. Mobile and location-based marketing are set to grow as marketers leverage location-based potential.

Will widget/app-based TV dominate?

'Widget or app-based TV is rolling out, and will be built into the majority of flat-screen TVs sold during the holiday season. Early adopters in the US are pulling their cable and dish now and downloading the shows they want to watch on their computers and Apple TV. When that occurs, networks will directly distribute their content to a large portion of their customers, who will pick and choose all programming they watch, when they want to watch it – sort of like it has evolved to now with DVRs and on-demand, but with much greater control by the viewer, who will buy or subscribe to the programmes they watch without having to buy bundled purchase packages. When any part of the old TV spectrum is released to transmit the internet, speeds will accelerate to the point instant real-time on-demand viewing will take place with minimal need for downloading.'

Forecasted by Rodney Mason, CMO, *Moosylvania Marketing* (2010) in the fifth edition of this book. Do you think it is finally happening now?

Mobile

Mobile should be seen as a normal approach to running a business. In order to leverage the best personalization and customer experience from geo-targeting technology, mobile should be seen as business as usual, rather than an optional extra in the marketer's armoury. Mobiles (and tablets and soon, wearable technology) are commonly used by customers across the world. They are a fundamental part of your customers' lives. So too marketers must ensure their customers can interact with their brands via whatever technologies they use, whether mobile or other devices.

Mobile, along with social media, content marketing and personalization will be the most heavily experimented areas. 'Targeting and personalization is the highest priority area for businesses in digital-related marketing' (eConsultancy, 2015).

Nearly six in ten consumers access the internet on their mobile

'While the proportion of households with access to the internet remains stable at 82 per cent, the ways in which people connect continues to evolve. Nearly six in ten respondents (57 per cent) said they personally used their mobile phone to access the internet (up from 49 per cent in Q1 2013), driven by growth in the smartphone market. Almost all UK adults who have mobile phone internet access also have access via fixed broadband. Only 4 per cent of UK adults reported that their household's only means of internet access was a smartphone.'

Ofcom (2014)

Location marketing and geo targeting

Geo-targeting signposts a new era in both mobile and marketing overall. The development of geo-targeting technology empowers those marketers that use it to arguably the most potent marketing tactic this century. Location-based marketing (LBM) is a significant development for the world of marketing. Early phase LBM delivered relevant ads into apps and browsers of mobiles when audiences moved into a specific geographic location (near a store or a high street). LBM V2 can do this and a lot more as it learns more about the user's physical 'geo' movements (as they physically travel around) plus their digital movements across websites and apps. See Chapter 13 for detailed examples.

Geo-targeting joy – boosting sales and loyalty without retail staff doing any work

'When utilized correctly, geo-targeting technology's implementation can increase sales value per customer, retention and brand loyalty without retail staff doing a single thing.'

eConsultancy (2015)

Apple's introduction of iBeacons Bluetooth Low Energy (BLE) targeting technology in late 2013 propelled geo-targeting technology into even more precisely defined geo targets. Within metres, ad messages delivered on mobiles and offers can change as consumers move around a store, an exhibition, a museum, or even perhaps a networking event. Despite the potential benefits, only a handful of companies are exploiting the technology (as is the case with most innovations as revealed by Everett Rogers' original analysis and prediction on how innovations spread into markets, first published in 1962 and still valid today, with its latest edition in 2003).

For examples on how location-based marketing actually works, see Chapter 13.

Remarketing

Sometimes also referred to as retargeting, remarketing lets marketers put ads in front of visitors to the marketers' website long after they have been on the website. In fact the ads can appear wherever the visitor goes online (as long as the website subscribes to an advertising network). Effectively marketers get a second chance to remind their visitors about the brand whose website they just visited. The brand can also deliver a call to action (CTA) to help the visitor reconnect with the brand. So retargeting delivers ads to an already interested audience (since they've already bothered to visit the website).

Apps

An app is simply a piece of software for an iPhone or iPad that can do anything from keeping up with the sports news, to following a favourite team or player, playing a game, reading free books, analysing a golf swing, taking better photographs, learning to speak French, finding the lowest prices, managing the household bills, Skyping the family, Twittering with friends, making rude noises, stopping snoring, consuming a mobile version of a media brand or consuming a new experience for any brand.

Some companies are using the App Store as a form of advertising, pushing their brands onto millions of devices worldwide. BBC, Time and Sky News are all available on iTunes, because they know that having their brand name (and services) on a screen that customers carry with them everywhere extends their reach and builds brand loyalty. If a brand can find something of value and something of relevance to its target market then users can continue engaging with the brand long after any particular ad campaign is over.

Building social media like Twitter and Facebook into an app is potentially very powerful. Other 'walled garden' experiences, such as the Xbox, are developing social media aspects to their games so that players can keep in touch with their friends and compare scores, etc, as they lean over the 'wall' into the social media networks. Others are also using apps as an added-value extension of the brand experience. Few brands as yet appear to be using apps as revenue generators (fees for downloads or additional brand advertisements).

Here is a selection of apps as examples:

- *Shazam:* Identifies music from the radio, TV, ads, soundtracks, clips by pointing a mobile at the music source. It then lists the singer, songwriter, band, lyrics, music to buy and

forthcoming concert tickets for the artist. How helpful is that?

- *Zippo:* The US lighter manufacturer created an app that replicates an image of a typical Zippo flame. Five million people downloaded it, many of whom don't even smoke. It is now popular at music concerts and 'the flame' is used to welcome artists.

- *Kraft Foods iFood Assistant:* A sticky iPhone app with 50 per cent of downloaders continuing to engage with it three months after first downloading it. This builds ongoing brand loyalty.

- *Bus Times app:* Saves travellers waiting time by telling them exactly when their bus will arrive at exactly which bus stop. Simple but brilliant. Another public travel app, the Avego app, gives updates on public transport and is used in 60 countries.

- *House-buying app:* *Irish Times*-owned MyHome.ie partners with Phoneware to show home buyers listings, floor plans, photos and agent contacts, all linked to Google Maps to see what schools, parks and motorways are nearby. Filters allow searchers to explore it by price, number of bedrooms and property type.

Will apps replace websites and social media platforms?

Is it possible that the World Wide Web may, one day, be deemed redundant as everyone uses their favourite apps online?

Apps extend TV reach and engagement

Here is how Fox TV network's app for *Glee* (the musical comedy series) works. It costs £0.59 to download, and within a few weeks of launch it had several hundred thousand users. These customers are engaging beyond the show, as they get extra information, or they sing karaoke to songs performed in the show and then share their work of art by posting their recordings to social networks. Of the first 200,000 subscribers, some 60,000 have been published. Thirty per cent high-level engagement like this is powerful (see 'The ladder of engagement', Chapter 1). Users can also buy additional songs. On average, the app is used once or twice per week for 8- to 10-minute sessions, mostly when the show is off air. Is this an ad or a product extension or both?

The app helps to restore a sense of being in an audience or in a group, particularly if it allows the audience to share their thoughts, feelings and, in this case, songs with each other. Apps that integrate with social media help get a brand quickly discussed.

Social TV and its supporting apps extend a brand's reach, enhance the customer experience, deepen the engagement and the brand relationship and simultaneously earn a new revenue stream from subscriptions. Such 'walled garden' experiences mean more 'marketing utopia' (see Chapter 1) – it's a great time to be a marketer.

Additional revenue streams may follow if additional brand advertising is added to the app. The *Glee* app developers are actively talking to brands about sponsorship opportunities, such as providing free songs to users.

New media categories: POEM (Paid, Owned and Earned Media)

Importantly, if we're truly entering a POEM media mix model, brand websites are key. They anchor the owned, reinforce the paid and incubate the earned. POEM represents paid media (eg promoted tweets and posts), owned (you control and own, eg your website, social media platforms, CRM/direct mail, packaging, exhibitions etc) and earned (word of mouth, discussions, chats, comments, shares, retweets, likes, reviews, user generated content and viral) media.

Sometimes called BOE (Bought/Paid, Owned and Earned), media has migrated to more interesting media mixes, sometimes multitasking media. We have 'moved from mass media to masses of media because the inclination of people to move from being passive consumers to active participants has risen exponentially. Interconnectivity between media

is the norm... media like TV, radio, newspapers all use platforms like Twitter and Facebook as back channels to extend audience engagement with their content' (McPartlin, 2011).

Traditional media

There is a shift in vision and philosophy amongst advertisers. Media owners now have to think differently. Consider Facebook: although it primarily earns revenues from selling engagement ads that drive people to brand pages, 'marketers and agencies want it to focus less on selling media and more on helping them solve problems and create big ideas' (Learmonth, 2010). Big marketers like Unilever, with its multi-billion advertising budget, have been visiting the Googles, Facebooks and Hulus (and lesser-known up-and-coming start-ups) of Silicon Valley for years, to understand 'new' concepts like social media, search-contextual advertising and geolocation advertising.

Press

Press gives an 'announcement feeling for an advertising campaign, and can be used at launch to play on the newsworthy angle. Today's technological advances allow low-cost entry into the world of publishing. This has reduced the publishing industry's traditional high-investment barrier to entry. In effect, this means that we are seeing new magazines, journals and newsletters appearing alongside multi-edition, tailor-made magazines such as the US *Farmers' Journal* (which produces over 1,000 different editions of each month's publication targeted at over 1,000 different types of farmer). The result? More accurately targeted media that allow advertisers and PR people to target their messages more effectively.

TV

TV is at the heart of 'Emotional Engagement' in advertising. It can deliver high-quality audio-visual messages to national audiences numbering in their millions. When respondents to Ofcom's Media Literacy Tracker were asked which medium they would miss the most if it were taken away, television continued to be the most popular response, with 42 per cent of UK adults choosing this option in 2013 (compared to 44 per cent in 2005).

FIGURE 7.5   Most missed media activity

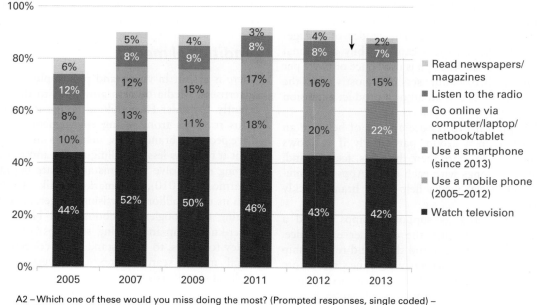

A2 – Which one of these would you miss doing the most? (Prompted responses, single coded) –
NB Showing the five most popular responses in 2013 at an overall level.
Base: All adults aged 16+ (3244 in 2005, 2905 in 2007, 1824 in 2009, 1823 in 2011, 1805 in 2012, 1642 in 2013).
Significance testing shows any change between 2012 and 2013 – where it is possible to make a comparison

SOURCE: © Ofcom. Ofcom fieldwork carried out by Saville Rossiter-Base in October to November 2013

There have been some notable changes over time. More than a fifth (22 per cent) of UK adults now say they would miss their mobile/smartphone the most – more than double the proportion giving this answer in 2005. Similarly, those citing going online via a computer (PC/laptop/netbook or tablet) has also doubled (approximately), from 8 per cent in 2005 to 15 per cent of UK adults in 2013. (Source: Ofcom research, fieldwork carried out by Saville Rossiter-Base in October to November 2013.)

The average minutes per day spent watching TV is still a surprisingly high 341 minutes for all individuals in the UK in 2013, representing a slight dip from the previous year, but still a surprisingly large amount of time to have the TV on.

As mentioned earlier in this chapter, media mashing, media stacking and media multitasking means that although the TV is on, many viewers are also watching/interacting with other screens/devices simultaneously.

Radio

Radio is a friend. Radio is a companion which people allow into their lives and become much closer

to as consumers than many other media. It is a secondary medium (people consume it while doing other things (driving, cleaning, working). Radio is an agile, cost-effective, low-advertising avoidance and high-impact media channel. Radio listening is the main media activity at breakfast time. Although television viewing dominates in the evening, and activities involving text communications thrive during the day, listening to the radio accounts for up to 58 per cent of all media and communications activities at the start of the day. Radio makes up 71 per cent of all audio-based activities. Considering music video channels, personal music collections, streamed music, personal digital music, on-demand listening and live radio listening, radio accounts for the largest portion by far (Ofcom, 2014).

Cinema

Cinema ads generate deeply emotional engagement with their very captive (uninterrupted) audiences who enjoy longer-form cinema ads. Many audiences consider the 'special' cinema advertisements to be entertaining and therefore part of the whole cinema

FIGURE 7.6   Average minutes per day of TV viewing by age: 2006–2013

			% change: 2013–2010
All Individuals			−4.4% (10min)
Children			−12.2% (−16min)
16–24			−14.3% (−21min)
25–34			−7.2% (−13min)
35–44			−8.3% (−18min)
45–54			−5.1% (−13min)
55–64			−0.7% (−2min)
65+			−0.5% (−2min)

Legend: Individuals — Children — Adults 16–24 — Adults 25–34 — Adults 35–44 — Adults 45–54 — Adults 55–64 — Adults 65+

SOURCE: © Ofcom, BARB, Network
New BARB panel introduced 1st Jan 2010. As a result pre- and post-panel change data must be treated with caution (see dotted line).

experience. Cinema delivers large captive audiences, and generally creates a dual viewing experience which fosters talk-ability between the viewers. Cinema accesses a hard-to-reach audience (young upmarket and light TV viewers). Although it delivers lower frequency (compared to TV), cinema does deliver deeper message out-take because of high attention and a focused environment which enhances the audience's ability to remember messages.

Outdoor posters

The most visual of all media, outdoor, is a confident, stature-building media for brands. Also called OOH (Out of Home), it cannot be turned off and hence some location marketers equate proximity with impression, ie if you are within five metres you are most likely to have seen the ad poster. Outdoor posters are used by 95 per cent of the top 100 UK advertisers, as outdoor continues to invest in its own improvement in quality, illumination, digital and now big data-driven responsive poster ads (that change according to data feeds). Surprisingly, OOH can reach 80 per cent coverage of a consumer market in a week. Digital outdoor can be dynamic with live content, news streams and social messaging. Near-field

communication (NFC) allows data exchanges and purchase with mobile devices.

Ambient media

Beyond TV, radio, cinema, posters, the press and the internet, there are many other advertising media, ranging from scented, mirrored or graffitied posters, to floor posters; from heated bus stops, painted train platforms, tunnel entrances, taxis, buses, trains and planes, to banners in space visible from earth, to aerial balloons, to the bottoms of beer glasses, to lottery balls, to screen savers, to the back of stamps (and around the front edge of stamps in the United States), to cutting fields into patterns (crop circles), to free bookmarks at the checkouts of bookstores.

The misery of choice

David Ogilvy once described the increasing array of choice as 'the misery of choice'. It applies to media planners and buyers today as well.

FIGURE 7.7   A more detailed market breakdown

Digital Classified* 6%   Press Display 12%

Digital Search* 22%

Press Classified 5%

H1 2014 Total Market £8.87bn

Digital Display* 12%

Television 25%

Outdoor 5%

Radio 3%   Cinema 1%   Direct Mail 10%

Digital = Online, mobile and tablet. Includes broadcast VOD and digital news / magazine brands revenue.
TV & Radio: H1 2014 excludes TV and radio sponsorship revenue, which will be added in for FY 2014 when published in 2015

SOURCE: IAB/PwC Digital Adspend Study 2014

Which media is most popular?

In the UK TV still takes the single biggest slice of the advertising spend (25 per cent), followed by digital search (22 per cent) with digital display ads and press display ads on 12 per cent each (IAB/PwC, 2014).

If you add digital display to digital search and digital classified ads, then 'digital advertising' took 39 per cent of the total ad spend market in the UK in 2014. And within digital, search ads take the biggest slice of spending, followed by display ads, followed by classified ads. Surprisingly, the majority (58 per cent) of digital display ads are 'In app' (appear in apps), although this is slightly less than 2013, when it was 61 per cent. Interestingly, display, overall, has the biggest growth/increase year on year.

Which media is growing fastest?

Whilst radio (12 per cent), TV (8 per cent), cinema (3 per cent) and outdoor/posters/billboards (2 per cent)

are all enjoying growth, digital enjoys the strongest growth (17 per cent). Falling behind are direct mail (−3 per cent) classified press ads (−7 per cent) and press display ads (−8 per cent) (IAB/PwC, 2014).

Media selection (overview)

Should the press and/or radio be used? How should a client or an agency choose which medium to use? Which TV stations and/or publications should be used? Which vehicles within a particular medium (eg the *Guardian* or *The Times*)? The press includes national dailies, Sunday newspapers, evening newspapers, daily and weekly regional papers, and magazines. Television, radio, cinema and posters are considered. The key points are as follows:

● Audience size (reach or penetration). Some media cannot carry national brands because they cannot offer national coverage. Media such as the regional press are generally considered to be local media, since they talk to the community. Television can get to large audiences quickly.

FIGURE 7.8   Display leads the way with like-for-like growth

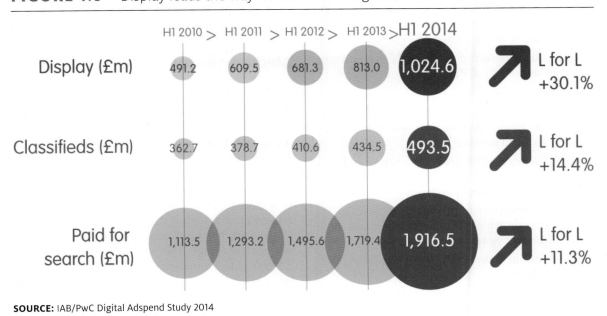

SOURCE: IAB/PwC Digital Adspend Study 2014

FIGURE 7.9   Digital shows the strongest growth

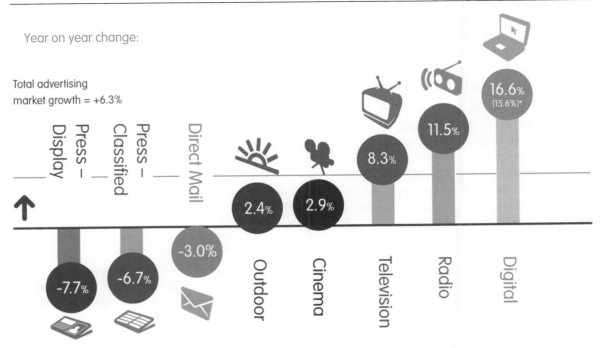

*Digital: Like for like growth (actual growth). Includes broadcast VOD and digital news / magazine brands revenue.

SOURCE: IAB/PwC Digital Adspend Study 2014

- Audience type (eg 15- to 24-year-olds don't watch much TV but do go to the cinema; on the other hand, not many over 45-year-olds watch the music station MTV).
- Budget (production cost, media cost and cost per thousand – CPT).
- Message objective:
  - Response required: is action required after the ad (eg filling in a coupon or phoning an 0800 number)?
  - Creative scope: are colour, sound and movement needed (eg TV's movement can show impulsive purchases)?
  - Demonstration: product usage is often best shown on TV, but all media can show product benefits.
  - Technical detail: TV is not good; the press is better.
  - Urgency: TV, radio and national papers can be topical and announce urgent commercial news.
  - Compatibility, 'rub-off' or image effect of media and vehicle on the product itself. For example, would Harrods advertise in the *Sun*? TV puts a product or company alongside the major players and therefore enhances the image, since many viewers think they must be good if they're on national TV.
  - TV adds credibility: 'as seen on TV'.
- Ease of booking:
  - Lead times for space: magazines, TV and cinema have long lead times or notice of booking.
  - Lead times for production: some press can be knocked out overnight, whereas a cinema production takes months.
- Restrictions. Some products, for example cigarettes, are totally excluded from all advertising, and certain media restrict the promotion of some products, such as alcohol in children's programmes.
- Competitive activity. Advertisers watch, copy and sometimes avoid the places where their competitors advertise.

See the Tactics Matrix on page 284 of Chapter 10 (taken from my SOSTAC® Guide To Writing Your Perfect Marketing Plan 2015) as it explores different tactical tools from advertising to mail shots. Although it is work-in-progress, it should help discussions when considering which media.

Media selection (detail)

Audience size

TV allows commercial messages to 'reach' large numbers of people on a national or regional level. TV used to be known as a mass medium, but, as the number of stations increases, more niche channels are emerging on cable, satellite and mainstream terrestrial TV, which means that TV is becoming less of a mass medium. Radio attracts smaller regional audiences, although it can offer national coverage. Cinema attracts small audiences and can offer slow national coverage, but can be great for 15- to 35-year-olds. The national and regional press deliver what they say – national and regional audiences respectively. Because posters can prove difficult to coordinate on a national scale, there are poster-buying specialists. Direct mail can address large national and international audiences, but because of its high cost per thousand the target audiences are likely to be tightly defined and targeted. Finally, TV's audience size is seasonally influenced, with the audience increasing in winter and reducing in summer.

Audience type

Generally, 15- to 24-year-olds are busy doing other things and don't have time to watch TV, whereas cinema can attract this target group. Radio is popular with housewives and commuters. The national daily newspapers tend to target specific socio-economic groups and political sympathizers, while magazines reach targeted groups defined by their lifestyles, income levels, ages and sex. Posters can target commuters who travel by car, bus and train.

Audience state of mind

Audience state of mind or receptivity to messages varies across the media spectrum. TV audiences can be relaxed and passive, sometimes viewing in a trance-like manner (the 'couch potato syndrome'). TV and its ads can become a form of visual wallpaper, sometimes used as company and sometimes to 'warm up' a room. Radio can also be used in the background, but listeners do tend to work with the radio, as they create visual images from verbal messages. The cinema delivers a captive audience that is happy to be involved in the suspension of disbelief and will not leave the room to make a cup of tea. In fact, many viewers thoroughly enjoy the special cinema ads. The national press is deliberately read, as information is sought. Some research reveals unconscious feelings of guilt (waste and/or inadequacy of knowledge) if a newspaper is left unfinished. Magazines are absorbed in a more relaxed mood.

Cost of production

The cost of producing a TV ad can range from £1,000 to £10 million or more, depending on the length, complexity and actors involved, whereas radio has a lower cost of production ranging from £500 to £20,000. Stationary pictures with a voice-over promoting the local Indian restaurant can cost just a few hundred pounds, while a more lavish 90-second full-production cinema advertisement could cost up to £1 million or more. Radio and the press sometimes provide free help with basic productions. Posters can be produced for as little as £125 for a six-sheet (1.83 × 1.2 metre) poster or £11,000 for a backlit 96-sheet (12 × 3 metre) poster campaign for two weeks. Direct mail can be as cheap as the cost of a letter, but if a four-colour brochure is specially designed and produced then the costs can be anywhere from several hundred to several thousand pounds for design and artwork alone.

Minimum cost of space

Advertising space is rarely bought in single units. A single ad is unlikely to achieve as much as a campaign or a series of ads would. Ads are generally scheduled and bought over a period of time rather than as one-offs. The cost of space is relatively high on TV compared to radio; a single off-peak 30-second spot on a regional radio station could be as little as £20, compared to £500 for TV. A national 30-second spot in the middle of Coronation Street could cost up to £100,000. A one-off, full-page, four-colour ad in the *Sun* or the *Financial Times* costs £45,386 and £50,151 respectively. Smaller space can be bought, right down to the square column centimetre (approximately £205 and £190 for the *Sun* and *Financial Times* respectively).

Cost per thousand (CPM)

Within a particular medium, say the press, there is a wide range of media vehicles available, from *Amateur Gardening* to the *Economist*. The CPM varies vastly across different media vehicles (eg from approximately £1 in the *Sun* to £70 in the *FT*) and across different countries (eg 50p in Bulgaria to £15 in Norway for 30-second peak-time viewing). Although CPT varies greatly, the actual selection of a particular medium (say, the press versus television) and a specific media vehicle (say, *Amateur Gardening* versus the *Economist*) is influenced by the quality of the media as well as the relative cost.

Some CPM/CPT (cost per thousand people reached with the ad):

- radio (30"): £1.95;
- OOH (out of home): posters £2.87;
- static media (posters): £6–£20 CPT;
- TV ad (30"): £5.76;
- press FP: £6.50;
- OOH digital: £11.32;
- interactive media: £18–£500 CPM;
- website display ads: £5–£500 CPM impressions/day;
- B2C e-mail data: £180–£500 CPM (including access and despatch to...);
- B2B e-mail data: £250–£1,000 CPM (including access and despatch to...);
- SME data: £150–£500 CPMT (including access and despatch to...);
- affinity CPC: £2–£10 (depending upon product and margin...CPP + commission to intermediaries);
- search CPC: 50p–£100;
- social media ads CPC: £1–£100+.

Message

TV has sight, sound, colour and movement, which makes it an ideal medium for product demonstrations and impulse purchases, but the time constraint and viewing mode make detailed messages almost impossible. Ads are viewed serially, whereas press ads compete with other ads and editorial, often on the same page. Remote control channel zapping has made TV more vulnerable as an advertising medium. TV, radio and cinema are highly transitory, in that the viewer cannot refer back to an ad once it has been shown (unless it is taped). On the other hand, the audience can refer back to press ads, posters and direct mail. TV's fleeting messages leave no room for detail but can grab attention, create

TABLE 7.2   Average response rates across different tactical tools

Media	CTR	Notes
Facebook ads	0.01 to 20%	
LinkedIn ads	0.01 to 20%	
Display ads	0.05 to 20%	Banner ad, average click-throughrate
E mail ad in Enewsletter	0.1 to 10%	
Paid search	0.5% to 2%	Highly dependent on targeting and bidding across campaign and proportion of brand/non-brand search phrases
E mail house list	1 to 10%	E-mail campaign response compilation

awareness and arouse interest. More and more ads across the media spectrum, including TV, are tying in with direct response mechanisms (0800 numbers, web addresses or coupons to fill in) so that more detailed information can subsequently be delivered to the audience.

Ease of media buying

Some popular TV programmes (and magazines) require long lead times for booking space. Advertisements are still pre-emptable (they can be outbid and kicked off a particular spot on the day they were booked to be broadcast). Big agencies generally do not get pre-empted. Different rates or prices can be bid; the top rate guarantees the spot, but agencies and clients want to avoid paying these extremely high rates, so they make bids at prices lower down the scales (giving various amounts of notice about pre-emption). Clearcast pre-approves most British television advertising. Clearcast is now owned by seven UK commercial broadcasters, and replaced the Broadcast Advertising Clearance Centre (BACC) in 2008. Approval takes time. Cinema can have longer lead booking times but shorter clearance time from the Cinema Advertising Association. Radio is the most flexible of all, with same-day clearance and short lead booking times. The national dailies tend to have flexible positions and size and short lead times, while magazines have longer lead

times. Certain positions cannot be booked in the short term, eg one-year lead time. TV and radio can offer a higher frequency, since an advertisement could theoretically go out every half-hour all day. The lack of national network coverage makes the regional press a tough task for media planners and buyers involved in national campaigns.

Response rates

Dave Chaffey of Smart Insights compiled an average response rate across different tactical tools (or channels) based on research across different sectors.

Some say it's meaningless to present average rates since there are so many sector and campaign factors that can affect response rates. However, Chaffey lists some of the factors that actually affect the response rate:

- **Creative** – the combination of visual imagery, branding, copy and call-to-action. Achieving AIDA – Awareness, Interest, Desire and Action – is still important here.
- **Relevance** – depending on targeting and creative. Relevance is the mantra in Google to boost quality score in pay-per-click.
- **Integration** – if the ad has been viewed in other media (higher frequency) a higher response is more likely (usually peaking at 3–4 impressions).

- **Targeting (and timing)** – probably the biggest factor to ensure a relevant ad. Digital offers day-parting to ensure ads are run at peak viewing times for different platforms and to coincide with ads.
- **Copy (and call-to-action)** – obvious, but the reason to respond often isn't stressed.
- **Attributes** – these are the technical attributes of the campaign like effectiveness on a mobile platform and response mechanism.
- **Landing page** – a relevant page like these tailored to the campaign will always make the campaign more effective compared to linking to the home page or a product page.

Chaffey (2012)

Mixing mass with niche media channels

Here is Millward Brown's Leonie Gate-Summers discussing how the media mix can work.

With a plan which already features **high-reach TV** (which the majority of campaigns do), the power of smaller channels can actually be more in the duplication and the reinforcement of campaign messaging, which these channels can deliver to a key target audience. While there is no such thing as the ideal media plan, there is clear evidence for the inclusion of **targeted, niche media** in multi-media plans as these channels tend to **deliver strong brand impact for relatively low cost.**

Our CrossMedia database shows that the **brand impact (per person reached) of low-reach digital activity (eg microsites) far exceeds that of higher-reach digital activity (eg.online display)** and other traditional media, justifying this trade-off of fewer people seeing your message with more powerful impact on those that do.

However, **online** as a channel holds a unique position in the media landscape, offering sites that are often **even more targeted than magazines,** behavioural targeting that can reach consumers who are at the right category involvement level, as well as high-reach sites and networks for mass reach.

On the other hand, if you are using digital as part of a multi-media plan where other channels such as TV and outdoor are delivering mass reach, then taking a more focused approach to your digital activity by making the most of behavioural or contextual targeting to communicate with a smaller group of specific consumers may be a more productive use of the digital budget.

Is the same creative approach going to work for a broad reach campaign as for a campaign delivering more targeted reach? Probably not – as with other media, broad-reach digital creative needs to have mass appeal and a simple message which will cut through with less-engaged consumers. For a targeted campaign you will be reaching more-engaged consumers, who already have a degree of knowledge about the brand or category, and therefore you need to tailor your message to their specific needs and interests.

Gaming, microsites and social media properties offer yet more chances for brands to experiment with targeted media campaigns. Millward Brown research has shown strong brand impact for all these channels, and a lot of that is down to their ability to reach the right people with tailored content which they will want to engage with – something which is a lot harder to do for the diverse mix of consumers delivered by more mass-reach channels. The challenge here is balancing the sometimes substantial production costs of developing such content, with their limited reach – something which can be overlooked in the excitement around experimenting with new types of content.

To truly **deliver brand impact** in a changing media landscape, there needs to be a readjustment of focus on to the importance of **delivering tailored messaging** and creative **to those consumers you value most.**

How much space, how often and when?

Having selected the media type, and specific vehicles within each media type, the next question is how much space and/or airtime should be booked. In what season, month, week, day or hour should the advertisement appear? How many times should the ad be seen? How many times is too many times? Can the audience become irritated? Frequency? This last question becomes more difficult when a campaign uses several different advertisements, particularly when each new ad builds on the last one. The creative side of the campaign can sell itself to the client, but the media schedule often requires much more detailed justification. Once the media schedule has been agreed, it can be passed on to the media buyer to start booking the space (within booking deadlines).

Which media and which vehicle?

Does the impact of a double-page spread (DPS) justify the cost? Would the reach be increased by placing two single-page advertisements in two different magazines instead? Should TV be supplemented by radio, by posters or by both? Is a personal media network worth creating so that the target audience is hit with a brand's message first thing in the morning on the radio, on posters in the neighbourhood area, in the appropriate paper on the way to work, on TV that evening, in the cinema that night and finally on the radio in the car coming home from the cinema?

Media buyers' computers churn out cost-ranking analyses that list the publications in order of their cost per thousand, with the lowest at the top. CPT offers a quantitative criterion, but does it reveal heavy-user information? Perhaps a high CPT conceals within it a large chunk of the heavy users, which may make the advertisement more effective? Qualitative criteria (audience size and how they use the media, targetability, message type, ease of booking, restrictions and competitive activity) all affect the choice. In the end, experience, judgement and a little bit of creative flair influence the decision to buy space.

Media plan/schedule

The media strategy is then refined into the tactical details specifying exactly what space should be booked where.

Media buying

It pays to plan carefully. Plan first; then buy. A skilled media buyer can save enormous sums by playing one media owner off against another. After all, there are many different routes (or media vehicles) to the minds of the target audience.

There are series discounts (10 inserts or ads for the price of 9), and volume discounts if you spend over a certain amount. Many agencies pool their media buying together to gain the maximum discounts. Negotiating and discounting vary from country to country. Countries such as Austria and Denmark allow very little negotiation with media owners. Media buyers and media planners or schedulers need to work closely together.

Programmatic buying

Programmatic Advertising automates the bidding, buying and placing of online advertisements in real time in order to continually optimize the return, or profitability, of the continuing stream of advertisements.

FIGURE 7.10   CPM remains the dominant charging model

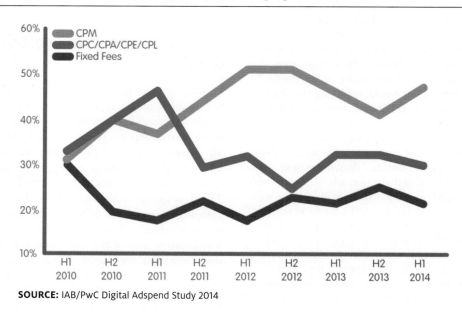

SOURCE: IAB/PwC Digital Adspend Study 2014

> ## Mad men, meet programmatic robots
>
> '...the shift towards auction-based buying of media formats such as search and video and automated trading of display media, has moved the industry to data-driven, technology-centric planning and buying modes. Mad men, meet algorithm.
>
> Decision systems applied to vast pools of media inventory allow humans to triumph over complexity and solve multivariate marketing inputs, in real time.
>
> Programmatic trading enables advertisers and agencies to make sense of data inputs in real time, and make instant buying decisions against target audiences.'
>
> Naughton (2015)

Media research

Media research basically tells the media buyer and scheduler which publications are read by what type of people, how many and what type of people are likely to watch a particular television programme, who listens to what on the radio, which kinds of films attract what kind of audience, which poster sites are passed by most people, etc. Media buyers can then decide if the particular media vehicle's audience profile matches their target market, and if the audience size proves to be cost-effective in terms of cost per thousand, coverage, frequency, opportunities to see (OTSs), TV rating points (TVRs) (see pages XX), etc.

How many people watch Neighbours or the ITV News? How many listen to Capital Radio's breakfast radio show? How many people read the *Sun*? Advertisers are even more interested in what type of people are in the audience and whether they are heavy, medium or light users of the product type or even the specific brand. Although the *Sun* is considered to be a working man's paper, 31 per cent of its readership are ABC1s. So some strange anomalies do exist, and media buyers must tread cautiously. Information concerning socio-economic groups, product usage types and lifestyle data all help to build a profile, which the advertiser can then use to target the most relevant audience.

An initial search into the British Rate and Data (BRAD) directory reveals a limited amount of information regarding circulation and audience type (socio-economic groups). This can be cross-referenced (or cross-tabulated) with the Target Group Index (see p. 177) to reveal, for example, types of audience according to lifestyles and typical product purchases, in addition to the usual demographic information.

The qualitative data explain how the media are used by target audiences – the role the media play in people's lives. Some advertising agencies use focus groups to research the obscure media used by a particular group of opinion leaders or to investigate how an audience uses the media.

Media research bureaux

TV audiences are measured by the Broadcast Audience Research Bureau (BARB), which monitors a sample of 4,500 homes through its people meter. The meter records what stations are turned on, and the hand-held remote control unit inputs data about who is watching the TV.

Radio audiences are measured by Radio Joint Audience Research (RAJAR).

Cinema uses Film Audience Research and Evaluation (FAME) to measure cinema and video audience size and profiles. Admissions are also measured by Gallup/EDI.

Newspaper and magazine readership is measured by National Readership Survey (NRS), which carries out 35,000 in-home interviews each year. The Audit Bureau of Circulation (ABC) audits the sales or circulation of over 2,000 different publications, including the nationals. ABC also audits and verifies website traffic.

Freesheets or local newspapers use the Verified Free Distribution (VFD) system.

Posters use Route (formerly Poster Audience Research) and the Poster Audit Bureau (PAB).

British Rate and Data (BRAD) is the media buyer's reference book, because it lists all the circulation or audience figures, as well as the costs (rate card costs). It also gives detailed information on deadlines, mechanical data and commissions on thousands of newspapers, consumer publications, business publications, new media, radio and TV networks, and much more. The monthly book, which contains over 1,200 pages, is subscription based. The information is also available online.

Media jargon and vocabulary

Cover and reach

'Coverage' is the percentage of the target audience reached by the advertising. If, for example, ITV News reaches 5 million viewers, 16 per cent of whom are ABC1 male, then an ad placed during the break will reach 0.8 million ABC1 males (16 per cent of 5 million viewers). If ABC1 men are the target audience and there are, in fact, 10.6 million ABC1 men in the UK, then although the advertisement reaches 0.8 million ABC1 men the coverage is only 8 per cent (0.8 million as a percentage of the total target market of 10.6 million).

Frequency

This is the number of times an ad is shown or placed in a particular period of time. How many times should an ad be shown and seen? Between four and six times? The optimum frequency is often really unknown. Should it be concentrated over a short period (a 'burst strategy') or spread steadily over a longer period (a 'drip strategy')? For example, an advertising frequency of 60 can be built up by either 1) having the same advertisement shown before, during and after ITV News every weekday for four weeks, or 2) having one advertisement every six days throughout the year.

Programmatic advertising

> Programmatic advertising is the automation of the buying and selling of desktop display, video, FBX, and mobile ads using real-time-bidding. Programmatic describes how online campaigns are booked, flighted, analysed, and optimized via demand-side software (DSP) interfaces and algorithms.
>
> Gurbaksh Chahal, Founder,
> Chairman and CEO, RadiumOne

Media tie-ups

Some marketers feel that the traditional press campaign does not deliver a 'deep enough' form of communication to meet the information-rich demands of certain product launches. So they therefore want 'media tie-ups' (which may include advertorial supplements and/or the creation of a series of supplements) from, say, a particular magazine or newspaper.

Opportunities to see (OTSs)

OTSs are the number of exposures or opportunities that a particular audience has to see a particular advertisement. In the previous example there would have been 5 million OTSs for adults and 0.8 million for ABC1 men. If the ad went out every night for five nights during the ITV News break, the total number of ABC1 men OTSs would be 5 × 0.8 million = 4 million OTSs.

Cost per thousand (CPT) – also CPM (cost per mille)

CPT calculates the average cost of reaching 1,000 of the population. If it costs, say, £100,000 to place a 30-second spot (advertisement) on national TV with a peak-time audience of, say, 10 million, then the cost per thousand or the cost of reaching each or any group of 1,000 people within the audience is £100,000 divided by 10,000 (10 million = 10,000 groups of 1,000 people). The cost per thousand here is £10. CPT allows cross-comparisons across different media types and media vehicles (although quality of media must also be analysed). For example, if a full-page advertisement in the *Sun* reaches, say, 9.5 million (bought by 3.5 million but read by 9.5 million) and costs, say, £45,000, then the CPT is £45,000 divided by 9,500 (9.5 million = 9,500 lots of 1,000 people), which gives a cost of £4.74 per thousand. CPM (cost per mille/thousand) is the same as CPT and is commonly used.

Ideally, cost per enquiry or order generated gives a truer picture, but this can only be measured after the advertisement has run (and if the advertisement was designed to achieve these kinds of responses rather than, say, increase awareness or change attitudes). Experience and knowledge provide useful insights into media scheduling and buying. CPT varies according to the actual selection of a particular medium and a specific media vehicle. The quality of the media affects CPT, as does the quality of the audience, ie advertising to high-income earners will cost more per thousand than reaching a larger, middle-income audience.

TV rating points (TVRs)

TV rating points are referred to as gross rating points (GRPs) in the United States and overseas. GRPs can be used across different media, whereas TVRs refer to TV in the UK. One TV rating point is

1 per cent of the target audience. The percentage of the target audience viewing a spot ('reach') multiplied by the average number of opportunities to see gives the TVR. Television companies will sell packages of guaranteed TVRs. For example, a target of 240 TVRs means that 60 per cent of the target audience will have, on average, 4 OTSs. It could also mean that 40 per cent have seen it six times. Reference to the media schedule quickly identifies the frequency. Four hundred TVRs (80 per cent seeing the message five times) is considered an average-sized one-month campaign. Eight hundred TVRs in one month is a big campaign. It has been suggested that some confectionery and record companies run a lightweight campaign and buy 100 TVRs so that they can tell the retail trade that they are running a television advertising campaign (the 'pull' helps the 'push').

Impacts

Impacts refer more to TV than the press. Impacts measure the total number of people who saw the ad multiplied by the number of times they saw it. In the ITV News case it would be 0.8 million × 5 = 4 million impacts (for ABC1 men). To make more sense of impacts, divide them by the universe (number of people within the target market) to get TVRs (television rating). Impacts are more useful when converted to TVRs.

Drip

Drip means spreading relatively small amounts of advertising over the whole campaign period. A 'steady drip' of advertising creates presence over a longer period of time.

Burst

Burst is the opposite to drip. Here the ads are concentrated into a smaller time-frame, creating a bigger impact but only for a shorter period of time.

Continuous patterns

Continuous patterns of advertising are a regular and uniform presentation of the message to the target audience. A rising pattern is where the ads are increased up to a particular event. A fading pattern is where the ads are slowly reduced after the event (or after a product launch).

Flighting patterns

Flighting patterns are where the advertiser spreads the ads over a longer period of time. It can mean boosting advertising at certain times to match seasonal demand, match a competitor's ad campaign, support a particular sales promotion, respond to adverse publicity or simply seize a one-off market opportunity.

Pulsing

Pulsing supposedly combines both continuous patterns and flighting patterns, ie to incur high levels of ad spend when required but also to maintain some advertising in between times so that the target audience does not forget the brand. This 'safe option' is an expensive one. Pulsing is also known as the 'long tail approach'. In conjunction with econometric modelling it can actually prove better value.

Pulsing can save money

A radio ad campaign in the Irish Republic found that it caused an uplift in awareness for three weeks after it was broadcast. As a result the agency recommended to the client to move from a bi-weekly burst to a three-weekly burst. This retained the impact of the campaign, saved a lot of money and allowed the campaign to run longer in a 'long tail' format. NB: This is not the same as the niche market long tail concept.

Position

Position refers to the place where the ad is shown. Back pages, inside cover pages, right-hand pages, TV pages and so on have greater readership and more impact than other pages (eg the third right-hand page has a bigger impact than the first left-hand page). Similarly, some positions on a page are more effective than others. Media buyers are aware of this and so are the media owners, since their rate cards (prices) reflect the value of, and demand for, certain positions. The Boddingtons beer media strategy was built around position, ie it concentrated its advertisements on the back page of glossy magazines to the extent that it 'owned' the back pages for a period of time.

Environment

The environment or context in which an ad is exposed affects the message itself. The types of features or editorial, and other advertisements that run alongside an advertisement affect the likely effectiveness of that advertisement. An advertiser can lose credibility if the programme is a parody of the product being advertised, for example the film *Airplane* with an airline ad in the break.

Summary

Media consumption patterns are changing, as are media. Great care is required in developing the right media mix and vehicle mix, as well as timing and pulsing, since this is arguably marketing's single biggest spend. Small savings here can free larger budgets for elsewhere (eg social media campaigns).

Key points from Chapter 7

- Media choice is growing continually.
- Media planning and buying have more of an impact on the bottom line than producing an ad.
- Different media have different advantages and disadvantages – careful planning is required.
- Evaluate media options according to consistent criteria.

References and further reading

Account Planning Group (1987) *How to Plan Advertising*, ed D Cowley, Cassell, London

Chaffey, D (2012) Marketing campaign response rates, *Smart Insights*, 11 Oct

Common Sense Media Research (2013) Zero to eight – children's media use in America, *Common Sense Media*, Fall

Davies, M (1992) *The Effective Use of Advertising Media*, 4th edn, Business Books, London

Douglas, T (1984) *The Complete Guide to Advertising*, Papermac, London

eConsultancy (2015) Quarterly digital intelligence briefing: digital trends 2015, *eConsultancy.com*

EIAA (European Interactive Advertising Association) (2010) Multi-Screeners Report 2010

Engel, J, Warshaw, M and Kinnear, T (1991) *Promotional Strategy: Managing the marketing communications process*, Irwin, Homewood, Ill

Gates-Sumner, L (nd) Sharpening the arrow: The value of modern targeting approaches, Millward Brown

IAB and Thinkbox (2008) Combine TV and online to boost brand perception, *Brand Republic*, 10 June

IAB /PwC (2014) Digital Adspend H1 2014 & WARC [online] http://www.iabuk.net/research/digital-adspend

IPSOS Canadian Interactive Reid report (2010) *ipsos.ca*

Kennedy, J (2009) App-fab, *Marketing Age*, November

Kohler, E (2007) Hyperlocal is more about ads than news, *Technology Evangelist*, 9 August

Learmonth, M (2010) Top marketers to Silicon Valley: Help us get ahead of consumer. Through visits to tech hub, big advertisers getting more than sales pitches, *Ad Age*, 17 May

Marketer (2008) Watching the coffee channel, May

McPartlin, Peter (2011) New Media Model, *Marketing Age*, 5 (2)

Markiewicz, P, Sherman, N and Jaworski, D (2008) *Millennials and the Digital Entertainment Age: A sourcebook for consumer marketers*, Digital Media Wire, West Hollywood, CA

Mason, R (2010) Moosylvania Marketing, *Advertising Age*, 4 November

Media International, Reed Publishing Services, London

Media Week, EMAP Business Publications, London

Naughton, E (2015) Mad men, meet the algorithm: the art and science of modern marketing, *Guardian*, 13 March

Nielsen Wire (2009) TV viewing among kids at an eight-year high, 26 October

Ofcom (2014) The Communications Market Report, 7 August

Patel, K (2010) Will growing crop of TV apps engage viewers, advertisers? *Ad Age*, 17 May

Pew Research (2009) Newspapers face a challenging calculus, 26 February

Rayman, N (2013) More than 33 per cent of kids under two use tablets so prepare for an army of robot babies, *Time Magazine*, 28 October

Rogers, E (2003) *Diffusion of Innovations*, 5th edn, Simon and Schuster

Signal (2015) How digital marketing will change in 2015: what marketers need to know now, *Signal* [online] http://info.signal.co/download-report-how-digital-marketing-will-change-in-2015

Smith, PR (2015) The SOSTAC® Guide to Your Perfect Marketing Plan [online] www.PRSmith.org/SOSTAC

TV Free America (2010) Invisible Children blog, 2010, TV's ugly stats

XPLANE (2009) Did you know? YouTube video [online] https://www.youtube.com/channel/UCZhxbU7zFAxi7K3B9dZ4oRQ

Further information

Audit Bureau of Circulation (ABC)
Saxon House
211 High Street
Berkhamsted
Herts HP4 1AD
Tel: +44 (0)1442 870800
www.abc.org.uk

British Audience Research Bureau (BARB)
20 Orange Street
London WC2H 7EF
Tel: 020 7024 8100
www.barb.co.uk

British Rate and Data (BRAD)
BRAD Insight
Zetland House
5–25 Scrutton Street
London EC2A 4HJ
Tel: +44 (0)20 8102 0904
www.brad.co.uk

Film Audience Measurement and Evaluation (FAME)
Pearl & Dean
Corinthian House
Tottenham Court Road
London
W1T 7RJ
Tel: +44 (0)20 7199 2400
Fax: +44 (0)20 7199 2401
www.business.pearlanddean.com

Joint Industry for Regional Press Research (JICREG)
c/o The Newspaper Society
2nd Floor
292 Vauxhall Bridge Road
London SW1V 1AE
Tel: +44 (0)20 7963 7480
www.jicreg.co.uk

National Readership Survey Ltd (NRS)
7/8 Market Place
London W1W 8AG
Tel+ 44(0) 207 637 9822
www.nrs.co.uk

Ofcom
Riverside House
2a Southwark Bridge Road
London SE1 9HA
Telephone: 0300 123 3000
www.ofcom.org.uk

Route
Route Research Limited
3rd Floor
35–45 Dorset Street
London W1U 7NA
Tel: +44 (0)207 317 2770
www.route.org.uk

Radio Joint Audience Research (RAJAR)
6th Floor
55 New Oxford Street
London WC1A 1BS
Tel +44 (0)20 7395 0630
www.rajar.co.uk

Verified Free Distribution (VFD) – contact
the Audit Bureau of Circulation (ABC)
Saxon House
211 High Street
Berkhamsted
Herts HP4 1AD
Tel: +44 (0)1442 870800
www.abc.org.uk

08
Marketing communications agencies

LEARNING OBJECTIVES

By the end of this chapter you will be able to:

- Understand the range of different types of agencies
- Draw the structure of a large agency and modify it with new marketing tools
- Discuss different methods of remunerating agencies
- Set up a selection process
- Nurture relationships between agency and client

Agency types   218
Introduction   218
DIY, full-service or specialist   218
Tomorrow's agency   219
The agency of the future   220
Are agencies currently a mess?   220

Agency structure   220
Planning department   221
Creative department   222
Media department   222
Production department   223
Traffic department   223
The account management team   223
The account executive   223

Agency remuneration   224
Commission   224
Commission rebating   224

Fees   225
Pay-by-results (PBR)   225

Agency relationships – selection and retention   226
Agency selection process overview   226
Issuing the brief   228
The pitch   230
Analysing the agency   232
Choosing an agency   233
Rejecting an agency   236
Firing the agency   236
Firing the client   238
Managing the relationship successfully   239
Life in an agency   239

Key points from Chapter 8   240

References and further reading   240

Further information   241

Agency types

Introduction

This chapter covers agencies, types of agencies, their structure, fees and working relationships, from shortlisting to briefing, selecting, hiring and firing.

There are many types of agencies, including advertising, sales promotion, direct mail, PR, corporate identity design, web design and more. Some call themselves agencies and others, consultancies. Regardless of title, the barriers created by the separate disciplines are falling. Corporate identity design consultants' services are spreading into advertising campaigns (to launch the new identities); sales promotion consultants are tempted into direct mail, as this communications tool requires a constant flow of incentives, premiums and sales promotions; advertising agencies are dropping the word 'advertising' and PR consultants are dropping 'PR', as these terms restrict them from developing and delivering the integrated marketing communications services their clients require. The overall approach by, and structures of, advertising agencies is changing. Most agencies have moved their total focus beyond the one-way 'tell' medium of traditional broadcasting, with its limited levels of interactive responsiveness. These agencies are now integrating more closely with the 'responsive disciplines', such as direct mail, sales promotions and social media. Moving from 'tell campaigns' to 'listening campaigns' requires a constant customer dialogue nurtured and integrated across many media.

Some agencies see new structures as an exciting challenge for the agency world. 'At the very least, the shaking up of structures and processes that pre-date the new technology by about 100 years can't fail to have a liberating effect that should be greatly to the benefit of clients', says Sir Martin Sorrell (1996), Chairman, WPP Group. Other agencies feel that the required changes in agency structure require not just new structures but new language. 'Impact' is being replaced by 'dialogue' (and even 'trialogue'), 'poster advertising' by 'street dialogue'. Perhaps 'direct mail and radio' should change to 'kitchen dialogue'. 'Engagement' has become the new mantra, replacing 'response'. The process of change among agencies is being driven partly by unsettled clients, visionary agency directors, the media explosion and new types of competition emerging.

One of the best-known ad agencies in the world, Saatchi & Saatchi, dropped the word 'advertising' from its title. It is now just plain Saatchi & Saatchi, the Lovemarks Company. It describes itself as a 'full service, integrated communications network'. It even commissioned a short video called 'The last ad agency on earth' (which can be watched on YouTube) to confirm that the old agency concept was no longer its concept.

DIY, full-service or specialist

As 'ad agencies' are by far the biggest type of agency, TV consumption is still going up and offline budgets are still far greater than online budgets (across the board), 'advertising agencies' will be used here (despite their restructuring into new forms of agency). The larger ad agencies offer a full service, including creative, research and planning, media planning and buying, and production and now social media planning. Some full-service agencies also have departments specializing in forecasting, market intelligence and business planning, together with support services for the advertising campaign, including point-of-sale design, sales literature, sales conferences and other below-the-line activities such as sales promotion, PR and direct mail. The agency, like any other business, also has other departments that are of little interest to the client, such as accounting and finance, personnel, administration, etc (see Table 8.1).

Advertisers can choose to use only their own in-house staff to run a campaign. Do-it-yourself or in-house advertising also varies, as some advertisers prefer to contract out some of their requirements to specialist services such as a media scheduling and buying agency known as a 'media independent'. Similarly, the creative work can be put out to a 'hot shop' or 'creative shop'. Saatchi & Saatchi started as a creative shop. Alternatively, the advertiser can go à la carte by picking and choosing separate agencies with specialist services for different parts of the process, eg using four different agencies for the research, creative, production and media planning/buying stages. There are other types of specialist agencies that focus on a particular industry sector.

A recent discrete development in the à la carte option is the agreement of a large, well-known, full-service advertising agency to subcontract its creative services to a small communications consultancy on an ad hoc basis. This may last only as long

TABLE 8.1   The pros and cons of different working relationships

Aspect	Full services (under one roof)	Specialist services	In-house
Management and control	Easier, since it is all under one roof	More work (coordinating)	Total control, but more work involved
Security	Limited risk – sensitive information is shared with agency	More risk – more people have access to information	Minimal risk – no outsiders
Speed/response	Reasonably good	Possible problems if à la carte = more coordination	Fast, since all decision makers are available
Cost	Expensive, high overheads, but lower media costs with agency buying power	Cheaper, fewer overheads	Cheaper, but less media buying power
Fresh views	Yes	Yes	No
Expertise	Yes (jack of all trades, master of none?)	Yes (fill in gaps in client's skills)	No (lack of specialized knowledge)
Stress	Less pressure/workload	Delegate some workload	More stress – more work

as the agency has spare capacity or is searching for extra revenue. Some clients demand that their full-service agencies work alongside the client's separate choice of media independents. Some full-service agencies get only a portion of the full job. A recession can force some clients to cut back their own in-house advertising department and operate a less costly and more flexible ad hoc project arrangement with various agencies.

Tomorrow's agency

Agencies, like all businesses, are living in a category-less and a border-less world. Hyper-competition is here to stay. Martin Sorrell says that agencies will be competing with software companies, search engine companies and many more as 'frenemies' or 'copetitors'. In this excerpt from an *Ad Week* interview with Sir Martin Sorrell by Noreen O'Leary back in 2013, exploring who will be occupying what space in the agency world in five years from

then (ie 2018), Sir Martin revealed the emergence of frenemies:

> You never know what will come out of left field, but what is different now is all these new layers of competition: our direct competitors; others, like Nielsen, Ipsos; companies like Adobe, Salesforce. com; the Google, Facebook, Amazon, Apple group. All the differences will become less and less – we will morph into each others' territory much more.
> O'Leary (2013)

This new wave of frenemies, copetitors, category-less competitors, hyper competitors – call them what you will – most likely also include management consultants such as Bain, McKinsey, Accenture, and the restyled IBM, as well as an array of smaller, nimble, highly creative yet mathematically capable digital consultancies who have sprung up, and who are, as Nick Watt (2013) suggests 'also being invited out to play. With all these new players in the market, it seems that agencies no longer have a monopoly when it comes to ideas or creativity.'

P&G integrate its agencies with a single 'throat to choke'

Several years ago, P&G undertook the task of refocusing their global agency relationships. They realized they had more than 2,500 different agencies and 3,000 pay points, with a huge duplication of resources, relationships and remuneration. Over the course of a three-year process, they launched a Brand Agency Leader Model – whereby a single person of a lead agency would have a single contact point for all integrated services on that brand at P&G. The BAL model has driven a new culture of accountability amongst lead agencies, and a new approach to an old problem. The model is not foolproof, and there have been a lot of kinks along the journey – but it's a quite unique step in the challenges of unifying communications.

The move also required fundamental changes on the P&G side – a single 'throat to choke' had to be established for each brand internally, with that person controlling the briefing and approval of all agencies globally. Not every company is ready for such a radical change, and not every P&G brand has migrated to the BAL model.

R3 (2015)

The agency of the future

In an excellent piece entitled 'The Agency Of The Future', Mike O'Brien predicts that as clients are already beginning to automate many of the less challenging communications processes in SEO, PPC, display, e-mail, mobile and social, agencies will deliver fewer and fewer of the following processes:

- content development;
- activation publishing;
- digital analytics deployment and reporting;
- social interaction propagation;
- mobile communications;
- web experience management;
- cross-channel testing and optimization;
- media optimization;
- campaign management.

Are agencies currently a mess?

Mike O'Brien (2015) continues:

At the moment most agency teams are split into management, client services, researchers, planners, creative, media, production, data, analytics, brand, direct, digital. Digital makes things even more complex, with specialist teams for SEO, PPC, display, e-mail, affiliates, UX, social, content, analytics, and so on. It is a mess. The wastage is extraordinary. The results are less than inspirational.

Agency structure

Different types and sizes of agencies have different structures. The structure of a large advertising agency is shown in Figure 8.1, which illustrates the many different departments, people and skills that have to work together to create an advertisement. Companies that have their own in-house advertising departments, and smaller, external agencies, will subcontract (or hire) any of the departments they do not have. Many of the bigger agencies also hire, or subcontract, directors, producers, camera people, photographers, film companies, print and production facilities. Any other agent, agency, consultant or consultancy – whether public relations, direct mail, sales promotion or corporate identity – also relies on the ability to bring together many different skill sets and departments, as shown in Figure 8.1. Although pure ad agencies are growing into integrated agencies offering an additional suite of social media services, TV advertising is not going away and still takes a disproportionately large chunk of any brand's budget. Therefore the original ad agency structure is still worth exploring.

Agencies have evolved from 'pushing advertising campaigns to nurturing communities of consumers around brands'. The new breed of agencies have greater data analytics, brand, direct and digital skills along with the required planning, creative and media skills. It is also possible that, instead of pitching for a brand's business, agencies may offer a new service – selling access to groups of consumers' groups with similar interests that they have nurtured (eg a Facebook or LinkedIn group, or see the example of Citroën gaining access to ASOS customers in Chapter 15 on sponsorship). Successful agencies

FIGURE 8.1   Structure of a large advertising agency

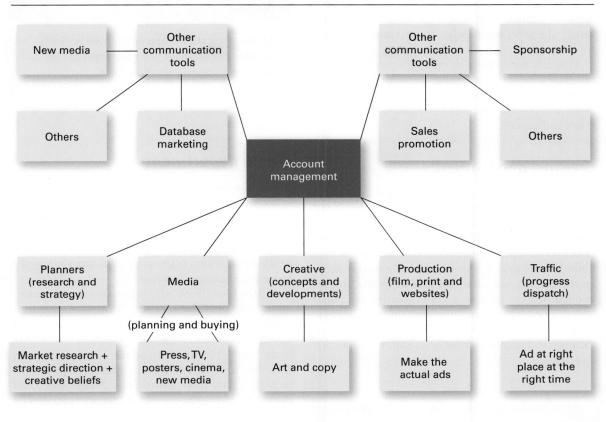

will probably connect themselves with clearly defined communities of consumers and 'cultivate insights into their behaviour' (Farey-Jones, 2008). These communities can be online and offline, eg an agency funding a community hall. So, many new skills and new departments need to be considered in addition to the basic Figure 8.1.

Agency structures have changed somewhat over the years, particularly recently with agencies wanting to position themselves as more nimble and quicker to react, many have developed flatter, less compartmentalized structures. We've seen the changing role of account management from intermediaries to project managers – witness the birth of Mother, where account handlers were re-christened mothers and morphed into quasi producers. The story here is that the ad agency structure is changing.

Let's have a look at a classic agency structure:

Planning department

Planners are more than glorified researchers. They have to know the right kind of questions to ask in the research, commission the research and interpret the results at two different levels. First, they have to absorb, summarize and translate large market research reports into simple lay terms for inclusion in the creative brief that they, in conjunction with the account director, give to the creative team. They also need to understand analytics, and of course digital potential. Second, the information has to be interpreted at a strategic and tactical level for discussion with the account executive, account manager, account director and often the client. Planners provide an objective voice, unhindered either by the account executive, who sometimes wants to 'sell' an advertising concept to the client simply because the creative director wants to get on with it, or by clients, who sometimes want to get on with it by quickly running some advertisements to satisfy the sales force, who are anxiously waiting for news on the new campaign.

Planners are experts in making sense of market research data and condensing the information into creative briefs. Marketing clients may also want more analysis and insights from customer communities and groups.

> ### Creatives' role will change
>
> 'Creatives will still be important, but will work less on one-way campaigns to a mass audience than on "ongoing dialogues" with individuals.'
>
> Kemp and Kim (2008)

Creative department

It is unfair to stereotype creative people as coming in late, lying around and dreaming up the big ideas and concepts that drive all advertising campaigns. They can work long hours under extreme pressure to deliver unique, creative ideas that grab attention, build brands and win customers. They constantly search for the big idea that has to fit the single-minded strategy presented in the creative brief that is developed by the planning department. Creative people usually work in pairs, covering words and pictures, ie a copywriter (or wordsmith) and an art director.

> ### Creative people – an appreciation
>
> 'Somebody finally has to get out an ad, often after hours. Somebody has to stare at a blank piece of paper. Probably nothing was ever bleaker. This is probably the very height of lonesomeness. He is one person and he is alone – all by himself – alone. Out of the recesses of his mind must come words which interest, words which persuade, words which inspire, words which sell. Magic words.'
>
> Leo Burnett, Founder, Leo Burnett Company

Creatives will work more on content required for generating ongoing dialogues with individuals and less on one-way campaigns to a mass audience. Outsourcing will include user-generated content (see Chapter 1), harnessing champions and brand advocates as user-generated content becomes more important.

Media department

The media department basically plans and buys the space where the advertisements are eventually placed (press, websites, posters, social platforms, apps, games, TV, radio, cinema, etc). Media planners and media schedulers can be separate from media buyers, who negotiate and ultimately buy the space from the media owners.

Maths Men (those who are involved in programmatic ads, algorithms, or any form of software or automation that helps to minimize media costs and optimize a client's budget) are becoming key players in the media department and media houses. Maths Men used to be called the Econometrics Department; now they tend to be called Data Analysts or Data Planners. However, as econometrics becomes a slightly dated term and data or 'big data' keeps its current appeal, data analytics and data planners are more commonly used terms. Rather than being a department in an agency, many planning departments now sit in media companies, albeit owned by agency holding group companies such as WPP.

Both media planners and media buyers can be further separated into those who specialize in TV, press or digital media, remarketing and programmatic advertising. As markets fragment and media explode into many more magazines, TV stations and websites, large audiences become more difficult to buy. Despite this, the media explosion presents new opportunities for schedulers and buyers, as these new media vehicles have access to more tightly defined target markets. **The media department now analyses the appropriateness and cost-effectiveness of much more media than ever before.**

This is quite a responsibility, as the bulk of the advertising spend is in media and not production (eg a £20 million campaign might have a £19 million media budget and a £1 million production budget). On top of this, media departments can deliver highly creative media strategies that find new ways of delivering advertisements to target audiences. See Chapter 13 for more examples.

You think you are overworked – try the media department or a media company. The explosion of blogs and other social media has opened new media channels which reach various target groups. If this is where significant numbers of the target audience spend time (consuming this media experience), then surely media buyers and planners now have an awful lot more work to do.

Production department

The production department actually makes the advertisement. Many agencies subcontract various parts of the production, eg hiring a studio, camera crew or photographer, director, editing suites, etc. This can involve long pre-production meetings finalizing all the minute details, flying around the world to shoot some film, and the less glamorous, lonely post-production – working around the clock in a dark and dingy editing suite.

Creating games, funny virals and some ads

Production departments (and outsourced production companies) will be full of clever people, some of whom can create great 60-second movies (and longer-form ads – see Chapter 13), as well as online games and of course contagious virals.

Traffic department

Although the traffic department is now usually part of the creative services department, dispatch, or traffic, is responsible for getting the right artwork or film to the right magazine or TV network at the right time. This becomes complicated where posters, cinema, radio and magazine inserts are included in the media strategy. Multiply this by several different campaigns for a range of different clients, and the need for a traffic manager becomes self-evident. Add in games and virals, and traffic gets busier.

The account management team

In a large agency this can involve an account director, account manager, account executive, planner, creative director, copywriter, art director, TV producer, media director, TV media scheduler, TV airtime buyer, press planner and press buyer.

The account executive

Sometimes also called an account representative, the account executive is dedicated to a particular client. The account executive wears two hats – the client's when talking to the agency and the agency's when talking to the client. Responsibilities include attendance at all client meetings, writing up 'contact reports' and general liaising between the many different members of the agency's team and the client so that projects get delivered on time (quasi producers). Many agencies write up contact reports (after each meeting), because they confirm and clarify all key points discussed, conclusions reached and any actions to be taken. This cuts out the opportunity for any misinterpretation further down the road when the client says 'I never said that' or 'I never asked for that.' When agreed by the client, vital documents, such as a summary of the agency's interpretation of the client's brief, or concept proposals, are sometimes required to be signed by the client as 'approved'. This keeps communication clear, reduces ambiguities and, if a row does break out over a particular strategic direction or over the details of copy (the words in the advertisement), the agency can pull out a signed 'approved by' copy. This is particularly helpful when a manager leaves a client company, because it confirms the stage-by-stage approval of the development of a campaign.

Account execs – new community managers?

Account people will evolve into 'community managers', who will help the community sell itself to certain brands. 'The agency would know which brand would be best to let in, which brands should be kept out, and what information can be shared and with whom it can be shared.'

Kemp and Kim (2008)

In summary the three key components of the agency are:

1 planning and strategy;
2 creative;
3 media.

Agencies prefer searching for big ideas to posting on social media

With the growth of social media many clients initially felt they were neither skilled nor knowledgeable enough to run their own social media, so they were happy to subcontract out to agencies. However, as social media is maturing (it is, after all, 10 years old now), more clients, like NIKE, feel more confident to bring it back in-house, within the marketing department, or customer care or CRM. Some agencies are simultaneously quite pleased with this development, since they feel that agencies are best at generating the 'big idea', the big creative concept, and not the detailed operational minutiae of writing 10 tweets, two Facebook posts, an Instagram, a Pinterest and a blog post every day. 'Three years ago most brands didn't really have a clear understanding of the impact social media would have on internal resources or their marketing strategies. Fast-forward and there are now roles in marketing departments focused solely on sharing and publishing content all the time. The smarter agencies have figured out that their value in the mix is on the idea rather than the day-to-day community management' said Roger Warner, director at social media agency, Beyond, in an interview with Sebastian Joseph (2013).

Agency remuneration

Agencies have three basic methods of calculating their remuneration: commission, fees and pay-by-results (PBR).

Commission

Although this has changed drastically, historically media owners have given recognized agencies a 15 per cent discount off the rate card price. Thus, in the case of a £10 million TV advertising campaign, the agency gets invoiced by the TV station at rate card £10 million less 15 per cent, ie £8.5 million. The client then gets invoiced by the agency at the full rate card price, ie £10 million (this can be checked with British Rate and Data (BRAD) or the media owner's published rate card). The 15 per cent commission really represents a 17.65 per cent mark-up, ie the £1.5 million commission is the mark-up which the agency adds on to its media cost of £8.5 million:

Agency invoiced by TV station less 15 per cent	£8.5 million
Agency invoices client at full rate card	£10.0 million
Agency mark-up	£1.5 million
Agency mark-up	17.65 per cent

The agency will also apply its agreed mark-up to other services that it subcontracts, such as market research and so on. Thus a piece of research that costs the agency £10,000 would be charged to the client (+17.65 per cent) at £11,765. One of the problems with the commission system is that it can tempt agencies to get clients to spend, spend, spend. Incidentally, the commission system does not necessarily cover all production costs, so these costs are often separately invoiced directly to the client by the agency. Over the past 10 years the number of clients using this method has declined significantly, in favour of a combination of the payment methods outlined below. In fact the 15 per cent commission has been slashed in half by some media owners. Back in 2006, Yahoo announced that it would pay 10 per cent commission to agencies that spend £80,000+ per month on search marketing, 5 per cent to those spending £20,000+ and nothing to agencies that spend less than that.

Commission rebating

Specialist media-buying companies – with much lower overheads – can work with commissions as low as 2 or 3 per cent. Some clients insist that the full-service agency only takes a smaller commission, say 10 per cent, with the balancing 5 per cent going back to the client. Commission rebating occurs when an agency passes on some of its commission to the client. There is no actual refund or rebate. The agencies simply invoice the client at rate card costs less the level of rebate, in this case 5 per cent. Commission rebating opens the door to agencies competing on price instead of on quality of service, as they have done traditionally. Most industries dislike price wars, and advertising is no exception. In 1984, Allen, Brady & Marsh (ABM) resigned its £3.5 million B&Q account after a request for rebates. It also took a large advertisement in the advertising trade press explaining that the 15 per cent commission left most agencies with 2 per cent profits after tax and any reduction would affect the quality of advertising. It fought against the tide of change, and refused to become involved in commission rebating. ABM was a fantastic agency generating some classic advertising campaigns, but, sadly, it no longer exists.

Many clients today are moving towards fees instead of solely commission-based remuneration.

> ### Rebates above and beyond their normal commissions based on all the money they spend for all their clients
>
> 'In most of the world (the United States excluded), ad agencies get rebates from media companies based on their "pooled buying" power. In other words, they get cash returned, above and beyond their normal commissions, based on all the money they spend for all their clients.
>
> Clients aren't routinely informed about exactly how much of these rebates is generated by their particular spending. Even when clients press for answers, they often allow agencies to keep the extra money so clients can continue to pay lower fees.'
>
> Crain (2013)

Fees

Smaller clients with smaller media spends do not generate sufficient commission, so a fee will generally

be agreed. Larger clients are also moving towards fees – an annual, quarterly or monthly retainer or, alternatively, a project fee. No commission means no media bias, since the agency is then free to recommend, say, direct mail, without losing any of its income (which would have been generated through commissions).

Many agencies receive a fee along with some level of commission, and/or some level of pay-by-results. The agency's remuneration essentially depends on how much work is involved and how much the client is likely to spend (on media). The trend, particularly with larger clients, appears to be moving towards a fee basis or a mixture of fees, commissions and results.

Pay-by-results can be mutually beneficial. It is sometimes disliked because of the lack of control that the agency may have over its own destiny.

Pay-by-results (PBR)

Not so long ago, major agencies would only dabble in some PBR, while the newer agencies, hungry for business, were prepared to put their heads on the block and offer most of their services on a pay-by-results basis. Today PBR has become the norm rather than the exception, with the majority of British advertisers remunerating their creative advertising agencies according to the results achieved. Media agencies had an even bigger majority, with 60 per cent being paid subject to PBR factors (ISBA, 2010). Media owners like Google offer another form of PBR: CPC (cost per click) and CPA (cost per action). If no one clicks on the sponsored phrase or no one buys (if that is the goal) then Google do not get paid a penny.

The problem with PBR is that some results are beyond the agency's influence, eg poor product quality control, late delivery or inadequate distribution, a price change, a strike at the factory or competitor activities such as doubling advertising and cutting prices. So if sales form the main criterion for payment then the agencies are vulnerable by the very nature of their dependency on so many uncontrollable variables.

If, on the other hand, the payment is linked to results directly influenced by advertising, say level of awareness or a shift in image or positioning, then the agency has more control over its own destiny. Results, of course, have to be measured through market research. **One area where PBR is relatively easy to manage is direct mail campaigns that deliver a certain number of enquiries, orders or customers.** Similarly, an SEO campaign can be linked to number of visitors generated by SEO. Another area where results are easily measured and are directly related to the agency's input is media buying. If an agency achieves media buying at a price that is better than average, then the saving can be shared between client and agency. For example, if the average advertising cost per thousand to reach, say, housewives with children is £3.50, and if the agency gets this for 10 per cent less, then the saving might be split 8 per cent to the client and 2 per cent to the agency. (Note: quality of the media is also taken into account.) Some agencies, like BBH, prefer a fixed bid with shared risk system. For example, if an advertisement is produced under budget, the production company keeps a percentage and the client receives a percentage. If the advertisement is 10 per cent over budget, the client pays; anything over 10 per cent and the production company pays.

PBR extends beyond advertising into other disciplines as far away as design. This can apply to new product design (as a royalty) or even packaging design, when the packaging design consultancy bases its fee (or a portion of its fees) on the client's increase in sales occurring after the launch of the newly designed pack. Although PBR appears attractive to the client, it can generate extra administrative work, as exact results have to be measured, royalties and contributions calculated, invoices requested and cheques raised for each agreed accounting period.

The method of agency reimbursement is fundamental to the client–agency relationship (both working and contractual). An agency's range of reimbursement packages can influence the client's selection process.

Agency relationships – selection and retention

The coordination of any campaign's development, launch and measurements requires time and management skills. Powerful personalities in agencies need to be managed. The ability to ask the right question is a valuable management skill. **The fatigue** factor in negotiations or discussions can also cause rash decisions to be made. Marketing people tend to be energetic, enthusiastic, action-orientated achievers. Sometimes steely patience needs to be exercised. Perhaps a decision has to be delayed until further research can answer some emerging questions. Painstaking attention to detail may sometimes seem irksome to the advertising agency, but it is often the mark of a true professional. On the other hand, a key resource, time, may be running out. More research reduces the risk but costs time and money. Can deadlines be moved? Is there money left for more research? Is there time before the competition launches its new offer? A decision made in haste is rarely the best one.

Agency selection process overview

Defining exactly what is required is the first stage of agency selection. This is because an appropriate choice is partly determined by a specific requirement. Some furniture retail chains may consider the strength of the media department the key criterion when choosing an agency, particularly if the store primarily wants maximum media coverage for its relatively straightforward black-and-white product information advertisements. Another client may be looking for a radically fresh approach and have a bias towards agencies with abundant creative talent. Either way, a clear brief should be prepared to identify exactly what – in marketing and advertising terms – the new advertising campaign is trying to achieve (see Chapter 2, 'The brief' at p. 52).

The agency selection procedure is as follows:

1 define requirements;
2 develop a pool list of attractive agencies;
3 credentials pitch (by the agencies);
4 issue brief to shortlisted agencies;
5 full agency presentation or pitch;
6 analysis of pitch;
7 select winner;
8 agree contract details;
9 announce winner.

Some clients prefer to get on with it by issuing a full brief to the shortlist of, say, six agencies without going through the agency credentials presentation. Other clients prefer to restrict the valuable research findings and strategic thinking to as few agencies as possible, because the unsuccessful agencies are free to work for the competition at any time in the future.

Pool list

Most advertising managers and marketing managers observe various campaigns by watching advertising and noting any particularly attractive campaigns. Agencies working for the competition need to be excluded or treated with extreme caution. Some desk research, both online and offline, can reveal the agencies behind the brands by reference to organizations such as Nielsen Media Research or Adforum.com, which allow advertisers to look for agencies using sensible criteria. Advertisers can create shortlists, preview creative work and explore an agency's profile, online and free of charge. Many marketing managers have a fair idea of who is doing what advertising in their sector by constantly reading the trade press. Other managers simply increase their advertising dosage by spending a few weeks watching more advertising than normal. Some clients sift through the agency portfolio videos, which can be bought from Campaign Portfolio or Marketing Week Portfolio for a few hundred pounds (the agencies pay a lot more to acquire this advertising space in the first place). In these videos, agency after agency present themselves in a sometimes surprisingly tedious fashion. Some clients prefer to do their own screening and request an agency reel (video) or an agency information pack directly from a particular agency so that they can view the agency's best work. Try some online sources (eg **www.adforum.com**) initially, where you can get some agency info, preview some of their creative work (peruse some ads) and sometimes see some interesting updates and communications articles and news alerts. Remember, selecting agencies is hard work and requires rigorous attention to detail. Bad selections are very expensive.

Another way of building a pool list is through the professional associations. Upon receipt of information about a potential client's basic requirements, professional bodies or trade associations such as the **Institute of Practitioners in Advertising (IPA), the Incorporated Society of British Advertisers (ISBA) and the Advertising Association (AA)** all offer to provide lists of agencies that they feel are suitable to handle a specific type and size of business. Similar services are offered by the relevant professional institutes of other service sectors such as public

relations, sales promotion, design, direct mail, etc (see 'Further information' at the end of each chapter). This service is normally free, and the associations are extremely helpful to the uninitiated.

There are also agency assessors, such as the Advertising Agency Register, and intermediaries whose business is agency selection. They can handle the development of the pool list, pitch list, pitch analysis, agency selection and even performance assessment of the agency when it starts working for the client.

Probably fewer than 10 per cent of agency hires in the UK are through intermediaries (Bashford, 2008). The assessor services are popular with international clients that need help in all aspects of their quest for the right agency. Similar services are available for PR, direct mail, sales promotion and corporate identity. Intermediaries can help agencies find new business by producing daily reports identifying potential new opportunities, eg when a new marketing or PR director is appointed, which could suggest the need for extra services. Some agencies interview any new senior decision makers, to explore their communications plans and then relay this information back to their clients. Retainer fees can vary, from single-user fees starting at £950 per annum to £60,000 per annum, which then provides an entire outsourced new business function from identifying opportunities to acting on them.

Credentials pitch

Some clients, before issuing a full brief, prefer to ask the pool of agencies to present their credentials. This includes examples of current and previous work, team members' profiles, and company history, structure and facilities. It is worth visiting the agency, and sometimes at short notice, as this gives the client a feel for the potential agency, and its atmosphere, organization, professionalism, etc. From this a final shortlist is selected and issued with a detailed brief.

Too-long agency shortlist

Some years ago, Westminster City Council invited 10 agencies to pitch for its communications work. A long shortlist creates an unnecessary amount of unpaid work for everyone concerned.

Briefing, pitching and selecting take time and skills. Apart from creating a lot of work, a large pitch list sometimes leaves sensitive marketing information with many different people. Some cynics see it as an opportunity to get free strategic and tactical ideas from the best brains in each agency.

Issuing the brief

Briefs vary in size, structure and level of detail. Some clients may summarize on to a single A4 sheet of paper; others issue a much more detailed briefing document (one Guinness brief was 100 pages). Essentially, the brief should incorporate at least the situation, objectives and strategy (SOS) and the 3Ms (men/women, money and minutes), part of the SOSTAC® planning system explained in Chapter 10. The brief tends to be brief, while a marketing communications plan has much more detail. Since the brief usually goes out to several agencies pitching (only one of which will get the business), a difficult dilemma emerges. How much confidential and strategic information should be revealed in the brief, given that the majority of the recipients will not work for you and may one day work for your competition? Food for thought.

At the bare minimum, the brief will usually include the following:

1 *Situation* – where you are now, including the market, channels, segments, target markets, trends, competition, market share, position, current and previous campaigns, strengths and weaknesses, unique selling propositions (USPs), features and benefits of the brand and the organization.

2 *Objectives* – where you want to go: marketing objectives and communications objectives (see Chapter 10, p. 277 for examples) plus specifically defining exactly what is the problem (or opportunity). Include the required positioning and tone of voice. Ensure also that effectiveness criteria and evaluation methodology are clearly specified.

3 *Strategy* – how you are going to get there (including how the marketing strategy fits in with the overall corporate strategy). This may also include a campaign strategy if this is already worked out.

4 *Control* – how you will know when you've arrived. Both the agency and the client should agree on what success and failure will look like. What are the key criteria, and how will they be measured?

5 *3Ms:*
   – Men/women: who makes the final decision, members of the team, who reports to whom, contacts for additional questions.
   – Money: key question for the agency – what is the budget?
   – Minutes: timescale and deadlines for pitch, agency selection and eventual campaign launch.

Control is sometimes included, as it outlines how the campaign will be measured, which in turn motivates the team to get it right. A smaller client may prefer to replace the advertising and/or marketing objectives with a statement of the problem and subsequently ask the agency to present a complete promotional plan. It is likely that the agency's first question will be: 'How much do you have to spend?' As mentioned, there are obvious dangers of releasing strategic information to several agencies, the majority of whom will never work for you (since there is usually only one winner or single agency selected). The corollary is that too little information reduces the quality (and possibly strategic direction) of the proposals. For that reason, it can be helpful to show examples of the kinds of ads that are preferred: this can help creatives to get a feel for what you want. So start collecting ads, sales promotions, web pages, packaging, etc now.

It is important to get the brief correct and concise. If there are specific requirements, spell them out, eg 'It must be clearly legible from eight feet away' or the 'The brand name must stand out from the crowd', etc. You must work hard at stating your positioning and of course benefits, USPs, etc. Remember, a casual brief will probably generate casual concepts followed by frustrations and accusations. Get the relationship off to a good start with a clear, concise, yet comprehensive, brief.

Pre-pitch agency efforts

The shortlisted agencies are invited to make a full presentation or sales pitch. This usually involves several members of the agency staff and is viewed by several members of the client company. The cost of a major pitch varies from £10,000 to £50,000 (up to six agency people involved for six weeks, £36,000, plus £10,000 for materials plus £4,000 for research). Preparation for a pitch is usually an intensive affair and can include researching the client's market, media, company structure and individual personalities (prior knowledge of who will attend the pitch and hopefully some background information on their personalities and interests), strategic planning, brainstorming, concept development (advertising ideas), slide shows, videos, rehearsals and even meditation. Without doubt, new business pitches increase the adrenalin flow inside agencies.

US-owned McCann Erickson is reported to draft in a professional teacher of meditation and relaxation techniques before every pitch. JWT practises its pressure presentation techniques with bizarre scenarios like asking its teams to imagine that they discover one of their art directors pushing cocaine and that, as they prepare to fire him, they discover his wife is dying of cancer and in need of private medical treatment. **Real empathy, sound strategy, exciting creative work and reasonable costs are often considered to be the key factors during a pitch,** but some agencies take initiatives before the actual pitch, as Table 8.2 shows.

Pre-pitch client's feelings

Other potential or prospective clients would deny any such self-imposed pressure. They may see the pitch as an exciting and stimulating process full of fresh ideas and strategic thinking presented by clever, articulate (and sometimes entertaining) people. Client egos are massaged, and generally the prospect is treated as a revered guest. Other

Will they love me?

'Our research has shown that, generally speaking, clients are not happy about changing agencies. Such events are usually a signal that they are unable to sustain a productive relationship with other people, which is something that none of us is pleased to accept, however difficult the other people might be... the prospect [potential client] is under pressure from his boss to get it right quickly... so when he steps from the bustle and stress of his own trade into the palm-fringed oasis of Berkeley Square or Charlotte Street or Covent Garden it is possible that he has two questions in his mind: "Will they love me?" and "Can they save my neck?"'

Brian Johnson, New Business Director, JWT

TABLE 8.2   Pre-pitch agency initiatives

Client	Agency	Stunt
Kiss FM Radio	BBDO	Delivered a framed poster to the Kiss MD bearing the legend 'We'll put your name on everyone's lips'*
Kiss FM Radio	Saatchi	Covered Kiss HQ with pink balloons on Valentine's Day
Guardian	Publicis	Booked a 96-sheet (40' × 10' poster) site opposite the newspaper's offices during the week of the pitch and ran flattering ads that changed each day*
Financial services company	Publicis	Sent a safe containing the agency's credentials
Toyota	Saatchi	Three Toyota cars suspended above Charlotte Street, hanging out of the agency's offices*

* Won the account

prospective clients see pitches as a more tedious affair, since they have to repeat their brief in detail several times over and then sit through the inevitable credentials bit before they get to the heart of the matter – the agency proposals.

Most selling situations, including pitches, are about the removal of uncertainty. So understanding the problem, and identifying clear solutions with enthusiasm and conviction, is a winning formula.

The pitch

After weeks of intensive preparation of exciting creative ideas, ingenious media plans and pitch rehearsals, copies of the proposal or pitch document are laser-printed, bound and made ready for client distribution after the main presentation. The pitch itself is where an advertising agency has the opportunity to advertise or sell itself. Given that most campaigns try to be different, grab attention and make an impression, it is understandable that some agencies should regard a pitch as a creative opportunity also. Some would say, an expensive opportunity as the cost of a pitch can be astronomical, eg £100,000 on a big global pitch say for British Airways or a global brand. Agencies often make test films for the pitch and costs quickly add up. Most agencies try and budget around £15,000 for a pitch but while this might cover material/travel and research costs, many more hours are burnt in overnight presentation preparations. As to clients paying for pitches, it is still too rare but they'd never pay more than £5,000 which is really just a token gesture. However, in an oversupplied market driven by the adage "speculate to accumulate if the prize is big enough", we will continue to see a thirst for pitching, with some being far better than others. There are many stories of daring pitch techniques, some of which work and some of which do not. Here are a few.

Legendary 1980s agency ABM created **the classic British Rail pitch, which purposely created client tension** when the top executives from British Rail were kept waiting in a smoke-filled reception area while the receptionist ignored them throughout her gossip-filled telephone conversation. Eventually a space was cleared among the empty cans and orange peels, and the executives were invited to wait, as the agency people were 'busy'. After some minutes the British Rail executives had had enough.

As they got up to leave, the agency chairman, Peter Marsh, clad in full BR uniform (complete with cap, whistle and flag), burst in and said, 'You don't like it. Why should your passengers?' He then invited them to listen to how he and his colleagues were going to solve their problems.

Don White, formerly of Benton & Bowles, is reported to have **dressed up as a redcoat** for a Butlins pitch. The client took one look, said 'Anyone dressed like that isn't suitable for my business' and left. David Abbott of Abbott Mead Vickers is reported to have **greeted Metropolitan Police Commissioner Sir Robert Mark with a high-pitched nasal 'Hello, hello, hello'** as he arrived to hear the agency pitch. Not amused, Sir Robert left the building.

Agencies pitching for the **Weetabix** breakfast cereal account were invited to make their pitches in a hotel. As ABM was the last agency to pitch on the final morning, it decided to **redecorate the function room in the ABM colours.** This required an overnight painting and carpeting exercise. A stage was built, and a special chair was delivered to the function room for Mr Robinson, the arthritic and ageing Weetabix chairman. As the Weetabix panel seated themselves the next morning, the lights dimmed until they were all immersed in an enthralling darkness. A spotlight burst a stream of light on to the stage, where **Peter Marsh knelt as he opened his pitch** with: 'As one of Britain's few remaining wholly owned independent advertising agencies, it gives me great pleasure to present to you, Mr Robinson, as chairman of one of Britain's few wholly owned cereal manufacturers...' ABM won the account.

One final ABM classic pitch was for **Honda.** ABM hired the **60-piece Scots Guards bagpipe band** to play the Honda jingle 'Believe in freedom, believe in Honda', while marching up and down London's Norwich Street (where ABM was making its pitch). Again, ABM picked up the account. Another agency, AMV, had Hollywood hero Bob Hoskins at its pitch for BT (which it won).

Strict adherence to the time and type of presentation (specified by the client) is essential. When **Burkitt Weinreich Bryant** was pitching for **Littlewoods,** it was asked to make a 'short and sweet' final pitch, since the then 92-year-old chairman, the late Sir John Moores, would be in attendance. The trade press reported that 'after over 30 minutes managing director Hugh Burkitt was asked to finish as it became obvious that Sir John's interest and attention was waning'. **A row broke** out as Hugh Burkitt persisted and a senior Littlewoods executive tried to stop the pitch.

Way back in the 1990s, **when British Airways moved from Saatchi & Saatchi to Maurice and Charles Saatchi's new outfit, M&C Saatchi,** all the agencies involved threw everything at this prestigious £30 million account. In an attempt to dramatize BA's global reach, Saatchi & Saatchi did the pitch in different rooms for different stages. Each room had been completely redecorated in the styles, natural habitat and climate of particular parts of the world – tropical rainforests, etc. When Bartle Bogle Hegarty (BBH) got its chance, it reassured BA about BBH's ability to create extremely satisfied clients by providing ready-made testimonials after the presentation – a wall went back and BA were surrounded by the key decision makers of every one of BBH's clients, who then had lunch with them. When M&C Saatchi got its chance, **Maurice Saatchi stood up and talked about the importance of music to the BA brand,** explaining that they had commissioned their own composer to create a unique blend of popular classical music that BA could own. A growing murmur of approval was heard. He went on to say that they would like the client to meet the composer, at which point **in walked Andrew Lloyd Webber.**

The worst, most painful and potentially career-busting ad agency presentation was presented by Saatchi & Saatchi's own Peter Levitan when pitching for the Adidas account. They had already been told by **Adidas** that the account was as good as theirs as long as they didn't $%&* up the pitch. They did.

You can read an extract of the full detailed and honest account of it, mistake by mistake, at **www.PRSmith.org/blog.** An extract is also printed here with the kind permission of Peter Levitan, of Peter Levitan & Co:

'A few weeks after that meeting, Maurice (Saatchi) told me that we were going to pitch the global Adidas account. Huge brand, global business, cool category, big budget, powerful competition and potentially great creative. Not much more for an agency to wish for... A couple of days later, Maurice and the reclusive Charles Saatchi and I met with Robert Louis Dreyfus, Adidas' new CEO and majority owner to discuss the pitch. Get this: Robert was a good man and close friend of the agency. Close? He had been the CEO of Saatchi & Saatchi Advertising Worldwide. He was one of us... I am working with Maurice and Charles Saatchi – the most famous advertising men in the world. They asked me to run a huge pitch for the global Adidas account. Adidas' CEO is a close friend of the agency and the management of Adidas America wants us... But wait, there's even more good news. During an early meeting, Robert leans over to me and says: "*Peter, you've won this business as long as you don't $%&* up the pitch.*"'

The pitch, however flopped. A video opening with scenes of baby seals being beaten to death as a way of demonstrating man's inhumanity to man contrasted with the big idea: 'the glory of sports', just didn't work. Compounded by a lack of rehearsals, big egos, no leader/manager, no control, no budgets, no real understanding of the clients' challenges and opportunities, loose creative brief and the pitch team roles based on seniority (not expertise), the pitch failed.

Dropping your guard

During an intense, high-profile, multimillion-pound pitch, the client called for a 10-minute break. Unfortunately for the agency (which will remain unnamed), a senior agency member had forgotten to remove his scribbled notes, which the client accidentally read. 'Watch out for the – in the glasses', it said at one point.

Not surprisingly, the agency lost the pitch. Some time later, the same agency was pitching for another piece of the business and, as the agency opened its pitch, all of the client team simultaneously donned pairs of glasses! The agency coped and went on to win this separate piece of business.

Pitches, like presentations for major campaigns, are now an ongoing process where effort is concentrated on developing a relationship (relationship marketing) with the client before the final presentation. This can sometimes involve client exposure to the strategy and even the advertisements before D-Day. One UK agency, Howell Henry Chaldecott Lury, has tried to appropriate this process on its own with what it calls 'tissue groups', ie a series of build-up meetings with the client. In the United States the most notable exponent, Chiat Day, has been doing this for a long time. Without doubt there is a cultural shift to ongoing pitches rather than a big finale.

An online pitch

'The British Interactive Media Association accepted pitches only via Facebook and Twitter. "We read about BIMA's agency trawl in *PR Week*, so one of our consultants became a follower of the BIMA Chair, Paul Walsh. Within minutes he came back to us with a brief and we started on the pitch", said Jennifer Janson from Six Degrees, the agency that eventually won the pitch.'

Williams (2008)

Post-pitch agency's agonizing wait

Post-pitch tension is agonizing. Awaiting the outcome of a pitch is a tense and worrying time. When the phone eventually rings and it turns out to be the prospect, everyone holds their breath. Rejection means total failure. All the brilliant ideas, the careful research, the buzz of excitement, the long hours – all down the drain. Selection means total success. The post-pitch wait makes the mind wander. Were there any clues as to what the client thought of the pitch? Len Weinreich, advertising guru, gives a nervous insight in 'Scratching an indecent living' (see Figure 8.3 on page 235) and an almost unbearable wait in 'No news is bad news' (see Figure 8.4 on page 237).

Occasionally the prospect client actually helps the agency by giving feedback that identifies where the client saw a real weakness. The agency can then eradicate the weakness before the next pitch. Similarly, a successful agency will be interested to find out why it was chosen, so that it can capitalize on its strengths.

Analysing the agency

As Nigel Bogle, CEO of Bartle Bogle Hegarty, says: 'The key questions today are less about an agency's ability to execute brilliantly and more about visionary strategic thinking, razor-sharp positioning, pinpoint targeting and ingenious media solutions.'

The order of importance of the following questions can vary, depending on what the prospective client really wants. Some clients may consider the agency's location and car parking facilities relevant, whereas other clients would discount this as trivial and irrelevant to good advertising. Here are the 20 most vital questions to help choose the right agency:

1 Does the agency really have a feel for my product and market? Does it really understand my brand's situation and potential?

2 Has it got strong research and planning capability?

3 Does it know the best media to use? Will its media-buying skills make my budget go a long way?

4 Has it got creative flair? Does it win awards? Does it suggest new ideas?

5 Is it full-service, or does everything get subcontracted out? Can it handle a pack redesign, public relations, sales promotion and direct mail if called upon?

6 How much integration experience with above-, through- and below-the-line as well as online does it have?

7 Is it international? Can its headquarters force it to resign the account should it decide to seek business in the same industry overseas? Alternatively, can it take on a lot of our coordination work through its own international management network?

8 What will it charge? And on what basis? How much time will it spend on the account?

9 How does it allocate resources in the planning, testing and evaluation process?

10 Does it display cost-consciousness?

11 How will it measure its effectiveness?

12 Are we a small fish in a big pond? Is it too small or too big for us? Do we have contact with the principal partners? Will it fire us if a competitor offers it a bigger account (should we insist on a five-year contract)?

13 Who will work on the account? Are we likely to get on together (chemistry)? Will the pitch team be involved? How stable will our account team be? Are the people who worked on the case histories

still with the agency? (This is a crucial question.)

14 Does it have a good track record? Do clients stick with it and place repeat business with the agency? If not, why not?

15 How is my investment going to be returned? (This should feature prominently in the agency's pitch.)

16 How much experience does the agency have in marketing integration (particularly with the internet)?

17 What is the agency process (not just a bunch of arrows in a fancy PowerPoint slide)? Ask how it intends to allocate resources (time and people) to particular aspects of the campaign, including planning, concept development, testing and evaluation, etc. This helps in making interesting comparisons with other agencies. If an agency is unclear about this, then perhaps it is running an inefficient business (which might cost you money).

18 Ask how much time it will devote to your account.

19 Also, what are the agency retention rates?

20 Check its references. References of past clients can also be requested.

Choosing an agency

The assessment form shown in Figure 8.2 can be weighted and scored as appropriate for each client's needs. A rating scale of 1–6 can be used. Agencies should be assessed using the same criteria. Few agencies perform so outstandingly that they remove all doubt in the client's mind as to which agency it should choose. The criteria should be agreed in advance by the team involved in the selection process. The assessment form shows one approach that attempts to formalize the selection by using consistent criteria. Each company obviously tailors its own approach.

And some agencies add a little extra hook, sometimes proprietary applications, widgets or iApps, for example the South Africa multimedia agency who won the UK Tourism account when it presented a digital workflow system that enabled regional offices to remotely customize English-language campaigns

to their specific needs. Called Dynamic Positioning Mode, it was a new system of profiling consumers and generating consumer relationships using digital marketing tools.

Brand activation – can the agency deliver?

By delivering engaging brand interactivity and experiences, online or offline, that capture customers' hearts and mind, brand engagement campaigns get customers to 'act' or do something. BA brings brands to life and ideally helps to form long-term emotional connections. It may be relatively easy to do this occasionally, but can agencies offer continual brand activation? Would ongoing activation dilute the impact of any campaign or sequence of events? Where's the commercial return, and what is this contributing towards the equity of the brands they represent?

It's also essential to understand the importance of a seamless, joined-up approach to activation, rather than a series of disconnected, tactical executions. Either one agency needs to manage all elements of activation or agencies need to work collaboratively and stop protecting their ownership of the client for the benefit of the wider brand activity. The answer ultimately lies in the ambition of the brand combined with the insight, expertise and planning unearthed by agencies from a strategic, data and creative point of view.

Perry (2015)

The pitch is never over – cars have ears

After making a good pitch, a well-known agency kindly offered a chauffeur-driven car to take the clients to the next agency on the pitch list. During the journey the client team analysed the previous pitch and commented that the media strategy appeared 'off-brief'. The next day the agency found a way of representing the media strategy – and it won the business. The limo driver was an account man at the agency. Ethical or not, it's reality.

FIGURE 8.2 Choosing an agency – an assessment form

AGENCY	Understand our product and company?	Commitment to our project?	Research, planning & strategic thinking	Media planning and buying including digital	Creative	Size, in-house resources, full service including digital	International	Location	Fee/cost	Will we get on?	Opinion of existing clients
1											
2											
3											
4											
5											

FIGURE 8.3   Scratching an indecent living

Scratching an indecent living

My ferrety acquaintance, Crispin Neat, intrepid slogan detective, telephoned recently. "Hello, Lenny," he burbled. "I thought you might like to know that I'm branching out. Diversifying."

"Excellent news, Crispin," I replied, feigning enthusiasm. "What other services will you offer the hard-pressed advertiser?"

"Scratch pad deciphering."

"What's that?"

"Simple, Lenny, old chum. You gather and despatch the scratch pads after a crucial meeting and we'll decipher the scribbles and the doodles. We'll interpret the curious, dubious squiggles that clients leave behind."

"Crispin, that is the most ridiculous scam I've ever encountered."

He paused to draw breath on the other end of the 'phone. "Lenny, Lenny," he admonished. "If cynicism is your only reaction to my new sca . . . I mean, venture, then I have to tell you that you've been ignoring one of the most invaluable sources of high-grade intelligence in the business."

"Talk me through it." I was compelled to listen.

"Well, look at it this way. You've got this captive audience. You're either presenting for the account, or pleading to retain the business. Either way, it's hypertension ad biz max stressworld for all participants and the anxious clients need to combust mega-kilojoules of excess nervous energy."

"Hence the doodling?"

"Correct. But (and here's the brilliance of the idea) it's their *sub-*

Len Weinreich

conscious that's doing the doodling. So, whatever materialises on the pad is an action diagram of the client's thought processes. See?"

"I see. But how do you decipher their darkest thoughts if they're only scribbly doodles? And anyway," I added, "some clients actually tear their encrypted messages off the pad and tuck them into pockets. What's your action then?"

"The rub, Lenny. The old brass rubbing lark. We massage the undersheet delicately with a 9B pencil and a palimpsest of the jotting appears, by magic. From then on, interpretation is everything."

"OK. I How do you interpret?"

"You mean you've missed my new book: *Corporate Doodling: The Direct Line To Your Clients' Intentions.* It reveals all."

"I missed the book. Supply the topline, please."

"Well, many symbols are clear. Sketches of knives, revolvers, bludgeons, barbed wire and strategic nukes mean that he or she

might be firing the agency."

"Crispin, what about clients who can't draw? Can you explain *their* scratch pads?"

"All in my book, old chap, £9.50 at leading booksellers. Since you ask, anything resembling a maze represents confusion on their part. Blurred shading or scratchy hatching means they think you're a shifty bunch of crooks."

"Crispin, in my experience, they generally scribble down a few low key phrases from the presentation or make a few critical comments for subsequent reference."

"Of course, Lenny, of course. But each one can be a telling pointer. In order to cope with that eventuality, we've cobbled together a computer program called SNOOP which correlates their scratch notes with the agency slides and overheads in order to present you with an Attention Rating Admiration Factor and Purchase Property Index on a scale of one to ten."

"What happens if they've only scribbled a 'phone number or an enigmatic address in SW10?"

Crispin was wounded. "Haven't you read *any* of my books?"

"Er . . . which of your *oeuvre* have I missed now, Crispin?"

"*Corporate Blackmail for Profit and Pleasure* one of my all-time chart-toppers and money spinners. A right little cash cow."

"Thanks, Crispin. Don't call us . . ." *Clickbrrrrrr*

Len Weinreich is a vice-chairman of Burkitt Weinreich Bryant Clients and Company

Rejecting an agency

A rejected agency's managing director has the difficult job of picking up the shattered team and building up the agency morale again. The rejected agencies usually ask the prospect for some feedback for future reference. Here are some answers that rejected agencies have recorded upon asking why they had failed:

- 'I just didn't like you.'
- 'I'm afraid you are not European.'
- 'You're too small.'
- 'They [the other agency] have more experience of this sector.'
- 'You have too much experience in this sector. We're looking for a fresh approach.'
- 'If it wasn't for the other agency you would have come first.'
- 'The final decision was evenly split and you lost 8–7.'
- 'Although we preferred your creative work, the other agency does have a place to park in London on Saturdays – and it's terribly handy for the shops.'

As managing directors are never told that their pitches are terrible and come last, having always been narrowly beaten into second place, there is a plea from the advertising industry to clients that they should tell it like it really is!

Firing the agency

A *Campaign* magazine survey identified the following reasons for sacking an agency (in order of importance to the client):

1 receiving no fresh input;
2 account conflict at the agency;
3 a new marketing director arriving;
4 a change of client's policy;
5 other accounts leaving the agency.

A derivative of number 2, conflict of interests, arises with mergers and acquisitions. After acquiring Gillette for $57 billion, P&G sacked Gillette's agency, Mindshare (part of the WPP Group). Gillette explained that it was removing its $800 million global media planning and buying business.

Mindshare already works for Unilever, P&G's arch rival (WARC, 2005c).

An example of number 3 above is when BA appointed its new CEO Willie Walsh. After 23 years, M&C Saatchi lost its prized BA account worth £60 million (and estimated to be between 6 and 7 per cent of Saatchi's turnover). Prior to that, Saatchi's had only one pitch, 10 years previously, when it retained the business by the skin of its teeth after Bartle Bogle Hegarty prematurely broke out the champagne (WARC, 2005a).

Agencies also get fired if the ads just don't get results. According to a study by White Ops and the Association of National Advertisers, marketers will waste $6.3bn on internet ads that aren't even delivered to humans! (Shields, 2015).

Ask agencies outrageous questions

'Too many agencies are wondering, "Am I going to have a job six months from now? What does my client really think?" When the agency doesn't know where it stands or if the client believes in it, it becomes dysfunctional. That's the biggest thing that's missing. If the client's not happy, get on with it. Tell them what's wrong and what they need to do. Marketers also shouldn't be afraid to challenge their agencies. The best teams ask outrageous questions of their agencies. And agencies love that. And when you answer those, you get great work.'

Stengel (2010)

In the international arena, business relationships (including agency relationships) are even more delicate, as WPP discovered when it was fired by China's largest advertising conglomerate (Citic and its Beijing Guoan Advertising arm). Citic's vice-chairman, Yan Gang, claimed that WPP's CEO, Sir Martin Sorrell, had treated him 'very rudely' during an April meeting in London to discuss management problems at the joint venture (WARC, 2006).

Although over 20 years old, *Campaign* magazine's '13 ways to be a loser' article identifies many recurring reasons why agencies still get fired:

1 **Control of brand's advertising switches to rival of client:** Gold Greenlees Trott lost

FIGURE 8.4   When no news is bad news

When no news is bad news

"Why don't they ring? It's been four, no, three, days since they were in for the presentation. Didn't they say they'd make their minds up the next day? God. No news is bad news. Or is it good news? I can never quite remember.

"Anyway, I don't think we won it. I mean, we would have heard, wouldn't we? That guy, the one down the end of the table with the woolly khaki tie, he never liked us. He asked the worst questions. Like that one about putting all their press money in TV. That was a stinker, maliciously inserted to distract me. Quite arrested my flow, log-jammed my drift. No sense of un-folding drama, silly sod.

"The woman liked us though. I had a feeling she'd marked us down because we had too few women in the presentation team. But I could tell she warmed to me. Smiled a lot when I projected in her direction. God! Why haven't they rung yet? It's not as if we really need their lousy business, after all it's only an account. Ad agencies are like re-volving doors: one account leaves and another one follows, I mean, enters. Have you seen this year's free-fall figures? The income from their billing would make good the loss of those bastards from . . .

"We won't get it. They hated the

Len Weinreich

creative work. Detested it. They sneered at the ads. You would've thought they'd never seen a real commercial before. On the other hand, they'd asked us to be radical. Their brief advised ignoring all re-straints. Still, I think it might have been wiser to check the script with the ITVA before the presentation. The naked couple and the golden retriever might be a little rich for today's audience.

"We spent a month assembling this presentation and now, a week, okay, maybe three days later, not a dicky bird. Not a peep. Not even a whimper. Not even one of those mysterious calls to the media de-partment dishing them undercover dirt. Nothing.

"Perhaps we should have bribed them. Maybe we should have taped a few large denomination notes to the inside covers of their docu-ments. Perhaps I really should have nobbled the top man when he dashed out for a pee.

"Quite frankly, I think they loathed the work. And my suit. And our media director. It didn't help that our creative (ho, ho) di-rector completely cocked up the or-der of the storyboards. Or that our dizzy planner addressed their com-pany by the wrong name, twice. This instant they obviously are ap-pointing someone else because they have no wit, taste, imagination, discernment or balls.

"I'm not so sure we'd be happy handling their business. They'd be terrible clients. Endless trips to their remote offices to niggle over a charity ad mechanical.

"Stuff their lousy business. Prob-ably seriously unprofitable. In fact, I shouldn't be surprised if they went belly up. I've heard some interest-ing City whispers concerning the bizarre hotel bedroom habits of their chairman. Apparently . . . ***, is that the phone?"

Len Weinreich is a vice chairman of Burkitt Weinreich Bryant Clients and Company

---

Fosters when Elders IXL and its Courage division took over control of marketing Fosters from Watneys, a GGT client.

2 **Agency produces irrelevant or inappropriate advertising:** Lowe Howard-Spink lost some of its prized Mobil account after its 'breakthrough' Dan Dare campaign failed. Insufficient planning was cited as a reason behind the fiasco.

3 **Client is unsettled over too many changes at agency:** Foote Cone and Belding lost £22 million worth of business – including Heinz and Cadbury – because of management upheaval.

4 **Client unhappy over excess negative publicity surrounding its agency:** IBM is uncomfortable over the widely reported lawsuits involving its agency and breakaway

Lord Einstein O'Neill and Partners. Could result in IBM choosing neither and picking a new shop.

5 **Takeover of agency infuriates client:** Goodyear, Philips, Pilsbury said goodbye to JWT after it was taken over by WPP. Most cite 'disruption' as a reason for leaving.

6 **Client rationalizes its agency roster:** Toyota chose its dealer agency Brunnings over its main agency Lintas London after a creative shoot-out. British Telecom reviewed its entire account and picked three main agencies – BBH, Abbott Mead and JWT.

7 **Total breakdown in agency–client relationship:** GGT resigns the *Daily Express* after repeated clashes and an inability to work with title's marketing staff.

8 **Agency fails to come to terms with account:** BMP got sacked by Comet, its first major retail client. Former vice-chairman Paul Leeves said BMP won the business 'one year too soon'.

9 **Lack of solution creatively:** Abbot Mead couldn't crack the *Daily Telegraph*. Later the agency admitted to producing tasteless series of press ads which aroused the ire of women, among others.

10 **New client arrives:** Allen Brady & Marsh's long-standing Milk account was reviewed after new NDC chief Richard Pears joined.

11 **Agency can't master the client's politics:** JWT lost British Rail. Agency was allied to the central advertising body while the chairman, Bob Reid, was committed to devolution. Network SouthEast chief Chris Green was not keen on JWT after it produced two poor ads, one in which it was in legal hot water with the Monty Python people.

12 **Agency merges with another, producing conflict and massive disruption:** difficulties surrounding the merger of Reeves Robertshaw Needham and Doyle Dane Bernbach resulted in massive client fall-out.

13 **Client is the subject of a merger or takeover:** Fast becoming a major reason for account moves.

Reproduced by kind permission of
Haymarket Marketing Publications Limited
and Laurie Ludwick

Firing the client

Agencies sometimes resign accounts, particularly if a larger competing account is offered to them. Occasionally, they are obliged to resign if an agency takeover or merger brings in some competing accounts and thereby creates a conflict of interest. New demands by a client sometimes become so difficult that the account becomes unprofitable or, as in the case of ABM, a reduced commission is considered unsatisfactory.

Arrogance and egos

Some years ago, a continually critical senior marketing manager commented at the end of yet another long, unsatisfactory meeting, 'If this were my company [which it wasn't; he was an employee], I would fire the agency.' The long-suffering creative director responded, 'If this were my agency, which it is, I would fire the client, which I am.' He left the room, with the marketing manager knowing he now had to face colleagues and break the news that there was no campaign ready to roll out, no agency, and an agonizing new pitch process required.

> ### How to upset the client and get sent to jail – overcharge them
>
> Thomas Early (former senior partner and finance director) and Shona Seifert (former president) at Ogilvy & Mather (O&M) New York were both reported by WARC to have been found guilty in 2005 of fraudulently overbilling the White House Office of National Drug Control Policy in 1999 and 2000. The guilty pair were allegedly responding to the anger of O&M North America's co-president Bill Gray at the loss of anticipated income. Gray was not among the accused. Early got a 14-month prison sentence and $10,000 fine. Seifert got an 18-month prison sentence and $125,000 fine (she was also ordered to write a code of advertising industry ethics). O&M extricated itself (but not its employees) from the affair with a $1.8 million settlement in 2002.
>
> WARC (2005b)

Managing the relationship successfully

Companies like P&G, Coca-Cola, Unilever, Nestlé and others are deemed to be the best-in-class brands when it comes to integrated marketing communications. 'All of the top players have their agencies evaluate them. Some even have their agencies evaluate each other. But all of them have built in a continuous learning loop to keep driving innovation and integration and keep asking "what's next?"'.

R3 (2015)

> ### Unilever stops paying for slow work and integrates communications via multi-discipline, better-trained integrated digital teams
>
> 'Unilever is often identified as a thought leader in integrated marketing communications. Starting with the business objectives for the brand and remaining agnostic to the channels used to deliver the big ideas, Unilever takes a consistently unified approach that is enabled by multi-disciplined teams and the environment of collaboration promoted among all Unilever brands. As a part of its "Crafting Brands for Life" strategy, Unilever seeks to strike a healthy balance between magic and logic – or in other words, creativity and sales. Unilever also doubled its spend on marketing training to keep up with the ever-changing digital landscape and build a stronger team that goes beyond sole marketing skills.
>
> From 2014 onwards, R3 has been consulting with the global Unilever team on Agency Integration, Management and Compensation. While this assignment is still confidential, the approach is to reward agency partners on outcomes, not on inputs. In a world where, under a fee structure, agencies are paid more based on the slowness of their work (more hours), Unilever is seeking a new path that will truly enable stronger alignment between their goals and the agency's ideas.'
>
> R3 (2015)

Life in an agency

Agency staff from all over have joined in a Twitter conversation about #AgencyLife revealing some insights that are not usually discussed publicly. Fuelled by the blog Adland, it suddenly spread as staff released their frustrations &/or humour. Here's a selection of tweets:

- **@jawaherdesign** Client loves concept but rejects it because 'the target audience isn't smart enough to get it' #agencylife
- **@theRowdee** Briefs that are never brief: l #agencylife
- **@CreativeTweets** Creative Director uses the non-words 'virality' 'sharability' and 'memification' in the same sentence. With a straight face. #agencylife
- **@Adland** You're trying to sell spaghetti-sauce with a hashtag on twitter. #agencylife
- **@Adland** When your ghost ad wins an award, it's the agencies best work that year. When it's exposed as a ghost, you're publicly fired. #agencylife
- **@sprads** Whining. Lots of whining. A tremendous amount of whining. #agencylife
- **@adland** Your new brand spokesperson has 900 followers on twitter in the first 5 minutes. They all work at the agency. #agencylife
- **@adland** They finally send you to Cannes. You're stuck jetlagged in a hotel room working for 3 days straight. #agencylife
- **@copybeard** You tell a non-adlander you're a copywriter and they ask you about copyright law. #agencylife
- **@bootstudios** Oxymoron #agencylife
- **@samobribri** Slightly worrying that none of the #agencylife tweets were positive.

Parekh (2013)

There is no doubt that agency work is intense, high pressure, challenging, creative (and analytical these days) but it is also rewarding, fun, exciting, stimulating, never a dull moment... #agencylife does give a small insight into this hectic world. Perhaps #agencyfun would generate a totally different stream of thoughts. Either way, be careful with your tweets as they can cost you a job (see over).

Sacked because of a tweet

'PR agency Redner Group lost its largest client, games company, 2K, in 2011, following a tweet by an agency staff member after seeing some negative reviews of the game they were promoting: "too many went too far with their reviews. We r reviewing who gets games next time and who doesn't based on today's venom." 2K issued a statement: "2K Games does not endorse or condone the comments made by @TheRednerGroup and confirm they no longer represent our products. We maintain a mutually respectful relationship with the press and will continue to do so. We don't condone @TheRednerGroup's actions at all."'

Bruell (2011)

How to ensure good agency relationships

1   Agree a system of remuneration – fees, commissions, mark-ups, time, expenses and method of billing – in writing. Remember, it is better to argue over a quote than an invoice.

2   Trust the agency team (share research and information with them, and involve them).

3   Make them become part of the marketing team. Use their expertise.

4   Ask relevant questions. Listen carefully to the answers. Do not be intimidated by strong agency characters. All propositions should be justifiable. The final decision is the client's.

5   Explain to the agency who makes what decisions, ie who has authority for which decisions.

6   Sign or approve in writing each stage from brief to concepts – finished artwork, running proofs and so on.

7   Keep briefs short and unambiguous.

8   Regular reviews help to plug any gaps in performance, whether creative, strategic or personal.

9   Write an occasional thank-you note to the team.

10 A stable relationship builds a real team, since the agency gets to know the client, the team, the company and the market inside out. In addition, the client does not have to worry about unfriendly, discarded agencies that have previously had access to sensitive information.

Key points from Chapter 8

- Clear communications between client and agency are important if the right messages are going to be successfully communicated to target audiences.

- Agencies, consultancies and consultants can become more than just suppliers of marketing services; they can become strategic partners of the client.

- Careful selection is crucial to ensure the development of a mutually beneficial long-term relationship.

References and further reading

Bashford, S (2008) The rise of the intermediary, *PR Week*, 4 July

Bruell, A (2011) Redner group loses biggest client over tweet, *Ad Age*, 15 June

Burnett, L (nd) Quote bank, WARC (World Advertising Research Centre)

Cowley, D (ed) (1989) *How to Plan Advertising*, Thomson Learning, London

Crain, R (2013) Agencies add data to boost fees, but whose data is it? *Ad Age*, 25 March

Farey-Jones, D (2008) Consumer relationships key to future agency success, *Brand Republic*, 8 February

IPA (2003) *The Client Brief: A best practice guide to briefing communications agencies*, Joint industry guidelines for young marketing professionals in working effectively with agencies, IPA, ISBA, MCCA, PRCA, London

ISBA (2010) in conjunction with the Advertising Research Consortium, *Paying for Advertising 5*, ISBA, London

Joseph, S (2013) Nike takes social media in-house, *Marketing Week*, 3 January

Kemp, M and Kim, P (2008) The connected agency, Forrester report

Learmonth, M (2010a) Do you know the ABCs of DSPs? Agency-relations teams pitch in, *Ad Age*, 26 April

Levitan, P (2014) *The Levitan Pitch. Buy This Book. Win More Pitches*. (2014) Portlandia Press, Portland Oregon

O'Brien, M (2015) The agency of the future, www.PRSmith.org/blog, 1 July

O'Leary, N (2013) Martin Sorrell talks candidly about mergers, mayhem—and his own demise, *Ad Week*, 10 November

Parekh, R (2013) The ad biz is yukking it up with the #AgencyLife hashtag, *Advertising Age*, 12 April

Perry, R (2015) So what is brand activation? *Guardian*

R3 (2015) Integration 40, a report by R3 on 40 of the world's most integrated marketing approaches, R3 Worldwide

Rijkens, R (1993) *European Advertising Strategies*, Thomson Learning, London

Shields, R (2015) The case for big brands taking ad tech in-house exchange, *Wire*, 6 May

Sorrell, M (1996) Beans and pearls, D&AD president's lecture

Stengel, J (2006) Top P&G marketer urges agencies to integrate planning, *WARC*, 7 February

Stengel, J (2010) How to save the troubled agency–marketer relationship, *Ad Age*, 26 April

WARC (2005a) British Airways ditches Saatchi Brothers after 23 years, 10 November

WARC (2005b) O&M's Early jailed for ONDCP fraud, 14 July

WARC (2005c) WPP's 'Chinese walls' fail to reassure P&G, 6 October

WARC (2006) Chinese ad giant drops WPP pact in favor of Omnicom, data sourced from *AdAge.com*, additional content by *WARC* staff, 16 June

Watt, N (2013) What are the challenges facing agencies in the digital revolution? *Squared* [online] www.wearesquared.com

Weinreich, L (2000) *Seven Steps to Brand Heaven*, Kogan Page, London

Williams, H (2008) Six Degrees lands BIMA retained brief, *PR Week*, 29 August

Further information

AdForum MayDream SA
112 Bis rue Cardinet
75017 Paris
France
Tel: +33 (0) 1 42 04 96 37
www.adforum.com

Advertising Agency Registrar Services
AAR Group
26 Market Place
London W1W 8AN
Tel +44 (0)20 7612 1200
www.aargroup.co.uk

Advertising Association
7th Floor North
Artillery House
11–19 Artillery Row
London SW1P 1RT
Tel: +44 (0)20 7340 1100
www.adassoc.org.uk

Agency Assessments International
100 Pall Mall
London SW1Y 5NQ
Tel: +44 (0)20 7321 3828
www.agencyassessments.com

British Rate and Data (BRAD)
BRAD Insight
Zetland House
5-25 Scrutton Street
London EC2A 4HJ
Tel: +44 (0)20 8102 0904
www.brad.co.uk

Incorporated Society of British Advertisers
ISBA
12 Henrietta Street
London WC2E 8LH
Tel: +44(0)20 7291 9020
Fax: +44 (0)20 7291 903
www.isba.org.uk

Institute of Practitioners in Advertising (IPA)
44 Belgrave Square
London SW1X 8QS
Tel: +44 (0)20 7235 7020
Fax: +44 (0)20 7245 9904
www.ipa.co.uk

09
International marketing communications

LEARNING OBJECTIVES

By the end of this chapter you will be able to:

- Understand the globalization of markets and the international opportunities arising
- List and explore the international challenges arising in international markets
- Avoid the classic errors in international markets
- Discuss the strategic global options available to marketers interested in growing on a global scale

The globalization of markets 244
The growing global opportunity 244
Respecting global complexity 245
Touching a global nerve 246
Forces driving globalization 247
The elite global players 247
Below-the-surface similarities 247
Below-the-surface external differences 248
Below-the-surface internal differences 248

International difficulties 248
Language 249
Search terms 249
Literacy 250
Tone 250
Sharing 251
Searching 251
Motivation 251
Colour 251
Design 252
Gestures 252
Culture 252
Original national identity 253
Devices 253
Media availability 254
Media overlap 254
Lack of media data 254

Lack of media credibility 254
Varying media characteristics 254
Different media usage 254
Different media standards 254
Different cost structures 254
Legal restrictions 254
Competition 255

International mistakes 255
Wrong names 255
Wrong strapline 255
Wrong product 256

Strategic global options 257
Global marketing strategy 257
Global advertising strategy 258
Four global advertising strategies 258
Anyone for a Facebook global page? 262

Agencies in the international arena 262
Choosing an international agency or
    independent local agency 262

In conclusion 264

Key points from Chapter 9 264

References and further reading 265

The globalization of markets

This chapter examines opportunities and the difficulties, strategic options and actual implications for implementation of international marketing communications, in particular global communications.

The growing global opportunity

Look around you. Yogurt, pizza, spaghetti, rice, kebabs, Indian cuisine, Chinese meals, Mexican food, Japanese Sushi and American burgers are popular and now available in most cities across the world. Not too long ago they were considered sophisticated luxuries. The Rolling Stones and Shakespeare also have a global appeal. Coincidentally, there are more people learning English in China than speak it in the United States.

Thirty years ago, back in 1985, the global village emerged when 1.9 billion people from different time zones across the world simultaneously watched, and donated funds to Live Aid, the charity concert for Ethiopian famine relief. And so we continue to connect and communicate more easily with free WhatsApp calls and video sharing as well as Skype video conference calls. The London to Brussels train is quicker than the London to Newcastle train. However, be forewarned: clichés like 'The world is getting smaller' oversimplify this growing global opportunity but remember it is one that is still wrapped in cultural complexity.

Some say that human beings have more things that bind them together than separate them; others argue that market differences are greater than market similarities. There are, in fact, what Young & Rubicam creative agency called 'cross-cultural consumer characteristics'. These identify the common ground. The person living in a smart apartment block in London's Knightsbridge probably has more in common with his or her counterpart living in a smart apartment block off New York's Central Park than with someone living in a drab south London suburb. There are indeed some common denominators and some common sets of needs and aspirations that can be identified, particularly in similarities of lifestyle.

Global markets are here. Al Jazeera's English-language TV news service has a 100 million audience worldwide. BBC World Service does what it says on the tin. Football clubs have global fans; Barcelona FC have 83 million fans on Facebook alone while Manchester United Football Club have 64 million Facebook fans but recently claimed they have 659 million around the world (source: **www.Kantar.com**) although this is disputed by BBC (Prior, 2013). Since media follow markets, media consumption is going global; therefore marketers must remember that brands with international ambitions must have a consistent global image – production should be international in mind, and content rights should be global. Creating content that users can pass on via their networks is an increasingly important channel of communication. But, as the Universal McCann (2007) report suggests, 'when using these channels it is fundamental that brands and media organizations think global.' Multiple local identities and/or conflicting brand identities simply will not work.

We are global – the internet says so. Although spread across the world, customers with similar interests can communicate and share thoughts through images, audio, video and text anywhere in the world:

> This means that clusters of customers with similar tastes and interests are connecting with each other to form new global niches and segments. The Internet, and broadband in particular, has changed business dynamics. It has created a level playing field for the smaller niche brands to compete with the established global players. Small brands have access to bigger, global markets and can communicate directly with customers across the world in new and more meaningful ways – ways never dreamt of 10 years ago.
>
> Chaffey and Smith (2008)

China alone presents a vast opportunity

'Sir Martin Sorrell was talking at the Millward Brown WPP Top 50 Most Valuable Chinese Brands conference and he mentioned that the population of China "could be 1.3bn or it could be 1.5bn". Think about out it. That error margin is two-thirds of the population of the United States.'

Orton-Jones (2013)

China alone presents a vast opportunity but one that needs careful attention, understanding, planning and long-term commitment.

Global marketplace – prepare for new markets and new competitors

'Consider this. A "relatively unknown" Chinese internet company, Alibaba, is the world's largest eCommerce company (*Wall St Journal*) which handled $240 billion worth of merchandise in 2013, with 7 million merchants. It had $8 billion revenues and $3.5 billion profits, with the largest IPO ever ($160 billion+). Some describe Alibaba as a marketplace, a search engine and a bank (it sells more than Amazon and eBay put together). What has helped make Alibaba so successful? Their customer-centric mission, "making it easier to do business across the world" followed by their motto, "Customer first, employee second, shareholder third."'

McGovern (2014)

Respecting global complexity

The total global concept suggests that the big global marketing players can accelerate the globalization process by transcending cultural boundaries and bringing their messages, goods, services and traditions to the markets they choose. There are some cultural norms that suggest that the total global concept will not happen everywhere, at least not in the next few generations. Lailan Young (1987) reported that the Barusho bride in the Himalayas has a tough time on her wedding night, as she has to share the bridal bed with her mother-in-law until the marriage is consummated.

Post-natal male exhaustion

'In the southern Indian state of Kerala, Puyala women return to the fields to tend the crops after the birth of their babies, while the husband goes to bed. The rest of the family ministers to his needs until he recovers. In the Andaman Islands, especially anxious husbands will stay in bed for anything up to six months.'

Young (1987)

The lost kingdom of the Minaros was 'discovered' in a mountain hideaway 16,000 feet up in the Himalayas by a French explorer in 1984. The Amazon-like women totally dominate their men, marrying several at a time and keeping them in line by brute force. The former Kwakiutl of Vancouver Island demonstrate what is almost a parody of industrial civilization: the chief motive of this tribe was rivalry, which was not concerned with the usual issues of providing for a family or owning goods, but rather aimed to outdo and shame neighbours and rivals by means of conspicuous consumption. At their potlatch ceremonies the people competed with each other in burning and destroying their valuable possessions and money. This is in contrast to the Dobu of north-west Melanesia. This culture is reported to encourage malignant hatred and animosity. Treacherous conduct unmitigated by any concept of mercy or kindness and directed against neighbours and friends is expected.

The Zuni (a branch of the Pueblos of New Mexico) are a people whose life is centred on religious ceremonial, being prosperous but without interest in economic advancement. They admire most those men who are friendly, make no trouble and have no aspirations, detesting, on the other hand, those who wish to become leaders. Hence tribal leaders have to be compelled by threats to accept their position and are regarded with contempt and resentment once they have achieved it. Even cultures that are relatively better known have their own intricacies over something as simple as a handshake, eye contact and the use of colours. For example, brown and grey are disapproved of in Nicaragua; white, purple and black are the colours of death for Japan, Latin America and Britain respectively.

Understanding other cultures – the oppressed male

'The Kagba women of North Colombia practise not only free love but free rape, and few men are safe.'

Young (1987)

If this is deemed to be strange, consider how other cultures might view the seemingly bizarre behaviour patterns of the tea-drinking, nose-blowing, ball-room-dancing and kissing population of Europe.

The reader may be surprised to know of a tribe where it is not uncommon for the men of the tribe to behave in a promiscuous manner with other men's wives and daughters in public. It is so popular it is even broadcast on their television networks. The country: the UK. The practice: ballroom dancing. Here is a description of this behaviour:

It is common in such dancing for the front of the bodies to be in constant contact – and they do this in public. In spite of the close physical touching involved in this type of dancing (a form of bodily contact not unlike that assumed in sexual intercourse), our society has defined it as almost totally asexual. Although ballroom dancing can involve high levels of intimacy, it is equally possible that there is no sexual content whatsoever. Many adult men in the United States have danced in this fashion with their mothers, their sisters, the wives of the ministers at church socials without anyone raising an eyebrow. Yet many non-American cultures view this type of dancing as the height of promiscuity and bad taste. It is interesting to note that many of those non-Americans for whom our dancing is a source of embarrassment are the very people we consider to be promiscuous, sex-crazed savages because their women do not cover their breasts.

Ferraro (2001)

The international marketer embraces other cultures, researching and respecting the local culture as being right and proper and perhaps adopts Geertz's (1983) insight:

the world... does not divide into the pious and the superstitious... there are sculptures in jungles and paintings in deserts... political order is possible without centralized power and principled justice without codified rules; the norms of reason were not fixed in Greece, the evolution of morality not consummated in England... We have, with no little success, sought to keep the world off balance, pulling out rugs, upsetting tea tables, setting off fire crackers. It has been the office of others to reassure; ours to unsettle.

Touching a global nerve

Despite the complexities of cultural idiosyncrasies, there are many common needs that manifest themselves into common wants and purchasing patterns, particularly where there are similar levels of economic

Cannibalistic disease: kissing

'A whole lot of people think kissing is not at all natural. It is not something that everybody does, or would like to do. On the contrary, it is a deplorable habit, unnatural, unhygienic, bordering on the nasty and even definitely repulsive. When we come to look into the matter, we shall find that there is a geographical distribution of kissing; and if some enterprising ethnologist were to prepare a "map of kissing" it would show a surprisingly large amount of blank space. Most of the so-called primitive races of mankind such as the New Zealanders (Maoris), the Australian Aborigines, the Pauans, Tahitians, and other South Sea islanders, and the Esquimaux of the frozen north, were ignorant of kissing until they were taught the technique by the white men... The Chinese have been wont to consider kissing as vulgar and all too suggestive of cannibalism... the Japanese have no word for it in their vocabulary.'

Pike (1966)

wealth. It follows that, if a manufacturer or service supplier targets roughly the same socio-demographic groups in different countries and touches a common nerve within these target markets, then the same product or service can be packaged and promoted in a uniform manner. The pricing and distribution may vary, but the branding, packaging and even advertising can be the same. The manufacturers of world brands can therefore position their products in a similar manner in the minds of millions across many different cultures. This is the result of careful analysis and planning by expert marketing professionals rather than a trial-and-error approach to market extension.

The next challenge lies in moving the rest of the communications mix in a uniform manner so that not just advertising and packaging but also sales promotions, direct mail, sponsorship, etc, reap the benefits of a global approach. This globalization issue has revealed itself through the increased use of the internet. Even local firms going on to the net attract customers from all over the world. A web presence can deliver a global presence. However, this does present challenges, as Pepsi discovered, with its European blue can being seen by its US customers, who much prefer the traditional red can. Similarly, Tia Maria, although it is consumed around the world, has different age segments in different countries, eg in the UK Tia Maria is about girl power, targeted at 18- to 24-year-olds, while in the Netherlands it's drunk neat by pensioners. Now this 'common nerve' presents a positioning challenge. Despite these difficulties, Coke and computers have proved that large, lucrative global markets do exist.

Forces driving globalization

It is not just a product-orientated corporate push for growth but more of a market-orientated reaction to the emergence of common global lifestyles and needs. These are emerging as cheap travel, combined with higher disposable incomes, allows travellers to leap across borders, visit other cultures and return home with a little bit of that culture's soul in their own. Television itself has brought into the sitting rooms of Europe's homes pictures and images of the United States' *Breaking Bad*, Australia's *Neighbours*, UK's *The Inbetweeners*, Africa's famines, Nepal's earthquake and ISIS atrocities. It has also brought stunning scenes from the depths of the oceans, the balmy beaches of the Caribbean, the rugged beauty of the bush and the once rich and fertile Amazon rainforest. This global awareness is exploited by the corporate push for growth, which has forced many suppliers to move beyond their already saturated local markets to overseas. Improved production, distribution and marketing techniques have accelerated the movement of products and services from all around the world into local markets. Professional buyers now scour the world in pursuit of new suppliers. The internet gives immediate access to a world of new sources. Political barriers are generally still falling in China and the eastern bloc and, of course, Europe's own internal political barriers are being dismantled also as Europe expands. The doors of the world's markets are opening. The key, it seems, is to identify core benefits that are common to different cultures, along with any relevant cultural idiosyncrasies.

The elite global players

The significant benefits derived from developing a global brand supported by a global communications strategy are currently reserved for a relatively small number of world-class marketers. This elite band of players recognize the right conditions and apply thorough research and planning to exploit the brand's assets on a global scale. However, it should be remembered that a single communications strategy (incorporating everything from branding to the complete range of communications tools) rarely works for all the players operating in international markets. The desire to harness the global opportunity is natural, because international markets offer huge rewards. They also present intricate problems. Careful cultural homework needs to be included in the detailed research and planning that go below the surface.

Below-the-surface similarities

Similar buying behaviour and buying patterns do not necessarily mean a uniform market with uniform needs, uniform communications channels, uniform decision-making processes, uniform decision-making units, or even uniform reasons for buying. Take the case of buying premium-priced water. In a Khartoum slum an impoverished family pays 20 times the price paid by families with water main connections, while half a world away a middle-class family buys bottles of mineral water. This demonstrates 'unreal similarities'. The buyers appear to behave similarly by purchasing expensive water. They are, however, very different; in fact, they are from totally dissimilar groups with different aspirations, motivations, lifestyles and attitudes, not to mention disposable income. On the surface there is a market for private water in both countries, but the distribution channels, communications channels, advertising messages and levels of disposable income are poles apart.

An analysis that goes below the surface (or below the sales results) will reveal a range of different motives, aspirations, lifestyles and attitudes to the same product. Surface information can create a false sense of simplicity. International markets can also suggest surface solutions that ignore the cultural complexities and intricacies of distant markets. As Sir John Harvey-Jones' popular business TV series once warned way back in 1988:

> Operating in this milieu requires much greater sensitivity to national differences than we are accustomed to having. The mere fact that one stays in the same sort of hotel almost anywhere in the world, that one arrives in the same sort of

car, that it is now possible to call by telephone or telex directly from almost anywhere in the world, all gives a superficial feeling of sameness which is desperately misleading and must never be taken for granted.

Globalization, intertwined with cultural idiosyncrasies, is emerging in many markets around the world. The marketing maxim 'Think global, act local' remains valid. Although the late great Professor Theodore Levitt's 'globalization of markets' is occasionally criticized by some academics, he was right; globalization is happening and it does offer huge rewards for those who seize the opportunity.

South Korea – 'Would you like plastic with your credit?'

'A completely different mindset applies to customers in other countries. In South Korea, the Visa credit card company will ask you on a new Visa card approval on the phone 'Do you want plastic with the credit?', as the credit card functionality will automatically be enabled on your cell phone and the old-fashioned plastic card for your wallet is a free optional extra, only really needed if you travel outside South Korea.'

Ahonen and Moore (2007)

Below-the-surface external differences

There are, of course, many differences below the surface also. In practice, the European Union is splintered by different levels of economic development (north and south), culture, attitudes and lifestyles, languages, retail trends, direct mail trends, sources of information, time taken to make a decision, and so on. Different marketing mixes and communication mixes are required for different European countries. For example, in the Netherlands, dentists derive 40 per cent of their turnover from the sale of products such as toothbrushes. In Germany, supermarkets are expected to sell only cheap, utilitarian brushes, while the pharmacies handle the premium brands. In Italy, a premium brush has to carry a fashionable, exclusive label. This makes any above-the-line (ad) campaigns

difficult. The communications mix was built around direct mail to dentists supported by point-of-sale and product literature, packaging design and sales presenters. Although these can all change over time, it underlines the necessity for detailed and thorough research before entering any market.

Below-the-surface internal differences

The marketer's challenge goes beyond communicating with new international customers and into working with international partners whose idiosyncrasies and languages pose many problems. To some, overcoming local customers' idiosyncrasies may seem relatively easy compared to overcoming local partners' working practices. Whether the local partners are suppliers, distributors, sales agents, advertising agents, strategic partners or prospects, it is essential for success to understand and work with very different approaches to business. Take nomenclature for a moment. The French normally refer to advertising as publicité, which can cause some confusion, while the Yugoslavian word for advertising is propaganda. Other cultures have difficulty translating 'marketing', 'marketing communications' and 'advertising', as they have not yet created such words.

Southern Europeans work to live and northern Europeans live to work

'Somewhere in the world there are people who think the Germans are messy and unpunctual. (The chances are they are in Switzerland.) There are countries where Greece is regarded as a model of efficiency. There are countries in which French bosses would seem absurdly egalitarian and others where Italian company life would seem oppressively regulated.'

Mole (1998)

International difficulties

International markets are riddled with hidden cultural differences that make global marketing an intriguing challenge even for the most capable international marketing expert. Positioning on a global scale is not easy. Apart from language, literacy, colour, gestures and culture, marketers now have to try to think how global audiences search for information – what words, what search engines along with a raft of other variables. Even if you do translate correctly, you probably have to redesign your web pages, as many other languages require more words and therefore more space to deliver the same message.

Here are some of the intricacies that contribute towards the challenge of global marketing:

- language:
  - search terms;
  - CTAs;
  - hybrid.
- literacy;
- tone;
- sharing;
- searching;
- motivation;
- colour;
- design:
  - form filling and privacy;
  - payments.
- gestures;
- culture;
- original national identity;
- devices
- media availability;
- media overlap;
- lack of media data;
- lack of media credibility;
- varying media characteristics;
- different media usage;
- different media standards;
- different cost structures;
- legal restrictions;
- competition;
- non-global names.

Language

Language obviously requires careful translating, whether it is straplines, product descriptions or instructions (see 'International mistakes' on p. 255). There are exceptions to the rule (where the language reflects beneficial cultural aspects of the product, eg Audi's Vorsprung durch Technik strapline). And some brand names simply don't work when used in foreign languages and thus restrict the brand's international growth potential or dilute the brand's presence through the need to have two brand names.

Beware of automatic translation as it does not always work perfectly. For example, the word 'home' is automatically translated into maison, the French for 'a home to live in' (as opposed to 'home page'). In Italy, machine translation for the word 'hi-fi' generates a machine translation of ciao-fi. Ciao means hi or hello. And even the most perfect word-for-word translations often do not match the real meaning as different countries use completely different words when online.

Swansea Council translation process gone wrong

A sign that read 'No entry for heavy goods vehicles. Residential site only' was sent, by e-mail, for translation into Welsh. As the translator was not in the office, an auto-response e-mail was returned to the sender saying: 'Nid wyf un y swyddfa ar hyn o bryd. Anfonwch unrhyw wiath i'w gyfieithu', which means 'I am not in the office at the moment. Please send any work to be translated.' Since the original message had two sentences, it was assumed the Welsh message was the translation, and the sign was duly printed and erected.

Search terms

A British white goods retailer launching in Germany discovered that the common English term 'Slimline' was simply never used. Instead, German consumers search for goods using precise measurements. A British sports retailer soon realized that Germans will never search for 'football kits'. They will only search for 'football shirts'. These small nuances make a big difference when it comes to an international search strategy.

Calls to action

Requests for more information can vary dramatically by country. The UK and United States prefer a more direct approach, such as 'Get Quote', while Australians are more likely to click on something citing 'Free'. The Chinese prefer a more respectful 'Request Quote'. Eastern cultures tend to be more polite and formal.

Hybrid language

The term 'cheap flights' worked well in most markets, but it was almost completely ineffective in Italy. Consumers there often use hybrid Italian/English phrases so 'voli low cost' is a far better fit.

Same language different words

Even the same language uses different words; for example, in the UK, PPC means 'paid media' yet Americans call it SEM while some other countries call it SEA.

Same language different spelling

Even when using the same language, spelling can differ; British and Americans might spell the same word differently, eg minimise/minimize or colour/color. When marketing in these countries your marketing communications must reflect (ie use) these 'incorrect' spellings.

Searching in one language for results in another language

For example, the term 'Hindi News' is used in English to find websites written in Hindi. Technology is another core area where key terms from another language are often used to find and talk about products and services.

Oban Digital (2015)

Language barriers can be expensive

Even the same language can have different meaning in different markets, eg a 'boot' refers to the rear of a car (in the UK) as well as a shoe. In the United States, the rear section of a car is called a 'trunk'. This is relatively minor, but how about exactly the same word having radically different business meanings? Take a trillion. In most English-speaking countries, including the United States and the UK, a trillion is 1 followed by 12 zeros: 1,000,000,000,000.

In most continental European countries, a trillion is 1 followed by 18 zeros: 1,000,000,000,000,000,000.

Be careful also with a billion, as it has different meanings – in most English-language countries a billion is 1 followed by 9 zeros (a thousand million) but in many other parts of the world it is 1 followed by 12 zeros (a million million).

Literacy

In many developing countries literacy is low (Dudley, 1989). This limits the amount of explanation in advertising. Even with high literacy, the reading of translated Western-style advertisements still causes problems, eg before-and-after toothpaste advertisements if they are not adjusted for Arabic readers, who read from right to left. In other low-literacy countries, pictures may be used to explain the contents. When Gerber first sold baby food in Africa it put a picture of a Caucasian baby on the label and didn't realize that, in Africa, companies routinely put pictures on the label to show what's inside, as there is a high rate of illiteracy.

Tone

Tone can be subtle. In mainland Europe and also in the United States, a luxury brand will approach its target audience online with bespoke, glossy, aspirational communications – more like a brochure than a transactional site. However, in China this may fail. Even for expensive purchases, and major high-profile brands, Chinese consumers prefer a no-nonsense approach – they want to know how to buy and what the options are, with all the information at their fingertips.

Sharing

A UK Premier League football club wanted to target fans across India, Mexico, Thailand and the UK with a social media campaign – four very different audiences. Research found that each wanted very different content, and to consume and share it at very different times. For instance, Indians are less likely to react to tweets or Facebook posts during match-time itself and often for hours afterwards, while others are hugely reactive in the immediate aftermath of a game.

> ### Social networks differ
>
> The same is also true of social media platforms with people in China using Sina Weibo, an alternative to Twitter, and Germans using Xing over LinkedIn.

Searching

Even though you have got international visitors on your website, you need to research their needs as they may be quite different to each other and hence a website will have to cater for these differing needs. A Nordics-based cruise company discovered many different nationalities visiting its site had many different information needs. The Brits were very interested in the Northern Lights, while the dog-loving Germans were far more interested in Husky-dog sledding; the Americans, meanwhile, wanted information on 'activity sports' while the French, with their own ski resorts, didn't want any information on Alpine sports.

Motivation

Motivation, or reason to buy the same product can, and often does, differ across different countries as Oban Digital (2015) explain:

> In Germany, price and quality are the most influential factors, while the Japanese most value

a high level of customer service. The Japanese concept of Omotenashi, described as its unique approach to hospitality, is one reason why customer service is highly regarded. Kawaii, the concept of cuteness, is another differentiating factor in Japan. Kawaii values innocence, beauty and fun and is used in many areas you wouldn't expect. Brands add cuteness to their product set by associating it with pastel colours and images of hearts, flowers, stars and rainbows. Even construction guard rails are infused with Kawaii elements!

> ### Google, Yahoo and Bing are not as big as Baidu
>
> Yahoo and Bing are far more important in the United States than the UK for instance, where Google overwhelmingly dominates. Baidu, in China, and Russia's Yandex, dominate their home markets with up to 75 per cent reach each, while Yahoo in Japan (now a separate entity) and Naver in Korea are also important considerations.

Baidu requires time and money

Baidu takes time to set up an account. It takes months, as opposed to hours or days. It has strict data controls, content standards and other idiosyncrasies about content. So plan well ahead of any launches and allow extra time (and knowledge skills) required.

You're also highly unlikely to make that vital first page of results organically, so Oban Digital suggest that your media spend is more vital on Baidu than on Google. Yet, once you're on, you're reaching the world's biggest online population.

Colour

Colour has a direct access to our emotions. Watch how red is commonly used in advertising in the West. Colour, however, does not have uniform meaning across the world. Asians associate red with prosperity and good luck. Consider a financial services website: if Asians see no red, they will leave; if Westerners see red, they might leave. Never wrap a gift in red in Finland, as it is associated with Russian

Google, Yahoo and Bing not enough in China or Russia

'Some marketers wanting to break into China or Russia might mistakenly believe a reach of around 25 per cent through Google, Yahoo and Bing might be a shortcut worth taking. Given the size of these markets, yes of course you might reach millions through such engines, but are they actually the people you want to reach? Restricting yourself to those three search engines means the audience you reach is likely to be mainly Western expats, internationalists and the elite. The aspiring middle class, the new consumers, probably the people you should be talking to, are still more likely to go local.'

Oban Digital (2015)

aggression during the Second World War. Blue in Iran means immorality. White in Japan means death (hence McDonald's white-faced Ronald McDonald has problems). Black means death, unlucky or morbid in some countries. Websites designed with black backgrounds may be seen as 'hip' in the West, but can suffer lack of traffic from China and Hong Kong.

Design

UK and US customers prefer a cleaner, uncluttered approach with lots of white space (signalling a re-assuring sense of order) and drop-down menu. Eastern markets, however, with less efficient languages (ie they require more space), prefer busy landing pages, with links down both the left and right side of the page. This is partly due to the sheer volume of characters making searching clumsier and therefore a poor CX. And even within Europe there are many nuances and differences, for example French retail sites are often busy, messy and can look old-fashioned to the English eye.

Form filling and privacy

Privacy is also important in China. There, consumers prefer real-time interaction rather than being asked to provide information such as e-mail addresses, using services such as 22. Though they love to comment and interact online they also want to preserve their privacy.

Payments

Only a small percentage of German consumers use credit cards. So if you can't offer a bank transfer service then consider using a service such as PayPal.

Gestures

When greeting or bidding farewell, physical contact beyond a handshake in South America, southern Europe and many Arab countries is a sign of warmth and friendship, but in Asia it can be considered an invasion of privacy. After a meal in Egypt it is considered rude not to leave something on your plate, while in Norway and Malaysia leaving anything on your plate would be considered rude. Basic body gestures are not global. In some parts of India, Sri Lanka and Bulgaria, shaking the head from left to right means 'yes'. Touching the lower eyelid may be just an itch, but it also suggests to a South American woman that a man is making a pass, or to a Saudi man that he is stupid. Scratching an earlobe has five different meanings in five Mediterranean countries: 'You're a sponger' (Spain), 'You'd better watch it' (Greece), 'You're a sneaky little...' (Malta), 'Get lost!' (Italy), while a Portuguese will feel really pleased. The A-OK gesture (thumb and index finger in a circle with the rest of the fingers open) means money to a Japanese, zero in France, 'OK' in the United States, a rude gesture in Brazil and 'I'll kill you' in Tunisia. Even the thumbs-up sign is deemed to be a devastatingly obscene gesture to a Sardinian woman and insulting in Iran. Thrusting your palms towards someone's face may be meant to be endearing, but to a Greek there is no greater insult, since this gesture is called a moutza and comes from the Byzantine custom of smearing filth from the gutter in the face of condemned criminals.

Culture

Culture creates a quagmire of marketing problems: religion, sex, eating, greeting, habits, lifestyles, the role of women – the list is endless. Ferraro (2001) points out nine critical dimensions that contrast the United States with the rest of the world's cultures. She says that US culture places a high value on 1) individualism, 2) a precise reckoning of time, 3) a future orientation, 4) work and achievement, 5) control over the natural environment, 6) youthfulness, 7) informality, 8) competition and 9) relative equality of the sexes.

Chinese breakfast: positioning's cultural challenges – breakfast comforting or breakfast crunching?

'A breakfast product in China should be soft, it should be reassuring, it should be comforting and NOT be about discovering your dreams as you crunch your way through the morning!

A food product manufacturer, many of whose products are consumed before noon, launched with cereal, a breakfast cereal. The Chinese don't like to crunch in the morning. The role of breakfast in the morning is fundamentally different than in America. This is a protective society; a mother's fundamental role is to protect her children with love as opposed to enable them to go discover their dreams. So breakfast in the morning should be soft, it should be reassuring, it should be comforting. This company had trouble recognizing that their lead product couldn't be what it would be in the United States. To own the morning would require a fundamentally different business model and through that they have tried to have relationships with an acquisitions strategy with domestic companies.

Madden (2012)

As always, online can complicate matters. For example, Scandinavians and Germans are reluctant to use credit cards, the currency of the internet; the French dislike revealing personal information; the Germans prefer to pay with a cheque, after delivery of the goods. In meetings, the Dutch and the Germans want to get straight to the point in business dealings, whereas in countries like Spain, Brazil and Hong Kong some general chat is the most important part. In France, family is private and not part of business discussions. In Hong Kong, expressing an interest in family, general health, and observations of the country help to nurture good relations.

Even protocol for follow-ups to a meeting varies from country to country, as some countries place more importance on the written word than the spoken word, and vice versa. As Julian (2009) points out: 'In Spain for instance, it's important to follow up an e-mail with a phone call, but in

Germany you must do the opposite and put your phone conversations into writing.' As for humour, use it sparingly, if at all. In Germany, humour is generally considered inappropriate in business. It is essential to take advice from expert export advisory services such as UK Trade & Investment in the UK.

Christmas in other cultures

Taking advantage of the Christmas opportunity requires an understanding of each international market. For example, in Brazil and Spain the celebration continues until 6 January (when festivities end). In Russia the celebrations start on 7 January. In India Christmas Day is called Bada Din (Big Day) in Hindi, and it is a national holiday that allows people from all religions to celebrate with their Christian friends. In China the main celebration occurs at the end of January (the Chinese New Year or the Spring Festival). In other countries Christmas does not happen (in fact the word is illegal in some countries).

Original national identity

National identity can be an asset or a liability. For example, Dudley (1989) reported that Marathon Oil makes a point of stressing its US association in Italy, where US high technology is beneficial, but in Germany Marathon avoids the issue of its US parentage because of the German concern over US control in the German energy industry.

Devices

In the mobile-obsessed UK, you'd probably turn to mobile. However, in Thailand, 16–34 year-olds are much more likely than the average Brit to access a social networking site via PC over a smartphone. In parts of Africa and Asia mobile is now the primary device through which to access internet, surpassing PC traffic. Rich media content will not deliver the optimum user experience in such a mobile environment... consider the ease and speed of internet access, or that their smart devices might be generations behind those in the West.

Ozon.ru – Russia's Amazon

In some markets such as Russia, consumers are loyal to 'local' and it might make more sense to launch via a marketplace such as Ozon.ru – the Russian Amazon equivalent.

Media availability

Television is sometimes unavailable, since 1) developing countries do not have a high penetration of televisions in domestic households, 2) some countries do not have commercial TV stations, and 3) others do but they restrict the amount of advertising time. Some countries, like Pakistan, do not allow YouTube, 'although we know a significant proportion of the population accesses the service via proxy servers, it would be impossible to know who was consuming what and when' (Oban Digital).

Unilever and BAT have made their own medium available in East Africa by running their own mobile cinemas.

TV helps

'The further away from a TV screen, however, the more difficult many experts say it becomes to create and to deliver a pan-European message.'

Mead (1993)

Media overlap

Television, radio and the internet from one market can spill over into other markets, for example half the Canadian population has access to US television. The Republic of Ireland receives the UK's BBC and ITV channels. In mainland Europe local TV is received by neighbouring countries.

Lack of media data

Great Britain and Ireland have well-structured and categorized media analysis data (audited data). Without reliable media data the optimum cost and effectiveness of the overall campaign are unlikely to be achieved. Properly structured media markets are easier to work in.

Lack of media credibility

Unregulated or poorly regulated media in some countries may flout the principles of legality, decency, honesty and truth, which in turn may make these media untrustworthy or create audience scepticism about the particular source of information.

Varying media characteristics

Coverage, cost and reproduction qualities can and do vary from country to country. Some countries are technically more advanced than others, eg they may have massive penetration of high-speed broadband, while other countries do not even have many cinemas.

Different media usage

Kahler and Kramer (1977) suggest that the British tend to see TV as a visual medium, while TV to the Americans is a visual accompaniment to words.

Different media standards

A lack of uniformity of standards means that different types of both film and artwork may be required for different markets, for example the United States and the UK have different standard page sizes that may require different artwork, which increases cost.

Different cost structures

Different countries have different forms of negotiation and bartering. The Americans and the Japanese are poles apart. In less developed countries cash may not be available, but barter, or counter-trading, can offer an acceptable alternative.

Legal restrictions

Whether voluntary codes or actual law, there is as yet no harmonized set of laws or regulations. For example, Lands' End's website in Germany cannot mention its unconditional refund policy, because German retailers successfully sued in court. (They normally do not allow returns after 14 days.) This presents the advertiser with different problems in different countries. In Sweden, misdemeanours by advertisers may be charged under the criminal law, with severe penalties.

Competition

Different markets have different key players using different strengths. For example, Ford's position of 'safety engineering' worked in many countries, but not in Sweden, where, of course, Volvo occupied the position. Competition may react in different ways in different markets.

Language, literacy and logic

Combine these three in the international arena and a new challenge emerges – writing instructions. It is a skill in one language, and attempting to translate instructions is complex. This is an extract from the translated instructions for assembling a 'knapsack':

1 Lead for hind leg in an opened position.

2 Lead the frame of the sack support up.

3 Insert the blushing for blocking in the proper split, push it deeply and wheel in an anti-time sense till it stops.

International mistakes

Here is a selection of global misses or mistakes made by brands attempting to sell into international markets. It includes wrong brand names, wrong advertising slogans or, worse still, a fundamentally unsuitable product for a particular international market.

Some marketers carefully choose names that work for their local domestic market but never consider that one day the successful brand could sell into several markets. This insular perspective more than likely restricts any future growth opportunities into international markets and almost certainly restricts the brand from developing into a global brand.

Wrong names

Here are a few examples:

- Sic (French soft drink);
- Pschitt (French soft drink);
- Lillet (French aperitif wine);
- Creap (Japanese coffee creamer);
- Irish Mist (in Germany 'mist' means manure);
- Bum (Spanish potato crisp);
- Bonka (Spanish coffee);
- Trim Pecker Trouser (Japanese germ bread);
- Gorilla Balls (American protein supplement);
- My Dung (restaurant);
- Cul toothpaste (cul means anus in France);
- Scratch (German non-abrasive bath cleaner);
- Super-Piss (Finnish car lock anti-freeze);
- Spunk (jelly-baby sweet from Iceland);
- the Big John product range was translated as Gros Jos (slang for 'big breasts') for French-speaking Canada.

Even sophisticated marketers get it wrong. General Motors discovered that Nova meant 'it won't go' (no va) in South America. Ford launched the Pinto in Brazil and soon realized that it was slang for 'tiny male genitals'. Coca-Cola's phonetic translation in China meant 'Bite the wax tadpole'. After launching into English-speaking markets, Japan's second-largest tourist agency was surprised to receive a steady influx of enquiries for sex tours. The Kinki Nippon Tourist Company soon changed its name.

These translation problems are not insurmountable. For example, Curtis shampoo changed its name from 'Everynight' to 'Everyday' for the Swedish market, since the Swedes wash their hair in the mornings. Mars changed its well-known 'Marathon Bar' to 'Snickers' to fit in with the worldwide brand name communications strategy.

Wrong strapline

The New York Tourist Board found 'I love New York' difficult to translate into Norwegian, since there are only two Norwegian verbs that come close: one translation is 'I enjoy New York', which lacks something, and the other is 'I have a sexual relationship with New York'. Scandinavian vacuum cleaner manufacturer Electrolux used this in a US campaign: 'Nothing sucks like an Electrolux'. When Parker Pens marketed its ballpoint pen in Mexico, its advertisements were supposed to read: 'It won't leak in your pocket and embarrass you'. Unfortunately, embarazar does not mean embarrass. It means impregnate, so the slogan had an entirely inappropriate meaning. The Mitsubishi Pajero had problems, since pajero in some parts of the Spanish-speaking world means a liar, in others a plumber and in others something much worse. Other expressions that have been imprecisely translated include US cigarettes with low asphalt (tar), computer underwear (softwear) and wet sheep (hydraulic rams). Attention to detail is required when translating, as even the smallest error, such as missing out an accent on a letter, can drastically change the meaning. For example, in the United States, a bilingual banner celebrated '100 ano of municipal history'. In Mexican Spanish, año is year but ano is anus.

'I saw the potato'

During the Pope's visit to Miami it was reported that some T-shirts were printed supposedly saying 'I saw the Pope'. However, the translation was 'I saw the potato', because *Papa* with a capital P means Pope, whereas *papa* with a small P means potato.

Wrong product

In the attempt to get the packaging, advertising and branding right, global marketers can sometimes forget the fundamental product and whether it is suitable for the market in the first place, leading to campaign failure. Here are some examples of international product failures arising from the basic product itself: Christmas puddings in Saudi Arabia (where the word 'Christmas' is illegal and 50,000 of the Anglo-Saxon population go on leave during Christmas anyway); and toothpaste to combat betel nut stains (stained teeth imply wealth in some cultures, as does being overweight in others). General Foods' packaged cake mixes found the Japanese market too small for them (3 per cent of homes had ovens). Coca-Cola had to withdraw its 2-litre bottle from Spain, because few Spaniards owned refrigerators with large enough compartments. Tennent's Caledonian, a successful Scottish lager, flopped initially in the UK because it came in 24-packs rather than six-packs. Philips had to change the size of its coffee makers to fit into the smaller Japanese kitchens and its shavers to fit smaller Japanese hands.

Microsoft pays dear for insults through ignorance

'Insensitive computer programmers with little knowledge of geography have cost the giant Microsoft company hundreds of millions of dollars in lost business and led hapless company employees to be arrested by offended governments.'

Brown (2004)

Even the major global players can get it totally wrong. Microsoft was reported (Brown, 2004) to have released its colour-coded world map with time zones showing the disputed Jammu and Kashmir region as not being in India. Under Indian law, this is an offence. Result: the Windows 95 operating system was banned, with hundreds of millions of dollars in lost sales. Office 97 was subsequently launched without colour coding.

Microsoft employees were arrested in Turkey when Kurdistan was shown as a separate entity, so Kurdistan was subsequently removed from all maps. 'Of course we offended the Kurds by doing this but we had offended the Turks more and they were a much more important market for our products. It was a hard commercial decision, not political' (Tom Edwards, Microsoft's senior geopolitical strategist quoted in Brown, 2004).

Another mistake that caused catastrophic offence was a game called Kakuto Chojin, a fighting-styled computer game with a rhythmic chant from the Koran. Despite being alerted by a Muslim staff member as to this insult to Islam, Microsoft still launched the game in the United States on the assumption that it would not be noticed. After a formal protest by the Saudi Arabian government, Microsoft withdrew the product worldwide. The list goes on. China, Korea, Spain and Uruguay have all been upset by various Microsoft products. In Korea its software showed the Korean flag in reverse and prompted government objections. In Spain, hembra means woman, but in Nicaragua and some other Central American countries it means bitch. In China, when Microsoft referred to Taiwan as a country, the police moved in and questioned staff. In Uruguay, a proud republic, Microsoft's Outlook referred to 30 April as 'the Queen's birthday', which offended the government.

Strategic global options

More and more businesses have to compete in the global arena. For many companies there is nowhere left to hide. Those that do not move into the global market will probably find that the global market will come to them, as new international competitors target their once-safe local market. There is a need to be proactive rather than reactive. Those that ignore this small part of the globalization process may not be around in 50 years.

A defensive strategy (eg consolidating the existing customer base, staying native, and blocking competition from entering with, for example, a series of flexible distributor promotions) may safeguard the company, at least in the short term. Offensive strategies are required if a company is seeking entry into new markets, eg increasing promotional spend in key national markets, supported by a flexible operations system. Strategic alliances and joint ventures offer a lower-cost, lower-risk (and possibly lower-margin) method of entry into these new, large and increasingly competitive markets. Global competition has even prompted global cooperation in the marketing communications industries. Advertising and PR independent networks are popping up alongside the global agencies that have expanded to meet their clients' global requirements.

Global marketing strategy

Keegan and Schlegelmilch (2001) identified five marketing (product/communication) strategies for multinational marketing. These were determined by the state of the various international markets, analysed by 1) whether the need (or product function) was the same as in other markets,

2) whether the conditions of product use were the same as in other markets, and 3) whether the customer had the ability to buy the product:

1 *Same product/same communications.* This applies to markets where the need and use are similar to those of the home market, eg Coca-Cola, with its centrally produced advertisements that incorporate local differences in language.

2 *Same product/different communications.* This applies to markets where the need or function is different but the conditions of product use are the same, eg bicycles in Europe and bicycles in Africa (recreation and transport, respectively).

3 *Different product/same communications.* This applies to markets with the same product function or need but with different conditions of product use, eg different petrol formulae but the same advertising image (eg Esso's tiger).

4 *Different product/different communications.* This applies to markets with different needs and different product use, eg greeting cards and clothes are held to be 'culture bound', but it should be noted that some clothing companies (like Levi's) use the same, centrally produced, wordless advertisements internationally.

5 *New product (invention)/new communications.* This applies, for example, in the case of a hand-powered washing machine.

It is highly unlikely that the complete communications mix can be standardized by centrally controlling and producing everything from advertising to sales promotions to point-of-sale to PR to direct mail, etc, because of, first, the differences in regulations and laws, which vary from country to country, and, second, the array of differences highlighted above. There are of course exceptions to the rule. IBM's Aptiva ran a 'win tickets to the 1996 Olympics' campaign across 12 European countries, while a new point-of-sale campaign rolled out to 15 European countries. Mars also developed a pack specifically for the Euro 96 football championships, featuring a green colour base with white netting effect, which appeared in shops in the UK, France and Germany.

Global advertising strategy

The question of whether at least the advertising can be standardized (across the world) is a source of great discussion. Kahler and Kramer (1977) original work suggests that successful standardization is dependent on the similarity of the motivations for purchase and the similarity of use conditions. For culture-free products such as industrial goods and some consumer durables, the purchase motivations are similar enough to permit high degrees of standardization. Culture-bound products, in contrast, require adaptation. Customs, habits and tastes vary for these products, and customer reaction depends on receiving information consonant with these factors. It has been argued that 'buying proposals' (the benefits proposed in the advertisement) have a good chance of being accepted across large geographical areas, whereas the 'creative presentation' (creative treatment) does not.

Essentially, if the international market had a similar set of needs and interests (to the established market), then a successful adaptation of the advertising message was more likely (as in the case of pattern advertisements – see 'Central strategy and local production (pattern advertisements)' below). Simon Majaro (1993) observed that the gap between the time a product reaches its decline stage in the most advanced market and the introduction stage in the slowest market is narrowing. If this trend continues, the point will be reached where the pattern of the life cycle in a domestic market will become identical with the pattern in the foreign markets. This will of course have a tremendous

impact on the communications strategy of firms operating internationally. It would mean that in time it would become possible for the communications objectives of such firms to become more and more homogeneous, thus allowing for a larger measure of standardization. In other words, if the trend continues, it should become possible for the same campaign, subject to the manipulation necessitated by linguistic and cultural variations, to be undertaken in all markets. This is indeed the kind of standardization that Coca-Cola has achieved in world markets. This strategy stems in the main from the fact that the product life cycle profit of Coca-Cola is pretty homogeneous throughout the world. Rijkens (1993) confirmed the trend towards 'greater international-ization and centralization', where basic creative ideas are centrally produced for international use. Kahler and Kramer (1977) felt that transferability of advertising was dependent on the possibility of a more homogeneous consumer, who might, for example, evolve out of the ever-integrating European community. If the European consumer showed a willingness to accept the products of countries within the community, and if that consumer was motivated similarly to consumers in other countries, a common promotional approach would be practical; but if national identities prevailed, separate campaigns would be more likely to succeed.

Four global advertising strategies

The four basic strategies available for global marketing communications are:

1 central strategy and production;
2 decentralized strategy and production;
3 central strategy and local production (pattern advertisements);
4 central strategy with both central and local production.

Central strategy and production

Advertisements are controlled and produced by the head office (or its agency). This includes message modification, such as translations and tailor-made editions for various markets. Examples of centrally controlled and centrally produced advertisements include Coca-Cola's emotion-packed 'General Assembly' advertisement showing the world's children singing happily and harmoniously together, which was similar to their classic 1971 'I'd like to teach the world to sing' (McCann) in that it was packed with emotion and carried a universal theme. The 21 language editions of this advertisement opened with 'I am the future of the world, the future of my nation' and ended with the tag line 'a message of hope from the people who make Coca-Cola'. Each country then edited in its own end shot of the appropriate child's face. Incidentally, the German edition was dubbed slightly out of synchronization, since Germans associate quality films with dubbed (slightly out of sync) US and British films. Scottie's nappies save production costs by omitting any dialogue and just using a different voice-over for each country. Levi's does not bother with voice-overs, dubbings or translations, as there is no dialogue – just music. Its unified logo and brand image does away with the need for different pack shots (close-ups of the pack/label) for each country, so its commercials are used throughout Europe.

Decentralized strategy and production

Advertisements are controlled and produced by each local subsidiary and its agency specifically for the local market. This approach generates lots of different advertisements by the same company. Each division or subsidiary works with its own local agency to produce tailor-made advertisements for the local market. As well as being an expensive approach, it can destroy uniformity and a consistent global presence, but it does allow more creativity to suit the specific needs of the local market. Different positionings in different markets do require different campaigns, sponsorship and retail strategies. For example, if Rolex epitomizes 'achievement' in New York and 'trendiness' in Tokyo, it must implement two of everything: two product lines (one stately, one flashy), two ad campaigns, two sponsorship series and two retail strategies (Doctoroff, 2005).

Central strategy and local production (pattern advertisements)

The pattern provides uniformity in direction but not in detail, which allows the advertisements to be locally produced but within the central strategic guidelines. This is where head office guides the

strategic direction of the advertisements but allows local production. These advertisements work to a formula, or pattern. In the Blue Band margarine advertisements, whether in Scandinavia or Africa, the appropriate happy mother could be seen spreading margarine on bread with her happy family sitting around eating it. Impulse fragrance used a 'boy chases girl' formula across Europe, but still allowed for cultural idiosyncrasies like eye contact, sex appeal and law-abiding citizens to be tailored into each country's different production. Renault's pan-European strategy was to 'endow the car with its own personality'. In France the car was shown with eyes. In Germany the car talked back. In the UK the end line was 'What's yours called?'

Central strategy with both central and local production

Centrally produced non-verbal commercials are used to build a unified identity, while local productions supplement this platform. This is demonstrated by the Levi's example given below. Although 'standardized' generally refers to production, it can also include centrally controlled media strategies, planning and buying. The centralized or standardized global campaign problems are discussed below. As Rijkens (1993) says:

> As far as advertising is concerned, the company will continue its policy of central production of non-verbal commercials and cinema films, to be shown throughout Europe and intended to establish a uniform identity for Levi Strauss as a business and for its products. Advertising produced locally by the Levi Strauss subsidiaries will respond to local circumstances and to the local competitive scene.
>
> This formula, also applied by other companies marketing a uniform product and using one advertising strategy on an international scale, has proved successful and may well be further developed once the single market really comes about.

Advantages of central strategy and central production

1 *Consistent image.* A consistent image (and positioning) is presented around the world, allowing consumer awareness and familiarity to prosper.

2 *Consolidated global position.* It leaves the brand in a stronger position to protect itself from any attack.

3 *Exploits transnational opportunities.* It reduces message confusion arising when advertising in one country spills over to another (eg boundary-bouncing satellite TV) or when migrants and tourists physically travel to another geographical area (geographical segment).

4 *Saves costs.* Economies are enjoyed by not having several different creative teams (and production teams if central production) working on the brand around the world (saves reinventing the wheel). There is the possibility of centrally produced (or at least centrally designed) point-of-sale material also. Levi's has found that it saves £1.5 million by shooting a single TV ad to span six European countries (at £300,000 production cost per each one-minute TV ad).

5 *Releases management time.* It may also reduce the size of the marketing department, which might otherwise be tied up briefing creative teams, approving creative concepts, supervising productions, etc. It may even save time invested with packaging designers, sales promotion agencies, etc, if pack designs and promotions are run from a central office.

6 *Facilitates transfer of skills.* It does this within the company and around the world, since in theory it is the same job anywhere around the world. It also stimulates cross-fertilization of company ideas if staff are moving around internationally.

7 *Easier to manage.* It is easier to manage centrally, since there is in total a smaller number of decisions and projects to manage:

   – One creative decision facilitates harmonization of creative treatments, particularly in areas of media overlap.

   – Media policies – manage the media overlap between countries to maximize effectiveness and recommend preferred media choice in specific territories.

   – Budgets – determine local budgets for each product in each market so that the method of allocating resources is balanced.

   – Agree an activity programme and a specific reporting system to facilitate easier management.

Disadvantages of central strategy and central production

1 *Stifles creativity.* It stops local creative contributions from both company staff and the local advertising agency (whether part of an international group or an independent agency). The account may be considered by the local agency staff to be dull and boring, and the supposed 'best brains' (from the creative department) may avoid being involved with it.

2 *Frustrated local management.* Although the local office may be accountable for its performance, it does not have control over its own destiny, since advertisements are centrally produced or directed. This may lead to a sense of frustration.

3 *Minimal effort from the local agency* (if using an international agency with its network of overseas branches). The high global advertising spend may put the brand high on the agency's head office list, but the local agencies may find it is uneconomic to spend too much time and top brains on it.

4 *Lost opportunities.* The opportunity to react quickly to changes in the local market is lost.

5 *Different product life cycles.* Different markets may be at different stages of their life cycle, which may make the standardized approach unsuitable. It may, however, still be possible to standardize each stage of the brand's development, eg Boots launch of Nurofen in the UK and northern Europe.

6 *Wrong idea.* Some central advertising concepts may simply not work as well as a locally created original idea. Sales therefore perform below their potential.

7 *Difficult translation.* Some ideas just do not lend themselves to translation, eg Pepsi's 'Come alive' was translated in some countries as 'Come from the dead' or 'Come out of the grave'.

8 *False savings.* Local language adaptation or modification costs may negate the cost savings generated by the centrally controlled creative work.

9 *Market complexities.* The many other local market differences (eg variations in consumer protection regulations and media availability) may make a standardized message extremely difficult.

10 *Inexperienced staff.* A lack of suitably qualified expert staff who can manage the coordination of transnational standardized campaigns may make the whole centrally controlled advertising concept too risky.

Rudyard Kipling's advice to McDonald's

'Asia is not going to be civilized under the methods of the west. There is too much Asia and she is too old.'

Rudyard Kipling (1891)

McDonald's India now offers tailored products for the Indian market – mutton, chicken, fish and vegetable products, not beef, pork or their by-products. Since Hindus don't eat beef, the Big Mac is called the Maharaja Mac and made from lamb.

Decentralized strategy

Successful marketers recognize a customer-centric world in which customers choose to do business with the brands that speak to them as individuals and are always relevant to their lives, jobs, families and cultures. As Ben David (2015) points out 'marketers are adapting their ad programmes to better relate to consumers on an individual level, but those targeting a global customer base still need to heed cultural differences to make their ads more effective across continents.'

Decentralized, localized and highly relevant ads perform better

Ben David (2015) observes that brand marketers create regional-specific advertising programmes (whether by country or even by city) because they

How North American and European ads differ

It's difficult to generalize advertising preferences across regions as each advertiser is striving to be more unique and innovative than the next, but we can extrapolate a few common themes. Consumers in North America are accustomed to forming a direct relationship with big brands, so ads tend to focus more on the brand experience. US marketers use the power of storytelling to help define the consumer's persona traits, and then create an ad story that places the consumer within that storyline.

On the other hand, European consumers don't tend to formulate that relationship with a brand. Consumers respond better to ads that contain brand messages around product cost and value. It's typical to see ad messaging in Europe touting the unique practical selling points of the product or service, versus emotional selling points. For instance, the underlying tone of a European ad might be, 'you should buy these shoes for their durability', versus the North American tone, 'you should buy these shoes so you can feel like LeBron James'.

know that the most effective ad experiences are those that are highly relevant to the customer and use an engaging medium, such as video. Marketers now have the capability to stop thinking by geographical segments – which still require assumptions about a large group of people to create one message that's intended to fit the entire target population – and truly speak to each customer as an individual.

Data helps:

By leveraging first-party customer data (both on-site historical and offsite behaviour) brands can deliver video advertising programmes that generate the content and creative in real time, and best connect with the consumer. Data-driven creative can be used across regions to pull in the most relevant assets, products and information for varying consumer cultures. Personalization and real-time relevance are the most important elements to deliver the most engaging experience for a consumer. Marketers are truly able to speak one-on-one with a consumer and highlight the unique and emotional selling points that matter most, whether it's cost and features in Europe, or brand lifestyle in North America.

Personalized online advertising, which first emerged in the North American marketplace, is gaining traction in the European market as well. Today, personalized video advertising is still developing in both regions, though it is, for now, more prevalent in North America. The reality is that no one wants to be approached like he is just another consumer, and brands are taking note.

Anyone for a Facebook global page?

Once again, the new currency, 'relevance' emerges as key in the ongoing attempts to continually engage and ipso facto strengthen customer relationships. Content simply has to be more relevant to target markets. This raises a question for global brands of whether to have a single global brand page on a social platform like Facebook or just have more relevant region-specific content?

Clara Shih in *Ad Age* (2013) suggests that 'Subscriptions, likes, and check-ins all count as implicit recommendations, and there is a risk that users will remove their connections (likes/check-ins/subscriptions) to brands that they do not want to be recommending.'

In order to maintain relationships, content and posts from companies will need to be more targeted and tailored to specific audiences, a task which, Shih suggests, will be increasingly difficult to accomplish with global brand pages.

> Instead, I expect to see the rise of the local page maintained by the local field representatives... Local pages could capitalize on keywords and data (like location and proximity) that are automatically incorporated into graph search results. Furthermore, the ability for local businesses to bring their relationships online, engaging with smaller, more focused communities gives them the opportunity to provide stronger relationships than the corporate marketer who is typically separated from the majority of their audience.

This is a discussion worth exploring further.

Agencies in the international arena

There are several different types of agency from which an international advertiser can choose:

- international agencies (multinationals);
- independent networks, associations or confederations of agencies;
- local independent agencies;
- house agencies.

In addition to deciding whether to centralize control over advertising (and effectively standardize it), the international marketing manager must decide whether to put all international advertising in the hands of one international agency or hand it out to local independent agencies. Many local independent agencies have grouped themselves into networks or associations, which means that they have a ready-made network of contacts with the other network member agencies in the various international regions. A fourth and less common option is for the client to set up its own house agency specifically to handle its own worldwide advertising. Two options will now be considered: whether to choose a single international agency or several independent local agencies.

Choosing an international agency or independent local agency

This question is linked to whether the communications should be controlled centrally or left to run autonomously. Should the marketing team at headquarters work with just one large multinational advertising agency or should it allow a range of independent agencies to use its unique skills on a local basis? A coordinated message can be developed in either situation. For example, centrally produced advertisements (with local modifications, translations, etc) and pattern advertisements (formula advertising) can work under either system. Although a centrally produced advertisement is more likely to be handled by a large international agency, there are exceptions where local independent agencies with local media buying and production skills (if pattern advertisements are required) may be preferred. It is possible to choose to work with a range of independent local agencies while adhering to centralized policies. These policies can help the client to manage the whole advertising process by giving specific guidance on creative directions, media strategies, budgets and activity programmes. As Majaro (1993) says, 'Obviously where the product profile justifies communications standardization, it may be advisable to use the services of an international agency with offices in all markets.' Majaro continues: 'Hoping to attain the same results by using a host of local agencies with no international expertise is a formula for waste in worldwide marketing.'

Advantages of using an international agency

Compared to local agencies, the international advertising agency claims the following advantages:

- Full service – because of the international agency's size, it can offer a full range of services, including research, planning and translation, under one roof.
- Quality – some clients feel reassured by the quality feeling of a large international agency (as opposed to taking a chance with a smaller local agency). Quality and standards should, in theory, be universal.
- Broad base of experience – training and transferring personnel is common among the international agencies.
- Presence in major advertising centres – the agency branches are located at the centre of most major cities or marketing territories.
- Cost saving – less duplication in areas of communication, creative and production departments.
- Easier to manage – a single central contact point combined with the points listed in 'Advantages of central strategy and central production' on page 259.

Disadvantages of using an international agency

It is arguably easier for a single international agency to standardize the message. The disadvantages of standardization (see p. 260) therefore apply where central control moves in. In addition, the overseas subsidiary may lack enthusiasm if the account was won elsewhere. It is as if, by necessity, various branches of the international agency are brought in. The lack of excitement may be compounded, particularly where all the creative work has been handled by head office. In a sense, the branch's job is relegated to media scheduling and planning.

The key to successful central communications

'If Shakespeare and the Rolling Stones can do it, so can advertising.'

Maurice Saatchi

Rather than engaging in high-risk new product development many corporations prefer to consider the lower-risk new market development approach. This doesn't mean international marketing is cheap. It's not. It requires resources to grow sales and market share internationally. Without this or with too little resources the propensity for failure increases. Adequate resources: budget (money), time (minutes) and skilled people (men/women) increase the likelihood of success.

However, making it all actually happen is another thing altogether. Take advertising: although more and more advertising is used in more than one country, only some of it works successfully.

Understanding the disadvantages in addition to the advantages is the first step towards implementing centralized communications. Identifying the barriers reveals the levels of resistance among distant marketing managers. It follows that internal marketing skills are also required. Before international communications are standardized (centralized), management thinking must first be harmonized internationally. Diminishing local autonomy without diminishing local responsibility requires skilful management handling. Indeed, maintaining management motivation requires people skills, particularly when their responsibilities for advertising budgets are being slashed.

Many local managers will perceive the central advertising campaign to be dull and disappointing because it is based on the lowest global common denominator – those common cross-cultural characteristics that somehow find commonality across borders that can result in dull ideas.

Inspiring managers to continue to excel under a blanket of apparently bland advertising is a challenging job. It becomes more challenging the longer internal communications are delayed.

> ### How to avoid some international difficulties when creating graphics
>
> Avoid:
>
> - text-based graphics;
> - visual puns;
> - gestures;
> - animal icons;
> - body parts as metaphor;
> - racial and/or gender stereotyping;
> - flags, maps, political and religious symbols.

Get the resources required for international growth

Scarce resources limit international growth plans (or any plans for that matter). It appears that scarce

digital marketing analytics resources seem to 'plague European and US companies' more than those based in Asia. Compared to their Asian counterparts, companies based in Europe and the United States are nearly twice as likely to suggest that they don't have the analysts they need to make sense of their data. A key theme emerging from the feedback we received in response to our open-ended questions is that most companies sit on heaps of data, but being able to turn all their data into actionable insights is something that few have been able to master (Source: Econsultancy, 2015).

International marketing communications require even more attention to detail than domestic marketing communications. But, even closer to home, care is required to ensure the correct translation processes are in place. A process is required to ensure copy is sent off for translating, translated, double-checked and then uploaded into the correct section of the foreign language site.

In conclusion

International markets present many challenges and many rewards. There are many similarities amongst customers around the world, but there are also many differences lurking below the surface. Even more attention to detail is required in international markets, as the opportunities for errors increase. Systems, processes and teams have to be harnessed to make it all work successfully.

Key points from Chapter 9

- The globalization of markets is ongoing.
- There are, however, technical and cultural idiosyncrasies that need to be accommodated.
- There are many other challenges that arise in international markets beyond just culture, including language, media, laws (or lack of them) and much more.

- The biggest challenge is to stay relevant to each region.
- The classic errors are made even by the big established brands. They can be avoided by thoroughly checking and researching each market.

References and further reading

Ahonen, T and Moore, A (2007) *Communities Dominate Brands*, Future Text, London

Anholt, S (2001) *Another One Bites the Grass*, Wiley, Chichester

Becht, B (2010) How I did it: Building a company without borders, *Harvard Business Review: The Magazine*, April

Ben David, E (2015) Relevant, personalized ads solve global marketing challenges, *The SmartVideo Blog*, 24 February [online] http://info.sundaysky.com/blog/

Brown, P (2004) Microsoft pays dear for insults through ignorance, *Guardian*, 19 August

Chaffey, D and Smith, PR (2008) *eMarketing eXcellence*, Butterworth-Heinemann, Oxford

Doctoroff, T (2005) *Billions: Selling to the new Chinese consumer*, Palgrave Macmillan, New York

Dudley, J (1989) *Strategies for the Single Market*, Kogan Page, London

eConsultancy (2015) Quarterly digital intelligence briefing: digital trends 2015, eConsultancy

Ferraro, G P (2001) *The Cultural Dimension of International Business*, 4th edn, Prentice Hall, Englewood Cliffs, NJ

Geertz, C (1983) *The Interpretation of Cultures: Selected essays*, Hutchinson, London

Harvey-Jones, J (1988) *Making It Happen: Reflections on leadership*, Collins, London

Inskip, I (1997) Marketing international brands in Asia needs fresh thinking, *Marketing Business*, May

Julian (2009) The 'lucky seven' tips when collecting payments from overseas companies, *Octempo: RM Blog*, 18 December [online] http://blog.octempo.com/

Kahler, R and Kramer, R (1977) *International Marketing*, South-Western Publishing, Cincinnati, OH

Kashani, K (1989) Pathways and pitfalls of global marketing, *Marketing Business*, June

Keegan, W J and Schlegelmilch, B B (2001) *Global Marketing Management: A European perspective*, Financial Times/Prentice Hall, Englewood Cliffs, NJ

Kotler, P (2002) *Marketing Management: Analysis, planning, implementation and control*, 11th edn, Prentice Hall, Englewood Cliffs, NJ

Lajoie, M and Shearman, N (2014) Defining Alibaba, *Wall Street Journal*

Madden, N (2012) Five questions with Tom Doctoroff, JWT's Greater China CEO, *Ad Age Global*, 27 June

Majaro, S (1993) *International Marketing*, 2nd edn, Allen & Unwin, London

Mazur, L (1997) Successfully managing cultural differences, *Marketing Business*, September

McGovern, G (2014) Customer-centric and easy-to-use is the new business model (The Alibaba story) *Gerry McGovern//New Thinking*, 18 May

Mead, G (1993) A universal message, *Financial Times*, 2 May

Mole, J (1998) *Mind Your Manners*, Nicholas Brealey Publishing, London

Morris, D (1988) Watch your body language, *Observer*, 23 October

Oban Digital (2015) Understanding your new global customer: 10 things you need to know about search and conversion when marketing to an overseas audience [online] www.obandigital.com

Orton-Jones, C (2013) Follow the money, *The Marketer*, March/April, p. 33

Pike, K (1966) *Language in Relation to a Unified Theory of the Structure of Human Behavior*, Mouton, The Hague

Prior, E (2013) Do Man Utd really have 659m supporters? *BBC News Magazine*, 18 February

Rijkens, R (1993) *European Advertising Strategies*, Cassell, London

Shih, C (2013) What's a 'Like' worth? Ask Facebook's graph search, *Ad Age Digital*, 14 February

Universal McCann (2007) Power to the people: Tracking the impact of social media wave, 2.0, May

Usunier, J C (2000) *Marketing across Cultures*, Financial Times/Prentice Hall, Englewood Cliffs, NJ

Winick, C (1961) Anthropology's contribution to marketing, *Journal of Marketing*, 25

Young, L (1987) *Love around the World*, 2nd edn, Hodder & Stoughton, London

10
The marketing communications plan

LEARNING OBJECTIVES

By the end of this chapter you will be able to:

- Write an outline marketing communications plan
- Understand the importance of gathering intelligence and research for the situation analysis before writing the rest of the plan
- Explore strategy, knowing that it is an area of weakness for most organizations
- Establish control systems

Introduction to the SOSTAC®
    marketing communications
    plan   268
The 3Ms   269
Budget setting   269

Situation analysis   271
Segmentation and target marketing   272
Decision-making units   273
Global segments   274
B2C (consumer) segments   274
B2B (industrial) segments   274
Segmentation requires careful
    analysis   276

Objectives   276
Marketing objectives   277
Communications objectives   277

Strategy   278
TOPPP SITE (nine key strategic
    components)   279

The benefits of a strong marcomms
    strategy   279
Three strategic examples   282

Tactics   282

Action   284
Critical path or project plan   285

Control   285
Some tactical tools/channels are better
    than others   287
Net promoter score, satisfaction score and
    recommendation score   289
Sentiment analysis – social conversation
    scores (social media monitoring)   289
Return on investment   289

Key points from Chapter 10   290

References and further reading   290

Further information   291

Introduction to the SOSTAC® marketing communications plan

There are many different approaches to building a marketing plan or, more specifically, a marketing communications plan. There is no single common approach, but there are essential elements that every plan must have. SOSTAC® was developed in the 1990s after 10 years of searching and experimenting: a simple aide-mémoire that helps managers to recall the key components of a marketing communications plan. SOSTAC® can in fact be applied to any kind of plan – a corporate plan, marketing plan, marketing communications plan, social media plan, direct mail plan or even personal plan:

S   –   Situation analysis (where are we now?).

O   –   Objectives (where do we want to go?).

S   –   Strategy (how do we get there?).

T   –   Tactics (the details of the strategy – marcomms mix).

A   –   Action (the details of tactics – implementation – how to ensure excellent execution – systems, processes, guidelines and checklists and internal marketing).

C   –   Control (specific measurement and metrics monitored exactly when to see if 'we are getting there or not').

+ 3Ms (the three key resources):

Men and women (human resources).

Money (budgets).

Minutes (timescales).

And now, if you so choose, you can see this on video, in a bit more detail, in four minutes at **www.PRSmith.org/SOSTAC**, or watch it later and continue reading.

SOSTAC®'s **simple structure is applicable at different levels.** In each chapter in Part 2 of this book, SOSTAC® is applied at a lower level for each of the communications tools, an advertising plan, a direct mail plan, etc. SOSTAC® can also be used to check other plans to see if they are comprehensive

FIGURE 10.1   Visit **www.PRSmith.org/ SOSTAC** and watch the 4-minute video

and cover the key items that every plan needs. You don't have to use the same terminology, but SOSTAC® should help the development of a logical structure combined with the key elements of a plan.

SOSTAC® provides an outline or a structure for a comprehensive plan. A real plan requires a lot of detail, and the first component, the situation analysis, is so important that it can take up half of the total plan (now this can be dumped into the appendices at the back of the plan or kept in the front half of the plan – but either way the situation analysis must be thorough). Objectives and strategies should be written in a concise manner, while the tactics and action plans can require a lot of details. Control, feedback and monitoring mechanisms should be built into the plan so that everyone knows what is going to be measured when, by whom, and most importantly, what happens when the numbers go up or down? Who takes action? Who reports to whom? Managers need to know if the plan is succeeding or failing early on rather than at the end of the year, when it is too late. So SOSTAC® and the 3Ms provide a simple structure for building an integrated marketing communications plan.

So SOSTAC® + 3Ms works for any type of product or service in both **consumer and business-to-business markets,** as demonstrated in the short case studies used in this book. Although the case studies provide only an outline plan, they show how easily SOSTAC® can be applied to either planning the overall marketing communications or just planning a campaign for a single communications tool such as direct mail. Let us consider now each SOSTAC® component in more detail.

Note:
Several extracts in this chapter are taken from the two SOSTAC® books by PR Smith:

> SOSTAC® Guide to Your Perfect Digital Marketing Plan (2015)
> SOSTAC® Guide to Writing The Perfect Marketing Plan (2013)

> **www.PRSmith.org/SOSTAC**

The 3Ms

As mentioned above, the 3Ms, the three key resources, consist of:

1 men and women (human resources);
2 money (budgets);
3 minutes (timescales).

Men/women are the human resources: who is required to do what? It means professional men and women skilled and capable of handling specific activities. Some can be drawn from within the organization; others have to be brought in from an agency or consultancy or recruited as full-time members of staff. Many organizations may not have this calibre of person or, if they do, these people may be kept so busy that they cannot do any additional tasks. Is it worth asking over-busy people to give half their attention to a project or asking under-qualified and underutilized people to have a go? Perhaps the marketing communications task is too important to be casual? There is no doubt about the importance and limited supply of the human resource.

Minutes, the third M, is the most limited resource – time. Is there enough time to do the job, to carry out the research, to develop credibility, to nurture a twitter following, to develop a new pack, to prepare properly for a good mailshot, etc? Crystal clear timescales and deadlines are critical. Without them any plan becomes uncontrollable, because there are no time-related milestones. Timescales for objectives, and deadlines for each activity (eg proposals, concept development, concept testing, regional testing, national roll-out, European launch), are required. How much lead time do you need if you want to launch a new toy at Christmas? The product has to be ready by February, for the New York Toy Show, when the major US retailers place their Christmas stock orders. A new pack can take three to six months. So you may still need a total of 12–14 months to develop the pack and exhibitions. On a separate note, many organizations are using 90-day plans, reviewing intently and revising the plan every 90 days.

Money means budgets, and senior management will tend to scan budgets first and foremost. There are many different ways of setting marketing communications budgets, and there is not a generally agreed methodology but rather a whole range of approaches that can be described as either scientific or heuristic.

Managers tasked with setting a budget ask themselves a series of 'What if?' questions about what would happen if a particular strategy and series of tactics are pursued. A combination of judgement, experience and rational evaluation is applied to develop an appropriate budgeting method for organizations.

Budget setting

Budgeting

Outlined below are the most common approaches to budgeting:

1 Objective and task – identifying the overall objectives and then breaking these down into specific tasks and calculating the budget accordingly. For example, to sell x million cans of Coke would require x per cent levels of awareness, which would require x number of impressions, which would require x amount of advertising, which would cost £x. This is sometimes called the 'ideal' or 'task' approach.

2 Modelling involves the use of a variety of econometric and simulation techniques to determine how various budget levels may affect performance (eg sales). An example of this is Unilever's AMTES area market-testing model.

3 Profit optimization tries to find the optimum marketing spend that would generate the most profit. It is based on ensuring that the marginal revenue derived from each

marketing communications activity exceeds the marginal cost.

4   Percentage of sales is a crude but quick way of calculating a budget. For example, taking 5 per cent of £1 million forecasted sales means the marketing budget is £50,000. In B2B markets, the percentage ranges from 0.5 to 2 per cent, and in B2C markets it ranges from 5 to 20 per cent.

5   Competitive parity analyses competitors' marketing communications spends. Basically, it suggests that if an organization wants to match a competitor it should spend the same amount as that competitor.

6   Affordability is usually driven by accountants, who draw up business plans, work out profitability and then allocate some budget to marketing based on what is left over or affordable. This is the opposite of the objective and task method. It is based upon what is affordable after taking all costs and an amount of profit away from sales.

7   Payback period is the time taken for an integrated campaign to pay back the costs (or budget) of the marketing communications.

8   Arbitration requires a senior member of staff to arbitrate between different views of the marketing team and the rest of the business.

9   Some academics categorize these different budgeting approaches as scientific and heuristic. Scientific planning approaches include: objective and task; modelling; payback period; and profit optimization. Heuristic planning approaches include: percentage of sales; competitive parity; affordability; and arbitration.

ROI

Marketers inevitably have to justify to the financial director the actual return on investment (ROI) of the marketing communications investment. ROI calculates the profit (created from the extra sales generated from the integrated marketing communications campaigns) as a percentage of the investment. This can be done for the whole mix or, more easily, for a specific marketing communications tool such as an advertising campaign or even a tool such as exhibitions (see 'costs' in Chapter 18, p. 491).

The usefulness of ROI is discussed in the section 'Control' later in this chapter.

In reality several budgeting approaches are used. Although a manager might use the ideal task approach, the review panel (of senior management) will immediately convert it into a percentage figure, compare it with the competition's spend and ask 'Can we really afford it?' and 'Does it deliver the required level of profits?' It is not unusual to find the initial budget request cut back by senior management as other divisions and departments compete internally for limited funds for the following year's marketing. Few companies have sophisticated optimum profit models that attempt to identify the optimum spend.

Allocating budget between online and offline marketing

The answer lies in where customers are spending their time consuming media, interacting with colleagues and engaging with particular types of brands. This determines where the budget should be allocated; for example if a particular audience spends 50 per cent of its time on online then 50 per cent of that target market's budget should go online.

Allocating budget between customer retention and customer acquisition

Another interesting question is how to split the budget between customer retention and customer acquisition. If selling to existing customers is supposed to be on average six to seven times more profitable than selling to new customers, there is a school of thought that suggests that marketers should spend at least equal resources on 1) keeping existing customers happy (eg CRM) and 2) acquiring new customers. Businesses like Amazon reportedly pay £50 to acquire a customer, and Virgin pays up to £150 (a free laptop), while Reichheld (2006) estimated the Dell average customer to be worth $210 (five-year net present value), with a detractor (someone speaking negatively about Dell) costing $57 and a promoter generating $328. In the world of online marketing it is increasingly easy to calculate the cost of customer acquisition. See the section 'Control' at the end of the chapter.

Allocating budgets to social media

A burning question emerging across all markets is 'How much resource should we allocate to social media?' It really depends on the strategy and how active an organization wants to be. At a minimum, any marketer needs to have someone listening to conversations, participating in ultimately driving the discussions.

The old 'shouting' model (advertising and PR) is no longer as effective as it once was. Today's marketing models involve careful listening to customers (and prospects) online (as well as offline) and giving fast responses to changing moods, identifying emerging needs, issues and trends that are occurring online continually. Marketers don't have a choice. This is not a luxury set of tools. Here's a selection of 'must have' approaches to listening taken from the PR Smith blog. The old marketing ship is sinking:

1 listen to customer service;
2 listen to customer feedback;
3 listen to customer communities;
4 listen to local chatter (Twitter);
5 listen to multiple websites (feed readers);
6 listening to influencers;
7 paid-for listening tools for sentiment analysis, such as Radian6 and SM2;
8 free listening tools (Social Mention, Twittersearch, BoardReader)

See Social Listening Skills (Smith, 2014a) for more information on each of the approaches.

FIGURE 10.2   As mentioned on page 21, the old marketing ship is sinking

Photo courtesy of DavyMac.com

Situation analysis

The situation analysis needs to be comprehensive. In-depth analysis of customers, competitors, distributors, channels, the organization's performance, strengths and weaknesses as well as external opportunities and threats including trends.

Arguably the greatest marketing book ever, *The Art of War*, was written over 2,000 years ago by the Chinese military strategist Sun Tzu (translated version Wing, 1989). Most senior marketers have a copy of it on their shelves. It has become a classic read, particularly for some enlightened marketing managers. Interestingly confrontation, or war, is seen as a last resort and the best military strategies win the war without any bloodshed. They win wars through intelligence.

Sun Tzu effectively confirms why the situation analysis needs to be comprehensive.

Here's an excerpt:

Those who triumph,
compute at their headquarters
a great number of factors
prior to a challenge.

Those who are defeated,
compute at their headquarters
a small number of factors
prior to a challenge.

Much computation brings triumph.
Little computation brings defeat.
How much more so with no computation at all.

By observing only this,
I can see triumph or defeat.

'Much computation' or much analysis is required.

The better the analysis, the easier the decisions will be later. Decisions about strategy and tactics become a lot easier when you know your customers, your competitors, your competencies and resources as well as market trends. That's why half your plan should be devoted to the situation analysis. It doesn't have to be at the front of the plan (you can dump a lot of it in the appendices) but the detailed analysis must be carried out if you are to succeed.

Smith (2015)

Hence almost half of the marketing communications plan should be devoted to the situation analysis.

The first year you do this analysis it will be particularly challenging, but as you find better (and often free) resources for highly relevant information, it gets easier, the intelligent information gets stronger and consequently, you make better-informed decisions. This ultimately boosts your results.

The marketing communications plan does not require a full **SWOT analysis,** which is usually found in the full marketing plan. The situation analysis in the marketing communications plan must keep the focus on communications aspects such as performance (identifying which elements of the communications mix work best), target markets and positioning. It should certainly include an explanation of the product or service's positioning – how the product is perceived in the minds of the target market. Lucozade was positioned as a sick child's drink until the marketing people saw a bigger opportunity and repositioned it as a healthy adult's drink. Perceptual maps plot where different brands and product types are positioned on certain criteria, as shown in Figure 10.3.

The situation analysis can include a **PEST** analysis specifically relevant to communications, eg political (what new laws or regulations affect communications); how economic fluctuations might affect media and messages; social trends and changes in attitudes and media usage; and technology's fast-changing impact on communications.

A vital part of any analysis is the market and its structure. How is it segmented? What are the most suitable segments that can become target markets? Are the target markets big enough? Are they profitable enough? Are they vulnerable to competition? Do the existing distribution and communications channels serve them properly? Are customers satisfied in each target market? Do they intend to repurchase? Who is involved in the decision-making unit (DMU)? Do the key opinion leaders and opinion formers support the brand?

Segmentation and target marketing

Segmentation and target marketing are so important that they appear almost everywhere in a marketing plan: in the situation analysis in detail, in the objectives briefly and in the strategy (as a fundamental component); they are also referred to in all tactical campaigns and events.

Target marketing involves the division of a large market into smaller market segments. Each segment has its own distinct needs and/or its patterns of response to varying marketing mixes. The most attractive segments are targeted according to the organization's resources. Attractive target markets are those that will generally be more profitable,

FIGURE 10.3   A perceptual map showing Lucozade's classic repositioning from a sick child's drink (when the UK had a disproportionately large child population) to a healthy adult's drink (when the UK demographic shifted to a disproportionately large young adult population)

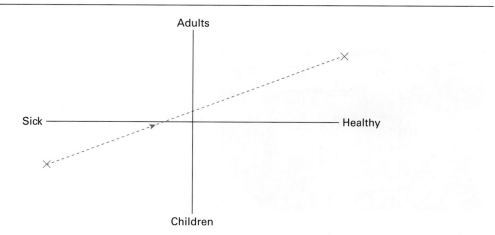

eg segments located closer to the organization, or loyal customer groups, or heavy users of a particular product or service. Targeting reduces wastage of resources (eg money spent on mass advertising) and, ultimately, it increases sales, since better-prospect customers are contacted. Segmentation and target marketing are absolutely fundamental approaches to marketing. Some communication channels are more wasteful than others, eg TV, but the **Target Group Index (TGI)** (see Chapter 6) helps to identify what kind of brands people buy, the papers they read, the programmes they watch, etc. As mass markets fragment and splinter into mini-markets or segments, and technology provides more tailored communications, there is less requirement for mass marketing and mass communications. The ability to segment a market accurately is a key skill that marketers need to spend time on again and again, revisiting their marketplace and thinking about how it can be broken into segments.

Segment attractiveness

Ideally, segments should satisfy the following criteria:

- *Measurable.* Is it quantifiable? Can buyers who fall into this category or segment be identified?

- *Substantial.* How many buyers fall into this segment? Is there a sufficient number of buyers in the segment to warrant special attention and targeting?

- *Accessible.* Can this group be contacted? Can they be isolated or separated from other non-targeted markets? Are there specific media and distribution channels that provide access to them?

- *Relevant.* The benefits of the product or service being offered must be relevant to the target. There is no point picking measurable, accessible and substantial segments if they have no interest in what is being offered in the first place. Know your own customers. Knowing the ideal customer's profile is fundamental to success. Some database companies actually carry out 'profiling' or an analysis of an organization's own customers into groups with distinctive profiles. This helps in targeting the appropriate message through the appropriate medium.

Some segments are obvious. Cat food is bought by cat owners, petrol is bought by motorists, and heavy-duty cranes are bought by both large construction companies and leasing companies. Other segments are less obvious. Expensive cars are bought by high-income groups, while cheaper cars are bought by both high-income groups (as a second or third car) and low-income groups. Who are the heavy users, eg who are the 9 per cent of the UK adult population who drink 65 per cent of the lager consumed? Who are the buyers? Gift boxes of chocolates are bought for women by men. Who are the deciders? Cola drinkers may tend to be young, but who does the buying, who makes the decision, who influences and who pays? This is where segmentation focuses on the decision-making unit.

£50 Rembrandt

A Rembrandt probably would not sell (even for £50) in the wrong target market, whereas in the right target market it would fetch several million pounds.

Decision-making units

The DMU is made up of influencers, advisers, deciders, users, buyers and payers. It applies to all types of markets (industrial, consumer, products and services). A baby's pram may be used by mother and child, bought by the mother and father, influenced by the grandmother, and decided on by the whole family. Similarly, the purchase of a new photocopier may have been instigated by a secretary who keeps complaining to the boss about the old machine breaking down. The end user may be several secretaries; the decider may be the financial director; the buyer may be the organization's professional buyer or the managing director. In some organizations the DMU may be a committee. In other organizations there is a central decision maker, or there may be a decentralized approach with each branch or region making its own decisions. The acronym SPADE (starter, payer, adviser, decider, end user) helps to identify some of the different members of the decision-making unit.

The DMU can consist of several people or committees, or it can sometimes be just one person. There is one other influential member of a business-to-business or industrial DMU, and that is the 'gatekeeper', who acts as a screen and sorts out unsolicited sales pitches from more important incoming communications. The gatekeeper is often a secretary or personal assistant, who may decide whether to interrupt a manager with a phone call or allow a direct mailshot to land on the manager's desk.

Global segments

Segments do not always have to be localized or defined on a geographic basis. Values, attitudes and lifestyles (VALs) can be used to identify cross-cultural common characteristics. For example, the advertising agency Euro RSCG identified the four main European psychographic segments as follows:

1 modern materialists: 117 million (acquire goods and services);

2 new radicals: 50 million (concerned with change and reform);

3 get what you deserve: 110 million (more conservative and resistant to change);

4 bygones: 83 million (oldest, most moralistic group, threatened by consumerism).

Global idiosyncrasies complicate the supposedly simple global segments. Chapter 9 looks at the international arena in more detail.

Global convergence

'So tastes are converging and to discover that all you have to do is talk to my teenage son. I have taken him with me on trips all over the world and I keep introducing him to a local boy who he can spend the day with to learn something about the life in those countries. And in every country he's visited, whether it is Jakarta, Indonesia; São Paulo, Brazil; Manila in the Philippines or a small town in The Netherlands, he has spent the day exactly the same way. They have gone to a local shopping mall, played video games and eaten a McDonald's hamburger.'

Kanter (2001)

B2C (consumer) segments

Segmenting markets into groups of buyers and targeting those groups that are more likely to be the best customers are absolutely vital if marketing communications are to be both effective and efficient. Markets can be broken into segments using many different criteria. Here are some typical consumer criteria:

- demographics:
  - age;
  - job type (socio-economic groupings);
- geodemographics: geographical location, type of neighbourhood and demographic data;
- psychographics: attitudes, beliefs, VALS (values, attitudes and lifestyles – see Chapter 6, 'The Target Group Index' on p. 177);
- behavioural: benefits sought (see Chapter 4, 'The toothpaste test' on p. 107); usage frequency; readiness to buy; loyal vs non-loyal.

The biggest improvements in segmenting and targeting are coming from social media and new commercial database companies that can offer extremely granular targeting facilities. Facebook can now offer several hundred criteria or 'filters' to tighten your targeting including: location, interests (business, hobbies, relationships, technology, fitness, food and drink, entertainment, sports, shopping and fashion), behaviours (travel, mobile device, digital activities), demographics (age, gender, language, education, generation, work, relationships) and a lot more. For the full list see 'How to Target Very Very Specific Audiences on Facebook', **www.PRSmith.org/blog**. Meanwhile, see how new databases can give access to very precisely targeted really hot prospects (in the next boxed story).

B2B (industrial) segments

In industrial markets and business-to-business markets, segmentation criteria are different but nonetheless vital. Here are some commonly used segmentation criteria for industrial markets:

- type of company (Standard Industrial Code – SIC);
- size of company;

How can you target frequent flyers who might take a train instead?

'If you were trying to sell train tickets to frequent flyers, who are the ideal prospects? Your ability to ask great questions, find databases and interrogate them in new ways to profile prospects is a great skill. Look away. Stop and think for a moment.

How about asking data owners of major mobile networks (eg WEVE) to find "mobile users who disappear in Heathrow and reappear in Edinburgh in the time a flight would take". Then segment these travellers and promote highly relevant offers via their mobiles. Add a mobile commerce component enabling prospects to directly purchase a rail ticket, or just wave their smartphone at the ticket counter or transport kiosk. Could mobile technologies be the future of retail?'

PR Smith (2015)

Floating targets

Many markets have a floating percentage who move in and out of the market. Take insurance. Like most financial services, it is considered to be so dull and off-putting that most people would rather not think about it. So, if customers reluctantly review, say, their insurance suppliers every four years, then you have only got 25 per cent of the market active each year. Divide this by 12 months and you have only got approximately 2 per cent of the market active in any particular month. That's why there is no point advertising specific product benefits when the 'active' market is so small. Instead, many brands just want to maintain awareness levels, so that they are at least considered when the customer becomes ready to buy.

- structure of company (autocratic vs centralized);
- location or geographical area;
- heavy or light users;
- existing suppliers;
- benefits sought;
- title or position of key decision makers.

Again, many marketers are creating new targets – their own lists of prospects – often created from visitors that land on a website and subsequently used in remarketing ad campaigns. Or their digital body language (see page 323) identifies each visitor having a particular level of interest (or readiness to buy) derived from their click behaviour. Marketing automation is increasingly being used to automatically send alerts, e-mails, or trigger telephone calls to offer help to visitors.

Most airlines start their targeting with two basic different segments on each plane: the business traveller and the leisure traveller. These segments can be further segmented, eg the business traveller may be divided into club class, executive class and so on. These can be further divided into different benefit segments, eg those who want a fast check-in, those who want frequent flights, those who want top-class in-flight service, those who want a reasonable price, and those who want 'seamless travel' (connections for the next flight, cars and hotels all booked for them). Most travellers want all of these benefits, but usually consider some more important than others, so much so that they choose one airline over another because of a particular key benefit. If this type of flier proves to be significant in number, then it is a valid segment. The organization then decides if it has the resources and sustainable advantages suitable to target this segment.

To continue the airline example, Transavia Airlines segmented various companies that might have had some connection with the Netherlands (and therefore might have had a need for its services) into five different target groups of business fliers and travel agents. As shown in Figure 10.4, a different communications strategy was developed for each segment. A gift/food hamper and a boxed presentation were delivered personally by the sales manager to those accounts (customers) that warranted this kind of attention (resources). Lighter users had a smaller mailing. Top travel agents got a boxed mailing, while other travel agents just got a mailing.

Now when you layer in click data (or a visitor's digital body language) you can see how automated marketing systems are growing so rapidly. Whether an e-mail is opened, clicked on, website page explored, next step taken, determines the next piece of communication – all set up by carefully laid sets of rules, built around behaviour (and non-behaviour).

FIGURE 10.4   Business traveller segments and communications mixes

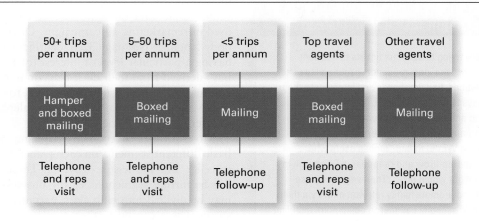

Segmentation requires careful analysis

In reality, all the target customers rarely fall neatly into one single segment, eg 67 per cent of the *Sun*'s customers might be C2DEs and 33 per cent ABC1s. As mentioned, not all buyers of small cars are in lower- to middle-income groups. Many small cars are bought by mid- to higher-income groups as a second or third car in the family. There is, however, usually a core target made up of heavy users or easily convertible prospects; Lyons Tetley's Quickbrew tea is targeted at women aged 35+ (core C1C2D). Some markets have several people involved in the decision making (DMUs). For example, the advertising campaign promoting Shell's free miniature classic sports car collection was aimed at ABC1 fathers aged between 25 and 64 with children aged three to nine; within this they also had to ensure high coverage of high-mileage drivers (heavy users). Other markets have customers who drift into the marketplace and then out again, as in the case of financial services.

However, sophisticated technology can help the marketer today by adding new segmentation variables on top of the traditional variables. For example, it will be possible to segment buyers by their brand purchases and their stockholding (in the fridge) as well as the usual age, income and geographic criteria. Infomediaries (owners of information), such as manufacturers of fridge-freezers with inbuilt online capacity to reorder automatically when products are taken out of the fridge, hold valuable data about customers' stock levels. If consumers agree to share this information with other third parties, this opens up interesting segmentation opportunities. For example, Pepsi might like to make a special offer to a ripe segment like Coca-Cola consumers who are out of stock. It's worth considering how this might apply in the B2B sector, eg office stationery or software supplied by an intermediary.

Objectives

After analysing the situation through secondary and primary sources (see Chapter 6), a clear picture of 'where we are now' emerges. The next step is to define as specifically as possible 'Where do we want to go?' Ideally objectives should be quantified in terms of success or failure criteria. Timescales should also be set. Clearly defined objectives make the management task of control much easier. Drawing up objectives for the first time is a difficult task. In future years, the previous year's objectives and corresponding results will help to make the planning job a little easier, as everyone has a better idea of what is realistic and what is not. Establishing clear objectives is necessary to give a focus to the organization or division. Clear objectives also give direction to subsequent creative efforts. Some marketing managers and agencies break objectives into many different types; other marketers use just one set of objectives (and sometimes without quantification or numbers attached). As a discipline it is useful to break up objectives so that performance can be measured more accurately. Objectives should be SMART:

S – specific

M – measurable

A – actionable

R – realistic

T – time specific

Two types of objectives are examined here: marketing objectives and communications objectives.

Marketing objectives

Typical marketing objectives refer to sales, market share, distribution penetration, launching a number of new products, and so on. For example, marketing objectives might be:

- to increase unit sales of product/brand X by 10 per cent over the next 12 months;
- to increase market share by 5 per cent over the next 12 months;
- to generate 500 new enquiries each month;
- to increase distribution penetration from 25 per cent to 50 per cent within 12 months;
- to establish a network of distributors covering Germany, France, The Netherlands and Italy during the first six months, followed by Switzerland, Austria, Belgium and Luxembourg in the second six months.

It is worth noting that not all marketing objectives are growth orientated. In Denmark, electricity boards no longer pride themselves on how much electricity they sell but on how little. Product withdrawals are another example where objectives are not attached to year-on-year growth. In very competitive mature markets, with new entrants appearing on the market, maintaining market share and consolidating sales might be more appropriate than expecting big growth. Given that marketing is shifting towards retention of profitable customers and deselection of unprofitable customers, the emphasis in some companies has moved from growth in turnover or sales to growth in profit or ROI.

Communications objectives

These typically refer to how the communications should affect the mind of the target audience, eg generate awareness, attitudes, interest or trial. Again, these tend to be most useful when quantified. DAGMAR (defining advertising goals for measuring advertising responses) and AIDA (attention, interest, desire, action) provide yardsticks for communications objectives by trying to separate the various mental stages a buyer goes through before buying. (The response hierarchy models are discussed in Chapter 4.)

The mental stages suggested by DAGMAR and AIDA are as follows:

DAGMAR	AIDA
Unawareness	–
Awareness	Attention
Comprehension	Interest
Conviction	Desire
Action	Action

Here are some examples of communications objectives:

- to increase awareness from 35 per cent to 50 per cent within eight weeks of the campaign launch among 25- to 45-year-old ABC1 women;
- to position the service as the friendliest on the market within a 12-month period among 70 per cent of heavy chocolate users;
- to reposition Guinness from an old, unfashionable, older man's drink to a fashionable younger person's drink over two years among all 25- to 45-year-old male drinkers;
- to maintain brand X as the preferred brand (or number one brand) of photocopiers among at least 50 per cent of current UK buyers in companies with 1,000-plus employees;
- to include Bulgarian wines in the repertoire of possible wine purchases among 20 per cent of ABC1 wine buyers within 12 months;
- to support the launch of a new shop by generating 50 per cent awareness in the immediate community one week before the launch;

- to announce a sale and create 70 per cent awareness one day before the sale starts;
- to reposition the *European* as an upmarket business paper (from a general mid-market newspaper) (see Figure 10.5).

The *European* newspaper positioned itself in new market space, where the management saw a gap in the market. But was there a market in the gap? No other paper was offering a high-quality, European business newspaper. However, we have to ask: was there a real need for a weekly European newspaper at that time? The *European* has now ceased publication.

Does a gap in the tea-drinking market always equal a market in the gap?

If 85 per cent of the world's tea drinkers like hot tea and 15 per cent of the world's tea drinkers like iced tea, it doesn't necessarily mean that there is a screaming gap for luke-warm tea.

Objectives can cover a variety of goals. It is useful to separate marketing objectives from marketing communications objectives. Detailed, specific objectives ensure that the subsequent choice of strategy is clearly focused.

Strategy

Strategy summarizes 'how we get there' – how the objectives will be achieved. Strategy drives tactics in the same direction. Strategy summarizes tactics. Communications strategy helps to harmonize and integrate all of the tactical communications tools. Communications strategy can include selection of target markets, positioning, selection of communications tools, sequence of communications tools (are different tools used at different stages?), and more.

Most of us are afraid of strategy...

'...because we don't feel confident outlining one unless we're sure it's going to work.'

Godin (2009)

Marketing communications strategies are hard to find. Often the strategy is retrospective in so far as the tactics are planned and then a strategy is created to make sense of the tactics. This is far from ideal. One aide-mémoire for the components of marketing communications strategy is TOPPP SITE taken from the SOSTAC® Guide to Your Perfect Digital Marketing Plan (Smith, 2015).

FIGURE 10.5   Repositioning the *European* newspaper from a medium-quality newspaper to an upmarket European newspaper

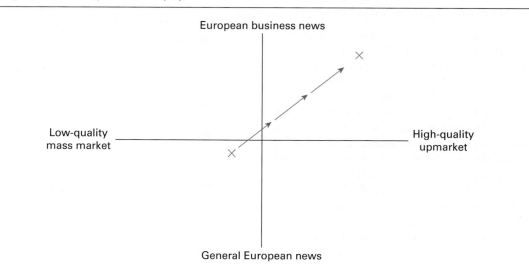

TOPPP SITE (nine key strategic components)

Here are nine key components to consider when building your digital marketing strategy. You do not have to use all of them in your digital marketing strategy. In fact, the strategy excerpts I'll show you later only include a selection of these nine key components. You may find some components overlap/integrate. This is good. Your strategy doesn't have to be in the same order as TOPPP SITE. Feel free to move the components around to suit your strategy. Now let's consider each of the nine components to help you to build a crystal clear digital marketing strategy:

- Target markets (essential).
- Objectives (it's helpful to summarize what objectives the strategy should deliver).
- Positioning (essential).
- Processes (strategy can involve new processes such as marketing automation, remarketing, split testing).
- Partnership (strategic alliances and marketing marriages can make marketing easy).
- Sequence (or stages, eg Develop Credibility before Raising Visibility).
- Integration (of data and marketing across all 10 communications tools).
- Tactical tools (or channels: list the priority tools: TV, PPC, SEO, e-mail or PR, social media and content marketing etc).
- Engagement (what level of the ladder of engagement is required?).

Ideally the communications strategy should consider all of these aspects and then succinctly answer the selected components. Objectives, by the way, don't have to be regurgitated, but do keep an eye on them, as any strategy that ignores objectives is a waste of time. Razor-sharp strategies are required now more than ever before. A lot of people work very long hours, and they are very loyal and committed people, but if the strategy is wrong all that hard tactical work is wasted.

Getting positioning wrong can destroy a business, and getting it right can save a business. Positioning is strategic. Careful analysis is required to find a positioning that is actually needed by customers

> ## Working harder won't save a bad strategy
>
> 'There's no point rowing harder if you're rowing in the wrong direction.'
>
> Ohmae (2000)

> ## Our biggest mistake was wrong positioning
>
> 'E-cigarette company Blu-e-cig CEO, Jacob Fuller, says "Our biggest mistake was to call it an e-cigarette – an alternative method to give up smoking." Blu-e-cig now want to reposition their product from: "an alternative method to give up smoking" to "a lifestyle choice for smokers".'
>
> Benady (2014)

and is not delivered by the competition; ideally, that the organization can genuinely deliver better than competitors. Brands are strategically positioned to fill different gaps in the marketplace.

Developing good marketing communications strategies requires careful consideration. Although occasionally frustrating, it is worthwhile because it delivers many benefits. It is important to remember this because developing and agreeing strategic decisions costs time, money and energy. Many marketers have an inner urge to get on with the job, get creative, develop wonderful advertising campaigns, wacky sales promotions, exciting websites and apps, delightful new sales literature, sensational seminars, webinars and events. Other marketers are under pressure to get out and talk to customers, bring in some sales, generate revenues and justify their existence. So seemingly self-indulgent navel gazing such as strategic contemplation may not always appear worthwhile – in the immediate term.

The benefits of a strong marcomms strategy

Strategy is not short term. It is medium to longer term. A good strategy reaps many benefits including:

- Gets 'more bangs for your buck' – delivers a stronger, clearer and more co-ordinated message as all tactics pull together.
- Saves time – speeds up tactical choices by giving direction to all tactical decisions.
- Saves money – Plan in advance and buy early (no 'rush rates').

Target markets

Target markets need to be defined very clearly. Today we have many new variables (or filters) to help marketers identify targets (see Targeting in Chapter 17, p. 464 and see p. 342). Time and effort spent carefully analysing and discussing who is/are the most ideal target market/s is time well spent.

Positioning

Positioning is so strategic that you really don't want to be changing this each year. Positioning means precisely how you want to be positioned (or perceived) in the minds of your target customers. Note: positioning is the foundation for brand propositions (what's in it for the customer) and ultimately, the customer experience (CX). In fact, defining the brand, the OVP and the CX are part of strategy. OVP and CX also influence the marketing mix (tactical decisions), for example exclusive products online; differential pricing; exclusive online promotions; prioritizing which channels; online distribution partners etc. These details are addressed in your Tactics section.

The classic repositioning: from sick child to healthy adult

Lucozade repositioned itself from a 'sick child's drink' to a 'healthy adult's drink'. They followed the market trends: the demographic shift from a massive child market (baby boom) in the '60s to a bulging 40-year-old market in the noughties (2000s). They also followed the trend towards 'healthy living'. This repositioning strategy drives changes across all of the marketing mix tactics from chemist shop distribution and 'mother and child' ads to sports celebrity ads and Coca-Cola-style distribution into shops, restaurants and offices.

Objectives

It is always worth double checking that your strategy actually delivers the 'big' objectives (Mission and Vision) as well as the typical sales, market share and ROI KPIs. Strategy without some reference to objectives is, not surprisingly, unlikely to achieve those objectives. Hence some organizations like to see the main objectives referred to when presenting their strategies. Deciding which is a priority objective – customer acquisition or customer retention – is a strategic decision (see more later).

Process

If you are introducing a new approach, a new process, a system or even new way of thinking, this can be strategic, eg introducing marketing automation or insisting analytics are used to measure, understand and drive all future decisions; nurturing a 'constant beta culture'; or introducing a new customer service process integrating telephone, Twitter and Facebook. See the Action section for the detailed process of producing great marketing content.

Finally, do you need a new marketing team structure or to employ external agencies to manage the process of marketing?

Partnerships

Partnership – introducing or strengthening or reducing strategic partnership/marketing marriages/ marketing alliances. Are there potential partners out there whose customers would welcome your organization's products or services? Selecting the right partner can firstly give you access to a much bigger target market and secondly, strengthen your brand. But remember partnerships have to benefit both parties, with clear goals, roles and responsibilities – 'the devil is in the detail'.

Sequence or stages

Develop credibility before raising visibility. How many businesses get that one wrong? How many major TV ad campaigns or content marketing and social media platforms drive traffic to websites that don't work? In addition there may be other steps such as building awareness, then brand preference before seeking sales, or other stages in a campaign such as acquiring endorsers, establishing relationships and advocates, followed by campaign rollout. Another approach to some of the stages you want to move customers through is Dave Chaffey's RACE (Reach means increasing awareness and encouraging visits; Act means initial interaction; Convert means conversion to sales; Engage means post-sales engagement designed to create long-term loyalty and advocacy). Customer acquisition vs customer retention decisions will be determined by the objectives you have set earlier.

Integration

Integrating customer data online and offline is a strategic decision. From click behaviour data (digital body language), to registration data, to social media data to CRM (Customer Relationship Management) to purchase behaviour, to post-purchase contact data. Layering it with external data from third-party databases. 'Having social data as well as a complete history of your leads' and customers' activity in one place is invaluable to your company, because it means you can finally stop wasting time on what doesn't work, as well as equipping your sales team with the information to help them close more deals' (Toner, 2014).

Process and integration

Integrate social data with your CRM or contacts database. Introduce an integrated customer profiling process into both outbound and inbound campaigns.

Tactical tools

Tactics (or channels) will be explored in more detail in the Tactics section. Your marketing strategy should, however, identify which are the major tactical tools (or channels) you will be using. Your brand, the customer experience you wish to deliver, the nature of your audience and the strategy you wish to adopt will define which tactical tools to use in your campaigns. Should you prioritize with a major PPC ad campaign, e-mail campaigns, nurture an affiliate marketing programme, or develop social media campaigns based on some great new marketing content delivered via social media? Which social media platform(s) will be prioritized? 'Sales promotion' has largely been replaced by 'content marketing' (free gifts of useful content). Content marketing may well be a major strategic component (assuming it supports the brand and the desired CX).

Engagement

There are different levels of visitor engagement. From encouraging visitors and customers to give ratings and reviews to nurturing advocates to collaborating and co-creating ideas and products. This is the ladder of engagement starting with low-level engagement (ratings and reviews) and at the top of the ladder is collaborative co-creation. You can download a complete chapter from the welcome page on the PR Smith Marketing Facebook page. But also remember that not everyone wants to engage all the time; sometimes visitors just want to complete a task, find some information or just buy something and leave your site. So don't ignore the basics of properly tested, quick, easy-to-use websites and apps.

Engagement boosts sales – social media first-in wins

'Bain found that customers who engage with companies via social media channels spend 20–40 per cent more money with those companies than other customers. They also demonstrate a deeper emotional commitment to the companies, granting them an average 33 points higher NPS® (Net Promoter® Score).'

Barry et al (2011)

What about the X factor (or the CX factor)?

The customer experience is at the heart of your business and your strategy.

What a brand says about itself (through its brand positioning and brand propositions) is less important than the actual experience the brand delivers to its customers across all touchpoints. So although positioning and brand propositions are important they are less important than the actual customers' experiences (CX). The CX establishes the brand experience which needs to be clearly defined. CXM (customer experience management) needs to be integrated and managed across functions, by all staff online and offline. So positioning drives propositions which influence the CX. Some marketers define the CX along with the positioning and propositions.

Others define them separately at the end and add them to their strategy. For those marketers the strategy acronym becomes TOPPP SITE X.

> ### Costco vs Apple customer experience
>
> Costco customers expect bare-bones service in return for low prices, while Apple customers expect high-quality innovative products at relatively high prices. Those are very different customer experiences, but they both delight customers (Brand and Hagen, 2011). And they are delivered to customers consistently online and offline.

Three strategic examples

Taken from SOSTAC® Guide to Your Perfect Digital Marketing Plan (Paul Smith, 2015).

HSBA

Drive prospective traffic via a blend of inbound and outbound marketing via automated marketing and subsequently building incremental profiling via data profiling to ensure added-value relevant offers and timely advice – reassure and reinvigorate customer relationships.

The Great Sportsmanship Programme

Reposition from a book (targeted at sports fans in UK and Ireland) to an educational programme targeting youths with challenges from Ireland, the UK and the UAE via the big five social media platforms: Facebook, blogs, Twitter, YouTube and LinkedIn, with an emphasis on Facebook, to allow youths to self-select their level of engagement for the continual delivery of user-generated content to satisfy the growing global network of schools, clubs, coaches and ambassadors.

XYZ cable TV

Develop credibility before raising visibility. Develop 'XYZ TV – Help' presence integrated across several social media platforms. Improve existing CRM system. Then create a range of social media campaigns over time (integrated with other online activities) to move customers up the ladder of engagement, ultimately including XYZ TV (user-generated content).

Develop 'XYZ TV – Help' website which primarily consists of dedicated video tutorials supported by a distinct 'XYZ TV – Help' Facebook, Twitter and video channel (YouTube) presence.

Develop a blog which is the central hub for all the social media tools (including Facebook, Twitter and YouTube).

There is no one single approach

There is no one single approach to building marketing communications strategies. In fact many companies do not put them together at all. A good communications strategy helps to keep all the subsequent tactical communications tools integrated and moving in the same direction, delivering bigger impacts and reducing costs. A simple way to practise writing marketing communications strategies is to generate several alternative strategies, so that strategic options can be considered. Try generating a bad strategic option so that you can begin to see, first, that there is always more than one strategy available to choose from and, second, that some strategies are better than others.

Tactics

Tactics are the details of strategy. In marketing, communications tactics are the communications tools and channels such as advertising, PR, direct mail, etc. The tactics in the marketing communications plan list what happens when and for how much. They are often best expressed as a Gantt chart, as shown in Figure 10.6. The Tactics section describes the themes, types of campaigns and whether the work will be done in-house (and whether upskilling is required) or out of house via agencies and consultancies.

The Tactics Matrix (Figure 10.7) is designed to help to choose which tactical tools are most useful at various stages of the customers' buying process. The matrix helps marketers to consider, discuss and eventually choose a particular tactical tool to achieve a specific objective. It is work in progress and designed to stimulate discussion.

FIGURE 10.6   Tactical timings of different communication tools

	Jan	Feb	Mar	Apr	May	Jun	Jul	Aug	£
Advertising – TV – Press – PPC									
Social media – Blog – YouTube – Facebook									
Website – SEO – Inbound links									
Sales promotion – Sample drop – Competition – Collection									
Direct marketing – Mailshot – Telesales									
Publicity (and public relations)									
Sponsorship									
Exhibitions									
Packaging									
Point-of-sale and merchandising									
Internet									
Word of mouth – Viral marketing – CRM NGN									

This is just a shortlist of some of the tactical tools employed by an organization.

Few social media strategies

'MarketingSherpa's US study (December 2008) found that the vast majority of those surveyed rated social media marketing effective at influencing brand reputation, increasing awareness and improving search rankings and site traffic. Although many organizations have a corporate blog or Facebook page, few have strategies in place and even fewer have written social media policies. In fact, only 33 per cent of larger firms had a written policy to manage brand communications, and a mere 13 per cent of smaller businesses had a written policy.'

eMarketer.com (2009)

FIGURE 10.7   Tactics Matrix

Tactics Matrix	BENEFIT →	Reach	Speed	Lead time	Message size	Targeting	Personal-ization	Cost: CPC/CPM	Control	Credibility (message)
OBJECTIVE ↓	TACTIC/CHANNEL ↓									
Awareness/ familiarity	Display ads	High	Medium	Long / Med	Medium	High	Medium	Medium	Medium	Low
	PR	High	Medium	Medium	Large	Low	Low	Low	Low	High
	Sponsorship	High	Low /Med	Long	Small	Low	Low	Medium	Low	Medium
	Social media (content marketing)	Low/Med/ High	Low / Med	Medium	Large	Medium	Med / Low	None	Low / Med	High
Consideration	Search ads & SEO	Low/Med	Medium	Long/Med	Small	High	Medium	Medium	High	Low / Med
	E-mail (AM)	Med	High	Short	Large	High	High	Low	High	Medium
	Website incentives	Low/Med	Low	Medium	Med / Low	Low/Med	High with Auto Marketing	None	High	Medium
	Social media	Low/Med /High	Low	Short / Med	Large	Medium	Med / Low	None	Low / Med	High
	Sales pitch	Low	Medium	Short	NA	High	High	High	High	Med / High
Decision	Search ads & SEO	Med / Low	Medium	Short	Small	High	Medium	Medium	High	Low / Med
	E-mail (AM)	Medium	High	Short	Large	High	High	Low	High	Medium
	Website incentives	Low	Low	Medium	Low	N/A	High with Auto Marketing	N/A	High	N/A
	Telesales	Low/ Med	High	Short / Med	Large	High	High	Low	High	Medium
	Sales pitch	Low	Medium	Short	Low	High	High	High	High	Med / High
	Exhibition	Medium	Medium	Med/Long	Large	High	Low	High	Medium	Med / High
Post-purchase relationship building	Direct mail/e-mail newsletter/ special offers added value	Medium	High	Short (eM) Med (Dmail)	Large	High	High	Low (eMail) High (DM)	High	Medium
	Social media	Low/High	Low	Short/Med	Large	High	Medium	None	Low / Med	High
Post-purchase repeat sales loyalty…adv..	Direct mail/e-mail	Medium	High	Med/Short	Large	High	High	High (DM)	High	Medium
	Social media	Low/High	Med	Short/Med	High	High	Medium	None	Low / Med	High

The Tactics Matrix www.PRSmith.org © PRSmith 2014 v2

Action

Excellent execution of tactics is surprisingly rare. In fact, execution, or 'action' can often prove to be the weakest link in many business's grand plans for success. Strategy summarizes, and gives direction to, 'How you are going to get there?' Tactics are the details of strategy and Action is the details of tactics. The Action section of your plan ensures that the tactics are executed to the highest possible standard.

The Action section includes:

- systems;
- processes;
- guidelines;
- checklists;
- internal marketing.

All of these help to ensure high quality execution (Smith, 2015).

Internal marketing is largely about internal communications and motivation to make sure everyone understands what the marketing activities are all about and everyone knows who has to do what, when and how. This can include mini action plans since each tactic is a mini project which needs professional execution. You don't have to include all the mini projects in the initial plan.

You can add systems, processes, guidelines and checklists, either into the body of the plan or in the appendices at the back, or you can simply issue them later. The Action section of your plan is about ensuring that your plan is executed to a high standard.

'Everything degenerates into work.'

Peter Drucker

In reality the action/implementation of the marketing communications tactics requires an ability to get other people (staff, agencies, printers, etc) to deliver on time and within budget.

Critical path or project plan

Any kind of project planning can be used here, whether critical path or just a Gantt chart. A detailed project plan is required for each tactical communications tool. For example, the production of a mailshot can be as shown in Figure 10.7.

This is just for one mailing. More detailed planning is required if there is a series of mailings. The response handling also needs to be planned carefully. With hybrid and automated marketing systems (see Chapter 17), the responses can be routed to an inbound telesales team, who filter respondents, rank them in terms of urgency, size and location, and pass the enquiry to a relevant salesperson or dispatch further information and update the database for future activities. All of this requires careful planning to ensure sufficient resources are available to make the strategies and tactics actually happen.

Control

Plans should include control systems – how performance will be monitored, measured and controlled. Managers need to know at an early stage (rather than when it's too late) how a campaign is running and whether it is an advertising campaign or a mailshot. If it is not working, it should be stopped. **Control systems need to be in place to help monitor any campaigns or activities** (see Figure 10.8). This is where clear objectives can once again help, since they can usually be broken down into more detailed objectives covering shorter periods of time. Once marketers are armed with clearly defined, precise objectives, money can be spent on measuring performance against the objectives (whether defined as sales, enquiries, awareness, or return on investment, etc).

Marketers can now measure and compare all activities: inbound (social media campaigns) and outbound marketing (ad campaigns), online and offline. If a campaign is focused on boosting brand awareness or repositioning a brand in the mind of the target audience, this can be measured separately through surveys. If the campaign is focused on engagement and/or sales, this can be easily measured by identifying if visitors, enquirers or customers are emerging from each communications tool – assuming the campaign is focused on generating engagement at some level, eg interaction on a website or Facebook page (posting a comment or voting), registering for a newsletter, taking a trial or making a purchase. The web analytics reveal where visitors are coming from, and telesales, reception and sales staff should also always log where new enquiries are coming from (how visitors heard about the business and what key phrases they used to find the website).

Cost per order, cost per enquiry and cost per visitor can be easily calculated. Other variables need to be closely monitored, including:

- cost per order and cost per customer acquisition;
- net promoter score, satisfaction score and recommendation score;
- reputation/social conversation scores (social media monitoring);
- return on investment.

Note that the figures in Figure 10.9 are not real. Over time, professional marketers learn what are realistic conversion ratios of enquirers or website visitors to customers. For example, in Figure 10.9, 1 per cent of visitors generated by search engine optimization (SEO) convert to customers, while only half of 1 per cent of visitors from a viral marketing campaign convert to customers. The figure would probably be higher for visitors generated from PPC campaigns.

Consider SEO. In Figure 10.9, it generates 20,000 visitors and costs £20,000. This gives a cost per visitor of £1 (£20,000 divided by 20,000 visitors). If the site converts 1 per cent of these visitors into customers, then the SEO generates 200 new customers (1 per cent of 20,000 visitors). The cost per order (CPO) generated by SEO is £100 (£20,000 divided by 200 orders).

FIGURE 10.8   An action plan for one communication tool – a mailshot

	Wk 1	Wk 2	Wk 3	Wk 4	Wk 5	Wk 6	Wk 7	Wk 8	Wk 9	Wk 10	Wk 11	Wk 12
Creative brief												
List brief												
List proposal												
Visual concepts												
Visuals approved												
List order												
Final copy/design												
Artwork brief												
Print quotes												
Set artwork proofs												
Receive lists												
Data preparation												
Finished artwork												
Printer brief												
Printer proofs												
Merge purge lists												
Print												
Computer bureau output files												
Live laser proofs												
Mail house brief												
Print delivery												
Laser print letter												
Mail house delivery												
Mail house sort/enclose												
Mail												

FIGURE 10.9   Control systems

Quantified objectives State each quantified objective and its time period	Means of measuring Sales analysis; number of responses; surveys	Frequency of measurement Daily; weekly; monthly; quarterly; annually?	Accountability Who does it?	Cost How much does it cost to measure?	Action? Who needs to be alerted if significant variances are found?

If a viral marketing piece costs £30,000 (to create and seed) and it generates 20 million players of which 10 per cent click through to the website, this generates 2 million visitors. Say only half of 1 per cent convert, because many of them are from international markets not relevant to this service. This generates 10,000 customer 'uniques' (unique visitors). Feel free to fill in the rest of the figures yourself.

The table in Figure 10.9 can be extended. You can create your own, more accurate, analysis by adding another column for percentage of visitors that convert to enquirers (and a percentage of them eventually convert to customers, and a percentage of them convert to repeat customers, at which point the costs decline significantly and large profit margins emerge). A longer list of tactical communications tools can be added, including different exhibition events, different e-mail campaigns, different virals, etc, so that the marketer can see what works best and ultimately do more of what works and stop what doesn't.

Some tactical tools/channels are better than others

Remember, some tactical tools (channels) are better at generating awareness (banner ads) and some are better at closing sales (e-mail with a sales promotion). So customer acquisition may not be the prime goal of some tools (like advertising, PR and sponsorship). Therefore they may have different criteria for success. Be careful not to make decisions, eg to stop using a certain tactical tool based on the wrong criteria.

In fact marketing can be like a football or basketball match. The 'assist' is as important as the goal. So if you can identify players (or tactical channels) that are part of the customer journey, these may be worth investing more in. Multi-channel funnel analysis does just this and helps you to make better decisions.

The lifetime value of potential repeat sales of a customer can give a truer picture of their real value. Remember, lifetime value can include 'share of wallet': other products or services that a customer might be prepared to buy from the same supplier.

You also need a rigorous structured approach to measuring relative satisfaction (compared to competitors) for each stage of the online experience – product search, evaluation, enquiring, purchases, post-purchase communications, after-sales support, etc. You need this more than once a year. Many organizations like to have 90-day plans and then review and modify them every quarter.

FIGURE 10.10 Cost per order/cost per customer acquisition

	Volume of people/ size of audience	Total cost	CPT/CPM (cost per thousand people reached)	Percentage CTR (click-through rate/visit website/ enquiry)	Unique visitors	Cost per visitor/ lead	Conversion rate of visitors to customers	Number of orders/ customers	Cost per order
SEO	n/a	£20,000	n/a	n/a	20,000	£1.00	1%	200	£100
Viral A	20,000,000	£30,000	£1.50	10%	2,000,000	£0.15	0.5 of 1%	10,000	£3
Blog	n/a	£20,000	n/a	n/a	10,000				
Banner ad	100,000	£1,000	£10	1%	1,000				
PPC ad	n/a	n/a	n/a	n/a	n/a				
Opt-in e-mail	10,000	£2,000	£200	2%					
Online sponsorship	50,000	£5,000	£1,000	1%					
E-zine/e-newsletter	1,000	£10,000	£10,000	5%					
Press ad	1,000,000	£5,000	£5.00	1/100th of 1%					
Direct mail List A	10,000	£5,000	£500	2%					
Telemarketing – outbound	5,000	£20,000	£4,000	10%					
Exhibition B	6,000	£18,000	£3,000	n/a					

Net promoter score, satisfaction score and recommendation score

It is important to monitor satisfaction scores (though remember that the satisfaction criteria can change and leave an old system irrelevant if not updated). Some blue-chip marketing directors like to keep a simple system monitoring just what percentage of customers would recommend the organization. Other marketers take advocacy and 'detractors' (customers who feel negatively about the organization or brand) and develop reporting systems that combine both variables to highlight a net promoter score (Reichheld, 2006).

Sentiment analysis – social conversation scores (social media monitoring)

Marketers need to keep abreast of what is being said about their brands, their organizations and their staff (as well as the competition) in the vast array of conversations in social media platforms around the world. Marketers need to know about the quantity and intensity of commentary about brand or product. In addition to the free services of Google Alert, there are other social monitoring tools, including Google Blog Search, Twitter Search, Yahoo Pipes, BlogPulse, BoardReader and BoardTracker. There are also some more comprehensive licence fee systems with their own scoring systems, which include Radian6, Market Sentinel and Precise Media. So I continue to ask: if a conversation takes place online and you're not there to hear it, did it actually happen?

Return on investment

As mentioned in Chapter 1, marketers must learn to speak the language of the boardroom. This includes ROI on marketing expenditure. Can marketers demonstrate rigorous professional discipline and track what communications campaigns deliver a better ROI than others? Can marketers convince the board that the return from investment in marketing is better than the return generated by investing the money elsewhere (eg in a high-interest deposit account)? It is possible to calculate the cost per order, profit per order and cumulative profit

> ### Social media control myth
>
> 'One of the most common fears I focus on defeating among executives and brand managers is that in new media brands lose control by publishing content and engaging in social networks. The general sentiment is that by sharing information and creating presences within public communities that they, by the nature of democratized participation, invite negative responses in addition to potentially positive and neutral interaction. By not fully embracing the social Web, many believe that they retain a semblance of control. The idea is that if brands abstain from providing a forum for hosting potentially disparaging commentary, it will prevent it from earning an audience – in this case, an audience that can impact the business and the reputation of the brand. However, retaining control, following the socialization of the Web, is nothing more than pure legend. While many companies retain control during the stages of defining and shaping messages, control is relinquished at the point of distribution. Once messages are published, they are at the mercy of consumers, peers, and influencers online and offline.'
>
> Solis (2010)

from a campaign. But remember customer acquisition may not be the main goal. For example, if boosting awareness is the main goal, then it may be worth calculating the correlation between brand awareness and market share, because then you can calculate the ROI of increased awareness.

Professor Tim Ambler (2006) explored four measurement mechanisms – return on investment (ROI) (or return on marketing investment (ROMI), or return on marketing expenditure (ROME)), discounted cash flow (DCF), return on customer, and net advocates (Reichheld, 2006) – and concluded that no single metric does it all. In fact, a combination of metrics is required.

Control includes various areas of market research and testing, so measurement systems need to be built into the plan.

Planning is really an iterative process. A manager puts together a plan and a budget. Senior management agree it or reduce it by way of budgets. The manager revises the plan in the light of the resources available. The plan is then rolled out, results watched carefully and action taken to change the plan if necessary (ie if it is not working). If something is not right, it is better to find out why, make corrections and move on – hence the importance of control mechanisms. They provide a manager with useful feedback as to whether the plan is working or not. Everything a manager does is a learning process since, assuming the desire for constant improvement, a manager is monitoring what works best and what doesn't. Each year, as experience is gained, improvements can be made through this longer-term iterative process. Procter & Gamble asks its managers to build on their 'learnings' (what they have learnt from the marketplace). They constantly learn from the marketplace and then incorporate those 'learnings' in their next marketing plan.

ROI is not the only measure

'Despite all evidence to the contrary, the belief that a single number can be used to assess marketing performance is persistent. Some say that top management can only handle a single number, or silver metric, so we must choose the least bad one. Others believe that ROI is so standard as not to be worth challenging. Others again claim modernity for customer concepts such as customer equity, customer lifetime value and Peppers and Rogers' new "Return on Customer". Yes, they are new and, yes, they have value, but these measures are not the silver metrics their promoters claim them to be.'

Ambler (2006)

Key points from Chapter 10

- SOSTAC® provides an effective structure for any plan.
- Market research and intelligence reduce risk and boost the likelihood of success. It is essential to gather key information before making any decisions about strategy or tactics.
- TOPPP SITE are the key components for writing a strategy. Write several options before choosing the best one.
- Build control systems into the plan.
- 90-day planning cycles can be useful.

References and further reading

Ambler, T (2006) Use a dashboard when driving your marketing, *Market Leader*, 33, Summer

Benady, A (2014) E-cigarette boss Jacob Fuller on comms and the industry's 'biggest mistake' *PR Week*, 25 June

Band, W and Hagen, P (2011) The right customer experience strategy, *Destination CRM* [online] http://www.destinationcrm.com/Articles/Columns-Departments/The-Tipping-Point/The-Right-Customer-Experience-Strategy-74691.aspx

Doyle, P (2001) *Marketing Management Strategy*, 3rd edn, FT Prentice Hall, Hemel Hempstead

Doyle, P, Saunders, J and Wright, L (1987) A comparative study of US and Japanese marketing strategies in the British market, Warwick University report

eMarketer.com (2009) Social media best practices, 29 July

Engel, J, Warshaw, M and Kinnear, T (1994) *Promotional Strategy: Managing the marketing communications process*, Irwin, Boston, MA

Forrester Research (2009) *US Interactive Marketing Forecast, 2009 to 2014*, Forrester Research, Cambridge, MA

Godin, S (2009) When tactics drown out strategy, *Seth Godin's Blog*, 7 August [online] www.sethgodin.typepad.com

Kanter, B (2008) How much time does it take to do social media? *Beth's Blog*, 1 October

Kanter, R M (2000) *Marketing CD 2: Segmentation, positioning and the marketing mix*, www.PRSmith.org

Kanter, R M (2001) *On-line Marketing Course 2: Segmentation, positioning and the marketing mix*, 2nd edn, www.PRSmith.org

Kotler, P (2001) In conversation with Paul Smith

Kotler, P et al (2000) *Marketing CD 3: Marketing planning*, www.PRSmith.org

Ohmae, K (2000) *Marketing CD 2: Segmentation, positioning and the marketing mix*, www.PRSmith.org

Reichheld, F (2006) *The Ultimate Question: Driving good profits and true growth*, Harvard Business School Publishing, Boston, MA

Smith, PR (1998) *Marketing Communication: An integrated approach*, 2nd edn, Kogan Page, London

Smith, PR (2004) *SOSTAC Marketing Plans* (CD)

Smith, PR (2013) SOSTAC® Guide to Your Perfect Digital Marketing Plan, www.PRSmith.org/SOSTAC

Smith, PR (2014a) Social Listening Skills Parts 1 & 2 [online] www.PRSmith.org/blog

Smith, PR (2014b) How to Target Very Very Specific Audiences On Facebook [online] www.PRSmith.org/blog, 21 Aug

Smith, PR (2015) SOSTAC® Guide to Writing the Perfect Marketing Plan, www.PRSmith.org/SOSTAC

Smith, P, Berry, C and Pulford, A (1999) *Strategic Marketing Communications*, Kogan Page, London

Solis, B (2010) The myth of control in new media, *Brian Solis*, 25 January

WARC (2006) Adidas to reposition Reebok from fashion to action, 26 January

Wing, R L (1989) *The Art of Strategy (*translation of Sun Tzu, *The Art of War*), Aquarian Press, Wellingborough

Further information

HAVAS Worldwide London
HAVAS PR UK
Cupola House, 15 Alfred Place
London WC1E 7EB
Tel: +44 (0)20 7240 4111
www.havasworldwide.co.uk

Euro RSCG
Havas Media
Privacy Office
Dr Fleming 17
08017 Barcelona
Spain
Tel: +44 (0)20 7257 6077
www.eurorscg.co.uk

International Organization for Standardization
ISO Central Secretariat
BIBC II
Chemin de Blandonnet 8
CP 401
1214 Vernier, Geneva
Switzerland
Tel: +41 22 749 01 11
www.iso.org

National Readership Survey Ltd (NRS)
7/8 Market Place
London W1W 8AG
Tel+ 44(0) 207 637 9822
www.nrs.co.uk

Target Group Index (TGI)
Ealing Gateway
26–30 Uxbridge Road
Ealing
London W5 2AU
Tel: +44 (0)20 8433 4000
www.kantarmedia-tgigb.com

11
The changing communications environment

LEARNING OBJECTIVES

By the end of this chapter you will be able to:

- Embrace the constant nature of change in markets and ergo marketing communications and recognize the integrated digital opportunity is now greater than ever before
- Be aware of the importance of checking the laws and regulations relevant to marcomms
- Consider building risk assessment into marketing plans, particularly including economic risks
- Accept the need to understand social change and integrate this change into marcomms to reflect changing social norms, values and roles
- Dispel any fears of technology and embrace technological changes as aids to marketing

Introduction   294
CX and the changing nature of competitive
    advantage   294

Politics (regulations
    and laws)   295
Some UK laws affecting marketing
    communications   295

Do consumers need more protection?   296
Increased EU consumer rights   297
Privacy   299

Self-regulation: codes of practice   301
Permission-based marketing   302

Code of Advertising Practice   302
Television advertisements and Ofcom   303
Macro-political effects on business and
    communications   304

Economics   304
Economic effects on markets and communications   304

Social change   305
Shrinking attention spans   305
Living in fear?   306
Companies that ignore Black Swan events
    will go under   306
Ethics   307
Demographics   308

Technology   309
Five big technological trends   310
The increasing pace of change   314

Summary   314

Key points from Chapter 11   314

References and further reading   314

Further information   316

Introduction

We are children of change. Right now business is going through 'the biggest change since the industrial revolution' (with the social media revolution 10 years ago, see Chapter 1), and marketing is going through its biggest change ever as finally, automation meets marketing. This is marketing's most radical time of change. This chapter looks at how marketing communications are affected by the rapidly changing business environment and its many uncontrollable factors (only one of which is technology).

Everything changes including customers, competition, channels, technology, trends, even regulations and laws. This chapter explores how changes in these may or may not affect marketing communications. We looked at how media consumption is changing in Chapter 7 (media buying and planning) and information processing is changing in Chapter 4 (buyer behaviour). Meanwhile whole markets are pulled and pushed in different directions by forces that are outside an organization's immediate control. New laws, changing regulations, fluctuating economic cycles, demographic shifts, new social values, attitudes and cultural norms, fast-changing technology, and aggressive, borderless and category-less competitors are some of the key factors that constantly move markets away from the status quo. As a result, yesterday's marketing communications strategy can soon become a lot less competitive and effectively therefore, obsolete.

This means that the marketing intelligence and information system (MIIS) should constantly feed back information on patterns, trends or sudden changes in any of these uncontrollable forces.

The 'OT' part of a SWOT (strengths, weaknesses, opportunities and threats) analysis monitors the external opportunities and threats that emerge in the business environment.

The PEST factors (political, economic, social and technological) or PESTED (add environment and demographics), need to be monitored to identify trends that can affect your business, presenting either an opportunity or a threat. PEST provides a useful acronym for scanning the external business environment for any of these change factors that directly or indirectly affect a business and how it communicates:

- Political (including legal and regulatory).
- Economic (global economic shifts and cycles of recession and boom).
- Social (new values, attitudes, lifestyles, ethics/environment and demographics).
- Technological (the internet, databases, digital TV and much more).

Competition can also be added as another key factor in an organization's environment which could stop growth, reduce it or even cause an organization to fail and die. Any of these change factors could ultimately push a business into extinction if seemingly subtle, yet significant, changes are constantly ignored. There is a tendency to resist change, perhaps because of the insecurities it heaps upon individuals. Some organizations wait until the last moment before changing. Others see an advantage in being proactive rather than reactive. We will now consider how these PEST factors affect the organization's marketing activities, and its communications in particular.

> ### New borderless, category-less competitors changing the marketplace
>
> Once upon a time, grocery stores sold groceries and petrol stations sold petrol. Today, grocery stores sell groceries and sell petrol while petrol stations sell petrol and groceries. Telephone companies sell broadband and TV, not just telephone services. All markets are constantly changing. Categories are blurring as competitors seek growth from share of wallet (if equipped with a strong brand and trustworthy customer relations, they can sell a wider range of products/services). Then some new players, such as network companies like Uber, are pushing markets into a new 'shared economy'. And on it goes – this is the borderless, category-less merry-go-round continually changing the structure of all markets.

CX and the changing nature of competitive advantage

All products and services continually tend towards becoming commodities as competitors copy whomever is winning. It follows that the design of the fundamental product or service, on its own, is less likely to deliver competitive advantage. Many feel that strong brands and a well-maintained customer database can be combined to deliver competitive advantage. As you monopolize your own mini market (through your own database) you create a protective wall (built on brand relationships) around your customers that stop competitors coming in.

Some say that content marketing can also create a new source of differentiation, in fact a new source of competitive advantage. It certainly can. At least, that is, until competition copies it.

Going back to the brand and the customer database. This only works as long as all of the customer touch points deliver a single consistent customer experience (CX). A unified CX is seen by many organizations today as a source of competitive advantage. And for many companies this means recreating themselves. What can deliver competitive advantage is a unified and consistent CX offline and online (across all platforms and touch points).

This presents a major challenge for most organizations. It also presents a major opportunity to develop competitive advantage over those that don't. When all staff are united around a clear customer experience it also motivates staff from all departments to work together to deliver a better CX. From strategies to tactics to detailed actions and priorities, a strong customer vision focuses everything. And ironically it can unleash creativity and innovation as the move to build a great CX will, in effect, demand creativity from all staff and all departments.

Let's get back to the PEST factors that marketers must also watch carefully. Let's start with politics. Consider briefly how laws and regulations can affect your business. In marketing communications in the UK laws are slow and expensive to enforce as they involve courts, whilst regulations are often self-regulating as in the case of both advertising and sales promotions. Let's have a look at politics and a few laws that affect marketing communications first.

Politics (regulations and laws)

UK business legislation provides laws that essentially support the principles of being honest and truthful. There is also a host of self-regulatory professional codes that draw on the same set of basic business principles, ie that marketing professionals should conduct their business in a legal, decent, honest and truthful manner.

Before looking at the laws, it is worth mentioning that short-term, dishonest deals that slip through any regulatory systems generate only short-term gains and do not tend to generate long-term sales, since repeat business will not come back. The 'everlasting customer' or the 'lifetime customer' concept is a long-term winning strategy, since the marketing perspective focuses on selling 10 cars, 10 fridges, thousands of cans of food or beer, or 50 years of office cleaning to one B2B customer over a long period of time instead of grabbing a one-off, short-term contract. The average of average estimates suggest that it costs six times more to sell to a new customer as it does to sell to an existing one. Fooling a customer is myopic. You can only cheat a customer once. Flouting the law or regulations restricts a business's long-term growth.

Meanwhile EU directives are subsequently adopted into UK law (and other European countries' local laws by each country independently). **In the UK a statute is a law (also called an Act) that has to be voted in by Parliament. Acts are the primary legislation. Regulations are refinements of an Act,** and they are brought into force by the Secretary of State (minister). Regulations form part of the law in the UK.

In the UK, television advertising alone has approximately 150 statutes and regulations that affect it. The Unfair Commercial Practices Directive 2005 harmonizes trading laws across the European Union and prohibits businesses from treating consumers unfairly. The directive was implemented through the Consumer Protection from Unfair Trading Regulations 2008 (CPRs). Business Protection Regulations are also known as BPRs.

Some UK laws affecting marketing communications

- The Trade Descriptions Act 1968 effectively stopped false claims and has mostly been repealed and superseded by the CPRs.
- The Sale of Goods Act 1979 (Section 13: Sale by Description) demands that goods sold match their description.
- The Business Protection Regulations 2008 replaces large parts of the Control of Misleading Advertisements Regulations

1988 in terms of B2B protections in respect of advertisements. These regulations provide a back-up for self-regulation. The Control of Misleading Advertisements Regulations 1988 provide legislation in respect of advertisements.

- The Telecommunications (Data Protection and Privacy) Regulations 1999 emerged from the Data Protection Act 1998.
- The EU Directive on Privacy and Electronic Communications Regulations (PECR) came into force in 2003.
- The Communications Act 2003 was driven by the Electronic Commerce (EC Directive) Regulations 2002.
- The Enterprise Act 2002 ensures fair competition.
- The Consumer Contracts (Information, Cancellation and Additional Charges) Regulations 2013, supersedes The Consumer Protection (Distance Selling) Regulations 2000, although they are basically similar in many places. It protects consumers by insisting marketers supply, in writing, full details of the goods or services offered, delivery arrangements and payment, suppliers' details and the consumers' cancellation right before they buy (known as 'prior information'). Consumers can cancel the order during the cooling-off period of 14 calendar days. These regulations apply when selling via the internet, TV, mail order, phone or fax.
- The Consumer Protection from Unfair Trading Regulations 2008 seek to tackle unfair sales and marketing.
- The Business Protection from Misleading Marketing Regulations 2008, combined with CPR, also provide protection for businesses.
- The Digital Economy Act 2010 regulates digital media and offers new protection against copyright infringement. Note: only some parts of the Act came into force in 2010; the main regime still remains unenforceable.

The overall guiding principles are the same in law as in voluntary regulations: simply be legal, decent, honest and truthful. If all else fails, the Office of Fair Trading (OFT) provides a safety net, and complaints about marketing communications (advertising, shop-window displays, etc) can be referred to the OFT for scrutiny. Some other laws affecting marketers in the UK:

- The Bribery Act 2010 – in the UK sales promotions, incentives and gifts to distributors and staff can now be seen as bribes if deemed excessive and carry a maximum fine of 10 years in prison. Marketers should issue guidance on corporate hospitality and have internal training, communications and procedures to back this up. Companies should keep a register of gifts and require employees to update it; review incentive schemes that may operate; consider changing supplier agreements to add or amend anti-bribery provisions; and review commercial practice to assess potential risk.
- The Trade Marks Act 1994 adapted UK trademark law to fit with European legislation. This means that a wider range of products and service attributes can now be registered as trademarks.

Over time, the EU laws are rolling out across Europe, in particular laws that offer even more stringent customer protection. The new EU Consumer Rights Directive, which has been implemented by The Consumer Contracts (Information, Cancellation and Additional Charges) Regulations 2013 ensures that consumers who buy online, in most circumstances, have considerably more rights than those who buy in stores.

Businesses must be extra transparent and ensure consumers can easily see (a) the identity of the business and the business registration details, (b) its geographical address, (c) an accurate description of the goods, and (d) full detailed returns policy, delivery information and terms and conditions.

Do consumers need more protection?

TTIP is the Transatlantic Trade Investment Partnership between the United States and the EU, criticized by some as it may allow US corporations to sue EU governments for loss of profits or revenues caused by a government's local laws or regulations. Anti-TTIP videos on YouTube suggest that American tobacco companies are already suing the Australian government for loss of profits since banning persuasive cigarette packaging. Is it possible for corporations to challenge governments for being over protective of their citizens? Will this open the gate for major corporations to sue governments for revenues lost due to protective laws and perhaps re-introduce colourful cigarette packaging and maybe tobacco sponsorship and, maybe even, one day, reintroduce cigarette advertising?

FIGURE 11.1   If corporations challenge governments for being over-protective of citizens, could this open the gate for law suits leading to the reintroduction of cigarette advertising?

Increased EU consumer rights

In 2014, the European Union passed a new directive on consumer rights that will effect B2C online businesses. Essentially, this new legislation protects consumers and also increases competition between enterprises across all 28 EU member states. There are many changes but here are the four biggest:

1   *Cooling-off period increases from 7 to 14 days.* The 'cooling-off window' (the time in which the consumer can cancel their order), is to be increased from 7 working days to 14 calendar days, thus bringing it in line with many other members of the EU including Germany who already have 14 days. It is worth noting that the

directive also states that a consumer can cancel the order and return the goods for any reason.

2   *Post costs included in the refund process.* Not only are consumers entitled to a refund if goods are returned within 14 days, consumers can also claim back any standard delivery charges incurred in returning the goods. Hence many eCommerce companies manage their own returns process via commercial parcel centres.

3   *An end to pre-ticked opt-in boxes.* No more pre-ticked opt-in boxes that cross-sell or offer extras during the sales process.

4   *No more 'Buy Now' buttons.* Once upon a time 'Confirm Order' or 'Buy Now' were acceptable CTAs (Calls to Action). Today, the consumer has to be protected from mistakenly entering into a contract by clicking that 'Buy Now' button. From now on, these buttons, tabs or panels have to clearly state that you are entering into a contractual agreement, eg 'Order with obligation to pay.'

Hope (2014) and European Commission, Consumer Rights (2015)

Since 2013 DG Justice (Director General) ensures a better harmonization of consumer laws by introducing important legislative initiatives, such as:

● The Directive related to sales and guarantees, covering certain aspects of the sale of consumer goods and associated guarantees.

● The Directive related to unfair contract terms protecting the consumers against unfair terms in consumer contracts.

● The Directive on consumer rights protecting the consumers in respect of distance contracts and contracts negotiated away from business premises as well as in respect of certain other aspects of consumer contracts.

● The Directives on distance selling and doorstep selling will be subsequently repealed.

European Commission, Consumer Rights (2015)

International financial reporting standards cost $54 billion

International financial reporting standards require companies to value their intangible assets (eg brands) on their balance sheets, subject to annual review for impairment, which means that the difference between the price paid and the current value of an acquired brand must be calculated. Any resulting write-downs can have a significant impact, as AOL Time Warner discovered in 2002. It had to write off $54 billion for the value lost when AOL acquired Time Warner at the end of the dotcom boom in 2000. See more on the financial value of brands in Chapter 2.

There are, as mentioned, many other laws and regulations, both national and international, which affect a business and its marketing communications. For example, the EU Telecommunications **Data Protection Directive (enforced by the Data Protection Registrar)** makes it illegal for companies to fax homes or businesses that have opted out. (See Fax Preference Service details on p. 316.) Some of the legislation may not appear to affect the marketing communications directly, eg product liability laws, but caution, coupled with expert advice, is required, particularly in the international arena. Product liability puts an increasing onus of responsibility on manufacturers, distributors and retailers to make sure that the products they market are safe and sound. It also affects marketing communications (and it even affects the instructions on a pack, as shown in the box opposite). The 'borderless world' knows few barriers when it comes to liability. Bloggers and twitterers take note (libel cases and breach of trade secrets cases will emerge).

Increasing law suits threaten marketers

Many industry sectors regulate themselves. In fact advertising has its own code of practice to which marketers must adhere. In addition, there are many laws that mostly protect the customer from being exploited by unscrupulous marketers, eg unfair or false advertising, or breach of their increasingly important privacy.

Ambush marketers London Olympics 2012

The London Olympic Games and Paralympic Games Act 2006 and the Olympic Symbol Act 1995 protects sponsors' rights by attempting to prevent ambush marketing and to protect exclusivity of official sponsors, which effectively means that only official sponsors, suppliers and licensees are allowed to use the Olympic marks, while the law prohibits non-official advertisers from the unauthorized use of:

- logos: the Olympic marks, such as the London 2012 logo, the Olympic rings or any other logo that can be confusingly similar to the Olympic marks;
- images: such as the Olympic torch, Olympic flames, athletic images and the colour combinations of the Olympic rings;
- mottoes: the Olympic and Paralympic mottoes;
- words: 'Olympic', 'Olympiad', Olympian', 'Olympix' and similar words;
- word combinations and phrases that falsely suggest an association between a business, its goods or services and the Games;
- sounds, designs, images and marks: advertising, marketing material, sales promotions, goods with words (spoken or written), sounds, designs, images and marks associated with the Games.

Sparkling wine shooting

The 20-year-old case of a US consumer suing a UK paint company (for alleged injurious effects of a lead-based paint) strikes fear into the heart of many potential exporters. According to Pohl (1991), a growing awareness that a manufacturer carries a heavy and detailed obligation to warn potential users about any dangers that might lurk in the use of its products has prompted some sparkling wine manufacturers to print disclaimers on the packaging warning against possible risks involved in uncorking their products.

Do customers need more protection from unscrupulous marketers? Or do all of these new laws and regulations slow business down and sometimes stop marketers entering a market?

Does Red Bull give you wings... or not?

Red Bull energy drink offered to refund $10 (with a maximum cap of $13m) to anyone who consumed their product after 2002 since their 'Red Bull Gives You Wings' campaign was sued as false advertising. There is a debate about the caffeine levels being less than a cup of coffee. So Red Bull settled out of court to avoid the distraction. Most marketers may now look even more carefully at the promises they make via their advertising.

Privacy

Breach of privacy regulations costs money and brand image

A television company in the United States was fined £3 million for flouting the Do Not Call laws. Five telemarketers allegedly called on behalf of Direct TV, contacting consumers registered on the Do Not Call database. One of the firms did not put the required live salesperson on the line within two seconds of the consumer answering the phone (Precision Marketing, 2006).

Poor data management leads to £980k fine from Financial Services Authority

Nationwide was fined £980,000 when an employee's laptop containing confidential customer information was stolen from the employee's house in August 2006. The FSA's action is based solely on Nationwide's breach of the FSA's Principles for Businesses, Principle 3: Management and control: 'A firm must take reasonable care to organize and control its affairs responsibly and effectively, with adequate risk management systems' (Anning, 2007).

Unsolicited e-mail individual sues sender £1k

Gordon Dick received an unsolicited e-mail and sued online IT product vendor Transcom in respect of this single e-mail, which it said it sent out once a year to customers and those who had contacted Transcom about its services. Dick denied ever being in either category and threatened to sue Transcom unless it 'treated for peace and made him an offer'. He won over £1,000 (Anning, 2007).

Unsolicited e-mail – ISP sues sender £45k

Adult site Nortycams sent salacious unsolicited e-mails to UK recipients who had not opted in to receive them. The ISP, Microsoft, claimed its image as a service provider was being damaged, and Nortycams settled for a combined damages and costs figure of £45,000 (Anning, 2007).

Facebook forget to ask permission

In 2007 Facebook Beacon turned Facebook users into product evangelists by posting their online purchases to their wall. Facebook neglected to ask for user permission first which resulted in one of their early privacy nightmares. It was a powerful concept, however, and today Nike uses Facebook Connect to do very much the same thing, only with user permission this time (Hubspot, 2011).

Google allegedly using cookies (without permission) to target consumers

Google has lost a Court of Appeal bid to prevent British consumers having the right to sue it in the UK over breach of privacy. They accuse Google of collecting private information without their knowledge and consent between summer 2011 and spring 2012, using cookies in order to target them with personalized advertisements (Press Association, 2015).

25,000 Facebook users demand compensation for privacy breaches

Facebook is being sued, allegedly, by about 25,000 of its users, as part of a case that says the site is conducting mass surveillance. The claim is part of a class action lawsuit being brought by European data protection campaigner Max Schrems, which says that Facebook's data collection and 'like' buttons breach privacy laws. More than 900 of the people bringing the case are in the UK. It will be heard in a court in Vienna and is being brought against Facebook's headquarters in Dublin, where all of its accounts outside of the United States and Canada are registered. Facebook has not yet commented on the case, but disputes the involvement of Austrian courts since it is registered in Ireland, according to reports. But Schrems and his legal team argue that the dispute is a consumer case and should be heard in his home country (Griffin, 2015).

€100m fines for data protection breaches

There will be significant fines for companies that do not comply with the proposed regulation of up to 5 per cent of annual worldwide turnover, or €100m, with the possibility for individuals and associations, acting in the public interest, to bring claims for non-compliance. These fines will make data protection a boardroom issue and will require companies to carefully review what they need to do to comply (Long, 2013).

No security policies, reviews, testing, audits or disaster recovery = negligence

Breaches of privacy and website security can end up in court. Organizations can be accused of negligence for breaches of privacy/security. In addition to damaging your customers' trust in your organization, 'security lapses can mean that company directors end up in court, if they are deemed to be negligent in their responsibilities towards good security' (Chaffey and Smith, 2013). In fact, Web 2.0 can actually make it easier for security breaches. Although usability and accessibility are popular issues, we don't see much about security.

Good website management must build in security policies, security reviews, security testing and auditing, as well as planning for business continuity in case of 'disaster recovery' and emergencies. 'Remember, the earlier security is discussed, the cheaper it becomes to manage risks. Also integrate security into any testing programmes' (Chaffey and Smith, 2013). Privacy will become more important.

Data security disasters

Memory sticks, discs, laptops, and files lost or stolen from homes or cars or left behind on a train have included information about the following:

- 10,000 prolific offenders – profiles and other information;
- 84,000 prisoners – profiles and other information;
- 30,000 people with six or more convictions in the last year;
- 100,000 personal details about members of the armed forces;
- 600,000 people interested in, or who had applied to join, the Royal Navy, Royal Marines and RAF;
- 25,000,000 child benefit claimants;
- Gulf War invasion plans stored on a computer stolen from an RAF officer's car in 1990.

BBC News Online (2008a, 2008b)

Quarantining Facebook to control tracking

'It's well worth keeping an eye on the realities of the world of online tracking from a personal perspective, which gives the term "the web" a rather different meaning.

Ghostery is a useful service that "provides a window into the invisible web – tags, web bugs, pixels and beacons that are included on web pages in order to get an idea of your online behaviour". They monitor over 1,000 trackers and "give you a roll-call of the ad networks, behavioral data providers, web publishers, and other companies interested in your activity".

The Electric Frontier Foundation's information on cookies and tracking continues to be a useful resource, and the University of Pennsylvania's office of audit, compliance and privacy video from late last year is a very clear overview of how to set up your Facebook privacy, presumably for their students and staff.'

Oliver (2012)

We are the last generation to know privacy as it was

American author, Brian Solis, suggests that we're 'still in the early stages of learning just what it (privacy) all means and doesn't mean. It is now something that will have to be taught.' He develops the 'we are what we share' angle by saying: 'And more importantly, what we share online, will now require thoughtful curation to deliberately construct a more accurate and desirable portrayal of who you are and how you wish to be perceived. Therein lies the inspiration for social networking; the understated, willful and dramatic leap between privacy and publicness' (Solis, 2012). It has also been suggested that your online profile is a window to your soul.

'Friend Get Friend' not recommended

Even FGF and NGN (Neighbour Get Neighbour) sales promotions that ask customers for a friend's e-mail address to pass on an offer are not recommended. In fact The Information Commissioner's Office (ICO) advice on viral marketing is that it is best to get a customer to confirm their friend's permission when giving another e-mail address.

The Information Commissioner's Office (ICO) guidance on PECR (the Privacy and Electronic Communications Regulations) highlights two forms of viral marketing: where a marketer asks a person to send an original marketing message to a friend; and where a marketer asks a person to provide them with their friend's contact details. ICO warns that, with the first type of virals, marketers are in fact encouraging their customers to break the law by sending unsolicited messages to others without prior consent in order to promote products or services. ICO therefore 'strongly advises' marketers to instruct customers only to forward viral e-mails to those individuals they are certain will be happy to receive them.

On the second viral type, ICO advises that marketers cannot use third-party e-mail addresses provided by customers or others, unless they are satisfied those forwarding the contact details know their 'friend' consents to receiving marketing messages from the marketer concerned. Best practice is for the marketer to ask customers to confirm they

have the consent of their 'friends' to pass on their details, and to tell customers they will let the 'friends' know how they received their contact details. Marketers should also check they have not previously been asked by the 'friends' concerned not to send them marketing messages (Williams, 2010).

Self-regulation: codes of practice

Various professional bodies draw up their own codes of practice to which their members must adhere. Failure to do so may result in expulsion and sometimes negative publicity, along with a form of blacklisting. In the case of advertising or a sales promotion, a breach of a code can also result in the withdrawal of an advertisement or sales promotion, etc. This can be expensive, as the development of any campaign costs money. The risks are arguably higher in television, where a 60-second advertisement can easily cost a million pounds. Most advertisers want to stand out from the crowd. To do this they sometimes have to be daring, bold and controversial. The advertiser's dilemma here is whether 1) to be so controversial that the advertisement teeters on the brink of being pulled off the air or 2) to play safe with a less controversial creative treatment.

Although marketing communications must adhere to the laws of the land (ie one cannot misrepresent or blatantly mislead), the voluntary codes are both cheaper and quicker to apply should any complaints or claims be made. The codes also offer useful guidance to the marketer, so that most problems are ironed out before an advertisement goes out on air or is published in the press. Essentially, advertisements should:

- be legal, decent, honest and truthful;
- show responsibility to the customer and society;
- follow the basic business principles of fair competition.

Professional bodies need to be vigilant in order to maintain the credibility of their profession. This is particularly true in advertising, where the consumer's scepticism and resistance to advertising are heightened or lowered according to the credibility of the advertising industry. This credibility is founded upon the industry's reputation and determination to maintain standards of legality, decency, honesty and truthfulness.

Permission-based marketing

Regardless of legislation and regulations, common sense and good ethics dictate that marketing professionals should adhere to permission-based marketing. This means that all e-mail campaigns and all telemarketing campaigns should be built around 'opt-in' lists or databases. These are lists or databases of customers or prospects who have readily given their permission for further contact by 'opting in'. However, the 'opt-in' can be included in the T&C (Terms & Conditions) when accessing 'Free wifi' services.

Consciously 'opting in' generates better-quality lists, in terms of subsequent response, than those lists that have discrete opt-ins (wifi) or those lists where you have to 'opt-out', where the customer or prospect has to consciously make the effort to tick a box to ensure there will be no further contact. 'Opt-in', by contrast, ensures that customers or prospects consciously make an effort (eg tick a box) to request further communications from the marketer. There is increasing resistance to intrusive online marketing (including SMS messaging). Arguably, this resistance is also spreading to offline marketing, including direct mail. Therefore it follows that best practice should be permission-based marketing.

In addition, marketers need to tread carefully when using new technologies. There is the well-publicized fine handed to a Leeds company, Moby Monkey, for an SMS promotion. This came about as the result of a mass SMS broadcast to hundreds of thousands of randomly generated numbers – it was inevitable that many of these included mobile phones owned or used by children (Murphy, 2003). Then, in late 2002, the Australian high court made history (in Gutnick v Dow Jones) by declaring that anyone publishing information on the internet could face legal proceedings anywhere in the world (Keegan, 2002). So, although caution is required, common sense and good ethics should prevail and act as useful guidelines for marketers.

Code of Advertising Practice

The Code of Advertising Practice (CAP) is for non-broadcast and covers ads that appear in a wide array of media including newspapers, magazines, cinema, billboards, mailings, leaflets, paid for space online, sales promotions (wherever they appear), texts, e-mails and on UK-based company websites. This Code must be followed by all advertisers, agencies and media. The Code is enforced by the Advertising Standards Authority (the consumer side of CAP, which is the advertiser side), who can take steps to remove or have amended any ads that breach these rules. The BCAP (Code of Advertising Practice – broadcast) applies to traditional 'spot' ads on TV channels and radio stations licensed by Ofcom as well as teleshopping, interactive services and text services.

This will affect all direct marketing activities, including telemarketing. Creating EU harmony in either regulations or legislation can be challenging; for example, cold calling is banned in Germany and some US states. Equally, sales promotions, incentives, premiums and free gifts are generally unacceptable in Germany but can cause problems in France. The European Advertising Standards Alliance (EASA) may provide a platform for promoting self-regulation and harmony across Europe.

Free advice

Help and guidance is readily available from **www.cap.org.uk**, with free confidential and expert advice on non-broadcast ads prior to their launch. They offer a free 24-hour-turnaround service advising advertisers if their promotions are within the regulations, and there is a chargeable service if a four-hour turnaround is required. The website also contains copies of the advertising codes, help notes and other online advice.

Anyone planning a TV ad for UK licensed terrestrial and satellite channels should submit it to Clearcast for approval. Radio advertisers should submit their ads to the Radio Advertising Clearance Centre (RACC).

Marketers can keep up to date with developments in advertising regulation by registering for e-mail news alerts from CAP and BCAP as well as the CAP Copy Advice team.

CAP principles

The main principles of the Codes which apply to all ads is that advertisements should not mislead, harm or offend. Certain products or services are subject to further specific rules. For instance, products or services that have the potential to harm or which are age-restricted, such as alcohol or gambling, are subject to additional restrictions above and beyond the general rules. The Codes also provide further clarity in some complex areas such as finance, the environment, and health and beauty.

The Codes are owned, written, revised and enforced by CAP and BCAP. They are developed in response to public policy, changes in legislation, emerging technologies and advertising trends, as well as in response to social or political concern. The Codes are regularly updated and are periodically reviewed to make sure they remain relevant.

Why Rooney's Nike tweet breached the rules

'When Wayne Rooney tweeted: "My resolution – to start the year as a champion, and finish it as a champion....#makeitcount gonike.me/makeitcount" it wasn't clear that it was a paid-for tweet from Nike, and the campaign was banned. Consumers must be protected from this in the same way "advertorials" must declare they are advertorials. Someone has suggested music celebrities mentioning brands charge £3k a tweet. Is this true? Can't celebrities use their Twitter accounts as an advertising platform? "No" says the ASA. Not even Rooney.'

Reynolds (2012)

CAP funding

The system is funded by a voluntary levy on advertising spend. This is collected at arm's-length on behalf of CAP, BCAP and the ASA by two bodies: the Advertising Standards Board of Finance (Asbof) and the Broadcast Advertising Standards Board of Finance (Basbof).

The levy is set at 0.1 per cent of advertising space costs and 0.2 per cent of Mailsort contracts, and is collected at arm's-length to maintain the independence of the system. It ensures that the system is properly funded, whilst ensuring that CAP, BCAP and ASA regulatory decisions are not influenced by who may or may not be funding the system. See **http://cap.org.uk/News-reports/FAQs.aspx**.

CAP and the ASA

The ASA (Advertising Standards Authority) is the independent watchdog responsible for administering the Codes. It responds to complaints from consumers and industry about advertisements that appear to be misleading, harmful or offensive. If a complaint is upheld, then the ad has to be withdrawn or amended.

Television advertisements and Ofcom

TV advertisements, on the other hand, must gain approval before broadcasting. **Ofcom came into being in 2003, having been created by the Telecommunications Act 2003,** and for the first time a single entity regulated what traditionally had been seen as disparate forms of media.

Initial scripts are approved by Clearcast, and a clearance certificate is issued. However, this does not guarantee that the finished production will also be acceptable, as the film's treatment is sometimes difficult to envisage from a script or storyboard, and so it is also screened for final approval by Clearcast before broadcasting. Even after an advertisement is cleared for broadcasting, it can still be pulled off the air if the ITC requests it. Its attention can be aroused by complaints from the public. If, after it has examined the material and considered the complaint, it feels that the complaint should be upheld, it can then pull the advertisement off the air.

In addition to advertising, other marketing services have their own regulations and codes. For example, the Code of Sales Promotion Practice is also published by the CAP and basically provides guidelines for sales promotion activities. The Institute of Practitioners in Advertising (IPA), Chartered Institute of Public Relations (CIPR), Public Relations Consultants Association (PRCA), Institute of Sales

Promotion (ISP) and other professional bodies all have codes of practice to which their members must adhere. Any breach of the code can result in a member being warned or ultimately struck off the institute or association member list. This may have some short-term negative publicity, plus, in the medium to longer term, exclusion of that member from pitch lists. Some clients refer to the appropriate institution or association when choosing a new agent or consultant.

Macro-political effects on business and communications

We now move from national and international regulations and legislation, which affect marketing communications, to international political negotiations, which affect the world economy. It should be remembered that the larger international trading companies need to monitor the results of worldwide political agreements. Plans are prepared to meet a range of scenarios built around possible results from, say, the current major economic disputes. *Fortune* magazine describes two scenarios used by an oil company.

Scenario 1: sustainable world and global mercantilism assumes that all the major international economic disputes are solved, there is European unity, the United States and Japan agree trading terms (and avoid a trade war), free trade prevails across the globe, and stable growth is maintained. As a consequence, environmental issues receive more attention. The implications for Shell are new emission restrictions and a reconfiguration of the energy industry in which less oil and more natural gas are used.

Scenario 2: global mercantilism, which assumes a gloomier world where regional conflicts basically destabilize the world, trade wars and recessions rage, trading blocs form, and consensus on environmental issues is never achieved. This scenario implies less regulation, a piecemeal approach to environmental issues and much more oil consumption.

Worldwide political agreements not only affect product portfolios (the range and types of products or services), but also the social agenda, which determines what are considered to be the most important social issues in the minds of customers. This, in turn, affects the organization's social responsibility policies and subsequent communications programmes. The social factors examined in 'Social change' also

indicate how the agenda can change over relatively short periods of time. First, we will consider how the national economy affects organizations and their marketing communications.

Economics

Economic changes affect markets and, in turn, a marketer's choice of marketing messages. Economies move in cycles, but few can forecast exact economic trends across different regions. Some market economies are more risky than others, particularly at certain periods or stages in their cycles. Marketers must be in tune with economic trends. **Since 2005, UK company reports must, by law, include a description of the principal risks and uncertainties facing the company** (as well as a description of the resources available to the company and a statement of the business's objectives and the strategies of the company). Businesses now need marketers to analyse the risks of various markets and of particular strategies. **In the United States, the Sarbanes–Oxley corporate governance legislation requires a risk management approach to business.** Interestingly, the 2004 Enterprise Risk Management Integrated Framework mentions the word 'customer' 71 times and the word 'marketing' 11 times. Marketers are well positioned to analyse risk and integrate at board level.

Shift to the East

'The dominance of the United States and the dominance of Europe – particularly Western Europe – is eclipsed. What we're witnessing is a sharp shift in wealth in a relatively short period of time from West to East.'

Martin Sorrell, WPP, at the 2006 World Economic Forum, Davos

Economic effects on markets and communications

Industrial and consumer markets are directly and indirectly affected by the state of the economy. The global shift in economic power from West to East is affecting many markets. Exchange rates, interest rates, unemployment, levels of disposable income, etc all affect how much money is around, how much will be spent and, in a sense, the size of many markets or industries.

During a recession almost everyone cuts back. Consumers spend less. Companies spend less. Many organizations cut back on all types of spending, including marketing (although there are exceptions, such as Procter & Gamble, which, according to Bill MacNamara (1991), ex-Asda divisional marketing director, 'automatically raise their marketing expenditure in a recession'). A classic fall in derived demand emerges: as primary consumer demand falls, the secondary demand (for the commercial products and services required to make and market the consumer products) also falls. This reduces growth in the marketing service industries like advertising and design. It becomes a buyer's market as prices tumble and better deals are demanded by clients. Several agencies and clients go into liquidation. There is therefore an increased need to check the financial stability of any agency, partner, supplier or customer.

Meanwhile, advertisers have to address the difficulty of encouraging people to buy during a serious recession. During a recession many buyers search for better deals, which include price cuts, extended terms and value-for-money sales promotions. These promotions do not necessarily increase brand loyalty. The scars of an economic recession may be permanently expressed in terms of buying patterns, attitudes, values and, ultimately, the advertising imagery, which reflect the changing norms, roles and values of a culture.

Recession-induced psychological change

Even a phenomenally strong economic recovery may not bring back the consumer spending patterns of the 1980s. Values, attitudes and lifestyles may combine to create lower levels of consumption, new buying processes and an overall pattern of trading down (away from premium-price brands). The worldwide recession brought job cuts and quality-of-life worries out of the headlines and into millions of homes. Some feel that consumer markets have changed because of a recession-induced psychological change that moved people away from the self-indulgence and excess of the 'me, mine, more' mentality of the pre-millennium to the 'learning to live with limitations' of the post-millennium.

This could affect buying behaviour and the supporting advertising messages, for example a move away from images of personal achievement to images about personal relationships, or even a move away from advertising that is built around the user imagery (from where 'the user is the hero' to where 'the product is hero'). This suggests that advertising will have to provide more hard information as consumers buy more carefully, seeking out the best deal, and display a price consciousness that rejects premium-price brands for better-value products that provide relevant benefits and excellent performance. Marketing messages change to match the mood created by the state of the economy. Equally, marketers must monitor the overall business environment for high-impact events such as a recession or banking crisis, to be ready to react and, ultimately, to reflect the changing set of needs that people acquire as their circumstances change.

Social change

Norms, values and roles change. Today, fathers change nappies, cook dinners and shop in supermarkets. Many women earn more than their male partners. Roles are becoming less clearly defined. It is no longer abnormal to have two working parents. Children are growing old younger, and many adults feel fatigue beyond their years as they suffer 'information fatigue syndrome' (too much information), which weakens the effectiveness of marketing communications, as audiences simply cannot digest all the information being thrown at them. Meanwhile roles continue to change.

Shrinking attention spans

And all the while customers' attention spans shrink, e-mail open rates plummet and social media engagement nosedives; the information fatigued, multitasked, semi-burnt-out customer has limited time and desire to give their personal data to 'other' companies. So first in (first to get the sign-ups) wins. The 'connected customer' expects the 'Internet of Everything' (everything connected) to deliver highly relevant, added-value content and experiences constantly.

Living in fear?

Although we have more material goods are we more secure individually and collectively? Do we feel content, comfortable and relaxed with ourselves and our surroundings? Or do many people avoid eye contact and social engagement on the streets, even around their own homes? It seems that people engage less on the street as they rush hurriedly from home to commute to work to commute to home.

Tweens (8- to 14-year-olds) seem to sense this. Fed with a palate combining TV news that tends to focus on negative stories and YouTube images of terrorism, it is almost inevitable. Over a decade ago this was observed by Lindstrom who suggested that research into tweens revealed they had common fears, including terrorism and family breakdown. Their view of the world around them is changing. Marketers must reflect these changes in their messages (Lindstrom, 2003).

Companies that ignore Black Swan events will go under

Black Swan events are almost impossible to predict. Instead of perpetuating the illusion that we can anticipate the future, risk management should try to reduce the impact of the threats we don't understand.

> We don't live in the world for which conventional risk-management textbooks prepare us. No forecasting model predicted the impact of the 2010 economic crisis. This crisis surprised many economists and academics. Moreover, as we all know, the crisis has been compounded by the banks' so-called risk-management models, which increased their exposure to risk instead of limiting it and rendered the global economic system more fragile than ever.
>
> Low-probability, high-impact events that are almost impossible to forecast – we call them Black Swan events – are increasingly dominating the environment. Because of the internet and globalization, the world has become a complex system, made up of a tangled web of relationships and other interdependent factors. Complexity not only increases the incidence of Black Swan events

but also makes forecasting even ordinary events impossible. All we can predict is that companies that ignore Black Swan events will go under.

> Instead of trying to anticipate low-probability, high-impact events, we should reduce our vulnerability to them. Risk management, we believe, should be about lessening the impact of what we don't understand – not a futile attempt to develop sophisticated techniques and stories that perpetuate our illusions of being able to understand and predict the social and economic environment.
>
> Taleb, Goldstein, and Spitznagel (2009)

Changing world – no longer black or white

Who would have thought the world's favourite golfer would be a black man and the world's favourite rapper would be a white man? Tiger Woods and Eminem have already been the world's best and who knows may one day be number one in their respective rankings once again.

Young men find a lot of pressure out there and are not sure what their role is (see Chapter 4 for more). Children are growing old younger. This is substantiated by the following statement from over ten years ago: 'Corporate brands are starting to replace character brands. Kids are starting to grow up at an earlier age and so move away from characters and into brands sooner. Their pocket money is spent on items such as mobile phones and branded merchandise' (Levy, 2003). Young people also prefer to text rather than talk when using their mobiles. They also see grammatically correct sentences in ads, on television or the internet, as outdated (Lindstrom, 2003).

This means the world's population is ageing. This has significant social and economic implications, as Harvard's Farrell, Ghai and Shavers (2005) observed:

> The world's population is aging, and as it gets even greyer, bank balances will stop growing and living standards, which have improved steadily since the industrial revolution, could stagnate. The reason

is that the populations of Japan, the United States, and Western Europe, where the vast majority of the world's wealth is created and held, are aging rapidly. During the next two decades, the median age in Italy will rise to 51, from 42, and in Japan to 50, from 43. Since people save less after they retire and younger generations in their prime earning years are less frugal than their elders were, savings rates are set to fall dramatically.

And older people's needs are changing too. They may flex their muscles with grey power votes or just demand younger lifestyles; for example, senior citizens considering retirement lifestyles and homes want Pilates, Chinese chicken salad and wireless-ready housing. Meatloaf, bingo and chair exercises are not required. 'In the past it was about healthcare and the nursing staff, but this group is saying I am not ready for that. I want Pilates, a lap pool, gourmet dinner and I want to lead my own life with flexible choices' (Dwight, 2007).

'Adults are changing too. They're overloaded with information. Their time and attention is being wasted... people no longer respond the way they used to' (Brøndmo, 2003). Impatience and intolerance of irrelevant information continue to grow today as customers juggle multiple tasks in their busy lives. This is partially why Google is so successful. It fits a need: to find information quickly. Google is 'in the business of revolutionizing the nature of knowledge; search has become integral in the way we think and act' (Andrew Keen, in Smith, 2008).

OK, Google, sort out my life, please

'We cannot even answer the most basic questions about you because we don't know enough about you. The goal is to enable Google users to be able to ask questions like "What shall I do tomorrow?" and "What job should I take?" This is the most important aspect of Google's expansion.'

Smith (2008)

Attitudes towards issues change. Once environmentalists were considered to be hippies, communists, anarchists or outcasts because of their lack of conformity with other people's beliefs, values and attitudes. Today, most political parties and major corporations recognize the importance of environmental groups.

Ethics

Social consciousness among buyers is important. However, the degree of importance can change over time. Perhaps it is linked to economic cycles; for example, during economic downturns does ethics fall down the ladder of importance? However, many customers want to know more about products and their producers. Do the products or producers damage the environment? What do the producers do in the community? Do they donate political funds? Do the organizations disclose information, and so on?

Many buyers are becoming aware that the supermarket is the economic ballot box of the future. And investors also are becoming increasingly interested in the corporate citizenship of organizations that they might consider funding.

Banks are becoming weary of lending funds to higher-risk, environmentally poor companies. Insurance premiums will also reflect the higher risk of non-green companies. The corporate responsibility record is now a criterion in joint ventures. For example, who wants to invest time and money in an organization that has a poor environmental record? To put it another way, who wants to inherit a green time bomb?

Some estimates suggest that a 'green screen', or false green claims by corporations, will last only a short period, since probing pressure groups, investigative journalists, scrutinizing financial analysts and information-hungry customers will eventually reveal a much bigger problem than that which was originally hidden. This implies that the marketing people have a vested interest in ensuring that an organization operates in a socially responsible manner. Corporate attitudes towards altruism and ethics are changing, as are personal religious beliefs.

Finally, one extraneous factor that affects the business environment is the environment itself. If the world continues to heat up, northern European attitudes, emotions and feelings about different stimuli (particularly colour) may change. This would affect almost all forms of marketing communications, and possibly even radio.

Demographics

The statistical analysis (or division) of a population or audience by age, sex and social status helps marketers to segment and target markets. This can be combined with location or geography (hence the term 'geodemographics') and contextual or behavioural information (see Chapter 13). In addition, there are demographic cycles, trends and movements that can help an organization to learn about its market many years in advance. Some years ago, forecasts (Gwyer, 1992) revealed that by 2030 the UK population would start to shrink and deaths would exceed births. The period total fertility rate (PTFR) is now at 1.8 children per family, which is below the replacement level of 2.1. By 2030 the over-80s market will expand to 3.4 million (3.5 times more than in 1961). Demographic shifts affect markets and consequently marketing communications.

For example, the demographic shift during the 1980s pulled the market away from Guinness, as a disproportionately large number of younger drinkers (20-year-olds) emerged after the 1960s baby boom. Guinness was positioned as an older, unfashionable drink. To chase the moving market, Guinness and the now extinct but then brilliant advertising agency Allen, Brady and Marsh repositioned the product as a younger and more fashionable drink. The 1990s saw the demographic bulge move on to create a disproportionately large number of 30-year-olds. Guinness chased this swell by using a maturing blond-haired man to help to position the drink appropriately. At-home drinking of wine and beer is a current social trend, which marketers reflect in their special offers for cases of beers. Perhaps in the future the ozone layer will completely crumble and the weather will warm up, followed by increased liquid consumption, including beers. Or will there be another baby boom (as fewer women use the pill because of cancer scares), creating a vast 18- to 25-year-old market two decades later? Or then again perhaps an even bigger health trend will curtail all regular drinking behaviour.

Or will the EU ban all alcohol advertising and 'promotion'? Maybe real estate companies will force pubs to increase their prices and thereby push drinkers back into their homes to consume canned draught beers. Or perhaps the decline of Western civilization will follow the decline of the Roman and Greek empires with over-indulgence and decadent lifestyles, including heavy drinking, and thereby create a short- or medium-term boost in the beer market before a major slump.

What are the implications of an ageing UK population? Bigger typefaces and print to help older eyes read commercial messages? Many products and services repositioned as the more mature person's choice? There will still be youth markets, but they may not be as attractive, since they will shrink in size and competition may become quite ferocious.

The falling marriage rate, the increasing divorce rate and the increasing number of births outside marriage contribute towards the sad term 'disintegrating family'. In addition, the number of single-person households is expected to increase. The traditional happy-family advertising formula is becoming obsolete, and marketing campaigns have been reflecting this for years. Oxo ads have shown the husband cooking the family lunch while the wife is out at play. Persil ads also reflect the changing demographics and roles, eg one ad shows a friendly grandchild who helps his grandmother to wash up with a top brand of washing-up liquid. The traditional 'housewife' (woman) shopper is no longer the sole key decision maker. Just take a look around a local supermarket on a Saturday morning, where you will see male shoppers buying Fairy Liquid, Ariel and Palmolive soap.

Decision-making units (DMUs) are changing (see Chapter 10, 'Segmentation and target marketing'). Over 60 per cent of mothers in the UK work either part time or full time, compared with 10 per cent in the 1930s and 20 per cent in the 1950s. Incidentally, it has been suggested that guilt-ridden working mothers may ease their discomfort by buying the 'best' brands for their families instead of buying the store's less expensive own brand. A Gallup poll suggested that 90 per cent of working mothers suffer some psychological discomfort in combining the roles of mother and worker.

The effects of the changing structure of DMUs apply to a broad sweep of products and services and not just FMCGs. Insurance, health care and double glazing target both partners instead of the head of the household or the main income earner. Many telesales phone calls fix an appointment to visit only when both partners or spouses are available for a sales presentation.

In 1990, futurologist Alvin Toffler forecasted that technology could facilitate vast demographic shifts as populations migrate from the cities to work in their own electronic cottages (complete with phone, fax and computer). Although there has been some movement, a major shift has not yet occurred. Technology, meanwhile, has relentlessly marched on into new realms of marketing.

Hanging out at the oxygen bar

Here is an IBM future vision from many years ago: oxygen bars offering 'nutraceuticals' (staple foods packed with vitamins and minerals) and gas for the jet-set hyperactive executives and fun lovers. Memory drugs, male birth control pills and remote-control surgery might all affect markets, their structure, the communications channels and communications tools.

Technology

With customer data trails being left everywhere, data storage costs falling, cloud wars breaking, content wars unleashing, the internet of everything emerging, digital body language and marketing automation growing it seems as if change in marketing is accelerating.

Customer data is everywhere

We leave digital trails everywhere when we browse, click, scan or fill in a form. This data can be cross-referenced with social media platforms to gather extra data. Additional third-party databases layer on more information. Search, social, and analytics combine with clever APIs (Application Programming Interfaces) allowing software components to interact with each other, helping marketers drill down into a gold mine of customer data.

Big data growing

Big data refers to relatively large amounts of structured and unstructured data that require machine-based systems and technologies in order to be fully analysed. 'The much-hyped term has inspired a slew of definitions, many of which involve the concepts of massive volume, velocity and variety of information. In other words, what turns data into big data is the amount of information, and the speed at which it can be created, collected and analysed' (Kaye, 2013).

Content wars unleashing

Meanwhile content wars are drowning customers in a rising sea of marketing content. Many marketers don't know why some content works and some doesn't, which creates a situation that 'leads to more content being created' (Belicove, 2013). In fact, Eric Schmidt, CEO of Google, effectively summarized the gigantic scale of new content and other information when he observed that every two days we create as much information as we did in the last two thousand years (Kirkpatrick, 2010). And content marketing is part of this as so many marketers churn out more content.

Data storage costs falling

As the cost of data storage comes tumbling down and data integration/analysis tools get cleverer, potentially large volumes of useful customer data are emerging almost everywhere.

Marketing automation coming of age

Finally, the last bastion of business to resist automation, marketing, is opening the gates ever since Eloqua's Steven Woods opened it all up with *Digital Body Language* (2009). In fact marketing automation is being applied to an increasing number of levels in marketing.

Here's John Horseley's (Digital Doughnut) list of marketing automation – what can be automated?

- design software;
- automated RTB (real-time buying) advertising;
- audience targeting for advertising;
- mobile advertising;
- advertising serving;
- content marketing;
- social media publishing;
- marketing asset management;
- form/landing page management;
- e-mail delivery;

- e-mail creation;
- a/b testing;
- CMS;
- campaign management;
- CRM;
- media optimization;
- affiliate marketing;
- e-commerce;
- customer experience management;
- community management;
- social media monitoring;
- website analytics;
- lead management;
- data warehousing;
- data analysis and reporting;
- payments processing;
- marketing resource management.

Boosting profits

The benefits of marketing automation: time saving, efficient, CRM single CX, consistent CX customer profiling (integrated data), personalization, content improvement (optimization via constant A/B testing).

Technology changes and integrating CX across all channels

Marketers in Europe, the United States and Asia rank technology-related opportunities very highly. In fact the CX is the hottest topic; the challenge of delivering a single consistent, relevant experience to the customer. An experience that somehow continually helps, informs, entertains and inspires the customer, an experience that continually adds value in a consistent manner whether online or offline. This is the challenge of real integrated marketing – delivering this continuous added-value experience across all platforms online and offline.

Content marketing, social media, mobile, personalization, big data, marketing automation, location-based marketing and multichannel campaign management are seen as the most exciting opportunities for marketers. It is interesting to see how the priorities vary across regions; however, the CX is top of everyone's list of opportunities as revealed by an eConsultancy/Adobe Quarterly Digital Briefing research study (2015).

Cloud wars breaking

The marketing cloud is a hub, where marketers automate and integrate all customer data, automatically analyse it then continuously and automatically serve highly relevant engaging content across multichannels at just the right time on the right platform to the right customer. Marketers use the marketing cloud (multichannel marketing automation, content management tools, social media tools and analytics platforms) to create a wall of service around their customers, which blocks competitors. This race towards automated integrated digital marketing hubs is on.

'The nature of marketing has exploded from an ancillary communications function to the Grand Central Station of customer experience' (Brinker, 2015).

The Internet of Things (IoT) emerging

After the fixed internet of the 1990s, came the mobile internet of the 2000s connecting 2–6 billion people. Then came the IoT, connecting 28 billion things from smartphones to watches, glasses, cars, clothes, your home, and your business (Jankowski, 2014).

CMOs will outspend CIOs on IT

With this kind of new opportunity (integrated digital hub) it's not surprising to see Gartner predict that CMOs will outspend CIOs on IT in 2017 (McLellan, 2012) as the 'race towards the automated integrated digital marketing hub is on' (Akhtar, 2014).

Five big technological trends

1 Cross-channel, multichannel and omnichannel are all terms that have been around for several years now and reflect marketers' priority for their strategies, campaigns, customer experience and customer journeys to span channels and devices.

FIGURE 11.2   Top priorities for marketers

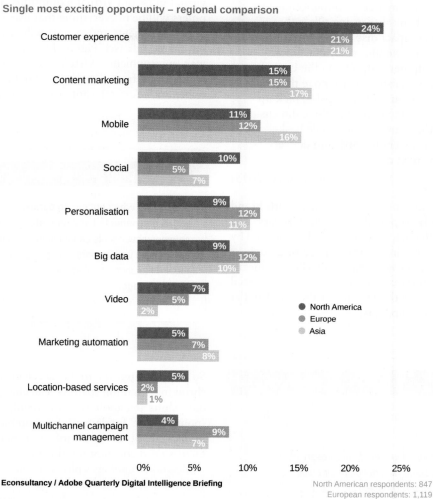

Single most exciting opportunity – regional comparison

Econsultancy / Adobe Quarterly Digital Intelligence Briefing

North American respondents: 847
European respondents: 1,119
Asian respondents: 384

2   Joining up data across channels (which in turn leads to better use of data) is a prerequisite of effective personalization and will be key in supporting this omnichannel vision.

3   Smartphone and tablet adoption continue to fundamentally change how brands engage with customers. In order to make the most of it in today's environment, mobile should be a core competence that can be built upon, rather than a stand-alone special feature.

4   Technology keeps changing the face of marketing communications. Web 2.0 (social media) has had a huge impact on marketing (see Chapter 1), and Web 3.0 (the semantic web) is emerging. Social change and technology change are driving new business models and new marketing models. It is a wonderful time for marketing, as these new opportunities allow marketing-driven business models to satisfy customers in new ways, deepen brand loyalty, spread messages and improve overall business operations.

This takes marketers into new territories and into the boardroom.

5 Think of customer care announcements, automatic bank dispensing tills, robot-operated compact disc stores, and outbound and inbound telesales voice machines. Home computer shopping in the United States allows customers to move their home computer's mouse to scan aisles, pick up products, examine them in three dimensions and put them into an electronic basket. Payment is by credit card, and delivery comes the next day.

eConsultancy (2015)

Pepsi can page groups of its customers with brand bleepers already supplied. In fact, bleepers and other items with computer chips can be triggered by simply moving within a certain range of a pack or product. Today, location-based marketing means that mobile phones can alert customers to special offers as they enter the vicinity of the retail outlet (see location ad campaigns).

The internet also provides virtual meeting places, virtual discussion groups, virtual greetings cards, virtual gifts and virtual exhibitions. Invisible computers will be in everything that uses electricity, and 3D environments and avatars will increase – both in virtual worlds (see Figure 11.4) and in traditional web environments. Virtual reality and augmented reality draw from a mash-up of data, allowing even richer and more relevant customer experiences.

Digital body language

'Marketers who continue to pursue their mission with a disconnected and non-integrated set of communication tools cannot gain the multi-perspective visibility into their prospects that is required to understand and leverage their digital body language.'

Woods (2009)

Moore's law

Every 18 months, processing power doubles, while costs hold constant.

Gordon Moore, founder of Intel, observed that each new generation of computer chips (semiconductors) doubled in power every 18 months. This has been valid for 30 years and is predicted to continue for the next 30 years... has held since the 1960s, and recent developments in so called 'molecular electronics' – arranging molecules in electronic circuits – suggest improvements are likely to continue for another 30 years.

Krugman (2000)

This means that in just over 30 years computer chips will be 1 million times more powerful than today. Note: today's modern luxury car has more computer power than the first human spaceflight craft that landed on the moon.

So change appears to be accelerating – whether shrinking attention spans (social changes), quantum data shifts (technology), new regulations and laws (political) or fundamental economic cycles (economics) that grow or shrink your market, the PEST factors need constant monitoring.

Behind technology's physical manifestations, more subtle advances are occurring. Witness marriages between technologies such as geographic information systems, analytical modelling market analysis and data mining. See the semantic web (on the next page) as well as digital body language in Chapter 12 (pp. 323–4) and location-based ad campaigns in Chapter 13 (p. 362 onwards). Google Alert and Google News can even do a lot of a manager's reading by scanning journals, newspapers and trade magazines for relevant material and printing out headlines, summary abstracts or complete articles. Robots make our lives easier.

PART TWO
Communications tools

PART TWO

12

Selling, social selling, sales management and key account management

LEARNING OBJECTIVES

By the end of this chapter you will be able to:

- Understand the purposes of different types of sales teams
- Map out the key stages and skills required of key account management
- Begin to manage the sales force
- Identify different ways of extending your sales force

Introduction   320

Functions of selling   321

Consultative selling   321

Key account management (KAM)   321

Integrating the sales force with
   the communications mix   322

Integrating sales with online activity   323

Digital body language and marketing automation   323

Social media, prospecting and social selling   323

Reverse forensics prospecting   324

Real-time conversation prospecting   324

Social web data prospecting   325

LinkedIn discussion-based prospecting   325

B2B social identity service improves
   prospecting   325

Managing the sales force   325

Types of salespeople   325

Recruiting   326

Training   326

Motivating   327

Controlling   328

Time – the scarce resource   328

Extending the sales force   329

Types of sales force   329

Advantages and disadvantages   333

Advantages   333

Disadvantages   333

Summary   334

Key points from Chapter 12   334

References and further reading   334

Further information   334

Introduction

The word 'sales' is conspicuous by its absence in job titles on business cards. 'New business development', 'Account manager', 'Key account manager', 'Relationship manager' and 'Marketing executive' are often preferred, yet selling's impact on most markets at some stage is vital. The 'selling' stigma is surprising, given the size and importance of selling. A study called Balancing the Selling Equation (Abberton Associates, 1997) indicates that there are approximately 470,000 professional salespeople in the UK alone. The London Business School's Associate Professor of Marketing, P J S Law, cites selling as a vital ingredient: 'I cannot think of a product or service which has not, at some stage on its journey from producer to customer, been the subject of face-to-face negotiations between buyer and seller.' The sales force budget allocation varies according to industry type, but generally, in B2B markets, more budget is spent on selling than on advertising or PR.

B2B markets depend on personal selling more than others. Winning an order for, say, a heavy industrial machine cannot be done by advertising, direct mail or telesales (telephone selling). This kind of selling requires a top-level sales professional. Consumer goods, on the other hand, rarely use personal selling to the end user or consumer because of the high cost per visit (ranging from £27 to £500, depending on the seniority of the salesperson, the frequency and length of the visit, etc). Nevertheless, consumer products need salespeople to sell or 'push' the product in the retail chains (and wholesalers).

There was an era when selling was all about short-term tactics, quick sales, in–out and on to the next unsuspecting prospect. This is short-term transactional marketing, which in the long run reduces sales and profits. It is probably best summarized by the well-known Heaven and Hell story.

Today, selling has moved away from the short-term, quick-sale scenario. Combative salespeople are being transformed into 'customer servants'. Selling today is more about 'partnering' and relationship building: 'You don't sell to people; you partner with them.' This is particularly true with key account management (KAM), which requires a more strategic approach to selling. Today selling is about building durable relationships that are dependent on satisfying the customer constantly. IBM today is following a growing trend towards paying the sales force salaries partly on customer satisfaction. Many companies are now measuring success not just by units sold but also by the far more rigorous yardstick of customer satisfaction. Selling has moved beyond the marketing and sales departments as companies realize that in today's heated competitive markets the whole company must sell.

A dead prospect

A man dies and arrives at the Pearly Gates, where St Peter tells him he cannot enter until Hell has been given an equal opportunity. Although the man knows he wants to go to Heaven, St Peter insists that he checks out Hell first. To his amazement, the man discovers that Hell is a party town, with free-flowing drink, good music, lots of friendly supermodel lookalikes everywhere, perfect weather, immaculate golf courses, football pitches, super-fast broadband and white sandy beaches. Best of all, everyone is friendly and concerned that the man feels comfortable in his new surroundings. St Peter appears and asks the man for a decision, upon which the man says, 'Hell's for me!' When he returns the next day, all he sees is bodies, scorched, burning and screaming. 'But this isn't the same place', he shouts at St Peter in the distance. 'Oh, yes, it is', St Peter replies. 'Yesterday you were a prospect. Today you are a customer.'

The changing salesperson

'I sold systems that people didn't want, didn't need and couldn't afford.'
Bill Gardner, IBM veteran with 23 years' service, now retired

'Forty-five per cent of the variable component of my pay cheque depends on how Jon Gorney at National City Corporation rates me.'
Don Parker, IBM salesperson

Functions of selling

The purpose of selling is not just to sell. Master salespeople gather intelligence and build relationships (which can, in turn, create competitive advantage). Research suggests that as little as 10 per cent of a salesperson's time is in fact spent actually 'selling'. In addition to prospecting, appointment setting, letter writing, travelling, training and administration, many salespeople are also responsible for some customer care, post-sales service, entertaining, intelligence gathering, forecasting, understanding customers, developing customized solutions, team selling, etc. Some managers say that 'Customers seek longer-term relationships with fewer suppliers than formerly, and in return for security of business ask their suppliers to do more for them.' Forecasts suggest that there will be a concentration of key accounts (large customers) and they will need suppliers who work with them as strategic partners instead of adversaries (see 'Consultative selling' and 'Key account management (KAM)' below). Team selling may become more popular as research and development, production, distribution, sales, marketing and even legal and financial people work with the customer.

The best salespeople are expert listeners. They ask intelligent questions and listen carefully. The best salespeople are masters at capturing data. Since the sales force is in the front line of the market, it provides a fast and accurate feedback mechanism. Competitor activity, customer needs, and new opportunities and threats can and should be picked up by the sales force and fed back, without delay, to the sales manager or marketing manager. Reasons why an old customer is lost or a new customer is won should also be fed back immediately.

Consultative selling

Looking at customers as partners with whom a company wishes to develop a long-term, repeat-business relationship requires a shift in the business paradigm from 'selling to them' to 'working with them'.

B2B selling is no longer just converting features into benefits. Selling is more to do with problem solving and strategy fulfilment (for the customer). 'What is your requirement and how can we fulfil it?' is not enough. Salespeople have to understand customers' business strategies and then see how

they can help. GE asked its largest customers what they expected from the GE sales team. Customers revealed: 'The number one thing we expect is excellent knowledge of our company, our industry and the environment in which we do business.'

Offering expert advice and consultancy demands an attitude shift where the customer is seen as a partner rather than just a sales target. The short-term 'win–lose' scenario (the seller gains at the customer's expense) is replaced by the longer-term strategic partnership 'win–win' scenario. This builds customer retention through enhanced customer satisfaction, which in turn creates a sustainable marketing advantage. These new partnerships may involve joint development programmes that might not bear fruit for five or more years. This may seem inefficient in the short term but highly effective in the medium to long term. This is a strategic shift towards KAM.

Master salespeople

Master salespeople are masters at gathering information. They are equipped with 'must know', 'useful to know' and 'nice to know' questions before every meeting.

Key account management (KAM)

Key account management means managing the most important customer relationships. It is strategically important and requires highly skilled senior salespeople or senior management. In addition to salespeople being able to sell on a personal level, KAM requires many other time-consuming skills, including:

- Solutions selling and collaborative selling, which generate tailored products or services, including ensuring customer retention, growing lifetime value and share of wallet. It is all about value creation for the client or partner. The initial sale (demonstration, pitch, handling objections, building trust, presenting proposals, closing the sale and after-sales service) is just the beginning. Intense collaboration is a complex, time-consuming joint effort. KAM must help the client to identify unique sources of value. Collaborative selling is a high level of customer engagement and generates collaborative co-creation offline (see Chapter 1 for the online version).

- Project management skills (to ensure tailored products and services are delivered on time and within budget).
- Relationship building at many complex levels right across the decision-making unit (this requires the ability to analyse clients' internal structures, systems and overall organization and continually widen relevant contacts).
- Research and intelligence gathering (and sharing information).
- Negotiating skills (to nurture the long-term relationship and deal with a large decision-making unit).
- Legal skills (an understanding of legal issues and contracts).

10 Steps to KAM

McDonald and Woodburn (2007) identified 10 steps towards developing KAM within an organization:

1 Select the right accounts.
2 Categorize them for their sales and profit potential.
3 Analyse their needs.

4 Develop strategic plans for (and with) each of them.
5 Get buy-in from all functions about their role in delivering the agreed value proposition (to the key account).
6 Get the right organization to serve the selected key accounts' needs.
7 Get the right people and skill sets in the key account team.
8 Implement the plans on an annual basis.
9 Measure success, particularly in respect of whether they create shareholder value added.
10 Reward individuals and teams for their success.

An alternative approach to seeing how KAM evolves through the following stages was developed by Millman and Wilson (1995). This overlaps with the above but also goes beyond it by including the 'uncoupling' stage when the partnership ends.

Integrating the sales force with the communications mix

An organization's own sales force, or a distributor's or agent's sales force, should be updated regarding any new advertising, sales promotions or social media campaigns. Some advertisements are wasted when they succeed in pulling customers into stores only for the customers to find out that the sales staff behind the counter are not familiar with either the

TABLE 12.1   Stages of KAM

Stage	Activity
Pre-KAM	Identify potential accounts (select the best clients – who's the perfect client?). Understand how they make decisions; key criteria; key players.
Early KAM	Tentative agreements and probing; identifying how the organization can help the client.
Mid-KAM	Account review and senior management involvement.
Partnership KAM	Joint problem solving and sharing sensitive information.
Synergistic KAM	Synergy of shared values and one-entity perspective.
Uncoupling KAM	A positive move recognizing that there is no further value in the relationship.

advertisement or the particular offer being made. Equally, salespeople may spend considerable time ensuring that wholesaler and retailer point-of-sale materials are in place and ready to support an advertising campaign. The amount and type of personal selling required changes as a product or service moves through its life cycle (see 'Types of salespeople' on p. 325). Using a sales force to create awareness is expensive (and slow and not recommended). The salesperson has more impact in the final stages of attention, interest, desire and action (AIDA), eg a salesperson in a retail store. Equally, salespeople can ask buyers what phrases they use when searching for the salesperson's products or services. This key phrase inventory should be fed back regularly to the marketing team who are optimizing the websites and any social media. Another level of integration is between the web analytics and the sales team (see the next section).

Integrating sales with online activity

Digital body language analysis can deliver a weekly alert to each global account manager and summarize all visitors' activity from an existing key account (or a major new prospect), whether a brief visit or a deeper investigation of a particular new product. This helps salespeople gain deeper insights into, firstly, what is of interest to their key accounts (and/ or key prospects) and, secondly, what buying stage they are moving towards. Alternatively, reports can analyse prospect interest levels by both region and product, allowing marketers to identify areas in need of additional focus and resources. These reports can save a lot of time and effort and build stronger rapport between the sales and marketing teams, as sales teams really appreciate these valuable insights. Marketers can also instantaneously see which campaigns are generating better visits and conversions. This helps to improve resource allocations to optimize ROI. See the next section for a brief perspective on digital body language, or Chapter 21 for more detail.

Digital body language and marketing automation

Professional buyers source and purchase products and services online all the time. The opportunities for a salesperson to get to meet the prospect are reducing. Once upon a time a salesperson could meet purchasers earlier in the buying process and gauge their reactions and, ultimately, their readiness to purchase by listening carefully to their questions and comments and, most importantly, watching their body language. Today, instead, marketers watch website visitors' digital body language to determine how interested a prospect visitor is, how ready they are to buy, and how they can help the prospects to make a purchase. If, for example, a prospect has returned several times to the site and downloaded three white papers, and some colleagues from the same company have also visited the site, this might indicate the visitor is at an advanced 'information collection' stage in the buying process. This can automatically trigger a tailored on-screen message via a web page or a pop-up message, an e-mail or a phone call from a salesperson offering help. See page 309 for more on marketing automation.

> ### A window to a buyer's mind but digital body language gained
>
> 'When the sales market switched from face to face to online, we lost a window into the buyer's mind. But we gained access to a compelling cookie trail of leverageable information, in the form of their digital body language.
>
> "Digital body language" is the catch phrase coined in 2009 by Steven Woods, co-founder and Chief Technology Officer at Eloqua, to describe trackable patterns in online behaviour of customers.'
>
> Blur group e-mail 2 June 2013

Social media, prospecting and social selling

The sales team should be well trained in networking both in offline and online. At offline events they are trained to open up discussions, move around a room, identify prospects and more. Online, salespeople have a great opportunity to use their networking skills across social platforms. Meeting new people, joining new discussions, new groups, helping other people – putting themselves about – in the right networks (or groups). Listening to discussions, joining discussions, starting discussions, and sharing genuinely useful information allows salespeople to get to know people having helped someone. Salespeople must identify the best social channels, ie where their target audience is communicating about topics relevant to your brand. If most of your customers and prospects are on LinkedIn and not Twitter, you should invest more resource on LinkedIn groups, discussions and maybe even advertising etc.

Incidentally, blog posts, tweets and any social media content can have a CTA (Call to Action) to get another report/video/tip or to have a salesperson call them to help with the next steps.

> ## Social selling enriches marketing database with social data
>
> Social information such as LinkedIn interests, groups, Twitter hashtags etc. can be added to the marketing database. Professional salespeople watch key customers'/prospects' social information so they can have more meaningful conversations. Social selling also allows salespeople to interact with customers 'socially'.

Reverse forensics prospecting

Some call it 'Reverse IP Look-Up Prospecting' as this approach to prospecting delivers a list of businesses that have just visited your site daily, weekly, monthly, or in real time. This prospect report is a hot list of companies that usually have an interest in your business and/or your products. The list comes complete with the company name, address, phone number, website and firmographic (industry type/sic code, number of employees) and optional credit rating, as well as what the visitor is interested in (what key words they used, which pages they visited, for how long). It does not, however, capture the individual's name.

A good salesperson can easily research LinkedIn and other databases to identify who might be that anonymous visitor. Some salespeople just pick up the phone and ask who is responsible for purchasing whichever product was being looked at. Prospects are often pleasantly surprised to get a call which can subsequently answer all the questions immediately.

This system can effectively help to identify the visitor's stage in the buying process from their digital body language – what they click on and dwell on including the length of the phrase used in the search, duration spent on product pages, repeat visits, duration spent on the pricing page and duration spent reading product reviews pages.

Rules, or filters can be added so that:

- a key account manager can be alerted when his key customers (or prospects) are crawling across his site;
- a particular product specialist sales rep can be alerted when businesses are looking at his particular product;
- an area sales rep can be alerted when businesses from the same geographic territory are visiting the site;
- repeat visits or groups of visitors from the same organization can be reported.

Reverse forensics (RF) only works for B2B businesses and when the visitor is using a fixed IP address (ie working from an office which has its own fixed IP address as opposed to a remote worker from home, or someone using an iPhone with 4G, or accessing via WiFi). This only covers a percentage of visitors. In fact, overall, RF estimate that approximately 5 per cent of visitors actually make an enquiry (e-mail or phone); 45 per cent of visitors are competitors or suppliers and the remaining 50 per cent are prospect opportunities. Companies like Lead Forensics charge between £250 and £5,000 per month (for between 50 to 5,000 visitors per day); this could generate up to 10–1,000 leads a day (based on only 20 per cent of visitors) or 200–20,000 leads a month respectively.

Most business people that visit a website will not pick up the phone and call, even though they may have a need for your services. However, some will gladly take a call from an expert adviser/salesperson from the business whose site they were recently exploring.

Real-time conversation prospecting

Some call it 'social web prospecting', either way it is a relatively new prospecting service primarily for B2B companies. Basically the system monitors conversations, posts, tweets, hashtags etc to find people talking about your product/service type or a related issue or a conference. Companies like crowdVu.com identify these people, collect their contact details, and then cross-reference this data with other online social platforms to build a better profile. They then cross-check this with a range of subscription databases (such as Dunn & Bradstreet) to deliver as much detail about as many people discussing your product type or a related issue as possible. It could be a group of people discussing a particular topic, or a group that attended a particular conference.

Social web data prospecting

As is often the case, the skill is in the ability to ask a good question. For example, 'Can you find me influential Twitter users, who are based in London and who work at companies in the finance industry where their revenue is greater than £200 million per year?' The answer is yes. Asking the right question is a great skill. For a relatively small budget targeted prospect names and contact details can be delivered. For example, if a sales team wanted to talk to everyone who attended a particular conference in a particular industry sector, listening tools can listen to the conference hashtagged discussions on Twitter and elsewhere and build a list of target prospects, and layer on top information from other databases.

Most prospects are ignored

'The tragedy is that most prospects fall through the cracks in the floor boards. Eighty per cent of B2B leads are not followed up. Of the 20 per cent that do get followed up, sales reps reject 70 per cent too quickly (even though the majority of these prospects eventually buy within 24 months and often from a competitor). Effectively, only 6 per cent of a business's hard-earned leads get followed up.'

Woods (2009)

LinkedIn discussion-based prospecting

Specialist social selling agencies spend a day clearly defining your ideal target customer profile and their interests. They then target 300 'perfect fits' and invite them to join your newly set up dedicated group which specializes in discussing the target group's interests. On average 100 of the 300 carefully targeted LinkedIn prospects sign up. After a few weeks or months of creating and participating in discussions, a tailored message is sent to each group member offering a one-to-one chat about a relevant sales topic. One agency in Dublin generates 10 well-qualified leads per month for its clients. And if the leads are no good, the client does not have to pay – ie the client only pays for good leads. At an approximate cost of £1k for set up, plus £1k per month, this means an average prospect lead (after the £1k set-up cost) costs £100. Sales and marketing teams will know whether £100 for a well-qualified lead is a good deal.

B2B social identity service improves prospecting

Social identity services can deliver the complete social media picture from your existing data. Social media data deepens insights into your own existing database of prospects and customers. When shared with the sales prospecting team it can help to qualify leads and also equips salespeople with information about what interests a prospect has. Basically this system enriches an organization's existing sales and marketing database with social web information. This can be used by salespeople or used in the CRM or marketing automation platform.

Managing the sales force

Types of salespeople

Some sales reps are excellent at winning new business ('order getters') and find the servicing of regular accounts to be dreadfully tedious compared to the exciting buzz of new business. Other reps are meticulous professionals who service an account ('order takers') with such professionalism, pride and affection that they create barriers for competition by building a 'wall of warmth' around their customers. In reality, most reps have to do a bit of both jobs. Shiv Mathur (1981) wrote an intriguing paper about 'transaction shifts', which suggested that different types of marketing managers (and salespeople) were required as a product passes through its life cycle, since the product requires different levels of service support at various stages.

In an increasingly impersonal world of faceless faxes and voicemail, face-to-face communications or personal selling can provide a reassuring, personal touch. In addition, the salesperson can respond immediately to a buyer's changing needs and moods. The salesperson can also provide instant feedback from the customer or marketplace (see Chapter 6, 'The intelligent rep'). On the other hand, a sales force can be expensive in terms of cost per thousand contacts, and sometimes it can prove to be uneconomical on a cost-per-order basis. This largely depends on the size and profitability of the order, the distance travelled to get it, the number of meetings required, etc.

The primary responsibilities of the sales force manager include recruitment, training, motivating, controlling and collecting feedback.

I perform better as a salesperson now

'I used to have a territory where I was a free agent... today the computer recommends which calls I should make... my sales aids remind me what to ask and say... my manager knows where I am and I spend half my time on training courses... but I do sell 30 per cent more per annum.'

A domestic appliance executive

Recruiting

Determining the right size and structure of the sales force is vital. What is the optimum call frequency? Who should service the account? As an organization changes or grows, so too the sales force and its responsibilities must change. Sales force attrition is a fact of life. Some salespeople move to new companies; some are promoted; others retire or are fired. This means that recruitment is a continual process that demands skills, cash and time. Recruiting the right salesperson is a resources-consuming management activity. The New York Sales and Marketing Association (2002) revealed that 71 per cent of customers buy from a salesperson simply because they like and trust them. Two out of three customers change suppliers because of a salesperson's lack of interest, attention or communication. Recruit the wrong people and sales can actually be reduced

instead of increased. Keeping the right sales team together is largely determined by levels of training, motivation, control and feedback.

Making noises like farm animals – sales training

Imagine a group of people walking around a room, making farm animal noises and trying to form a circle with their eyes closed. This is part of a rigorous selection process of a field marketing team whose job is to help major marketing player Unilever to launch new varieties of an established snack product. Top marketing companies recognize that the more time they invest in selection and training, the better the result. Preparation is rigorous, including dealing with hecklers. As mystery shoppers check on the team, nothing is left to chance.

Training

Training is an ongoing affair, not a one-off activity. It is a continuous process. Like thinking, it requires practice. Tony Buzan's classic books (1988, 1989, 2003, 2013) emphasize that thinking is a skill that needs development and exercise. Basically, the sales force has to acquire and maintain three pieces of knowledge and one set of skills – selling skills. The three pieces of knowledge that the professional salesperson must have are:

1 product knowledge (marketing mix, features and benefits, and unique selling propositions – USPs);
2 market knowledge (customers and competitors);
3 company knowledge (history, structure, etc).

The 7P approach to selling skills

There are several different stages involved in selling. The 7P sequential approach identifies areas for skill improvement. The seven stages are:

1 prospecting (looking for potential customers);
2 preparation (objective setting, continual customer research, etc);
3 presentation (demonstration, discussion);
4 possible problems (handling objections);

5 'please give me the order' (closing the sale or getting the order);

6 pen to paper (recording accurately all relevant details);

7 post-sales service (developing the relationship).

Increasingly today, more and more sales come from past customers and through growing the share of wallet of existing customers. Both employees and past employees can help to prospect for new business. For example, McKinsey Consultants harnesses a network of its ex-employees – recognizing that the alumni can help to generate new business. Similarly, PwC discovered that 60 per cent of new business came from ex-employees or via ex-employee contacts.

Each stage requires a certain amount of training and practice. Training should also include non-selling activities (information-gathering techniques, time-management skills, personal expense control, etc). Preparation is continual and includes an initial analysis of the customer's business, issues and objectives, clarifying exactly what the customer wants to achieve as well as identifying its compelling reason to act. In fact, most major sales in large B2B situations involve a huge needs analysis. This involves analysing the customer's situation and includes needs, benefits, barriers and ways forward. The decision-making unit is analysed in great detail to ensure that all key decision influencers are addressed at the appropriate stage in the selling process. The customer's financial position, access to funds and decision-making units are also carefully studied. Eventually a risk analysis will be completed, identifying potential problems, their sources and their likely impacts.

Motivating

Maintaining the sales force's motivation is a vital part of sales management.

It can be as easy as publishing the monthly sales figures against targets for each sales rep and circulating the figures among the sales team. This can lead to competition among members, which may inhibit them from sharing ideas, contacts, leads and even closing techniques. On the other hand, it can keep everyone focused on targets, with peer pressure as a source of motivation. It is the sales manager's job to build a team feeling and get everyone working together, sharing ideas rather than hiding them from each other.

'Psychic income' is often a stronger motivator than financial income, yet it does not need to cost the company any more money than the traditional financial incentive. Psychic income offers rewards aimed at the higher levels of need, such as being valued, recognized, rewarded and challenged (see Chapter 4, 'Motivation', and Maslow's hierarchy of needs).

This is how it works. A bonus cheque for £1,000 tends to get spent on dull and boring things like reducing the overdraft or paying the mortgage. On the other hand, the same £1,000 spent on a holiday for two or a spectacular piece of Waterford glass acts as a constant reminder of a job well done. Even a clap on the back, a thank-you note, a presentation ceremony or a photograph in the newsletter (or in the annual report) can arouse feelings that satisfy the higher levels of Maslow's hierarchy of needs. This contrasts with the £1,000 used to satisfy the dull, boring and soon forgotten lower levels of need.

Closing techniques: how to use problems (objections) to close a sale

'Julie says: "I don't like the way you dress, I don't think you make enough money, and you drive like a maniac."

Frank hears: "I don't like the way you dress [*buying signal*], I don't think you make enough money [*buying signal*], and you drive like a maniac [*buying signal*]."

Frank's response: "If I let you pick my suits, if I double my income, and if I promise never to exceed the posted speed limits, then will you marry me?"'
Frank Pacetta, Xerox sales manager

Psychic income – two holes of golf with Jack Nicklaus

The Maritz Corporation specializes in psychic income packages. They even give out pyramid-shaped paperweights that list Maslow's needs. They tailor their awards so that individuals are offered an appropriate range of stimulating options. Some of their choices have offered trips to the moon, ballooning across the wine fields of Burgundy or two holes of golf with Jack Nicklaus. As you approach the 18th green there is an 80-piece orchestra perched on scaffolding, playing the tune of your choice.

The reward itself is soon forgotten here, whereas the psychic income reward tends to linger longer and therefore offers better motivational potential.

The annual sales conference should be a motivator and act as a forum for sharing ideas ('how I made a sale' contest), identifying and solving problems, improving techniques, and recognizing and rewarding achievements. The conference should also provide a pleasant environment that reinforces feelings of being glad to work with the company.

Controlling

Controlling the sales force involves analysing sales:

- by product;
- by market or region;
- by salesperson.

Sales can also be analysed by profitability or the 'contribution' each order makes towards the overall profitability of the organization. This encourages the salesperson to sell higher-margin products or services rather than succumbing to the temptation of 1) giving discounts and 2) pushing easier, low-margin items. The bottom line tends to be turnover or sales, number of new accounts (customers) won and old accounts lost, and the quality of those accounts (size and creditworthiness). Further analysis reveals number of orders (and average order size), calls-to-orders ratios, etc. Even miles driven give some indication as to whether reps are chasing their tails or leaving room for improvement. Good planning helps control.

Good sales forecasting provides targets and yardsticks for measurement. Sales forecasts can be drawn up by sales reps for each customer for each month and eventually put together to form an overall sales rep forecast. This can be modified to allow for low forecasts that reduce target sales figures, thereby reducing pressure on the reps and making it easier for them to attain their daily, weekly, monthly, quarterly and annual targets. There are also more sophisticated forecasting models that take into account a host of factors, including prices, competitors, state of the economy, etc.

Typical quantitative standards are as follows:

- sales volume as a percentage of sales potential;
- selling expense as a percentage of sales generated;
- number of customers as a percentage of the total number of potential customers in the territory;
- call frequency ratio, or total calls made divided by total number of customers and prospects who are called (or visited) by the salesperson.

The extinguisher

There is always room for creativity in marketing, and particularly in selling. Whether it is a new form of presentation, a new way of prospecting or a new way of showing determination to win the business, the list is endless. The extinguisher's creative approach below is not to be recommended. This story is recalled from a marketing magazine of many years ago.

Having recognized the weary tread of a door-to-door salesman coming up the stairs, the giggling office staff scrambled behind doors and under desks to avoid the approaching salesman's eye contact. I only realized that a salesman was looming when I noticed the sniggering bodies scattered behind the furniture. Too late. I turned around to see a shabby little man with a greasy raincoat and coffee-stained briefcase move towards me. Before I knew it he had opened his briefcase and poured a jar of petrol over himself. Out of his inside pocket he drew a lighter and set fire to himself. Then, while standing in the classic salesperson pose (right arm holding out a spray can and left arm pointing to the label), he said 'And this, ladies and gentlemen, is the FlameZapper miniature fire extinguisher.' As he proceeded to spray himself, he continued, 'You can carry it anywhere.' He left several cans lighter and several pounds heavier.

Time – the scarce resource

Salespeople are spending less and less time in front of customers (Dixon *et al.*, 2011). Some previous estimates suggest salespeople spend less than 10 per cent of their time engaged in face-to-face selling (Abberton Associates, 1997). The rest of the time is spent filling in report forms, travelling, setting up appointments, attending internal meetings, etc. Is this the optimum use of a key resource? Definitely not, so some companies use other communication tools (such as a direct response advertisement or a mail-shot) to generate enquiries and then categorize or qualify the quality of the enquiry or lead into 'hot, medium or cold' prospects. An online form or an offline telesales team can then further qualify the lead by determining how urgent, immediate or serious the enquiry is (see Chapter 17 for further examples). They can even set up appointments in a way that minimizes the travel between appointments. 'The extinguisher' (in the box opposite) is an extreme example, where the salesman seizes the relatively rare face-to-face opportunity and makes a sale every time (although he may also soon be locked up!).

Servicing existing customers with a mixture of telephone calls and personal visits, instead of visits only, allows sales reps to become more efficient by reducing the frequency of their visits but maintaining the frequency of contact or service by phone. There is obviously a fine line between the less personal telephone call and the more personal visit. Some buyers may prefer to avoid the interruption of a sales visit and appreciate a courtesy call ('just checking to see if everything is all right or if there is anything you need'). This minimizes time wastage (for both parties) while maintaining the customer service facility. Getting the balance between calls and visits is vital, since the competition is also out there, every day, knocking on the same doors. Optimum call frequencies need to be carefully planned.

Extending the sales force

Types of sales force

The three key resources, the 3Ms (men/women, money and minutes), are limited. Selling soaks up all three resources. There are various combinations of types of sales force. An organization's field sales force can be supported by an in-house telesales team who do the prospecting and appointment setting, thereby freeing the field salespeople to do what they are best at – selling. Resources can also be invested in agents, distributors, wholesalers, retailers and their reps so that they become an extension of the sales force. Alternatively, a temporary sales team can be contracted in to screen prospects and make appointments (telesales teams) or to go out and sell or give

free samples away (see 'Field marketing' below). There is no single correct sales force mix; for example within the commercial tyre market one company achieves 200 calls per executive per annum, while its largest competitor achieves over 1,600. The former company has focused on large accounts and uses agents to service the independent trade. The latter sells direct to customers of all sizes. Both companies are highly profitable, and both have highly efficient sales organizations.

The correct approach is, of course, to monitor constantly the effectiveness of each sales force mix (customer satisfaction, sales, market share and profitability) and the efficiency (number of calls, cost per call, conversion rates of enquirers to customers, etc). There is always room for improvement.

Own sales force

Although a sales force creates a large overhead, it does allow direct control over recruiting, training and motivating. The section 'Managing the sales force' (p. 325) explores the processes involved in getting the best out of this key resource. First consider alternative extensions of the sales force, both online and offline, including field marketing, multi-level marketing, affiliate marketing and distributors' sales assistants.

Field marketing

It is possible to hire flexible sales forces for ad hoc tactical activities or regular repeat activities. Reduced cost, flexibility and direct measurability make a contract sales force or field marketing team attractive compared to a full-time, in-house field sales team. Cost can be further reduced by using a syndicated or shared team as opposed to a dedicated team devoted to one particular product only. There are, of course, risks, particularly if the salespeople have a tendency for hard selling, misrepresentation or even rudeness. Careful scrutiny and supervision can usually identify these potential problems before they develop into a full-blown crisis. Field marketing tends to be used by FMCG or impulse goods manufacturers, but can be used by a wider range of organizations.

Typical field marketing activities include:

1 selling into independent retail outlets, eg field sales teams sold Christmas charity cards to almost 18,000 outlets during January, February and March;

2 merchandising and display – arranging stocks and literature in retail stores and other outlets, eg 25,000 newsagents and doctors' surgeries had the Department of Social Security's Family Credit information point-of-sale material placed in them within 14 days;

3 sampling and promotions – providing teams (eg the Pepsi Challenge) in shopping precincts and superstores and at national events and exhibitions;

4 market research into shelf facings, stocking levels and positions in store (including number of shelf facings or number of units that can be seen);

5 monitoring customer care and service – with mystery shoppers who are employed to observe service and report back details of the specific levels of in-store service and customer care.

Field marketing's main advantages are widening the reach without acquiring the overhead of a full-time sales team. The disadvantages, in addition to the fees, are that training, motivation and constant monitoring and feedback are required to get the best out of the field sales team.

Telemarketing

In addition to direct selling, telemarketing (telephone marketing) is used for appointment setting, lead generation, list building or cleaning, market research, customer care, and even shareholder communications. An outbound campaign requires telemarketing professionals to make the calls, as opposed to an inbound campaign, which receives calls generated from 0800, freephone, local, standard or premium-rate (which act as 'self-liquidating', ie generating revenues that pay for other costs) phone numbers listed in direct response advertisements, mailshots or websites. Telemarketing is a flexible tool. Depending on the previous day's results, a telesales campaign can change on a daily basis, with the telesales script being rewritten overnight and tested the following day.

Telemarketing can be part of a contact strategy that includes mailshots (letters, brochures and vouchers), e-mails, visits and calls. Equally, telemarketing can qualify prospects to determine which particular contact strategy is best, eg prospects with less immediate needs might be mailed a brochure,

while telemarketing contacts the more immediate buyers with a view to setting up an appointment. Another stage will emerge when the not-so-urgent prospects who received the brochure start to mature into the buying mode. The database can prompt some telesales action, and so on. Detailed objectives for the campaign, such as total number of calls, number of calls per person per hour, conversion rates, minimum amount of information to be collected, etc, must be agreed.

Once again, sales and marketing need to work closely together; the telemarketing manager needs to know when the mailings go out or when the sales team are available for appointments. Script development draws on the features, benefits and USPs. It will also include open-question, presentation, objection-handling and closing techniques. The telemarketing team can then be briefed and trained. Lists, scripts, incentives, prices and timing can all be tested. The results will be carefully monitored and used to develop the optimum combination for the full roll-out of the telemarketing campaign. These results should be analysed to continually build on previous success.

Telemarketing is an expensive way to boost awareness on a cost-per-thousand (CPT) basis, but it is flexible and quick and can be cost-effective if targeting the right customer profile. It can also save costs by maintaining customer relationships with telecalls bolstered by fewer actual visits from a sales rep.

Multi-level marketing

Multi-level marketing is a system of selling goods directly to customers through a network of self-employed salespeople. The manufacturer recruits distributors, who in turn recruit (or sponsor) more distributors, who in turn recruit more distributors, and so on. Each distributor is on a particular level of discounts (depending on the size of stock purchased). Distributors effectively earn income on their own direct sales to the distributors they have recruited. Distributors also earn a percentage of the earnings of all of the other distributors connected through their chain or line of distributors.

Multi-level marketing is sometimes called network selling, retail networking or pyramid selling. Several companies have proved that network selling can be a legal and successful method of marketing. Pyramid selling has a bad image because it was exploited unscrupulously, with new distributors being promised fortunes in return for large investments in stock that never sold. In addition, these selling systems tend to exploit personal contacts and networks, which can cause individuals to view all their friends and family (or anyone with whom they come into contact) as sales prospects. This mercenary perspective is sometimes enveloped in a kind of corporate evangelism, which gives this sales and distribution method a poor image, despite the several legitimate and successful systems that thrive in the United States.

The Trading Schemes Regulations 1997 allow a maximum initial fee of £200 (within the first seven days) to be charged for enrolment as a distributor. Goods are then purchased at a discounted wholesale price, which allows newly enrolled distributors to add their own margin of profit when selling the goods to an end user. Goods are returnable (and 90 per cent of the cost recoupable). Any training fees must be clearly stated in the written contract, and training must not be compulsory.

The advantage of multi-level marketing is acquiring a vast distribution network with no direct overhead, although margins are reduced as commissions are paid. Disadvantages include that some countries do not accept multi-level marketing and ban any form of 'pyramid selling'.

Affiliate marketing

Although it does not employ salespeople *per se*, affiliate marketing extends the reach of a brand's sales potential through a form of multi-level marketing online. Affiliates generate sales on a commission-only basis. Affiliate partners usually have access to specific communities or target markets. The affiliates basically refer visitors to the brand's website, and every time the referred visitors buy the brand the affiliate gets paid a commission. The affiliates use banner ads (usually supplied by the brand), e-mail and PPC ad campaigns.

The relatively risk-free concept is straightforward:

- Affiliate networks generate traffic to the client's website via banner ads, PPC and e-mail.
- Affiliate networks track this traffic closely (via tracking codes) and supply reports.
- Commission is paid against whatever the agreed goals are: traffic, leads or enquiries, or actual sales, eg if sales conversions are the goal and no sales are generated then no commission is paid.

- The only investment a marketer needs is 1) the copy about the company or product to attract affiliates and 2) the banner adverts for affiliates to use on their sites.

The original form of affiliate marketing was selling through clubs, associations and networks, whether online or offline. Members within networks, clubs or associations tend to trust relevant offers from within the group. For example, an insurance company might ask a football club to encourage its members to buy its credit card. Each time a football fan buys a card, the club gets a commission and the member gets a discount or a gift instead (eg a club baseball cap that costs £2 could have much greater value, as a club baseball cap is so relevant). The insurance company can do the same online, except on a potentially much bigger scale and with multiple clubs, associations and communities. As well as boosting sales, this also increases brand awareness. In fact, affiliate marketing can get a brand's ad carried by hundreds if not thousands of websites; for example, Marriott Hotels use Commission Junction to reach into over 700 highly relevant websites with a range of banner ads and special offers.

Amazon has an estimated 400,000 affiliates or 'associates' who offer Amazon books to their networks; a horse-riding website can have a book about horse riding promoted on the website in an Amazon banner that takes the buyer directly to Amazon. Everyone wins. The customer is offered very relevant books only. The website owner adds value to its website by adding highly relevant books and subsequently earning a revenue or commission on each book sold. There is no risk to the website owner, as no stockholding investment is required, and no resources are required for logistical operations (dispatch, post and packaging, and invoicing), as this is all handled by Amazon.

Essentially affiliate marketing extends a brand's reach across hundreds and sometimes thousands of websites (and search engines), generating extra sales on a commission basis (approximately 30 per cent). However, the affiliate may be competing for the same traffic that the brand's own website wants (or it may reach way beyond the brand's own reach). Heavy use of PPC ad words (including the brand name) by affiliates can push up bid prices for the brand itself. Some brands have strict guidelines about the use (and even restrict the use) of their brand name by affiliate PPC campaigns. Brands need to check out the quality of the affiliate's website and how it portrays the brand to ensure no damage to the brand. There are two types of affiliate programmes: in-house affiliate programmes and affiliate network programmes. Ask how the brand is being portrayed and whether the brand is effectively competing with affiliates to attract the same visitor.

In-house affiliate programmes

Some brands like to have their own affiliate networks. Amazon has over 400,000 partners who place highly relevant Amazon banner ads on their own sites, delivering visitors who buy and simultaneously earning a steady stream of revenue for themselves. Many major brands list their affiliate programmes on their websites under 'Affiliate programme', 'Associate programme', 'Referral programme' or 'Partner programme', giving a full explanation of how it works, including log-in, tracking, banners available and frequency of commission payments. Commissions range from 5 per cent to 30 per cent.

Affiliate network programme

A network is a collection of companies that have affiliate programmes but are managed by one company, eg Commission Junction, Affiliate Future, Trade Doubler or UK Affiliates. A lot of companies want affiliate programmes but they don't want to manage them (commissions, payments and queries), which can be costly in terms of time, money and systems. An affiliate network company like

Commission Junction recruits relevant new publishers (websites), checks the quality of each new affiliate, activates existing publishers, and motivates them to boost performance and ultimately grow sales. Some affiliate networks have a set-up fee (up to £2,000) and a monthly management fee, and all have a commission override, on top of the commission paid to the affiliate (say 20 per cent of the affiliate commission). For example, if an item sells for £100 with an affiliate commission of 30 per cent, £30 goes to the affiliate and £6 goes to the network (20 per cent of the £30 commission), so the brand pays a total of £36 from the £100 sale.

There are three parties involved: the merchant (eg a brand owner), a publisher (affiliate, eg a website owner) and the affiliate network (eg Commission Junction). Consider the retailer Argos ('the merchant') using Commission Junction ('the affiliate network') to reach different target markets via different publishers, eg it could target cheap furniture into its network of student sites (publishers) and camping equipment into its network of festival sites (publishers) from the 16,000 affiliate publishers that are in Commission Junction's network.

Distributors' sales assistants

In both B2B and B2C markets, most brands sell to distributors, who in turn sell to wholesalers and/or end users (ultimate customers). Winning the battle for the distributor's 'mindshare' (or share of mind) can be an important part of sales force management. Mindshare means the amount of attention

FIGURE 12.1   In-house affiliate programme

FIGURE 12.2   Affiliate network programme

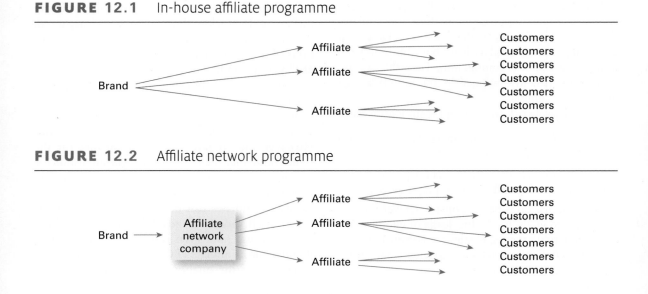

and effort that a distributor's sales force gives to a particular manufacturer's product. A distributor often carries many different product lines supplied by several competing suppliers. The mindshare concept aims to develop the distributor's sales force into an extension of the supplier's sales force.

All suppliers would obviously like to have the distributor's sales force recommend, select or push their particular brand to the end user. Mindshare can be won by creating and maintaining a partnership approach that develops a mutually beneficial business relationship. This means the manufacturer must supply:

- a reasonable quality of product (and price and delivery);
- creative and frequent sales promotions (eg a distributor sales rep club where the top distributor's reps are presented with awards, in front of the distributor's own management, once they attain a certain level of sales; there might be a silver, gold and platinum club for 50-, 100- and 200-unit salespeople, respectively);
- product training;
- joint visits (the manufacturer and distributor visit the end user together);
- cooperative advertising (where the manufacturer shares the cost of the distributor's advertising when it promotes both the parties);
- merchandising and display services.

Mindshare requires a longer-term approach to selling, since the sales reps' efforts do not necessarily result in an immediate order. But mindshare will contribute to longer-term sales. It is therefore management's responsibility to develop a suitable time horizon and a mindshare strategy that works.

A US marketing consultancy, the Richmark Group, claims that a mindshare strategy has been found to be more powerful than strategies based on product differentiation and other more traditional market strategies. Manufacturers who successfully implement this strategy can build a market position that it is almost impossible for competitors to duplicate. Mindshare can make a competitor's marketing communications totally ineffective. Imagine the manufacturer makes electrical cable Z100, the distributor is an electrical wholesaler and the end user is the electrical contractor who will buy and install the cable under the floorboards of a new house.

An end user (electrical contractor) customer asks a distributor's sales rep (electrical wholesaler's rep) for a competing brand, say brand A1000. The distributor's rep recommends and offers the Z100 cable instead. The end user seeks advice in selecting a specific brand. The distributor's rep recommends the manufacturer's brand Z100. The distributor's rep effectively becomes part of the Z100 brand 'unofficial' sales force.

The advantage of mindshare is spreading the sales force wider without acquiring the fixed overhead of the additional resource. The disadvantages are, once again, that training, motivation and constant monitoring are required. Note that organizations must pay heed to the new Bribery Act 2011.

Advantages and disadvantages

Here are some of the advantages and disadvantages to consider when deciding whether to increase or reduce the communications tool.

Advantages

Salespeople are great (when trained and motivated) at getting key messages across to buyers. Messages can also be changed (though it requires some training) in a relatively short lead time. If the product or service requires a personalized presentation then investing in salespeople rather than just advertising makes sense. B2B markets invest more in sales teams than advertising. Salespeople are also great at collecting intelligence and market research, as well as building relationships and, of course, getting sales.

Disadvantages

A sales force cannot spread a message as quickly and as widely as advertising, sponsorship, PR or perhaps a piece of viral marketing. Sales teams require investment in training, motivation and monitoring. It is important to spend time carefully recruiting salespeople, as they are the organization's brand ambassadors. On a CPT basis, sales teams do not compete with advertising, sponsorship or PR, but on a cost-per-order basis they may very well do better than other promotional tools.

Summary

The sales force is a key marketing resource that can determine the success or otherwise of any organization. Sales teams and marketing people need to work together more closely to share intelligence and leads in a systematic process. Managing the sales resource requires clear management skills. There are many different options to extend the sales force: through its own sales team or using field marketing, multi-level marketing, affiliate marketing or mindshare through distributors' sales teams.

Key points from Chapter 12

- There are different types of sales teams, including in-house, telemarketing, multi-level marketing, affiliate marketing and distributors' sales assistants.

- KAM requires a variety of management skills, including consultative selling.

- Managing a sales forces requires recruitment, training, motivation and monitoring.

References and further reading

Abberton Associates (1997) *Balancing the Selling Equation*, CPM Field Marketing, Thame

Buzan, T (1988) *Make the Most of Your Mind*, Pan Books, London

Buzan, T (1989) *Use Your Head*, revised edn, Pan Books, London

Buzan, T (2003) *How to Mindmap*, Thorson Publications, London

Buzan, T (2013) *Modern Mind Mapping for Smarter Thinking*, e-book, Proactive Press

Constable, J and McCormack, R (1987) *The Making of British Managers*, CBI/BIM, London

Denny, R (2000) *Selling to Win*, Kogan Page, London

Dixon, M, Frewer, S and Kent, A (2011) Are your sales reps spending too much time in front of customers? *Harvard Business Review*, 8 February

Francis, K (1998) What is KAM?, *Winning Business*, January–March

Hancock, M, John, R and Wojcik, P (2005) Better B2B selling, *McKinsey Quarterly*, 16 June

Jobber, D and Lancaster, G (2000) *Selling and Sales Management*, Financial Times/Prentice Hall, Harlow

Mathur, S (1981) Strategic industrial marketing: Transaction shifts and competitive response, City University Working Paper 33, City University, London

McDonald, M and Woodburn, D (2007) *Key Account Management: The definitive guide*, 2nd edn, Butterworth Heinemann, Oxford

Millman, T and Wilson, K (1995) From key account selling to key account management, *Journal of Marketing Practice: Applied marketing science*, 1 (1), pp 9–21

New York Sales and Marketing Association (2002) Tips and advice in selling, *Sense and Sensibility*, 22 April

Woods, S (2009) *Digital Body Language*, New Year Publishing, Danville, CA

Further information

Institute of Sales and Marketing Management
Harrier Court
Lower Woodside
Bedfordshire LU1 4DQ

Tel: +44 (0)1582 840001
Fax: +44 (0)1582 849142
www.ismm.co.uk

13
Advertising

LEARNING OBJECTIVES

By the end of this chapter you will be able to:

- Understand the evolutionary nature of advertising
- Explore cutting-edge new advertising tools
- Appreciate the potential for integrations with social media and other marketing communications tools
- Know how to plan the stages of an ad campaign

From Mad Men to Maths Men – the changing
    nature of advertising   336
Video and the Big Idea are still important   336
The end of advertising or start of a new era?   336
Does advertising really work? Strong and weak
    theories of advertising   337
The second screen   338
Analytics, big data and ads   338
The rise and fall of owned and earned media
    but not paid media   339
The magic marketing formula   339

Data-driven ad campaigns   340
Data delivers competitive advantage   340
A data-driven campaign type: location-based
    marketing   340

New data-driven targeting tools for
    advertising   342
Contextual advertising and behavioural
    targeting   343
Location-based advertising variations   343
Behavioural mapping (location and
    movement)   344
Remarketing   344
Programmatic ads   345
Beacons   346
Apps ads   346
Native advertising   347
Integrating mobile, apps, TV and social TV   348

New forms of advertising   348
Where creative Mad Men meet Maths Men   348
User-generated ads   349
Long-form ads   349
Short-form ads   350
Postmodern ads   350
Creative ads   351
Sponsored TV   351

Managing a 'traditional' TV ad campaign   352
The situation   352
Objectives (including the 'brief')   354
Strategy   354
Message development (strategy and tactics)   354
Media developments (strategy and tactics)   359
Action   362
Control   362

Managing a location-based ad campaign   362
How location-based marketing works   362
Location-based marketing – data flow, bids and ads   363
How visitors are tracked   365

Advantages and disadvantages   373
Advantages   373
Disadvantages   373

Key points from Chapter 13   374

References and further reading   374

Further information   375

From Mad Men to Maths Men – the changing nature of advertising

Advertising is changing all the time, and in the last five years it has seen some massive changes that challenge the nature of advertising itself. It is morphing into dialogues, social media, user-generated content, native advertising, and a myriad of wonderful new ways of communicating with customers. These include contextual advertising, behavioural advertising, location-based advertising, long-form and short-form ads, apps, social TV, postmodern ads and of course creative ads and even contentious ads. This chapter explores these and uses a selection of mini cases to demonstrate these changes in action.

The pre-digital ad business for the big brands was all about 'The Big Idea' that made a TV ad special and sometimes leveraged across three or four media (radio, press, cinema and posters) as demonstrated by the Mad Men TV series about ad agencies in the 50s and 60s. However, it is interesting to see that the less glamorous communications agencies, those working in direct mail and integration have proven to have the right fundamental skills for the digital age advertising (analysing and manipulating databases) to continually optimize results. It's the bigger Above the Line agencies who've been wrong footed by the digital explosion.

The post-digital ad business has become multichannel delivery and consumption, moving from mass messages to individual targeting, as Big Data and analytics (Maths Men) shake the ad world up and introduce programmatic ads, remarketing/retargeting, data enhancement and automated marketing. Then the social media revolution with its reviews and recommendations, likes, shares and comments is shifting message control from the advertiser to customer. We see the emergence of Owned Media (your social media platforms and content marketing), Earned Media (shares/likes/comments/word of mouth and reviews) and Paid Media (ads and native ads).

Video and the Big Idea are still important

Despite all of these changes, two things remain: firstly, the big medium of exchange is still film (video) – maybe not a 30-second TV ad but perhaps a video targeted at mobile devices and perhaps also aimed at another 20 different social channels which ends up going viral. And secondly, the Big Idea (creative idea/message) is still required by Mad Men as they work with the Maths Men to target more precisely and optimize continually their advertising ROI. The growth of analytics has helped data planners become king as they now have the tools to slice and dice this data to target 'individual tastes on a mass scale'.

However, creative ideas are valued more than ever – except now they need to cross channels and come alive in many more forms. Great advertising still comes from great briefs except now they are media neutral as brands are no longer 'products' but experiences created from all touchpoints not just consumption.

The end of advertising or start of a new era?

Many critics believe advertising is on its way out; Regis McKenna (1991) announced that we are 'witnessing the oblivion of advertising'. More recently, some other marketers have said that location-based services remove the need for advertising. To date, the fortunes of advertising have risen alongside the growth of the mass media. Now that this growth has stopped, questions are being asked. Mass media has fragmented (thousands of TV stations, millions of websites and an explosion of new magazines, radio stations, podcasts, blogs and new apps). Martin Sorrell (1996) of WPP said: 'Massive audiences become more and more difficult to buy.' Some suggest that it is the end of lavish advertising productions, which used to depend on mass audiences to make them cost-effective.

Who said this about advertising, and when?

'Advertising [is] one of the most fundamental ways to sort out information. And that's the gift of advertising: to connect with people in a human way, to make the kind of emotional connections that are at the core of storytelling.'

'Advertisements are now so numerous that they are very negligently perused.'

Which of these statements is the more recent? One is by Google's CEO, Eric Schmidt, in 2009 and the other by Samuel Johnson 250 years earlier.

So some feel advertising is a maturing industry. Although it does have a unique ability to simplify and condense a complicated selling message into an emotionally charged 30-second piece of film, media proliferation has meant that the traditional 30-second TV advertisement is no longer the answer to everything. But brilliant advertising, particularly if it integrates with social media, has a significant role to play. Customers will consume them if they cut through the clutter, are relevant and available at just the right place at the right time.

More TV and radio stations, newspapers and cinemas still need advertisements to fill them. Social media platforms still need video to fill them. But the days of media owners just selling ad space are over. 'Marketers need media owners to think creatively about using the media for reaching out and also building stronger relations, as well as selling more product X.' Learmonth (2010) refers to this in more detail (see Chapter 7); also see how Citroën partnered with ASOS's media and database to access the ideal target market (Chapter 15).

There is a shift in vision and philosophy amongst 'advertisers'. Interruption marketing (ads shouting at customers) has less of a role today. Marketing campaigns are no longer just about cost per thousand (CPM) and page views and more about learning how to interact with customers and participate in their activities as they spend more time online. Customers want to be engaged with relevant added-value content. They want to find relevant information only when they want it and share it with whomever they

desire. Despite the hype, advertising is not going away. It's just reinventing itself to meet the demands of social media. Contextual advertising, behavioural targeting and location-based advertising are clear examples of advertising reinventing itself.

Media owners and advertisers are thinking more creatively and, in some cases, thinking way 'outside the box'. They understand customers' needs for interaction and involvement and are developing strategies to maximize them. This is demonstrated in the integrating of social media, new variants of advertising (see below) and radical rethinking by companies like Coca-Cola, which is shaking up its view of marketing by not relying on traditional advertising and, instead, investing serious money into ideas that bring entertainment value to brands. It is developing content and partnerships with media companies, as it sees its brands such as Coca-Cola as 'portals' offering a 'network' or means of distribution in their own right. This concept has been dubbed 'brand entertainment', and companies such as Coca-Cola, Nike, Orange and Mercedes-Benz are busy integrating brands into such varied areas as sport, entertainment, music, travel and gaming.

Old ads advice still works today

'In planning an advertising campaign, the first step should be to clear the decks of all opinions. The next step should be to find a scientific method of testing.'
John Caples (1932)

Half of my advertising is wasted

'The days are over when clients politely smiled when anyone used the John Wanamaker (1838–1922) quote: "I know half my advertising is wasted. I just don't know which half." Today, better-disciplined clients demand more measurement, more integration and more dialogue from all of their communications.'
Advertising Age (1999)

Today, as mentioned in Chapter 8 (agencies) it is suggested that 'Marketers will waste $6.3 billion on internet ads that aren't even delivered to humans!' (Shields, 2015), according to a study by White Ops and the Association of National Advertisers. Is this possible?

Does advertising really work? Strong and weak theories of advertising

The strong theory of advertising suggests that basically advertising works. It suggests that it helps to move customers through a series of hierarchical stages towards purchase (see Chapter 4). The ultimate proof of strength is where advertising can persuade customers to buy something they have never bought before. This is challenged today, as it assumes that customers are passive and unable to process information properly. Andrew Ehrenberg (1974) challenged this and proposed **the weak theory of advertising,** which suggested that customers are driven by habit and that advertising reinforces rather than drives initial sales. Advertising could, he suggested, increase the frequency of purchases, as it could stimulate habitual buyers into more frequent choice of the advertised brands against a repertoire of considered brands. **He developed the awareness–trial–reinforcement (ATR) model** (see Chapter 4). He maintained that advertising could increase or maintain awareness and improve the customers' knowledge, but only for those brands that customers were already buying (or at least had some prior knowledge of). Some academics went further and suggested that advertising could not convert customers who had reasonably strong beliefs that contradicted the messages in the advertisements. The truth is that no one is 100 per cent sure of exactly how every aspect of advertising works. The same applies for every aspect of marketing. The winners will be those who have inquisitive minds and a willingness to continually learn how marketing communications work.

Coca-Cola continually learning

'"When it's something new, it's hard for publishers to know what the value is," she said. "We didn't know how it would work out but we wanted to learn in that space. It could have completely flopped. They [Twitter] also wanted to learn with us."'
Carol Kruse, Vice-President for Global Interactive Marketing at Coca-Cola, which is an official sponsor of the World Cup, in Bradshaw (2010)

The second screen

Advertisers now look for PR and social media conversational opportunities. The media consumption trend towards 'two screens' is still growing as the audience multitask (see Media chapter) and simultaneously use TV and social media (via mobile or tablet or laptop). It delivers a second audience for advertisers, since people watch the main event on TV while social media 'lengthens the shelf life of an advertisement'. Witness how Budweiser's 60-second Clydesdales 'Brotherhood' ad has had 9.1 million views on YouTube to date, as well as 1.5 million shares on Facebook and 10,000 retweets on Twitter (Dalton, 2013).

As audiences continue to migrate from offline to online, the second screens are growing in importance. In fact, the UK will reach a major media milestone this year, as it is set to become the first country in the world where digital media will take a 50 per cent share of advertising spending (eMarketer, 2015). Norway and China are following close behind. The UK will retain its lead by this measure until 2018, when digital's portion of total ad spending in China will become the largest worldwide.

Fifty per cent of all advertising is digital

Total media spend in the UK is split equally between digital and all other traditional formats combined – TV, print, outdoor and radio. Ad spending on mobile and online devices will attract more than twice the ad spending that goes to TV, which will account for a 24.9 per cent share this year (eMarketer, 2015).

Analytics, big data and ads

What exactly is the impact of big data in advertising?

The impact is massive on all fronts. For planners, there will be more data to understand consumer behaviour. For creatives, the barriers of the real world will be broken down allowing them to impact the consumer in accordance with time, real time. For media, increasingly it will be more power segmentation. We can now forget about just demographic data or the IAB standard formats. Now we have full access to everything. The Big Data will bring us to a level of sophistication in communication never before achieved.
Adriel (2014)

We are the humans and we are the data

The reshaping and changing of communication will be an ongoing process always taking one step forward and never having to take a step back to review success or failure. With all of this technology and data we can finally forget about packaged solutions, about defined channels and about thinking of communication inside pre-determined formats. We are finally able to work with something that never changes: our perception, our emotion and our passion in dealing with humans and creating for them. I believe this is because we are the humans and we are the data.

Emotional data for emotionally targeted ads

Imagine an advertising engine that monitors people's emotional states based on their search queries, e-mails, instant messages, use of online games, as well as facial expressions, tone of voice, speech patterns and body movements?

> Kinect is the motion-sensing input device that was released for Xbox but now also has a version for Windows. A user who screams or paces back and forth, when observed by Kinect, could be assigned a negative emotional state by a currently hypothetical advertising engine... and ads aren't wasted on people who are temperamentally unsuited to them. For example weight-loss product advertisers may not want their advertisement to appear to users that are very happy. Because, a person that is really happy is less likely to purchase a self-investment product that leverages on his or her shortcomings. But a really happy person may purchase electronic products or vacation packages. "Party" advertisers do not want to appear when the user is sad or crying.'
>
> Delo (2012)

The rise and fall of owned and earned media but not paid media

As marketers remix their communications mix and have been shifting resources generally towards social media the question emerges: 'at what point does social media become less effective?' Perhaps the last World Cup was the turning point as brands compete as publishers, as sponsors and advertisers to try to dominate the discussions, the awareness and preference levels and, ultimately, the sales.

Owned media, or own channels, such as your website, your YouTube channel or Twitter stream give you a certain amount of control over your message. Earned media means engagement which means word of mouth (or mouse) generated by discussions, likes, shares all triggered by your content. Going viral to a marketer is arguably akin to winning a World Cup Medal for a footballer but with little control over your message. While 'paid media', whether banner ads, pay-per-click ads, promoted posts, promoted tweets or, some argue, sponsorship offer more control and can be a much faster way to spread a message.

More free content = more expensive attention

If all brands become content publishers and engage in conversations simultaneously, surely this makes it more difficult to grab attention?

More content = less attention

More free content = more expensive attention

If owned and earned keep taking a larger share of the communications mix, at what point does it become less effective? The World Cup has generated a frenzy of high-quality content. Why? We think the potentially powerful viral component of reaching out and connecting with customers via an emotionally charged, shared experience, tempts a lot of marketers to become publishers. But can it scale as fast and efficiently as 'paid for' media?

Connecting via an emotionally charged shared experience

YouTube executives talk about viral videos as always having a 'shared experience' component, whether this means riding the right trend, mood, public holiday or major event. The World Cup has elevated 'notions of connectedness and shared experiences to new levels' (Benady, 2014). Competing brands will use sponsorship, guerilla marketing, content marketing and of course ads of paid media (ads when required to get scale and impact quickly. You can explore the rise and fall of owned and earned but not paid media at **www.PRSmith.org/blog** (Smith, 2015).

[Note: First published in Smith, PR (2015) The Rise and Fall of Owned, Earned but not Paid Media, **www.PRSmith.org/blog**: 27 June.]

The magic marketing formula

Always apply the magic marketing formula – IRD – to boost results:

- identify needs;
- reflect these needs (through ads, sales presentations, search engines etc.);
- deliver a good customer experience (ie fulfil your promise consistently at every touch point).

If Coca-Cola identify that people need to be loved, they reflect this by showing ads of people drinking

Coke and having a good time (whether polar bears or people); there is a good feeling that love exists. If a B2B technology supplier identifies a segment's main need is, say, security, then it reflects 'security' in its ads, exhibitions and social media, and optimizes for these key phrases.

A simpler example is obvious with the search engines and the magic marketing formula when you search for a very specific multi-word key phrase and then you see the exact phrase appear in the search engine results. It is a 'eureka' moment. It's like a fusion of your specific need with a supplier's offering. The perfect match. This is the formula reflecting your needs (phrases) through SEO.

In the case studies at the end of this chapter you will find a shocking example of how the magic marketing formula can be used in advertising to save lives. The anti-speeding campaign has reduced road deaths in Northern Ireland. The key to its success came from the in-depth research, when convicted speed drivers who still felt it was their right to break speed limits, were asked: 'What about if you killed someone?' No, this would not stop them. 'What about if you killed a child?' A resounding chilling silence. The idea was born. The eventual ads showed children in a garden being killed by a car. The shocking ads reflected the horror of killing a child. The video went viral and road deaths have decreased. The magic marketing formula works. See the full ad in the case study at the end of this chapter or the full video and the full story of this shocking, yet successful, TV ad at **www.PRSmith.org/blog**.

Data-driven ad campaigns

Data delivers competitive advantage

The digital advertising landscape has rapidly changed over the last few years. Not long ago, digital marketing, and digital targeting had its limitations – it was based on content behaviour, search and cookie data and that's all there was. Today, that data environment has opened up with vast and varied data sets providing all sorts of deeper audience insights and contextual user information.

Advertisers and their agencies now seek richer, multi-layered sets of data to give information on location, history, demographics and other sources that enable advertisers to serve the right ad, to the right audience, at just the right time.

Location data will become more powerful (for more on this see Chapter 6). It is crucial in understanding, segmenting, contextualizing, and actually predicting customer behaviour.

In what would have been double Dutch just a few years ago, here's BlisMedia talking about how data can create competitive advantage in advertising:

> Using device recognition augmentation methods, such as device usage profiles, geo location clustering, cross-device/screen analytics or ID linkage, improves digital marketing programs. Exclusive strategic data partnerships with say major wifi providers O2 and Sky are also important. The mobile environment is expanding fast. The proper use of data is delivering competitive advantage to those that seek it.

A data-driven campaign type: location-based marketing

You are where you are and have been

Once upon a time marketers used to say '**you are what you shop**', meaning the brands that you buy represent who you are, or who you aspire to be, ie revealing your real motivations and desires. So analysing a brand's customers' other purchases could give marketers additional insights into the desires and aspirations of a particular target market from observing their shopping baskets. Then ACORN came along and said '**you are where you live**', as they categorized customers into geo-demographic segments all based on postcodes or types of residential home. Online consumer businesses deliver to homes (with postcodes), help to determine where similar types of customers are and where to locate hubs for deliveries. Then came mobile location marketing which said '**you are where you are, and where you have been**' (eg a 6-star hotel versus a local café). Adding 'You are where you have been' enriched location-based advertising (on mobiles). Most digital advertising is based on the sites you visit and the searches you make. But now you can also add in the locations, or places, you go (in the offline real world) and watch the ROI rise.

The early version of LBA (location-based ads) back in the early 2000s was all about 'proximity', ie pushing ads at people depending on where they were. For example if you are walking towards a

Burger King then McDonalds can serve you an ad or a special coupon for a McDonald's burger across the road.

They know where you are

If any of your apps or social media platforms have 'location' enabled in the settings (as most people do have them on), then your device (mobile) triggers information to be sent to an ad network telling it that this device owner with a particular profile is within a few metres of a Burger King (based on physical places and websites you have visited and apps you have been using).

These push-based ads can be sent by a media company once the customer has (a) opted in to receive relevant ads (often while signing up for a mobile phone service) and (b) is in a particular location (and has opted in for ads when downloading an app or signing up for free wifi).

They know where you've been (physically and digitally)

Today LBA V2 also uses data about where a user has been (rather than just where they currently are). This information builds a more accurate profile of a user, even when the user has gone back to their home. A deep analysis of behaviour can include (within milliseconds) both where you've been visiting/browsing online and where you've physically been visiting/travelling in the real world offline. Effectively, LBA can improve a customer's experience by delivering just the right message at just the right time in just the right place. For example, before LBA V2, the system might have assumed that someone visiting cooking websites was a 'stay at home' mum. But if the data also shows that the same person goes to an international airport once a week and visits the business lounges, we could assume he or she is a business traveller who has cooking as a hobby. Add in even more data points and you begin to get a very accurate picture of what kind of person they are. You can also target users who have been in, say, a particular store any time within the last six months, excluding, of course, regular everyday customers to avoid wasting ads targeted at the already converted.

Using data to find more potential mortgage customers

TSB Mortgages need to continually improve the effectiveness of their ad campaigns. Working with Manning Gottlieb OMD and Talon, BlisMedia analysed data generated from over 200 million daily ad impressions across a two-week period to map the actual real location of people in the market for a new mortgage. They geo-fenced estate agencies in Cambridge, so they could look at the devices that were inside this area and then tracked where they went afterwards. Equipped with this data, Talon, an out of home (OOH) media specialist agency, planned the OOH advertising based on these movements. Geo-fencing is drawing a border around a target location which enables marketers to detect target devices within this location.

Tracking those who visited estate agents and then used property-related mobile apps and websites, helped to identify where these property hunters' travel routes were. This meant that TSB could buy OOH advertising (out of home billboards) in the most effective locations (and not necessarily the most expensive ones). Rich location data can help you to put your posters in the best possible locations. Mobile location ads are disrupting a 50-year-old advertising model.

Location-based ads vs geo-targeting ads

Location-based ads (or proximity ads) should not be confused with geo-targeting which Google, Facebook and other platforms have been using for many years to target specific areas based on where the user is geographically located – either recognized by the locations of his internet service provider or the registration details which include their address (home/office address). Early LBA, on the other hand, uses location-tracking technology in mobiles to target customers with specific ads that are relevant to their actual location as they travel around

The future of LBA

LBA will target the user rather than the device so they can serve omnichannel ads across multiple screens (laptop, desktop, smart TV, tablet). Some firms have invented fingerprinting technology that attaches itself to a single user. Others, like BlisMedia, are using location-based mobile advertising data to identify the same user across various devices.

Mobile wallets

As mobiles are used to pay for many transactions, then even greater data will become available. Imagine mapping and matching online ads with purchases at the till. This vision is what drives projects like Google Wallet.

Hijacking competitors

It's the dream of some brands to put a cookie on a rival's home page. With location-based mobile advertising, they can come close. For example, fast-food brands can already track users who visit their competitors' stores and then serve them ads at key times of day. Once BlisMedia know the device ID, they can see what the user looks at, has looked at and where they've been as well as where they are.

Hyper-local targeting ads

While a potential investor was on holiday in Bali, BlisMedia crunched his data to determine his location and served a 'Happy Birthday Harry' banner on each mobile site he visited that day.

BlisMedia geo-fenced W Hotel, Bali. So each time his device ID appeared on a website that used programmatic ads, Blis got a notification of an invitation to bid to serve an ad (or, in this case, a very personal message).

FIGURE 13.1   BlisMedia birthday banner

SOURCE: BlisMedia

Set up time and budgets

These LBA can be set up and ready to run in three days. Typical budgets range from £10,000 to £100,000. This will grow as advertisers realize the potential of clever LBA campaigns.

Measuring LBA

Marketers can take a sample group but show only half of them an ad for a particular store. Any uplift in store footfall by the group that saw the ad can then be compared against the group that did not see it. On a separate note, click-through rate can be anywhere from 0.5 per cent to 2 per cent (it can be higher – sometimes as much as 5 per cent – but on average across times, locations etc, CTR is between 0.5 per cent and 2 per cent).

Note: There is more on location-based marketing in the next section and in the penultimate section, 'Managing a Campaign' (see p. 352).

New data-driven targeting tools for advertising

Customers still want relevant advertising to inform them, entertain them and challenge them just as it always has. After all, advertising does inform, persuade and remind. It can still, very quickly, help to build brands, raise awareness and nurture brand relationships, and all in a relatively controlled environment (compared to the vagaries and uncontrollable nature of editorial exposure generated by

PR, sponsorship and social media campaigns – see Chapter 14, 'Lack of control'). So, although it will not be the same as before, there is a future for integrated advertising. This means that managers will still have to be able to manage the development of an advertising campaign, which will be explored after considering the new forms of advertising:

- contextual advertising and behavioural advertising;
- location-based advertising;
- behavioural mapping (location and movement);
- remarketing;
- programmatic;
- beacons;
- apps ads;
- integrating mobile, apps, TV and social TV.

Contextual advertising and behavioural targeting

Marketers are now free from the limitation of segmenting and targeting customers with 'monochrome' classifications such as 18- to 25-year-old ABC1s. In addition to age and sex, location, workplace and college, today marketers can target customers according to their actual behaviour, interests and passions (by keywords used).

If, say, you are advertising on Facebook, you can see, as you add a filter or segmentation variable, the approximate number of Facebook users that fit the profile.

Other online organizations, such as newspapers, can now serve very specific ads to readers online determined by the words on the pages they read, the number of pages they read and how often they read these pages. Ads can be selected according to a customer's changing status or status updates on Facebook. For example, a man who announces to his network of friends that he is getting married or updates his status with 'I'm getting married' or 'I've just got engaged' will find that he is subsequently served ads about wedding photographers, suit hire, limousines, romantic honeymoon holidays and maybe even wild stag venues. This is contextual advertising.

It is also called **behavioural targeting.** For example, if a 23-year-old male living in a major city is online comparing car prices, Microsoft can serve (or target)

him with an ad for a Mini Cooper, while a 40-year-old suburban businessman with children might be served an ad for a people carrier.

It gets more interesting. Ads can be made even more relevant according to the geographic location of the customer. This is location-based advertising (LBA).

Location-based advertising variations

There are many types of LBA ads, such as a text message display ad. Push-based ads are sent by a media company once the customer has (1) opted in to receive relevant ads (often opting in while signing up for a mobile phone service) and (2) is in a particular location.

Sharing your location data

A restaurant, pub or night club may incentivize customers to share a special offer whilst sharing their location to attract their friends into the venue. Other customers might value knowing that a friend is having a coffee around the corner – as long as they are happy for all their network to see what they are doing and with whom. Sharing of location information with your network may become as common as sharing your status update.

Targeting locals

Another variation of LBA can integrate with other data. For example, if a local newspaper collects postcodes as part of its registration process and has, say, 10,000 readers in a certain postcode area, it could serve local restaurant ads and special offers to just those 10,000 customers who live near those particular restaurants. The paper can still cover national, international and local news whilst delivering very relevant local ads.

Transactional banners

Interestingly, many banner ads are now '**transactional** banners' or, alternatively, branded applications (apps), which means customers can buy directly from the banner without being taken away from their preferred platform to a website. Customers on Facebook can order a pizza delivery while still on Facebook.

Behavioural mapping (location and movement)

Behavioural mapping is a type of systematic observation research that tracks behaviour over space and time. The tracking may focus on a particular place or be based on an individual's movements. These two techniques are also called place-centred and person- or individual-centred mapping. Here's how Mini (cars) used behavioural mapping to raise awareness and engagement (brochure downloads and boosting the number of test drives) for the two new models, the Mini Countryman and the Mini Paceman.

Many websites, some apps and most free wifi systems opt users into this type of advertising (permission is often granted when accepting the terms and conditions of free wifi, so read the small print), or when accepting cookies. Each device is given a unique identifier which can then be tracked.

Through behaviour mapping and/or IP location, Mini served ads in real time to ABC1 device owners who were either visiting: 4/5* hotels; Michelin-starred restaurants; business-class lounges in airports;

or who were in proximity to a Mini dealership, or in a competitor dealership. It took two days to set this up. The £20,000 campaign ran for five weeks and delivered the following results:

- Average campaign click-through rate (CTR) 0.55 per cent (industry benchmark CTR 0.5 per cent).
- Average daily impressions: 160,843. Mini Paceman ads delivered greater volume impressions (63 per cent) but Countryman ads delivered better CTR (0.60 per cent); iOS out-performed Android on device OS CTR – 0.97 per cent vs 0.75 per cent; CTR peaked at mid-morning (10:00), mid-afternoon (14:00) and immediately after work (17:00) – break periods and commuting times; CPM (or CPT) was between £5 and £8.

Remarketing

Remarketing, or retargeting is the practice of delivering display-advertising to either previous visitors to your site (site retargeting), or to web searchers

FIGURE 13.2   Selection of Mini ads

SOURCE: Blismedia

seeking out products and terms similar to yours on major search engines (search retargeting). So for example, if you put a shiny new Nikon D800 in your shopping cart, but don't buy it, Google (and others) will offer advertisers the opportunity to put ads for the D800 in front of you and others who have done the same. The challenge, highlighted by Lynne (2012) is 'not that retargeting is hard to implement, but rather that most web marketers don't know how to make it work with their already existing web marketing efforts'. The Topline case study in Chapter 16 blends remarketing into the advertising mix and boosts the return on marketing investment (see pp. 448–52).

How does remarketing work?

Here's Google's own explanation: Remarketing can help you reach people who have previously visited specific pages on your website as they visit other sites on the Google Display Network. To start using remarketing, add the remarketing tag (a small snippet of code that you get from AdWords), across all your site pages. Many sites have an identical footer for all pages, and this remarketing tag could be placed there. Once you've added the remarketing tag to your site, you can create remarketing lists for any of your webpages – effectively a list of visitors (without their names) who are interested in product X (if they visited product X page). So when a visitor visits this page, their cookie ID is added to the re-marketing list (google 'How remarketing works'). If that visitor (or that browser) with the unique cookie appears on another site the original site is invited to bid to serve an ad to that already interested visitor – even though they are on another site.

Remarketing = stalking?

'Some consumers are being bombarded by these ads. Poorly executed campaigns make ads stick to you like flypaper, following you everywhere you go, sometimes weeks after visiting a marketer's website. While retargeting can create a lift in direct-response metrics, what is the long-term impact on branding from being relentlessly stalked like this? It's a question that smart brands are considering carefully.'

Straz (2012)

Note: remarketing, along with targeting Facebook 'lookalike' audiences (similar profile to your customers or fans) and Facebook custom audiences (customers you already know), are used in the Topline Christmas ad campaign in Chapter 16 on sales promotion.

Programmatic ads

Programmatic advertising or programmatic marketing use data to basically automate the buying and selling of media inventory (ad space). This helps marketers firstly to target more relevant audiences, secondly to tailor and personalize ads and thirdly to remarket or serve an ad to someone who was previously on your website (but has now gone somewhere else online). PA uses real-time first- and third-party data to identify the best online audience for a campaign.

Advertisers used to buy thousands of impressions or blocks of impressions. Everyone saw the same ad. Today, PA and its RTB (real-time buying) functionality creates an automated online auction for space to place your ads.

PA effectively replaces manual or human-based methods. This is why the 'Maths Men' have become a lot more important in the ad world. They create clever algorithms to place ads in real time in front of more relevant audiences. Those clever Maths Men that used to work in the city are now needed by ad agencies and are being lured by agencies with very large salaries. The 'Maths Men meet the Mad Men' (classic ad agencies).

The most common form of programmatic buying is real-time bidding (RTB) which uses automated auctions to sell display impressions to the highest bidder. One impression at a time. Publishers (media companies or website owners) list their inventory (and their audience profile). Advertisers specify which ad inventory (audience profile: demographics, geography, interests, behaviours, time of day, device etc.) that they wish to purchase.

When an advertiser is matched with their target audience, ad exchanges use automated auctions to sell individual impressions to the highest bidders, whose ads are then served to the individual. This is all done in about 1/10th of a second.

How to set up programmatic marketing

Implementing RTB is relatively easy but optimizing it is a bit more challenging. However, it is worth it as continual small improvements add up over time to become significant savings and significantly higher conversions.

Here's Zowie Skelton (2015):

> So, when a consumer visits your website, the browser communicates with an ad server – the technology that places adverts on websites. The server then sends a message to an ad exchange with information about that user, such as the IP address, location and details of the website the consumer is visiting.
>
> A web page has space on it for ad space which is available for real-time bidding. Information about the web page, and the user viewing it, is passed on to an ad exchange, a platform which then auctions off the available ad space to the highest bidder. As an advertiser, you – or your media buyer – send a bid electronically to the ad exchange via a demand-side platform (DSP).

Beacons

iBeacon technology allows unprompted messages on your mobile as you move around either outside or inside a store. Apps installed on your iPhone effectively listen out for the signal transmitted by these beacons and respond accordingly (eg display a special offer) when the phone comes into range of a beacon. So if you pass a beacon (which is effectively a small, cheap Bluetooth transmitter) in a shop and if you have already installed that retailer's app, your mobile will display a special offer/alert.

Virgin Atlantic is testing iBeacon at Heathrow airport (Ranger, 2014a), so when passengers are walking towards the security checkpoint their phone automatically pulls up their mobile boarding pass ready for inspection. Relevant special offers, such as commission-free currency exchange, can be displayed as passengers walk by. Upon entry into the Virgin lounge you can be greeted by name (as the beacon technology presents Virgin with information on who you are and where you are) and presented with your favourite cocktail.

iBeacon is also more accurate than GPS (which can also detect a device's location). However 'iBeacon is not the only game in town – PayPal is working on its own "PayPal Beacon" technology' (Ranger, 2014b). You can, of course, opt out by changing permissions under Location Services for the relevant app (accessed via Settings > Privacy >

Location Services) or by switching off Bluetooth, or if worst comes to worst, uninstall the particular app.

Apps ads

'Apps' are useful software applications that provide, or allow users to do, just about anything on a mobile phone, for example a calculator, petrol prices locator, music identifier (point the phone at a radio and it lists the name of the track, the album and the band), sports news, weather forecasts, golf swing analysis, stock market feeds, managing bills, learning a language, and 'On this day' (famous people's birthdays). Kraft Foods' iFood app offers help and reinforces the brand value. One of the most popular is Zippo's app, which displays a flickering flame (popular at concerts). Skype, Twitter and Facebook all have apps that allow customers to use their services even more frequently. Some brands commission their own relevant apps; other apps are created by developers and sold to organizations that find them useful for their customers and, ideally, relevant to their brands. Few brands are actually using their apps as revenue generators (see the Glee exception below). Apps or widgets (used on websites), by extending brand usage, add value to customer experiences, brand awareness and brand affinity.

Apps or widgets can effectively put a brand name on to millions of devices worldwide. Each time they are used they boost awareness; 50 per cent of those who downloaded the Kraft Foods app continue to engage with it three months after first downloading it (Kennedy, 2009a). Apps are putting brands back on screens (mobile phones) that were previously stealing attention from TV viewership.

Some call it a form of 'screen wars hyper-competition'. Regardless, the challenge remains to keep app audiences engaged (how many apps do you enthusiastically download but rarely use?).

As mobile continues to steal audiences from TV, Apple TV also challenges cable TV (see Chapter 1) and cable TV is challenged by social media. America's CNN TV US president, Jonathan Klein, said many years ago that they see Facebook as its major threat: 'although rival Fox is currently winning the ratings war in the US, their real threat comes from Facebook' (Whatmough, 2010).

See Chapter 19 to explore the critical nature of retailer in-store apps and also Chapter 1 to see how apps add value to the user experience.

> ### Apps, like any asset, need maintenance
>
> Do remember that apps need to be maintained as operating systems and security are updated. Without maintenance the app performance weakens, reviews become negative and the downward spiral emerges where a marketing asset becomes a marketing liability (like an unclean database is a liability but once was an asset).

Native advertising

Native advertising (or 'in-stream' advertising) is a form of online advertising that looks like editorial, (it has the 'look and feel' of the platform on which it appears (so it blends in)). For example, an article written by an advertiser to promote their product, but having the same look and feel as the articles written by the editorial staff. Media owners and publishers are increasingly looking at sponsored content as a way to replace lost traditional ad revenue. The *Daily Mail* recently invested $3 million in a native partner. Interestingly, its North America CEO Jon Steinberg, put it in context by saying 'We're all competing against Facebook, ultimately' (Heine, 2015). Meanwhile *Forbes* blends in native ads on its cover.

The founder of the Content Marketing Institute, Joe Pulizzi, defines native advertising as:

- **A directly paid opportunity.** I hate to bring out the obvious, but native advertising is 'pay to play'. If a brand or individual did not pay for the spot, it's not native advertising.
- **Usually content based.** The information is useful, interesting and highly targeted to the specific readership. So, in all likelihood, it's not an advertisement promoting the company's product or service directly.
- **Delivered in-stream.** To truly be a native ad, the user experience is not disrupted. The advertising is delivered in a way that does not impede the normal behaviour of the user in that particular channel.

There's a debate about just what, exactly, native advertising means. 'Many believe that native advertising is just a digital euphemism for the classic advertorial (ads that look like editorial but with a declaration that they are an advertisement) that would frequently fill a page in your local newspaper or national magazine – only with less of a wall between the traditional church-and-state structure of editorial and advertising' (Joel, 2013). David Weinberger (2013) describes how 'a new bestiary of ways to get paid-for content directly into the media stream has been developed, some of which directly assign authorship to the company bankrolling them'. 'Some of which directly assign' suggests that not all advertisers declare the native advertising as ads. 'Critics suggest that, at best, native advertising is a form of trickery and, at worst, a gross violation of journalistic standards' (Pulizzi, 2014a). But either way, with native advertising brands pay for someone else to distribute and (ultimately) own your content.

Paid media vs owned media – readers trust owned media

Sponsored content is not everything a brand publishes because 'there's a huge distinction in readers' minds between paid media and owned media... readers trust earned media (shared, likes or comments) whether it comes from a brand or not, but they're suspicious of paid media no matter whose name is on it' (Slaughter, 2014).

> ### Owned and paid media = great teacher and a substitute teacher
>
> 'Here's an analogy: owned and paid media are kind of like a great teacher and a substitute. You see a great teacher every day; and most days you learn something new and useful from them. You build up trust with this teacher over time, you listen to what they have to say, and as with the best teachers, the relationship continues even after you've left the class. That's the kind of relationship brand publishers can create with owned media.
>
> A substitute (a sponsored story), on the other hand, doesn't have that earned trust, and anything they say is going to naturally be viewed with more suspicion. Here's the thing though: sometimes the substitute is awesome. In the best cases, they can bring new perspectives, new information and new energy to a classroom. The best sponsored content can bring those things to an audience in the same way.'
>
> Slaughter (2014)

Native advertising vs content marketing

Content marketing is an ongoing process that is best integrated into your overall marketing strategy, and it focuses on owning media, not renting it. In content marketing, you own the media. It's your asset. In native advertising, marketers pay someone else to distribute and (ultimately) own your content. Writing for the Content Marketing Institute, Joe Pulizzi defines content marketing as 'a strategic marketing technique of creating and distributing valuable, relevant, and consistent content to attract and acquire a clearly defined audience – with the objective of driving profitable customer action' (Pulizzi, 2014b).

Native social ads are dressed up to look (almost) exactly like normal tweets, Facebook posts, and LinkedIn updates from your friends and followers. Marketers can use free social media analytics to beta-test their paid social ads, ie by seeing which posts, tweets and updates get most traction and promoting or sponsoring these posts.

Integrating mobile, apps, TV and social TV

Apps extend the user experience beyond the TV with a much wider array of engagement activities and, although the TV programme may be over, prolong the sense of being in an audience or group, thereby adding value, extending the customer experience, deepening engagement and boosting satisfaction levels, awareness levels and, ideally, recommendation levels (see Chapter 10, 'Net promoter score, satisfaction score and recommendation score' on p. 289).

Fox TV network's app for *Glee* (the musical comedy series) is a good example. It costs £0.59 to download and within a few weeks it had several hundred thousand users. Customers use the app once or twice per week for 8- to 10-minute sessions, usually when the show is off-air. The app combines karaoke and social singing. Sing to the app, and the pitch indicator tells customers if they are on the note or if they're sharp or flat. The app corrects the pitch and optionally adds harmony. Saved recordings can be uploaded and used to create a band of like-minded 'gleeks' who follow customers' tracks and share them via Facebook, Twitter or Myspace feeds. The 'Broadcast' button allows users to add their performance to Glee's global sing-along, which also allows other users to add their own voices on to another user's – effectively extending the virtual glee club. *Glee* has several other apps such as 'Unofficial Glee Trivia' and 'Unofficial Glee Facts', both selling on iTunes for £0.59.

Social singing: singers wanted – no talent required

'"The thrill begins once you start singing into this app. You cannot sound bad. Period." – David Pogue, *NY Times*. Sing your favourite songs with friends, strangers or the cast. Glee will enhance your pitch and harmonize your voice while you sing. Share your top songs with friends to get Gleeks and earn more free songs, like just-added "Bohemian Rhapsody"!'

The official App Store

New forms of advertising

Where creative Mad Men meet Maths Men

There is no doubt that Mad Men (traditional ad agencies) need to deliver more creative ads to cut through the clutter, engage customers and nurture communities. Equally, advertising needs the 'Maths Men' to creatively use data in new ways so that marketers can reach audiences that actually need the information (ad) at just the right time in the right place. Chapter 1 discusses the ongoing need for creativity.

More user-generated ads will emerge (as mentioned in Chapter 1), and more apps, games, virtual worlds, massively multiplayer online role-playing games (MMORPG), intelligent media units, UGC ads, long-form ads, short-form (one-second) ads, as well as postmodern ads and plain old contentious advertising. Let's explore some of these:

- user-generated ads;
- long-form ads;
- short-form ads;

- postmodern ads;
- creative ads;
- sponsored TV.

User-generated ads

The ladder of engagement in Chapter 1 explained how UGC added a dimension to customer engagement. Chevrolet's Tahoe opened up the concept by placing the winning user-generated TV ad during the Super Bowl. It is increasingly popular, arguably because it employs the magic formula (identify needs, reflect them and deliver them). Users (customers, prospects and sometimes even non-prospects) are invited to create an ad, whether TV or press. The PR machine works hard behind the scenes helping to spread the word of mouth as the final selections are narrowed down to a winner. Social media communities ideally buy into it and spread the word even further. Naturally, there are some disadvantages, as negative ads can be created and posted for public viewing. It can be moderated, but as with most aspects of social media it is best to be transparent. Another interesting development of UGC ads is UGC films or UGC long-form ads.

Google's perfect ad

'I've always argued that the correct ad in YouTube is itself a YouTube story. Once you start watching, it's so good you can't stop – don't have a 30-second limit in principle – and the best ads may be an ad about a refrigerator that is so compelling you will drop everything in your life and drive at full speed to get to the refrigerator store. That's the job of advertising companies: to come up with that narrative that will get you to really want that refrigerator.

That's what they compete over; our job is to host them.'

Eric Schmidt, in Kennedy (2009b)

Long-form ads

Long-form ads can help a brand stand out from the clutter and do not necessarily cost more than a traditional 30-second or 60-second ad, as, firstly, they can be repurposed and, secondly, there is less need to buy media space. Nike created a three-minute ad about the art of dropping beats using sneakers. Waitrose's mini-cooking show with celebrity chefs giving cooking tips used the whole three-and-a-half-minute ad break. Absolut Vodka created a 15-minute documentary commercial featuring Jay-Z called NY-Z; Kraft Foods' Greek chocolate brand Lacta created a 27-minute user-generated branded movie initially for online consumption but eventually seen on local TV (free), as it generated so much buzz. An extension of long-form ads is sponsored TV programmes (when major soap powder brands sponsored TV dramas, the 'soap opera' was born).

Lady Gaga's nine-minute ad and product placement

'Lady Gaga's nine-minute video included product placement for Virgin Mobiles, Wonder Bread (unpaid) and Miracle Whip (paid). It has had "28 million views on YouTube, been watched on MTV.com nearly 500,000 times and shared on Facebook and tweeted directly from the pop star's site some 150,000 times".

Featured throughout "Telephone" are shots of a Virgin Mobile cellphone, a nod given to the mobile sponsor of Gaga's Monster Ball tour, as well as a Polaroid camera and photo booth as part of Gaga's new role as the camera company's creative director. Several characters are also seen listening to music on Heartbeats by Gaga headphones from Interscope Music and surfing the internet on the "Beats" laptop from Hewlett Packard, all of which were unpaid extensions of Gaga's marketing partnerships.

Online, music-video site Vevo bought a slot on the YouTube home page that referred users to the "Telephone" page on Vevo.com, which crashed the morning of the clip's premiere. The video broke all Vevo single-day traffic records and had already generated close to four million views on YouTube in less than 24 hours.'

Hampp and Bryson York (2010)

Short-form ads

Somebody had to do it sooner or later, and Miller beer did it – a one-second TV spot during the Super Bowl 2009 (the American football final). The ad cost a fraction of the $3 million normally charged for 30-second spots during the Super Bowl. The ad, starring actor Windell Middlebrooks, gave one second of inspiration and reminded viewers that 'High Life is common sense in a bottle'.

Postmodern ads

A new style of advertising, postmodern advertising, may at first seem a little abstract, and certainly unconventional, as neither the user nor the product is the hero. Old-fashioned ad people find it difficult to understand how an ad that doesn't appear to address a brand's values or have any apparent link to the brand can work. Perhaps this is best explained by Cadbury's drum-playing gorilla ad. This post-modern ad has no apparent link to the brand, as drums, music, gorillas and animals are not part of the brand equity. However, there is a link between the brand and the ad – it is fun and enjoyment. It is 'feeling good', which is how people feel when they

eat chocolate. What engages people better than a gorilla sitting behind a set of drums waiting as a really well-known piece of rock music builds up to the climax, where the drums come blasting in and the gorilla thumps perfect drums? The ad didn't tell people to feel good; it simply made them feel good. Results: 2 million hits on YouTube; 100 Facebook groups; bloggers who tried to identify why they liked the ad so much and whether the gorilla was Phil Collins (the singer) in a gorilla suit; and a 9 per cent sales increase year on year. In addition, all five variants were back in growth for the first time since the beginning of 2005.

> ### Postmodern ad brief
>
> 'People feel uplifted when they eat it [Cadbury's chocolate]. One of the things I believe passionately is that the advertising should be as enjoyable as the product. The brief was not to tell people to feel good, it was to make them feel good and the "gorilla execution" is an expression of that.'
>
> Phil Rumbol, former Marketing Director, Cadbury, in Jones (2008)

FIGURE 13.3   Cadbury's drum-playing gorilla

Creative ads

Marketers need even more creativity. Some websites can be information heavy, and therefore a quick creative ad can be a quick pleasurable experience. As Saatchi CEO Kevin Roberts' (2010) blog says, 'Marketers bring optimism and joy amidst doom and gloom. Marketers need to bring optimism and joy to people. We've 60 million unemployed in the world. This is the age of the idea... Invest in the unreasonable power of creativity. If we've got a great idea, people will tell it. Humour, love, emotion and music.' So marketers have to be relevant and increasingly creative, challenging and sometimes contentious to break through the clutter. The Paddy Power ad in Figure 13.4 certainly cuts through the clutter.

Sponsored TV

As already mentioned, a natural extension of long-form TV ads is sponsored TV programmes, including soap operas, sport and entertainment. Interestingly, BBC (a non-commercial broadcaster) now only considers commissioning new TV pro-

Great moments in copywriting: Ogilvy and the beggar

'During one of his morning walks to work in New York City, David Ogilvy encountered a man begging with a sign around his neck. The sign read: "I am blind", and, as evidenced by his nearly empty cup, the man was not doing very well. Ogilvy removed the man's sign from around his neck, pulled out a marker and changed the sign to read: "It is spring and I am blind." He hung the sign back around the beggar's neck and went on his way. On his way home he was pleased to notice the vagrant had a full cap.

Daye and VanAuken (2008)

grammes that satisfy their 'find, play, search' criteria. This includes finding the programmes or user-generated content (UGC) related to them across several social media platforms, sharing them with friends, drilling down to new depths of knowledge,

FIGURE 13.4 This six-week outdoor campaign broke through the clutter but received consumer complaints via the Advertising Standards Authority towards the end of the campaign; the ads were subsequently withdrawn slightly earlier than expected

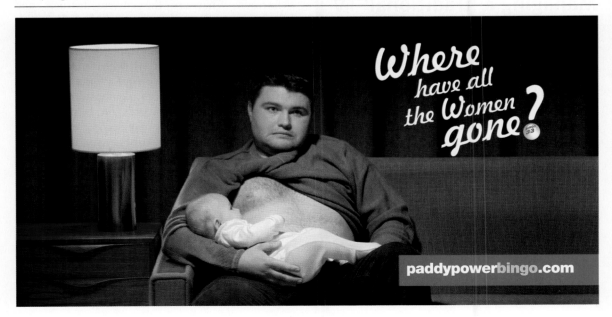

and encouraging user-generated creativity in everything from apps and widgets to more traditional user-generated content. New-styled sponsored TV programmes, like 'Bud House' (see the box below), draw on social media and UGC.

Budweiser experiment with World Cup sponsored reality TV and social media

Budweiser created a World Cup online reality TV show and social media integrated web series with 32 fans from 32 countries living, eating, breathing and watching World Cup matches together. Fans were grouped together in rooms based on the actual World Cup groups of countries. Fans were sent home as their teams were eliminated. The last-standing fan presented the Man of the Match trophy to the final team's most valuable player after the last game of the World Cup. New episodes were uploaded to the Bud United channel on YouTube several times a day. Viewers kept in touch and shared content with their favourite 'Bud House' fans via Facebook and Twitter. Viewers also influenced events in the house via the 'You Decide' polling tube on Bud United's YouTube channel.

Managing a 'traditional' TV ad campaign

Here's how an advertising campaign is planned and managed. SOSTAC® + 3Ms (discussed in detail in Chapter 10) is a flexible system that can be adapted to any plan, whether a full marketing plan, an advertising plan or an integrated social media plan. A general approach to each stage will be considered, and then it will be applied to several short cases of cutting-edge ad campaigns at the end of this chapter.

First, consider what each SOSTAC® stage contains:

- Where are you now? (Situation – S)
- Where do you want to go? (Objectives – O)
- How will you get there? (Strategy – S)

The advertising campaign planning process incorporates an analysis of the current situation (research)

and a clear definition of the overall communications objectives, as well as the specific advertising objectives. Only then can the advertising strategy be devised. The strategy summarizes broadly what to say (message), how to say it (execution, tone or creative strategy), who to say it to (target audience), where to say it (media choice or media strategy), when to say it (timing) and, sometimes, how much it will cost (budget). Strategy can also guide the integration or links between advertising and all of the other communications tools.

The situation

There is a lot of research to be done before any exciting creative work can be started. What are the current sales trend, market share trend and overall market trend? Are there any regions or segments that buy more than others? How big are the competition's sales (per region and per distribution channel)? What is the profile of the customer and of the non-customers who might be converted? Who is the target market now and in the future? Who are the heavy users? When do they buy? Where do they buy?

How is the brand positioned in the minds of various target markets? Why do people use or not use the brand? This can be the most difficult question to answer, because real reasons are often deeply hidden beneath apparently rational buying behaviour. What are the current features and benefits of your product or service? A feature is translated into a benefit by using three words: 'which means that'. For example, 'This car has a crush loading of over 5 tons, which means that it can roll over without the roof caving in.' Many advertising campaigns can demonstrate benefits without having to use words (in fact, wordless advertisements like Levi's may become more popular as satellite television grows – see Chapter 9), but it is the application of this three-word formula that helps to identify real benefits that can then be demonstrated. Spending time 'interrogating the product' is a good investment.

Product interrogation

In addition to the previous question, further questions, or product interrogation, can sometimes reveal hidden benefits, which advertising can subsequently highlight. Is there anything unique about the product (a unique selling proposition – USP)? Product (or service) interrogation explores and examines every angle, including product characteristics, user characteristics, ways of using, benefits of using, disadvantages of non-usage, competitor comparisons, product heritage, customer cases, newsworthiness and more. How does it compare against the competition's features and benefits both in people's imaginations and in reality? Or have they even heard of it? (What percentage are spontaneously aware of your product or service? Is it top of the mind or front of mind, ie do customers include it in the first three brands they think of when considering your product type?) What is important to the target customers? Or perhaps there is a high level of awareness but a low level of preference, possibly because of a poor product or poor image. What do customers consider to be the most important factors (key buying criteria) when making a choice? What is their ideal product?

Social media potential

Most campaigns today will be mindful of what arouses discussions and chatter in social media when it comes to ad campaigns. Topicality and trends will be monitored from a discussions perspective to see what is hot and generating a lot of buzz. Are there aspects of certain types of campaigns that lend themselves more to social media and user-generated content? Some social media tools can be used to identify hot topics, phrases and even words (eg Google Zeitgeist and Google Trends).

Trend identification

What new values, trends, attitudes, lifestyles or business styles are emerging that may affect the organization's product or service? Individualism, self-exploration, materialism, environmentalism, ageism, sexism, interaction: once the advertisers identify a relevant trend, they can then reflect it through advertising imagery.

Review of past advertisements

An analysis of competitor advertising campaigns can trigger ideas and, more importantly, provide some insights into competitor strategies, thereby helping the strategic thoughts of the advertising for the brand in question. Even the brand's past campaigns can give some guidance as to how they reflect the state of the market, what the objectives are, and what works and what does not.

Trends change advertising

'Another major exercise was embarked upon to understand the consumer environment that the new advertising executions would have to operate in.

The central thesis was quite simply that in the early and mid 1980s consumers felt most comfortable following the crowd and feeling a collective sense of involvement. In this context advertising that showed session drinking in the pub (men making wisecracks) was quite appropriate. Brands in the main lager arena prospered. The role these brands occupied was to lubricate the session drinking of the male-dominated pub. In the late 1980s this climate changed, and the process of change continues. Now consumers wish to stand out from the crowd and express their individuality much more. They do this by demonstrating their discernment in the clothes they wear and the brands they choose.

The implications for the advertising were fundamental: a more sophisticated audience, a change in the pub environment, less session-drinking orientation and a different attitude to premium brands. Indeed, it presented a significant opportunity for draught Guinness, which was already moving in the more fashionable image arena, to catch the crest of this wave and exploit it fully. In order for it to do so, this social change needed to be confirmed and understood in some detail.'

Ogilvy & Mather

Answers to all of the questions raised in the situation analysis and review are required before setting advertising or communications objectives. In a sense, researching the current situation reveals the objectives for the campaign. Good research makes objective setting easier.

Research, however, costs time and money (and people), so it needs to be budgeted for or, ideally, built into a continual system of information gathering (see Chapter 6, 'Marketing intelligence and information systems') to help both objective setting and subsequent measurement of the campaign's effectiveness.

Objectives (including the 'brief')

After you have analysed the situation through primary and secondary research sources (see Chapter 6), a clear picture of where you are emerges. The next step is to define exactly where you want to be. Ideally, objectives should be quantified in terms of success or failure and timescale. This makes control easier, since actual results can be measured against quantified objectives. The previous year's objectives, and corresponding results, help to make setting objectives a little easier, as experience provides a better idea of what are realistic objectives for the future.

Objectives should be **SMART**:

Specific
Measurable
Actionable
Realistic
Time specific

A clear strategy (how to get there) is not possible without clearly defined objectives (where you want to go). Without a clear strategy, a loose set of tactics, lacking cohesion (and sometimes pulling in different directions), is likely to emerge.

Establishing clear objectives is necessary to give a focus to the organization. Clear objectives also give direction to the subsequent creative efforts. The Situation Analysis, The Objectives and the 3Ms can become the agency brief. Some marketing managers and agencies break objectives into many different types. We focus on just two types here: 1) marketing objectives; and 2) communications objectives.

Marketing objectives

Typical marketing objectives refer to sales, market share, distribution penetration, launching a number of new products, and so on. See Chapter 10, 'Objectives'.

Communications objectives

You will find examples of these in Chapter 10, 'Communications objectives'. As mentioned in there, communications objectives typically refer to how the communication should affect the mind of the target audience, eg generate awareness, attitudes, interest or trial. The defining advertising goals for measuring advertising results (DAGMAR) and awareness, interest, desire and action (AIDA) hierarchical models reveal some of the mental stages many buyers have to move through before buying. Again, these objectives (eg 'to increase awareness') are more useful when quantified ('to increase awareness from 35 per cent to 45 per cent within a six-week period').

Another way of looking at communications objectives in a competitive market for, say, the purchase of a car is that shown in Figure 13.5. A particular campaign's objective may be to move a significant number of prospects from one set to the next. Some advertisements go further by seeking to reinforce or reassure existing buyers.

Strategy

Once the situation has been fully researched and clear objectives identified, the campaign or advertising strategy can be developed. It will include positioning, objectives, target audience, key benefits, secondary benefits and often a statement of what kind of media will be used. The strategy will not get bogged down in detailed tactics or any specific creative messages. It should offer strategic direction to the client and agency team. Some clients will work with the agencies to develop this key statement. Other agencies do all the work and present the campaign strategy to the client for approval.

The campaign strategy forms the foundation for the more detailed planning and development of the actual message (or the advertisement itself) and the selection of the media. Figure 13.6 illustrates how the initial situation, objectives and strategy (SOS) form the basis for the subsequent development of the message and media plan.

Message development (strategy and tactics)

Creative briefs

With the review complete, objectives set and strategy agreed, the creative team can finally be called in

FIGURE 13.5 A way of looking at communications objectives in a competitive market for the purchase of a car

and briefed. The creative brief is a key document. Each agency has its own style (see top advertising agency BMP DDB's style in Figure 13.7). It is here where all the volumes of research findings and weeks of discussions have to be concentrated into a single-page creative brief that translates the details and research jargon into relatively simple lay terms that explain exactly what the advertisement should do.

This is the brief that the planner or account manager gives to the creative team. It succinctly covers all the key information, such as: the target audience and its perceptions, motivations and buying criteria; advertising objectives, proposition, tone and how the audience should feel after the advertisement; and constraints and choice of media. It is an important document and should be signed (or approved) by an account director before being passed to the creative team. Sometimes the client wants to approve it also.

Both the agency and the client need to have a clear focus on exactly what the advertising should say or what it should achieve. Many creative people don't want too much detail ('Just tell me exactly what you want!'). They will then set about delivering a creative idea or concept. Figure 13.7 shows the summary creative brief that BMP DDB used for the award-winning Hovis campaign.

Concepts

Ideas or concepts are roughly designed into 'roughs' or 'scamps', which can be developed into a storyboard (see Figure 13.8). The idea can then be further developed into better-quality visuals known as key frames (see Figure 13.9). These, in turn, can be shot on video to create an animatic (moving cartoon of the advertisement complete with music, voice-over and sound effects). Any of these visual presentations of the advertising concept (concept board, storyboard, key frames and animatics) are discussed and/or researched before the idea is allowed to go on to the expensive production stages and eventually to the even more expensive media stage (buying space and actually advertising). If the concept 'researches well', ie gets good feedback from the focus groups, it can be taken forward for further refinement and eventual production. Even with poor research findings (ie the focus groups do not like the concept), some clients and agencies sometimes pursue an idea regardless. For example, Heineken's long-running 'refreshes the parts other beers cannot reach' campaign did not research well but was, nevertheless, produced. It eventually went on to become a successful campaign.

Advertising agency BMP DDB's rough concept idea for the Hovis campaign (Figure 13.8) was developed from the initial creative brief (shown in Figure 13.7).

FIGURE 13.6   The remaining stages of the campaign planning and execution

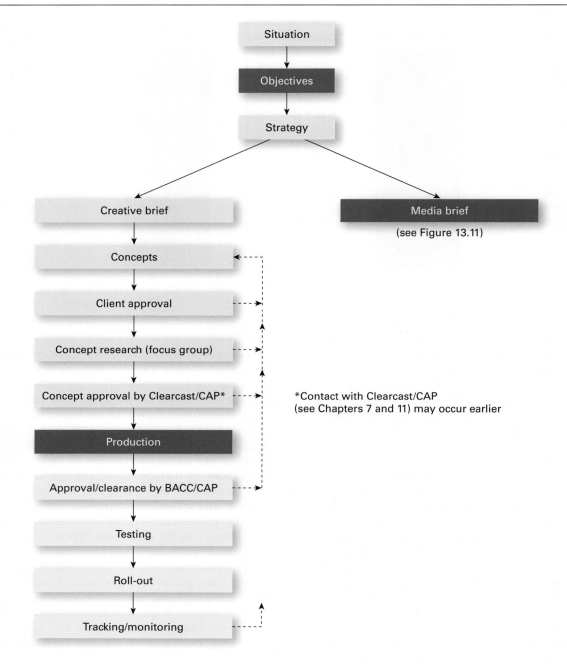

FIGURE 13.7   BMP DDB Needham's creative brief for Hovis

CLIENT	British Bakeries	INTERIM REVIEW
PRODUCT	Hovis	FINAL REVIEW
JOB NO.		PRESENTATION

What is the advertising required to do?

To convince Mums that their family will love Hovis

MEDIA BUDGET   PRODUCTION BUDGET

REQUIREMENTS (Please select by formatting requirements in **bold**)

One off ads   Ad in existing campaign   **New Campaign**
TV   Cinema   Press   Radio   Poster
Size/Timelength:

Any possible links between media channel and message?

What is the **single** most important thing we want to say?

Hovis is the one good thing you can do for your family everyday

Why should people believe this?

People believe that Hovis is full of goodness – more so than other brands of bread. Its name even means 'strength of man' and, even though we are talking white bread, its brown bread credentials help give it a healthy feel.
Hovis has always been associated, via its advertising, with things being done properly in an idealised world. Hovis today still does things properly (they still make their bread in essentially the same way) but the reality of the world in which it is operating has changed & these idyllic images are becoming increasingly irrelevant to today's bread buyers.

What tone of voice should we use?

Down to earth, honest, of the people.
Hovis might take bread seriously, but it shouldn't take itself too seriously

What are the mandatory requirements?

Campaign must be able to work across the Hovis product range.

Who are we talking to?

Almost everyone eats bread & Hovis is a mass market brand, so our idea must have broad appeal.

Primarily, however, our audience is Mums with kids (0–10). They get through a loaf a day on sandwiches for packed lunches, toast when the kids come home from school etc. Kids prefer white bread. Mums have all heard of Hovis & it is one of the first brands of bread that they think of. However, recently it has become more distant – a bread for other people. Kingsmill has taken over as the best bread for families.

As a group, Mums share a common trait, they all believe that looking after the family is roller coaster of positive and negatives and that looking after the family is harder today than ever before. Anything they can rely on for a spot of 'goodness' is appreciated.

Our secondary audience are the kids themselves – whatever our idea, it must have playground currency. If Mum can see that the kids like the ads it will go a long way in giving her the confidence to start buying Hovis

What do we want them to think or feel having seen the advertising?

If I buy Hovis for my family, then, whatever else might happen, at least I know I've given them a damn good start.
And my kids will enjoy eating Hovis.

What is the cleverest bit of thinking on this brief?

This is really about owning a category generic. Despite not having any tangible reasons to believe, there is much in people's emotional associations & beliefs in the Hovis brand to allow Hovis to credibly own this territory.

Issued by

Date

Signatures:

Client   BAD   Olivia Johnson   DOC

_____   _____   _____   _____

FIGURE 13.8

Hovis 'roughs' of new characters

Client approval

Concepts have to be justified or explained to clients. Agencies support their concepts with a message rationale, which basically explains why the concept is brilliant and guaranteed to achieve outstanding results!

The concept is developed into key frames, which are then presented along with the message rationale to the client. The key frames can also be shown during focus group research. Figure 13.9 shows a Hovis key frame.

FIGURE 13.9   Hovis key frame

Media developments (strategy and tactics)

More money is spent on media than on the production of the advertisement itself. It is here that large savings can be made. Media planning is becoming increasingly scientific as press and TV proliferate. Although media buying, some argue, is an art in itself, some media planners understand the qualitative side of the media as well as the quantitative side and can therefore use media in a creative manner. The awards in *Media Week* give an insight into the creative use of media.

Expert media planning and buying can also save vast sums of money, which can be either redeployed to buy more advertising space or saved and used elsewhere in the communications mix. There is, of course, the temptation to keep the saving and add it on to the bottom-line profits (by taking it away from the bottom-line expenses). Figure 13.11 shows the process of media planning.

Media selection

Media people should not be briefed to book space after the advertisement has been created. They need to be involved early on, as their creative media input can influence the finished creative message. Carat Research shows that placing advertisements in unexpected positions can boost the likelihood of seeing them. From ads appearing upside down, to perfume ads in finance pages, to a McDonald's ad in *Vogue* magazine, to buying all the back pages of specific colour supplements for a year (Boddingtons), to buying an entire newspaper for one day (Microsoft and the *Times*), to an entire 3½-minute commercial break (Waitrose's mini-cooking show), the media planners have plenty of creative scope. And they have plenty of new media to play with, from video vans (with large computer screens and mobile billboards) to floor posters, to laser-beamed buildings (see Chapter 7, 'Ambient media' on p. 203), to long-form ads, to user-generated ads and right through to social media.

Message and media selection

Eric Meyer some years ago reported that up to 30 per cent of US ads actually damage the brand. Today, perhaps some marketers get distracted by the exciting allure of highly ambient opportunities and technology interactivities rather than first checking the quality, relevance and context of the message. For example, is putting your logo on a rubbish bin appropriate for a brand like Rolex? Even if the message says something like 'Bin your old watch and buy a Rolex', it is simply not appropriate.

Here are some additional examples of how media selection can work creatively and effectively.

FIGURE 13.10   Finished Hovis commercial

CONVERSATION

Harry: Pooh.
Alfie: Bra.

Harry: Bogies.
Alfie: Er ...

FVO: When the witty conversation
        starts to drag ...

FVO: give them a break with peanut butter
        and banana in fresh White Hovis.

Harry: Mmm.

Alfie: Mmm.
FVO: Things'll soon start to pick up again.

Alfie: Belly button.
Harry: Pants.

MVO: White Hovis.
        Get something good inside.

FIGURE 13.11   The media planning process

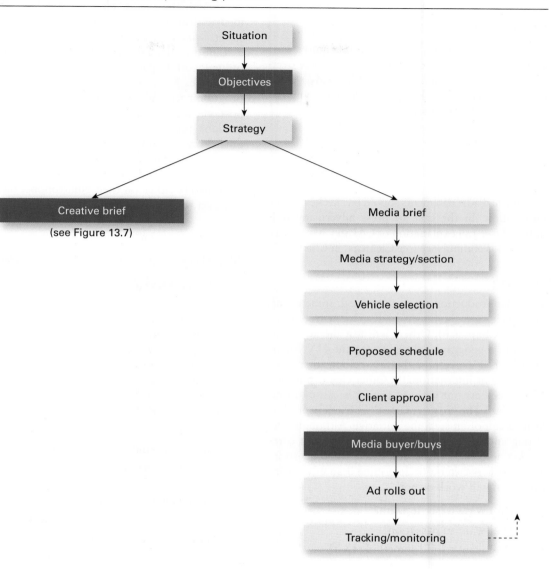

Häagen-Dazs ice cream used the weekend press to allow the advertisements to be savoured and enjoyed at leisure, while 'the intimacy of the experience could be hinted at better through the personal communication of the press'. Part of Guinness's media strategy was to use black-and-white 'fractionals' (ads within a small space) in newspapers, which, as the *Media Week* awards explain, meant that they 'effectively dominated the mono newspaper world with fresh and extensive copy rotations, so that no reader would see any one execution more than once over a period of seven months'. Chapter 7 looks at media research, planning and scheduling.

Media schedules

In addition to the creative use of the media, careful analysis can identify the optimum media schedules. A media plan is then developed and presented to the client. This plan shows the types of places where the advertisement could be used. The space is then negotiated and bought (see Chapter 7).

Action

Production

The production of an advertisement requires time and careful attention to detail. It may involve overseas locations, casting, contracts, rehearsals, special effects, weeks or months of sophisticated computer graphics, studio shoots, editing and more.

Control

Clearance

The finished advertisements should be checked before publication. **In the case of press advertising it is optional** (see full explanation of CAP in Chapter 11). For TV it is compulsory (see Clearcast in Chapter 7).

Testing

With the production stage completed, some clients or agencies test the finished advertisement in a hall test (see Chapter 6). Others will test the advertisements in a geographical region (eg the ITV Anglia or Ulster TV regions) before rolling them out nationally or internationally. Other clients put their advertisements out without testing because of time constraints. The 'first to market' with a new product or idea can often steal the initiative. Although both strong and weak theories have some validity, some marketing professionals simply ask three questions about success criteria to determine if an advertising campaign will work or not:

1 Do I want to see it again?
2 Do I want to pass it on?
3 Do I want to add something to it?

Roll-out

After rigorous testing the finished ad (eg Figure 13.10) can be released, or rolled out, across its whole market.

Tracking

The advertising campaign can and should be monitored, or tracked, to see how it is working, eg what level of awareness it is generating or whether it is affecting attitudes or even sales. This allows any problems to be corrected sooner rather than later.

While the advertising messages are being developed, the media planners are busy devising media strategies and plans to ensure that the advertisements get the optimum exposure.

Call tracking helps identify which ads (online or offline) work best even when the customer responds by phone, for example if a consumer sees your programmatic ad on a smartphone, on a blog post, via social media (or even on the radio, TV, or outdoor posters) but responds by phone instead of clicking on a link or a website.

By assigning a unique ('tracked') telephone number, you would then know whether a caller saw your advert either on their smartphone, on a blog post, via social media or on their television set.

Managing a location-based ad campaign

At this stage in the evolution of location-based advertising campaigns and programmatic advertising, it is probably easiest for many marketers to use expert companies in the field, eg use a data-driven programmatic, ad-buying solutions company, like BlisMedia. To work with these kinds of solutions companies, marketers must understand:

- how location-based marketing works (target markets, publishers, advertisers);
- how layered data reveals additional insights about target markets;
- how DSP (demand-side platform), exchanges and SSPs (supply-side partners) interact;
- data flows, bids and ads;
- adding unique identifiers to each device IP;
- tracking visitors;
- micro LBA cases: Gillette and Thomson Holidays.

How location-based marketing works

The target market

If you, a consumer, are browsing via your mobile (or tablet) and you click onto the sports page of the *Guardian* newspaper online, a ping (it's called a bid impression/bid stream) is sent from the publisher (the *Guardian*) to an online ad network. This effectively announces 'a viewer is looking at the sports page on the *Guardian* and invites bids (in real time, ie right now) from advertisers (or their agencies) to serve an ad to this consumer (say car intenders/buyers). Marketers can see what the viewer is looking at that time via the bid impression (if they work with the right supply-side partners). They can also cross-reference that device ID into their own database and see what that person generally looks at/has looked at in the past and where they usually go location-wise. The advertisers gain access to buying this impression and then have an ad served via a DSP (demand-side platform) which is offered by providers like BlisMedia (see column opposite).

The publisher/the media

Site owners and app owners are called publishers since they publish the site or the app which can host ads. Some sites (like newspapers or news stations) offer their ad space inventory to advertisers as their main source of revenue. So these ad exchanges are serious business. To participate in the Ad Network, the publishers sign up as an SSP (supply-side partner).

The advertiser

Brands seek to get in front of their prospective customers (and even their existing customers and sometimes their competitors' customers), ideally when that customer is either already aware of the brand and/or is moving towards making a purchase. This is where LBM can deliver much more relevant ads to customers by targeting only those customers whose behaviour has already expressed an interest in the product or service by either visiting a physical location (in the real offline world) and/or visiting a website or app online. Brand advertisers access the demand-side platform while SSPs are the publishers (websites and/or apps) that provide data and the ad space (or ad inventory).

How layered data can help

Data companies like Experian can delve into their databases to reveal additional insights about target markets. No names are given. It is hashed anonymized data. Experian can reveal if there are people in the postcode area that you have geo-fenced that

have applied for a credit card. This data could be used to target a credit card ad that may be useful to them to help them buy, say, a new baby buggy.

Data-driven, **programmatic**, ad-buying solutions companies like BlisMedia help advertisers. They could ask Experian: 'We are looking at these postal codes for people interested in mortgages. Have you got any information on people looking for mortgages in that geographical area? They might deliver aggregated anonymized data (not individual information) which gives an insight; for example they may reveal that there are approximately 8,000 people looking for mortgages in a particular area where previously Blismedia were only targeting say 1,000 mortgage customers.

Here's the number of people in this postcode who have recently had 'mortgages in principle' enquiries made on their credit file. In other words, people that have applied for mortgages already. BlisMedia could start to look at other people that they haven't yet targeted, in addition to that original target group. BlisMedia would then delve into its own database to look at browsing histories of other devices in that area. The target audience might grow from 1,000 to 3,000 based on the Experian data.

Experian basically deliver insights into the target market. They provide info on ABC1 in a particular area. Some of that information might include a postcode, in which case BlisMedia can start looking at residential IP addresses on that postcode. And then they can start seeing devices that are attached to that IP address. And then we can start to see the devices when they are leaving the home. Just another way of developing behavioural location user IDs. BlisMedia can get a residential IP address once their potential customers connect via wifi.

Location-based marketing – data flow, bids and ads

Location-based marketers continually collect data

As already mentioned, if your apps or your social media platforms are 'location enabled', your device location can be detected via the information passed back to the exchange from the publisher (the website) and sometimes via GPS. However, exchanges/SSPs often 'wrap up' very basic estimated location

FIGURE 13.12   BlisMedia location demographics audience

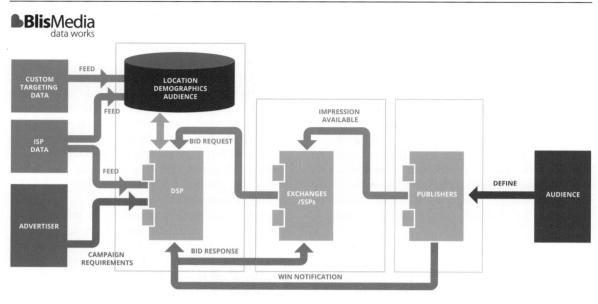

SOURCE: BlisMedia

data into GPS lat/longs and try to sell it on. This is where some specialist agencies clean and filter the data so that only precise data (lat/longs with five decimal points of accuracy) get used as the user passes locations such as football stadia, hotels and tube stations. This creates a footprint of where you have physically travelled in the real world over the last two months (if the device ID is in a particular database and, if the device, at that time, is using either apps or visiting websites that subscribe to the SSP Ad Network).

A unique identifier is added to each device IP

A brief history of where you physically went in the offline world plus where you have visited online can be added to the unique identifier. This data can be used to infer your gender, age and interests; for example, if you visited Mothercare and young women's fashion sites, it will infer you are a young mother (or about to become a young mother). But cross-referencing with other data could actually reveal that this particular user is actually a young father so the ads served would be different. Agencies can also layer additional data, for example from Experian or the DVLA databases.

If a user is logged onto a BMW wifi point in a dealership, they may be in the research mode or actual purchase stage. Their level of interest can be identified from their click behaviour (or digital body language). Location and demographic data can be combined to define digital audiences, and then serve tightly targeted display ads (via real-time bidding) to users across mobile, tablet and laptop.

So they can serve timely geo location offers to individuals in a retailer or in a supermarket. Like the McDonald's example earlier – they can target people within five metres of a location. They can also then link the device footprint (where else the device owner physically walked, eg to Ladbrokes to place a bet and took a bus home). They can also layer on additional data.

> ### Advertising is now as much about Maths Men as Mad Men
>
> 'Advertising is now as much about Maths Men as Mad Men' says WPP ad supremo Sir Martin Sorrell.
> (Note: 'Mad Men' is an AMC television series about advertising agencies in the 1950s.)

You can see why ad agencies employ mathematicians (many of whom previously worked in the City developing algorithms to optimize the buying and selling of stocks and shares in real time). Their USP is the way they crunch the data, which is gathered from various partners such as wifi networks, supply-side platforms and so on.

Unique device identifier (UDID)

Each smartphone has a unique device identifier (UDID), which is a sequence of 40 letters and numbers that is specific to each device and looks like this: 2b6f0cc904d137be2e1730235f5664094b831186. This unique device address/identifier is created by the manufacturer. When you turn on the device the software creates a device ID or IDFA (identity for advertising) so publishers can recognize devices when they connect.

About 16–24 pieces of information are attached in the 'bid stream' (which is a bid request announcing that an ad impression is available for auction) from the publisher, via the exchange. Information within the bid request includes minimum price CPM, lat/long data and gender and the device ID for example. This piece of information gives the bidder location and content behavioural data so they can decide on the amount of their bid.

Blis uses the same device ID that the phone software creates when you turn it on to create a tracking device ID, as the identifier (or tag) it uses to store that device profile in their database. Mobile web cookies are what the publisher drops into the device browser to understand what kind of content they are using. Device IDs are not passed through the exchanges when the user is on mobile web – only when they are using apps. The mobile web cookies last for a month and then delete themselves.

How visitors are tracked

If you are (a)using public wifi, (b)using an app, or (c)browsing a website. After asking your permission, each device lodges a bit of code or a user ID (websites call them cookies) invisibly onto the user's browser (or app). The device ID is sometimes also called a user ID and is used as a unique identifier, which allows marketers to create groups of devices/users (or segments) so that they can, for example, compare different groups' behaviour after exposure to an advertising campaign. Device manufacturers like Apple or Samsung/Android/Google have specific device IDs but only they can see those on the network and they are used for their own mobile advertising and app store purposes. Note: cookies are for desktops. Mobiles use the term user IDs. (See box on p. 366.)

On pp. 367–73 are some cases showing:

- Pay-per-click ads boost sales for Halfords tyres.
- Pay-per-click ads boost ROI by optimization for cab company.
- Shock tactics viral TV ad reduces deaths.

BlisMedia were asked by Gillette to deliver rich media ads incorporating dynamic weather info to identify female mobile users in the designated age range across the UK.

The immediate results showed an uplift of more than10 per cent who identified Gillette Venus as a trusted brand and an 11 per cent-plus uplift in those who thought it was a brand for people like them.

BlisMedia were also asked by Thomson Holidays to increase footfall (traffic into their stores). **Using Path (a retargeting solution) and footfall attribution**

(measures footfall in a location related to an ad) they helped Thomson combine remarketing and OOH (out of home) billboards. By comparing a control group against a group served with the ads it tracked path activity through to store footfall up to seven days later.

They delivered an increase in store footfall. Ads served in OOH sites: **121 per cent uplift**; previous travel site or App users, **135 per cent uplift**; Thomson store visitors, **138 per cent uplift.**

This subsequently helps to reallocate budget more efficiently.

FIGURE 13.13   Gillette ad with dynamic weather information

SOURCE: Blismedia

FIGURE 13.14   Thomson remarketing ad

SOURCE: Blismedia

CASE STUDY 13.1   Pay-per-click ads boost sales: Halfords Autocentres

Situation/brief

Nationwide Autocentres was bought out and transformed into Halfords Autocentres. Whilst Halfords was well known primarily for selling car parts and bicycles, it was important to build brand awareness of its new services following the acquisition. As the business changed, so did its priorities and ClickThrough agency was asked to begin work on a paid search campaign for Halfords Autocentres' new 'tyres' services.

Halfords Autocentres asked ClickThrough to increase their paid search traffic, tyre bookings and conversion rate, and decrease their cost per booking to less than £45.

The main aim was to raise awareness of Halfords Autocentres, educate consumers about available tyre services, and highlight competitively-priced services, such as tyre checks and replacements, to drive traffic and conversions.

Objectives

- Increase paid search traffic, tyre bookings, conversion rate.
- Decrease their cost per booking to less than £45.
- Build brand awareness.

(Actual KPIs (Key Performance Indicators, or numbers) are not available)

Strategy

Expand key phrase list to include major tyre brands which Halfords are now offering.

Deliver tailored landing pages for key phrases (particularly tyre brands)

Tactics

Search ads and suitable landing pages were developed for each ad group. An ad group is a group of related words that searchers might use when looking for the same item. For example if they were searching for Continental tyres, some people might search for 'Continental 195' and others might search for 'Continental tyres prices'. Here's a typical ad group for Continental Tyres:

- continental 195;
- continental tyres prices;
- continental tyre;
- continental eco contact 3;
- continental tyres online;
- continental car tyres.

The number of keywords in an ad group (six in the above ad group) all depends on the different themes or variations of the product. The number of ad groups in a campaign also depends on the number of products. In this Halfords case, there will be ad groups for each of the different tyre brands so you can tailor the ad text (and the relevant landing page).

So when any of these phrases are used to search, then this ad will be served to the searcher (the ad will appear according to how high the bid is and the relevancy of the ad):

Continental® Tyres Halfords
£10 Off Each Pair Of Tyres Online.
Buy On Your Mobile Today.
m.halfordautocentres.com/Avon

When visitors click on the ad, they will be taken to the dedicated landing page for the Continental tyres (see over) and never to a general tyre page or a general home page. Ads should not create more work for the weary searcher. The more relevant the landing page is to the search term, the more likely the visitor is to like what they see and this increases the propensity to purchase.

A similar-styled ad group can be created for each of the other tyre brands stocked by Halfords. So Goodyear tyres will have their own ad group of phrases used by people searching for Goodyear tyres. The Goodyear ad will then be served:

Goodyear ® Tyres of Halfords
£10 Off Each Pair Of Tyres Online.
Buy On Your Mobile Today.
m.halfordautocentres.com/Tyres

Action: create relevant word/phrase list

First of all ClickThrough identified with Halfords Autocentres which tyre manufacturers they stocked, looking at car makes,

FIGURE 13.15   The dedicated landing page for Continental tyres

halfords
autocentre
MOT | service | repairs

Sign in | Register | Find a local Autocentre

Your Autocentre: Select   Your Vehicle: Select

Enter keyword, product or part code   Search

Your Products
0 item(s)   £0.00

| MOT | Car Servicing | Tyres | Brakes | Car Repairs | Air Con | Car Care | Advice |

Quality Guarantee   £ Price Promise   9/10 Customer Satisfaction   Need help? 0800 096 4216

WIN 2015 BRITISH GRAND PRIX TICKETS
Buy two or more Pirelli tyres for your chance to win our Grand Prix prize draw   PIRELLI   Find **Tyres**

FREE Podium Cap with every qualifying purchase

Home » Advice & News » Tyres Advice » Continental Tyres

Advice & News

Continental Tyres

German expertise and cutting edge design makes Continental tyres one of the largest and most respected brands in the world for performance tyres. Their selection of car, van and 4x4 tyres offer outstanding performance, even in wet conditions, while a wide range of winter tyres provides enhanced traction in icy conditions.

There is nothing more important to Continental than safety. Thanks to the innovative ideas of their research and development team, and their several decades of experience, every Continental tyre is able to combine maximum safety with individual requirements and optimum ride comfort.

Continental tyres available at Halfords Autocentres

Eco Contact 3
- An excellent summer tyre for mid-range cars that also provides enhanced grip in the wet
- Circumferential and lateral grooves provide good water evacuation to give shorter braking distances in wet conditions

ContiSportContact 5

The ContiSportContact 5 is the latest tyre in Continental's sport family for both cars and 4x4s (pure on-road applications). The ContiSportContact 5 utilises Black Chilli Technology to offer extremely short braking distances whilst still maintaining high mileage and fuel economy. The macro-blocks on the outer shoulder help ensure the contact area is maximised so that the

RELATED PRODUCTS

Tyres
£10.00 OFF every pair of tyres
Ends 13th May

Find Tyres

Free Tyre Check

Book Online

SOURCE: ClickThrough Agency

tyre brands and sizes. This was then used to create seed words lists (such as: tyre brands; misspelling variations, eg 'Continental', 'Continental tyres' and 'Continental tires' (misspell); and the Top 10 most-used phrases to find your site).

They then used the following tools and techniques to create a keyword and landing page plan:

1 AdWords keyword planner. Using these seed words they extracted from AdWords a list of keywords, the

search volume, cost per click and competiveness of the keywords to help drive the strategy of landing page priorities.

2 AdWords search query reports. This shows the actual keywords that people are searching with so you can add the keywords into your portfolio of key phrases (that are currently being used) to drive up relevancy and drive down cost.

FIGURE 13.16   Key phrases

	Search term	Match Type ?	Added / Ex ?
☐	michelin tires	Exact match	Added
☐	goodyear eagle f1	Exact match	Added
☐	goodyear eagle f1 asymmetric 2	Exact match	Added
☐	pirelli scorpion zero	Exact match	Added
☐	hankook tires prices	Exact match	Added
☐	michelin tyres price	Exact match	Added
☐	pirelli p6000 tyres	Exact match	Added
☐	continental 195 55r16	Phrase match	None

3   On-site search. This shows the commonly searched terms on Halfords Autocentres' own website and helps to maintain and grow the keyword list. These keywords and the specific tailored landing pages were prioritized according to search volume, demand and competiveness. ClickThrough worked with Halfords Autocentres to scope out a number of dedicated manufacturer landing pages, so when users were searching for tyre brands such as Continental, Goodyear, Avon, Pirelli or Dunlop they came to a useful and dedicated Halfords Autocentres landing page about these particular brands.

Results/control

ClickThrough continually improved the performance of Halfords Autocentres' PPC campaign for tyres. The PPC team employed industry-leading bid management software to ensure the campaign was consistently profitable, bringing down the client's CPL (cost per lead) whilst increasing conversion and PPC sales.

The results were as follows:

Sales: 351 per cent increase (in sales generated by Google AdWords) in 12 months.
Conversion rate: 9 per cent increase.
Cost per Lead reduction of 22 per cent.

CASE STUDY 13.2   Pay-per-click ads boost ROI by optimizing: Cover my Cab

The situation

Cover My Cab has more than 30 years' experience providing specialist insurance products to taxi drivers, fleet owners and taxi operators. The brand is part of J&M Insurance, a 'business-to-business' insurance firm that has served the taxi industry for longer than any other specialist broker.

ClickThrough Marketing began working with Cover My Cab in April 2014, helping to manage and optimize its PPC campaigns.

The challenge: After four months working on Cover My Cab's paid search campaigns, results were good. However, ClickThrough suspected more gains could be made by opening the monthly budget caps (ie removing the daily cap or monthly budget) and opting, instead, for an 'always on' PPC strategy, to get 24/7 visibility (since users search 24/7).

Ian Boyden, paid search manager, says: 'The risk with capping your spend is that you could "go dark" too early in the day. In other words, your ads stop appearing because you've spent your allocated budget, but your audience may well still be searching for your services. You might even find that you're missing out on peak search activity by capping budgets.'

When optimizing a Google AdWords account it is always worth seeing what impression share each of your campaigns has. There are two types of impression shares:

1 *Impression share lost to budget.* This is the percentage of time your ads weren't shown on Google due to insufficient budget.

2 *Impression share lost to rank.* The percentage of time your ads weren't shown on Google due to a low position in the AdWords auction.

ClickThrough used their proprietary forecasting tool to perform a deep-dive analysis of Cover My Cab's AdWords account.

The tool showed that the account had around 5 per cent impression share lost to budget in August 2014. It forecasted that, if budget caps were removed so there were no impressions lost to budget, Cover My Cab could have spent approximately 11 per cent more and seen conversions increase by 11 per cent also. This analytic forecasting tool suggested that by switching to 'always on' ClickThrough

TABLE 13.1   Analysis of Cover My Cab's Adwords account

Metric	Current Performance	Performance with Open Caps (0% Imp Share Lost to Budget)	Delta Change	%Change
Imp.	200,000	210,000	10,000	5.00%
Clicks	16,000	16,800	800	5.00%
CTR	8.00%	8.00%	0.00%	0.00%
Conv.	1,000.00	1,110.00	110.00	11.00%
Cost	£25,000.00	£27,650.00	£2,650.00	10.60%
Cost/Conv.	£25.00	£24.91	−£0.09	−0.36%
Conv. Rate	6.25%	6.61%	0.36%	5.71%
Avg. CPC	£1.56	£1.56	£0.00	0.00%

Forecasted results by changing from a budget cap to 'always on' campaign
SOURCE: ClickThrough Agency

could generate (or deliver) an extra 10,000 impressions, which could generate an extra 800 visitors of whom 110 will convert, reducing the cost per conversion from £25 to £24.91.

Objectives

To reduce conversion costs below £25 and boost sales/conversions beyond previous months' (exact numbers are not available).

Strategy

Remove the budget cap and become 'always on'. Because the spend increase meant increasing the daily budget caps rather than pushing the position of the keywords up through the maximum cost per click they were willing to pay, Cover My Cab would not pay any more per click – as they would if they were jostling for higher positions. The tool showed simply and effectively how gains could be made by raising budget to allow the client to be visible 24 hours a day.

Tactics

ClickThrough's paid search executive Dave Earnshaw said:

> This might sound like a simple thing, but many clients we take on have a limited budget and are worried about overspending. Ian created this tactical tool to show clients in a clear and simple way how they could improve their number of leads, and still remain within their cost-per-lead target without the risk of wasting budget.

ClickThrough presented the findings to Cover My Cab, who agreed to trial this new approach and raise the budget for the next month.

Action

Removing the budget cap and becoming 'always on' was easy to execute. In fact it was set up in minutes, with no additional bid management or optimization. No additional costs nor time required.

The results (control)

In September, Cover My Cab spent 24 per cent more on clicks, and saw:

- number of conversions increase by 25 per cent;
- number of clicks increase by 23 per cent;
- cost per conversion decrease to £24.72.

Cover My Cab were very pleased with the results and have since decided to be 'always on' (although they do monitor it closely). Meanwhile ClickThrough's Ian Boyden says:

> The next time you see impressions lost to budget, we recommend opening up the budget as you may be restricting additional volume of traffic and conversions. We recommend an 'always on' strategy with PPC, and if you find your account is spending too much then you should reduce CPCs until you see spend hit your target.

TABLE 13.2   Actual results after starting 'Always On'

Month	August	September	Difference
Imp.	200,000	250,000	25.00%
Clicks	16,000	19,680	23.00%
CTR	8.00%	7.87%	−1.60%
Conv.	1,000.00	1,254.00	25.40%
Cost	£25,000.00	£31,000.00	24.00%
Cost/Conv.	£25.00	£24.72	−1.12%
Conv. Rate	6.25%	6.37%	1.95%
Avg. Pos.	3.49	3.00	−14.15%
Avg. CPC	£1.56	£1.58	0.81%

CASE STUDY 13.3   Shock tactics: viral TV ad reduces road deaths

The situation

Since 2000, speeding has killed a classroom of Northern Irish children. Every increase in speed increases the risk of death. Research shows that just a 5 per cent increase in average speed increases the risk of serious injuries by over 15 per cent and road deaths by over 20 per cent.

Although 'speeding' is understood to be dangerous, there is a gap between the reality of what speeding is and how drivers interpret their own behaviour:

- Drivers perceive that they engage in safe speeding.
- They go over the limit but are in 'full control'.
- Seen as different to the type of speeding that results in serious collisions. They choose their speed not by what the law dictates, but by their own feeling of safety, how in control they feel.
- Particularly on rural roads/motorways.
- Feeling that in 30mph zones there is a reason for the limit, but on faster roads this reason is lacking.
- Much more likely to stick to speed limits in urban areas.

Drivers underplay the consequences of speeding, believing that they will not be as serious as people make out and that it will never happen to them anyway. Speeding is enjoyable and pleasurable, with many drivers even showing the classic signs of addiction.

There is an increasing belief that speeding is acceptable, almost normal, and common to everyone.

Objectives

To propel speeding to the forefront of the public's mental agenda and to reduce speeding and road deaths caused by speeding.

Strategy (message strategy)

To propel speeding to the forefront of the public's mental agenda by disrupting and challenging false perceptions through deep emotional engagement of road users as to the truly horrifying consequences of speeding.

Targeting: drivers responsible for speed-related KSI (killed or seriously injured) collisions: (a) males 17–24; (b) males 25–34; (c) females 17–24

Strategy (media strategy): campaign in TV, cinema and digital

Tactics

Create an intensely shocking 60-second ad and buy 1200 TVRs (TV Ratings).

Action

Research – focus groups to find what would motivate speeding drivers to slow down. During the intense research carried by ad agency Lyle Bailie focus groups revealed that 'speeders' feel it is their right to drive at whatever speed they want. They won't change this for anything. 'What about if you killed someone?' No this would not stop them.

FIGURE 13.17
DOE road safety classroom

FIGURE 13.18   An intensely shocking 60-second ad to promote road safety

'What about if you killed a child?' A resounding silence. A possible angle! The idea was born.

This research opened up a potential creative strategy. How can we challenge these misperceived beliefs?

Cognitive dissonance – drivers understand that travelling at speed means that they are less able to react to unexpected events. However, they enjoy speed and believe that they are safe and in control when speeding. The natural response to cognitive dissonance is to reduce it by changing one of the beliefs/behaviours. The problem is that rather than reducing speed, drivers are instead using false rationalization, misattributing the consequences of speed to other factors. Individuals have become more sophisticated at rationalization and can now rationalize factors that were previously disrupting.

A deeply emotional approach is vital to disrupt this rationalization, to create a discomfort that can only be reduced by changing speeding behaviour. 'The temptation with unexpected events is to attribute blame to the unexpected event or to state that any speed level would have the same effect. The strongly felt exception to this is when a young (and therefore innocent) child is involved – the moderating influence of the child cannot be underestimated here.' This was without exception across all of the groups.

Children are powerless and as drivers we feel a responsibility for their safety. It is our human nature to protect children. The thought of hurting a child is universally horrifying and is the most powerful trigger for challenging misperceived beliefs.

Action (ad roll out)

The 60-second advertisement was first shown on a Tuesday night during a programme called 'Dentist' with no social media reaction. It was shown again at half time during an England vs Uruguay game (19 June). It immediately received 7,000 YouTube hits. Rang ad agency (20 June) – by the end of the phone call, 23,000 hits; 53,000 by the end of the day. Four days later there had been 2.2 million views. Further results are shown here:

- ad shown Tues 17 June during Dentist – no reaction;
- played again at half time during England vs Uruguay game;
- 19 June generated 7,000 YouTube views;
- 20 June 11am 23,000 YouTube views;
- 20 June midnight 53,000 YouTube views;
- 24 June 2,200,000 YouTube views;
- 1 July 4,000,000 YouTube views.

Control

The cost of a road death is £1.43 million (Oxford Economics, 2012). This figure is taken from the Department for Transport Highways Economic Note No.1 (2005), and is made up of lost output, human costs and medical and ambulance costs.

Advantages and disadvantages

Here are some of the advantages and disadvantages to consider when deciding whether to increase or reduce advertising as a communications tool.

Advantages

Advertising is great at getting messages out to large audiences quickly. Today ads can also be targeted at niche markets, as there are media vehicles (magazines and TV programmes) that target niche audiences. And of course PPC ads can now be tailored to audiences with particular interests. Location-based advertising takes this a stage further. Advertising is good for building awareness (and growing brands) but not so good at closing sales. On a CPT basis it can be quite effective. And the message can be controlled (as it cannot be in PR or social media).

Disadvantages

Message credibility is less than that of PR or social media, as it is seen as 'advertising trying to sell something', though credibility can be enhanced by source credibility. Some media advertising, such as TV ads, has a long lead time if changes are required. Such advertising also requires relatively large budgets for creating the ads. (Note that PPC ads can be small and flexible, and ads can be changed within minutes.) Advertising is less engaging than social media or an interactive website, although some ads now seek to change this, as they integrate with social media. It can be difficult to cut through the communications clutter, as ads generally cannot be personalized.

Key points from Chapter 13

- Media planning can be creative.
- Creative ads are designed to break through the clutter, but by default may be deemed contentious.
- Research can be used at all stages of the development of a campaign.
- Advertising needs to be integrated with social media and other marcomms tools.

References and further reading

Aaker, D and Myers, J (1987) *Advertising Management*, 3rd edn, Prentice Hall International, Englewood Cliffs, NJ

Adriel, I (2014) Are we human, or are we data? *Digital Times* 11 February

The Advertising Century (1999), *Advertising Age*, 29 March

Belch, G and Belch, M (2001) *Advertising and Promotion: An integrated marketing communications perspective*, 6th edn, McGraw-Hill, London

Benady, A (2014) The 20th World Cup: social media strategies and brand war rooms, *PR Week*, 10 June

Bradshaw, P (2010) Coke sees 'phenomenal' result from Twitter ads, *FT.com*, 25 June

Brannan, T (1998) *A Practical Guide to Integrated Marketing Communications*, Kogan Page, London

Broadbent, S (1994) *The Advertising Budget*, Admap Publications, London

Caples, J (1932) *Tested Advertising Methods*, Harper Brothers

Cowley, D (ed) (1989) *How to Plan Advertising*, Cassell in association with The Account Planning Group, London

Dalton, J (2013) 24.1 million Tweets posted during Super Bowl XLVII, *Media Matters*, 5 February

Daye, D and VanAuken, B (2008) Great Moments in Copywriting: Ogilvy and the Beggar, *BrandingStrategy.com*, 17 January

Delo, C (2012) Microsoft Files Patent to Serve Ads Based on Mood, Body Language, *Ad Age Digital*, 12 June

Douglas, T (1987) *The Complete Guide to Advertising*, Pan Macmillan, London

Dwek, R (1997) Who's got the net by the eyeballs?, *Revolution*, October

Ehrenberg, A (1974) Repetitive advertising and the consumer, *Journal of Advertising Research*, **14** (2), pp 25–34

eMarketer (2015) UK to achieve world first as half of media ad spend goes digital, *eMarketer*, 27 March

Fanning, J (1997) Is the end of advertising really all that nigh? *Irish Marketing Review*, Marketing Institute, Ireland

Hampp, A and Bryson York, E (2010) Singer's manager dishes on all those product-placement deals (and lack thereof) in the nine-minute video, *Ad Age*, 13 March

Hart, A and O'Connor, J (1990) *The Practice of Advertising*, 3rd edn, Heinemann, London

Heine, C (2015) Daily Mail Invests $3 Million in Native Partner Taboola, *Daily Mail*, 4 June

Howell Henry Chaldecott Lury and Partners (HHCL) (1997) *Marketing at a Point of Change*, HHCL, London

Joel, M (2013) We Need a Better Definition of 'Native Advertising', *Harvard Business Review*, 13 February

Jones, H (2008) Gorilla tactics, *Marketer*, May

Kennedy, J (2009a) App-fab, *Marketing Age*, November

Kennedy, J (2009b) A wave of optimism: Interview with Eric Schmidt, *Marketing Age*, **3** (6), November/December

Kohler, E (2007) Hyperlocal is more about ads than news, *Technology Evangelist*, 9 August

Learmonth, M (2010) Top marketers to Silicon Valley: Help us get ahead of consumer. Through visits to tech hub, big advertisers getting more than sales pitches, *Ad Age*, 17 May

Learmonth, M and Bryson York, E (2010) Facebook poised to take geo-networking mainstream, *Ad Age*, 10 May

Lynne, C (2012) Social media and retargeting: a perfect match, *Business 2 Community* 18 October

McKenna, R (1991) Marketing is everything, *Harvard Business Review*, January–February

O'Neill, M (2010) Budweiser celebrates the World Cup with Bud House reality series, *Social Times*, 14 June

Oxford Economics (2012) Economic payback of road safety advertising in Northern Ireland, commissioned by Lyle Bailie, www.lylebailie.com

Parekh, R (2010) Why long-form ads are the wave of the future, *Advertising Age*, 3 May

Patel, K (2010) Will growing crop of TV apps engage viewers, advertisers? *Ad Age*, 17 May

Percy, L, Rossiter, J R and Elliott, R (2002) *Strategic Advertising Management*, Oxford University Press, Oxford

Pulizzi, J (2014a) The ultimate guide to native advertising, *Linkedin Pulse*, 7 January

Pulizzi, J (2014b) Hey WSJ – content marketing is not native advertising, *Content Marketing Institute*, 6 November

Ranger, S (2014a) Virgin Atlantic tests Apple's iBeacon at Heathrow, *ZDNet*, 1 May

Ranger, S. (2014b) What is Apple iBeacon? Here's what you need to know, *ZDNet*, 10 June

Roberts, K (2010) Creativity, *KRconnectblogspot.com*, 21 January

Schmidt, E (2009) A wave of optimism, *Marketing Age*, 3 (6), November/December

Shields, R. (2015) The case for big brands taking ad tech in-house, *Exchange Wire*, 6 May

Slaughter, S (2014) The success of native advertising hinges on earning readers' trust, *AdWeek* 26 August

Skelton, Z (2015) How to power up with programmatic marketing, *Digital Doughnut*, 24 June

Smith, PR (2014) Research-driven shock ad uses magic formula and goes viral, www.PRSmith.org/blog, 23 August

Smith, PR (2015) The SOSTAC® Guide to Writing Your Perfect Plan, www.PRSmith.org/SOSTAC

Smith, PR (2015) The rise and fall of owned, earned but not paid media, www.PRSmith.org/blog, 27 June

Smith, PR, Berry, C and Pulford, A (2000) *Strategic Marketing Communications*, 2nd edn, Kogan Page, London

Sorrell, M (1996) Beans and pearls, D&AD president's lecture

Straz, M (2012) The remarkable rise of retargeting, *Online Spin, Media Post*, 22 October

Weinberger, D (2013) The ethics of using paid content, *Harvard Business Review*, 22 July

Weinreich, L (2001) *11 Steps to Brand Heaven*, Kogan Page, London

Whatmough, D (2010) Facebook threat, *PR Week*, 19 March

Further information

Advertising Standards Authority Limited (ASA)
Mid City Place
71 High Holborn
London
WC1V 6QT
Tel: +44 (0)20 7492 2222
www.asa.org.uk

Committee of Advertising Practice (CAP)
Mid City Place
71 High Holborn
London
WC1V 6QT
Tel: + 44 (0)20 7492 2222
www.cap.org.uk

Incorporated Society of British Advertisers
ISBA
12 Henrietta Street
London WC2E 8LH
Tel: +44(0)20 7291 9020
Fax: +44 (0)20 7291 903
www.isba.org.uk

Institute of Practitioners in Advertising (IPA)
44 Belgrave Square
London SW1X 8QS
Tel: +44 (0)20 7235 7020
www.ipa.co.uk

Ofcom
Riverside House
2a Southwark Bridge Road
London SE1 9HA
Tel: +44 (0)300 123 3000
www.ofcom.org.uk

14
Publicity and public relations

LEARNING OBJECTIVES

By the end of this chapter you will be able to:

- Understand how PR is changing and its expanding range of PR tools
- Appreciate the potential for integration with social media and other marketing communications tools
- Plan an outline PR campaign knowing the advantages and disadvantages of PR tools

Introduction   378
What is PR?   378
Public relations and marketing   378
Product PR and corporate PR   379
PR is more than communications   379
The PR mix   382

New and old PR tools   382
Media relations and publicity   382
News releases   383
Press conferences and interviews   384
Video news releases   384
Syndicated radio interviews and down-the-line
   interviews   385
Photography   385
Publicity stunts   386

Viral marketing   390
Social media   392

Advantages and disadvantages of PR   392
No media cost   392
Higher credibility   393
Lack of control   393

Advantages and disadvantages
   summary   404
Advantages   404
Disadvantages   404

Key points from Chapter 14   404

References and further reading   404

Further information   405

Introduction

Positive publicity nurtures good relationships with the media (media relations). This is only one of the responsibilities of public relations, as it deals with a range of different 'publics' or stakeholders. Public relations integrates with public affairs, corporate affairs, community affairs, community relations, corporate relations and corporate communications. The first part of this chapter explores what exactly PR is and where it fits with marketing; then it examines various PR tools and finally the advantages and disadvantages of PR over other marcomms tools. The golden rule, 'Develop credibility before raising visibility' underpins this chapter.

What is PR?

Public relations is regularly, and sometimes worryingly, referred to as 'PR', which is often confused with 'press releases' or 'press relations'. These are, in fact, only a part of real public relations. **A simple definition of public relations is: 'the development of and maintenance of good relationships with different publics'.** The publics are the range of different groups on which an organization is dependent. These include employees, investors, suppliers, customers, distributors, legislators, regulators, governments, pressure groups, the community, the media and even the competition. Most of these groups have different (sometimes conflicting) interests in any particular organization. The UK's Institute of Public Relations (IPR) uses the following public relations definition: 'the planned and sustained effort to establish and maintain goodwill and mutual understanding between an organization and its publics'. In 1978 in Mexico, the World Assembly of PR Associations agreed what is now known as the 'Mexican statement': 'PR practice is the art and science of analysing trends, predicting their consequences, counselling organization leaders and implementing planned programmes of action that will serve both the organization's and the public interest.'

Public relations and marketing

While marketing traditionally focuses on markets or just three of the publics, ie customers, distributors (the 'trade') and the competition, public relations is concerned with many more publics. Add in the emergence of globalism (eg websites can be viewed around the world), increased media interest (including social media) in business, new investor criteria (eg ethical policies), more effective pressure groups, information-hungry customers and the constant search for cost-effective communications tools, and you can soon see why PR has grown in importance. In fact, PR-driven communications has proved its worth with the emergence of major global brands like Google, Facebook and LinkedIn without any significant advertising. The new understanding of the power of PR is demonstrated when business analysts suggest that both management and unions, before embarking on a dispute, now ask: 'How will this play in the media?'

Some organizations insist on public relations, advertising, direct mail people, and sales promotion people sitting in together on various project meetings so that they cross-fertilize ideas and create synergy through integrating the marketing communications at an early stage.

Who reports to whom? Is PR part of marketing or marketing part of PR? Product publicity is part of the marketing communications mix and therefore should be under the control of the marketing director or manager. Corporate PR, on the other hand, often reports to the board or CEO directly. However, Martin Sorrell (2015) recently said: 'PR can cast off its self-doubt, build its influence and take the

---

The death Of PR?

When the editor in chief of UK's *PR Week* announces 'The death of PR agencies – as we know them', the PR industry has to listen to it. 'Advertising and PR are increasingly the same thing', says Danny Rogers. 'PR was about editorial persuasion; selling stories to journalists. And while the distinction between bought media and earned media still exists, you now find their executives working across both.' Rogers continues, 'So now is the opportunity for those with earned (media relations) and owned (company websites, magazines or events) media skills to completely rebrand their business. Alongside endeavours to reinvent themselves according to today's transforming media, they may finally need to cast off those two deadly letters – P and R.

Rogers (2014)

lead on social media, content-led campaigning and reputation... PR can place itself at the centre: data, social and content present great opportunities.'

Product PR and corporate PR

The previous definitions give an indication of the diverse nature and far-reaching effects of public relations. We need to separate product PR (product or brand publicity) and corporate PR (corporate image enhancement). Product PR (sometimes called 'marketing PR') promotes a product or a brand and is the responsibility of the marketing manager, while corporate PR promotes a company and is the responsibility of the corporate communications director. A manager responsible for product PR would ultimately report to the marketing manager, whereas a manager responsible for corporate PR would probably report to a board director or the board itself. Both types of PR do, however, integrate with each other. Jon White, in *How to Understand and Manage Public Relations* (1991), suggested that:

> public relations is a complement and a corrective to the marketing approach... it creates an environment in which it is easier to market... public relations can raise questions which the marketing approach, with its focus on the market, products, distribution channels and customers, and its orientation towards growth and consumption, cannot. Public relations concerns are with relations of one group to another, and with the interplay of conflicting and competing interests in social relationships.

Publicity objectives can vary from promoting a product (product PR) to promoting a company (corporate PR) among employees, customers, investors, the community, local government, etc. The simplest way of expressing the difference is to 'discriminate between brand or product image and corporate or company image' (Hart, 1992). Marketing will tend to be sales or market share orientated, while public relations can, but not always, be sales or market share orientated; for example a PR objective may be to recruit the best employees, to win permission to build a new factory or to influence government. Nevertheless, today's PR people, like any marketing professionals, have to be fully versed in blogs, micro-blogs (Twitter), wikis, online networks, RSS feeds, social bookmarking, tags and podcasts, as well as optimized news release (social media press release, newsroom with social media functionality, social and professional networking sites such as LinkedIn, Myspace and Facebook, communities, forums, Yahoo groups, Google groups, Ning, virtual worlds such as Second Life, crowd-sourced news aggregators like Reddit and Digg, and e-zine articles). Today's PR is often measured less by press coverage (press clippings) and more by web traffic, registrations and sales, sentiment and brand engagement.

The influence of public relations stretches far beyond product marketing and into corporate strategy, particularly where long-term decisions affecting choice of markets, products, factory locations, production processes, etc are concerned. External groups are becoming more demanding, and organizations are beginning to have to demonstrate their social responsibility on a global basis. Ethics and social responsibility have traditionally been the bastion of public relations. Today all managers need to develop their awareness and understanding of at least the PR implications of both boardroom and marketing decisions, strategies, policies and actions (or the lack of these).

Integrated reporting

There is a massive opportunity for corporate communications in adopting 'integrated reporting'. The International Integrated Reporting Council (IIRC) has seen Coca-Cola, Microsoft and Sainsbury's 'jumping on board with the concept', which is basically intertwining non-financial reports (eg CSR reports) with financial reports. Integrated reporting has been mandatory in South Africa for some time.

Farey-Jones (2014)

PR is more than communications

Publicity and visibility should not be raised before a solid platform of credibility has been developed through decent, safe products, friendly customer service, caring ethics and socially responsible policies. The PR mix (see Figure 14.1) gives an indication of the diverse nature and far-reaching effects of public relations. It is more than just communications; it is part of the broader business disciplines such as corporate planning, finance, personnel, production and marketing. It cannot work effectively unless it is integrated into these areas and unless it also links with product quality, customer care and design management (corporate identity). These are the credibility elements that build a platform for subsequent publicity, which, as can be seen from Figure 14.1, is just one of the many visibility tools.

Corporate responsibility

Survey after survey reveal that the public feel that industry and commerce don't pay enough attention to their **corporate social responsibilities (CSR)**. People feel that a company that supports the community is a good one to work for. People believe that companies have responsibilities to their employees and communities that go beyond making profits. Today ethical issues are highlighted by new pressure group techniques.

Although Naomi Klein's challenging book *No Logo* (2000) was criticized, she did highlight issues and the need for constant corporate social responsibility. Amnesty International, which defends the human rights of individuals, departed from its normal focus on prisoners persecuted for either their religious or their political beliefs and, as Klein reported, 'is also beginning to treat multinational corporations as major players in the denial of human rights worldwide'.

Corporate responsibility is not just an overseas responsibility but starts in the corporations' own back gardens. A few years ago, the *Chicago Tribune* reported that Sears Roebuck had hundreds of elderly protesters picketing its store as a result of a decision to reduce pensioners' life insurance benefits. Any amount of press releases, or even advertising, announcing Sears' caring ethics would have a negative effect until this basic credibility problem was sorted out.

Shell in Nigeria

'The most significant landmark in the growth of anti-corporate activism also came in 1995, when the world lost Ken Saro-Wiwa. The revered Nigerian writer and environmental leader was imprisoned by his country's oppressive regime for spearheading the Ogoni people's campaign against the devastating human and ecological effects of Royal Dutch/Shell's oil drilling in the Niger Delta. Human rights groups rallied their governments to interfere, and some economic sanctions were imposed, but they had little effect. In November 1995, Saro-Wiwa and eight other Ogoni activists were executed by a military government who had enriched themselves with Shell's oil money and through their own people's repression.'

Klein (2000)

Nike

'According to Campaign for Labor Rights, the largest ever anti-Nike event so far took place on October 18, 1997: 85 cities in 13 countries participated. Not all the protests have attracted large crowds, but since the movement is so decentralized, the sheer number of individual anti-Nike events has left the company's public relations department scrambling to get its spin onto dozens of local newscasts. Though you never know it from its branding ubiquity, even Nike can't be everywhere at once.'

Klein (2000)

Even companies with a great tradition of social responsibility and, ergo, high credibility, like Cadbury Schweppes, sometimes score PR own goals when mixing marketing and social responsibility without carefully thinking through the implications. Some years ago it offered nearly £9 million worth of sports equipment to UK schools if schoolchildren bought lots of chocolate (millions of bars of chocolate had to be bought to get all the equipment). The media quickly picked up on the negative spin associated with the prospect of a teenager 'needing to consume thousands of calories before being able to play with a new basketball'. Using cause-related marketing to boost sales and corporate image is popular but needs, first, to be thought through carefully and, second, to be screened to ensure that there is a clear and positive strategic fit between the brand and the cause.

Good business is not just about achieving financial targets; it is also about behaving with a sense of responsibility. Over 50 per cent of the value of the Fortune 500 and the FTSE 100 comes from intangible assets, such as management, leadership, vision, innovation, customer loyalty, product and service quality, intellectual property, brand equity and reputation (Larkin, 2003). In September 2001 the US stock market was worth an estimated $24 trillion; by summer 2002 it had collapsed to $11 trillion. The events of 9/11 and economic uncertainty had a significant impact, but so too did the collapse of Enron and a wave of other scandals that raised fundamental questions over corporate governance.

At the time, the vast majority (84 per cent) of Americans thought that the people who run their companies are trying to do what is best for themselves rather than the company (Accenture, 2004). Years later, after another major economic crisis and an environmental crisis (BP), organizations now, more than ever before, need to engage in, and provide evidence of, solid ethical policies.

Companies can take positive steps such as being transparent and carrying out environmental impact studies, talking to communities, addressing their issues and finding solutions. An Irish renewable energy company, Mainstream Renewable Power has wind farms and solar parks across the world and they work closely with each community to ensure harmonious co-existence. Other companies join the per cent club and promise to donate 1 per cent (or half of 1 per cent) of profits to the local community. There are even 2 per cent and 5 per cent clubs. Another way is by ensuring regular ethical and/or environmental audits and, of course, taking appropriate action.

Shell trigger protests in Ireland

Shell continues to be embroiled with controversy, by way of environmental protest when in 2010 an award-winning documentary called *The Pipe* highlighted Shell's attempt to pipe gas under fields in Rossport, Co. Mayo, Ireland. Five locals 'The Rossport Five' were jailed, which caused a national outrage. The ShellToSea.com, is an attempt to stop the proposed construction of a raw natural gas pipeline through a parish, as locals feel this puts local residents at risk.

FIGURE 14.1 'Shell to Sea mural', courtesy of Lapsed Pacifist (talk)LP

Imagine your funeral

'I went on this training course (at Procter & Gamble) where you had to imagine what the minister might say about you at your funeral. When I realized that mine would say I was the leading expert on housewives' toilet cleaning products, I realized it was time for a change.'

Hamish Taylor, Managing Director, Eurostar

It is not just about making good business sense. Marketing, PR and corporate communications professionals are in the exciting position of being able to help improve their local communities, support valid causes, improve the environment, and much more. The bottom line is that it makes long-term business sense to be ethical, as it creates a platform of credibility that enriches all subsequent communications. As Bob Leaf of Burson Marsteller, succinctly says in the award-winning PR film *Actions Speak Louder than Words*, 'Ethics is good for business' (PRTV, 1991).

Cancel the Christmas party

'As CEO of Electronic Data Systems, Mort Meyerson made an unpopular decision and cancelled the Christmas party when he realized it was going to cost $360,000. Instead, he insisted, "We'll take the $360,000 and buy food and clothes and toys, and we'll get our employees to take those things personally and deliver them to the inner city, to people who don't have anything." The result was, initially, outrage that the party was cancelled, then depression, then recognition that the company was doing something different and then elation for those who actually took part in the project. This project "made them more human... made them better employees... better family members... it did a whole bunch of things". When Meyerson was CEO, he used to give 10 per cent of his time to community and philanthropic projects.'

Colvin (2003)

Harry Potter's anti-marketing magic builds the PR hype

'Review copies were withheld from interviews, no author interviews were allowed, and foreign translations were deferred for fear of injudicious leaks... printers and distributors were required to sign strict legally enforceable confidential agreements. Subtle hints that there weren't enough copies of the book to go around... fake TV footage of heavily armed security vans delivering Potter books to online book stores... Twenty advance copies were "accidentally" sold by an unnamed Wal-Mart in deepest West Virginia and one of the "lucky children" was miraculously tracked down by the world's press and splashed across every front page worth its salt... Another copy "accidentally" found its way to the news desk of the Scottish Daily Record.'

Brown (2001)

The PR mix

Figure 14.2 also shows how the 'visibility' or publicity-generating activities such as news releases, news conferences, publicity stunts, conferences, events, exhibitions, sponsorship and sales promotions can all integrate. Before we look at publicity in more detail, it is worth mentioning again that the key to long-term success is to develop credibility before raising visibility. Credibility is created by a proper product and/or quality of service. This means that the product must match the promise made by the marketing communications, ie do not sell a Rolls-Royce and deliver a Ford Ka. False expectations only lead to disappointment, frustration and extremely high post-purchase dissonance. This kills off any long-term repeat business. Good customer service makes doing business a pleasurable experience for all parties. Having the right sort of people or institutions associated by their using or endorsing a product improves credibility. So too ethics, social responsibility and corporate image all contribute towards building a credible image.

There is no point waving a flag or raising an organization's visibility if it does not have a solid platform of credibility supporting it. The days when the two aspects were held separately are gone. Spending thousands or millions of pounds on raising a profile is not just wasteful but actually damaging if a lack of credibility is exposed. So today, more than ever before, it is worth investing men/women, money and minutes in getting the credibility right before raising visibility. And credibility must also be evident on websites and blogs, as journalists use these as their first port of call for gathering information.

New and old PR tools

Media relations and publicity

Take a look at the local and national newspapers, trade journals, radio programmes and television. Spot the commercial news items or features that have made news. Although they appear to be written by an editor or journalist, many of them have been written by skilled PR professionals. Like advertising, editorial publicity can achieve many similar communication goals, such as increasing awareness, repositioning a brand, generating enquiries and boosting sales. Busy editors do not have time to scout around for all the items they use. They depend on a constant feed of professionally presented news items and news releases from organizations. Despite this, sackfuls of press releases get thrown into editors' bins continually. Many of them are badly written and inaccurately targeted (sometimes even addressed to people who have long left the newspaper).

Publicity can be generated through written press releases and feature articles for the press, video news releases for television programmes, syndicated radio recordings for radio programmes and digital press packs for all and sundry. Publicity is also generated by press conferences, press receptions, media events (what the media less reverently call 'stunts') and public speaking at conferences, lectures, seminars, dinners, chat shows, etc.

News releases

News by definition is new – a new idea, a new process, a new product, a new service or even a new use of an old product. News should 'defy expectations' and provide a new way to understand the world we live in, so it has to be newsworthy. A news release should make it easy for a journalist (and a search engine) to make news. All the key information should be in the first paragraph for the journalist, and key phrases, if relevant, should be used in the title or headline and also in the opening paragraph (to optimize it for search engines). The press releases can then be distributed to the news wires, top-ranking free publicity websites, news aggregators, relevant social news sites such as Digg, and relevant online and traditional media outlets. Press release services like Pressbox, PRWeb, Free Press Release and ClickPress can do it all in one go.

Ensure the organization's web URL is included and any other links to relevant sections of a website, as not only does this help readers but it also acts as inbound links, which boost search engine rankings.

As the proliferation of online news aggregators (eg Google News) increases, the debate continues as to whether PR staff are writing news releases for people or machines – a human editor or a robot. The reality is both. A select few organizations bother to write different news releases for human editors and online aggregators.

The debate rattles on with Ryan Singel's (2006) comments:

> Standing up for the human intellect, upstart Digg is betting that its formidable legion of users can find better and more interesting news faster than any algorithm Google – or a number of upstart companies – can code. On the machine side, the purest algorithmic news finder is Google News, which made waves in the media world when it debuted. With Google News, it's code, and not a team of editors, that decides which stories make it onto the front page.

This boring headline is written for Google

Journalists over the years have assumed they were writing their headlines and articles for two audiences – fickle readers and nitpicking editors. Today, there is a third important arbiter of their work: the software programs that scour the web, analysing and ranking online news articles on behalf of internet search engines like Google, Yahoo and MSN. The search engine 'bots' that crawl the web are increasingly influential, delivering 30 per cent or more of the traffic on some newspaper, magazine or television news websites. And traffic means readers and advertisers, at a time when the mainstream media are desperately trying to make a living on the web.

Online newsroom

If building an online newsroom or media facility on a website, make it easy to make news by considering what journalists need when writing up a story:

- news releases and press releases (easily searchable and sortable by date, by topic and by department);
- photos (linked to each news release, plus an archive or library of high-, medium- and low-resolution images);
- video (can be linked to a new release if it is a launch event, a press conference, a speech, an interview, a product demonstration, vox pops or endorsements);

- media kits to support news (all of the above in one downloadable file);
- general corporate information (corporate background, corporate financials, corporate statistics and executive team information);
- research and study data, white papers, links and related resources (including blogs, which journalists use increasingly);
- awards and recognition;
- upcoming events;
- contact information.

Note that all media assets, including videos, photos, news releases, white papers, etc, should be easily searchable, sortable and shareable. An effective online newsroom invites visitors to go deeper into the site for additional background information on the organization, its corporate social responsibility, its people and its media assets, so that journalists get to know the organization and form a healthy relationship.

Embeddable digital press kit

Buena Vista International's film *Starship Troopers* had an innovative 'digital press kit' available to support its launch. The kit comprised a ready-made mini-site packed with material related to the film. It was designed in such a way that it could be incorporated into other media sites. This made a convenient package for media partners, distributorships, agents and promoters to link the mini-site to their own website.

Press conferences and interviews

Press conferences are an efficient way to release information to a large number of journalists, newspapers, blogs and radio and TV stations. They should include pre-prepared press packs and, ideally, rehearsed Q&As (the likely questions and sensible answers), although there is not always time to prepare Q&As.

Key staff need to be trained for press interviews. Avoid jargon, tell the truth and be topical, relevant and unusual if possible. A story that stirs up some trouble can be attractive to an editor. However,

some caution is required to ensure the facts are 100 per cent correct, as journalists will investigate rigorously and any inaccuracies will subsequently cause damage. Finally, the human angle (human story) always appeals at an emotional level. Paint a picture with words; as Scott Chisholm (2010) says, 'Imagine is the most powerful word you can use in an interview.'

Virtual press conference in Second Life

For those international bloggers and journalists who could not physically attend the launch of Northern Ireland's creative digital hub in Belfast's Science Park, a virtual press conference was held the next day, with some 50 bloggers attending. The Minister for Enterprise's avatar and PR Smith's avatar presented the hub and took questions for an hour afterwards. This resulted in a buzz of discussions on key international blogs, raised awareness, a new network of bloggers and a surge of valuable inbound links.

Video news releases

A video news release (VNR) is conceptually the same as a written press release, except that it is produced on broadcast-quality digital video. A key factor is that it must be newsworthy or highly relevant as a feature item. VNRs also save broadcasters from having to send their own busy camera crews out to cover a story. The VNR consists of two sections: a 90-second 'A' roll, which carries a commentary designed to show the editor and/or journalist how the story could run on air, and a three- to five-minute 'B' roll, which is a selection of loosely cut shots ('rushes') designed to be re-edited by the broadcasters into their own style, ie the broadcasters use their own commentary, graphics and captions so that as far as the viewers are concerned the story has been originated by the broadcaster. As with a press release, **a VNR is paid for by the organization that is looking for some positive publicity. The TV stations receive VNRs free of charge.** Again, as with press releases, there is no guarantee that the material will be used, since a bigger story can break at any time. Equally, a VNR can be used negatively, since, unlike advertising, there is no control over the final message. And these videos can also eventually be used on social media sites, websites and blogs as well as form part of the press resources.

Syndicated radio interviews and down-the-line interviews

A syndicated radio interview is, on average, a three-minute recorded interview about a person, event, company, product or service. The audio file and script are distributed (or syndicated) to radio stations. The same principles as apply to VNRs apply here, ie it should be newsworthy and not a blatant plug. For just a few thousand pounds, a syndication supplier's basic package usually includes:

- preliminary discussion;
- interviewer – selecting, booking and briefing;
- structuring the interview;
- studio session (one hour);
- recording (three minutes);
- editing the master tape;
- two spare copies for the client;
- cue sheet preparation (written introduction to the taped interview);
- selecting 30 relevant radio stations (only one per area where stations overlap);
- monitoring – three to four weeks after dispatch a written report is produced, giving details of which stations broadcast the information, which is sometimes followed up with a more detailed report.

A 40 per cent take-up of a professionally produced, newsworthy, accurately targeted syndicated radio interview is considered to be an 'average success rate'. There is usually a range of optional extras (eg localized cue sheets or overseas distribution).

Syndicated producers usually offer an alternative service – 'down-the-line interviews'. This is where the interviewee is brought into the studio, linked up live to local radio stations one at a time, and interviewed on a one-to-one basis. On average the interviewee does about 10 separate interviews per day. Some interviewees have been known to do up to 15 separate interviews in one day. This is exhausting, and sometimes the later interviews are not as good, as interviewees cannot remember if they have said something before or not.

Photography

A picture paints a thousand words. A cleverly crafted photograph can catch a photo editor's eye. Some of the same criteria as for a news release apply – is it newsworthy, is it different, does it tell a story, does it catch the reader's eye and does it add value to the publication? If the photo has someone famous in it, then it is even more valuable. Ideally photos can be stored in three file sizes: high, medium and small resolution. They can be stored securely for press, or distributors only. Social photo sites like Flickr.com can store the images, embed them on the company's or individual's blog and embed them as part of an electronic press kit. Again tagging makes the images searchable and sortable. Here is a list of some great publicity photos that generated vast audiences:

- *Jarvis Cocker's blue beard for Oxfam* was part of a series taken by Rankin to promote Oxfam's 'blue faces' campaign, which was to raise awareness of the effects of climate change on poor people around the world, and was carried out across the UK festival season.

- *Dom Pedro and the 15 Second Film Festival.* Dom Pedro is the iconic character used by the 15 Second Film Festival to promote the concept of 15 Second Movies. Each movie has a beginning, a middle and an end, and Dom Pedro is the front man, deal maker and do-er who catches the picture editor's attention. **www.15SecondFilmFestival.com**.

- *No 10 Downing Street.* Plan UK created this image to put pressure on the prime minister to help 72 million extra children into primary school across the world. This was part of an ongoing advocacy/PR campaign to ensure the government delivered on promises to fulfil the Millennium Development Goals (MDG) at the MDG summit in New York in September 2009.

- *Projection on parliament.* Don't forget planes! – Friends of the Earth took its successful campaign for aviation emissions to be included in the Climate Change Act to parliament and mobilized huge public and political support for action on climate change, engaging a mainstream public audience, as well as environmental activists and politicians.

- *MPs support Friends of the Earth's rainforest-free lunches for planet-friendly farming.* Andrew George finds out that there's no such thing as a rainforest-free lunch if you're eating meat or dairy. He's one of 160 MPs who backed Friends of the Earth's call for government action to reduce the environmental impact of livestock farming.

- *Admiral Lord Nelson.* The stunning skyline around Nelson demonstrated the total commitment of the whole of London, its authorities and its people as part of the campaign for the London 2012 Olympics bid.

Publicity stunts

Publicity stunts are at much higher risk of error and 'egg on the face' than issuing a news release with a photograph, since the media are invited to wait and watch. Didier Pasquette promoted Vanguard while walking high above the River Thames on a tightrope, meeting Jade Kindar-Martin heading in the opposite direction. The two had to climb over each other midstream in the first ever double tightrope crossing of the Thames – a stunt that was publicized worldwide.

FIGURE 14.2   Jarvis Cocker's blue beard

PHOTO: Rankin/Oxfam

FIGURE 14.3   (Dom) Pedro El Magico, silent investor of the 15secondfilmfestival.com

FIGURE 14.4   The 10 Downing Street image for the MDG summit

PHOTO: Plan UK/Mark Read

FIGURE 14.5   The 'Don't forget planes!' campaign

PHOTO: Friends of the Earth

FIGURE 14.6   Andrew George supporting Friends of the Earth's rainforest-free lunches

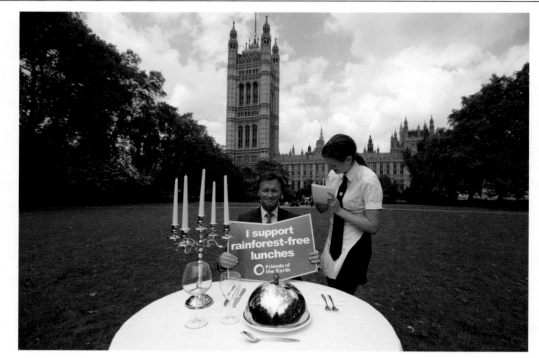

PHOTO: Warren Allot

FIGURE 14.7   Admiral Lord Nelson supporting the London bid

PHOTO: On Edition

Legendary publicity stunts

'The most celebrated was by a New Yorker called Jim Moran, who once contrived a bar-room brawl between a fairly well-known band leader and a bystander. When the judge asked what they were fighting about, the band leader told him it was over the recipe for Pimms Cup. Pimms had hired Mr Moran because they were having trouble establishing the brand name in the United States. The "brawl" received so much publicity that he solved the problem with a single blow.'

Independent on Sunday, 1 April 1990

Other stunts include:

- **The Archaos fish diet:** A classic 'What the –?' photo, this is a brilliant example of life mimicking art. Photographer Gavin Evans was sent to shoot a fish-throwing act. Stuck for a workable angle, Gavin stuffed a fish in the performer's mouth. Archaos subsequently made the stunt the grand finale to its routine.

FIGURE 14.8   The Archaos fish diet

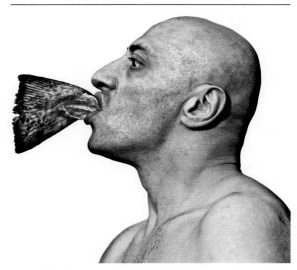

PHOTO: Gavin Evans

- **Friends Of The Earth one-off gig with Razorlight at the Science Museum:** Razorlight played a one-off gig at London's Science Museum to back Friends of the Earth's call for aviation emissions to be included in the forthcoming Climate Change Act.

- **Fuel poverty stunt outside the Royal Courts of Justice:** Friends of the Earth and Help the Aged took the government to court over its failure to tackle fuel poverty.

- **Mortascreen's Funeral Procession:** Mortascreen has a consumer database of over 7 million deceased individuals, with 50,000 UK deaths being added each month. Brands use the Mortascreen database to remove deceased people from their mailing lists, firstly, so families are not upset in bereavement with unwanted mail and, secondly, to improve the effectiveness of the brands' marketing campaigns. The PR agency Eulogy set up a photo opportunity using a traditional horse-drawn funeral procession, complete with four mourners, walking across Westminster Bridge and Parliament Square and finally coming to rest behind the London Eye. The funeral cortège contained a coffin filled with the amount of direct mail Londoners receive in one day addressed to deceased loved ones. This publicity stunt achieved 90 pieces of coverage across key national, broadcast, trade and online media (within an hour it was on YouTube and probably even more quickly on Twitter), delivering 35,000,000 Opportunities To See (OTS), with a Publicity Value Equivalent (PVE) of £578,000. On a small budget of £8,500, this generated an ROI of £68:£1 or 6,800 per cent. It also generated £60,000 worth of licence sales, which gave a sales-to-fee ratio of 7:1.

A photograph's unconscious messages

With the accelerating rate of declining attention spans, images become more important. Your organization's images send out many unconscious messages. It is worth checking your images match your company's core objectives. Even head and shoulder shots can send all sorts of messages, as shown in the selection over the page. Note that although folded arms can suggest insecurity or nervousness, if the subject can relax the shoulders it reduces the defensive impact and can look quite confident, as shown over:

FIGURE 14.9A–D   Selection of head shots and the messages they send

- Low key images with plenty of shadow create mystery and interest.

- Triangular shapes created by the pose give a sense of strength and reliability.

- Direct, questioning stare suggests an individual who will 'get to the heart of the matter'.

- Inclusion of cufflinks and watch convey high status.

- Slight tilt of the head towards the viewer is a friendly, welcoming gesture.

- Loose scarf protects the neck, balancing the openness of expression and head tilt.

- Camera angle enhances an elegant feminine neck whilst lighting carves out high cheekbones.

Photos by Grey Corporate

Viral marketing

Viral marketing devices include videos clips, TV ads, cartoons, funny pictures, a short poem, a political or social message, or a news item, games or widgets, but they can also be a game, a photograph, a graphic or just a piece of text, as long as it is enlightening (informative), entertaining (shocking or funny), engaging (people must play or interact with it) or simply so good that you just have to pass it on to a friend or colleague. That is the acid test: is it worth looking at again, and is it deemed valuable if it is passed on? Anything that enhances the value of the sender (or person who passes it on) has viral potential.

Viral criteria

The viral object has to be so amazing that it makes people want to pass it on. The best ones simply make compulsive viewing. Here are some tough criteria:

- Is it good enough to make people pass it on?
- Is it on trend with whatever is trending?
- Does it create a 'shared experience'? (eg Father's Day, St Patrick's Day, Christmas time – people want to share the experience, so suitable virals can be propelled by a shared experience).
- Is it emotional (does it make you smile/laugh/ feel enraged/shocked/happy/sad/sentimental)?
- Does it have the wow factor?

FIGURE 14.9A–D   *(Continued)*

- 'Young entrepreneur' status reinforced by light grey suit, tie and pocket handkerchief.

- Shot outside to enhance green credentials and natural products.

- Hint of blossom on trees and budding green leaves creating a fresh, spring like impression.

- Expression is relaxed and confident. Head is balanced and upright, being neither aloof nor 'over-friendly'.

- Glasses as a prop (rather than on the face) suggesting seniority and someone who works with detailed documents rather than their hands.

- Pose, with the glasses, suggests a college lecturer: someone with professional knowledge.

- Open shirt and lack of tie exposing neck: showing trust and openness.

Photos by Grey Corporate

For an example of an image that went viral, see the photo of the back of the US President's seat in Chapter 16 on page 443.

Seeding

However, great creative material ('the viral agent') is simply not enough. It needs to be seeded, branded and measured. Seeding means identifying websites, blogs and influential people and sending them the e-mail, or posting the viral on their Facebook wall to start the virus spreading. Some agencies offer seeding services, where they have databases of people who like virals and tend to pass them on. Other marketers tend to build their own lists of their champions or brand advocates and influencers who like to be the first to see a new idea and therefore get credibility amongst their networks when they pass on useful virals. There are also websites that host virals for their audiences who like to view them, for example **www.viralmonitor.com** and **www.viralbank.com**. Branding means clear branding and a URL ideally, not just at the beginning and end where they can be cut out before being passed on. Although they cannot be controlled, virals should be measured as to what traffic they generate and what conversions come from this, as on an ROI basis.

TV channel E4's 'Stack Da Police' viral mixed real video, animation, sound and gaming technology to create a viral that promoted its new TV programme. It generated 3.8 million uniques and a 14 per cent click-through, which is about 0.5 million click-throughs. The cost per click (CPC) was 6p (approximately £30,000 divided by 500,000). Kerb viral agency created and seeded it for £30,000. See the full case study at the end of this chapter.

Social media

Blogs can be for individuals or they can be corporate blogs with several authors. In either case, a content strategy needs to be worked out, to ensure the postings are relevant and of value to the target audience. A content strategy also helps reduce the workload, as it identifies content that can be tweaked for the blog, eg a speech, a white paper or a book.

Remember that, although blogs tend to be informal, they do count as legal published documents in cases of libel, disclosure of trade secrets, breach of copyright, etc, so a certain amount of caution is required. In the case of a corporate blog with several contributors, this means that an overall editor is required, along with a workflow management process for approval of postings and responding to comments.

Resources are required to moderate and respond to various comments made by the audience. As with Twitter, blogs will probably require an increasing amount of time from the marketing department or PR department. This is where resources need to be integrated.

Blogs do help to nurture relationships with target audiences. Blogs and Facebook can also extend the brand experience into another dimension. In the case of www.GreatSportsmanship.org, readers of the book can see videos relating to the stories, participate in discussions about certain topics of interest, send in their stories for future editions of the book and future postings on the blog, hear radio interviews with the author, and much more.

The brand experience can further be enhanced by embedding applications or widgets in blogs, Facebook pages and most social media platforms. In fact, the embedded video player in the sportsmanship site is a very basic widget that adds enormous value to the blog, which adds value to the book. See Chapter 13 for more about widgets and apps.

The other visibility tools, such as advertising, sponsorship, exhibitions, sales promotions and direct mail, are all dealt with as separate chapters elsewhere in this book. Positive editorial is usually the result of carefully managed media relations.

Organizations and/or individuals must take time to understand what the journalist or editor wants, the news angle, the relevance of the piece, the appropriate time to deliver it to a news organization, the correct format or layout of the press release, and so on. One point to bear in mind is that PR campaigns, and particularly media relations campaigns seeking editorial exposure, do not have to be short-term, one-off news events.

Advantages and disadvantages of PR

As mentioned, editorial coverage can achieve many objectives similar to those of advertising, but there are three important points that differentiate editorial coverage from advertising:

1 there is no media cost;

2 the message has higher credibility;

3 there is no control over the message.

No media cost

There is no media cost since, with editorial coverage, unlike advertising, the space is not bought. There are, however, other costs, since news releases have to be written, carefully targeted and distributed to the right editor at the right time in the right format. This can be done by an in-house press officer or public relations department, or it can be handled by an external public relations agent or consultancy. There are news release distribution companies that specialize in getting releases physically or electronically to news editors' desks at the right time. This kind of editorial coverage creates valuable positive publicity, as **it has higher credibility than advertising copy.** No space was bought, and therefore no media costs were incurred. However, whether it is in-house PR people or an external consultancy, it does cost someone's time and expertise:

● to select the right target media (appropriate press and editors) at the right time;

● to write the news releases;

● to distribute the news releases;

• to handle any press enquiries. (There are, of course, other minor costs, some of which are hidden: photographs, stationery, stamps, phone calls, and wear and tear of the word processor, laser printer and so on.)

Editorial coverage is used increasingly to stretch the above-the-line advertising campaigns. Good press officers push the knock-on PR potential of advertising. Bruno Magli shoes enjoyed an uncontrolled estimated $100 million worth of free exposure during American football star O J Simpson's trial. The calculation is simple: add up the column inches of coverage, times by the amount of broadcast coverage and find the equivalent cost for the same amount of advertising space. There are more sophisticated methods of evaluation, which include: positive and negative comments; the position on the page; whether a picture is shown; the number of times a brand name is used, etc. Forte Hotels' constant quantitative report on editorial coverage is outlined in the box 'Scoring your PR performance' further on in this chapter.

Higher credibility

Editorial coverage has higher credibility than advertising because it is perceived as being written by an editor or journalist and not by an advertiser trying to sell something. There is arguably less resistance to the message. Some estimates suggest that a message carried in a piece of editorial has three times more credibility than a similar message carried in an advertisement. Despite the attraction of the message credibility factor, editorial coverage is risky because there is no control over the message. An editor can take a news release and criticize the sender for sending it. Advertisers, on the other hand, can control the message, since they buy the space and publish exactly what they want to say (within the law and advertising regulations). Despite this, editorial clippings and their associated levels of credibility are often compiled and used as endorsements in direct mailshots, sales literature, advertisements and exhibition stands. You can even see them above theatres promoting a show, where extracted comments from the press are highlighted in bright lights outside the front door. The third-party editorial coverage adds credibility to the claim that this is a good show. Equally, a reviewer can severely criticize a show and therefore damage the credibility (and viability) of that show.

Lack of control

The uncontrollable element of media relations is demonstrated by the montage of press clippings (editorial coverage) generated by PR Smith's 'nuclear missile' news release (Figure 14.10). This shows how the same news release gets totally different editorial coverage from two different editors. On the one hand, the *Wall Street Journal* gives it brief but positive front-page exposure, while *Personnel Today* treats the same news release with a lot of cynicism and, arguably, negative editorial coverage, despite a lot more detail about the promotion. It can be argued, in the case of PR Smith's award-winning PR video, that 'any publicity is good publicity', but this is certainly not the case with Ratners, IBM and McDonald's. These examples demonstrate the dangers of uncontrolled publicity (see the next section). Even carefully controlled media events such as annual general meetings can go wrong (see the box below). Every media event has an element of risk attached to it, since if things do go wrong the press are waiting – with cameras perched and pens ready.

Fat cat pig

'The production of a pig at the British Gas annual general meeting helped give the bandwagon against "fat cats" (overpaid directors) a memorable push.'
Andrew Bolger, *Financial Times* (date unknown)

Uncontrollable publicity – any publicity is good publicity?

The adage 'any publicity is good publicity' is not always true. Although the PR training video's negative editorial coverage (mentioned in the previous section) is, arguably, useful publicity, this is not always the case. Retail jewellery giant Ratners discovered this when it fell foul of the power of negative publicity. Its chairman, Gerald Ratner, told the press that his jewellery was 'crap'. This gained national coverage, but it also kept customers away from his shops and lowered morale among his employees. He relinquished his joint position of chairman and managing director, and the Ratners shops have since disappeared. On the other hand, unexpected

FIGURE 14.10   PRTV News Release: The same news release can generate totally different types of editorial coverage, from positive coverage on the front page of the *Wall Street Journal* to negative coverage in a training magazine editorial coverage can sometimes help, as shoemakers Bruno Magli observed when their sales jumped 50 per cent because of references to their shoes during the trial of O J Simpson. Uncontrolled editorial exposure, and particularly negative publicity, can somersault out of control, as IBM discovered during the 1996 Olympics when one of its official Olympic computers started churning out incorrect information. 'The press reported the story *ad nauseam*, even blaming IBM for things it had nothing to do with. In the aftermath of the tragic bombing in Centennial Park, for example, the *Philadelphia Inquirer* erroneously reported that an IBM system may have contributed to security lapses' (*Fortune* magazine, 9 September 1996). How a company handles the spotlight is a test for its company values. When 21 customers were shot dead in California in 1984, McDonald's knocked the restaurant down within days and eventually donated the land to a local community college. Continued publicity and association with such a tragedy are certainly not 'good publicity'. More recently, BP's negative publicity threatens the very survival of this highly profitable global success story. The negative coverage has been exacerbated by extremely poor crisis management (see 'Crisis management' overleaf for more).

Reducing the lack of control

Red faces can be avoided by checking to see if any events clash with a particular news release or event (such as launching a new hamburger bar on a national vegetarian day). There are directories available that list events and categorize them by type, region, date, etc. There are other directories that list editors' names, addresses and numbers (again categorized by type of magazine or programme). Editorial risk can be further reduced with the help of companies (such as Echo Research) that compile lists of journalists who have written articles on a particular organization or on its products, or on any particular issue, together with a favourable or unfavourable rating for each article. A further analysis compares the incidence of solicited and unsolicited press coverage, which can be cross-referenced with the ratings to identify any apparent bias in specific journalists' relationships with organizations. When a journalist calls the press office, the staff can punch in a few keywords into a desk terminal, and effectively see the profile of the caller on the screen almost instantaneously, even before the preliminary

greetings are completed. So the pressurized PR manager is briefed automatically.

Despite the best preparation and briefing, things still go wrong. In advertising, the organization gets a chance to approve the final copy (or wording), but with editorial coverage deadlines are too tight even for the friendliest of editors to allow the PR manager sight of the copy and layout before it is published: hence a bad day for Mr Pimlott (below).

Controlled integration of publicity

Publicity should be integrated with other elements of the marketing communications mix. Chapter 1 explained how many major advertising campaigns are now supported by press launches and followed up with a press and publicity campaign to maintain the visibility generated by the public relations people. An integrated packaging, PR and sales promotion campaign maintains the brand's share without any traditional above-the-line support. In other cases, blown-up press cuttings can be used (once permission is gained from the copyright owners) at trade fairs and exhibitions. Third-party endorsements can be used in advertising, news releases, sales literature, packaging design, sales promotion and so on. A single photographic shoot can produce a range of material suitable for advertising, packaging, exhibitions, direct mail, press packs, etc. Strategically, the marketing communications tools should all work together (consistent positioning) rather than pull in different directions. Ideally, each activity should be planned for maximum integration.

A bad day for Mr Edward Pimlott

'Mr Pimlott's letter to the *Grantham Journal* led to this apology: "In a letter printed in our July 25 issue, Mr Pimlott apparently described himself as 'a pillock of the community'. This was our error. Mr Pimlott described himself as a pillar of the community."'

Independent, 28 August 1997

Unforeseen opportunities and threats invariably emerge that make it difficult to plan for everything. For example, editorial is difficult to forecast. (Even if an editor promises to use a news release, it often gets 'spiked' or replaced by some other news item at the last moment; at other times the news release gets used later than expected.) Successful positive publicity can trigger all sorts of ideas for mailings, promotions and further press coverage. Crises and negative publicity are equally difficult to forecast and plan, although top companies invest in crisis management programmes before crises occur. This allows them to respond in the most effective manner. A well-handled crisis can actually leave an organization in a stronger position, for example Johnson & Johnson's excellent handling of the 1982 Tylenol poisoning crisis (when seven people died of poisoning from cyanide that had been inserted in their headache tablets) in Chicago.

Crisis management

Accidents happen, sometimes on a massive scale. Crisis management is standard procedure when a nightmare occurs. Top companies have crisis management procedures in place in case of a crisis – whether of their own or someone else's making. Key speakers are agreed, with key messages about the company, and specific messages for a series of different disaster scenarios. These are reviewed immediately if a crisis occurs. Media training includes a questions-and-answers document (tackling all the most frequently asked questions, including the tricky ones). Key to it all is simply to be human and decent. Show concern. Visit the site or the customers. Answer the questions. Pay for any damage (after the legal people have approved it). Communicate to all stakeholders. Avoid threatening legal action if possible. Legal options can be part of the solution, but rarely all of it. Note that legal action takes time (and money), and time is a very scarce resource during a crisis. Company spokespeople must tread with caution. As Alex Wollfall (2010) points out, 'After the global banking crisis and the politicians' expenses scandal, public distrust of politicians, company spokespeople and big brands is at an all-time high.'

There is a process, which usually includes the following steps. First, survey the scale of it. Is it just a handful of moaners or something more significant, and have they good reason to moan? Second, don't deny it. Acknowledge the issue if it is an issue. Be open and honest and give useful information where possible. When the toy company Mattel faced a number of product recalls, the **CEO tackled the issue head on with a video message that was**

Footballer takes on the press

'John Terry was granted a super-injunction to stop newspapers reporting details of his alleged affairs. But when the judge overturned the ruling a week later, the scorned media went in for the kill.'

Luckett (2010)

---

posted on Mattel's corporate website, spread virally across the internet and appeared on some TV news bulletins. Compare this to TV images of queues of concerned customers trying to withdraw their savings from a crippled Northern Rock for several days, while no one really knew what was happening and rumours spread uncontrollably. Third, be genuinely concerned. It seems ridiculous to spell this out, but a lack of sincerity will be sniffed out by an angry press corps very quickly. Witness the BP CEO's now infamous comment 'I want my life back', which displayed a concern for his own personal circumstances at a time when others' livelihoods were being destroyed by a massive environmental disaster. Fourth, be open with employees. Inform

---

Yacht holiday while Atlantic burns

'BP's Gulf of Mexico crisis is a case study in how poor communications skills will only magnify a corporate crisis. Avoid any photographs transmitting the wrong message. Of course everyone needs some time off but to be snapped enjoying yourself on your yacht in blue seas – when just across the Atlantic a BP field continues to spew oil into the ocean – is tantamount to reputational suicide. It was just the latest mistake by Hayward, who, despite correctly apologizing on 30 May, stupidly added: "I would like my life back", demonstrating a lack of judgement... His performance in front of a Senate committee was evidence of this. While one sympathizes with the pressure he was under, and the fears of his legal advisers, he came across as overly defensive and unemotional, playing into the hands of aggressive US journalists.'

Rogers (2010)

them as much as the press. Fifth, fix it so it is better than it was before the crisis. Make sure processes are reviewed so that the accident can never happen again. Finally, repair or compensate for any damage done or replace any faulty products.

It may be difficult to avoid financial losses, but crisis management can, if handled properly, strengthen relationships with all stakeholders. In this way it not only repairs damage but is an investment in the future. It is worth remembering that good corporate social responsibility gives a platform of credibility, particularly during a time of crisis.

Control – measuring media relations

Free publicity, news coverage or editorial can be monitored, measured and analysed. The old approach was just 'column inches' and TV minutes of press coverage. Today news releases are also measured by impressions, shares, reads, traffic and engagement. News clippings can be compiled in-house, by an agency or by a specialist news clipping company that monitors, cuts out, pastes up and delivers the clippings daily, weekly or however regularly the client wants. Google Alert can also highlight any references to a brand or organization online.

Similar media monitoring services are available for television, radio and the internet (scanning newsgroups, online editions and search engines), such as **www.ewatch.com**. The size of file, number of references, and quantity of space or time devoted to a chosen product, organization or issue are, again, a simple method of measurement. More detailed analyses give a breakdown of: front-page mentions; exclusive mentions; size of mention or cutting; number of beneficial credits; neutral credits; adverse credits; and opportunities to enquire (includes reach of article, circulation, and whether a contact address and/or phone number, enquiry card, coupon, etc was included). Various formulae attempt to calculate the quality of the coverage rather than the quantity. These can include photographs or diagrams, position on the page, etc.

Online measurement includes the following:

- 'Reads' measures how many times a news release has been read every day.
- 'Impressions' measures how often a news release headline was displayed to how many people visiting PR websites and RSS feeds.

- 'Activities' reveals who read the release, who skimmed the headline and how many 'shares'. Social media sharing is important, and the number of times a release was shared on Facebook, LinkedIn or Twitter can be measured.
- Keywords that were used to find the news release.
- Search engines that were used to find the release can be reported on as well.

All of these are hard facts, which could provide a simple format for pay-by-performance.

These factually based reports will make it easier for more PR consultancies to accept pay-by-results from their clients. The PR industry has not fully embraced pay-by-results (probably because of the large number of uncontrollable variables that affect the results).

Paul Miller, Strategic Planning Director at Porter Novelli Europe, has observed that 'the PR business is not the most sophisticated or advanced about setting good objectives. But this is now being recognized as a weakness, and what we like about performance-related fees is that they make clients really focus on what they want, so they are not wishy-washy.' In 2002, Hill & Knowlton, a leading PR agency, launched the pre-school animation series *Engie Benjy* using the TV stars Ant and Dec, and 30 per cent of its fee was contingent upon the programme achieving audience reach targets.

These forms of analysis measure what gets into the press; they do not measure what gets into the minds of the target audience, ie whether the editorial has changed or reinforced the target audience's attitudes and intentions, voting patterns, shared values, sales levels, etc. This has to be measured separately by researching attitudes and behaviour patterns. Sales can be measured, but it can be difficult to isolate PR from other communications activities when attempting to gauge the effect of any aspect of public relations. Perhaps this is the reason for the apparent resistance to payment-by-results. But, despite the difficulties of isolating and measuring PR's results, performance-related fees do encourage clients to set very clearly defined, measurable objectives.

In summary, PR punches above its weight. It can be a very cost-effective communications tool that nurtures and strengthens relationships with key stakeholders.

CASE STUDY 14.1 The gnome story that went viral

FIGURE 14.11 The start of the gnome going viral

SOURCE: OgilvyPR

Situation

Kern, a precision scales manufacturer, needed to build its brand, differentiate itself and grow market share within the science and education sectors. However, with millions of schools and laboratories around the world to reach, Kern faced the challenge of a highly commoditized marketplace and a disinterested media. Subsequent audience analysis by Ogilvy PR (surveys, perceptions audit and analysis of Kern's historic sales data) revealed: low brand recognition for laboratory grade balances; a highly commoditized marketplace; no significant discussion of measurement and accuracy outside of specialist titles; and few independent views on quality, reliability or precision. Recognizing that Kern's targets represented a global audience, from school teachers to Nobel scientists, this extremely diverse group was influenced by equally diverse sources, including friends, peers, and media. They are highly active online; inquisitively seeking out, discussing and sharing information they 'discover' from a host of influential and specialist cross-media sources.

Objectives

Ogilvy PR London and OgilvyOne were challenged to deliver an engaging business campaign that would effect behavioural change within the target audience, encouraging them to recognize brand 'Kern' for the first time and make purchases based on familiarity and preference. These translated into:

1 **Drive sales** of scales to the education and science sectors by enhancing Kern's brand visibility and preference amongst these key markets.

2 **Generate conversations** internationally around gravity's influence on weight measurement – explaining the importance of Kern's USP; calibrating scales for local gravity.

3 **Raise awareness** of Kern's reputation for accuracy within and beyond its existing customer base – securing coverage outside of specialist media.

Strategy

Make complex science accessible, harnessing Kern's gravitational calibration USP. Give the public a reason to talk about Kern and 'accuracy in measurement'. Conduct in-depth research into education and science influencers, delving into scientific theories on weight and measurement to find a unique, engaging concept that had viral potential. The Gnome Experiment was born – a global research project aimed at proving the scientific theory that gravity varies from place to place affecting weight. This would:

- harness compelling science surrounding gravitational anomalies to engage new audiences;
- give Kern a personality that would speak to all media channels;
- transform the way Kern reaches buyers, targeting influencers via new channels and encouraging interaction with the brand;
- go beyond traditional media, amplifying flagship coverage and developing engaging sharable content.

Tactics

Chip-proof gnome: Create a chip-proof garden gnome (also called Kern), providing the campaign with a universally appealing personality. Gnomes are famed for their love of travelling and originate from Bavaria, where Kern scales are manufactured.

Create local stories: Offer local stories anchored in international activity targeting territories including; Switzerland, South Africa, the UK, the United States, Canada etc. for physical activity to spark local conversations yet attract international attention.

FIGURE 14.12   The gnome pack

SOURCE: OgilvyPR

Stage 1: Endorsements/develop credibility

Packed in a flight kit containing a set of Kern precision scales, the gnome was then circulated between scientists and existing Kern customers globally. This provided profes-

sional endorsement of the Gnome Experiment as individuals weighed the gnome at their location before passing it on.

Stage 2: Initiated media and influencer engagement/raise visibility

- The Gnome Experiment Blog – a blog and website (gnomeexperiment.com) was created to host the experiment's results and directly engage volunteers and fans. Through these channels, and across other social media, the gnome's own personality emerged; scientifically irreverent.

FIGURE 14.13   The gnome in famous locations

SOURCE: OgilvyPR

FIGURE 14.13   *continued*

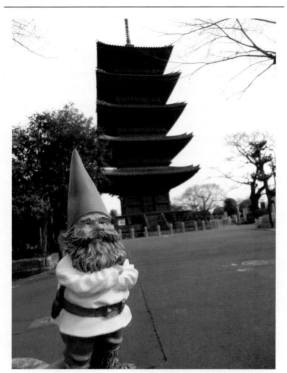

- Social media news releases targeting global media as well as science and education influencers brought consumer and target business attention to gnomeexperiment.com – requesting volunteers and engaging millions.
- Participants were given the tools to share their involvement with local media and friends.
- Content was shared including travel snaps of the gnome, video and facts about gravity to encourage further sharing.

Action

The creative use of little-known gravitational facts and a travelling gnome brought together academics, scientists and the media, sparking global conversations through the world's first mass-participation gravity experiment.

- Dispatching gnome packs. Following up to ensure safe receipt.
- Creating website/blog, testing and release.
- News releases and blog post creation.
- Monitoring reactions, press coverage, social media engagement, on a daily basis.

Control/measurement/results

Lauded by Oxford scholars and science geeks alike the campaign resulted in schools incorporating Kern's experiment into lessons, a TED presentation, *National Geographic* feature articles, and TV production companies around the world vying to feature Kern in shows.

One week after launch

News, science and education shows globally ran dedicated Kern segments.

GnomeExperiment.com saw 52,425 views, with a new participant enlisting every 20 seconds. 16,386 websites linked to Kern's gnomeExperiment.com

Two weeks after launch

Coverage reached an audience in excess of 355,378,000:

- Analytics revealed coverage reached 152 countries.
- 1,042 per cent ROI achieved based on new distributor sign-ups alone.
- Schools around the world added Kern's story to the curriculum.
- The experiment became a TED talk.

Drive sales

- Product sales to target groups increase by 22 per cent.
- 2,200 former customers get back in touch.
- 1,445 new leads generated: 40 per cent schools, 25 per cent scientists.

Generate conversations

Kern and its USP were debated amongst scholars, scientists and the general public across all media. Its experiment increased global understanding of the issues of gravity and weight measurement reaching an audience of over 350 million.

Corporate website visits increased 256 per cent and Gnome Experiment volunteers ranged from schoolchildren to internationally acclaimed scientists.

Raise awareness

Globally, people became enthralled by the Gnome Experiment as it brought science to life. For the first time Kern drew the attention of popular science publications, national newspapers, influential online publications, broadcast news and social media, eg *New Scientist*, Fox News, BBC, the *Metro*, *Le Monde*, *National Geographic*, etc.

Today

The experiment continues... Kern's Gnome visited Newton's apple tree in the company of BBC's Newsround, followed swiftly by a trip into earth's upper atmosphere in NASA's zero-G flight trainer. The campaign has taken Kern from laboratories and schools into people's daily lives. Millions learned about gravity, tens of thousands shared Kern's content, and thousands volunteered to take part in the experiment.

Men and women/human resource required: Kern worked with Ogilvy PR London and OgilvyOne. Ogilvy PR team was led by Blair Metcalfe and Allan Edwards who worked intensely with the Kern marketing manager.

Money/budget required: All of this was done for a surprisingly small budget of £10,000. Other non-OPR costs, including shipping, cases, web design and some advertising placement to showcase the campaign in trade press, added another £25,000 giving grand total of £35,000. Many people, for example the US Army at the South Pole, and SnoLab in Ontario, found the project so fascinating they simply gave their own time and even paid to move the gnome on once they had weighed him.

Minutes/time required: From brief to launch, campaign ran for two weeks but still has momentum and continues to engage its target market, maintain awareness, preference and sales.

CASE STUDY 14.2   The Snack Dash viral game

This is another more detailed viral case regarding the serious issue of obesity and healthy eating (created by KerbGames.com). The client, Digital Public, proposed a viral game to the School Food Trust to promote its healthy eating message, raise awareness of the School Food Trust and drive traffic to its site. The target market is a cynical age group, and the task of creating a game with such a nannying message without alienating the target market is a minefield.

Objectives

The brief was to build a game that conveyed the message of healthy eating to a target market of children aged seven and over in the UK, drive traffic to the site and also for the game to sit on the site as a flagship piece of game content for the site's newly established game section.

Strategy

To create more than just a game with a logo on it, or with information regarding healthy eating embedded in it, the strategy required the creation of a game with pure game play and humour that would appeal to children but that would actually illustrate the benefits of healthy eating within the game play.

Tactics

The tactics were to design and build a game that requires the player to guide the main character from start to finish in the shortest possible time, whilst collecting as many points as possible along the way. In order to fulfil the brief, one of the game's key features is the inclusion of healthy and unhealthy food. Collecting healthy foods (such as apples, water and carrots) increases the player's score and protects the player from danger. Conversely, the consumption of unhealthy food (such as crisps, sweets and fizzy drinks) causes the character considerable instant weight gain. The player can still move but is unable to move quickly enough to negotiate features like the loop-the-loop or to jump over the baddies. A little bit of exercise is required to lose the excess pounds (toggling the A and S keys will make the character perform a number of press-ups in order to lose that puppy fat). However, this all takes up precious time. The only way to get a good score and speed is by avoiding the fatty foods altogether.

Action

Week 1: design.
Week 2: develop.
Week 4: test.
Week 5: seed.

Control

Results: As expected from an engaging viral, it got huge worldwide traffic; 70 million uniques, with 3 per cent coming from the UK, which equals 2 million UK uniques, without any media spend. In the first two weeks alone, the game achieved over 3 million visits, with no budget spent on media buying. It subsequently spread like a true viral. The game has been independently tracked by MemeCounter and Viralchart. 'Out of over 400 campaigns this is the fastest-moving viral that we have ever tracked' (Viralchart.com). MemeCounter recorded over 340,000 visitors in one day, which beat the previous record by over 80,000 (MemeCounter.com). The cost per thousand was £8.33, and the reach was 3 million, with a cost of £25,000. This may seem expensive, but it was a highly engaged audience. The cost per click was less than 1p (£25,000 divided by 3 million).

Men/women

Created and seeded by Kerb Viral Agency.

Money

£25,000.

Minutes

Eight weeks to create, seed and spread to 70 million users.

CASE STUDY 14.3   Virgin Mobile's new tariff

Situation

Tariff announcements are essential for mobile phone providers, as they are one of the key factors affecting consumer purchase. It's a cluttered marketplace where a formulaic approach to PR is typically used. The campaign used innovative techniques in digital media to promote Virgin Mobile's new, very cheap, 30p tariff, engaged a hard-to-reach audience and delivered coverage that surpassed all client expectations for a new tariff announcement.

Objectives

- Engage Virgin Mobile customers, potential customers and key online influencers with the data tariff story – Virgin Mobile offers unlimited mobile internet for 30p a day.
- Find a creative way to get people talking about a dry news story.
- Increase inbound links to the tariff's homepage at **www.virginmobilepeople.com/30p.**
- Secure at least 60 pieces of coverage between online national news and blogs in three weeks.
- Increase average monthly new customer acquisition by 4 per cent.

Strategy

To build an online PR and social media campaign using innovative digital techniques to engage Virgin Mobile's customers, prospects and influencers. The campaign had to be developed with the essence of the brand in mind, so elements of youth, fun, funkiness, vibrancy and edginess were critical in positioning Virgin Mobile as the 'challenger' brand within its competitor set.

Tactics

The '30 peas' campaign was the first ever online PR and social media campaign for the launch of a new mobile phone tariff. The creative concept was to use '30 peas' in different, digitally enhanced ways to illustrate the new 30p tariff in a fun and quirky way. A stop-motion animation film of 30 frozen peas dancing through black holes, climbing mountains and playing Pong fully encapsulated the fun of the Virgin Mobile experience, with the subtle messaging 'If you can get all of the internet for 30p a day, just imagine what 30 peas could do.' The *30 Peas* film premiered at London's first interactive blogger event for the launch of a viral video called the Voscars (Virgin Mobile Oscars).

Action

The premiere of *30 Peas* took place at the Curzon Theatre in Mayfair, where a group of 30 of London's most influential bloggers were invited to showcase their favourite viral videos. Bloggers across all categories, including tech, coolhunting, mobile, social media, marketing, transport, London, food and news, took part, bringing an eclectic and vibrant energy to the event.

At the end of the screenings, the bloggers voted on their favourite videos. The winning video was packaged as a story and sold at a 'Virgin Mobile's 30p per day Mobile Internet Tariff' premiere.

The Voscars also saw the opportunity for Virgin Mobile to engage directly with online consumers. Members of the Virgin Mobile communications team were on hand to chat about the campaign, the data tariff and Virgin Mobile's plans for the future.

What was not covered in national news was covered by the bloggers in attendance at the event. Each of the 30 bloggers wrote his or her own post about Virgin Mobile, the Voscars, *30 Peas* and the mobile data tariff plan, often linking to or embedding the *30 Peas* clip.

Additional online outreach was conducted to bloggers who were not able to make the event, as well as to non-London-based bloggers on mobile, creative, entertainment, coolhunting and technology blogs.

Control

Results

- Monthly new customer acquisition increased 5.5 per cent (over 37 per cent over target).
- There were 99 pieces of coverage, including a feature in *Metro* online and print.

Minutes

Here are the timescales required for this campaign.

- Over 80 per cent of sites linked to virginmobilepeople.com/30p.
- There was OTS of over 20 million across non-mobile blogs and websites.
- There were 10,000 video views in 10 days.
- In total, 75 per cent of placements linked to or embedded the *30 Peas* video.
- Over 95 per cent of placements mentioned Virgin Mobile.
- For every £1 spent, 952 people were reached.
- Outcome: over 80 per cent of sites linked that wrote about the plan and/or the campaign created inbound links to Virgin's site.

Men/women

Account executive, managers and senior managers.

Money

This amounted to £21,000 for all PR activity, including agency fees and third-party costs.

FIGURE 14.14 Virgin mobile campaign timescale

Week commencing	24 November	1 December	8 December	15 December	22 December
Brief delivered	■				
Campaign planning	■				
Video production		■			
Event planning		■			
Blogger engagement		■	■		
Event confirmation			■		
Video approval			■		
Event			11 December		
Top virals story developed				■	
Top virals story sell-in				■	
Campaign evaluation					■

Advantages and disadvantages summary

Here are some of the advantages and disadvantages to consider when deciding whether to increase or reduce this communications tool.

Advantages

PR has higher credibility than advertising, as it is deemed to be a journalist's opinion or at least vetted by a third-party news source. Equipped with a good platform of corporate social responsibility, PR can work wonders. It also has much lower costs (on a CPT basis) than advertising. PR is good at generating awareness, building preference and overall brand building. It often delivers more 'bangs for your buck'.

Disadvantages

PR has no control of the message once editors receive it. They can rewrite it any way they want, whereas advertising controls its message. Editors, journalists and bloggers often dig deep under the surface to expose any inconsistencies. Also the message can spread beyond target areas. PR cannot close sales.

Key points from Chapter 14

- PR and marketing are not subsets of each other, although they do integrate.
- Editorial coverage has lower costs, higher message credibility and higher risks because of lack of control over the message.
- Social media is a natural fit for PR.
- Integrated PR contributes to marketing communications synergy.

References and further reading

Accenture (2004) *The Business of Trust*, White Paper referencing the World Economic Forum 2004

Bernays, E (1923) *Crystallizing Public Opinion*, Boni & Liveright, New York

Bernays, E (1969) *The Engineering of Consent*, 2nd edn, University of Oklahoma Press, Norman

Bland, M (1987) *Be Your Own PR Man*, Kogan Page, London

Brown, S (2001) Marketing for Muggles, *Journal of Marketing Management*, **17** (5), 5 July

Chisholm, S (2010) Getting your message across, *PR Week*, 16 April

Churchill, D (1992) The power behind the image, *PR Week*, 15 October

Colvin, G (2003) Value driven – think about this as you don your tuxedo, *Fortuna*, 18 December

Cutlip, S, Center, H and Broom, M (1999) *Effective Public Relations*, 8th edn, Prentice Hall International, Englewood Cliffs, NJ

Farey-Jones, D (2014) The Bigger Picture, *PR Week* March

Hart, N (1992) Is there a new role for PR in marketing? *Public Relations*, **11**, 1 September

Haywood, R (1990) *All about PR*, 2nd edn, McGraw-Hill, London

Jefkins, F (1998) *Public Relations*, 5th edn, FT Management, London

Klein, N (2000) *No Logo*, Flamingo, London

Kosky, H (2008) Howard Kosky on PR and digital broadcasting, *Independent*, 16 June

Larkin, J (2003) Reputation under fire, *Profile*, **35**, April, IPR, UK

Lohr, S (2006) This boring headline is written for Google, *New York Times*, 9 April

Luckett, T (2010) Crisis communications, *PR Week*, 26 February

Murphy, D (1992) Don't forget the hype, *Creative Review*, October, p 16

PRTV (1991) *Actions Speak Louder than Words*, PR training video by PR Smith, Chartered Institute of Public Relations, London

Rich, F R (2003) There's no exit from the Matrix, *New York Times*, 25 May

Rogers, D (2010) Poor comms skills just magnify a crisis, *PR Week*, 25 June

Rogers, D (2014) PR Week leader, The death of PR agencies, *PR Week*, July–August

Ross, D (1990) *Surviving the Media Jungle*, Mercury Books, London

Singel, R (2006) Man vs machine in newsreader war, *Wired Magazine*, 14 March

Sorrell, M (2015), founder and CEO, WPP, Bright Future, *PR Week*, May

White, J (1991) *How to Understand and Manage Public Relations*, Business Books, London

Wollfall, A (2010) Crisis communications, *PR Week*, 26 February

World Advertising Research Centre (WARC) (2005), excerpt from a subscription-based article archive

Further information

CIPR Public Relations Centre
52–53 Russell Square
London WC1B 4HP
Tel: +44 (0)20 7631 6900
www.cipr.co.uk

Communications Advertising and Marketing
Education Foundation Limited (CAM Foundation)
Moor Hall
Cookham
Maidenhead
Berkshire SL6 9QH
Tel: +44 (0)1628 427120
Fax: +44 (0)1628 427158
www.camfoundation.com

Public Relations Consultants Association (PRCA)
PRCA
82 Great Suffolk Street
London
SE1 0BE
Tel: +44 (0)20 7233 6026
www.prca.org.uk

15
Sponsorship

LEARNING OBJECTIVES

By the end of this chapter you will be able to:

- Consider the unlimited range of sponsorship opportunities online and offline
- Assist in managing a sponsorship programme
- Discuss the advantages and disadvantages, including what can go wrong
- Monitor a sponsorship programme

Introduction   408
Immature sponsorship   408
Mature sponsorship   409
What is sponsorship?   410

New and old sponsorship tools   410
Other (unusual) types of sponsorship   411

Managing a sponsorship programme   412
Situation – the target audiences   412
Objectives   412
Sponsorship strategy   413
Tactical plans   414

Action   414
Control – monitor, measure and evaluate   415

Advantages and disadvantages of
    sponsorship   417
Advantages of sponsorship   417
Disadvantages of sponsorship   417

Key points from Chapter 15   424

References and further reading   425

Further information   425

Introduction

So is sponsorship worth investing in? Can it work as a short-term tactical tool? Probably 'yes' to the former and almost certainly 'no' to the latter. Certainly major brands see sponsorship opportunities as strategic opportunities and hence longer-term agreements, ie 10- and 15-year sponsorship agreements are becoming more popular. Adidas recently extended their kit sponsorship with Bayern Munich until 2030 for a reported €900m (£645m). Even though the contract had another five years to go, the German sports kit manufacturer moved quickly to extend the sponsorship and secure a further 10 years with the Bundesliga champions. This figure is dwarfed by the Adidas 10-year sponsorship of Manchester United's kit for £750m which ended Nike's 13-year sponsorship deal (Lusbec, 2015). Brand managers understand the power of sponsorship and therefore see sponsorship as an in-term strategic marketing tool. Take Coca-Cola, who sponsored the FIFA World Cup back in 2005 and committed $500 million to extend its sponsorship until 2022. This gave Coke exclusive rights as non-alcoholic beverage supplier to all major competitions, including the World Cup tournament, and sales rights for TV and stadium advertising. It also extended its Olympic Games sponsorship for 12 years to 2020. The Coke deal covers the 2010 Winter Olympics in Vancouver, the 2012 Summer Games in London, and the games of 2014, 2016, 2018 and 2020 (WARC, 2005). Note that even the signing of a sponsorship contract provides a PR opportunity – Coke took it and signed the contract on the Great Wall of China. Although this is based on anecdotal evidence, it is from one of the world's best marketing machines, which considers that its sponsorship management ('know-how') gives it a distinct competitive advantage.

Immature sponsorship

The European Sponsorship Association (ESA) describes yesterday's approach to sponsorship:

> In the early days of sponsorship, arrangements were made for simplistic and one-dimensional reasons. There was little, if any, media proliferation; advertising was very much the dominant marketing discipline of choice (due

Some brands get more out of sponsorship than others?

'We do not sponsor sports. It's a very cluttered market where you can spend millions without getting much return.'

David Goldesgeyne, Head of Sponsorship for Lloyds Bank

'Each World Cup has proven even more rewarding than the last, in terms of global name exposure, premium positioning, sales promotion results, cementing relationships with trade customers.'

Gillette World Cup News

to a lack of alternatives) and gaining awareness for company or brand names was the strategic priority. It was considered enough just to attach your brand name to an event title and place your branding in front of the TV cameras. Partnership choices were often made on the likely volume of TV coverage alone, with no other considerations or priorities. Success was likely to be assessed by attaching a TV equivalent advertising value to the exposure of the company or brand name and whether this seemed to be good value for money when compared to advertising.

ESA (2015)

Align with new communities' passions through sponsorship

'While advertising is excellent for generating awareness, public relations informs and influences, and sales promotions stimulates trial, they all compete with each other to cut through the marketing clutter. Brands have found that the best way to get our attention is to identify the passions of new communities and align with them through sponsorship.'

Collett and Fenton (2011)

Today expert sponsors leverage the sponsorship opportunity to maximize the return on their investment. It is much more than just 'badging an event';

> In a community-less society sponsorship can give supporters a greater sense of belonging

In an increasingly impersonal world (where e-mail, texting and 'social' media platforms replace talking), while the pillars of society crumble (as trust plummets for churches, politicians, banks, police and communities) and work pressure and time increases, changing gender roles reduce a sense of order. ESA suggest:

> *Our sense of community and belonging is increasingly under threat; this has led to the adoption of new allegiances and relationships, often passionate ones, with a range of interests. Increasing numbers of media outlets and digital channels are offering more compelling, in-depth and personalized content than ever before. It is no surprise that these stronger and more intimate affiliations across a range of sports, arts activities, live entertainment, charities, environmental concerns, politics and educational activities are offering their followers (supporters) a greater sense of belonging and association.*
>
> ESA (2015)

for example if a mobile phone company sponsors a summer music festival, it will seek to be allowed to collect and distribute backstage gossip, generate exclusive video content, interviews and jam sessions, and share this with its audiences, with its own customers getting extra benefits. These may include VIP access, parties and intimate performances from artists. Some phone companies loan phones so people can share their partially branded photos and videos with their social media networks.

Mature sponsorship

Sponsors have got a lot more professional about leveraging their investment in sponsorship. EAS continue:

> Time has moved on and sponsorship has matured and now plays an integral role in an increasingly

sophisticated marketing environment. While achieving significant media coverage is still important, it is now likely to be only one of many objectives set by the company. Some sponsors select properties with no, or at least very limited, media coverage because their objectives do not require it. Sponsorship is so versatile that a relationship can be used to fulfill a broad number of strategic marketing objectives. Selection of the most appropriate property to satisfy specific objectives is, therefore, often the most crucial part of the sponsorship process.

> ESA (2015)

Think of sponsorship as an enabler of marketing's broader objectives and strategies. It is not an end in itself. Today marketers look beyond the old objectives of reach and affinity and try to leverage the sponsorship to create value for consumers in a way that can firstly, drive behavioural change and secondly, reinforce the brand. As Rosen and Minky (2011) say, sponsorship can 'create unique opportunities for experiences, access, self-expression, entertainment, connection, or contribution to the social good.'

So what should be sponsored? How does one choose what to sponsor and what to reject? Maybe arts are good for computers and sports are bad for banks? If sports sponsorship is so good for Gillette, why does it bother to advertise at all? Or perhaps its advertising doesn't work, which means any meagre improvement would be deemed to be a success? Do sponsorship funds come out of the above-the-line budget, ie does it always mean reducing the advertising budgets, or can they come out of some corporate

> The power of sponsorship

Tiger Woods is Nikes's $650 million man. His contract stipulates that he wears Nike clothes when doing other brands' promotional work, so its brand piggybacks other sponsorship programmes and advertisements.

However, just like PR, sponsorship is uncontrollable as sponsors' brands can be damaged by behaviours of the people they sponsor. Woods' well-publicized personal problems a few years back resulted in the loss of several sponsorship deals.

communications or corporate social responsibility (CSR) programme? How much should be spent? How much is too much? When does it become less value for money? How is it measured? Finally, what exactly does sponsorship mean? These are some of the questions this chapter answers.

> ## Sponsorship shifting from brand exposure to brand activation
>
> 'In a little less than 20 years, the focus of sponsorship has shifted from the valuation of brand exposure (eg jerseys, boards, etc) to the sponsor's brand activation by focusing attention on the organization's relationship with the people interested in the event.'
>
> Ferrand, Torrigiani and Povil (2007)

What is sponsorship?

Sponsorship is more than patronage, altruism or benefaction. **It can indeed help others while simultaneously achieving specifically defined communications objectives.** Some sponsors see sponsorship as a form of enlightened self-interest, where a worthy activity is supported with cash and/or consideration in return for satisfying specific marketing or corporate objectives. As sponsorship matures, its diverse range of programmes, objectives, advantages and disadvantages requires a relatively sophisticated level of management understanding.

The target audience must be researched in detail, crystal-clear qualitative and quantitative objectives must be set, and appropriate types of sponsorship vehicles must be agreed, considered and selected. A programme of integrated communications has to be planned with precision, and sufficient budgets have to be allocated to allow for 'leveraging', stretching or maximizing the overall sponsorship impact.

New and old sponsorship tools

All sectors of society can be targeted and reached through sponsorship. Just about anyone or anything can be sponsored. You can even sponsor 'the possibility of an event'; Granada TV once sponsored Manchester's bid to host the 2000 Olympics. The range of sponsorship opportunities is limited only by one's imagination. The obvious areas are sport, the arts, education, community and broadcast.

Whether the events are large or small (eg blind golf and blind cricket), sport offers an effective route into the minds of various target markets. Even within a particular sport there is a range of different sponsorship opportunities. Take football, for example. It is possible to sponsor a title, eg the Carling Cup or the Barclaycard Premiership, or a stadium, eg the Reebok Stadium. Perhaps a more interesting example is where Maxwell House coffee's Taste of Chicago sponsorship maximized the off-site potential by buying all 37,000 tickets to a game and then giving them away free in return for two empty Maxwell House jars. It is also possible to sponsor: a club, eg Emirates and Arsenal, Doritos and Wolverhampton Wanderers (incidentally, since the 1980s, five of Japan's baseball teams have been owned by railway companies, four by beverage companies, two by newspapers and one by an automobile company); a match day (eg York City gave 12 stand tickets, free buffet, free bar, free ads in the programme, hoardings in the car park and the opportunity to present the Man of the Match award and join players in the bar after the game – all for approximately £1,000); a kick-off (in the United States, Anheuser Busch sponsors NFL kick-offs, and they are referred to as 'Bud kick-offs'); a ball, eg Crystal Palace FC match ball sponsorship costs £250; a fair play award, often tied in with another sponsorship package; a sin bin (the Northern Ireland police force wittily sponsored the 'sin bin' at the Belfast Giants hockey team – essentially made up of neutral Canadians); a player (players receive individual sponsorship and in return they open stores, meet employees and acknowledge the sponsor in the programme); a pass, a tackle, a goal, a save or a miss – the Pizza Hut and American Express examples in the boxes opposite show US baseball creating such exciting opportunities. Score updates, gossip about players and even free betting can be sponsored. It is even possible to sponsor a fictitious team in a kids' comic.

Effectively anything can be sponsored, including golf on the moon. A golf equipment manufacturer asked Russian cosmonaut Mikhail Tyurin, who was

Sponsor anything: sponsor a catch – fan catches 33,000 pizzas

Pittsburgh Pirates fan Ted Bianucci was picked at random out of a crowd at Three Rivers Stadium to take the field to try to catch three pop-ups (balls shot out of a gun used to help catchers practise defence). Sponsors Pizza Hut promised every spectator in the park a free soft drink at Pizza Hut (by showing the ticket stub), a jug of soft drink or a small pizza if the fan caught one, two or three respectively of the pop-ups. No one had ever previously caught all three. Bianucci, to the cheers of 33,789 people, caught all three balls – and $150,000 worth of pizza generates a lot of good feeling and probably extra business as 33,000 customers enter Pizza Hut's premises.

based on the International Space Station, to take a golf club and ball outside to tee off into space for what was likely to be the longest golf shot ever (IOL, 2006). It is the marketer's job to spot the opportunity and determine if it is really just a publicity stunt sponsorship or if it is a medium- to longer-term sponsorship programme.

Sponsoring a miss

American Express and Best West International Hotels jointly sponsored a programme that donated $300 to children's baseball league every time top baseball pitcher Nolan Ryan bowled or pitched an opposition player out. If Ryan pitched a 'no-hitter' (bowled the whole team out for nought), then a whopping $1.25 million would be donated by the sponsors to the league. AmEx and Best West also donated three cents every time an AmEx card was used to pay for a Best West hotel. In addition, $2 was contributed for every newly approved AmEx card member application that came from a 'take-one' box at each Best West hotel.

Arts sponsorship can be even more diverse – from sponsoring the opening of Disneyland Paris, to a

film premiere, to a particularly obscure type of play to gain access to an otherwise difficult target market. Education is a sensitive area, and sponsorship can come in cash or in kind, such as a computer company donating computers to schools. **Community sponsorship** is becoming increasingly important as businesses recognize the importance of their community and their corporate responsibility. The corporate citizen is alive and well within the 'per cent club'. (In the UK, corporate members of the per cent club promise to spend one-half of 1 per cent of their profits on community programmes. In the United States, there are also 2 per cent and 5 per cent clubs.) In the UK, it is possible to sponsor the police, the fire brigade and the coastguard. Off-licence chain Thresher has sponsored a van for Avon and Somerset police force, while Newcastle Breweries has sponsored a mobile police station.

Sponsoring a possibility and then asking FIFA for money back

Morrisons supermarket chain sponsored the England 2018 World Cup Bid. After the bid was lost, they called on FIFA to donate £1 million to charity for compensation for an 'unfair' bidding process. Morrisons said: 'We think the decision-making process was unfair. We hope FIFA will do the right thing and offer £1m to be invested in grassroots football.' *PR Week* 17 Dec 2010

Here we are in 2015 and FIFA is now being challenged over exactly the same issue.

Other (unusual) types of sponsorship

Here are some other forms of sponsorship, which give an indication of the variety and potential available. An organization can sponsor an expedition (Mercury has sponsored a walk to the North Pole). British Aerospace, Memorex and Interflora signed as sponsors for a voyage into space (the package was subsequently cancelled). An organization can also sponsor a species (Systematics Association, a scientific group involved in classifying organisms, named seven wasps after the directors of Salomon Brothers when they waived a $300,000 debt arrangement).

The 'Ugly Bartender' contest sponsored by the Multiple Sclerosis Society is its second-biggest revenue generator. Some years ago, cows wearing Vladivar Vodka jackets in a field near the London-to-Brighton railway line were sponsored during the Brighton festival. Akai sponsored bullfights at £10,000 a fight. BP sponsored Eugène Ionesco's play *Journeys Among the Dead*. Sponsoring a war? It is possible to sponsor sections of the US Army (eg the Medical Corps). On the other hand, sponsoring peace initiatives is also possible. For example, during the height of the Cold War the *Irish Times* sponsored an official televised arms debate between Soviet and US diplomats. It is even possible to sponsor an Amnesty International tour.

Broadcast sponsorship offers possibilities ranging from sponsoring other people's advertisements (Midland Bank's £50,000 and Cancer Research), to the weather, specific programmes and themed weeks on cable television.

Online events in virtual worlds or online community events (webcasts, discussions, video walls, etc) can be sponsored. Effectively any event anywhere, online or offline, presents sponsorship opportunities that can be leveraged in many ways.

Managing a sponsorship programme

The SOSTAC® + 3Ms acronym (see Chapter 10) can be used to develop and manage a sponsorship programme.

SOSTAC® + 3Ms involves:

1 defining target audiences;

2 defining sponsorship objectives;

3 analysing and summarizing the current sponsorship situation (including competitive review, previous sponsorship experiences, sponsorship strategies, etc);

4 clarifying the strategy (how the sponsorship programme contributes towards the overall corporate or brand mission, marketing objectives and communication objectives);

5 developing the tactical details of how it all fits together;

6 building in measurement or evaluation to see whether the programme is worth repeating;

7 identifying the resources required to leverage a programme to give the maximum return.

Situation – the target audiences

There are two different audiences. The first is the one immediately involved with the programme; the second is the one that can be reached through advertising and media coverage. Although there are many spin-off objectives that offer benefits to different target groups, the primary objective should be linked clearly with the primary audience. This involves some research into the lifestyles, attitudes, behaviour patterns, leisure activities, issues and demographics relevant to the primary target group. Previous research should have identified the current situation, ie how the sponsor is positioned in the target audience's mind. This will reveal the kinds of specific communications objectives that need to be set.

Objectives

After defining the target audiences, objectives must be fully clarified to focus both the spin-off activities (eg sales promotions linked with the core sponsorship programme) and the marketing support activities (eg advertising and publicity announcements around the sponsorship programme). A sponsorship programme can satisfy many objectives simultaneously. The range of objectives is varied:

1 *Increase awareness* – eg Canon sponsored the Football League to create a presence, become a familiar household name and generally raise awareness of a previously relatively unknown company in the UK marketplace. Its sponsorship gave it a foothold in the UK market.

2 *Build/enhance an image* – this can help to reposition or strengthen a brand or corporate image through association with particular types of sponsorship activities, eg a caring image through community programmes. The sponsorship must support the brand values.

3 *Activating a brand* – there is a shift in sponsorship from building brands to 'activating' brands.

4 *Customer engagement* – there are many spin-off engagement benefits that can be shared with customers such as free gifts,

tickets, photos in return for participation in a sales promotion.

5 *Content generation* – part of the sponsorship package can be the brand's own content creators generating content, eg behind the scenes interviews, photos, videos etc.

6 *Differentiate a brand* – create a unique association with a particular passion point of a target audience.

7 *Strengthen brand personality* – associate a brand with an 'activity area' with which the target audience has a positive, and ideally, a passionate, connection (often referred to as a 'passion point'). This adds value to the overall brand proposition and allows a more personal, passionate and a more connected form of communicating.

8 *Improve or maintain relations* – with customers, the trade, employees and even investors through hospitality and entertainment at a sponsored event. Rumbelows department store sponsored English soccer's League Cup. Part of the agreement allowed the sponsor to appoint its own employee of the year to meet the teams and present the cup to the winning captain. Community relations can also be enhanced by supporting appropriate local activities.

9 *Increase sales and open closed markets* – Coca-Cola was banned in Arab markets because it had built an Israeli bottling plant. Sponsorship of the 1989 Arab Youth Football Competition in Riyadh helped to open the door again.

10 *Increase sales (sampling and direct sales)* – action-orientated sampling opportunities abound in a captive market where the buyer is in a relaxed frame of mind, for example buying and drinking Victoria Beer at a touch-rugby competition sponsored by Victoria Beer. Some market research can also be carried out. Sponsorship can create a dialogue, whereas a lot of advertising is a monologue (although there are some campaigns that engage the customer in more than just a monologue).

11 *Attract distributors or agents* – for example sponsoring a radio station's weather forecasts to build awareness and attract enquiries from agents in other markets.

12 *Employee motivation* – offering employees special access to the sponsored event, or team.

13 *Create promotional material* – some events offer wonderful photo opportunities with scenes, sights and stars. One climbing equipment company sponsors climbs primarily to secure stunning photographs with branded climbing gear featuring prominently.

14 *Circumventing advertising bans* – sponsorship, particularly of televised events, allows sponsors a way around mainstream above-the-line advertising bans, for example tobacco companies sponsoring sports events such as snooker. Incidentally, the famous Steve Davis vs Dennis Taylor snooker final kept one-third of the British population glued to their TV sets until 3 am.

15 *Cost effectiveness* – more bangs for your buck when comparing CPT (Cost per Thousand) reached vs CPT for advertising.

16 *Miscellaneous* – ranging from, for example, the generation of new product ideas (new product educational competitions) to graduate recruitment.

Sponsorship strategy

The strategy statement briefly explains which types of sponsorship programmes are preferred, why a particular sponsorship programme is selected, how it will be exploited and integrated, and at what cost. To maximize the effect, sponsorship must be integrated with other elements of the communications mix, eg advertising, sales promotion, direct mail and public relations. It should also be explained internally and sometimes used internally as part of psychic income (see Chapter 12) as a means of improving employee relations.

A sponsorship policy helps the programme selection process by defining sponsorship parameters such as the preferred types of sponsorship that fit with the overall mission statement and the marketing and communication objectives. Questions to ask include the following. Is there any relevance between sponsor and subject, eg a chess competition and a computer company share values of intelligence. Is there a consistent message or objective behind all the organization's chosen sponsorship programmes?

Does the association add value to the company or product? Does the sponsorship support the brand values? Is the association internationally acceptable? Think global; act local (sponsoring bullfighting is globally unacceptable, although Pepsi has sponsored it). Are there certain types or areas of sponsorship that are preferred? It is often felt that it is better to concentrate in certain areas. What is the ideal time in terms of seasonality and length of commitment, eg a three-year minimum? When should a sponsorship programme be dropped, changed or simply reviewed? Are both solus and shared or joint sponsorship programmes acceptable? Can staff involvement be incorporated? Does the sponsorship lend itself to leverage by offering potential for spin-off promotions and publicity? Does it lend itself to sales promotions? Can customers become even more engaged? Is it unique? Is it protectable from ambush marketing? (See p. 418 for more on this.) What is the competition doing? Are 'me-too' sponsorship packages (the competition follows with a similar sponsorship programme) preferred to unique (and uncopiable) sponsorship programmes? What kind of budget is required? What is defined as value for money?

Tiger Woods and a watch

Does the sponsorship support the brand values? The watch company TAG Heuer sponsored Tiger Woods for £1.5 million and he didn't even have to wear one of its watches while on the golf course (their sponsorship arrangement has now expired). Both brands, one might argue, are very similar. The trick is to balance the person and the product. Arguably, there was a good balance between Tiger Woods's and TAG Heuer's brand values: timing, focus and commitment.

Tactical plans

Squeeze as many benefits as possible into the programme. Sponsorship does not involve just adding the organization's name to an event, team or situation and waiting to see if awareness takes off overnight. A well-planned sponsorship programme involves attracting media coverage, corporate entertainment, new client recruitment, miscellaneous spin-off promotions and staff motivation schemes. (See Chapter 10, 'Tactics', to help develop a whole communications plan around the sponsorship package or to help integrate the sponsorship programme into the rest of the marketing communications activities.)

The launch is the easy bit. The real work starts then, as years one, two and three need constant attention to detail. A series of checklists and detailed plans (including contingency plans) have to be developed.

Action

The agreement

Agreements need to be carefully checked, as sometimes, in the frenetic search for funding, those sponsored may promise the world to potential sponsors. The potential sponsor needs to exercise some caution. Here are some points worth considering:

1 Have the contract checked by an expert. In particular, check the exit clause and exit arrangements, since it may be harder to get out of sponsorship than to get into it. For example, it is easy to start supporting a local theatre, but when the sponsor wants to switch into a different type of sponsorship the eventual withdrawal of funds may prompt the local paper to print a headline that reads 'Company X Pulls Plug on Theatre' or 'Company X Leaves Theatre in the Dark'. Consider exit strategies also.

2 Can those sponsored deliver on their promises? Can they provide proof? Have they done it before? Have they any references? Are they financially secure?

3 Is it fair and reasonable to all parties? Sometimes razor-sharp negotiators agree a deal that is too good for the sponsors, which eventually creates problems. A good example is Nike's sponsorship deal with the Brazil football team (see 'Sponsor being too clever' on p. 416).

4 Are there other opportunities for brand exposure via the sponsored person or organization's other marketing activities (see the box over)?

Nike piggyback on Tiger Woods's other endorsements

'Nike's association with Mr. Woods has worked wonders for the company. After signing him in 1996, Nike redid the deal in 2000 for a reported $105 million. That may sound like a lot of money, but not only has Mr. Woods single-handedly built Nike Golf, his apparel deal means that even when he appears in ads for his other partners, he wears Nike clothing. The swoosh is clearly visible in ads for American Express.'

Thomaselli (2006)

Pilot scheme

Pilot testing is where 'action' overlaps with 'control'. In an ideal marketing world, all risks are reduced by testing and researching everything. Extra research costs resources, primarily time and money. Sometimes the nature of a sponsorship programme does not lend itself to testing, eg sponsoring the English Football League, but customers can be asked what they would think of it (before signing on the dotted line). Alternatively, a local league can be sponsored to allow management to move up the learning curve. Telstra was reported to have jointly sponsored the 2003 Rugby World Cup so that it could learn about how sponsorship worked. The cautious or delayed approach arising from testing can also cause opportunities to be lost, since the competition may snap up the best sponsorship programmes. It may however identify some opportunities and avoid some nasty problems.

Roll-out

This is the exciting side that everyone sees without fully realizing the amount of work that goes on beforehand. Nevertheless, it is deceptively hard work since, even though the sponsors are enjoying entertaining their clients, it is still work. In smaller sponsorship programmes sponsors have constantly to think on their feet while entertaining, as minute problems inevitably crop up from time to time. In larger sponsorship programmes the constant alertness, attention to detail and readiness to react can be shared between members of staff (or a consultancy).

Staff will be interested in high-profile sponsorship programmes. Keep staff informed about how the programme is working and whether it is on target and generating results. Where possible, include programme prizes as staff incentives. Marks & Spencer sponsors projects that attract staff involvement.

Control – monitor, measure and evaluate

This is where the clearly defined sponsorship objectives make life easy, since results can be compared with predetermined targets. Once the result has been measured, further analysis as to why a programme was particularly successful or unsuccessful will help future sponsorship programmes. The first three objectives listed above, awareness, image and relations, would normally require some formal market research activity such as a survey. **There is, in addition, an interim method of evaluating sponsorship** – by the amount of media coverage or name mentions. There are many monitoring companies that provide such services.

35 days' continuous monitoring

When Npower sponsored cricket, media monitoring services revealed it received:

- 350 hours of TV coverage (Channel 4 and Sky);
- 12,500 banner sightings;
- 625 references in the national press.

Cost: £18 million over three years.

Result: spontaneous awareness up to 45 per cent.

Although cricket is on TV for long periods, its audience is often quite small. Sponsorship research company AGB divides broadcast time by audience size to give cricket a ranking of 67, less than half that of ice skating. There are other, sometimes simpler, approaches to measuring the effectiveness of sponsorship. For example, Volvo calculated that its $3 million tennis sponsorship generated 1.4 billion impressions (number of mentions or sightings times audience size), worth about $18 million in advertising.

It is worth noting that this measures only the amount of media coverage or output. It does not measure the ultimate objectives of, say, increasing awareness, changing attitudes or improving relations with different groups. This is where money may have to be spent on commissioning a piece of research that looks inside, instead of outside, the minds of the target audience.

The other objectives can be relatively easily measured if a system of measurement is set up in the first place, eg everyone is briefed to log or identify the source of any enquiries from customers, agents or distributors. Then again, a common-sense approach may help to identify results, eg new distributors or increased sales, without changing any of the other elements of either the marketing or the communications mix (and assuming the competition has not had a strike or a factory fire).

Waffles or lager?

In 1979 Belgium was 'better known for its waffles than its lager'. When TV ads were beyond budget, sponsorship of the Queen's tennis tournament beckoned. TV exposure and tennis's 'aspirational and achievement' image matched Stella's objectives. Stella rose to number 1 in Britain's premium lager sector. Sales increased by 400 per cent.

Observer, 1 April 1988

Canon got good value for its money when it sponsored the Football League for a limited period only. As Frank Jefkins (1991) observed, 'Hardly an office in Britain is without a Canon machine. It only took £3 million and three years – peanuts in that sort of business when you think what the sales are valued at.'

Sponsor being too clever

There was a legislative inquiry into Nike's sponsorship deal with the Brazilian football team. [Nike had negotiated a $400 million, 10-year kit sponsorship deal with the Brazilian Football Federation.] A sense that Nike had too much control over the country's affairs was magnified by original provisions in the contract allowing the company to promote 50 Nike-branded Brazil-friendly matches involving eight first team players... With World Cup qualifiers and other friendlies to organize, it became clear that the original number of Nike friendlies was too large. In November 1999 Brazil found itself double booked to play two matches. This led to a second-string Brazil team playing in Australia, while most of the country's top stars featured in a game against Spain. Consequently last April Nike reduced the contractual number of games it would promote to two a year. Also under the initial contract – since changed – legal disputes with the CFB were to be settled outside of Brazil. 'The CFB transferred part of its autonomy as a public entity to Nike', said Aldo Rebelo (head of the 25-member committee of Brazil's Lower House of Congress investigating Nike's sponsorship deal).

Colitt and Garrahan (2001)

Budgets

Budget allocation may in fact determine programme choice rather than the other way around. The formulae for determining the sponsorship budget vary, but a rough rule of thumb suggests that the basic sponsorship fee should be at least doubled to get maximum leverage from the programme (Coca-Cola allows 16 times the sponsor fee to generate maximum leverage).

This then leaves a budget for supporting marketing activities such as advertising and publicity, and maybe even some direct marketing. It also allocates some money for other spin-off activities. For example, sponsors of the Olympics will tend to milk the sponsorship to the maximum by running sales promotions offering Olympic prizes and donations in addition to simply carrying the 'official Olympic sponsors' logo. Payment can be in cash or in kind. A sponsor's services or facilities are likely to have a much greater value than cost; for example a newspaper sponsoring a boxing match can offer the fight promoter free advertising space in return for exclusive sponsorship rights. The cost may be minimal if the newspaper is not selling all its advertising space, while the value to the promoter is, of course, much greater.

There are also various government sponsorship grant programmes that contribute significantly towards the cost. (Check for any government subsidies; Arts and Business for example have different subsidy programmes.)

The 3Ms (men/women, money and minutes) need to be budgeted for and built into plans. Who is responsible for what – the supporting advertising, the spin-off sales promotions, the hospitality tent, the invitations, the publicity, etc? Is it all handled by an agency or controlled and administered by the in-house team? Time can be the greatest constraint to leveraging a sponsorship programme fully, since there may be lots of great ideas for exploiting the opportunities to the full but each one takes time to plan and ultimately put into action. Some estimates suggest a minimum of nine months is needed to develop a proper sponsorship strategy and programme plan.

Advantages and disadvantages of sponsorship

Advantages of sponsorship

Sponsorship can be cost-effective (compared to advertising) in terms of reaching a particular audience. It does allow access to very specific targeted audience that otherwise might be difficult to reach. Sponsorship can achieve many different objectives (see 'Objectives', p. 412), including:

- increased awareness;
- image enhancement;
- customer engagement;
- content generation;
- brand differentiation;
- strengthened brand personality;
- improved relationships;
- increased sales;
- sampling and database building;
- creating a platform for new promotional material;
- beating advertising bans, etc;
- employee motivation;
- cost effectiveness.

It also offers creative opportunities, including the engagement of an audience in a relaxed atmosphere of goodwill. Hospitality events open doors and create a dialogue that conventional media simply cannot match. As Alan Mitchell (1997) says, 'sponsorship reaches the parts conventional advertising cannot'. Sponsorship lends itself to integrated communications and the cost-effectiveness of integrated activities.

Sponsorship packages can offer brands an opportunity to communicate regularly. Finally, the effects of a sponsorship programme are measurable.

Even the uncontrollable nature of sponsorship is measurable. Consider the now classic case of the 1996 Olympic sponsors (who paid $40 million each). They were pleased to have the rights to the Winter Olympic Games in Lillehammer thrown in free of charge. The US figure skater Nancy Kerrigan was violently attacked six weeks before the Games began. The attack was masterminded by the ex-husband of her chief rival, Tonya Harding. However, interest in Kerrigan's recovery created an avalanche of media coverage before, during and after the event. The extra, unplanned coverage was carefully measured and valued by the sponsors.

Disadvantages of sponsorship

Sponsorship cannot close sales; it only creates awareness. It can carry only a very limited message (for the masses), usually just a brand name, although some brands leverage the sponsorship into many diverse aspects, which allows more detailed brand value messages. The message cannot be controlled; a football hooligan wearing a club shirt with a sponsor's brand might appear on the front page of a newspaper attacking a police officer. Guerrilla marketing can also damage the sponsor's impact. It is not so easy to change a message or to exit a sponsorship programme quickly (unless carefully planned). As with PR, there is a lack of control, as strikes, riots, weather and media all affect the impact of sponsorship.

Some say that sponsorship is insidious and that it undermines artistic integrity. In areas such as health and education, some feel that the issues involved are too important to be left to the whim of a corporation. Although sponsorship can deliver extremely cost-effective benefits, it can be misunderstood as an excessive indulgence by employees if they are kept in the dark about it and if there are redundancies occurring at the same time. In both cases sponsorship, particularly high-profile sponsorship, needs to be presented to the employees as a cost-effective business tool that can help the business to survive and thrive in the future. Sponsorship of a competitive activity, such as a football club, can alienate the company or product from the opposition fans, eg a national audience if the teams are involved in an international competition, or an even larger audience if the team or player behaves badly.

Global media coverage may not be a good thing if what is being sponsored in one country is unacceptable in another country, for example bull-fighting, camel wrestling, dwarf throwing, etc. If the medium is the message (ie the choice of sponsorship reflects the values of the sponsor), the message can become tarnished through its association with a socially unacceptable event. Some sponsorship deals can alienate a whole nation, particularly if the sponsor is perceived to have negotiated too good a deal for itself (see the box 'Sponsor being too clever' on page 416). The uncontrollability of so many variables from weather to fans to strikes to riots makes sponsorship more risky than advertising. Even pop concerts are risky, as Naomi Klein (2000) points out: 'Celine Dion's concert tour was picketed by human rights activists in Boston, Philadelphia and Washington, DC. Although she was unaware of it, her tour sponsor – Ericsson cellular – was among Burma's most intransigent foreign investors, refusing to cease its dealings with the junta despite the campaign for an international boycott.' Finally, ambush marketing allows non-sponsoring competitors to soak up some benefits without paying full sponsorship fees.

Ambush marketing

Ambush marketers attack official event sponsors by running competing promotions, events and advertisements close to the official sponsors' activities. This way they create an aura of being official sponsors without paying the official sponsor fees. An example is the classic 1984 ambush by Kodak when it sponsored the ABC TV coverage of the Olympics despite Fuji being the official sponsor. In 1988 Kodak was the official Olympics sponsor while Fuji sponsored the US swimming team. Nike managed to 'ruin the 1996 Olympics for the official sponsors by ruthless advertising and by exploiting its star names' (Boshoff, 1997). The International Olympic Committee stepped in next time round by ordering that all poster sites in Athens be bought up and fairly distributed. For the 1998 World Cup, Adidas paid £20 million to be an official sponsor and, among other things, built a football village under the Eiffel Tower, while Nike responded with a site

on the outskirts of Paris. Adidas signed up Paul Gascoigne, Paul Ince and David Beckham, as well as sponsoring the kit of nine teams, including Germany, France and Spain, while Nike sponsored six squads, including the favourites, Brazil (which cost £250 million over 10 years). The *Daily Telegraph* reported that 'rumours have it that Nike is willing to spend £20 million to hijack its arch-rivals Adidas during the competition in France'. Adidas planned a series of 'counter-stunts' and intended to 'ambush their ambush by having our own stunts and tricks'. Both companies supposedly had £20 million to spend on the five months up to and including the competition (on top of Adidas' sponsorship fee).

There is nothing really new in this, as ambush marketing has been around almost as long as sponsorship itself. Measurement of the 1991 Rugby World Cup broadcast sponsorship demonstrated its ability to influence consumers and override the main event sponsors. Spontaneous brand awareness of Sony rose among Rugby World Cup watchers by eight points to 61 per cent (between September and November). Despite the recession, the company went on to record sales in December. Although Sony was not a sponsor of the event itself, it did sponsor the ITV coverage. ITV report that invariably the first name mentioned as sponsor of the Rugby World Cup and overwhelmingly seen as the main sponsor was Sony.

However, overzealous policing can backfire. Pepsi was one of the official sponsors at the 2003 Cricket World Cup in South Africa. The drinks company had to distance itself from the embarrassment of the publicity surrounding the ejection of a fan caught drinking a can of Coca-Cola. Previously, Coca-Cola had been the official sponsor of the Football World Cup in Japan, where organizers had stopped fans from taking Pepsi into the stadium. This kind of action is not necessarily protecting sponsors from mainstream ambush marketing but is an indication of the attention to detail and the lengths that event organizers will go to in order to protect the interests of sponsors. It can, however, backfire in publicity terms.

Shani and Sandler's (1989) study of ambush marketing revealed that it works. For example, Wendy's got what it wanted for about $20 million or so less than McDonald's spend. McDonald's didn't leverage its sponsorship well at all, advertising its super-value meals and Double Big Macs instead of its Olympic sponsorship.

For some 20 years now, the Olympics Committee has had clear anti-ambush guidelines, including the registering of all trademarks and emblems, co-ordination with city authorities to control the skies above venues, and ensuring that sponsors have first option for any broadcasting and advertising rights for the event in each country where the

Olympics is shown on TV. In 2010 a beer company tried ambush marketing tactics inside the stadium by introducing a group of women wearing similar shirts. The women were ejected. The laws and regulations have become more stringent (the UK has specific Olympic legislation in place to stop ambush marketing).

Unpredictable sponsorship results from an ambushed knee

'When US skater Tonya Harding's associates hammered her main competitor Nancy Kerrigan's knee, they performed a dastardly deed – which happened to boost the fortunes of Kerrigan's sponsors, Campbell's Soups, for the first time in a decade. Campbell's was also a sponsor of the US Figure Skating Association. After the incident Campbell's placed ads everywhere, and when Kerrigan recovered and came

back to win silver Campbell's sales skyrocketed. Which just goes to show that no amount of planning could have produced the publicity it received from the wounded-knee incident and the sales bump that accompanied it. Campbell's was even mistakenly perceived by the general public as a full-fledged Olympic sponsor in 1994, even though it wasn't.'

Schlossberg (1996)

CASE STUDY 15.1   Liberty Insurance and GAA

What is the GAA

The Gaelic Athletic Association is the largest sporting body in Ireland; Gaelic games are among the most-watched spectator sports in Ireland, with over 1 million people attending matches live in any given year. The GAA has 600,000 registered members and over 2,300 GAA clubs nationwide. Every parish/community in the country has an historically established GAA club, allowing sponsors to reach all points in the country. Supporters of the GAA are deeply loyal to sponsors with a high level of the population agreeing that they would look favourably on a brand that sponsors GAA.

Situation analysis

In May 2013 for the first time ever in Irish sporting history, a sponsor, Liberty Insurance (LI), brought together Ireland's two oldest field games: hurling (a male sport) and camogie (a female sport), in a unique and ground-breaking sponsorship. Part of the sponsorship planning process included qualitative research among hurling players, camogie players and supporters. This research revealed key insights

around the Gaelic Athletic Association (GAA) engagement and participation. These outputs underpinned the strategic planning and activation of the sponsorship over 18 months. LI wanted an innovative programme that positioned hurling and camogie on an equal platform, and for LI to stand out in a cluttered market; bolstering the image of Liberty Insurance (part of a global insurer) as committed to the Irish market and understanding of the passion of the Irish for sport, while also delivering a return on business objectives, driving sales and quote volumes.

Objectives

1   **Awareness and brand building:** Drive sponsorship awareness; deliver minimum increase in two or more image statements; achieve higher consideration of Liberty Insurance among those aware vs unaware of the sponsorship; drive social media engagement through value-added content; maximize all opportunities for PR and media exposure.

2   **Acquisition and retention:** To increase insurance quotes and sales through the use of incentives targeted towards GAA hurling and camogie clubs.

FIGURE 15.1

Summary of Sponsorship

In May 2013 for the first time ever in Irish sporting history, a sponsor, Liberty Insurance, brought together Ireland's two oldest field games: Hurling (a male sport) and Camogie (a female sport), in a unique and ground breaking sponsorship.

Through an innovative campaign that positioned Hurling and Camogie on a equal platform, we achieved stand out in a cluttered market; bolstering the image of Liberty Insurance (part of a global insurer) as committed to the Irish market and understanding of the passion of the Irish for sport, while also delivering a return on business objectives, driving sales and quote volumes.

SOURCE: Liberty Insurance

3 **Fan engagement:** Deliver an enhanced fan experience for hurling and camogie supporters through experiential match day activations.

4 **Commercial relationships:** To develop a comprehensive programme to build meaningful relationships with brokers and commercial partners, including delivery of corporate hospitality to key insurance brokers currently engaged with Liberty Insurance.

5 **Employee engagement:** Increase excitement and awareness amongst staff through the development of an inclusive employee engagement programme.

Strategy

LI used careful audience and media research to identify a previously untapped sponsorship opportunity and integrate it with PR to gain access to a traditionally difficult target market. The selection of 'the bringing together' of Ireland's two oldest field games is a unique and ground-breaking

sponsorship. It also complements and reinforces LI brand values of integrity, inventiveness and fairness. The sponsorship has increased both awareness and reputation, driven positive engagement with Liberty Insurance and delivered a significant commercial return on investment.

Tactics

The LI approach was underpinned by an innovative campaign, positioning camogie/hurling on an equal platform across multiple consumer touchpoints.

Awareness and brand building:

- TV, print and online creative featuring hurling/camogie players provided a point of differentiation and showcased Liberty Insurance's shared passion for both sports.
- Live Twitter Q&As with camogie/hurling players.
- Innovative digital and print media partnerships with Today FM, Newstalk, journal.ie, the *Irish Times* and the *Irish Independent*.

- PR strategy 'One Game: One Family' was developed with players from both sports.

Acquisition and retention:

- GAA Club affinity programme via dedicated micro-site.
- €50 to a nominated hurling/camogie club for every insurance policy purchased.
- Entry for your nominated club into a draw for €10,000 with every insurance quote.
- Customer opportunities for sons/daughters to be flagbearers on match days.

Fan engagement: match day activations including:

- Complimentary branded shuttle buses bringing supporters to matches.
- Best Banner and 'Supporter of the Match' competitions; face painting and ice creams in Family Fun Zones.
- Flagbearer opportunities for children at All Ireland Finals and Semi Finals.
- Distribution of supporter 'Scór' scrollers; use of Liberty Insurance 'blimps'.

Commercial relationships:

- Provision of tickets, hospitality and events to foster relationships with Liberty Insurance's broker partners and stakeholders.

Employee engagement:

- 'Liberty's Big Day Out', Croke Park's largest ever sponsor-run event, for employees and families.
- Staff competitions for match tickets and mascot opportunities.

Action/execution

Careful attention to detail, staff training and project management ensures that all aspects of this innovative sponsorship programme are executed professionally, including: LI employees benefiting from LI's association with both hurling and camogie (900 employees and their families celebrated LI's sponsorship at 'Liberty's Big Day Out' in Croke Park, and 60 per cent of staff regularly attend matches during the Hurling and Camogie Championships).

Match day activation was carefully carried out to ensure all activation was carried out smoothly for: the complimentary shuttle buses to key fixtures; once-in-a-lifetime opportunities for children to be flag-bearers at the All Ireland Hurling and Camogie Finals; and contributing to the drama and theatre

on the day with 'Best Banner' and 'Supporter of the Match' competitions.

Several selected players were encouraged to tweet.

Control/evaluation

Awareness and brand building:

- Increased sponsorship awareness among GAA fans.
- Uplift achieved across six brand image attributes.
- Established a substantial consideration gap (aware vs unaware).
- Considerable PR and media exposure.
- Significant social media reach and engagement across Hurling and Camogie Championships.

Acquisition and retention:

- GAA activation affected significant uplifts across business metrics including acquisition, customer retention and Net Promoter Score (NPS).

Fan engagement:

- Match day experiential activation programme delivered to significant percentage of supporters on match days and in stadia.

Commercial relationships:

- Tickets and hospitality provided to a significant percentage of Liberty Insurance's broker partners and commercial stakeholders.

Employee engagement:

- 900+ employees and their families participated in 'Liberty's Big Day Out'.

Men/women

The ongoing management of Liberty Insurance's sponsorship is maintained through a partnership arrangement with regular meetings and engagement with rights holders, as well as fortnightly inter-agency meetings with advertising, creative, PR and social media agencies. Employee involvement is important too with over 50 per cent of Liberty Insurance employees directly engaged in the sponsorship, entering competitions, attending matches, participating as flag bearers and other related events. The sponsorship is activated through internal communications and ongoing face-to-face briefings including opportunities to have photographs taken with the All Ireland Hurling and Camogie Trophies. Staff are actively encouraged to participate in live Twitter Q&As with match players.

Money

The sponsorship fees and the budget for promoting the sponsorship across a range of tactical tools and channels are not available for release at this point in time.

Minutes

A five-year partnership with the GAA and Camogie Associations was announced in May 2013.

FIGURE 15.2A–B   Liberty Insurance sponsorship at work

CASE STUDY 15.2   Citroën and beauty

FIGURE 15.3
Citroën and Benefit collaborate

Situation

OMD UK was challenged by Citroën to launch a new range of female-focused collaboration vehicles which they had co-designed with global beauty brand, Benefit. Market research revealed two interesting insights (1) the target demographic (women) dislike the dealership experience as they feel they might be patronized and that 75 per cent would bring a man to a dealership to ensure they got the best deal (so OMD had to come up with a new promotional channel where they could speak directly to them); (2) women found 'aesthetics' as important as 'practicalities' when it comes to purchasing an automobile.

Objectives

The challenge was to:

- generate sales of 500 units by the end of 2014;
- drive reappraisal of the car-buying process so that it felt relevant to our key demographic;
- engage our audience in an environment where they were looking for inspiration.

To achieve these objectives Citroën had to create an experience outside of traditional automotive environments that would at once surprise and delight, but crucially empower female car buyers to feel comfortable to explore the car functionalities and appreciate the aesthetics of the Citroën DS 3 by Benefit.

FIGURE 15.4   Citroën wanted female car buyers to feel comfortable and enjoy the aesthetics

Strategy

OMD identified ASOS as the ideal partner to work with on this campaign – initially established as an online retailer it had become a huge media channel in its own right, with over 8 million 18–34-year-old female unique monthly visitors and 3.5 million customers per month in the UK alone.

Citroën didn't just build a partnership – it created a totally new channel for Citroën to promote Citroën DS 3 by Benefit to women, all in one place, turning an online retailer brand into a media channel and a sales boutique.

Tactics

- **Must-join waiting list:** To pique the Citroën audience's curiosity before launch, Citroën created a must-join waiting list, which teased consumers by letting them know 'something amazing was happening'.
- **Incentivized daily prizes:** Sign-ups were further incentivized by daily prize give-aways.

- **The online 'boutique':** Features included Spring/Summer style fashions inspired by the model and make-up tutorials by Benefit. The collection was inspired by the newly launched Spring/Summer collections which meant as visitors immersed themselves in the Citroën range they were able to shop the new season's look.
- **Virtual test drive:** We created a 'virtual test drive' – a video co-created with ASOS in a style and tone that made the experience more immersive and relevant. The partially animated video showcased the vehicles alongside the Benefit make-up product which had inspired their design as well as aligning 2014 fashion trends and new ASOS garments – all of which the consumer was also able to purchase. The opportunity to take the first step towards buying or arranging to physically try the Citroën DS3 by Benefit online outside of the normal automotive online experience – a revolutionary step by ASOS.com.
- **Consumer promotion:** A competition for an ASOS customer to win a Citroën DS3 by Benefit resulted in over 23,000 entries and became the most successful branded competition ASOS have ever run.
- **Look book brochure:** Moving beyond digital, ASOS created as stand-alone bespoke booklet for Citroën. This 'Look Book' brochure showcased the car collection (Benefit were also featured – as they were across the campaign) – one million were distributed in ASOS magazines, ASOS orders, Benefit retail stores and Citroën car dealerships.

Action

Internal marketing was deemed critical to get all staff on board. All head office announcements, regional/field updates and staff briefings were also included in the newsletter and internal briefings. This included everything from brand affinity to where to buy, nearest dealer and dealership events. All teams were made aware of the social media campaign, hashtags and more.

#drivenbybeauty was the campaign hashtag.

Control/measurement

- **Impressions:** Overall impressions were close to 64 million which was +325 per cent on the campaign KPIs.
- **Visitors:** The online car boutique was visited by 92,828 women – 86 per cent more than target.

- **Registrations:** Pre-sign up to the teaser campaign generated an astonishing 10,000 registrations from our core audience in just two weeks.
- **Sales:** With two months left in the promotion Citroën had surpassed the sales target with 517 vehicles sold. By early September all four models in the range (800 vehicles) had completely sold out, generating revenue of over £12 million (€15 million+).
- **Performance tracking:** ASOS' pre- and post-campaign brand performance tracker showed positive results across key metrics – a 16 per cent increase (to 51 per cent) in 'fun to drive' and a staggering 80 per cent increase (to 36 per cent) 'for active, lively people'; an unprecedented result for Citroën.
- **Referral visitors and referral conversions:** Citroën hosted the test drive booking page in a DS3 by Benefit hub on their own website. Unique traffic to this page from ASOS.com was 13 per cent; however, we knew the referred traffic was hugely more engaged following exposure to the ASOS car boutique – and of those who progressed to the confirmation page to take the car for a test drive booking, 65 per cent were referred from ASOS. This is a clear indication that ASOS was the perfect partner for the vehicle launch.

With no other media activity beyond the ASOS boutique and co-created media support we know it has been driven by creating a new sales channel that connects with female car buyers in a way no other car manufacturer has ever done before.

Men/women

Citroën sponsorship management had a team comprised of one Citroën marketing professional who co-ordinated the activity across the various Citroën Marketing, PR and sales teams plus agency OMD UK who had eight staff involved. The partnership between Citroën and Benefit was arranged directly between the marketing directors of the two companies. After that the teams were challenged to think outside the box to effectively launch the vehicle to the target demographic.

Money

ASOS were utilized as an innovate media partner and platform to launch the product.

Minutes

With the partnership **between Citroën and Benefit set up**, the sponsorship partner programme, first discussed December 2013, went live in February 2014 and ran until end of July that year.

Key points from Chapter 15

- Almost anything can be sponsored.
- Almost any target audience can be reached through sponsorship.
- Choose sponsorship programmes carefully, and separate the initial excitement from the numerical analysis.
- Sponsorship can provide a cost-effective marketing communications tool, satisfying a range of different objectives.
- Maximize leverage by integrating sponsorship with other communications tools.
- Sponsorship does not have total control over the message. Have contingency plans in case things go wrong.

- Think global, but act local (today's satellite communications may highlight a sponsorship programme that is acceptable overseas but unacceptable at home and vice versa).
- Budgets should be secured to leverage the programme and maximize impact through other communications tools.
- Keep employees informed. Sometimes getting them involved increases the leverage.
- Run a small pilot scheme, if possible, to iron out any teething problems.
- Beware of ambush marketing.

References and further reading

Atkinson, S (2007) Why just a logo is now a no-no, *BBC News*, 21 June

Boshoff, A (1997) World Cup's battle of the boots, *Daily Telegraph*, 4 December

Colitt, R and Garrahan, M (2001) Nike finds Brazil deal a bad fit, *Financial Times*, 12 January, p 19

Collett, P and Fenton, W (2011) *The Sponsorship Handbook*, Jossey-Bass

ESA (2015) European Sponsorship Association, ESA DIPLOMA 2015 (Study Notes – Module One Section 1.8.1)

Giles, C (1991) *Business Sponsorship*, Butterworth-Heinemann, Oxford

Ferrand, A, Torrigiani, L, Camps, I and Povill, A (2007) *The Routledge Handbook of Sports Sponsorship*, Routledge

Head, V (1981) *Sponsorship: The newest marketing skill*, Woodhead-Faulkner, Cambridge

IOL (2006) The year of golf in space, *IOL.com*, 7 December

Jefkins, F (1991) *Modern Marketing Communications*, Blackie & Son, London

Klein, N (2000) *No Logo*, Flamingo, London

Lusbec, K (2015) adidas all in with Bayern Munich until 2030 for €900M, *Football Marketing XI*, 30 April

Mitchell, A (1997) Sponsorship works, *Marketing Business*, September

Rosen, W and Minsky, L (2011) Six Steps to Successful Sponsorships, *HBR Insight Center Marketing That Works*, July 28

Schlossberg, H (1996) *Sports Marketing*, Blackwell, Oxford

Shani, D and Sandler, D (1989) Olympic sponsorship versus ambush marketing, *Journal of Advertising Research*, August/September

Shank, M (2002) *Sports Marketing: A strategic perspective*, 2nd edn, Prentice Hall, Englewood Cliffs, NJ

Thomaselli, R (2006) Dream endorser: Tiger Woods as a giant of marketing ROI, *Ad Age*, 24 September

Turner, S (1987) *Practical Sponsorship*, Kogan Page, London

WARC (2005) Coke pours $500 million into soccer sponsorship, 24 November

Further information

Arts & Business
[formally Association for Business Sponsorship of the Arts (ABSA)]
Business in the Community
137 Shepherdess Walk
London N1 7RQ
Tel: +44(0) 20 7566 6650
http://artsandbusiness.bitc.org.uk/

Business in the Community
137 Shepherdess Walk
London N1 7RQ
Tel: +44 (0)20 7566 8650
www.bitc.org.uk

European Sponsorship Association (ESA) Office
Suite 1
Claremont House
22–24 Claremont Road
Surbiton
Surrey KT6 4QU
Tel: +44 (0)20 8390 3311
Fax: +44 (0)20 8390 0055
www.sponsorship.org

Ofcom
Riverside House
2a Southwark Bridge Road
London SE1 9HA
Tel: +44 (0)300 123 3000
www.ofcom.org.uk

16

Sales promotions, gaming and content marketing

LEARNING OBJECTIVES

By the end of this chapter you will be able to:

- Discuss the difference between strategic sales promotions and tactical sales promotions
- Separate brand-enhancing sales promotions from brand-diluting sales promotions
- Understand the importance of content marketing as a socially driven sales promotion
- Grasp the emergence of gamification as a potent sales promotions tool
- Integrate sales promotions with other elements of the communications mix
- Work in a team developing sales promotions and understand the campaign management process
- Develop a content marketing process
- Avoid the typical costly trial and error
- Embrace creativity, amidst the vast range of collaborative opportunities

Introduction 428
Successful promotions 428
Unsuccessful promotions 429
Creative sales promotions 432

Gamification 433
What exactly is gamification? 433
Who uses gamification? 433
Gamification disaster – the mistakes to avoid 434
Gamification – getting it right: know your audience 434
Gamification – the business benefits 435

Virtual promotions 435
Joint promotions 436
Social media-driven promotions 436
Integrated promotions 437

Managing sales promotions 437
Situation analysis 437

Objectives 437
Strategy 438
Tactics 441
Action 441
Control 442

Content marketing 442
Managing content marketing 442

Advantages and disadvantages 456
Advantages 456
Disadvantages 456

Key points from Chapter 16 456

References and further reading 456

Further information 457

Introduction

Sales promotion is big business. In fact, it has traditionally been bigger than advertising in the UK. And if content marketing is included (giving free content away as a gift) as well as gamification (getting customer and prospects and trade and staff playing brand related games) then you can see why sales promotions are going to continue to grow. Brand activation and customer engagement are two big buzz words in marketing, as is content marketing. To date, the growth of sales promotion has been fuelled by several factors, including:

- the movement towards brand activation, customer engagement and strengthening of what was called 'relationship marketing' (and rewarding loyal customers);
- the growth of content marketing and the growth of gamification;
- the still-large spend on direct mail and e-mail (supported by incentives/sales promotions);
- the emergence of promotion-literate customers who expect promotions with certain product types;
- during recessions, price-conscious customers searching for value-for-money promotions;
- powerful retailers favouring suppliers whose products sell quickly (because of heavy advertising, exciting promotions or both);
- the constant search for more cost-effective, 'below-the-line' tools such as sales promotions.

Isolating and calculating the exact industry figures is difficult since, first, forfeited revenues from price promotions (discounts) are included in the size of sales promotions expenditure and, second, some companies categorize promotions as part of PR, ie they pay for a sales promotion such as free information booklets out of their sales promotion budget, while others see it as part of public relations. Whichever way it is looked at, sales promotion is a below-the-line activity that can be used externally with end users (customers) and intermediaries (trade distributors) and also internally with an organization's own sales force.

Sales promotions, premiums, incentives and motivation schemes are used for both products and services in consumer and business-to-business markets. There are three main categories:

1 customer promotions (premiums, gifts, prizes and competitions, eg on the back of breakfast cereal boxes);
2 trade promotions (special terms, point-of-sale materials, free pens, diaries, competition prizes, etc);
3 sales force promotions (incentive and motivation schemes; see Chapter 12, 'Motivating' for an explanation of how these become a form of psychic income).

Successful promotions

Whether they take the form of competitions, price reductions, free gifts, coupons, samples, special demonstrations, displays or point-of-sale, consumer sales promotions tend to affect the later stages of the communications and buying process (see Chapter 4, 'Models of buyer behaviour'), ie they trigger action such as a purchase or increased usage of a particular brand, whereas advertising tends to affect the earlier stages, such as awareness, interest and desire (there are exceptions, particularly where direct response advertising is concerned). Content marketing is often used, particularly in B2B markets, as a sales promotion to identify and build a list of prospective customers by collecting an e-mail address, in return for giving the gift of content. However, sales promotions are an expensive way of generating awareness and need to be supported by advertising, PR and social media. Sales promotions are often action orientated, particularly as they can tempt the buyer to buy, or at least try, a product or service. These kinds of promotions often provide the final nudge that moves a customer towards making a purchase.

Sales promotions consumers = Skinner's rats vs Pavlovian dogs?

In terms of learning about brands and learning to use them frequently, many sales promotions, and the engagement they create (by filling in forms, collecting coupons, posting application forms, trying a free sample, etc), are a form of **operant conditioning** (demanding active engagement) as demonstrated by Skinner's rats (see Chapter 4). Advertising, on the other hand, is thought by some to help buyers to learn and remember brands and their benefits by repeating the message and building associations between

---

Free Ladas boost football club sales by 36 per cent

After several seasons of declining gates, Russian football club Zenit used a simple sales promotion to boost attendances up to 26,000. Entry costs 1.5 roubles and tickets for the Ladas lottery cost 1 rouble. Ladas cost 8,000 roubles (equivalent to three years' salary for the average industrial worker). The biggest roar of the evening comes not as the two teams run out on to the pitch but when the three cream-coloured Ladas are driven on to the running track. The opportunity of winning a Lada just pulls in the crowd.

---

brands, logos, images and benefits, a form of **classical conditioning** as demonstrated by Pavlov's passive dogs' engagement (see Chapter 4). Well-thought-out sales promotions that embrace the brand values and deliver real customer benefits can be enormously successful. For example, Tesco's Computers for Schools sales promotion has been running for several years, and in that time two-thirds of UK schools have actively participated, with millions of consumers. Promotions must establish a clear and desirable proposition for the target audience. Then ask: does the promotion support the brand's longer-term strategy (support the brand values)? Promotions should strengthen or add value to the brand image.

These types of promotions build 'consumer franchise'. This means that the gift is in some way related to the brand, its image or its properties. Franchise-building promotions contrast with price and discount offers which can dilute brand values and do not enhance brand loyalty, despite boosting short-term sales.

Freebies not always required

Loyalty schemes (promotions) do not have to constantly give gifts away. Extra special service can build loyalty, as can engagement in competitions and games. Brand activation and customer engagement strengthen the relationship and build loyalty, without actually giving gifts.

Unsuccessful promotions

Many sales promotions fail for two reasons: 1) they have no link to the brand values and long-term branding; 2) a lack of attention paid to detail, so problems emerge, such as fulfilment (eg pubs and bars find SMS promotions offering money-off vouchers to be labour-intensive, since staff have to be trained). See 'Disaster promotions', for major disasters by, surprisingly, major brands.

There is much room for more creative flair in sales promotions (see 'Creative sales promotions' on p.432). Effective sales promotions can creatively build the brand franchise while achieving many other objectives, such as increasing sales, cementing loyalty, building databases, generating publicity and more. However, more than half of trade promotions fail: 59 per cent of global promotions do not break even (and in the United States that figure is even higher, at 71 per cent with the UK at 58 per cent and Italy, the lowest failure rate at 41 per cent) (Nielsen, 2015).

Disaster promotions

Despite the phenomenal size of the sales promotions industry and the data available for analysis, there are a frightening number of sales promotions that are relatively ineffective, and some are actually damaging in terms of branding, sales and cash flow.

Price promotions can damage brands

Take price promotions such as discount vouchers, two for the price of one, a free extra 10 per cent: they can help to boost sales in the short term, but what do they do to the brand in the long term? Discount the price and you discount the brand down to a point where it loses its brand value and competes solely on price (which is not a protectable competitive advantage). So many sales promotions damage the core values, the image and the positioning of the brand. Other promotions attract only promiscuous consumers who switch back to another brand as soon as the promotion is over.

Temporary boost reduces subsequent sales

Some promotions create a temporary boost in sales followed by an immediate drop, as customers who

FIGURE 16.1   Some promotions boost sales temporarily as customers stock up but don't come back for twice as long

initially bought and stocked up on more product then stop buying until they have used up their extra stock (as shown in Figure 16.1). Other promotions actually damage the brand image and even the holding company's corporate image, sales, profits and cash flow (eg Hoover's £48 million fiasco – see more later).

Here are a few classic cases of promotions that went horribly wrong, even for the biggest and the best of marketing companies:

- *Typhoo Tea's Cash Pot promotion.* In 1984 Cadbury Typhoo was reported to have had to make cash payouts of more than £1 million. According to *Marketing Week* Cadbury Typhoo's insurers were reported to have issued a High Court writ against the company seeking a 'declaration that some claims made by Cash Pot competitors are outside the rules of the competition'. Nevertheless, the expensive promotion apparently increased its market share to its 'highest level since its relaunch in 1982', but at what cost?

- *Coca-Cola's MagiCan.* In 1990 Coca-Cola's US promotion was supported by a massive $100 million push. The MagiCan looked, weighed and felt (even when shaken) like a regular can. When the tab was pulled, the winning cans had a mechanism inside that pushed real rolled-up dollar notes through the hole in the top of the can. Cash prizes, inside the can, ranged from $5 to $200. The winning cans had some extra liquid to ensure the weight of all cans was the same.

Murphy's Law

What can go wrong will go wrong with sales promotions. As with most marketing communications tools, things can go wrong with sales promotions and destroy many excellent ideas that have apparently been meticulously planned. Sample packs may burst open and destroy other goods (or carpets), or premiums may be pilfered. There can be problems of misredemption (non-buyers acquire other buyers' coupons), malredemption (large-scale fraudulent coupon redemption), over-redemption (with millions claiming their prizes), or door-drop samples that the dog or child gets to before the adult. The possibilities of a mini-marketing disaster seem endless. In addition, the *Competitors' Companion*, a monthly subscription magazine (www.competitorscompanion.com), publishes news and views on which sales promotion competitions are running, what prizes they offer, exactly where to get entry forms, which qualifiers are required (eg a label) and the closing dates. According to the magazine, 'You receive advice on the answers to their questions plus a regular list of winning slogans and tie breakers... that way, you can read what's catching the judge's eye today and make them work for you tomorrow.'

Inevitably there were a few duds. Most of them just didn't work, but in a few cases the seal that held the 'liquid that gives the can the feel of the real thing' had broken. Although it was not harmful, one small boy (who was not aware of the promotion) drank the liquid and public health officials were called in. Massive media attention followed; 750,000 cans were held back while each one was shaken to determine whether the seal was broken or not. An immediate TV and press campaign was put into action to explain the promotion and to warn customers not to drink the liquid if the seal was broken (*Marketing*, 31 May 1990).

- *Pepsi's special bottle top* was offered by its Philippine subsidiary with a 1 million pesos (£26,000) prize to anyone finding a bottle top with the number 349. Pepsi paid out £8 million before it realized that thousands of winning bottle tops were appearing everywhere. When payment stopped there were public demonstrations; then Pepsi plants were attacked with grenades, and Pepsi lorries were burnt (three people were killed). Pepsi executives hired bodyguards before fleeing the country.

- *Heinz recipe book* was a printed recipe book promotional offer on its Pickering Fruit Pie Fillings. Heinz forgot to print a reply address, so no one could participate in the promotion.

- *KFC plastic figures* seemed like a good idea (giving a free plastic figure in some of its meals as a promotion). Although they tested the plastic for proximity to hot food, they did not test it for children sucking off the plastic and poking their eyes with the remaining wire. Personal injury claims followed.

- *Macy's department store talent promotion* was designed to find an Annie for a new production of the Broadway show. The lucky 12-year-old winner later made even bigger news when she sued Macy's after she was 'dumped' from the production.

- *Hoover's free flights to New York* were offered to anyone purchasing any Hoover over £100. Wrong comparisons with response rates from dissimilar 'two flights for the price of one' promotion, prompted wildly inaccurate forecast response rates for this new promotion. (The company forecast 5,000 responses and received 600,000!) The fixed-fee limit of £500,000 was agreed with the relatively small travel agent. When the agency went bust, Hoover was exposed to a massive response (note sales promotion insurance is essential). Meanwhile the trade increased prices of the cheaper Hoover models to over £100 so that effectively any Hoover purchase qualified for free flights (Hoover should have restricted the offer to certain models). The promotion cost £48 million, careers and corporate image.

- *Kraft Foods' 'Win a free camper van'* promotion had a computer error that generated hundreds of winners. As the prize-winners' claims kept coming in, Kraft realized there was a problem. Some disappointed customers vowed never to buy the firm's food products again. Others sought legal action.

- *Vidal Sassoon shampoo samples.* According to *Marketing Breakthroughs* (1991), half a million special free sample minipacks of Vidal Sassoon shampoo were distributed throughout Poland. When news of the promotion spread, around 2,000 mailboxes (mostly at apartment blocks) were pillaged. The sample packs then started appearing in street markets and soon sold out. The extra costs incurred by the damaged mailboxes added a new dimension to the sales promotion review process.

- *Alamo Car Hire's free car hire* flopped in Germany. Alamo normally offers one free day's car hire with every 30-day hire. This was fine until it discovered that it is illegal in Germany to give anything free after just one transaction. The international arena further complicates the life of the sales promotion professional, as regulations vary enormously.

- *Coca-Cola and McDonald's* got into trouble with Coca-Cola's special-edition round bottle, which was a potential 2006 World Cup collector's item – available from McDonald's outlets in the host country Germany as well as Austria, Hungary and Poland during the tournament. This fell foul of Germany's strict waste recycling regulations. Although it was stamped with the word Mehrwegflasche, indicating it was returnable, McDonald's did not charge the customary deposit meant to ensure the bottle was returned for recycling. The environmental lobby threatened legal action if McDonald's continued to advertise or sell the bottles.

The moral of the story? Check all possible disaster scenarios. Get advice from third parties. Test the promotion. Take out promotional insurance: professional indemnity insurance covers an agency's duty of care to its clients; product recall insurance protects against the cost of a recall of products or promotional gifts; over-redemption insurance protects against an unexpectedly high response. Whether the client pays or the agency pays is an issue that needs to be clearly agreed long before any sales promotion campaign rolls out.

There is, arguably, a worse scenario. No one responds to the sales promotion. Large stocks of premiums are left in the warehouse, and teams of order fulfilment staff (who dispatch the prizes) sit around with nothing to do.

Creative sales promotions

There is always room for creative innovation. Whether it's a trip to the moon or a party in an underground nuclear shelter, the only limitation to potential sales promotion creation is one's imagination. If it is stunningly successful, it is likely that the competition will follow, unless the innovative promotion relates uniquely to the brand in a creative way. This is demonstrated by the *Sunday Sport* tabloid newspaper.

Is your mother-in-law an alien?

Although no longer in circulation, the *Sunday Sport* newspaper once offered a free test kit that helped readers to determine whether their mothers-in-law were, in fact, aliens. The paper sold out within hours.

This 'alien mother-in-law' type of promotion is arguably just a stunt designed to generate publicity that may, at least temporarily, increase levels of awareness, boost sales and also reinforce readers' loyalty by rewarding them with a gift that appeals to their mentality. Because the gift is relevant to both the target reader's sense of humour and the newspaper's image, it adds to the paper's branding. In a way it adds to the brand franchise or builds consumer franchise.

One sales promotion that might have impressed mothers-in-law was for Cadbury. When it launched its white chocolate, Snowflake, agency Triangle achieved significant consumer trial by negotiating a covermount of a free bar on *OK!* magazine. When it discovered that the same issue was featuring Anthea Turner's wedding, it persuaded *OK!* to give

free bars to all the celebrity guests. The additional brand exposure enabled Cadbury to hit the media headlines, gain an estimated £1 million worth of editorial coverage, and ensure a spectacular launch success as a result.

London's Victorian and Albert Museum created an open source participative promotion that engaged audiences by inviting them to create their own art which became part of the exhibition and simultaneously promoted the exhibition online and offline (see Case Study on p. 453).

Creativity and originality can work well together, as when NatWest Bank's sales promotions and direct marketing were combined as a 'direct promotion' (most mailshots use an incentive). NatWest moved away from the traditional clock/radio/calculator/travel-bag type of incentive used by the banks from time to time. Instead it offered the choice of one of 10 limited-edition prints that were specially commissioned from five artists. It mailed to 65,000 names (who were thought to have over £25,000 to invest) and received a 12.3 per cent response (instead of the targeted 5 per cent response level). Another highly creative and popular promotion was Guinness's inflatable armchair, which formed part of its campaign as sponsor of the Rugby World Cup. An application for the armchair was even received from Buckingham Palace!

Highly creative sales promotions may involve an element of risk. Insurance (indemnity insurance, redemption insurance, etc) is advised with all sales promotions, but particularly recommended with highly creative and high-risk ones. Incidentally, creative thinkers will spot the PR opportunities that can be exploited when creative sales promotions are developed. These can spread through social media networks, and the press are usually also interested. See how Ulster Rugby and Canada's TD Bank use creative promotions to 'literally blow their customers away', on video at **www.PRSmith.org/blog**.

Social media-driven sales promotions are explored in the case studies at the end of this chapter, with three promotions where users generate poetry and music (rap), digital art and a musical soundtrack (for a film). But first there is an interesting Christmas sales promotion case driven by advertising on social media platforms.

One other dimension that creative thinkers can explore is the huge synergies and creative potential released by joint promotions with other brands,

FIGURE 16.2   Two creative promotions on video – watch the recipients' reactions: www.PRSmith.org/customer-retention-isnt-boring-heres-wow/

sometimes known as marketing marriages (note: alliances can work across all 10 communications tools/channels/tactics; see Citroën and 'Benefit' brand in Chapter 15). Before all of this, consider gamification and virtual gifts as sales promotion tools in the online world.

Gamification

What's it all about?

We feel a sense of achievement upon completing tasks, whether building a boat or going for a swim. Gamification taps into this human characteristic, particularly if there is:

1 reward;
2 recognition;
3 progress.

What exactly is gamification?

Gamification can be defined as: 'The use of game thinking and game mechanics in a non-game context in order to engage users and solve problems. Gamification is used in applications and processes to improve user engagement, return on investment, data quality, timeliness, and learning.' The word was created by computer programmer and inventor, Nick Pelling.

More than entertainment and engagement

Gamification is much more than entertaining and engaging customers. Watch how gamification will become embedded into relatively mundane business processes to add sparkle to repetitive tasks. Gartner forecast that by 2015, 25 per cent of redesigned business processes will be using gamification to implement new improved processes. Given that Forbes suggest 75 per cent of staff (in the United States) are not engaged, then it's easy to see how gamification might help. But it's more than staff who benefit from gamification.

Who uses gamification?

Arguably all stakeholders can benefit from gamification. As it helps to deepen learning of brand awareness, brand aspirations, brand features, brand preference, brand relationships as well as entertaining and engaging the user/stakeholder in a meaningful and relevant way. Let's look at two stakeholder groups split into three: customers and staff (salespeople and cashiers).

Customers

Nike+ is a potent example of the power of gamification. As its membership grows, the brand relationship strengthens, which, in turn, help to boost sales in the running category. They estimate that as membership increased it has helped boost revenues in the company's running category by 30 per cent. And today 'Nike Missions' continues to grow (see **http://missions.nike.com/en_US**) as does its UK Facebook page which urges its 200,000+ fans to 'forget public transport' and 'make the commute home your racecourse'. Their creative approach to gamification also allows customers and prospects to race against themselves or a worldwide community.

Salespeople

Salespeople are competitive people by nature. Internal sales league tables have been around since the year dot as a way of motivating the competitive nature of the sales rep. One thing salespeople don't like doing is the mind-numbing repetitive administrative experience of recalling and entering data and filing reports into a database. So some organizations' sales reporting systems have been 'gamified' by rewarding accuracy and frequency of data entry with the scoring of points complete with a leader board and monthly prize – 'morphing mundane into motivation' by making a tedious task surprisingly exciting.

Cashiers

Here is the ultimate tedious task made surprisingly exciting by gamification, and how it currently helps bored, gum-chewing, cashiers in retail stores. Since the retail checkout is a chicane for customer emotions, in fact a lengthy queue, or a perceived delay in a queue can destroy, what was up to that point, a reasonably positive consumer experience. You can see why retail are exploring how gamification can help to improve this (and many other processes). American retail chain, Target, gamified the check-out process to help engage staff. As items are scanned the cashier sees red or green based on whether the item that was just scanned was within the 'optimum time'. They can also see their immediate score and compare it to the ideal time to see if they are 'in-time'. Getting the scan process right first time, every time, can shave a minute or more off the check-out procedure. And we all know the gift of time is one which customers welcome.

Gamification disaster – the mistakes to avoid

Given that most staff are not engaged – Gallup suggest only 13 per cent are engaged (Crabtree, 2013) – then it follows, surely, that gamification could boost efficiency and effectiveness by even just a few per cent. This can sometimes be the difference between profit and loss – survival and extinction – success and failure.

Poor gamification design

However a *Forbes* forecast (Burke, 2013) suggests that by 2014 poor gamification design will have nullified the potential and that up to 80 per cent of gamified applications will fail to meet business objectives (because of poor design).

Deloittes also suggest that '80 per cent of current gamified applications fail to meet business objectives primarily due to poor design'. Perhaps this is a similar to the lack of 'instructional design' in the many failed elearning projects in the '90s and beyond.

Don't leap into the game

So don't leap into gamification (without understanding good design) like many business people who jumped into elearning (without understanding instructional design). It's as if they felt they ticked that box 'yes we do gamification' or 'yes we have a Facebook page'. As Gartner's Brian Burke (2013) says 'remember not to confuse activity with success'.

Gamification – getting it right: know your audience

First of all know your audience. So who are the gamers?

The average gamer is 35, married, earns £23k pa; games 12 hours a week; owns two consoles, 18 games and takes a month to complete one game; rows with their partner twice a week over their pastime (Source: Pixwoo.com). Note this will change as gamification spreads to customers, call centres, cashiers, salespeople, other staff, suppliers and other stakeholders.

Eight gamification success factors

1 Narrative – that guides, challenges and changes as the player progresses.

2 Feedback – immediate re success or failure, and most importantly, progress.

3 Competitive – we like to compete with others – even in a different location – make it social.

4 GUI (graphical user interface) – must be easy and fun to use.

5 Test with a view to usability, security, scale, local or global roll-out.

6 Rewards, recognition, awards – it's a motivation programme (that involves changing behaviour, knowledge and or skills) NB: major staff motivators are 'progress' and 'psychic income'.

7   Achieve business objectives (not just entertainment).

8   Promoting gamification – avoid using the 'g' word and focus on bottom line results (ie don't promote the word gamification, do promote the benefits of gamification).

Add in some psychic income

Get gamification right and add 'psychic income' into the rewards programme – now that could deliver some interesting results. Psychic income is non-financial rewards that fulfil your dreams. Instead of giving £100 bonus which gets lodged in the bank and forgotten, give two tickets to see the person's favourite band or team (see the TD bank 'wow' video in the 'Creative sales promotions' section earlier). Psychic income specialist companies like Maritz in the United States offer a wide variety of 'amazing' rewards from shop floor workers to CEOs; for example, instead of giving a CEO a £40,000 bonus why not, if he or she really loves golf, give them instead, two holes of golf with Jack Nicklaus and on the 18th green there's an orchestra perched on a scaffolding playing the tune of your choice.

Add in some earned media/social sharing

Children's retailer Step2 use gamification and give points to users depending upon their social media interaction and activity within the BuzzBoard community. Customers are rewarded with points for different levels of engagement (see the ladder of engagement in Chapter 1) from sharing Facebook content, to uploading videos and photos, writing reviews, following fellow reviewers and subscribing to have reviews sent to their Facebook news feeds.

> ### Your customers are your greatest marketeers
>
> 'The amount of user interaction that Nike have created really is outstanding and will lead to the Holy Grail for any organization: customer loyalty. Your customers are your greatest marketers.'
>
> Yardy (2015)

Gamification – the business benefits

- customers – have fun, see progress, get rewards;
- staff – boosts product knowledge, processes efficiency, customer service skills and engagement;
- business – boosts awareness of brand and/or features/benefits, recruitment, retention and advocacy;
- business cost reduction (cost-effective tool to embed key messages and boost operations efficiency);
- business data capture – build your own customer database for future engagement and relationship building;
- boost to customer engagement = boosted revenues eventually.

So gamification can be a powerful type of sales promotion, but caution, care and a considered design are all required for successful gamification so that customers, trade staff, own staff or other stakeholders can be engaged, motivated, and rewarded via gamification as their relationship with your brand strengthens through this increasingly important and high-growth sales promotion tool.

[Note: this gamification excerpt was first published in **www.PRSmith.org/blog** in Oct 2013 in an article entitled 'Gamification – the good, the bad and the ugly'.]

Virtual promotions

Although some are puzzled by why consumers pay real money for non-existent goods (virtual goods), there is an element of conspicuous consumption involved. Marketers understand how this influences both offline and online buyer behaviour, particularly if it either is a collectable item or has status symbol attachment, or both. The virtual American Greetings case (see case study in Chapter 21) demonstrates how the difference between the virtual world and the real world is blurring all the time. The now classic film, *The Matrix*, explained this in a more dramatic manner. This is all brought back down to earth by Michael Zeisser with a useful analysis of virtual gifts (read on).

> ## So why do consumers want online objects that don't actually exist?
>
> 'While the notion of virtual goods – nonphysical objects used in online communities and games – still puzzles many executives, it's quite apparent that consumers love them. People acquire or compete for virtual items obsessively on Foursquare, Zynga, and many other sites. It is estimated that virtual goods have become a very real $5 billion industry worldwide.
>
> So why do consumers pay real money for online objects that don't actually exist? Their motives reinforce our notion that users seek online importance: they purchase virtual goods primarily for self-expression (such as virtual houses or virtual gifts) and for recognition (such as virtual badges for becoming, say, the 'mayor' of a bar on Foursquare). These behaviours are too widespread and intense to be fads, and marketers need to recognize them as meaningful. Brands should actively experiment with ways to use virtual goods as catalysts of word-of-mouth media.
>
> In the context of a social network, it is not a stretch to conceive of virtual gifts as important objects, especially as their availability can be strictly limited. Just think about the fervor consumers accord collectibles of all kinds, from baseball cards to dolls to coins. If virtual items prove similarly desirable, they are likely to be a big deal for consumers and marketers, as well as a great tool to create useful word-of-mouth media.
>
> We've also found that basic laws of consumer behaviour still apply: consumers love a bargain, and companies should take full advantage of social networks as powerful notification tools. Users can be alerted to sales or to the expiration of a promotion, but companies must be mindful that these feeds and tweets are designed as catalysts to generate virtual word-of-mouth media. They are not social media junk mail, but legitimate content objects – actual pieces of media that we want the initial recipients to distribute to their friends.
>
> One final recommendation: no gimmicks. Forget dancing monkeys, artificial contests, or stupid tricks; they add no value and waste people's time. A commitment to being useful in social media activities means a commitment to creating only high-quality interactions.'
>
> Zeisser (2010)

Joint promotions

Joint promotions, cross-promotions or marketing marriages offer economical routes to target the same customers with relevant offers.

When Coca-Cola led its army of soft drinks brands into a joint promotion with Cadbury, it was followed by their arch-rival Pepsi announcing another mega-brand deal, in this case, with Kellogg's. When Deep Pan Pizza created a joint promotion with Lego, giving children free branded toys, sales of children's meals inevitably grew. In fact they doubled. To maintain repeat purchases, the choice of toys was changed every quarter. However, caution must be exercised when choosing a partner. Equal-standing brands, budgets and branding details need to be clarified, with nothing left to chance. Stuart Hardy, Managing Director of WLK (which married Mothercare and Lever's Persil in a joint promotion), says, 'In any true relationship each side is going to have 50 per cent of the say. A lot of marketing people want 100 per cent of the say and only 50 per cent of the costs.' Although there are lots of opportunities, relatively few joint promotions seem to get off the ground. It must be agreed and specified who actually does what and gets what, including databases, space allocation, preferences, etc.

Social media-driven promotions

Social media has become an essential element of any sales promotion campaign, as word spreads fast across social media platforms. Social media is 'social', and that means people like to be sociable, by keeping in contact, sharing relevant (useful or fun) information. In fact, people's image or status is increased if they have sourced 'free stuff' or special offers, particularly if the offers are limited. Spreading useful information about sales promotions adds value to the connection, and people are deemed more worthwhile the more good stuff they have to share, so sales promotions naturally lend themselves to social media. See 'Virtual gifts' above and the three case studies later in this chapter, which demonstrate how user-generated promotions for poetry and music (rap), digital art and a soundtrack for a movie can make attractive sales promotions, which in this case are mostly driven purely by social media.

Integrated promotions

Sales promotions naturally integrate with other marketing communications tools, particularly packaging ('on-pack' promotions), point-of-sale, merchandising, sponsorship, PR, advertising, direct mail and selling and, of course, social media. It is no surprise that advertising-supported promotions do better than ones that are not supported. There are, however, many occasions when media support cannot be afforded or where point-of-sale materials promoting the offer are considered to be more cost-effective than above-the-line support. In fact, this chapter shows three sales promotions that work entirely through social media channels and platforms. But even a great sales promotion fails if no one knows about it. Some support, whether advertising, point-of-sale, PR or social media (and even space on 'owned media' such as a website can be kept for sales promotions), helps get promotions up and running. Creative promotional ideas command press coverage, so some budget should always be left for PR requirements (stocks of photos, transparencies, websites and social media platforms with downloadable images and news items, etc).

Coke auctions

'Coke's innovative Coke Auction campaign combined sales promotions and packaging with the unique online facility of online auctions, offline radio and TV advertisements, and online e-mail viral marketing. Online auctions harness some of the internet's unique functions. With innovation at the helm, Coke has somehow converted the normally discarded ring pulls into online currency called, unsurprisingly, "Coke credits". These credits are then used to bid for items from sports tickets to becoming stars in Coke ads (having their faces on the Coke signs) in major advertising venues. That was fifteen years ago!'

Smith and Chaffey (2001)

Managing sales promotions

Going back to mainstream sales promotions where gifts, prizes and competitions are popular promotions, the SOSTAC® + 3Ms planning process can be used to build a sales promotion plan.

Situation analysis

The situation analysis requires research into past promotions (including those of your competitors), present and possible future campaigns, combined with a clear analysis of the target market. An initial review can be followed by further research into the target market including concept testing, and eventually test marketing.

In addition to the usual demographic and psychographic information, further analysis may reveal what Philip Kotler (2000) identified as three types of new triers who are attracted to (and respond to) sales promotion offers: 1) users of a competing brand in the same category; 2) users in other categories; and 3) frequent brand switchers. These 'deal-prone customers', the brand switchers, tend not to be loyal and are likely to switch away to the next low-price or free-gift offer that comes their way. The group at the other end of the target market loyalty spectrum are called 'the immovables', who are locked into brand loyalty. Do not waste resources targeting them. The real target group within the target market are called the 'loyal susceptibles'. These are there to be won (or lost if they are your brand customers). Once their loyalty is broken, their new-found loyalties can be nurtured and relationships strengthened through regular relevant communications and engagement.

Knowing exactly who these people are and why they are more susceptible is the key to the sales promotions tapping into their susceptibilities, which in turn will increase market share beyond a short-term temporary boost.

After the real target market has been analysed, the eventual sales promotion concept should be researched in focus groups or at least with sample customers. When the idea or promotional tool is agreed, it is still worth testing it in a limited area or customer group to reveal any hidden problems or even opportunities before launching it nationally or internationally.

Objectives

As the name suggests, a promotion is a limited-period offer. It is therefore not surprising to find that sales promotions tend to have shorter-term tactical objectives (although, as previously explained, this need not be the case).

As well as boosting brand activation and customer engagement, some typical sales promotion goals include:

- increase sales (although it may be only a temporary increase, because customers can simply stock up with the goods or temporarily switch brands while the promotion is running) by:
  - rewarding loyal customers;
  - locking customers into loyalty programmes (where they have to keep buying the product or service over a period of time in order to collect the right number of coupons, vouchers, or items in a collection);
  - increasing the repurchase rates of occasional users;
  - generating trials among new customers (by triggering an impulse purchase).
- brand activation and customer engagement;
- demonstrate new features or modifications or introducing a new product or service;
- develop new uses;
- image development (awareness or repositioning);
- deseasonalize seasonal sales (eg skiing holidays in the summer);
- develop new sales leads;
- satisfy retailers with a complete package – gain trade acceptance;
- move excess stock;
- block a competitor (by offering incentives to customers to stock up);
- match a competitor (eg petrol tokens);
- build a database (some promotions also act as database builders: see how the Rothmans offer of a free pack collected 750,000 customer names, in Chapter 3, 'Database opens up £billions of new sales' box);
- generate publicity.

Strategy

All promotions should be part of a bigger and longer-term strategy. Longer-term sales promotion strategies are about building and reinforcing brand image, strengthening user loyalty, and even inviting new users to join the club, as opposed to short-term tactical sales boosts. Whether planned on a one-off tactical basis or on a more structured strategic approach basis, the sales promotion can have an impact on the brand or organization's overall image (eg Hoover). Corporate image is central to the longer-term strategic communications of the organization. Tracking studies (or continual market research) can monitor changes in specific aspects or dimensions of an organization's corporate or specific brand image. Content marketing works best when a sequence of pieces of contents are scheduled to be given to prospects or customers at various points in their buying cycle.

Matching types of promotions with specific objectives

Some sales promotion tools are more appropriate than others in achieving certain objectives (Table 16.1).

Some efforts have been made to rank the effectiveness of specific tools ('mechanics') against various objectives. Cummins (2003) identified how certain sales promotion techniques match up with various objectives (Table 16.2).

Strategic impact of sales promotions

'Years ago, Heinz used to say that they saw more far-reaching effects on image dimensions of their tracking studies from their sales promotion schemes than they ever saw resulting from advertising campaigns.'

Castling (1989)

Some organizations only see promotions as a short-term tactical tool, eg 'Get 50,000 people to see my store opening'. So strategic sales promotions are not always possible to achieve if clients do not want them in the first place. The difficulty is compounded by the fact that strategic promotions may sometimes not generate immediate customer response. So the questions is: should the longer-term image-building capability of a sales promotion be forfeited for the shorter-term tactical sales objective? Today, the desire for content marketing is forcing many companies

TABLE 16.1   Matching promotions with objectives

Objective	Promotional tool
Consumer	
Trial	Sampling; couponing; free draw; price-off; self-liquidator (send in some money, which pays the costs of the promotion); premiums; in-pack; on-pack; near-pack; reusable container; personality promotion
Retrial	Coupon for next purchase; price-off
Increase usage	Collections; games; competitions; extra-quantity or bonus packs; price-off multiple purchase
Develop new uses	Companion brand promotions; publications; workshops
Image development	Publications; sponsorship; charity
Trade	
Increase distribution, shelf facings or displays	Discount; extended credit; point-of-sale materials; tie-in with advertising
In-store promotion	Discount; extended credit; point-of-sale materials; tie-in with advertising; consumer offer; promotion allowance
Increase sales	Sales competitions and rebates (mostly independent stores and wholesalers)
Cement good relations	Gifts, holidays and awards
Sales force	
Sales and distribution	Psychic income and financial income

to think more strategically; for example, after a prospect downloads the free ebook, what do we do next, perhaps a webinar, followed by a free trial etc.

A strategic approach is preferred, as explained by Cummins (2003):

- It enables one offer to build on the previous one, and to establish a continuity of communication.
- It makes it possible to communicate image and functional values, so promotions work harder.
- It can produce considerable savings in time and money.
- It enables offers to be fully integrated into the other activities in the marketing programme (eg linking with advertising and PR).
- It facilitates a better approach to joint promotions (see above).

- A strategic approach does not exclude the use of tactical promotions, since it can provide a framework within which shorter-term tactics can be determined. In this way a sales promotion strategy makes the tactical planning easier and more productive.

How to develop a strategic approach

1 Identify what customers (and prospects) really want (in terms of promotions).

2 Identify the long-term strategic marketing and communications objectives.

3 Create guidelines for each product or service, showing the style of sales promotion that is most appropriate to the brand's long-term health. Ensure that this style contributes towards the strategic marketing goals (as opposed to sometimes going in the opposite direction).

TABLE 16.2   Linking the objective to the mechanics: how they match up

Objectives / Mechanics	Immediate free offers	Delayed free offers	Immediate price offers	Delayed price offers	Finance offers	Competitions	Games and draws	Charitable offers	Self-liquidators	Profit-making promotions
Increasing volume	9	7	9	7	5	1	3	5	2	1
Increasing trial	9	7	9	2	9	2	7	7	2	1
Increasing repeat purchase	2	9	2	9	5	3	2	7	3	3
Increasing loyalty	1	9	0	7	3	3	1	7	3	3
Widening usage	9	5	5	2	3	1	5	5	1	1
Creating interest	3	3	3	2	2	5	9	8	8	8
Creating awareness	3	3	3	1	1	5	9	8	8	8
Deflecting attention from price	9	7	0	7	7	3	5	5	2	2
Gaining intermediary support	9	5	9	5	9	3	7	5	1	1
Gaining display	9	5	9	5	9	3	7	5	1	1

Each square is filled with a rating from 0 (not well matched) to 10 (very well matched). Use it as a ready reckoner for linking your objective to the mechanics available

SOURCE: J Cummins (2003)

4 Determine exactly how much of the total marketing communications budget is available for sales promotions.

5 Ensure that there is support and commitment from senior management (eg the marketing director) so that sufficient management expertise and funds are available for the promotions to be professionally carried out.

6 Develop a method of evaluation so that longer-term performance can be measured against longer-term objectives. Ideally, this might then be compared to other types of marketing expenditure. Agencies and consultancies can review the effectiveness of their activities at the end of the year. Some agencies and consultancies are then asked 'Which communications tool is more effective and why?'.

7 Develop a promotions file that compiles ideas and costs throughout the year. These can then be reviewed closer to the time of planning.

8 Plan and forecast the sales promotions' results. This is obviously difficult to do, particularly the first time. Usually a best, worst and medium range of forecasts help to build some kind of management control and criteria for success or failure.

Tactics

The general short-term, 'immediate action', tactical nature of sales promotion contrasts with the longer-term image and brand-building capability of advertising. This need not be the case, because sales promotions can be planned on a strategic level. But, first, why is there a tendency towards short-termism?

Perhaps the short-term focus is a result of:

1 management pressure to boost quarterly sales, which therefore encourages the use of quick-response sales promotions;

2 shortening product life cycles, which demand quick sales results;

3 increased competition and increased new product introductions, which increase the need for tactical defensive sales promotions;

4 the speedy response required to handle business problems when they arise;

5 full-service agencies trying to sell the client additional services such as sales promotion on an ad hoc, 'add-on' tactical basis.

Action

This is where attention to detail and proper processes and resources are required to ensure the smooth running of any sales promotion. This is where you avoid the 'disaster promotions' mentioned earlier in the chapter (see p. 430). The choice of promotional tool can be directly affected by the availability of resources. The three key resources, men/women, money and minutes (the 3Ms), are tied up with a promotion. Careful contingency planning should cater for an unexpectedly large response. Insurance can help here, because things do go wrong

and costs can rapidly escalate. Although creating a promotion is exciting, finishing it is dull and boring, yet this is the mark of a true professional.

Cut-off dates, logistical arrangements (returning unused stocks) and even announcing the end of the promotion cost time and money. Shell wanted to avoid the flush of irritation that would undoubtedly rise up if its customers failed to cash in their carefully collected gift tokens before they expired and became worthless, so it advertised the end of the promotion.

Here is a checklist covering some key sales promotions issues:

1 Does the promotion exploit key strengths and unique selling propositions (USPs)?

2 Is it a franchise-building promotion? Does the gift, incentive or premium relate to or enhance your product or service or the organization's image? Does it carry a selling message or at least a subtle reminder of some selling message? Unrelated premiums, contests, refunds or price discounts do not reinforce the brand or enhance corporate values.

3 What can go wrong? Contingency planning, crisis management and insurance are worth considering.

4 Has the promotion got legal clearance? Should it be checked with the Committee of Advertising Practice (CAP) sales promotions department?

5 Will the promotion generate only a temporary gain while customers stock up and do not repurchase for twice the normal period? (See Figure 16.1.) Will existing or old stocks (not carrying the promotion) waste?

6 Does the promotion need advertising and PR support? Is it newsworthy? Great promotions fail if no one knows about them. How can it be spread into social media networks? In B2C markets, will the retail trade demand some above-the-line support for the promotion?

7 What other communications tools are required – new packaging, point-of-sale materials, new literature or contract field sales teams? Are these in the budget (time and money restrictions)?

8 Is there an administrative burden created by new order forms, coupons, judging, choosing winners, dispatching gifts, etc? Or will this all be handled by an external agency?

9 Is there a cut-off date, and is it clearly stated when the offer closes? Has the lead time (the period required to set up the whole sales promotion through to launch date) been established?

10 Is the sales promotion going to be costly? Does it fit the budget available? Is it cost-effective? Can it be measured?

Control

Control, measurement and monitoring form the loop in the management system. How can the success or otherwise of the promotion be measured? The number of respondents, redemptions and increased sales are all relatively easy to calculate, but these are only the surface figures. They may be hiding the fact that many of the responders are the wrong people (promiscuous nomads), or existing customers who simply buy twice as much this week (stocking up) but do not buy next week. In fact, it may be that less than one-quarter of the respondents actually represent new business.

The promotion may have worked well in one respect but failed in another. The purpose of measurement and monitoring is twofold:

1 to control current campaigns;

2 to improve future campaigns by learning about what did and did not work with the current campaign.

Each promotion has to work successfully across a number of communications stepping stones for it to succeed. As Holloway (1989) puts it:

It has to be: seen, interesting, understood, believed, relevant and compatible, persuasive, and produce the desired response among the right target audience... to be seen may require the promotion to be in pack, on pack, off pack, POS, etc, while the design of the visual elements has to cut through the clutter as many on-pack flashed offers are often never 'seen' by the target market. The middle criteria of communication effectiveness relate to the nature of the offer, the platform involved and the visual/copy elements of the promotion. Persuasion and response are dependent

on the combination of all of these variables. There are few promotions that emerge from pre- or post-testing which don't leave considerable room for improvement somewhere in the mix of essential ingredients.

At the end of the chapter there are four case studies that demonstrate the diverse nature of using social media both to spread a message and to engage stakeholders at the highest level – collaborative co-creation. Firstly, let's explore Content Marketing, what is it and how it works.

Content marketing

Content marketing is a hot topic in many organizations. It is a major component of many organizations' strategy. It can be a source of differentiation. It can give them an edge. It can attract visitors, help to nurture them into customers and help to retain them.

What exactly is content marketing?

Content marketing is all about creating and distributing, at the right time, really relevant content (videos, webinars, infographics, power point slides, tweets, posts, articles, white papers, books and even games) that helps prospects and customers to achieve their goals (eg enhancing their skills, being informed, entertained or just providing them with high-quality content they want to share with their own networks). Your choice of content ('content strategy') is influenced by your mission, your brand values and brand personality and also what your customers want or would value, that your competitors don't currently create.

Managing content marketing

Researching, creating, producing, distributing and engaging in any subsequent dialogue, makes content marketing an ongoing process requiring resources from within (trained staff) or external (agencies). Either way, managing content marketing requires a new set of thinking and processes.

In addition to analysing a lot of analytics, the US president's election campaign required a lot of

FIGURE 16.3   Time spent thinking creatively helped to generate this highly engaging photo during the hugely successful Obama campaign

Photo courtesy of Teddy Goff

FIGURE 16.4   The 'staff egg timer' (many staff contribute during brainstorming; then reduce staff during production, and then many staff help distribute content)

high-quality and extremely relevant content marketing. This required a lot of creative thinking. They worked hard to continually find creative ideas to engage their followers. The president's digital marketing was led by Teddy Goff and he told me that the photograph above surprised everyone by being one of the most popular pieces of content.

As was discussed in Chapter 14, this simple photograph generated a very high level of engagement and went viral. The caption was 'This seat is taken'. Obama's digital marketing team spent a lot of time with creative brainstorming to find content ideas that would continue to engage their followers. This is a constant challenge, as customers drown in a sea of content marketing. This type of free gift (or sales promotion), only works when it is relevant, engaging, interesting and is immediately understood as being some valuable content.

Think like a publisher

You have to think like a publisher, discover hot topics that are not well served by competitors, brainstorm, create content concepts, select the best ones, produce them, distribute them and measure their impact. You need a team that looks like an egg timer (large at the start, thin in the middle and large at the end – see Figure 16.4). A cross-functional group at the beginning (for brainstorming), then a small editorial team and small production team to produce the content, and finally a large team mobilized to help

the distribution (and engagement) at the end. Why not ask your partners, resellers and suppliers to spread your content? GaggleAmp alerts these groups every time you post, makes it easy for them to share and rewards them for sharing. It also integrates with marketing automation systems, and costs $100 pcm if you regularly post content (or less if you are infrequent).

See the range of content in the content pyramid as shown in Figure 16.5, below.

FIGURE 16.5   The content pyramid

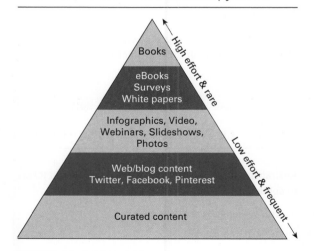

SOURCE: Adapted from curata.com

As shown in Figure 16.4 on p.443, many staff can help brainstorm new content ideas, then a single editor decides and manages production and then everyone is invited to help share the new content.

Leverage other content

Your marketing and advertising team probably have a lot of material that they can share on Instagram, Pinterest, YouTube, Vimeo, Vine, Facebook and LinkedIn. Sharing advertising collateral and any marketing content (PR photos with an added caption) in an organic way simply gets you 'more bang for your buck'. It's inevitable. Any speeches, presentations, articles can also be leveraged across many channels. Sift through your marketing collateral. Amongst these assets, you will find components that need polishing or some components that just need a caption and then, release them in an organized process (or schedule).

For a full insight into how a team of two generated content that went global and connected with a very specific universe of HR Directors, see the Kelly HR case study below.

Content calendar

A content calendar is used to schedule what content will be published in which month, week or day. Some calendars also specify type of content (post, video, infographic, eBook, webinar etc). Relevant key phrases that can be used to optimize the content and url links are sometimes added. Organizations adopt their own calendar style, some with a lot more detail than others.

Content wars

It is worth remembering that customers are drowning in a sea of content. Competitors are churning out content – some good and some bad. Customers' ability to consume content is finite because there are only so many hours in a day to read/watch/listen, even to really interesting content.

Mark Schaefer (2014) describes this as the 'Content Shock' when 'At some point, the amount I am "paying out" will exceed the amount I am bringing in and at that point, creating content will not be a smart business decision for me and many other businesses.

We may have to pay customers to read our content! In fact we already are (indirectly as we spend, say, six hours writing a blog post at a nominal cost of £100 per hour = £600 spent producing the piece!).'

Measuring content marketing's effect

Content marketing should be designed so that it is easy to measure its impact (is it driving traffic, or is it boosting registrations or sales?). It also must have feedback mechanisms beyond KPIs and analytics, which allow customers to give direct feedback. Build 'content pathways' so that when prospects or customers show interest in (open) a particular piece of content, they automatically get sent another, even more relevant, piece of content (or a link to a piece of content).

For more on measuring content marketing, watch the video 'Measuring the Effectiveness of Content Marketing' by Erin Robins O'Brien in an interview with Steve Farnsworth of the Steveology group, posted on **www.PRSmith.org/blog**.

Content marketing can be a major component in your strategy. But in a hyper-competitive environment you need to have processes in place to identify what's needed, produce it, release it and monitor which kind of content works best.

CASE STUDY 16.1   Content marketing delivers competitive advantage – Kelly HR

Australian company, Kelly HR, are doing all the right things re content marketing:

1 create engaging content;

2 produce the content;

3 measure content effectiveness.

Plus, they are doing an awful lot more with their content marketing. They create, promote and distribute their content marketing in a consistent format, in an integrated marketing communications process. This 'integrated content marketing' is now their number one lead generator, number one brand awareness builder and it is now delivering a competitive advantage that is rapidly becoming a sustainable competitive advantage.

Situation: the company

Kelly Services is a recruiting staff organization with two core audiences:

1 companies who will pay Kelly money to recruit staff for them; and

2 staff looking for a new job.

Kelly are effectively in both B2B and a B2C.

Target market

Instead of dealing with traditional staffing/recruitment companies, Kelly targeted the more traditional consulting firms including McKenzie's, the Banes, the IBMs, PWCs; all of whom have a lot bigger budgets. Kelly wanted to break into this market and demonstrate its capability to play in the outsourcing space where the deal size is typically $20 million to $1 billion and where it takes 18 months to two years to close deals.

Content, competition and the opportunity

Already a lot of the players were quite well advanced in thought leadership content but many of them were not taking it to a real content marketing approach integrating and leveraging the content to the maximum. Kelly saw this a really good opportunity to create competitive advantage and, frankly, they didn't have enough money to do anything else.

Step 1: content audit

Kelly's marketing content director, Todd Wheatland, talked to a lot of staff and identified 600 pieces of content that had been developed by someone somewhere for some purpose (eg promotional materials for events, exhibitions, conferences, collateral literature, reports, etc.) all of which were potential marketing content. Kelly found that the process of looking back (at existing content) in order to look forward to be very useful. This process helped the team to learn how to structure content. 'We understood a lot more about who we're trying to speak to, and what we're trying to tell them. What value Kelly is trying to add, what questions they're asking' said Wheatland. A huge underutilized resource was discovered.

Step 2: content selection

Out of those 600 pieces of content two were selected that could be used. Kelly are good at leveraging research. Eighty per cent of all their content, including blog posts, has a unique original research component to it.

Step 3: develop personas

Personas help Kelly to understand the audience, which tends to be typically C suite plus some HR and procurement audiences.

Step 4: identify five buckets, 200 key words and 2,000 pieces of content

Five buckets (themes) of content were identified along with some 200 relevant keywords that searchers would use. For each of those 200 keywords Kelly produced 10 pieces of content per year, optimized for that keyword. Effectively Kelly produce 2,000 pieces of content in English a year, based on these five buckets.

Step 5: secure budget: 3Ms resources

Kelly made a strategic decision to focus on content marketing, subsequently cancelling some major events that they normally attend and using the money to develop content and run a pilot programme to demonstrate value.

Resources required

Content has now become about 50 per cent of the total marketing spend. In terms of structure Kelly's content marketing team is lean – lead by Todd Wheatland who spends 50 per cent of his time with another content marketer in Germany who is basically the head of B2B content marketing and distribution channels. Kelly have one other person in the United States who is in charge of B2C content, which is now a big focus for Kelly since they have introduced the Kelly Service side of the business. The US team member spends 20 per cent of their time (annualized) on content marketing (0 per cent in the quiet months, and up to 40 per cent in the busy months), and there are many individuals both within and outside the company who play varying roles in Kelly's highly successful content marketing. This includes translations, videographers, animators, illustrators, etc. Beyond that, everything is outsourced.

Tactics: leverage content

The research report may be 80 pages in a general term; you may do a spinoff ebook that's 2–3 pages long and is very specific and targeted to a different audience. The research is repurposed into different elements beyond a research report to deliver eBooks, blog posts, infographics, social memes, animated infographics and more. In fact Kelly Global Workforce Index (survey) was leveraged to deliver:

- 1 × survey or ebook;
- 6 × topics/chapters (mini ebooks);
- 1,000+ content pieces;
- 200+ news releases;
- 20+ company events;
- 40+ external events;
- 30 × countries' languages.

Kelly also generate white papers over consecutive years and sometimes look at the same topic, going back to reinvent and refresh older pieces. Books still have a high degree of credibility when being considered for events.

Generate leads and integrate

Integrated marketing communications and integrated lead generation content marketing requires more than content generation. It's a naturally integrated process involving everything from undertaking the research through to analysis, content development, PR, events, staff mobilization and measurement. The website's front end has free content supported by a lot of social distribution around that, but then there is a lead registration or capture model for the really juicy pieces of content that Kelly think people are willing to go through and sign up for. Marketo is the lead nurturing platform used which integrates nicely into Sales Force, with auto alerts sent to sales reps when qualified leads interact with specific content.

Action: leverage, repurpose and produce

The production process can be the lengthiest part of content management, particularly if running a properly structured survey with time allowed for testing the questionnaire, rolling it out/fieldwork, analysis, report presentation and the array of design and editing required to generate a suite of marketing content. Atomizing content means breaking it into different formats and/or tailoring reports into very specific regional or industry type reports (relatively easy to do once the survey questions have covered some regions and sectors). For example, a global survey can be split and sliced in many ways, such as gender, jobs and geography, so that tailored reports for engineers in Queensland, or creative services people in New York, etc can easily be generated.

Integrate, mobilize and distribute

The task was producing so much content around specifically defined keywords, with frequency, and circulating and distributing that content, both on Kelly's own channels (slide share and YouTube), plus mobilizing staff and partners. Kelly wanted many people from within the organization to have an external profile. They didn't just want it to be the top 10–20 employees, the same old people who have the senior titles. So the content management team (of two) fought very hard to get people right down the basic operational level involved in being part of this mission. Kelly now leverage their content via staff social networks supported by a huge amount of internal content plus internal webinars. The sales teams are always briefed and equipped so they can offer added-value content (eg sample reports, memes, infographics and even mini ebooks) at exhibitions/conferences/events. Popular posts are also promoted (they find it delivers a healthy ROI).

Hot new content is also regularly leveraged via PR (news releases). Most surveys make interesting news.

Apps

Kelly believe in apps as part of their content marketing and they cannot overestimate the value of such things. 'People like shiny stuff.' People internally get very excited about things that maybe aren't that strategic but that actually have some sort of cool factor that they can share with their network, so they talk about it with clients. That funky factor, that thing that's a bit lighthearted, or a bit cool or a bit new; having something like that every few months, or whenever it is justified, has really helped sustain interest, momentum and a sense of excitement that stuff is happening within Kelly.

Action: systematic content marketing

Kelly now has one of the fastest-growing groups on LinkedIn with 25,000 members and another 350–400 new members a week, because LinkedIn promotes it and because Kelly manages it diligently. It literally takes only 10 minutes a day to manage the LinkedIn platform and yet it generates more traffic than search. Kelly's proactive weekly e-mail to any member of this group brings people back and says 'there's

FIGURE 16.6   Variety of content created from one piece of research

SOURCE: Kelly HR

three hot new discussions here, can you help out these guys?'. Todd believes that Linkedin Company pages is becoming, and will become more of the hub for any content and will become a much bigger channel.

With research Kelly do a lot of annual, quarterly and monthly stuff. It's like a self-perpetuating cycle. It's very easy to calenderize, it's very easy to find a process around and it gives you that layer of those core things that can help set your content. Calendarization around that gives you some predictability throughout the year.

Kelly try to stream the same visual look across the family of content.

Control/measuring results

In addition to its 25,000 LinkedIn members, Todd Wheatland's tiny team's continual stream of great content is now reaching a tightly targeted global audience which has, in turn, lifted the monthly unique visitors by over 350 per cent within the first 12 months. So from Kelly's own channel through to their SlideShare channel, through to YouTube, through to other communities it's not uncommon for those 200 key-words to have multiple Kelly results on the first pages of search results. Todd is very clear about the tight connec-tion between content marketing, marketing objectives, bringing in leads and closing sales.

Ongoing results – the knock-on effect

Events companies now invite Kelly to attend for free because they have become an influential content compa-ny. Some companies invite Kelly back because of their blog power. Events organizers see Kelly's growing database, their growing audience, all of their content and often ask them if Kelly can come and cover an event. Maybe even host the event? Kelly then get given behind-the-scenes access to talk to the different speakers, interview them and run that through various blogs. They now increasingly make connection between topics, spokespeople, content assets and events – a self-fulfilling cycle. Kelly's successful content marketing has moved them out of being the vendor, the guys in the trade hall booths and up to being the guys doing a lot of hosting, but also a lot of keynote speaking around topics that are important to Kelly's target market.

Conclusion

So through their dedication to relevant quality content, repurposing and promoting in an integrated process, Kelly have created an ever-strengthening competitive advantage – which is rapidly becoming a sustainable competitive advantage.

CASE STUDY 16.2   Topline's advertising boosts Christmas promotion

Situational analysis

With over 150 retail stores in Ireland and Northern Ireland, Topline is Ireland's largest DIY/building materials buying group (retail and trade chain of stores).

Traditionally, Topline's digital tactics focused solely on Facebook competitions and campaigns using a mix of organic posts and paid advertising targeting a broad user base in Ireland. This organic social media promotion tactic mixed with paid traditional advertising by Topline had worked reasonably well. Previous Topline competitions were also promoted via Twitter with scheduled tweets and profile background imagery; however, it was difficult for Twitter followers to use the competition page in order to enter the competitions, especially on mobile devices. Campaigns were not cross-platform nor cross-device so a large percentage of potential customers were neglected.

As of October 2014 Topline's Facebook following was 11,000. Topline came to Dublin-based agency, Continuum, looking for assistance on a digital campaign strategy with a view to driving traffic to their website and improving brand engagement online. An advertising budget was made available for a specific online campaign.

Objectives

The Topline digital marketing objectives were as follows:

- Primary objective: improve customer data collection for future Topline communications.
- Secondary objective: improve brand engagement on social media.

- Tertiary objective: generate website traffic to the corporate Topline site.

Exact target numbers are not available.

Strategy

Topline came to Continuum with a Christmas-themed social media competition – '12 Stoves of Christmas' – consisting of a giveaway prize of one Topline stove product each day for 12 days. Topline required Continuum to assist in the implementation of their proposed strategy to achieve targets and maximize the potential results of the campaign. This strategy needed to include cross-platform and multi-device capabilities to reach all of Topline's target audience.

Tactics

Google AdWords

- Standard display/text adverts were created for appropriately researched strategic keywords and placement such as the keyword – 'Stanley Stoves' with placement on Elledecor.com and Housebeautiful.com.

- A re-marketing campaign targeted people who had recently visited the Topline site. This audience then received Topline ads when they landed on other sites. The remarketing AdWords campaign performed significantly better than the standard display advertising and text ads. Remarketing campaign had a cpc of 0.43c versus 0.80c for text ads and 0.98c for placement ads.

FIGURE 16.7   Topline ran a Christmas-themed giveaway social media competition

Facebook

- Pre-defined target audiences (describe profile) based on previous Topline campaigns. 1) Lookalike audience, and 2) Custom audience for interior design/diy interest targeting, were targeted via sponsored posts.

- A separate lookalike audience was also targeted by sponsored posts for the competition to entice new engagement. This campaign performed the best by far with a cost of 34c per follow compared to previous cpf of 42c per like of a custom audience.

- Any remaining budget for Facebook was used to boost the standard organic posts.

- Lookalike audiences help you reach people who are similar to your current customers.

- Custom audiences let you reach customers you already know with ads on Facebook.

Twitter

- Sponsored tweets were used to amplify posts.

Action

A third-party application, 'ShortStack' was selected, implemented and used to host the competition page and data collection. This app allowed Topline to create a landing page without any coding or development dependence, and collect the entrants' contact details for each of the 12 daily competitions seamlessly across all channels including the Topline website, Facebook page and Twitter profile. An opt-in to further marketing promotions 'tick-box' was included on the landing page and provided a post-campaign final opt-in rate of 83 per cent.

A two-week campaign calendar that outlined all deliverable elements of the campaign from the set-up of the

FIGURE 16.8   Topline's Christmas sales promotion appearing on Facebook

Topline
December 1, 2014 ·

The 12 Stoves of Christmas officially starts today! Today's lucky winner will win
this fabulous Waterford Stanley stove, and will be announced here tomorrow.
#12StovesOfChristmas Enter now: http://a.pgtb.me/MZv6jT

Like · Comment · Share ·   👍 1,225   💬 354   ↪ 677

competition page using ShortStack to the selection of
competition winners was created and used as a point of
reference throughout the campaign.

Control

The Topline '12 Stoves of Christmas' social media campaign
was a success surpassing expectations for social media
engagement, e-mail communication sign-up and website
traffic generation.

Both Topline and Continuum made daily checks of the
campaign. These checks resulted in tweaks to the advertising spend throughout the campaign based on best
performing ads.

1   Customer data collection for future communication:

- Total competition entrants = 19,313

- Total competition entrants after duplicate removal
  and unwanted countries = 18,000

FIGURE 16.9 The campaign calendar

Activity	21st	22nd	23rd	24th	25th	26th	27th	28th	29th	30th	1st	2nd	3rd	4th	5th	6th	7th	8th	9th	10th	11th	12th	13th	
Competition Page Set-up and Testing																								6
Competition Page LIVE																								1
Facebook Advertising Set-up																								4
Facebook Advertising LIVE																								2
Graphic Creation																								7.5
Teasing Posts																								0.5
Embeding Competition Page to Facebook																								1
Embeding Competition Page to Website																								2
Uploading Graphics to Channels																								7.5
Competition																								2.5
Winner Announcement and Facebook Post																								

- Final opt-in competition entrants = 15,003
- Opt-in rate = 83.4%

2 Brand engagement on social media (Dec 2013–Dec 2014):

- Facebook following December 2013 = circa 1,000
- Facebook following November 27th 2014 = 20,300
- Facebook Following December 13th 2014 = 35,454
- Growth over 16-day period = 72%
- Growth since this time last year = 3,440%

3 Increase in website traffic (Dec 2013–Dec 2014) compared to previous month:

- Overall up 47%.
- Social media traffic up 147%
- Organic traffic up 11%
- Referral traffic up 134%
- Direct traffic up 82%

Other:

The ShortStack app competition page received 45,000 page views.

FIGURE 16.10   Topline overall traffic

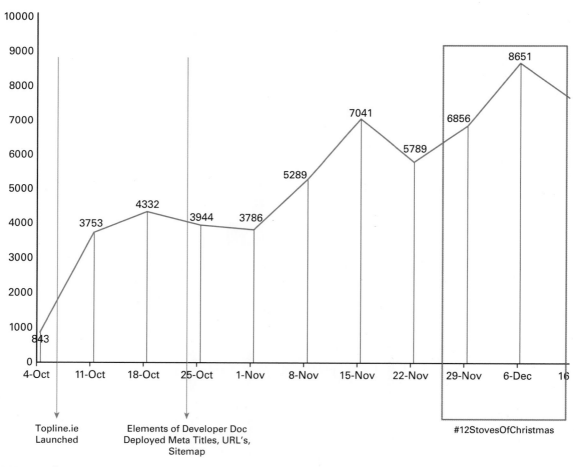

SOURCE: Topline

CASE STUDY 16.3   V&A activate young tech-savvys in collaborative digital art

Situation

The Victoria and Albert museum (the V&A) opened Decode: Digital Design Sensations as a special sales promotion. Decode showcased the latest developments in digital and interactive art and design from around the world. The V&A required an online and offline marketing plan to promote the exhibition/promotion over a four-month period.

Objectives

- To raise awareness of Decode: Digital Design Sensations at the V&A.
- To increase footfall and drive at least 40,000 visitors to the exhibition.
- To inspire people to get involved.
- To create a cultural buzz around digital art.

Strategy

The central aim was to activate a predominantly young, tech-savvy, male audience with a campaign idea that was in line with the core values inherent in digital art – openness, fluidity, collaboration and playfulness. The idea was to create a truly open-source participative campaign that would not just promote the exhibition but also enhance and extend it. By tapping into the natural creativity of its audience, the campaign would inspire and enlist them to help market and promote Decode through both online and offline channels.

Tactics

Karsten Schmidt, one of the world's most respected digital artists, worked with digital agency Saint to create a generative piece of art for exclusive use on the exhibition website. Schmidt's work was to be made open-source and available for 'recoding' (user modification). Recode Decode was born.

Via the Recode Decode microsite, visitors were invited to download, modify and submit their own creative interpretation of the work. These user-generated 'Recodes' were then showcased on the Decode website, and the best

'Recoded' works were used as part of the marketing and promotion of the exhibition across the London Underground and within online banner adverts.

In addition to this, Saint created an augmented reality (AR) platform for people to get an advanced look at Karsten Schmidt's work. The AR marker was included on all printed material and e-newsletters to encourage people to visit the website and find out about Recode Decode. The exhibition was also promoted via a dedicated Twitter hashtag discussion.

To ensure maximum exposure, the team worked with a third-party seeding agency to target online influencers within the world of digital art. They were enlisted to blog about and share Recode within their core networks. This created organic word-of-mouth growth. In addition, the V&A ran a bloggers' event giving them an exclusive preview of the exhibition.

Action: identifying opinion formers

Media partner Agenda 21 uses its own bespoke tool to identify opinion formers online. It tracks a number of related keywords within the blogosphere, eg 'digital', 'art', 'V&A' and 'museum', as well as the names of the artists, the names of the art on show, etc. Agenda 21 starts to follow bloggers who regularly post articles that feature one or more of these keywords, and it determines how big their blog audience is and how active (comments). With this information, Agenda 21 is able to identify who the real opinion formers are – the 100 bloggers it invited to attend the preview at the V&A, and the 300 bloggers it wanted to drive to the website.

Influencer engagement comprised two phases: 1) One hundred influencers in the London and Greater London area were identified and invited to a preview of the event in early December. This was to encourage excitement and coverage of the event within their online communities. 2) Three hundred influencers, including the hundred above, were invited to visit the Decode Recode site and to download the piece of code submitted by Karsten Schmidt for the chance to have their artwork displayed on the London Underground as part of the V&A's above-the-line promotional activity.

Control

Exhibition attendance completely exceeded the client's expectations, achieving 88,000 visits, more than double the original target. The Recode application was downloaded over 3,500 times in the first three months of the campaign, demonstrating an eagerness from the audience to get involved directly. Fifty-four 'Recoded' entries were chosen for display on the website, of which three were selected to be used to market the exhibition.

Social media successes included:

- 157 blog mentions;
- 69 news mentions;
- 942 tweets;
- 23 message board posts.

Men/women

Saint developed the project entirely in-house, using a core creative team (a creative director and creatives), a planner, an information architect, two designers, a symphony programmer, an action scripter, and a question-and-answer team for testing. Saint invited people to test, review and feed back on the various elements of the campaign (website usability, augmented reality performance, etc).

Money

The total cost for the campaign was £40,000, which included creative development, building, testing and all media costs (including printing).

Minutes

Saint pitched for the V&A work in August 2009. The website went live in October (four weeks' development), and the exhibition ran from November 2009 until April 2010.

CASE STUDY 16.4   Muzu.TV film soundtrack adds value and boosts engagement

Situation

Muzu.TV is a vast free online music video service that churns out videos by artist, random selection or jukebox (selected by others). It is fully social media enabled. Growth has come purely from social media, as it does not advertise. In fact, its success comes from a combination of factors, including always high-added-value events, and promotions (exclusive videos and competitions) for its stakeholders. Muzu.TV has been using win–win social media multiplier campaigns built around simple sales promotions concepts such as exclusive tickets to see artists perform in an intimate studio environment plus an exclusive video feed of the private gig for a national daily's website, in return for editorial coverage promoting the competition prize.

Objectives

Muzu.TV constantly seeks new sales promotion and PR concepts to raise its profile but also help bands boost their profile and fans get closer to the performer they love.

Strategy

The strategy was to create a new user-generated social media concept for movies that mashed music and video together in a unique manner, delivering huge added value for all stakeholders (musicians, songwriters, movie makers, Muzu.TV audiences and, last but not least, Muzu.TV), and creating a real soundtrack for a real movie. The winning track would be used in the movie. The process was:

1 Watch 10 clips from an independent movie (which is currently in the editing stage).
2 Select a scene from 10 scenes from the movie.
3 Write a song or select one from your own repertoire.
4 Attach the soundtrack to the movie clip.
5 Upload the song to a particular movie clip.

A new feature for the Muzu.TV music-loving audience was to see dramatic music clips. Movie makers benefited from the buzz built around a movie, through new ways to raise their profile. New ways to source a soundtrack for a movie would lead to financial savings. It was a new way to promote singer-songwriters.

Tactics

The concept was promoted through Muzu.TV, the usual social media channels, news releases and partners' social media channels and news releases. In addition, Muzu.TV invited songwriters (from a songwriters' database of 400,000). This created opportunities for unsigned musicians to get a position in the charts (with a track in the movie getting additional airtime and additional sales). Artists could also boost their own 'likers' and friends and generate traffic for their own websites.

Action

The judging criteria combined scores from social media popularity ratings and a panel of judges from the music and film industry, including the head of sync publishing at EMI and the lead actor/singer and guitarist from the Oscar-winning musical film *Once*.

Control

BuzzRadar monitored the social buzz (using its own proprietary tool originally created to measure Red Bull's social media performance).

The Buzz Chart measures the activity relating to a band across the internet and over a range of social media to work out the buzz around a band. This includes:

- the number of views on a page;
- the rating on the band page;
- the comments on the band page;
- tweets sent that mention your Twitter ID eg @yourband;
- page views on Myspace;
- number of plays on a Myspace music player;
- number of fans on Facebook;
- number of plays and shares a video has had on Facebook.

Note that number of views was an insufficient criterion, as some people write scripts that keep viewing the video without anyone watching it but keeping the 'views' score high. Hence a number of variables are factored in.

And the winner gets...

The real songwriter's prize was getting the music in a movie, and also getting a 'sync deal' (the artist gets a percentage royalty every time the movie is shown or played).

FIGURE 16.11   Muzu.TV focuses on music videos

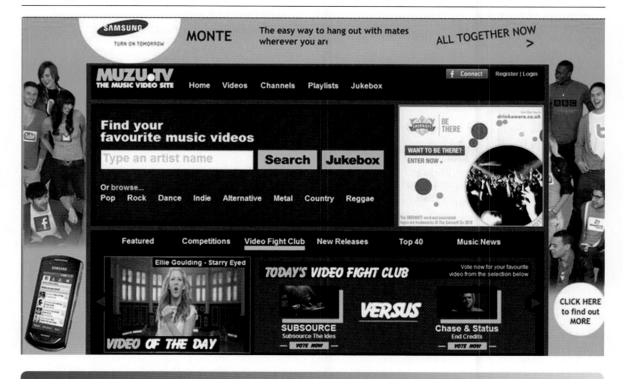

Advantages and disadvantages

Here are some of the advantages and disadvantages to consider when deciding whether to increase or reduce this communications tool.

Advantages

Sales promotions are useful when trying to close the sale or push the customer through the last stage of the buying process. They can also help to keep a relationship alive with existing customers by rewarding their loyalty. Sales promotions can support the brand and customer relations. They can be developed strategically to strengthen relationships over time. Increasingly content marketing is used in B2B marketing to capture e-mail addresses, develop leads and constantly nurture the customer relationship.

Disadvantages

Promotions require other tools to promote them, eg advertising, PR, direct mail or social media announcing the promotion. What can go wrong will go wrong, hence the need for insurance. Some promotions actually damage the brand. Promotions can be expensive to set up, procure, administer and wind down, although third parties are generally contracted to do so. On a CPT basis, promotions are expensive, although they can prove to be more cost-effective on a cost-per-order (CPO) basis. Content wars make content marketing a more challenging type of sales promotion.

Key points from Chapter 16

- Sales promotions can be used strategically rather than simply as short-term tactical tools.
- Sales promotions must integrate with other elements of the marketing mix.
- Attention to detail is required, as sales promotions can go horribly wrong.
- There is room for enhanced creativity, as social media has opened up a vast range of collaborative opportunities.

References and further reading

Bird, D (1990) No mileage in frequency marketing, *Marketing*, 10 October, p 12

Bird, J (1997) How to keep them faithful the world over, *Precision Marketing*, 26 May

Bond, C (1991) Marriages of some convenience, *Marketing*, 10 October, pp 23–26

Britt, B (1990) Coke's magic spells trouble, *Marketing*, 31 May

Burke, B (2013) The Gamification of Business, *Forbes*, 21 January

Castling, J (1989) Buying strategic sales promotion, *Sales Promotion*, July, p 11

Chapman, N (1985) Cadburys pays up in Typhoo game, *Marketing Week*, 17 May

Crabtree, S (2013) Worldwide, 13% of employees are engaged at work, Gallup, 8 Oct

Cummins, J (2003) *Sales Promotion: How to create and implement campaigns that really work*, 3rd edn, Kogan Page, London

Douglas, T (1987) *The Complete Guide to Advertising*, Pan Macmillan, London

Ehrenberg, A, Hammond, K and Goodheart, G (1991) *The After-Effects of Large Consumer Promotions*, London Business School, London

Farrell, J (1989) Which countries allow which promotions? *Marketing Week*, 16 June, pp 75–77

Grobel, W (2013) Marketing and insights practice manager, Deloitte, CIM Gamification webinar, July

Hollinger, P (1996) Electronic age raises ghost of Green Shield stamps, *Financial Times*, 9–10 November

Holloway, P (1989) Getting it right in the 90s, *Sales Promotion*, February, pp 23–24

Hyslop, R (1989) Round table discussion, *Sales Promotion*, July, p 14

Kotler, P (2000) *Marketing Management: Analysis, planning, implementation and control*, Millennium edn, Prentice Hall, Englewood Cliffs, NJ

Marketing Breakthroughs (1991) Polish give-aways struggle to reach target, December

Nielsen (2015) Trade promotion doesn't have to be a guessing game, Neilsen's Trade Promotions Performance Visualisation report

Pelling, N http://www.nickpelling.com/

Schaefer, M (2014) Content Shock: Why content marketing is not a sustainable strategy, *Businessgrow*, 6 January

Schnaars, S (2013) General manager EMEA, Badgeville, CIM Gamification webinar July 2013

Smith, D (2008) Google, 10 years in: Big, friendly giant or a greedy Goliath? *Observer*, 17 August

Smith, PR and Chaffey, D (2001) *eMarketing eXcellence*, 2nd edn, Butterworth-Heinemann, Oxford

Smith, PR (2013) Gamification, the good, the bad and the ugly, www.PRSmith.org/blog, 9 Oct

Smith, PR (2014) Customer retention isn't boring, here's wow, www.PRSmith.org/blog, 22 August

Yardy, R (2015) Your parents were wrong! You were not 'wasting your time' playing computer games' Digital Doughnut, 15 July

Zeisser, M (2010) Unlocking the elusive potential of social networks, *McKinsey Quarterly*, member edn, June

Further information

British Promotional Merchandise Association (BPMA)
52–53 Russell Square
London WC1B 4HP
Tel: +44 (0)20 7631 6960
Fax: +44 (0)20 7631 6944
www.bpma.co.uk

Content Marketing Institute
Z Squared Media LLC
HQ 17040 Amber Drive
Cleveland
OH 441111
USA
www.contentmarketinginstitute.com

Institute of Promotional Marketing Ltd (ISPM)
70 Margaret Street
London W1W 8SS
Tel: +44 (0)20 7291 7730
Fax: +44 (0)20 7291 7731
www.theipm.org.uk

Marketing Agencies Association (MAA)
4 New Quebec Street
London W1H 7RF
Tel: +44 (0)20 7535 3550
Fax: +44 (0)20 7535 3551
http://www.marketingagencies.org.uk/

Promota UK (Promotional Merchandise Trade Association)
Concorde House
Trinity Park
Solihull
Birmingham B37 7UQ
Tel: +44 (0)8453 714335
Fax: +44 (0)8453 714336
www.promota.co.uk

17
Direct mail (including e-mail)

LEARNING OBJECTIVES

By the end of this chapter you will be able to:

- Be aware of the changing trends in direct mail and opt-in e-mail
- Integrate direct mail (snail mail) and opt-in e-mail into both acquisition and retention communications campaigns
- Understand the advantages and disadvantages of both types of direct mail compared to other communications tools
- Appreciate the importance of integrating all direct mail as part of an integrated communications campaign or part of a contact strategy

Introduction to direct mail (and e-mail)   460

Tailor-made technology   460

Profiling technology   460

The list explosion   461

Integrated systems   462

Cost-effectiveness per order   462

Opt-in e-mail and mobile messaging   463

Success factors   464

Customer retention   465

Customer acquisition   465

Mobile messaging   466

Managing a direct mail campaign   467

Situation analysis   467

Objectives   467

Strategy   467

Tactics: creative mailings   467

Action   468

Control   469

Advantages and disadvantages   479

Advantages   479

Disadvantages   479

Key points from Chapter 17   479

References and further reading   480

Further information   480

Introduction to direct mail (and e-mail)

Direct marketing includes any marketing communications tools that interact directly with customers. This includes direct response advertising, telemarketing and direct mail (including e-mail). This chapter explores direct mail and opt-in e-mail. See Chapter 3 for more on contact strategies, data mining and profiling.

The growth of direct marketing, in general, and direct mail, in particular, has been fuelled by:

- big data;
- tailor-made technology;
- profiling technology;
- the list explosion;
- integrated marketing;
- the constant search for cost-effectiveness.

Tailor-made technology

Online newsletters and e-mails as well as offline newsletters, newspapers and letters can be personalized by name and also by relevant needs, eg many years ago the US *Farmer's Journal*'s 825,000 circulation received a tailor-made magazine with a minimum of 2,000 and a maximum of 8,896 different editions per issue. Essentially, the pig farmer's edition

FIGURE 17.1   Any product, service or communication can be tailored specifically for a customer

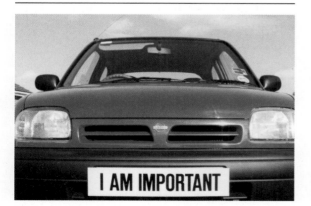

would not carry features or advertisements about cereal farming, etc. Farmers prefer their magazine to carry relevant material. The advertisers like it, because it offers better targeting. The magazine saves money on paper and post. The environmentalists might prefer it too. Personalized interactive TV programmes are already running in Spain and France, while online we have tailored newsletters, personalized ad tailored e-mails, messages and even tailored individualized mobile screen ads (see location-based ads in Chapter 13).

Profiling technology

Basic technology allows different mailing lists and databases to be added together and even superimposed on each other. Lists can be merged, and any overlap or duplications can be deduplicated ('deduped'). Geodemographics mix geographical location, type of neighbourhood and demographic data such as age, income and family life cycle. Other fields or layers of data can be added (see Chapter 13 also). Everyone fits into a cluster; from the keying of an address the database identifies the neighbourhood's cluster type or profile. This geodemographic typecasting uses shorthand names to identify cluster types. For example, a US database company classifies people with mature families living in affluent suburbs as 'pools and patios', whereas poorer rural areas are called 'shotguns and pickups'. People living there may have aspirations to move towards 'golf clubs and Volvos'. In the B2B space social media comments, profiles can be added to profiles.

It is said that demographics say 'You are where you live' (meaning your neighbourhood is a good indicator of your lifestyle and the kinds of products you are likely to buy) and psychographic databases say 'You are what you do' (meaning your behaviour patterns and buying preferences can be estimated from collected data on your (or similar people's) lifestyle, eg whether you are likely to own an iPod). In the UK, geodemographic packages such as ACORN, Pinpoint, Mosaic and SuperProfile are easily cross-referenced with media usage, product usage and lifestyle statements. Contextual layers can be added according to online behaviour on a specific site (see Chapter 11 on digital body language for more and Chapter 13 for more on 'you are where you are and where you have been' in 'Location-based ads').

They know you better than you do

An investigative journalist decided that he wanted to find out about himself, as he was soon moving to south-east San Francisco. Having keyed in his new address, he was told by the database company that he was classified as a 'young influential'. He was moving into a 'thirty-something childbearing neighbourhood'. It also told him that 'he may still be in a town house or a row house and may not have graduated to the detached single home but they were definitely starting to have children, making the transition from a couple-orientated lifestyle to a family-orientated lifestyle'. Furthermore, the 'young influentials' typically were aged 20–35, had a median income of $39,500, enjoyed jogging, travelling, new wave music and investing, read magazines like *Rudder*, *Scientific American* and *Town and Country*, and liked to eat yogurt, wholemeal bread and Mexican food and drink low-fat milk. This profile almost exactly matched the journalist's profile. That was over 20 years ago. Contextual advertising (Chapter 13) is even more interesting.

What profile do you want to target?

Here is a small selection of lists that could be relevant for the three types of target customers shown below:

- *Prominent people:* Rolls-Royce, Lamborghini and Jaguar owners, UK millionaires, rich ladies, tennis court owners, private plane owners, racehorse owners, greyhound owners and even cat owners.

- *Entertainment seekers:* Theatre goers, Shaftesbury Theatre goers, club goers.

- *Improvers:* Named clergy, buyers of self-improvement books, house improvers, house movers, and even a list of owners of Black & Decker drills.

- *Frequent flyers from London to Glasgow* identified via the following profile: mobile device in Heathrow area, switched off for 50 mins and appears back in use in Glasgow airport.

There are many other unusual lists that can fit target customer profiles like a glove (the skill is matching the two): people who have aerial photos of their homes, personalized car number plate owners, buyers of military prints and memorabilia, tall ladies, people in prisons, borstals and detention centres, women executives, hypochondriacs, management consultants, librarians, educational children's book buyers and so on. And, of course, the electoral roll is also publicly available.

The list explosion

The fourth factor fuelling the growth of direct marketing is the proliferation of lists or databases available both online and offline. The only restriction is imagination, or one's ability to define a target market or customer profile in a range of different ways. For example, home decorators could be redefined as 'home movers'. The million or so UK home movers could then be reduced to those moving into certain geographic locations or even neighbourhood areas, which might indicate their propensity to undertake the decorating themselves (as opposed to hiring someone to do it for them). See Chapter 16 and how layering data from ACORN in a geofenced area (specific area) can identify a much bigger market for mortgages (note this is aggregate data as opposed to individual data on a list/database).

A list, or a section of the list, can be hired or bought, and tested and/or refined by using certain software packages. It is important to select and check lists carefully, since the quality of many of the UK's 'cold' lists can be a problem, although data integrity is now much improved, especially with newer lifestyle databases.

The diversity of the lists available is intriguing and sometimes bewildering. The lists range from 'cynical humorous intellectuals' (18,000 *Punch* magazine subscribers) to 'slimming pill buyers who read the *Sun*' to 'young mothers' to 'fork-lift truck buyers'. Just about anything can be targeted. Even lists of 'right-wing, money-orientated gamblers who are influenced by advertising, react to new ideas and have disposable income' can be created (eg the original list of 3 million British Gas shareholders was available from the British Investor Database).

It is worth phoning list brokers and list owners to request a catalogue of lists (consumer or business-to-business) and spending an hour browsing. It is also worth exploring new data companies that deliver lists like 'attendees at conference X interested in Y' from crowdVu.com (see Chapter 12). A compiled list is collected from public records, directories, trade show registrations, etc. According to *World List News*, a mail-responsive list can produce a 300 per cent increase in response over a compiled list. The best list is an organization's own house list of customers, enquirers, visitors, employees, shareholders, etc. Make sure you invest resources to maintain this asset.

Integrated systems

Direct marketing can, and should, integrate with other communications tools. It can link different direct marketing tools to create a more cost-effective method of marketing communications. Depending on the quality of the lead, it can be followed up by mailing a brochure, or hot prospects might be telephoned to set up an appointment or to invite them to an event.

The lead generation might be created in the first place by a direct mail offer that invites readers, viewers or listeners to send in for a free gift (perhaps some high quality marketing content). Some marketers maintain that 45 per cent of business enquirers will buy within 12 months. The challenge then lies in identifying the hottest prospects and directing the sales force to them, and then following up the other leads over time. Note: RFM (recency, frequency and monetary spend) can be used to target the hotter prospects on your own database.

Identifying the hottest prospects or 'screening' can be carried out by following up with an outbound telephone interview to determine the prospect's status. Alternatively, the analysis can be carried out directly from the coupon if it was designed to capture the required detailed information. The outbound phone call can screen and ultimately fix an appointment for the sales or progress to the next appropriate stage in the buying process. Alternatively, an inbound phone catering for an 0800 or freephone number can accommodate enquiries generated from either a direct response advertisement or a mailshot.

This is only the start. **After the initial sale, database marketing can help to keep in touch with customers as they move towards a repeat purchase.** Conservative estimates suggest that it is six times easier to sell to an existing customer than to a new one.

Cost-effectiveness per order

Ideally, costs should be measured against results, not simply outputs. The cost of testing say a telesales campaign (1,000 names at roughly £10 per call) might be, say, £10,000, but the result might be 2 per cent success or 20 new customers. The cost per order or cost per customer in this case is calculated as £500. How does this compare with the current cost per new customer generated by other marketing techniques, such as direct mail, exhibitions, advertising or even the field sales team? The results, and costs, may vary if, for example, the telesales team is focused only on appointment setting and the field sales team handles the rest. This may result in, say, 15 per cent appointments (150); the sales team then convert, say, 30 per cent of these into 45 new customers. The telesales cost of £10,000 is added to the field sales cost of, say, £8,550. Then £18,550 divided by 45 gives a cost per new customer of £412. Alternatively, say a mailshot to 1,000 people costs £2,000 and 1 per cent convert to a sale, that cost per order is only £200 (£2,000 cost divided by 10 orders).

The lifetime value of the customer can then be calculated by multiplying the average value of expected orders per annum by the number of years the customer will exist. The cost per order of subsequent orders will be significantly less than the cost of the initial order because, as already mentioned, estimates suggest that it is at least six times cheaper and easier to sell to an existing customer than to a prospect.

Telesales can be used to support a sales force by servicing accounts over the phone instead of having a sales rep visit every month. Telesales can also be used to generate or even screen leads. At a cost of anywhere between £7 and £70 per appointment set up, a telesales campaign can release the salesperson from prospecting and even administration into doing what most reps are best at, face-to-face selling. Some estimates show that salespeople spend less than 20 per cent of their time actually selling; the rest is prospecting, travelling, form filling, etc. The average cost of a single sales visit might be, say, £200. This can be reduced if salespeople are released from other duties and can therefore make more visits. Some telesales campaigns link in with computer models that select the optimum call plan to minimize travel time. All of these activities, including order fulfilment, can be handled by an outside agency if needed.

Not surprisingly, TV ads and mailshots can link together both activity-wise and image-wise; awareness for an airline's TV ad four months after screening was 50 per cent higher among those who had received a mailshot that featured a scene from the TV ad than among a similar panel who had not received the mailshot. The database can also be used to research the impact of, say, a TV advertisement or a sponsorship package among different types of audiences.

A challenging data-mining brief

Find meaningful patterns in the data, target potential consumers, retain existing consumers more effectively, predict who would buy certain products, anticipate the volume of high sales of specific high-margin products and discover and capitalize on opportunities for cross-couponing.

Opt-in e-mail and mobile messaging

Opt-in e-mail is a useful online communications tool primarily for customer retention programmes rather than customer acquisition programmes. Despite this (and falling e-mail open rates), some organizations buy huge databases of 'opt-in' e-mail addresses, personalize a relevant offer and, despite the very small percentage response rates, still find it works for mass markets. However, opt-in e-mail campaigns are best used as part of a contact strategy for prospects who have enquired or customers who have bought. The contact strategy can include

e-mail, snail mail, telemarketing and personal visits. The mailings (online or offline) can be short messages or letters, newsletters, vouchers or full brochures (or links to a website section: video, eBook or web pages).

Although it is similar to direct mail, e-mail is most widely used for direct response (as opposed to brand building or brand awareness), although e-newsletters in particular can also support brand awareness. E-mail enables a targeted, and personalized, message to be pushed out to customers to inform and remind. They will, at worst, see the subject line within their e-mail inbox, even if only to delete it. Contrast this with the web, which is a pull medium where customers will visit your site only if there is a reason to do so. Nevertheless, unsolicited e-mail (spam) is illegal in B2C markets and damaging to a brand (see Chapter 11 for the regulations and laws).

Opt-in is the key to successful e-mail marketing, whether B2C or B2B. E-mailing only those who have opted in is simply best practice. Before starting an e-mail dialogue with customers, companies must ask them to provide their e-mail addresses. Privacy law in many countries requires customers to proactively opt in by checking a box (showing consent in some way). In the UK it is all right to e-mail prospects either if they have been customers or if they have made enquiries and have given their e-mail address. With every subsequent e-mail, however, marketers must offer customers an easy way to opt out at any time.

Opt-in e-mail

'E-mail is an effective push online communications method. It is essential that e-mail is opt-in, otherwise it is illegal spam. Consider options for customer acquisition including cold e-mail, co-branded e-mails and placements in third-party e-mails. For house list e-mails, experiment with achieving the correct frequency, or give customers the choice. Consider automated event-triggered e-mails. Work hard on e-mail design and maintaining up-to-date lists. Stay within the law.'
Chaffey and Smith (2013)

Success factors

Regardless of the type of e-mail, the direct mail variables have an even bigger impact on response rates. Once again, relevancy prevails.

Offer and creative execution

If the offer, or fundamental proposition, is not relevant it will not get a response. If the subject line in the e-mail is not deemed relevant it will not even get opened. Continual customer research helps to keep offers relevant. The creative execution can vary. The key part is, as mentioned, a subject head-line that catches attention and interest. Once opened, the e-mail has to be very short (it should have links to further information such as see, try and buy. Layout, colour and image need careful attention, as they affect the perception of the crea-tive message, which itself has to be carefully crafted (in fact usually a series of messages has to be crafted as part of a contact strategy). **The incentive should become a strong call to action:** to act now and not wait until later. Split testing and multivariate testing help identify what works best before rolling out the mailing. One final check for branding is to ask: 'Are the creative content and copy consistent with the brand?'

The e-mail copy should:

- grab attention in the subject line and in the first sentence;
- be brief and relevant to the target segment (use links to the website for more information);
- be personalized – not 'Dear Valued Customer' but 'Dear Ms Smith';
- have a clear call to action at the start and end of the message;
- provide an opt-out or 'unsubscribe' option by law;
- contain full address and contact details;
- operate within legal and ethical constraints for a country;
- send out multipart or MIME messages that display HTML or text according to the capability of the recipients' e-mail readers. Offer a choice of HTML or text to match users' preferences.

Timing

E-mail response rates vary according to the time of day, week, month and year. External events also affect response rates, as themes can match topical events. Some organizations find that Friday after-noon e-mails don't work whereas Tuesday mornings do. Marketers now note what particular time works best to get maximum open rates. And, as with any mailing online or offline, split tests before the campaign roll-out help, and careful monitoring thereafter is required.

Timing a sequence of e-mails

MAD (**www.mad.co.uk**) is a marketing-specific portal accessed through online subscriptions. It offers a trial one-month subscription to its service. During this period, a series of e-mails is used to help convert the prospect to a full subscription. E-mails are sent out at approximately 3, 10, 25 and 28 days to encourage a subscription before the trial lapses.

Targeting

In list or database selection, the variable that has the highest impact on success or failure is targeting: matching the right profile of customer with the right offer. The higher the relevance to the target market, the higher the response. This can be continually refined, as customer profiling can be continually improved as more data are captured over time and preferences are identified.

Response mechanism

Have a relevant landing page (or microsite). Do not send customers to a general home page where they have to start searching for the e-mail offer. Some e-mails when clicked through for the offer present an online form to profile the customer. Simplifying the form can have a dramatic impact, as can varying landing pages to boost sales.

Testing: split testing and multivariate testing

A/B testing allows marketers to test different headlines, different offers, different photographs and even different background colours to see which perform the best. From the creation of two versions of one variable (say two different headlines), A/B tests reveal which works better. Multivariate testing is a process that tests more than one component, effectively testing numerous A/B tests at the same time. By analysing different test results, marketers can spot which variables consistently deliver the best results.

> ### Test all devices!
>
> 'For example, mobile devices are increasingly used for e-mail access. Marketers need to adapt and tailor their message and interaction to take into account pixel width, image-to-text ratio, the placement of the offer in the message, call-to-action buttons and subject line, as well as the content and mobile-friendly links.'
>
> Hilpern (2013)

Customer retention

As mentioned, e-mail marketing is best for customer retention, as part of an ongoing contact strategy to keep in touch with customers and deliver them relevant updates, offers, tips and advice. It also provides a response mechanism for customers to air their views and give valuable feedback. Every contact creates an opportunity to continuously add data to the customer profile. It is therefore important that marketing integrates with the rest of the organization's operations, particularly if there was a sudden surge in responses but there was no system in place to manage responses (whether asking a question, making a complaint, looking for advice or trying to buy the product or service). Any glitches in the system can damage the customer relations that have been built up over time. **Well-managed systems test campaigns before roll-out and build in**

the facility of continual customer profiling to identify which customers are likely to want which products or services. (See the grandfather clock story in Chapter 3 on CRM, 'Catch the at-risk customer defectors', p. 82.)

Customer acquisition

For those companies that use opt-in e-mail for customer acquisition, there are three main options for customer acquisition programmes as highlighted in *Emarketing Excellence* (Chaffey and Smith, 2013):

- *Cold e-mail campaign.* In this case, the recipient receives an opt-in e-mail from an organization that has rented an e-mail list from a consumer e-mail list provider such as Experian, Nielsen, Claritas or a business e-mail list provider such as Mardev, trade publishers, event companies, or data companies like crowdvu. Although the recipients have agreed to receive offers by e-mail, the e-mail is effectively cold. For example, a credit card provider could send a cold e-mail to a list member who is not currently their member. It is important to use some form of 'statement of origination', as otherwise the message may be considered spam. Cold e-mails, unsurprisingly, tend to have a higher cost per acquisition (CPA) than other forms of online marketing, but different lists should still be evaluated.

- *Co-branded e-mail.* Here, recipients receive an e-mail with an offer from a company with which they have a reasonably strong affinity. For example, the same credit card company could partner with a mobile service provider such as Vodafone and send out the offer to their customers who have opted in to receive e-mails from third parties. Although this can be considered a form of cold e-mail, it is warmer, since there is a stronger relationship with one of the brands, and the subject line and creative will refer to both brands. Co-branded e-mails tend to be more responsive than cold e-mails to rented lists, since the relationship exists and fewer offers tend to be given.

- *Third-party e-newsletter.* In this visitor acquisition option, a company publicizes itself in a third-party e-newsletter. This could be in the form of an ad, sponsorship or PR (editorial) that links through to a destination site. These placements may be set up as part of an interactive advertising ad buy, since many e-newsletters also have permanent versions on the website. Since e-newsletter recipients tend to engage with them by scanning the headlines or reading them if they have time, e-newsletter placements can be relatively cost-effective.

Mobile messaging

Whether text messages, vouchers, downloadable podcasts, video clips or photos, mobile messaging is going to get bigger (location-based advertising is covered in Chapter 13). Suffice to say here that special offers made only to the relevant target market as they pass by a relevant venue will work, at least in the short term. Longer-term success will be determined by how well the industry regulates itself and the need for privacy (which is an issue that will continue to grow in importance also). If too many location-based mobile messages appear and clutter inboxes, customers will bar such messages and may also take legal action.

E-marketing best practice checklist – practical tips for e-mail marketing

E-mail marketing brings its own peculiar set of challenges that need to be managed. Your e-mail programme will fail if you are not managing these issues adequately:

- *Deliverability.* All e-mails are not delivered in the same way through different internet service providers (ISPs), corporate firewalls and webmail systems. Make sure you check your deliverability into the inbox using e-mail tools. Your carefully crafted e-mail may be classified as SPAM (1) due to use of spam words within the e-mail subject or body (use the content checker/test to see whether your copy is classified as SPAM) or (2) if the reputation of your e-mail sender is poor due to complaints or the broadcast characteristics are consistent with spam

(high volumes, sent rapidly). Check your reputation using SenderScore (**https://www.senderscore.org/**). The better your reputation then the less likely you are to be blocked for using copy such as 'free' or 'limited offer' which have proven effectiveness.

- *Renderability* refers to the difficulty of displaying the e-mail message as intended within the inbox of different e-mail reading systems. If the e-mail is all image-based, the images are not always displayed in the e-mail (an anti-spam measure). The e-mail will be meaningless unless it is has a powerful subject line. Response rate will fall. Best practice is to ensure the body copy gets your message (and CTAs) across even when images are blocked. Alternative text (tags behind the images) can also highlight offers and what the e-mail is about. An additional problem is that different e-mail readers display e-mails slightly differently, so they need to be coded and tested to look their best across different e-mail readers, which are even less standardized than different web browsers!

- *E-mail response decay.* E-mail recipients are most responsive when they first subscribe. It is difficult to keep them engaged. A carefully planned welcome strategy will include a series of pre-prepared e-mails with a variety of relevant messages, coupons, gifts and news, scheduled to be sent out over a period of weeks and months. Response will also affect which e-mail gets sent (see PayPal case study at the end of this chapter).

- *Communications preferences.* Recipients will have different preferences for e-mail offers, content and frequency which affect engagement and response. Some list members will naturally prefer more frequent e-mails and others prefer once a month. These can be managed through communications preferences.

- *Resource intensive.* Although e-mail offers great opportunities for targeting, personalization and more frequent communications, additional people and technology resources are required to overcome issues such as testing, deliverability and renderability. Having said that, most e-mail services like Mailchimp include deliverability and renderability testing. In addition, marketing automation systems and rules can be set up to link e-mails with click behaviour (whether click behaviour on a website or with an e-mail – opening it and/or clicking a link).

Source: Chaffey and Smith (2013)

Rain-triggered e-mails

'In the United States, bowling company AMF works with engagement marketing specialist, Silverpop, to take advantage of sudden changes of weather. Live weather feeds are used to trigger e-mails. So if rain is forecast for the weekend, e-mails are sent out to opted-in bowlers on AMF's database, offering discounts on and vouchers for the days in question. By making it clear that rain is likely and outdoor activities won't be as much fun, AMF has been able to boost participation and revenue.

Silverpop also works with Air New Zealand, putting live weather feeds into travel confirmation e-mails. Suggested activities for travellers to undertake once they reach their destination, provided by the airline's partner's, are tailored depending on the predicted weather conditions.'

Gray (2011)

Managing a direct mail campaign

Whether an organization is planning an advertising campaign or a direct mail campaign, a similarly disciplined approach should be taken, ie researching the situation, message development (creative mailing), media planning (list selection and timing), testing and monitoring, etc.

A direct mail campaign can be planned in the same way as an advertising campaign, ie by using SOSTAC® + 3Ms (see Chapter 10). However, six factors – timing, list selection, creative mailings, budgeting, operational implications and testing –

will be examined in more detail using the SOSTAC® structure (**www.PRSmith.org/SOSTAC**).

Situation analysis

The usual product interrogation, trend identification and soliciting customer feedback help build a bigger picture as to where the brand is.

Objectives

Crystal-clear objectives can eventually be broken down to ensure that everyone knows where the brand is going. Ideally, marketing communications objectives should be numerical for sales, enquiries and even brand awareness.

Strategy

Use STP (from the TOPPP SITE components of strategy discussed in Chapter 10). Segmentation creates customer profiles from the database (or just select profiles from a mailing list). Target or select the best profiles. Positioning ensures the message is right. Is there a marketing automation process (or manual), are there any partnerships (see Citroën's clever partnership with ASOS in Chapter 15), a sequence of e-mails? How does the data integrate with your main database? Any other tactical tools used to support the e-mail campaign (see PayPal case at the end of this chapter).

Remember list selection is the most important stage in the whole direct marketing process. Sixty per cent of any project's time should be spent on list selection. 'There's no point fishing in the pool if the pool ain't got any fish.' See 'Action' section for a 'list-buying checklist'.

Tactics: creative mailings

Opportunities for creativity abound. Most mail competes with bills and statements. Many of the top creative people still feel television advertising is more glamorous, so perhaps most mailings are restrained either by the people who create them or by the managers who commission them. Here are some odd exceptions:

● A plastic green cucumber was mailed by the Direct Mail Sales Bureau to all UK media buyers to raise awareness of the direct mail option.

● The Prince's Trust, when targeting company chairmen, mailed a box containing a ceramic bowl created by one of the businesses the Trust had supported (the bowl provided a gift for the chairmen's secretaries, to encourage them to pass on the pack; it also brought the achievements of the Trust to life for the chairmen).

● A briefcase was mailed to car distributors. When opened, the briefcase resembled a car dashboard complete with audio system and car phone. The recipient inserted a CD and lifted the phone to hear a sales pitch about why that particular car phone was outstanding. The briefcase further doubled as a point-of-sale item for the distributor.

● The mailing piece and the incentive can affect the budget significantly. Not all creative mailings need anything other than a few clever words. One recent mailing simply said 'Good morning'. This generated a lot of interest, anticipation and eagerness to get the next mailing in the sequence.

Action

List buying/hiring

Here are some questions that should be asked before using a list:

● Where do the names come from (eg compiled, previous mail responsive, subscription lists, etc)?

● When was the list built?

● How often is it cleaned (updated)? Is it Mailing Preference Service (MPS) cleaned?

● When was the list last used (and by whom) and what was the percentage of gone-aways (redundant names or addresses that the post office return to the sender)? Are there any known results or any references from past users?

● What is the rebate per gone-away that is returned to the list owner for future cleaning?

● What proportion of the target's total universe does the list represent, eg does the 1 million list of home movers represent all the home movers, or half, or what?

● What selections are available (eg geographic split, job title, etc)? Are there any additional costs?

● What net names percentage is quoted (ie net usable names after deduping with other lists)?

● Are there any rental restrictions (minimum quantities, competitive products subject to the list owner's approval, etc)?

● Assuming the list has an appropriate profile (similar to your specified target market), clarify whether:

  – it has named individuals as opposed to job titles or 'the occupier';

  – it is in an appropriate format, ie labels, disk, etc; if disk, check that the disk format suits the letter shop's requirements;

  – it is postcoded (for post office mailsort discounts).

● How much does it cost? What is the lead time from order to delivery?

If the list is hired, permission is usually given for one use only. Sleeper names are planted in the list to ensure that it is not used more than once (the sleepers immediately notify the list owner if they receive two mailings). Hiring charges vary from £50 to £350 per thousand. Many lists are not available for purchase, but those that are available are often priced at least four times higher than the rental price.

Integrated systems

If carefully thought out, the operational requirements clarify how the campaign will actually work. For example, what happens to the information that is collected during a telephone conversation? How do the sales representatives' diaries get updated, and who monitors their availability? Research by Euro RSCG Direct found 'an irresponsible use of response-handling mechanisms', with only a 70 per cent chance of respondents receiving information. The majority of this 70 per cent were never contacted again. Only 5 per cent ever received a follow-up telephone call. Is there a plan or system that ensures follow-up?

Automation can deliver both cost savings and increased effectiveness of marketing and sales follow-through. Hybrid systems help salespeople by reminding them which customers need attention this month, next month and so on. Enquiries generated through an array of marketing efforts are all dealt with (a brochure is dispatched along with a letter; telesales follow up for an appointment; an appointment is made for the salesperson). Nothing slips through the system. No enquiries are lost. All are followed up. The system has to accommodate returned goods and cancelled orders. Up-front investment in an integrated system is falling as more and more sales-tracking software packages come on to the marketplace.

Direct mail – a strain on your office?

'Even if the response is fairly modest it can still be a strain on your office resources. Could your telephone system handle thousands of calls in an hour? Could your staff still treat customers with enthusiasm at the end of a whole day of frantic answering? Do you have space for sackfuls of mail? Do you have time to answer every reply quickly? If not, a specialist fulfilment company can help.'

Royal Mail (2001)

Timing

The faster you need something done the more it will cost and the more likely there will be mistakes. Deciding whether the campaign should be multi-stage (generate enquiries, screening, follow-up phone calls and sales visits, etc) or single-stage (straight order), cross-platform or single media, and so on, is arguably less important than determining strategically how each mailing forms part of an overall communications programme that develops a cumulative effect.

One-off large mailings should gradually be replaced by smaller, more frequent mailings as the database identifies what is needed by whom and when. Many direct mail agencies can develop a campaign in four to six weeks, but ideally the campaign should be researched and planned strategically, and with a greater emphasis on creativity, to achieve 'cut-through'.

Timing also refers to identifying when a target market buys and how often. Markets are constantly moving. Buyers drift in and out at different stages. Some markets are seasonal, and others again have peaks and troughs on different days of the week.

Are target respondents more receptive to a mailshot that lands on a Friday morning or a Monday morning?

The development and scheduling of the campaign are shown in Figure 17.2. Essentially they follow the normal campaign development sequence: brief, concept development, research artwork, production and roll-out (note that research can be supplemented by continual testing).

As in an advertising campaign, a creative brief is followed by concepts that are subsequently approved, amended, researched and eventually developed into final copy and design. This is turned into artwork that is checked, proofed and eventually turned into final approved artwork that goes to the printer. Prior to this (or sometimes simultaneously) a list brief is agreed. This defines the target market. Lists are carefully researched and checked.

A list proposal is subsequently approved for ordering (purchase or hire). The letter shop puts the required letter into the system ready for laser printing on to personalized letters. Proof letters are checked and approved while the lists are prepared, merged and purged (duplicate names withdrawn). The printer dispatches the brochure to the letter shop, which then presses the button. The letters are lasered, folded, collated and inserted with the brochure or mailing piece into lasered (or window) envelopes (sometimes pre-printed with teaser messages or images) and posted. Then a dreadful quietness descends as the bags of mail are driven off into the sunset and the wait begins. Pre-mailshot tension can run riot, with nightmares about postal strikes, redundant lists, a printing error, a wrong expiry date or, worse still, a nil response level.

Good planning ensures that the best lists are used (perhaps based on test results), print, proofs, dates, etc are checked, and acceptable results are projected. Even in a situation where a lot of variables are unknown, careful planning can reduce the chance of failure.

Control

Budgeting 'money'

One way of budgeting is by asking: '**How much can the organization afford to spend to recruit a new customer?** How much is a new customer worth or what is the allowable cost per customer? What is the customer's lifetime value?' Then multiply this

FIGURE 17.2   Example of a mailing schedule

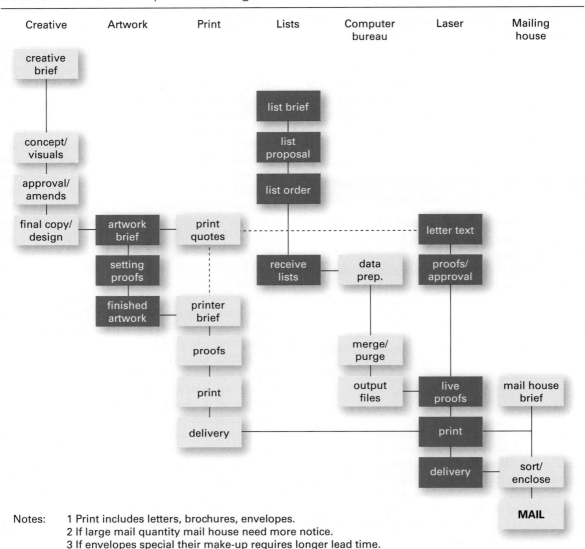

Notes: 1 Print includes letters, brochures, envelopes.
2 If large mail quantity mail house need more notice.
3 If envelopes special their make-up requires longer lead time.

SOURCE: Institute of Direct Marketing

by the number of customers required and, bingo, a budget emerges. Another way to build a budget or at least a ballpark cost figure is to calculate 50p per shot. Thus if an organization is running a 20,000 mailshot, then ballpark costs to cover everything (design, artwork, print, list, letter shop, insertion or collation incentive, envelope and postage) would be £10,000; a 500,000 mailshot would enjoy economies of scale and cost less than £250,000.

Cost per response and cost per order give the bottom line of success or failure. Percentage response levels vary from 0.5 per cent to 5 per cent, although there are many examples now of much higher rates – as high as 60 per cent – especially when targeting existing customers with strong creative combined with highly relevant incentives. (Note that enquiries, as opposed to orders, are easier to get and therefore pull higher response levels.)

How much would you spend on winning a customer? What kind of incentive would you offer a customer to take action and place an order? Here are a few examples: $50 Amazon voucher; Alliance & Leicester (bank) £50 (to open an account); Virgin, £400 (free laptop to selected customers); FedEx, £1,000 (free PC); Streamline.com, $1,000 (free fridge-freezer).

Test, test, test

One of the advantages of direct marketing is the ability to test, retest, change, monitor and learn what works best. Everything can be tested, including the colour of the signature. A white envelope will do better than a manila envelope, and a brightly coloured envelope will do better than a white one (but will it damage the long-term corporate image?). If 10 per cent of a direct marketing budget is allocated to continual testing, then response levels will be continually higher.

Test and optimize

There's nothing new in optimization. Drayton Bird (2000) tested 12 different 'appropriate' lists, three different prices, two different ways to pay, different times for the mailings, alternative ways of responding and several creative approaches. He found that the best combination of all these factors produced a result 58 times better than the worst combination. By identifying the best and worst responses for each variable, the maximum response variation (difference between best and worst) was found. Table 17.1 shows the results.

TABLE 17.1 The impact of different direct-mail variables on response levels

Variable	Different response between worst and best
List	× 6.0
Offer	× 3.0
Timing	× 2.0
Creative	× 1.35
Response	× 1.2

Ideally, everything should be tested in isolation to give more realistic results. There are sometimes so many combinations that testing might appear endless. However, the big variables (those likely to have a significant impact on the bottom line) should be tested. Work down the list, but stop when the cost of testing outweighs the benefits. As mentioned, direct mail lends itself to testing. It allows the marketing manager to become more scientific and more precise – basically a better manager. Testing the colour of a signature may yield only one-twentieth of 1 per cent difference in response, but even so it still generates increased revenues, so it is worth testing everything.

CASE STUDY 17.1   PayPal – helping Britain's online retailers to go mobile

Situation

In the space of one year the volume of mobile payments processed by PayPal tripled. As smartphones became more common, there was a change in the way consumers were making purchases. This was a massive opportunity for online merchants – and therefore an opportunity for PayPal to reinforce its position as the leading online pay-ment brand by talking to merchants about how they could optimize their sites for the 'mobile boom'.

Two problems: PayPal faced two main problems. Firstly, there was a general perception amongst merchants that going mobile was complicated. Secondly, many of them felt that it was not important to them. PayPal therefore had a twin objective of instilling a sense of urgency and explaining the value of the mobile opportunity, whilst also reassuring them by explaining the simple steps that could be taken now, while they start thinking and planning for the future.

Objectives

The commercial benefit to PayPal was to reinforce the benefits of its own mobilized payment solution. But of course, this proposition was not compelling to merchants who were reluctant to first optimize their own sites. So PayPal had to, firstly, spread the m-commerce gospel to the non-believers and, secondly reinforce benefits of PayPal's mobilized payment solution.

Strategy

A two-phased automated e-mail campaign supported by banner ads and telemarketing and a 'fully mobile optimized' microsite using high-quality content that not only helped merchants to understand the mobile opportunity, but which also helped them to begin their own mobilization process.

Tactics

This content was presented in a variety of formats:

- housed on a purpose-built microsite;
- promoted by an e-mail campaign;
- web banner adverts;
- supported by telemarketing.

As the microsite's content centred on mobile optimization it was critical for the site itself to be fully mobile optimized.

While responsive design is often the best approach to optimization, striving to develop web content that renders well on numerous devices often results in pages that are not truly optimized for any of them.

In this case the user interface on mobile devices needed to look and feel like a native mobile application. With more screen space available, it made sense for the interface on desktops and tablets to be very different and include much more information on each page.

To achieve this level of device optimization, two versions of the microsite were developed. Custom client-side coding enabled the user's device to be detected so that the correct version could be loaded automatically for each visitor. From the visitor's perspective the same site would appear to be dramatically different when viewed on different types of device.

The microsite showed visitors:

- why optimizing their websites for mobile devices is so important;
- how to approach mobilization (guidance and advice) together with an overview of PayPal's;
- mobile optimized payment solutions.

The high quality content comprised a series of:

- articles and links;
- interactive visual guide on the key five steps;
- video providing an overview of PayPal's mobile checkout service and benefits.

Action

Typically includes the details of implementation, ie how to ensure excellent execution of the strategy, and tactics. From internal marketing (ensuring all staff understand, and have the opportunity to share, the campaign), to detailed action plans re automated e-mail marketing.

Control/measurement

Reporting was a key requirement to be able to measure the success of the campaign. The microsite was hosted in the Eloqua MA platform, which meant that visitor activity on the site would be logged, either anonymously for visitors arriving from web banners or telemarketing, or by e-mail address for visitors arriving from the e-mail campaign.

Alongside common reporting metrics such as e-mail open rates and page visits, custom tracking was deployed so that campaign reports were able to provide a view of where microsite visitors arrived from and which devices they were using.

Survey data gathered before and after the campaign also served to highlight the campaign's effectiveness.

Results

- **Open rates 25–35 per cent:** The campaign had a very positive impact. E-mail open rates were between 25 and 35 per cent, driving 6 per cent of the customer base to the microsite.

- **CTR 20 per cent:** Of those merchants who received an e-mail from PayPal about mobile optimization, 20 per cent clicked on the articles/links provided.

- **Awareness almost doubled:** Of the merchants surveyed before and after the campaign, the effectiveness of the campaign awareness that PayPal provided mobilized payment solutions had nearly doubled – 11 per cent awareness increased to 20 per cent during the campaign.

- **Include mobile in their business plans: 24 per cent:** A quarter of merchants surveyed (24 per cent) were encouraged to include mobile as part of their overall business plans after seeing the information on PayPal's website and 57 per cent of all merchants surveyed had a positive view of PayPal as an enabler of mobile payments. The video on the microsite proved to be the most popular asset within the microsite proving a good way to display to content to the audience.

- **Brand preference from 70 to 78 per cent:** For merchants intending to offer mobile payments, PayPal remains the preferred solution. The proportion of merchants preferring PayPal increased by 8 percentage points from 70 to 78 per cent.

3Ms (men and women – human resource required)

PayPal worked with two agencies; Base One, a specialist B2B Agency and CleverTouch, leading experts in marketing automation. The two agencies worked together combining their specialist expertise to manage the project: Base One creating the content, microsite and communications material, while CleverTouch managed the planning and delivery of the communications and campaign measurement across Eloqua.

Success being carried forward

PayPal saw US $14 billion in payments through mobile last year and are expecting US $20 billion this year. The microsite continues to be used as collateral across the business and as part of other campaigns. PayPal continue to work with Base One and CleverTouch, creating and implementing a variety of innovative online campaigns to build on this success.

CASE STUDY 17.2   Acronis automated marketing campaign

Situation

Acronis is a software company that helps small to medium businesses manage their back-up and disaster recovery operations. The automated marketing agency CleverTouch launched a campaign entitled 'Digital assets' in the UK, which targeted senior IT contacts in organizations of up to 500 employees.

Objective

The objective was to target new customers in the UK with the aim of achieving about 65 attendees per webinar for real educational engagement. From these attendees, an estimated 10–20 opportunities per event would evolve with an average value of typically £5,000, ie £50,000–£100,000 revenue generated from each event.

Strategy

CleverTouch marketing deployed a five-stage strategy to inform identified organizations' IT managers about the latest practices in storage, back-up and recovery whilst meeting the objective to confirm that any existing contact still existed and was relevant. The focus was on helping prospects along their buying cycle or journey of understanding and not purely selling to them or securing a sales appointment.

Tactics

Acronis commissioned market research to identify the key pain points for IT managers implementing storage back-up and disaster recovery solutions. The results were presented in an Acronis white paper, which became the call to action for the first e-mail, an Acronis white paper entitled 'Digital assets research findings: Unveiling backup and recovery practices across Europe'.

- *Stage 1:* E-mail 1 was sent to 24,000 contacts. It had a secondary purpose of cleansing the database of contacts that were no longer in the role or relevant. The initial e-mail was re-sent to all those who had not clicked through or registered, whose e-mail address was still valid (c. 21,500). Duplicates were suppressed at all stages.

- *Stage 2:* E-mail 2 was sent to those who had opened the initial e-mail, with an invitation to download an Acronis blueprint in back-up and disaster recovery. The blueprint e-mail was re-sent to those who had not opened it and whose e-mail address was still valid (c. 2,125). Simply put, this e-mail was sent to everyone who downloaded 'Digital assets research findings'.

- *Stage 3:* E-mail 3 was sent to respondees of the first two e-mails inviting them to attend a market-research-led webinar – again highlighting the findings from the market research conducted and linking the findings into Acronis best practice (c. 4,600). Simply put, this e-mail was sent to everyone who downloaded e-mail 1 or 2.

- *Stage 4:* Throughout the campaign a link was included that enabled the recipient to forward the e-mail to a friend, providing Acronis with the possibility to acquire relevant contacts for this and further campaigns.

- *Stage 5:* Marketing engagement was used to follow up on those contacts who registered and attended and those who registered but did not attend the webinar, to identify any immediate sales opportunities. The qualified sales leads were passed to the Acronis sales team for closure (80 leads).

Action

The campaign ran across a five-week time frame, with typically five working days between e-mail distributions. This meant that contacts who were out of the office for a week would not miss the follow-up e-mail. When resending an e-mail the identical e-mail was sent with a different subject line. Recipients' e-mail addresses that were no longer valid (hard bounce) were removed from the contact database.

Marketing automation technology increased efficiencies in the whole process and workflow and reduced costs (see Figure 17.6).

Control

The goal was to get 65 attendees to a webinar (based on previous history and experience). The result was over 140 attendees, with 10 immediate opportunities (worth over approximately £50,000 in year 1) and one initial sale of £10,000. As a result of the campaign's success, the same process was applied to a secondary campaign within a three-week time frame. This second campaign had equally successful results, with again over 140 contacts in attendance.

As a result of the success, the campaign has now expanded to other languages and regions within Europe. To supplement the campaign with additional coverage, a channel partner version was developed, which was used by Acronis channel partners to enhance their marketing activities.

The key to this campaign was to nurture the prospects through the campaign and create a pool of engaged contacts to be used in future, more targeted campaigns, eg direct mail. This method of continued, ongoing activity aimed at educating and engaging contacts is far more beneficial than a single campaign that is executed in isolation.

Men/women, minutes and money

This campaign required an estimated 10 days from Acronis and an estimated five days from CleverTouch. It was a digital multi-step campaign, with each step requiring ever-increasing degrees of commitment and engagement on both sides. The campaign took eight weeks to research and plan and was rolled out in eight weeks. The budget for this campaign, including imagery and CleverTouch's development, build and delivery time, was estimated at £25,000. Currently the ROI is 4:1, and it is expected to peak at 10:1.

FIGURE 17.3   The amount of time IT managers could lose in the event of data loss (e-mail 1 with 'Digital assets research findings' attachment)

THROW AWAY EVERYTHING
YOU DID YESTERDAY
THEN TELL YOUR WHOLE COMPANY TO DO THE SAME.

Dear Phil Crawley,

Recent research indicates that a massive two thirds (63%) of IT managers would take a day or more to recover their company's data in the event of system downtime, leading to lost revenue, lost productivity and huge frustration of both employees and customers.

If you're not backing up regularly, one minor disaster could mean that everything everyone in your organisation did yesterday, the day before and last week...could be lost.

Read the Digital Assets Research Findings: Unveiling Backup & Recovery Practices across Europe.

✓ What you fear most about system failure

✓ How confident you are that you could recover in the event of a disaster

✓ How quickly you could recover

✓ How stressful data loss is in comparison to other events

▼ Download the Acronis complimentary White Paper 'Digital Assets Research Findings: Unveiling Backup & Recovery Practices Across Europe'

Best Regards,
Acronis Team

Get your Free Research Findings!

DOWNLOAD NOW

Acronis® Digital Assets
Research Findings:

Unveiling Backup & Recovery
Practices across Europe

March 2010

Acronis. Move. Manage. Maintain. Seamlessly.

FIGURE 17.4   A guide to back-up and recovery for small and medium businesses
(e-mail 2 with 'SMB guide to backup and recovery' attachment)

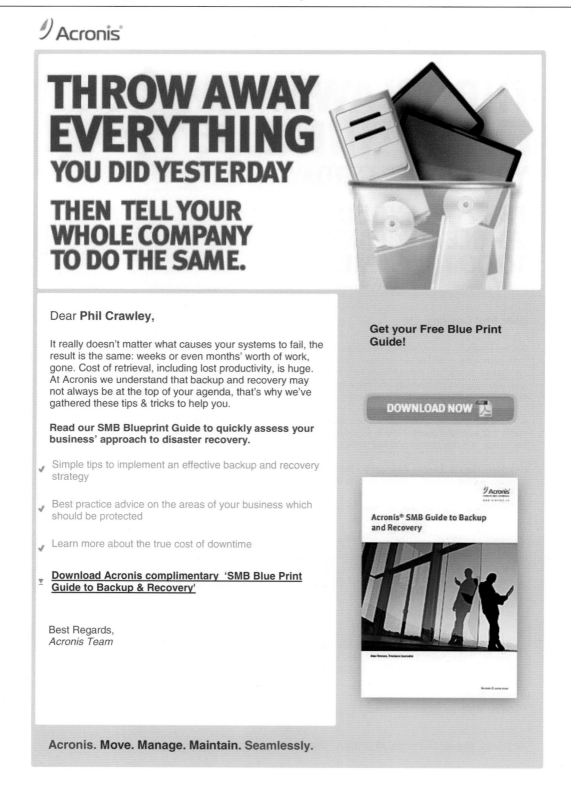

FIGURE 17.5   Invitation to a webinar exploring the challenges and pitfalls of protecting virtual server environments (e-mail 3)

Join us for an exclusive webinar to gain actionable insight from **Lauren Whitehouse**, Senior Analyst, <u>Enterprise Strategy Group</u>, about the challenges and common pitfalls of protecting virtual server environments. **Michael Lee**, Acronis Principal Solutions Architect, will demonstrate the award-winning <u>Acronis® Backup & Recovery™ 10</u> solution.

We will address such questions as; are you encountering stumbling blocks as you deploy virtual machines? Are you looking for better ways to protect data and mission-critical applications as virtual machine counts increase? Are you re-evaluating best practices to secure data across physical and virtual environments?

Topics we will cover:

- How to optimise virtual machine backup and recovery

- How to gain efficiency of a unified approach to protecting physical and virtual machines

Webinar Details: Thursday June 3rd, 2:00 - 3:00 PM London Time
Duration 45 mins.

Don't miss out <u>register now!</u>

Best Regards,
Acronis Team

Register now for our exclusive webinar!

"Virtualisation is about more than deploying virtual machines"

Date:
Thursday, June 3rd

Time:
2:00 - 3:00 PM, London Time

Presenters:

Lauren Whitehouse,
Senior Analyst
<u>Enterprise Strategy Group</u>

Michael Lee,
Principal Solutions Architect
<u>Acronis, Inc</u>

Acronis. Move. Manage. Maintain. Seamlessly.

FIGURE 17.6   Contact workflow strategy

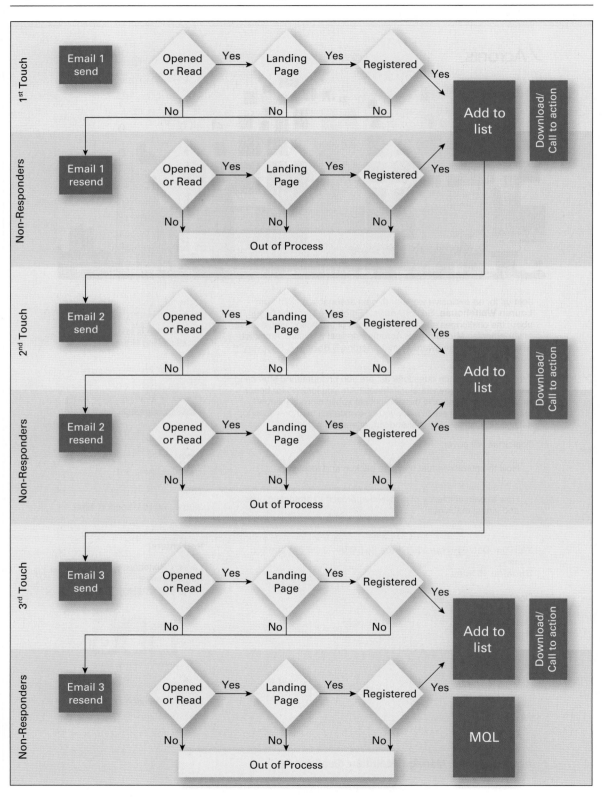

Advantages and disadvantages

Here are some of the advantages and disadvantages to consider when deciding whether to increase or reduce this communications tool.

Advantages

Direct mail can be tightly targeted (as can opt-in e-mail). Although the cost per thousand (CPM) for direct mail is high, the cost per order (CPO) or cost per acquisition can be a lot lower than for other communications tools. It can also be used for customer retention and nurturing customers over their lifetime. Direct mail is arguably better for customer retention than for customer acquisition. Ideally, direct mail (and opt-in e-mail) should be integrated into an overall contact strategy that is tailored according to the customers' preferences. This achieves high levels of satisfaction, because the mailings are always totally relevant to the customers' needs (remember the magic marketing formula). A well-targeted mailing in a jiffy bag or gift wrapped, with an attractive incentive inside, can generate unexpectedly high response rates, trigger word of mouth and sometimes generate publicity in the press.

Direct mail has always been more easily accountable/measureable than many other communications tools. It also lends itself to testing, split testing, and multivariate testing, with very quick response times. All direct mail presents an opportunity to build or enhance a database and subsequently use it to tailor and personalize offers. You can see why many direct mail agencies have grown into successful digital marketing agencies as the disciplines overlap. Finally, international direct mail can offer an alternative route for new market entry. Direct contact by mail or telephone may be cheaper and faster than a personal visit at the early stages of the buying cycle.

Disadvantages

In addition to sometimes upsetting intermediaries (through selling directly to customers), direct marketing has a problem with its image. Direct mail has connotations of 'junk mail' and is therefore vulnerable to criticism from environmental pressure groups. Opt-in e-mail has connotations of spam. Although research shows that a large majority prefer to receive direct mail, there is a percentage who consider it to be an intrusion or invasion of their privacy. Online, an unsolicited e-mail is considered even more unacceptable – a breach of netiquette (net etiquette) and therefore spam. In consumer markets this is now against the law. It is not surprising that spammers get 'flamed' by angry customers who send abusive messages back, sometimes repeatedly and sometimes with a mailbomb (a massive file) that may effectively close down the spammer's system. Database maintenance is also critical (and costs resources). This is an increasing problem, as e-mail lists are offered at very cheap prices, eg $35 per million (compared to £200 per thousand 'snail mail' addresses). The initial customer acquisition costs in snail mail can be high (subsequent transactions are much cheaper). Direct marketing has a high CPT compared to advertising. An average response of 1 per cent suggests, by definition, that 99 per cent of mailings get chucked in the bin. Poorly targeted mailings might one day be considered a threat to trees and the environment. There can also be a heavy investment cost in developing a database. Direct marketing can prove to be expensive for a one-off sale. Used effectively to develop repeat sales, gain 'lifetime value' and nurture relationships, it can prove extremely profitable. Finally, there is the risk involved with any marketing communications activity. A bad mailing, for example, can not only lose money but reduce sales and damage the company's corporate image. In fact a spam mailing would be considered irresponsible by any well-run company.

Key points from Chapter 17

- Direct mail and opt-in e-mail can be used to generate new business. Opt-in e-mail can, ideally, be used for customer retention (or as part of a CRM contact strategy) rather than just for customer acquisition.
- Direct mail is highly targetable and relatively easy to test and control.
- The systems and database behind any campaign must be fully integrated into the campaign or ongoing contact strategy.
- Organizations that ignore direct marketing and database techniques will suffer a competitive disadvantage.

References and further reading

Bird, D (2000) *Commonsense Direct Marketing*, 4th edn, Kogan Page, London

Brann, C (1984) *Cost-Effective Direct Marketing: By mail, telephone and direct response advertising*, Collectors' Books, Cirencester

Chaffey, D and Smith, PR (2013) *eMarketing eXcellence* 4th edn, Routledge

Considine, R and Raphel, M (1987) *The Great Brain Robbery*, The Great Brain Robbery, Pasadena, CA

Exhibition Venues Association (2000) *UK Exhibition Facts*, Vol. 12, Exhibition Venues Association, Mayfield, East Sussex

Gray, R (2011) Here today... *The Marketer*, July/August

Hilpern, K (2013) How to personalise your customers experience, *Marketer* March/April p 42

Howard, M (1989) Telephone marketing vs direct sales force costs, Commissioned by Datapoint (UK) Ltd, London

McCorkell, G (1997) *Direct and Database Marketing*, Kogan Page, London

Moriarty, R and Moran, U (1990) Managing hybrid systems, *Harvard Business Review*, November–December

Moriarty, R and Swartz, G (1989) Automation to boost sales and marketing, *Harvard Business Review*, January–February

Royal Mail (2001) *Getting More from Integrated Marketing and Making Direct Mail Work for You*, MBO, London

Schlosser, J (2003) Looking for intelligence in ice cream, *Fortune*, 17 March

Stevens, M (1991) *The Handbook of Telemarketing*, Kogan Page, London

Tapp, A (2001) *Principles of Direct and Database Marketing*, 2nd edn, Financial Times/Prentice Hall, Englewood Cliffs, NJ

Toffler, A (1980) *The Third Wave*, Collins, London

Watson, J (1989) The direct marketing guide, *Marketing Magazine*, 9 February

Worcester, R (2002) Customers: Handle with care, *Purple Issue*, 30 October

Further information

Direct Marketing Association
DMA House
70 Margaret Street
London W1W 8SS
Tel: +44 (0)20 7291 3300
Fax: +44 (0)20 7323 4426
www.dma.org.uk

Federation of European Direct Marketing (FEDMA)
Avenue Ariane 5, 4th Floor
1200 Brussels
Belgium
Tel: +32 2 779 4268
www.fedma.org

Institute of Direct Marketing (IDM)
1 Park Road
Teddington
Middlesex TW11 OAR
Tel: +44 (0)20 8977 5705
Fax: +44 (0)20 8943 2535
www.theidm.com

Mailing Preference Service (MPS)
DMA House
70 Margaret Street
London W1W 8SS
Tel: +44(0)20 7291 3300
Fax: +44 (0)20 7323 4226
www.mpsonline.org.uk

Information Commissioner's Office
Wycliffe House
Water Lane
Wilmslow
Cheshire SK9 5AF
Tel: +44 (0)303 123 1113
Fax: +44 (0)1625 524510
www.ico.org.uk

18
Exhibitions, conferences and events

Introduction   482

Conferences, summits and events   482

Virtual worlds   483

Managing exhibitions   483

Situation – to exhibit or not to exhibit?   483

Objectives – prioritize exhibition
  objectives   484

Strategy – develop an exhibition
  strategy   484

Tactics – determine pre-show promotional
  tactics   486

Action – train exhibition staff   487

Control – evaluate post-show   489

12 reasons for poor performance   492

Advantages and disadvantages   494

Advantages   494

Disadvantages   494

Key points from Chapter 18   495

References and further reading   495

Further information   495

Introduction

Imagine bringing a whole market together, under one roof, for a few days. An exciting idea? An explosive concept? It happens all the time. Exhibitions are unique in that they are the only medium that brings the whole market together – buyers, sellers and competitors – all under one roof for a few days. Products and services can be seen, demonstrated or tested, and face-to-face contact can be made with a large number of relevant decision makers in a short period of time. Relationships can be strengthened and opportunities seized if planned carefully. Exhibitions are a powerful marcomms tool, but they are expensive and require detailed planning; whether offline, online or in virtual worlds (see Chapter 11, p. 314) the same rules apply – they must be leveraged and integrated with several other marcomms tools. Thorough planning and training is required.

Conferences, summits and events

In fact some organizations are exploring parallel areas such as conferences and summits (their own or third-party conferences where they can exhibit and/or speak) and events which can expand into experiential marketing where brands are activated and brought to life by creative experiences in both the real world and virtual worlds.

When Jaguar Land Rover launched the Range Rover Sport, guests were invited to attend a live film of the upmarket car being driven all the way from New York docks to the venue. Not very exciting you might think; however, when the actual car was driven into the venue the driver, James Bond 007, Daniel Craig stepped out from the driver's seat. This event engaged and enthused 750 VIP guests and simultaneously connected with 20,000 others who had already registered to watch this event live also. Some four million viewers have since watched the recorded video while the many hundreds of mobile

FIGURE 18.1

Mazda North American dealer meeting

Prudential real estate national sales meeting

RNC welcome event

Gaylord Opryland Hotel Grant reopen

Photos courtesy of CorporateMagicInc.com

photos snapped at the event have been shared and reshared across thousands of networks (see the power of social media maths in Chapter 1).

JCB, whose yellow machinery is seen on construction sites, created a global roadshow that delivered a 300 per cent boost in sales. A three-day event ran 13 times in four weeks as more than 3,000 customers attended. Marquees, fireworks, dance diggers ensured that delegates had a fully immersive experience and orders were placed there and then.

As Claire Gascoigne (2015) says: 'The message is stop thinking about your next business event and start imagining your next business experience.'

Virtual worlds

Virtual worlds have changed but they are still growing. You won't have to step into them (eg log into Second Life) via your laptop or tablet or mobile. They will come to you in the form of augmented reality and eventually 3D hovering holograms helping us through our busy day. Augmented reality will present layers of additional data as text, video or 3D projections. We've seen some developments in Korea where virtual stores are created at train stations so that commuters can scan shelves (illuminated photos of shelves packed with products) and buy with their mobile phones, so that the delivery awaits them as they arrive home from work. The authors have both been approached by beautiful women in airports reminding us to declare any liquids in our carry-on luggage – only to find out the ladies in question were just animated cardboard cut-outs. So virtual worlds will grow. Virtual events too. The same principles apply when managing a virtual event (see p. 314 at the end of Chapter 11). For now let us explore what it takes to manage an offline, real-world exhibition.

Managing exhibitions

Exhibitions offer an array of opportunities, problems and challenges to the keen marketing manager. They can be leveraged to the maximum effect by integrating them with other communications tools and developing a longer-term perspective incorporating an overall exhibition strategy. Detailed exhibition planning skills require the manager to work through the following:

- Situation – to exhibit or not to exhibit?
- Objectives – prioritize exhibition objectives.
- Strategy – develop an exhibition strategy including:
  - selecting the right shows;
  - agreeing a design strategy.
- Tactics – determine pre-show promotional tactics.
- Action – train exhibition staff:
  - finalize the exhibition operational (daily action) plan;
  - ensure follow-up.
- Control – evaluate post-show.

Situation – to exhibit or not to exhibit?

Many marketers find exhibitions to be very expensive investments in terms of money required for renting the space, building a stand, promoting it, entertaining customers, travel and accommodation. They also find it expensive in terms of human resources and time required. Sometimes it's disproportionate in terms of return on investment, and marketers have to make tough decisions as to whether to continue attending all the usual exhibitions and conferences, particularly if customers are migrating online and doing business there instead of visiting trade shows. For the marketer who wants to attend some exhibitions, whether online or offline, here are the stages of planning that will help to boost return on investment, save time and, ideally, reduce workload through better planning.

Objectives – prioritize exhibition objectives

If you don't know where you are going, how do you know when you have arrived? How do you know if it is a good show or a waste of time and money? How do you know if you have had a good day or a bad day? How can you achieve if you don't know what you are trying to achieve? Clearly defined objectives are required to focus the effort. Typically, enquiries and orders can be easily quantified and broken into daily (or even hourly) objectives. A sweepstake among staff (guessing the numbers of enquiries and orders) can help to focus everyone's attention. Although exhibitions are hard work, they are dynamic in the variety of objectives they provide:

- Sell – generate sales and enquiries from new and existing customers, agents and distributors.
- Launch new products.
- Raise profile or maintain a presence in the market.
- Press coverage – internal (newsletter) and external PR opportunities.
- Reinforce relationships with customers, distributors and agents through hospitality and introductions to senior managers and directors. Taking care of customers at exhibitions can be part of a contact strategy (including e-mails, snail mail, telemarketing, sales team visits, etc).
- Enthuse and support local distributors, agents and sales team.
- Market research – customers, non-customers and distributors.
- Test new ideas – product testing and informal creative discussions.
- Competitor analysis and intelligence gathering.
- Staff motivation – some exhibitions can be the focal point of the year. They allow staff to come to the show or exhibition and feel a certain amount of pride in their organization.
- Meet new staff or potential recruits.

Strategy – develop an exhibition strategy

Ideally, exhibitions should not be used as a one-off, ad hoc activity. They can be used more effectively when: 1) they are viewed as a possible series of exhibitions; 2) they are integrated carefully with other communications tools; 3) they are selected and planned well in advance; and 4) their effectiveness is constantly measured. An exhibition strategy summarizes the frequency and types of show selected (eg national, international, real or virtual; see 'Selection checklist' below). Perhaps different segments of the market are served by different exhibitions, different product or service sectors, different geographical regions and different buying cycles (eg Christmas products have exhibitions in January for the coming Christmas season). Considering the bigger picture requires a knowledge of what exhibitions are available, suitable and affordable. This means continually collecting exhibition brochures and keeping them safely in an exhibition file for regular review.

An exhibition strategy can also give guidance about the kind of integrated marketing support provided and the total level of spending. Remember that the cost of hiring space at an exhibition is often only a small proportion of the total exhibition costs (between 20 and 25 per cent; see 'Costs' below).

Select the right shows

As with advertising or any marketing activity, exhibitions need careful targeting. There is an increasing number of exhibitions available, usually more than an organization can attend. Some are better than others. All of them have sales staff dedicated to promoting and selling their exhibition space. The exhibitor must choose carefully. The skill in selection is somewhat similar to that of the media planner (who must choose which media and specific media vehicles, except that media planners have access to considerably more audited information; see Chapter 7, 'Media selection'). There are various listings giving a diary of exhibitions and events for up to two years in advance.

Selection checklist

1 *Type of exhibition.* Local, national or international; vertical (tight focus of interest

for buyers or sellers) or horizontal (wide range of interest for buyers or sellers); general public; trade events; private events; symposia or conferences where a limited amount of exhibiting facilities are available.

2 *Target audience.* Type and number of visitors; audited figures should be made available, for example Audit Bureau of Circulations (ABC) figures are approved by the Association of Event Organisers (AEO) (the use of ABC figures is also a compulsory requirement of membership of the AEO, largely because ABC's figures are reproducible for checking and testing).

3 *Timing.* Does it meet buyers' purchasing patterns and can the organization prepare for it in time? For example, foreign shows may need to be planned 18 months in advance.

4 *Facilities.* Any limitations or constraints; how the organizers intend to promote the event; supporting contact events, such as dinners, award ceremonies, seminars, breakfast receptions, etc.

5 *Costs.* Compare 'cost of space' and 'size of audience' ratios between different exhibitions. The space cost is useful for comparison, but it represents only a small proportion of the total cost of exhibiting. The cost of the stand design is generally excluded if the exhibitor already owns a mobile stand unit, but miscellaneous items (see Figure 18.1) rapidly cause costs to escalate.

6 *Previous success.* How long has the show been running? Has it been a success previously? Is it enjoying year-on-year growth? Are there any customer (exhibitor) testimonials or references available?

7 *Endorsements.* What official bodies are supporting it? There are independent surveys that list visitor numbers, visitor quality, sales enquiries and a summary of exhibitors' results (see 'Evaluate post-show' below).

Agree on a design strategy

The stand design is a key factor in the overall exhibition strategy. It should present the right corporate image (see Chapters 14 and 21), announce the product or service, visualize benefits (arising from the product or service), attract interest and look aesthetically pleasing while providing for other functions such as display, demonstration, discussion, hospitality and storage (of spare samples, literature, coats, etc). **Identifying measurable exhibition success criteria** such as sales or orders, number of enquiries, cost per enquiry, cost per order, qualified contact names for a database, visitors' recall or level of awareness of the particular organization's stand, key messages intended by the stand, etc helps to guide the overall design of the exhibition stand.

A visitor may have less than three seconds to scan and decide whether to enter a particular stand instead of one of the many others competing for that same visitor's attention. Buyers have only a limited amount of time to visit a limited number of stands (the US Center for Exhibition Research suggests that the average visitor attending a show barely calls on 13 stands, regardless of the size of the exhibition). Buyers have to choose quickly whether to enter or not. Many exhibitions provide a computer printout of the exhibitors that fall into a particular category of suppliers of interest to a particular visitor. The printout usually includes a map identifying the location of the specific organizations listed in the category. This means that buyers can pause and decide what route they will take and which stands they will visit before entering the main exhibition hall. Despite a pre-planned schedule of visits, a busy buyer can still be attracted by an excellent stand design or promotional stunt to make an unplanned visit. However, a stunt can also attract time-wasting, stand-congesting, non-target market visitors. Some stunts have been found to deter senior decision makers, who may feel that they are aimed at lower-level visitors.

The 'three-second' test

When you next visit an exhibition look around you and see how many (if any) stands clearly tell you what they offer. How many exhibition stands actually explain what business the exhibitors are in and their benefits? How many stand designs actually help visitors by answering this question within three to five seconds before they pass by?

It is surprising to observe the number of organizations that promote their name first and foremost, perhaps followed by a product name, and somewhere, almost hidden, the product and product features are displayed. Product benefits (what buyers really seek) cannot be seen easily. Most buyers have to make the psychological leap and commit themselves by walking on to a stand to engage in a discussion that may eventually reveal the hidden product benefits. Larger organizations may feel that they have too many products to highlight any one individually, or that their name is associated with the product area so strongly that all visitors (including those from overseas?) actually look for the company name since they already know the exhibitor's business. Perhaps some exhibitors do not want to reveal their benefits to the competition too readily. Perhaps others simply don't ask their stand designers to consider this issue.

The design should be consistent with the organization's corporate identity guidelines (the design manual specifies the logo style, typefaces, and primary and secondary colours). **It should attract visitors and facilitate a simple selling sequence of attracting a visitor,** providing a comfortable space and facilities to demonstrate products, and fostering an environment for detailed discussion and negotiations if appropriate.

The design brief for an exhibition stand can use the basic SOSTAC® + 3Ms discussed in Chapter 10. Essentially the designer needs to know: who the target audience is; in what kinds of exhibitions the stand might appear; the locations and preferred stand locations (within the exhibition); stand size and function (display, demonstration, hospitality area, access and service facilities required); and whether the stand needs to be reusable. Information on competitors and their stands is also useful. Additional information such as the design manual and the dimensions of any display items is also important. The success criteria must be listed and objectives prioritized, eg presenting an image, attracting new business, meeting old customers, launching a new product, etc. The designer also needs to know the overall exhibition strategy (discussed above). Tactical information is sometimes included. This includes any promotional ideas, specific numbers of staff and visitors on the stand at any one time, whether any promotional off-stand activities will be attracting visitors on to the stand, whether the stand will be used for photo opportunities, and what

kinds of electronic gadgetry (data projectors, laptops, sound, etc), products and sales literature need to be displayed. **The designer also needs to know about the 3Ms, the three key resources of men/women, money (budget) and minutes (time).**

The whole exhibition design should focus on key, measurable objectives (are all the elements linked up to and consistent with the overall exhibition strategy, etc?). Sound, sight, space and even smell can be used creatively by a designer (there are, however, likely to be some constraints imposed by the organizers). Good designers exploit both two-dimensional design (eg graphics) and three-dimensional design (eg the use of space).

Tactics – determine pre-show promotional tactics

To maximize effectiveness, exhibitors do not depend on stand design alone to attract visitors. Careful pre-show promotions can ensure a steady flow of visitors on to a stand. Direct mail, linked with an incentive or sales promotion, free tickets, inserts, advertising, publicity, etc, can all be used to get visitors to decide to visit a particular stand before they arrive at the exhibition in the first place. Given that the average visitor visits only 13 stands, it is important to get on to the appropriate target visitor's 'must visit' list. Pre-show marketing helps to identify who to expect and who to chase up. It also provides a fresh opportunity to talk to customers and prospects on the back of the urgency and excitement created by the show.

Given that exhibiting is a resource-consuming activity, pre-show activity aims to maximize the effectiveness of the investment. Some types of show, such as conferences and seminars, are almost totally dependent on pre-event activity, as attendees will not walk in off the street. Advertising and editorial opportunities range from the usual trade, professional and domestic press, local and regional media, and transport (taxis, trains, buses and stations) through to the exhibition catalogue itself. Sponsorship of guides, maps, promotions, teaser promotions, free gifts and competitions can all be offered to the target visitor through advertising, editorial, inserts, mailings and even telemarketing. Good exhibition planning can integrate with other communication activities at an early stage. This means that the costs of sales promotions and incentives can be reduced significantly by increasing the organization's buying power when sourcing many different sales promotion gifts simultaneously. Delivery and invoicing can also be staggered or delayed so that cash flow bottlenecks do not occur. It might be possible to run a joint promotion with a non-competing exhibitor so that your product or service (or even just the incentive) is combined with someone else's to promote both sites as 'must see' sites.

In summary, pre-show promotional activity can involve:

- social media activity (announcing event; inviting visitors; updates (photos, videos, tweets, posts) during the build-up (plus thank-yous after the event);
- content calendar (see Chapter 16) can include marketing content created for and by the events;
- snail mail invitations (with an incentive?);
- e-marketing invitations and reminders;
- telesales key customers or prospects;
- field sales force briefing (to invite their key customers);
- press activities;
- sponsored activities;
- perimeter advertising (around the venue) and location-based advertising (see Chapter 13);
- press advertising (trade magazines and exhibition manual);
- joint promotions.

Action – train exhibition staff

After all the hard pre-show work, when a stunning stand has been created, the promotion has been publicized and a good flow of traffic on to the stand has been generated, what a shame it is to lose business through staff who don't know exactly how to deal with people. Staffing an exhibition stand is hard work. The day becomes even longer when staff have no goals, no targets and no exhibition training. The team needs to be briefed about why the organization is exhibiting (including specific objectives broken down into daily objectives). **Exhibition training helps staff to know: how to physically stand** (the importance of body language); **how to approach a visitor** (never with a closed question such as 'May I help you?' – try open-ended questions like 'What caught your eye?'); **what kind of information should be gleaned from visitors** (see the box below); **when a senior manager should be called over; how to demonstrate** (product knowledge and skills); **how to close a sale; and how to present records.** It is possible to practise before the show starts each day (or during quiet moments).

Six essential questions for qualifying a prospect

1 'Thanks for stopping. How are you familiar with...?' or 'What attracted you to our display?' or 'What do you see that you like?' (This gives the history of the prospective buyer and tells you where to start selling.)

2 'What's your situation now?' (This tells you if the prospective buyer actually has a real live need.)

3 'What would you like to achieve [or change]?' (This further defines the prospective buyer's application of your product.)

4 'What are your concerns as to budget?' (This tells you if the prospective buyer has the money.)

5 'How does your timetable look on all of this?' (This gives you the prospective buyer's timetable for buying or acting.)

6 'How would you like to proceed from here?' (This lets the prospective buyer take over.)

Engebretson (2000)

Increase newsletter signups

Staff can be trained to ask prospects what they need to know about the staff's business, then show the prospects some really relevant content from the blog or white papers and invite them to get regular free updates via signing up for the newsletter. This boosts the size of the prospect database.

Boost social media engagement with a social butler

Some events have social butlers who, equipped with their iPad, take photos and videos of visitors and then offer to post them immediately to the visitor's social platform with the appropriate hashtags. All the visitor has to do is hit their own 'share' button.

Finalize the exhibition action plan

Everything, from staffing to samples and sales promotions, has to be meticulously planned. Never underestimate the importance of attention to detail. Even contingencies should be allowed for. Exhibitions are hard work. A staffing roster schedules staff so that they can have a break and a chance to look around the exhibition (and report back on their observations). More importantly, the roster ensures that the stand is never understaffed or overstaffed with inexperienced staff. How many visitors are expected? How many staff will be required? How many junior and senior staff? Who staffs the stand and when? Comfortable shoes, regular breaks and solid rest between exhibition days are also essential. Individual performance on the stand can be measured against preset criteria (number and quality of enquiries, etc). Social media integration: are all the staff aware? Are there guidelines regarding tweeting and retweeting? Does everyone know the event hashtag and key messages? Here's how some organizations integrate Instagram and other social media into their exhibition activities.

10 ways to integrate social media into exhibitions, events or conferences

1. **Add a photo-sharing social network to your exhibition, event or conference checklist** so that you can increase engagement with your visitors and maybe even grow your database with more leads.

2. **Get the event hashtag** before exhibiting or attending, or establish one if you are the event host.

3. **Search using the hashtag to find your prospects' photos** and ask them to visit your stand (maybe add a small incentive): like their photos to start establishing a

relationship with these prospects; post your own photos using the hashtag also. You can also add geo-tags using the venue name and even add 'visit stand number 301' or 'main lobby' so visitors can find you.

4. **Add a tailored event landing page on your website** and paste the URL into your Instagram profile information (you can change it after the event). So when someone finds one of your Instagram photos (hashtagged to the event) and they click your avatar or your name to get to your information they will be able to click the link to take them to your tailor-made event website (well, landing page!).

5. **Grow your prospect database by giving them a reason to add their details.** Only ask them to fill out a short form so they can receive some information or maybe a prize or password to collect a prize from the stand. They are now added to your database.

6. **Amplify your reach.** Share your Instagram photos onto other social media platforms. Note photos shared from Instagram to say, Twitter appear as a link instead of a photo preview (and therefore have lower engagement rate). There are some 'hacks' to post as photos.

7. **Create a visually engaging backdrop** (with your brand name/url and maybe the event hashtag) with plenty of room for visitors to stand into your attention-grabbing image (note this will attract other people onto your stand also). The backdrop could be a cliff edge (and the visitor appears balancing on a cliff edge (photo)) or stepping into a philosophical quote with the text on one side and room for visitors to step into the text to create their own visually engaging (branded) selfie to share. Ideally the image should relate to your business benefits, values or mission.

8. **Run a contest** by asking attendees to repost, tweet, and share their own photo with your own hashtag, eg #PRSmithGiveAway. It could be the above visually engaging photo. Whomever gets the most likes or shares wins a prize. You can monitor entries by refreshing the contest hashtag. Ensure the prize whether offline or online can only be collected at your stand – so that you get even

more personal engagement (and another photo opportunity of presenting 'today's prize'). Be sure to check Instagram rules regarding competitions. Also request permission to re-use photos posted in the competition.

9 **Re-use these photo assets** across multiple platforms. Set up a photo feed to the website to show as a slideshow or display as a grid (during or after the show). Then after the show make some photo montages and share cross-platform including maybe a creative blog post featuring lots of photos.

10 **Finally measure the results:** (a) increase in the number of your followers; (b) increases in engagement levels (likes, shares, comments); (c) database growth; and (d) how much traffic was generated to the main site and whether any conversions were generated.

Small exhibitors can be beautiful

NCH Action for Children charity had to break through the clutter with a small two- by two-metre stand. Its stunning backlit graphic of children's faces, supporting the 'All Children Dream' theme, did the trick. The stand staff were fully trained in exhibition techniques and fully briefed to communicate key messages and collect key information. They fulfilled their 'key contacts hit list', snapped publicity photos with visiting MPs and shone out from the heaving masses.

What can go wrong will go wrong

The 'What can go wrong will go wrong' law runs rampant in exhibitions. Contingency planning reduces risks, but inevitably something unforeseen still occurs. One of the authors has had two such experiences, both of which happened at international shows: the first was in Birmingham, where a new electrical product set itself on fire while being exhibited; the second was in New York, where the freight company lost all the samples and display units. Other exhibition nightmares include a stand that was built upside down (because the architect read the plans upside down) and neighbouring stands encroaching on each other's areas (sometimes by accident), or breach of trade union regulations by using a hammer or screw driver!

To minimize risk of errors, checklists can be used to ensure execution is professional at all times. Here's a simple daily checklist used at the end of each day in preparation for the next day.

Ensure follow-up

The exhibition is not an end in itself, although by the end of the show the exhausted staff probably feel as though it is. Careful follow-up work must start almost immediately. This is where the organization can earn its return from the exhibition. Leads, enquiries, quotations, sales and after-sales discussions need to be followed up in a professional manner. This requires a follow-up meeting where all the staff go through the cards they collected, the people they talked to and the projects or jobs that were discussed. This prevents the duplication, contradiction and conflict that can arise where two people from the same prospect organization have asked two different members of staff for a quotation for the same job, or where two different enquiries have emerged for the same job from two different prospects. Worse still are unfulfilled enquiries. How many times have you left an enquiry with exhibitors never to hear from them again? Lack of post-show follow-up makes all the previous exhibition efforts a waste of time.

The manager can determine who follows up what, with a report-back meeting date set to see what sales are actually generated. More detailed evaluation of the true exhibition results can be carried out so that future efforts are improved. It is worth formalizing the evaluation process so that the trend, individual performance and competitor performance can all be measured.

Control – evaluate post-show

Post-show evaluation measures performance against the preset objectives. It also examines whether the objectives were realistic, whether the show was the right show, and what was good and what was bad about the organization's performance. A competitor's performance can also be evaluated to a certain degree. How can the performance be improved?

FIGURE 18.2   This checklist needs to be checked at the end of each day so that everything is in place for the next day

Daily Checklist

Appointments diary _____

Visitors book _____

Enquiries log/lead form _____

Badges _____

Business cards _____

Brochures _____

Press packs _____

Samples _____

Spare parts _____

Display screen _____

Laptop/s _____

Scissors, adhesive tape, penknife _____

Fishbowl _____

Water _____

Clean glasses _____

Insurance _____

First aid kit (including aspirins) _____

Other? _____

Should the exhibition be run again next year? Was it value for money?

Some post-show questions:

1 What percentage of the potential number of visitors to the whole exhibition (that fitted the target market profile) visited our stand?

2 What percentage stopped but did not visit our stand?

3 What percentage saw but did not stop at our stand?

4 How many leads or enquiries were created?

5 What was the cost per contact or visitor?

6 What percentage of contacts or visitors plan to buy the product or service?

7 What was the cost per 'serious' visitor?

8 What was the cost per order?

9 How effective was each staff member's performance? (According to Harry McDermott of Exhibition Surveys, 'Stand

staff should indoctrinate every visitor they meet on a stand. When those visitors think of the types of product shown they should think of the exhibitor. Research can get visitors to rate individual staff because the visitors' comments can be linked back to the stand record of contacts'.)

10   Did we overspend or underspend (too large or too small a stand, or too many or too few staff)?

Exhibition value analysis

Exhibition value analysis is a type of survey that includes both a multi-client survey and a confidential private survey so that comparisons can be made between the performance of the client company and that of its competitors. The survey covers visitor potential, the percentage that saw, stopped or visited a particular stand, visitors' perceptions, intentions to buy, and the stand's strengths and weaknesses based on a sample of known visitors to it (supplied by the company). Some research findings suggest that companies do not attend trade exhibitions to sell, but rather to build corporate and brand awareness.

Costs

Exhibition costs need to be looked at carefully. Various sources suggest that the cost of hiring the exhibition space represents as little as one-fifth of the total costs of exhibiting. This obviously depends on whether the cost of the stand design is included, whether there is much integrated promotional activity and whether the opportunity cost of taking members of the sales team 'off the road' are included. The most important thing is to be consistent, so that year-on-year comparisons can be made. Cost per enquiry, cost per order, percentage of sales, return on investment (ROI) and experimental non-attendance are now considered. Note that, in the ROI calculation, costs are treated as an investment (as opposed to an expenditure), which, technically speaking, is not correct.

Cost per enquiry. Cost per enquiry can range from £25 to £500. However, the bottom line for many organizations is still 'How much business did it generate?'

$$\frac{\text{Total exhibition costs}}{\text{Number of serious enquiries}} = \text{Cost per enquiry}$$

Cost per order. Total exhibition costs can be divided by the number of orders taken to find the cost per order. There are some difficulties here, however. First, there is the timescale (some orders instigated by contact at a trade show or exhibition can take several months or longer to be finally confirmed). Second, the regular orders (which would have been brought in by the normal sales force visits anyway) should, ideally, be separated from those incremental orders generated solely by attending the show. Third, there is a school of thought that suggests that exhibitions do not generate sales; they only allow the exhibitor to meet a useful target market, but whether the target market buys depends on a number of factors totally divorced from the show (eg the product, competitors' products, and prices). An average of averages shows a cost per order in UK and overseas exhibitions of £75 and £125 respectively (EIF, 2002). This ignores both the size of the orders and their profitability. The size of the orders could be expressed as a percentage figure in the same way as a marketing communications budget is sometimes expressed, ie marketing expenses as a percentage of sales. In this case, exhibition costs as a percentage of sales generated can be calculated as:

$$\frac{\text{Total exhibition costs}}{\text{Number of orders}} = \text{Cost per order}$$

Percentage of sales

The difficulty here lies in isolating the sales generated exclusively through the exhibition, ie ignoring sales that would have been taken by the sales force regardless of the exhibition. Nevertheless, the cost of taking the same number of enquiries or sales by routine sales visits should be compared to the costs of enquiries or sales taken during the exhibition.

Return on investment

The long-term profitability of the sales is probably the most important of all the criteria. This is difficult to calculate, because the lifetime value of a customer is often difficult to calculate, particularly in industrial markets. However, the short-term ROI can be calculated by dividing the profit or contribution made from the orders by the total cost of the exhibition.

For example, if the orders taken during a show amounted to £200,000 and the total cost of investment in the exhibition was £20,000, the calculation would be as follows:

Sales	£200,000
Less cost of sales (say 50 per cent)	£100,000
Contribution	£100,000
Less cost/investment in the exhibition	£20,000
Return or profit on the investment	£80,000
This can then be expressed in percentage terms	$\dfrac{£80,000}{£20,000}$ = 400 per cent

The real ROI should in fact only be calculated from additional or new sales that were generated by the exhibition. Say the exhibition generated only five new customers, who in total bought £50,000 worth. The real ROI (on new business) would be 25 per cent. The word 'investment' is a bit misleading, since if the exhibition stand cannot be used again it is not an investment but an expense. If the exhibition produced only one new customer, who bought £10,000 worth, then the ROI would be negative.

Press coverage

One simple gauge is to collect the press clippings from the show. How important publicity and press coverage are as exhibition objectives determines how important this criterion is. See Chapter 14, 'Control – measuring media relations' for more on evaluating press coverage.

Experimental non-attendance

Some organizations decide to stop exhibiting and use the opportunity to measure the impact of non-attendance on their sales and on their competitors' exhibition results.

The many other functions exhibitions provide are not included in the costs or revenues used in the previous calculations. Other, non-selling exhibition activities such as maintaining a presence, projecting an image, entertaining customers, marketing research,

competitor analysis and product testing all, in a sense, save costs that would have been incurred if they were commissioned outside the exhibition. Arguably, these 'saved costs' could be subtracted from the other costs in these calculations. Real costs can certainly be saved by careful coordination throughout the whole exhibition planning cycle.

12 reasons for poor performance

James Dudley (1990) highlighted research findings indicating the 12 main reasons for poor performance. How much has changed?

1 Inadequate statements of purpose and objectives – nobody quite knows what they are supposed to do.
2 Poor-quality visitors.
3 Bad location of the stand.
4 Ineffective quality and design of the stand.
5 Undistinguished performance of personnel running the stand, because of poor selection, training, motivation or management.
6 Lack of follow-up of leads and enquiries.
7 Ignoring the competition and letting them steal your prospective visitors.
8 Poor recognition of company by buyers.
9 Poor corporate identity, leading to low recall of the stand by visitors.
10 Breakdown in organization and control, leading to last-minute panics, such as an unfinished stand on the opening day of the show or late arrival of literature, give-aways and so on.
11 Inadequate arrangements made for staff working on the stand, such as locating their accommodation too far from the event, failing to obtain car park permits or not organizing meal vouchers.
12 Inadequate control of costs and budgets, leading to over-expenditure and consequently a poor return on investment.

CASE STUDY 18.1   Sedgwick at RIMS Monte Carlo

This case study demonstrates the kind of detailed and integrated planning required to run a successful exhibition.

Situation

With 60 European offices, Sedgwick is the largest European-based insurance broker and risk management consultancy (and ranked third in the world). Although Sedgwick is well respected, the similarity of competitor products and services makes professionalism, quality and expertise vital in adding value to the 'invisible' service. The credibility of the whole company is largely dependent on the credibility of the sales and support staff. Exhibitions provide a platform for staff visibility and customer contact. The Risk and Insurance Management Society (RIMS) Monte Carlo conference is a focal point for the European risk and insurance market. It takes place every two years and consists of a three-day, high-level conference and exhibition that attracts all major companies and buyers in the sector. It is therefore essential for Sedgwick to be there.

Target audience

The target audience is risk managers of medium-sized to large companies and managers responsible for buying insurance (finance directors, company secretaries and heads of administration) across Europe.

Objectives

The marketing objectives are:

- to introduce the new European client service network;
- to introduce several pan-European products (including the multilingual service and the Eastern Europe network);
- to create an opportunity for cross-selling (new products to existing customers);
- to attract 100 visitors to the stand per day.

The communications objectives are:

- to reinforce Sedgwick's position as the foremost European-based broker with the best European network (including eastern Europe);
- to demonstrate true pan-European expertise (eg multilingualism);

- to project a visibly European image (and not UK dominated);
- to create a totally cohesive 'one company' (single European company) in a clear visual statement;
- to improve internal communications by creating a focal point for the meeting of staff from across the continent to break down barriers between divisions or trading companies.

Strategy

The above objectives would be achieved in a cost-competitive manner by developing an outstanding pan-European exhibition involving: a press conference and press lunch; senior speakers at the main conference dinner; hosting a major dinner; and an innovative exhibition crowd-pulling concept, all integrated into the creative theme 'One Europe, first in Europe'.

Stand design

The nature of the industry and the economic environment was such that lavishly designed stands could create a worry in the minds of clients that 'We are paying for all this'. For these reasons the stand looked smart, professional and European but was not a luxurious extravaganza. Visually, the stand took its style from the *ERA 2* magazine to create a cohesive look. All graphics were in French and English.

Tactics

Given that most of the RIMS exhibition visitors fell into the target group, it was essential to create a hub of activity around the Sedgwick stand. A new product demonstration was placed alongside a crowd-pulling cartoonist who sketched visitors on pre-printed, branded paper, giving full service and address details on the back. This allowed both client and prospect visitors to take away something that was personal to them but was also Sedgwick branded. The same artist drew European cameos of many countries for a competition. The production of Sedgwick's European magazine, *ERA 2* (published in six languages), was carefully planned so that it was available for the exhibition. The first article in *ERA 2* focused on Sedgwick's eastern European operations.

Action

The stand was staffed by an international team at all times.

Control

A post-exhibition meeting was held to arrange a follow-up schedule for all enquiries and to evaluate the overall exhibition performance. The new products and services helped to develop existing clients and attract new ones. One indicator of the stand's success was the front-page coverage of the stand and Sedgwick's keynote conference speaker in a magazine sponsored by a direct competitor. All stand members felt that the exhibition was a morale booster, and it helped them to feel more confident with their clients. The staff began to feel part of one European company. In fact, a subsequent pan-European slogan competition received 400 entries from company staff (nearly 20 per cent of the European workforce). Arguably, the winning slogan was born out of the new post-exhibition mood: 'One Europe, one broker. Sedgwick.'

Men/women

The entire project was planned by an in-house team with both international and exhibition expertise. Senior management support and commitment to the exhibition were evidenced by the constant presence and involvement of the managing director of the French operation (the local host). The UK-based European PR manager controlled the overall plan and execution.

Money

A basic three- by three-metre unit of exhibition floor space costs between £3,000 and £9,000, depending on the exhibition. At RIMS, the three- by six-metre space (two units) cost £6,500. An additional £5,000 was budgeted for all other items, such as the cartoonist, contractor, transport, graphics and telephone lines. The high-quality, lightweight, flexible, reusable exhibition kit was tailored for the RIMS exhibition and subsequently built into the 18 square metres of rented space. The standard shell scheme option was rejected ('too bland'), as was the purpose-built stand option ('too expensive', with a cost anywhere from £10,000 to £30,000). The budget did not cover travel and accommodation, which, as is customary in a large organization, was paid for by each individual trading company.

Minutes

RIMS is a biennial event. Sedgwick's planning started 18 months in advance. Early commitment and good relationships with the exhibition organizers helped to secure the best stand location (and choice of halls), speaker opportunities and details of attendees, especially the press. Quarterly meetings were held with French colleagues. Planning meetings immediately before the exhibition were held on-site. Daily planning meetings for all staff members (around 70) were held early each morning to agree the day's strategy before the exhibition doors were opened to the public.

Advantages and disadvantages

Here are some of the advantages and disadvantages to consider when deciding whether to increase or reduce this communications tool.

Advantages

Exhibitions contain a whole market under one roof in an engaging environment where the message can be controlled: prospects, customers, distributors, competitors, the media and many more. While exhibitions do create a presence (or awareness in the mind of key customers), they do generate business. Orders can be taken (sales can be closed), and new customers can be introduced to the brand. Enquiries can be taken and customer needs explored in conversations that otherwise might be difficult to engage in.

Disadvantages

Many exhibitors are looking at the total cost of exhibitions (including pre-promotion, attendance, design and build, staff, sales promotions, gifts and 'freebies'). Some exhibition traffic is falling, and hence exhibitors see their costs rising. Lastly, exhibitions are hard work and require pre-show training and motivation, which are also time-consuming.

Key points from Chapter 18

- Exhibitions are hard work. They can work well for the exhibitor if they are planned and integrated with other marketing tools.
- Exhibitions can form part of a contact strategy.
- Exhibitions need visitors – pre-show promotion is critical.
- Every element of exhibition performance can be monitored and measured with a view to making improvements in the next exhibition.

References and further reading

Black, S (1989) *Exhibitions and Conferences from A to Z*, Modino Press, London

Cotterell, P (1992) *Exhibitions: An exhibitor's guide*, Hodder & Stoughton, London

Dudley, J W (1990) *Successful Exhibiting*, Kogan Page, London

Engebretson, D (2000) *Exhibiting in the USA* (video), Trade Partners UK, Department of Trade and Industry, produced in association with Multimedia Marketing.com, London

Exhibition Industry Federation (EIF) (2002) *The UK Exhibition Industry: The facts and how to exhibit*, EIF, London

Gascoigne, C (2015) Engage your audience – and make it special, Raconteur Business Events, 28 May

Seekings, D (1996) *How to Organize Effective Conferences and Meetings*, Kogan Page, London

Talbot, J (1989) *How to Make Exhibitions Work for Your Business*, Daily Telegraph/Kogan Page, London

Further information

Association of Event Organisers
119 High Street
Berkhamsted
Hertfordshire HP4 2DJ
Tel: +44 (0)1442 285 818
Fax: +44 (0)1442 875 551
www.aeo.org.uk

ESSA Event Supplier and Services Association Limited
119 High Street
Berkhamsted
Herts HP4 2DJ
Tel: +44 (0)1442 285 819
Fax: +44 (0)1442 875 551
www.essa.uk.com

Society of Events Organisers
29A Market Square
Biggleswade
Bedfordshire SG18 8AQ
Tel: +44(0)1767 312986
Fax: +44 (0)1767 316255
www.seoevent.co.uk

19
Merchandising and point of sale

LEARNING OBJECTIVES

By the end of this chapter you will be able to:

- Appreciate the impact of merchandising techniques
- Empathize with a retailer's strategies and merchandising policies
- Discuss retail strategies and how they incorporate store image, store layout, merchandise ranges, colour blocking, point-of-sale, promotions and a range of miscellaneous items
- Ensure that a culture of constant analysis and improvement is employed so that results can constantly be improved

Introduction   498

New digital challenges and opportunities   498
Stores = mobile showrooms?   499

Retailer empathy   501

Retail strategy   502
Store image   502
Store layout   502
Merchandise ranges   503
Colour blocking   504
Point-of-sale displays and retail sales
   promotions   504
Sounds, scents and mindshare   504

Merchandising tactical tools   504

Measuring merchandising
   effectiveness   506

Advantages and disadvantages   510
Advantages   510
Disadvantages   510

Key points from Chapter 19   510

References and further reading   510

Further information   511

Introduction

There was a time when below-the-line point-of-sale (POS) materials were considered relevant only to cosmetics, perfumery, confectionery and other impulse purchases. Today merchandising techniques apply to a broader spectrum of markets, from consumer to industrial. Although vast budgets can be spent above the line on advertising to gain the customer's attention or change an attitude, fewer resources are sometimes allocated to that crucial moment in the buying process – the point in the buying cycle where the customer is physically in front of the product or service and is about to make a final decision – to buy or not to buy – this is why it is also called the 'point-of-sale' (or 'point of purchase'). Indeed, merchandising techniques have spilt over into websites where goods and services are carefully displayed. In a sense, merchandising and point-of-sale are even more important in the online world (see also Chapter 21).

In many consumer markets the consumer's final decision to buy is often made inside, and not outside, the store. There is, however, some debate as to exactly what percentage of decisions are made inside the store. Although '70 per cent of decisions are made inside the store' appears to be used widely, Court *et al.* (2009) suggest that these figures may vary according to sector. Neff (2010) suggests that retail stores have more impact than TV when generating awareness for new products. However, many buyers showboat, using retail stores to find what they want, leaving the store and buying online later.

Shopping for happiness

In the offline world, going shopping is still a popular leisure activity. In fact some tourist resorts offer shopping facilities as a USP. This is also evident in the United States, where retail centres almost double as leisure centres. 'Mall walking' is a significant activity. In the north of England, customers are transported by the coachload to spend a day at one of Europe's largest retail centres, Gateshead's Metro Centre.

Websites, mobile phones and apps may affect these figures significantly, as all of these tools are vying for the consumer's attention and attempting to secure the decision making before point-of-sale can persuade or dissuade a customer. See how Dulux is actively shifting the decision from inside the store to outside the store online (Chapter 4, 'The buying process' on Dulux). And mobile devices can influence a customer before, during and after a shopping trip. Paperless couponing, special promotions, and information via SMS and location-based advertising are likely to have a significant impact on the customer decision journey.

Merchandising techniques such as display and store design are therefore vital communications tools that can guide a buyer towards making a purchase. They are often the last chance to communicate with the buyer. Merchandising does not apply just to the traditional retail outlets of supermarkets, garages and department stores, but also to DIY stores, brown-goods retailers (stereos and TVs), corner shops, office-equipment showrooms and cash-and-carry wholesalers.

The merchandising opportunity lies relatively untapped in industrial wholesale outlets such as electrical wholesalers and builders' suppliers, where a lot of merchandising tends to look dusty, dirty and uninteresting. There is room here for creative, intelligent and effective merchandising. It does require a delicate balance, since a hard-working electrician in search of some 2-core 3-millimetre cable might assume a distributor to be too expensive if it looked too glitzy and comfortable. On the other hand, merchandising and free coffee here can provide customers with useful information and a pleasant shopping experience, for example reminding the buyer about other relevant products and any special offers.

New digital challenges and opportunities

Marketers have got to get technology developers, app engineers, virtual engineers, social media creatives, content marketers and mobile marketers to come up with even more clever ways to engage, entertain, inform, save time, and add fun or knowledge to today's shoppers. Can they make shopping fast and fun? How can they use the interactive potential between store, merchandising, mobile and the customer – a much sought after experience?

See the Campbell's soup case at the end of this chapter for more.

Stores = mobile showrooms?

Are stores becoming just showrooms for mobile? That is, are stores becoming changing rooms where customers try on clothes and then buy online elsewhere later? It's known as 'showboating'. Some retailers encourage customers to use iPads supplied in the changing room so that if they find the same product at a cheaper price, the store will give the customer a special gift that compensates for the price difference, if they still buy from them.

> 'Stores are becoming as much showrooms for mobile and online shopping experiences as they are active shopping environments', says Blippar CMO and founder Jessica Butcher.
>
> Gray (2013)

Shop windows connect via wifi, databases and geo targeting

Shop windows can integrate offline with online seamlessly. Shop windows can offer real browsers an engaging 'buy now' moment even when the shop is closed by connecting the shop window display with a mobile app, QR code or various social platforms.

iPads pop up like mushrooms in retail stores

> iPads are popping up like mushrooms in retail stores, where they're usually about as useful. The place I get my hair cut has one sitting next to the register, always displaying their Facebook page, which by now must be seared into the screen because no one ever touches it.
>
> Grey (2013)

An American retailer in Japan has been testing the iPad to take something very simple – the paper sign which displays the price for, say, a line of bags – and turn it into 'a bottomless pool of product

> ### O2 and House Of Fraser: retailing, wifi and geo targeting
>
> 'Retailers that offer free wifi have an opportunity to collect data, build lists, highlight the retailer's own in-store app and geo target messages to users whenever they are in the area. For example O2, has been working with House of Fraser stores across the UK to offer its customers free O2 wifi. As well as giving customers the benefits of good internet access, this clearly presents geo-targeting opportunities, including pointing wifi users to House of Fraser's own department store app to showcase deals, offers and planned in-store activities.'
>
> Gray (2013)
>
> See Chapter 13 for more on geo targeting.

information, video and social integration capable of sucking in shoppers'. The iPad can also help customers with product information, product walk-throughs, loyalty points and prizes. In fact the iPad's top priority was to make the store less about selling and more about what retailers call 'dwell time' (time spent in the store).

Competitors lurk in customers' pockets

Both Amazon and eBay want customers to use their apps when physically shopping in other retail stores. They want customers to scan any product's barcode and the app will tell them if they can get a better price and free delivery which will save them having to lug home some heavy products. So hyper-competition is in your pocket. Retailers now have to motivate customers to use the retailer's app instead of that of the competition.

Mobile and merchandising

In-store marketing (or merchandising) has to cater for customers' desire and preparedness to expand their experiences somehow onto mobiles. So how can a retailer add value to their customers' experiences when inside the store? That is the question for many retailers.

CASE STUDY 19.1   Useful shopping apps can help

Situation/problem

Opportunity: the target consumer (brand-loyal women grocery shoppers) is overwhelmed with the grocery shopping task and meal planning. Market research customer insights (graphic) reveals customer issues and concerns: busy lives, time, managing kids, [food] waste, and crowded stores.

Objective

Help customers by finding a solution to address their concerns and consequently boost sales and brand loyalty.

Strategy

Create an innovative grocery shopping experience and provide a helping hand to the consumer, while utilizing the CRM and branded promotions (and create consumer engagement). Basically the app helps the customer manage their busy life.

Tactic

Design a mobile grocery shopping application that gives the consumer the ability to plan weekly shopping, plan meals, get recipes, have ingredients added to the shopping list, and provide the consumer with brand coupons and meal suggestions.

FIGURE 19.1   Shoppers' considerations for grocery shopping time

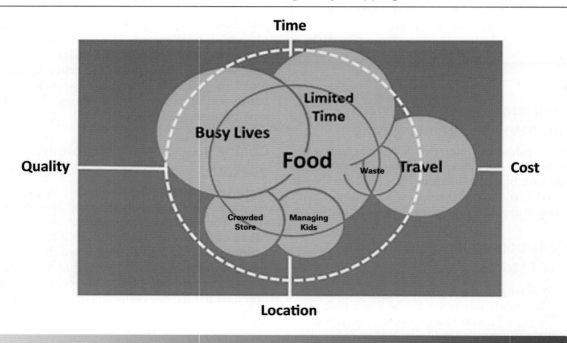

Dwell time decreases if companion/ child accompanies shopper

When working on a strategy to bring digital experiences to life in-store for Bloomingdales through CRI, one of the surprising insights had nothing to do with the customer's shopping behaviour in Bloomingdales, but more with the dwell time and attention span of customer when she bought a companion or child. Her dwell time decreased when she had a male accompanying her and decreased even more when she had a child or children with her.

When the customers are alone they accomplish their shopping. When observing a customer with a companion or child the flow of the shopper is interrupted.

The customer enjoys focusing on her shopping mission when alone or with an engaged shopping companion, and this is less likely when someone is in tow who is not engaged. When the unengaged shopper or child doesn't want to be there then the tension stirs within the shopper causing her to lose focus and want to tend to the care of her unengaged companion or child. These two men sitting on the uninspiring bench in the photo don't know each other. The man on the left was tapping his foot patiently waiting while his wife was looking for a new outfits; he said he does this every weekend. The man on the right had been waiting for the past 20 minutes for his wife to finish her shopping. He brought his iPad.

FIGURE 19.2   These two waiting men offer an opportunity to retail stores

Photo courtesy of Teri Sporato

This is an opportunity for a luxury retail store, or any store, to engage the shopping companions with the brand. The longer the attention of the unengaged shopper is occupied the longer the engaged shopper will continue on her shopping mission.

The Gap 1969 store took a leap and borrowed from the Apple Store. They placed a table in the centre of the store with several iPads for shoppers to use. On the iPad, the customer can browse assortments from Gap 1969 while the unengaged shopper could play games, check Facebook, movie times or simply browse. Gap 1969 created a feeling of wellbeing and comfort for the shopper, and for the unengaged shopper a positive brand experience.

Retailer empathy

Skilful supplier merchandising requires an ability to empathize with both the customer and the retailer/ wholesaler (distributor). Understanding customers is one thing. Understanding distributors and their perspectives, goals, strategies and tactics is another. It is easy to grasp the importance of maintaining the theme of an advertising campaign inside a store with carefully designed point-of-sale displays. It is not so easy to understand when, why and how a retailer will allow its space to be used for such in-store promotions and display, ie what its merchandising policies are and how to operate within that framework.

This '**distributor empathy**' helps suppliers to make their product or service (and the relevant marketing communications) fit in with the retailer's plans. The retailer relationship is even more important in today's UK retail market, since market power has moved from the manufacturer into the hands of a few major retail chains. It is therefore necessary to understand the various distributor strategies and their approach to merchandising techniques.

Some retailers do not enter into any merchandising arrangements with suppliers, as the retailers prefer to control all aspects of product presentation centrally to ensure commonality and consistency in all their stores. This is managed by carefully supervised store personnel and/or a roving display management and merchandising team. This does not mean that the supplier can have no involvement in the merchandising. Many stores encourage proactive contributions from their suppliers. Some suppliers gain permission to use their own display teams to ensure that their particular products or services have optimum display on their allocated shelf at all times.

Retail strategy

Every retailer has its own retailing strategy, which exploits its source of competitive advantage (eg exclusive products, lower prices, location or customer service). A department store exploits location, its quality of service and its range of products. A small independent grocery cannot compete on product range or price but can compete on its convenient location, opening hours and its personal service, friendly relationship and rapport. A takeaway restaurant may promote its unique home-delivery service. Competitive advantage is relative to competitors' unique selling propositions (USPs) and customer needs. A constant monitoring of the uncontrollable variables that affect markets reveals how competitive advantage can emerge or erode over relatively short periods of time. Strategies can change. Merchandising strategies are also affected by corporate cultures. For example, some distributors and retailers are more profit orientated than turnover orientated. This, in turn, affects their pricing, promotion and merchandising strategies and policies.

The more common low-tech merchandising tools are now summarized and discussed under six key headings:

- store image (external and internal);
- store layout (customer traffic flows);
- merchandise ranges;
- colour blocking;
- point-of-sale displays and retail sales promotions;
- sounds, scents and mindshare.

Store image

The human eye is more sensitive than is sometimes imagined. Clues about a shop are absorbed, often sometimes without our knowing it. Psychologists call these 'cue patterns'. They help shoppers to decide what kind of a shop it is before actually entering (if entering at all). The store's exterior offers an opportunity to communicate with customers, to invite them into the store or to reinforce a desired corporate image. Inside the shop the concept of the 'retail theatre' becomes evident. It has been suggested that a retail design concept lasts only three to five years, hence the need for the adaptable retail theatre that allows the store's interior layout and design to be changed easily. It is worth remembering that products, service and store design all contribute towards the overall store image, but if a customer has no prior experience of a particular store, or any word-of-mouth reference from peers, then the decision to enter or not to enter may be made solely from the store's visual image. The store's exterior is a bundle of cues. Even the psychological barrier or obstacle, the door, is removed or minimized wherever possible, thereby facilitating an even easier store entry.

FIGURE 19.3   Detailed attention to store layout is crucial

Photo courtesy of James Whelan

Store layout

Customer traffic flow can be directed around a store through detailed attention to layout. For example, 9 out of 10 people are right-handed and naturally prefer turning to the right, so most supermarkets have the primary doors on the left-hand side so the shopping is done to the right in a sort of clockwise manner. Flow-modelling time-lapse photos analyse which people go where in the store (and at what times, days, weeks or months). Further analysis reveals where the high-density areas are and whether they match the high-turnover areas. Customer movements can be predicted by model questions like 'If a customer were here (in the store), where would he or she go next?' This is important because, as a general rule, if the goods are in the wrong place they won't sell: 'out of sight, out of mind'. Primary and secondary visual points (as opposed to clutter) are used to pull the customer around the store or to 'shop the full shop' (visit every part of the store). Lighting, signage, photographs, software packages and even popular products like known-value items in a food supermarket help the customer to shop the full shop ('the more you see, the more you buy'). It is estimated that, out of the 25,000 food lines on display in a superstore, only approximately 250 are essential key value items such as tea, coffee, bread, etc.

Merchandise ranges

Once inside the store the customer is faced with a bundle of retail cues that are never neutral. Fruit or perfume is positioned at the front of a store (supermarket and department store respectively). This helps to create images and feelings of freshness and luxury respectively. Impulse products are placed at key positions. Cross-merchandising reminds the customer of related end-use products, which are carefully positioned beside each other, eg shirts and ties together, or pasta and pasta sauce. **The maxim 'Full shelves sell best'** is valid for FMCG (fast-moving consumer goods) retailers but not necessarily for some clothes boutiques. Although eye level is buy level, shelf positioning can reflect the current product life cycle stage. The larger retail chains use merchandising display software packages to determine the right allocation of space to a particular product or brand. An 'optimum shelf layout' printout (see Figure 19.4) shows what mix and quantities of packs on a shelf maximize a store's objectives (maximize sales,

FIGURE 19.4   Optimum shelf stocking printout shown from two angles minimize over- and under-stocking, maximize profitability). It presents a print-out of what the recommended shelf layout would look like. Some retailers like to have their own brands placed alongside the main brands, often on the left-hand side (since the Western eye reads from left to right and therefore spots the own brand first).

Colour blocking

A supermarket customer scans shelves at the rate of four feet per second from a distance of eight feet away. Packaging, therefore, has to work very hard to attract the customer's eye. Retailers and packaging designers sometimes use colour blocking to attract attention by placing similarly coloured items close to each other to create a stronger shelf presence. Colour blocking can also link colours to product-use associations; for example blue, green and white can be associated with stimulating and refreshing surf. This in turn might be built into the shower gel section.

Point-of-sale displays and retail sales promotions

This includes displays, sampling points, dump displays and so on. Many retailers will not allow suppliers this free space, since every square foot of retail generates a certain amount of revenue. In the appropriate store space, a retailer may allow the supplier the privilege of using extra space. Prime selling space can be bought by suppliers. A product's sales can be boosted depending on its location and shelf positioning. In-store sales promotion can tie in with advertising, cooperative advertising, publicity and perhaps even trade discounts and rebates. It should be designed to boost sales without creating any conflict with overall store image. Balance, proportion, lighting, colour and display units should be used to create the optimum impact on a consistent basis (perhaps across many hundreds of stores). Once the store grants permission, field marketing agencies can then provide merchandising teams to maintain proper POS displays or shelf facings.

Sounds, scents and mindshare

In-store sound effects can be used to make announcements (for example to direct shoppers' attention to a special offer), to add atmosphere (crowd applause in sports shop video walls), to relax the buyer or to stimulate the buyer to move faster (varying the types of music) and so on. Some POS tools engage customers in a dialogue by asking questions.

Scents are also used inside a store to change shoppers' moods and buying behaviour. The Monell Chemical Senses Center in Philadelphia has found its pilot projects highlight how the use of smell affects sales. For example, certain scents (in this case, a fruity floral scent) caused casual shoppers at a jewellery store to linger longer. An individual's brainwaves and moods (eg relaxed and trusting) can be changed by extremely low levels of certain scents. In the UK one home furnishings retailer uses a bakery and café to entice customers into the store to buy non-food-related products such as clothing and lighting.

In supermarkets it is interesting to note how odours are carefully managed; the smell from the fish counter will not be as strong as the wafting smell of freshly baked bread at the bread counter. London-based DigiScents can create a particular atmosphere in a retail store or evoke associations in the customers' minds through a variety of dispersion techniques, from central ventilation systems to hand-held sprays, liquids, granules, gels or powder (or even pressure-sensitive micro-encapsulated strips). All of these can help to produce specific moods or simply neutralize unpleasant odours. Effectively they create an 'aromatic logo' by impregnating a product or a service environment or just corporate literature with an aroma.

Finally, 'mindshare' (discussed in Chapter 12) combined with merchandising techniques provides an extremely potent communications package as the store's sales staff, space and display promote a particular supplier's goods.

Merchandising tactical tools

In addition to store design, layout, and merchandise ranges and policies, there are a number of in-store merchandising tools:

- leaflets and dispensers ('take one' boxes);
- stickers;
- posters;
- showcards and cardboard cut-outs;

- branded racks or display units;
- dump bins;
- three-dimensional:
  - injection-moulded characters (note that the toolmaking process required takes too long for some campaigns);
  - holograms;
  - free-standing floor displays.
- electronic gadgetry:
  - spotlighting systems;
  - video walls;
  - plasma screens;
  - illuminated display systems with fibre optics;
  - lenticular technology;
  - magic mirrors;
  - interactive POS systems, eg product advice systems, personal consultation systems, smart card POS suggested items.
- shelf space, eg number of facings, colour blocking (see p. 504) and integrated pack design (how all the packs look beside each other on the shelf);
- shelf positioning (premium locations, cross-merchandising, etc);
- in-store sampling;
- window displays;
- digital imaging and web-based merchandising analysis tools.

These systems have been available for many years. One possible problem with high-tech POS is that customers end up admiring the POS material instead of buying the product. On the other hand, products can benefit from POS support, as many products can get lost among the 25,000 lines of food that the average superstore displays. An innovative POS attracts attention – a key stage in the AIDA communication model (see Chapter 10). Although it is important to present fresh images to repeat-visit customers to maintain their interest and loyalty, many retailers' obsession with product density and profit per square foot means that they instantly dismiss most of a supplier's branded merchandising tools. In fact the majority of stores do not have the flexibility or the luxury of space to dedicate to one-off 'stunts' with in-built novelty obsolescence.

Whispering windows

'Britain's high street took a step closer to the dystopian future of science fiction movies, with shop window advertisements that talk to passing shoppers. The new technology conjures up visions of scenes like that of the 2002 hit movie *Minority Report*, in which Tom Cruise's character is assailed by talking billboards that hail him by name and plug their products.

The whispering windows being installed by John Lewis aren't yet so advanced – but the company says it has already shown impressive results in trials. "After installing whispering windows into our storefront, the number of people who stopped to view our window displays increased by nearly 50 per cent", said Kevin Scully, the visual merchandising manager of the company's Peter Jones store in Sloane Square, west London, where testing has been carried out on the system since June.

The technology originated from sonar work developed for the US Navy and is being applied for John Lewis by Newlands Scientific, a spin-off company from Hull University. It effectively turns a shop window into a giant speaker, using vibrations through a "bug" attached to the window to project sound.

So far, John Lewis has used the device to project the sound of music playing on DVD players and high-end plasma television sets in its store window – although the developers boast that it can also be used to make dummies speak. The whispering window is able to monitor the level of external street noise and set its sound output just above the ambient level.'

Adams (2003)

Virtual interactive POS

Many years ago, Brian Oliver wrote in *Marketing Magazine*:

Imagine walking into a high street department store and being greeted by a three-dimensional lifelike copy of John McEnroe's head. As you walk past, it starts to move and even speaks to you... pointing out the features of a tennis racket suspended in mid-air in front of you with no apparent means of support. Then a giant pair of moving lips mounted on a glass display suddenly start talking to you, inviting you to try on the store's winter fashions without even undressing. All you have to do, say the lips, is stand in front of a 'magic mirror', select an item of clothing and, before you can say 'Bruce Oldfield', your reflection is wearing it. Today many websites engage customers by inviting them to upload their head and shoulders photographs (for trying on spectacles on an optician's website) or a full photograph for a boutique (to see what certain clothes look like on the customer).

Bumping into 3D images

Reebok has developed 3D images that can be projected through shop windows and into the street. Using 'mirror technology' the image literally hangs in space in front of pedestrians. Pedestrians will be bumping into lots of 3D images as soon as production costs fall.

Lenticular displays

Lenticular displays present more than one image, which changes and catches customers' eyes as they walk by. Power sneakers and smart shoes are capable of uploading advertisements as people walk by a store (like a sort of digital chewing gum).

Location-based advertising and paperless coupons can be triggered by the actual location of a customer, so that, as customers walk through a shopping centre, their mobile rings, or a text message appears and mentions a relevant special offer in a store that is beside them at that precise moment. In-store screens and video terminals positioned at checkouts can transmit special relevant offers (based on previous purchase data) to customers as their store cards are swiped through the checkout.

Finally, virtual reality can allow all of this (walking, browsing, examining, buying and prompting) without customers having to leave their home or the safe confines of a local secure virtual hall or mall. And if you get bored you can nip over to the Louvre or to the cinema for a break without ever leaving your seat.

Measuring merchandising effectiveness

The bar code scanner at the checkout records what is being sold instantaneously. It can record the sales effect of allowing a product more shelf space, a different shelf location, special displays and so on. **Electronic point-of-sale (EPOS) scanners also measure sales responses to new advertising campaigns and price changes, as well as providing operational stock control data to central warehouses.** As suppliers and distributors work more closely together and become strategic partners, some suppliers are given access to a selection of EPOS data that measure sales results, store by store around the country, on a daily, weekly or even hourly basis.

This is similar to best practice web management, where the marketing team studies the analytics to see if there is any unusually busy activity on any particular product or service. Anything with a significant uplift in visits or sales can be highlighted on the home page to leverage the emerging popularity of the product or service. This gives the particular item an even bigger lift – until the next emerging popular item is identified and highlighted on the home page. Finding the most profitable mix of offers on the home page is similar to finding the most profitable mix of offers at key locations in-store. A constant process of analysis and improvement yields bigger and better results.

CASE STUDY 19.2   Campbell's Soup: where packaging and point-of-sale form a foundation for an integrated campaign

FIGURE 19.5   Campbell's limited edition cans soup

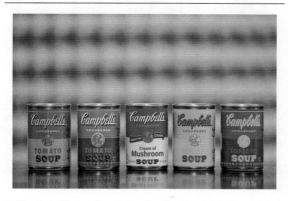

© The Andy Warhol Foundation for the Visual Arts, Inc / Artists Rights Society (ARS), New York and DACS, London

Situation

Campbell's Soup decided it was time to introduce its products to a wider market.

Objectives

- to build awareness for Campbell's new range of condensed tomato soup;
- drive sales and increase household penetration;
- to support retail listings drive.

Strategy

Create a limited edition Campbell's Condensed Tomato Soup featuring labels derived from original Andy Warhol artwork. Integrate a unique Warhol packaging with point of sale, and sales promotions generating UGC content, via the website supported by the PR campaign.

Unique POS creation

To encourage word of mouth and social media buzz once the product hit the shelves, renowned artist Stuart Murdoch was commissioned to create an **exclusive two-metre art installation,** built using over 2,000 cans, with both the original and the limited edition range. The use of the iconic

FIGURE 19.6   The limited edition cans were eye-catching

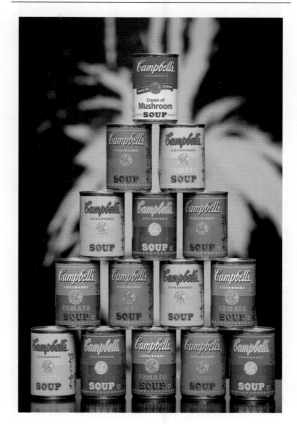

© The Andy Warhol Foundation for the Visual Arts, Inc. / Artists Rights Society (ARS), New York and DACS, London Table 1.1: The communications mix

red and white cans provided a platform of recognition for consumers, raised awareness of the new limited edition range and ensured both press and the public fully appreciated the relationship between the original Campbell's Soup can design, which many have an emotional association with, and the new limited edition cans.

The installation featured a well-known image of Andy Warhol on the front, made out of Plexiglass, framed by the brightly coloured new limited edition cans, raising visual awareness of the brand new range.

FIGURE 19.7   Campbell's two-metre art installation offered selfie opportunities

The installation was positioned in London's renowned Leadenhall Market for a closed photo call. National newspapers and news wires attended.

PR

In the months leading up to the launch, Campbell's targeted food, art, lifestyle and media news desks with details of the launch. Additionally the team approached key media and opinion formers through an intensive sampling campaign, also offering product for photo shoots. On the day of the photo call, samples were delivered to selected radio DJs and TV shows, resulting in coverage appearing on The Wright Stuff and This Morning, and Phillip Schofield tweeting about his love of the cans from both his personal and food-focused accounts!

Website

Working closely with the Andy Warhol Foundation for the Visual Arts in New York, Campbell's PR Agency, Wild Card, 'Warholized' the classic Campbell's website, redesigning the entire site to reflect classic Warhol styling.

User-generated content

A 'Warholizer' tool was built enabling visitors to upload images and transform themselves into works of art. Wild Card supported this through social media channels by

FIGURE 19.8   Campbell's 'Warholized' their website

designing a Facebook tab on the Campbell's page, encouraging fans to 'Warholize' their profile images.

Sales promotion

The 'Fifteen Minutes of Fame' competition on the website encouraged fans to submit appetizing recipes which include Campbell's soup, raising awareness of the benefits of the ingredient in many popular dishes. The competition was supported through Campbell's social media channels and sold across the digital landscape through bloggers and influencers. The winning recipe was professionally photographed and features on the Campbell's website.

POS and UGC

Post launch the installation travelled to three key regional Tesco stores in Watford, Coventry and Purley. The installation was situated at the front of store, engaging and educating consumers about the new limited edition range and providing a further photo opportunity for them (creating Campbell's-branded user-generated content). A team on site issued campaign collateral, money-off coupons and invited consumers to 'Warholize' themselves using iPads.

Control/results

Over 80 pieces of branded coverage have appeared to date, offering over 289,726,245 people the chance to view.

CASE STUDY 19.3   Thomson Tours

This case study demonstrates how vital merchandising is and how a field marketing agency manages the whole operation.

Situation

Major travel operator Thomson Tours enjoys a dominant market share and offers a wide range of long- and short-haul holidays to prospective customers via the travel agent in the competitive, and currently economically vulnerable, travel sector. 'Racking' (the display of a brochure in travel agents) is crucial to the success of all tour operators. Holidays are rarely booked without a comparison of the product offering from several competitors. Over 75 per cent of holidays are booked from a brochure that has been picked up and read. Few consumers ask counter staff for a brochure. It is therefore essential to ensure that the 30 different types of Thomson brochures are positioned in the right store, on the right shelf, at the right time of year. Stock of replacement supplies has to be ready so that the appropriate brochure is available at the point-of-sale at the right time. The several thousand travel agents mean that this is too big a requirement to be handled by Thomson's in-house marketing and sales team. Three thousand nominated UK travel agencies were targeted.

Objective

To ensure that the right brochures are available to the 3,000 nominated travel agents at all times.

Strategy

A comprehensive brochure management and merchandising support programme was developed and contracted out to the field marketing agency.

Tactics

Stamping, racking and ordering brochures as required and where stocks allow. This includes use of BOBCAT – a computerized brochure-ordering system based on Psion technology developed by Thomson with CPM Field Marketing. The system allows the merchandiser to transmit daily via a handheld computer to the brochure distribution house, thereby ensuring a speedy, accurate and effective stock control and delivery system.

Carrying out short sales presentations, highlighting key selling points to counter staff.

Action

Supporting brochure launches with additional tactical activity during key periods. Blitz operations such as these involve the team making 3,000 calls in two days, with the final results presented to Thomson three weeks later. Three thousand agents are visited, normally every two weeks.

Control

Thomson previously sent off batches of brochures to travel agents without really knowing which agents were running out, which agents placed them on which shelves and which agents had them thrown in a pile in the store room. The new merchandising system gives online data, which reduce wastage, as the team ensures the right brochures are on the right shelf at the right time. This has helped to increase sales by ensuring that the brochures are available at all the targeted agents. At the same time it has helped to reduce costs incurred by inappropriate print runs, unnecessary deliveries, etc.

Men/women

CPM allocated a team of 65 field staff, eight supervisors and one account manager to the ongoing field marketing activity. A team of 150 merchandisers and eight supervisors supports blitz operations at key times such as brochure launches. Both teams are headed by a national field manager who reports to Thomson's marketing department.

Money

Comprehensive field marketing activities range from £50,000 to £1,000,000 annually, depending on the size and scope of the operation.

Minutes

All field marketing staff attend a fortnightly half-day briefing. This is supplemented by six-monthly one-day sales conferences where major briefings and reviews are presented. The normal call cycle, which covers every one of the 3,000 travel agents, is two weeks. This means that every targeted travel agent gets visited and updated once a fortnight. Alternatively, a faster blitz can be completed within two days by using the extra 150 merchandisers.

Advantages and disadvantages

Here are some of the advantages and disadvantages to consider when deciding whether to increase or reduce this communications tool.

Advantages

Merchandising and point-of-sale are present at the point a customer makes a decision to buy, the very last opportunity to communicate with a customer before the decision is made. The message can be controlled, and it can range from ensuring customers are aware of the brand through to encouraging them to buy now. Special offers and sales promotions can be highlighted.

Disadvantages

Retail space is premium, and brands compete to get this space. It is therefore limited and expensive to secure. It is also expensive to create, deliver and install point-of-sale materials into the retail trade. Sales teams have to work hard and also try to motivate the busy retailer. Reverse logistics can be incurred at the end of a promotion if the POS has to be removed. Also the lead time has to include the retailer's time horizons as well as the time required to produce, deliver and install any POS.

Key points from Chapter 19

- Merchandising techniques not only offer a last chance to communicate with the buyer, but they can have a major impact on the customer's choice.
- Manufacturers need to empathize with their distributors' strategies and merchandising policies.
- Retail strategies incorporate store image, store layout, merchandise ranges, colour blocking, POS, promotions and a range of miscellaneous items.
- Constant analysis and improvement boost results.

References and further reading

Adams, R (2003) The whispering windows, *Guardian*, 8 August

Bryson York, E (2010) Shopping aisles at cutting edge of consumer research and tech, *Ad Age*, 15 March

Court, D *et al* (2009) The consumer decision journey, *McKinsey Quarterly*, Q3

Danger, P (1968) *Using Colour to Sell*, Gower, Aldershot

Engel, J, Warshaw, M and Kinnear, T (1991) *Promotional Strategy: Managing the marketing communications process*, 7th edn, Irwin, Homewood, IL

Erlichman, J (1992) How hidden persuasion makes shoppers spend, *Guardian*, 11 August

Gray, R (2013) Retail Revolution, *Marketer*, March/April

Grey, C (2013) The most ambitious in-store retail iPad integration we've ever seen, Fast Company Labs

Neff, J (2010) This upfront, P&G may want to boost spend on Piggly Wiggly, *Ad Age*, 3 May

Further information

British Promotional Merchandise Association (BPMA)
52–53 Russell Square
London WC1B 4HP
Tel: +44 (0)20 7631 6960
Fax: +44 (0)20 7631 6944
www.bpma.co.uk

Institute of Promotional Marketing Ltd (IPM)
70 Margaret Street
London W1W 8SS
Tel: +44 (0)20 7291 7730
Fax: +44 (0)20 7291 7731
www.theipm.org.uk

Marketing Agencies Association (MAA)
4 New Quebec Street
London W1H 7RF
Tel: +44 (0)20 7535 3550
Fax: +44 (0)20 7535 3551
www.marketingagencies.org.uk

POPAI UK & Ireland Ltd (Point-of-Purchase Advertising International)
Highfields Farm
Huncote Road
Stoney Stanton
Leicestershire LE9 4DJ
Tel: +44 (0)1455 271856
Fax: +44 (0)1455 273918
www.popai.co.uk

20
Packaging

By the end of this chapter you will be able to:

- Understand the three functions of packaging and the importance of packaging at the point of sale
- Explain how packaging design can create competitive advantage
- Appreciate the six design variables
- Outline the stages in the packaging design process

Introduction   514

The importance of packaging   514

The packaging opportunity   514

The three basic functions of packaging   514

The communication functions of the pack   515

The silent salesperson   515

Overprotective packaging   516

The long-term commitment   517

Brands, packs and corporate identities   518

The designer's tools   518

Shape   518

Size   519

Colour   520

Graphics   521

Materials   522

Smell   523

The packaging design process   524

Why redesign?   524

A packaging design brief   524

The packaging design process   525

Advantages and disadvantages   530

Advantages   530

Disadvantages   530

Key points from Chapter 20   530

References and further reading   530

Further information   531

Introduction

Once called 'the silent salesman', packaging has many purposes. It also presents opportunities to create competitive advantage and save money. Packaging designers work with six variables (shape, size, colour, graphics, materials and smell). Managing the packaging design process is similar in many ways to managing other marketing communications tools.

The importance of packaging

Since many sales assistants have been replaced by self-service systems, packaging today often has to act as a silent salesperson, helping customers by bringing a particular brand to their attention, highlighting unique selling propositions (USPs), giving friendly tips on usage and, ultimately, helping them to break through the misery of choice created by the increasingly vast range of seemingly similar brands. The plethora of 'me-toos' (similar products and brands) and the relentless fragmentation of markets mean that pack designs have to work very hard in these highly competitive, shorter life cycle markets of today.

The design of the pack can create competitive advantage by adding value, improving the product (eg improving the freshness or making it easier to pour, etc), developing stronger shelf presence, positioning a brand in a particular way, and creating or strengthening the brand's relationship with the buyer. The pack should be what top designer Michael Peters calls 'a visual magnet' that entices the customer to purchase and, eventually, become loyal to a particular brand.

Packaging can also be an extraordinarily effective advertising medium, particularly in terms of cost and penetration, and reach or cover of a target audience. On the shelf and in the home it continues to work, day in, day out, for 52 weeks of the year. In some ways it is a free medium.

No single element of the communications mix comes under as much environmental scrutiny as packaging. In a sense, packaging will reduce as oversized cartons and unnecessary layers of packaging are stripped away by environmental pressures (and some cost pressures). Good pack design also pleases the distributor and retailer by helping to make distribution, warehousing and use of shelf space more efficient. In fact, many warehouses are becoming fully automated distribution centres, demanding packs of a size that suits the warehouse handling equipment. Good pack design also saves manufacturing costs.

Falling in love with a pack

Packaging facilitates choice. Choice is rarely made on a rational basis. In fact, the consumer is faced with several thousand packs screaming 'Buy me'. A well-designed pack offers relief from the misery of choice. Ernest Dichter (1964) suggested that 'this relief may be derived through being permitted to like a product, almost to love it indiscriminately and irrationally'. A well-designed pack can offer this permission and so assist in the choice.

The packaging opportunity

Packaging is an area of opportunity, as some sectors are laden with impenetrable packs, inadequate labelling and messy packets such as boxes of tea that leak leaf dust, sugar packs that spill sugar and bottles that dribble after pouring. In a market where pack design is weak, a new design can steal the advantage. It is worth remembering that, although pack design at worst is just a recognition symbol, at best it can offer so much more. As the cost of advertising rises, product life cycles shorten and hyper-competition becomes fiercer, marketers need to get more from their packaging. Creative packaging can create competitive advantage. Even dull and seemingly staid pack designs can be redesigned to create a competitive, cost-effective edge (see the box 'Creative industrial packaging can also gain competitive advantage' on p. 523).

The three basic functions of packaging

The three basic functions of packaging are to:

1 protect (and contain);

2 offer convenience;

3 communicate.

First and foremost, a pack must protect its contents during storage, transport and usage. Some packs have to protect the user from the contents (as in the case of children with weedkillers, medicine, chemicals, etc). Sadly, some packaging today must also protect the contents from tampering. Six people died in Chicago when Johnson & Johnson's Tylenol pain relievers were laced with cyanide. There is a market for tamper-proof packaging and tamper-evident packaging.

Second, the pack must offer convenience in pouring, squeezing, storing, stacking and consuming (in cars, in the garden, on the beach, in the home and, one day, in space). Sugar and milk have yet to be mastered in terms of truly convenient packaging. Even a minute improvement in convenience can create competitive advantage, as demonstrated by Schlitz beer's pop-top can, which helped to boost sales from 5.7 million in 1961 to 15.1 million in 1970. On the other hand, some pack designs are so poor that they cause their own problems. In 1985 the Norwegian company Elopak had to use TV advertising to try to explain how to open Elopak cartons.

Third, the pack must communicate. Before concentrating on the communications aspects of packaging, it is worth mentioning that all three packaging functions are interdependent. The first two, protection and convenience, both communicate indirectly. For example, if the product is damaged, tarnished or stale, then a negative image is what remains, despite advertising, publicity and sales promotions that claim otherwise. Equally, if the instructions for storage or pouring are not communicated clearly, then the pack loses its protective and convenience capabilities.

Some products prioritize some functions over others. Some design solutions (or redesigned packs) cannot optimize all three functions simultaneously because of constraints such as cost or overall pack size limitations. Trade-offs, or compromises, between functions will then occur. Surprisingly, some optimum functions can be forfeited for other reasons.

The communication functions of the pack

The communication function breaks down into several different sub-functions:

1 grab the attention of the passing shopper;
2 persuade and convince the viewer that the contents match the promise made by advertising or the pack itself (the pack should say 'Buy me');
3 build brand personality and forge links with the buyer;
4 build loyalty with a pack that:
   – looks nicer on the table;
   – is easy to find in the garden shed or in the warehouse;
   – is distinctive and easily recognizable in a shop carrying 9,000 separate items;
   – is easier to use than the competition's.
5 instruct the user about how to use the product to optimum benefit;
6 inform the user of mandatory requirements such as warnings, source of manufacture and/or ingredients (buyers tend to want more information today).

The silent salesperson

The pack is the last and sometimes the only opportunity to communicate with and sell to a customer. All the other elements of the communications mix can get lost in the competitive and noisy jungle of commercial messages where each appeals for your attention. The pack is the silent salesperson. Initially it has to shout boldly to grab attention and then fade into the background and let the product benefits come forward. A well-designed pack can stop customers dead in their tracks and invite them to have a look, pick it up and pause for a few valuable moments while they are engaged at the point-of-sale. It is here that the pack can develop a dialogue by attracting, intriguing, arousing unconscious aspirations, informing, reminding, involving, entertaining and, above all, persuading.

The pack can arouse or trigger stored images from a television advertisement that have been lying dormant in the memory bank either if the advertisement includes a 'pack shot' (close-up of the pack) or if the pack includes some of the images from the advertisement. The brand can reflect images and aspirations. The pack can help the customer to recall those aspirations and develop associations between the aspirations and the brand. The hand lifts the pack off the shelf, allowing the customer, his or her other aspirations and the brand to move closer together.

Packs like Heinz are sometimes called **'trigger packs'**, because there is little dialogue other than the announcement of a strong, confident tone. The pack design concentrates on being recognized through its unique visual identifiers, colours, keystone, name and lettering, while heavy advertising communicates the brand values and aspirations. It is interesting to see Campbell's Soups dispense with Andy Warhol's legendary red and white livery and replace it with another aspirational soup setting. The Campbell's graphics portray product values that are arguably less protectable from the inevitable 'me-toos' sometimes produced by the retail stores' own labels. The Heinz pack and image are unique and therefore more protectable (in terms of branding).

Having said that, Campbell's introduced a limited edition Campbell's Soups can recently and integrated the new design online and offline across several communications tools. See the full case study in Chapter 19 on merchandising.

Overprotective packaging

There is a balance between protective packaging, sales, returns and overall costs incurred. Here are three examples from James Pilditch's outstanding book on packaging design, *The Silent Salesman* (1973). They demonstrate how over-packaging can be identified, reduced and subsequently used to boost sales and/or profits:

1 An electric light bulb company had a breakage rate so low that it prompted

FIGURE 20.1   Campbell's soup limited edition new designs

'Everybody must have a fantasy'   'Everybody must have a fantasy'

SOURCE: Wildcard

the question: were the bulbs over-packaged and too well protected? It subsequently reduced the grade of cardboard, and returns (of damaged bulbs) went up. The overall saving in packaging costs was greater than the increased costs of breakages and returns.

2 A detergent company used stronger boxes than its competitors. The distributors were aware of this and liked the better boxes, because they were able to put them on the bottom of the pile without their collapsing. The product was hidden at the bottom instead of being at eye level, which is the optimum 'buy level'. So the box weight was reduced. The boxes started to collapse and the detergent was soon freed from the bottom of the pile. Sales soon increased.

3 A London discount house was concerned over the lack of stealing. It thought, 'Maybe we make our goods too hard for people to get at', so the packs were redesigned.

The long-term commitment

The pack design needs to develop and change as markets constantly move away from existing products (and their packs). The pack may have to reflect changes in the customers' aspirations, incorporate demographic shifts such as an ageing population, exploit new technologically driven opportunities (such as microwaves, which require new food packaging) or simply highlight a new improvement in the product itself. There needs to be a constant review of customers and their perceptions, motivations and aspirations, and, of course, a constant review also of competitive packs. Sometimes customers simply get tired of a design.

One of the problems with packaging design is that it never shows up in a normal media budget. A major redesign involving a change of shape as well as a change in graphics can cost anywhere from £25,000 to £250,000 for the design stages. The tooling cost (the machine parts that the production line needs to produce the new pack shape) will probably double the cost. Packaging design is an evolutionary rather than revolutionary process. But not all designs involve three-dimensional

FIGURE 20.2   Spot the difference: subtle design tweaks increase shelf presence

changes; often it is simply a two-dimensional change of graphics. Sometimes this is so subtle (a 'design tweak') that the consumer is not even aware of the change, yet the new design will be working harder for the manufacturer. Look at the Heinz beans cans in Figure 20.2 and the subtle design tweak. Packaging design often does not sit comfortably in the marketing budget at all, but failure to get a pack right is tantamount to possibly wasting millions of pounds' worth of above-the-line advertising.

A constant design analysis looks at ways in which design can help to strengthen a brand's position. Heinz had maintained market share, but only at the expense of margin. Pack design gave it a lift. Turquoise is rarely associated with food except for Heinz. Subtle alterations were made to make the product more appealing and give it a stronger image for the future. The Heinz lettering was changed from a thin typeface to a fuller, more generous style; the keystone was broadened and a white in-line used to sharpen its impact; the lettering of 'oven' and 'with tomato sauce' was changed from turquoise to gold; and the tone of the turquoise background was enriched to create added warmth.

It is possible, as Dichter (1964) suggests, to fall in love with a pack. It is also possible, even for babies, to form extremely strong trusting relationships with a pack. The relationship-enhancing pack can also help to strengthen branding and even the corporate profile of the manufacturer or distributor that controls it. The next section of this chapter suggests how.

> ### Would you pour a pile of white powder over your new baby?
>
> 'Would you have the confidence to pour an unknown pile of white powder over your new baby? Put the powder inside the pack called Johnson's, and emotions are immediately evoked of the caring mother–child relationship. You would certainly trust the product with your baby. You would not be willing to pay much, if anything, for the powder alone. You would be willing to pay a premium for a brand you trust and believe in.'
>
> Lewis (1996)

Brands, packs and corporate identities

Some brands, and their packs, are inextricably linked with the corporation that owns or makes the brands (eg Heinz, Honda or BP). Others keep a lower profile with a more subtle form of corporate endorsement (like ICI's Crown Paints). Others still prefer to keep the freestanding brand or pack identity very separate from the corporation, which remains anonymously behind the scenes (eg After Eight chocolates and Nestlé). There are advantages and disadvantages to all three approaches. The corporate culture and diversity of products and markets can determine the specific approach. Packs can work in exactly the same way – linking the brand to the parent company. However, this may be restricted by the diversity of products and markets. For example, think of Esso ice cream, Lada airlines and Beecham's beer. If any of these products existed, the corporate link would not support the brand proposition; it would, arguably, detract from it.

The strengthening of the link between a company and its brands or packs can help the company by facilitating new product launches and brand stretching or brand extension (eg Heinz Weight Watchers). **It can also reinforce corporate presence** and, in turn, reassure different audiences, eg existing customers, new customers, investors and even employees. On the other hand, the link can create a design straitjacket that, as Lewis (1996) pointed out, 'inhibits the active development of sub-brands

aimed at different target markets'. Since different target markets often require radically different images, these images may pull in different directions, thereby detracting from the consistency of the overall corporate identity and image. In addition, if a particular brand has a problem (such as product tampering or a faulty production batch), it is immediately associated with the parent company. This negative reflection can, if the link between brand and parent company is clearly established, affect all the other brands operating under the same corporate umbrella. As James Pilditch (1973) said, '**The pack can contribute to instant consumer recognition of the company or the brand.**' Now let us consider the other communication functions of the pack.

The designer's tools

The six variables or tools a designer can use are:

1 shape;
2 size;
3 colour;
4 graphics;
5 materials;
6 smell.

Shape

Some brands have such distinctive pack shapes that they are recognizable from the shape alone, eg Baileys, Mateus Rosé, Perrier and Jif Lemon. Other pack shapes communicate conscious and unconscious meanings.

Ask a group to draw the first image, abstract or otherwise, that comes into their minds when the word 'love' is mentioned. If they struggle with this, ask them to imagine they are a design consultancy whose job is to design a logo for a new political party called 'the Love Party'. After a minute ask them to do the same for 'hate'. (Close your eyes or make a doodle yourself before reading on.) Over 95 per cent of the drawings tend to conform to the same perceptions about shape. The love image usually has softer edges, curves and maybe heart shapes, while the hate image tends to have jagged edges and sharper shapes like swastikas and daggers.

We may not consciously associate these meanings with shapes, but they are there. **During the Second World War, US paratroopers were tested to find whether they were shape orientated or colour orientated by being shown a film of abstract shapes and patterns.** The shapes moved from right to left and the colours moved from left to right. The paratroopers were then asked which way the design was moving. Shape-orientated men were supposed to be more intelligent, more stable and less emotional. The Thurstone test can be used for packaging design. It has revealed that younger children respond to colour more than form, while adults, and men in particular, react more to form.

Pilditch (1973) suggested that a rectangular box created images of sharpness, neatness and cleanliness, while a round box had associations of security, plentifulness and generosity. Go into a chemist's shop and observe the different packaging shapes used for adult and children's bubble baths. Some shapes give the product a value much greater than its contents. Shapes can also be masculine or feminine. Whisky bottles tend to be masculine in shape, while some perfume bottles are feminine.

FIGURE 20.3   This product can be recognized in the dark by feeling it

Shape affects the protection and convenience functions in holding, pouring and storing. How a pack fits into the hand is part of the study of ergonomics. A well-designed pack fits the hand more comfortably and creates what Coca-Cola proudly calls 'in-hand embellishment' (it feels good in the hand). In 1910, part of the packaging design brief for the now-famous Coca-Cola bottle read: 'We need a new bottle – a distinctive package that will help us fight substitution... we need a bottle which a person will recognize as a Coca-Cola bottle even when he feels it in the dark. The Coca-Cola bottle should be so shaped that, even if broken, a person could tell what it was.'

False ergonomics communicate unreal values to customers. For example, dimples (for fingers to grip) are sometimes placed down the side of a bottle, when in fact the bottle is rarely held by the two dimpled sides; instead, it is held by the two flat front and back sides of the pack. The subtle impression created by these false ergonomics is one of 'This pack looks slightly better or friendlier.'

Customers do not consciously choose one brand instead of another. Ergonomics can help to express that one brand is nicer to use than another. Real ergonomics help the user to have a more pleasant experience with the pack and therefore encourage repeat purchasing.

Some shapes reinforce product values by designing product features into the pack, as with the honeycomb effect on the base of a honey jar or the dimpled plastic two-litre beer bottles associating the product with a dimpled beer mug. Other shapes reinforce brand values, for example the historic liqueur bottle designed in the shape of a monk. The ultimate brand shape is arguably Jif Lemon's lemon-shaped pack. The Law Lords granted Reckitt & Colman exclusive rights to this shape; only Jif can use this unique get-up or shape to package lemon juice.

Can manufacturers own monopoly rights to a pack shape? The test, it seems, is 'whether the shape serves mainly to distinguish a product from its rivals and whether a competitor using the shape is seeking to mislead purchasers' (Warden, 1990). There are an infinite number of shapes. Pack shape can form a valuable property of the brand. It can become part of the brand or the brand equity.

Size

Size communicates. Would you give your loved one a perfume packed in a two-litre bottle? The corollary, ie large pack communicates better quality, is true in product sectors such as breakfast cereals. Consumer perceptions about cornflakes have been found to change according to size of pack. Large cereal packs build feelings of plentiful, expansive, energy-giving food, whereas a smaller pack may make the cornflakes seem heavy, solid and no good. Size can be used to communicate in different ways.

For example, a 33-centilitre bottle of premium beer cannot be fully poured into a half-pint glass. This forces the drinker, after filling a glass, to carry the bottle away from the bar and over to the table, where the unemptied bottle continues to work both as a badge and as an advertisement.

Different sizes are aimed at different segments, for example the family pack. Pack size can determine target markets, or is it that target markets can determine pack size? This may be similar to Ehrenberg's philosophy of marketing, which states that marketing means excluding many customers from a particular product (target marketing excludes the mass). Certain segments exclude certain sizes, as Coca-Cola discovered when it had to withdraw its two-litre bottle from the Spanish market after discovering that few Spaniards owned large fridges. If the colour were changed, would the pack then fit the fridge? Warm colours like red and yellow seem to advance or make the pack appear larger, while cold colours like blue recede and make the pack appear smaller. Although a change of colour would not have saved Coca-Cola's large bottle in Spain, colour does communicate in many different ways.

Colour

Colour communicates. Albert Kner, former design chief of the Container Corporation of America, said 'Colour is the quickest path to the emotions'. Words have to be translated into images in the mind. These images, in turn, have to be assembled, organized and categorized to give them meaning. This may be followed by an emotional response, which may subsequently trigger a physical response. Colour skips all this and goes straight into the emotions, often creating a physiological response. Colour is physical. Russia's Pedagogical Institute has found that most people can feel colours. Eyeless sight or 'bio-introscopy' suggests that all one's skin has seeing power. Red, green and dark blue have been found to be sticky. This may have something to do with electromagnetic fields. There have been claims that the Chinese can teach children to see with their elbows. Many years ago the US Color Research Institute found that the colour of walls in an office could make people feel sleepy, excited or healthy. More recently, a British police force has experimented with pink cells for prisoners. Red

increased blood pressure and pulse, while blue had the opposite effect.

The Lüscher colour test uses colour cards to analyse the reader's psychological, and specifically emotional, state. Green is 'the colour of the environment in Europe and a significant colour for all Muslims. It has religious significance in Malaysia and is popular in Mexico as a national colour' (Ronay, 2005).

Colour codes

Some product sectors, particularly food, appear to have colour codes. For example, within the carbonated drinks sector, red is cola and yellow is tonic. Freezer meat is red, fish is blue and anything low-calorie or diet is white. Pilditch (1973) has suggested that in the wake of health scares many of the world's cigarette packs now emphasize white: 'They hope white is associated with cleanliness and purity.'

Colours have meaning for people. Many people associate colours with images, eg 'garden fresh', 'mountain cool' or 'rugged manliness'. There was a group of people for whom 7UP's green bottle had almost medicinal links and therapeutic overtones: 'the thing to take when you had the flu and the doctor told you to take a lot of liquid'. Whether it is an annual report, a reception area, some sales literature or a piece of packaging, colour communicates. This applies to products and services in both consumer and industrial markets.

Colour affects perception. This is probably best demonstrated by Ernest Dichter's research (1964) into how packaging colour affects people's perceptions of taste. Unknown to the respondent, the same coffee was put into four cups. One of four different-coloured coffee cans was placed beside each cup. Respondents were then asked to match the statements below with each cup tasted. The research revealed strong perceptions linked with specific colours:

- dark brown can: 73 per cent 'Too strong aroma or flavour';
- red can: 84 per cent 'Richer flavour or aroma';
- blue can: 79 per cent 'Milder flavour or aroma';
- yellow can: 87 per cent 'Too weak flavour or aroma'.

More recent research into packaging colour and perceptions of washing machine powder provided interesting results. The same powder was put into three different-coloured packs. The respondents tried them on delicate clothing for a few weeks and were then asked which was best for delicate clothing. Respondents thought the performance (of the same powder) was vastly different. Statements below demonstrate the striking finding:

- largely yellow pack: 'too strong', 'ruined clothes';
- largely blue pack: 'did not work', 'clothes were dirty looking';
- blue and yellow pack: 'fine', 'wonderful'.

This differs from previous US research reported by Terrell Williams (1982) that tested identical washing powders in three different-coloured boxes; yellow, blue and red. The yellow detergent was 'mild, too mild really'. The blue detergent was 'a good all-round laundry product'. The red detergent was 'good for stains and the like'.

Colours may not be international, since different colours have different meanings in different cultures. For example, white is life, purity and diet in the UK, but it means death in Japan. Softer pastel colours and brighter colours are perceived differently around the world. In China, bright colours symbolize quality. Scott entered the Taiwan market with its US blend of pastel-coloured toilet tissues; the launch flopped. Sales took off when it changed the colours to bright red, yellow and gold. Can you imagine UK toilets with bright red toilet paper? Pilditch (1973) remarked, 'Not only do simpler folk like stronger colours, but people who live under bright sun have different values from those whose outlook is dimmed, say, by England's "leaden" skies. Think of this when designing packs to sell to Italian wine-growers, or Glaswegian dockers.' This is important, because cross-border packaging may become more common than cross-border advertising.

The cost of colour

Four colours obviously cost more to print than two colours. Can one be economic with the use of colour, the number of colours and the kind of inks? Is single colour too downmarket? Are four colours really needed? Has anyone tested a change in colours?

Graphics

Graphics communicate on different levels. The two-dimensional design on a label can help to create and protect individuality and uniqueness, reinforce a brand name or image, help to reposition, increase shelf presence, etc. The use of graphics is arguably the easiest of the designer's tools to analyse, as marketing managers are reasonably design literate as far as graphics are concerned. A naked body on the label of a bottle of beer will attract attention. However, not every brand manager wants this kind of attention. Graphics can use other images to make a pack stand out from the crowd. In terms of branding, the visual image should be distinctive and should make the pack immediately and easily recognizable. Even an ordinary tin box can become a valued item once some attractive graphics have been applied. **Graphics add value by adding aesthetic quality.** This creates 'stay-after value', which allows the branding to keep working inside the home for many years, sometimes generations. Graphics are sometimes used as a kind of sales promotion by becoming a limited-edition or collector's item, as in the case of the Guinness centenary Christmas label. Graphics can add value by offering, for example: additional features such as games (eg a box of matches with matchstick puzzles); intrigue; a room-enhancing, stimulating plaything rather than just a dull necessity (baby lotion with colourful children's toys); or quality associations with images of far-off places (coffee with palm trees).

Good graphics can create a mood or trigger lifestyle aspirations that reflect the often latent desires of the target market, for example a shampoo label showing an English country scene for one target market and a rugged desert for another aspiring lifestyle segment.

Attention to detail combined with an understanding of the cues and symbols that are relevant to a particular target market allow the designer to play with the unconscious meaning of symbols and images. In the case of a cooking fat, according to the psychologists, the positioning of a wooden spoon made it 'possible for the housewife to rehearse the use of the product while it was still on the shelf'. Pilditch (1973) explained that 'the spoon also served to inject the product with some of the reliability of grandmother's honest-to-goodness, my doesn't that smell good, old-fashioned kitchen'. In a separate piece of research the analysts turned to the number and layout of biscuits on a package. A picture showing biscuits scattered all over created psychological dis-comfort, or dissonance, because it suggested gaiety, disorganization, permissiveness and irresponsibility ('never know how many were eaten by the kids'). A different picture showing the biscuits in a neat line triggered associations with orderliness, parsimony, and fear of disrupting the line by taking a biscuit, which again resulted in unconscious psychological tension or discomfort. The third image of just a few biscuits on a plate cut out the chaos and the irresponsibility and invited the viewer to feel free to take a biscuit. The number of biscuits was, however, limited to demonstrate authority and control.

Graphics affect taste

In the same way as colour, graphics also affect taste perceptions. In fact, packaging designers can test different label graphics by asking focus groups or consumer panels to give their opinions on the taste of (unknown to them) the same product. The more elegant bottle will tend to have a refined taste, the macho label might have a stronger flavour, etc.

Graphics integrate with other packaging variables to create effective communications. Lewis (1996) suggested that 'if the form [shape and size of the pack] makes the statement then the graphics should step back'. The Lewis Moberly consultancy worked on Yves Rocher aromatherapy oils and created a tactile experience prompted by graphics 'by running the typography [letters] right round the bottle to encourage the viewer to turn it, touch it and begin to experience the product through the pack'.

Many years ago Coca-Cola discovered that its dynamic white contour curve (the flowing white ribbon underlining the Coca-Cola and Coke logo) reminded observers of the famous profile of the hobble-skirted contour bottle.

The graphics should be developed only after some other key questions have been asked. These include: Does the pack use the logo effectively? Can the graphics make space for future on-pack promotions? Do the graphics leave space for inter-national copy translation (usually requires more space than English)? Will the graphics lend them-selves or at least link with point-of-sale materials? Are the graphic images unique and protectable, or can someone else design something similar, leaving customers confused and unaware of their own brand-switching decision?

The other pack functions are also helped by good graphics; a blend of visual and verbal instructions

FIGURE 20.4   Bar codes provide useful marketing information

can make a product and pack much easier to use and store (convenience and protection).

Graphics can also indicate production processes or corporate caring values such as 'recycled' or 'free from animal testing'. There is some confusion currently because of the lack of central agreement on appropriate logos.

Finally, bar codes linked with electronic point-of-sale (EPOS) scanners at retail store checkouts help internal communications between the retailer and supplier by updating stock levels, reorder infor-mation and other sales analysis (eg by product, by store, by day, etc).

Materials

Materials communicate. Certain materials, like glass or metal, have an intrinsic value. Glass still seems to be associated with higher quality. Many wine drinkers would be suspicious of a supposedly top-quality wine if it was presented to them in a plastic bottle. Nevertheless, the packaging of wine has gone through the most radical of shake-ups. Thirty years ago, if someone had forecast that people would soon be drinking wine out of card-board boxes it is likely that the comment would have been taken as an insult – with hints of socially unacceptable behaviour. Yet today the wine box is arguably packaging's greatest innovation, with a nation happily drinking from cardboard boxes.

The materials used in packaging affect percep-tions of product quality. A good example of this was discovered in the United States, where, ironi-cally, the better product was perceived to be in the more difficult-to-open package. Crisps of equal freshness were packaged in wax paper bags and polyvinyl bags. The crisps in the polyvinyl bag were perceived (by 87 per cent) to be 'superior in taste and freshness' despite being more difficult to open.

Guinness found that packaging materials, and tins in particular, affected taste perceptions. There were comments like 'too gassy, it taints the flavour and it tastes of tin' (Nicholas, 1991). Pre-launch research of the Guinness draught can showed that in blind taste tests equal numbers preferred the pure draught Guinness and canned draught Guinness. Subsequent sight tests (showing the source, ie can or tap) revealed the hidden associations of tin cans: there was a 70:30 split in favour of the draught Guinness. Pretty Polly used tin as an innovative piece of packaging for its nylon tights.

Certain overseas markets have different packaging material expectations from what is considered to be the norm in the UK. For example, in Europe, meats, fruit, vegetables, pet foods and fruit juices are packed in glass. This means that if UK manufacturers want to enter these markets they will have to work with a new packaging medium, which may well be glass. In the UK, tin has an emotional quality. It can become even more emotional when mixed with shape and colour, eg a red, heart-shaped tin box of chocolates for St Valentine's Day. Today tin box packs are used for boxer shorts and children's clothes as well as food.

Technological developments allow relatively sophisticated printing techniques to be used on almost any kind of surface, as demonstrated by the attractive graphics used on today's cardboard wine boxes and tin boxes.

Some packaging materials have to work very hard. For example, microwave packs have to be able to protect and store the food at temperatures below zero and then have to offer convenience cooking by being able to be put into the microwave at very high temperatures. Some packs are then used to eat out of. Self-heating and self-cooling cans offer new levels of convenience. Apart from the convenience and communications implications of packaging materials, the final materials choice is integrated with a host of other factors such as optimum size, weight, strength, cost and filling speed, together with other features such as colour, closure, secondary packaging, shelf life, barrier properties, tactile characteristics and shelf impact.

Finally, material is the variable that is affected directly by environmental pressure groups. New legislation is putting pressure on manufacturers and retailers to use more environmentally friendly packaging. In the US, garbologists now probe landfill sites to determine the state of decay of various materials. In Europe, Germany leads the way in environmental legislation. A company's overseas growth may be stifled by packaging and materials that do not meet legislative criteria. Despite the logistical nightmare, the refillable pack is here to stay. The environmental factor has a direct impact on packaging and, in particular, on packaging materials. Warner-Lambert is developing a new disposable plastic made almost entirely out of biodegradable starch derived from potatoes, corn, rice and wheat.

Smell

Smells can change shopping behaviour. In a Philadelphia jewellery store some years ago, casual shoppers lingered longer than usual because, claims the Monell Chemical Sense Center, scents change shoppers' moods. In this particular case it was a fruity floral scent. Mood-changing odours change people's brain patterns. The *Chicago Tribune* reported the renowned, neurological director of the Smell and Taste Treatment and Research Foundation in Chicago, Dr Alan Hursch, as saying, 'Eventually we will be able to influence in a much more powerful way. By making people more relaxed or more trusting you could sell them more.' Scented packaging is becoming more popular.

Creative industrial packaging can also gain competitive advantage

The design resource is not exclusively reserved for FMCG goods. There is always room for design, creativity and innovation in industrial markets. Electric cable manufacturer BICC used pack design to stand out from the competition in the commodity cable market and to offer USPs to a traditionally conservative market. It moved from the traditional reel of cable to a newly designed box. This helped the electrical wholesaler by making stacking, storage and identifying (holes in the pack allowed the different colours of cable to be seen) a lot easier. The pack, however, was not allowed to look too upmarket, as the conservative buyers assumed it would be more expensive. Before phasing out the old cable packs (reels), they were used to advertise the imminent arrival of the new packs – the box of cable.

The packaging design process

Why redesign?

'If it ain't broke, don't fix it.' Perhaps, but some pack designs can become tired or dated, or the market simply moves away, making the pack's current position a liability. On the other hand, valuable brand equities or properties such as names and logos are assets worth maintaining. They may need 'tweaking' from time to time, but rarely need to be disposed of. Perhaps a creative brand manager and a professional printer can produce an updated or even new graphic design for a pack. Jan Hall, formerly of Coley Porter Bell, says this would be like 'putting together the Pope and a paint company to paint the Sistine Chapel'. Alan Topalian (1984) suggested that the designer's interest (or input) into the pack increases progressively during the course of the product's life cycle (see Figure 20.5). In other words, the pack design has an increasingly important role as competition becomes more intense.

A packaging design brief

The SOS + 3Ms can be used as a checklist when writing a design brief, which can be modified for packaging.

Situation/background

- Company (history, production facilities).
- Product (range, features and benefits, material properties, eg liquids, gases, chemicals).
- Market (size, growth, competitive structure, positioning, specific requirements such as pallet configuration).
- Target markets: segments, targets, decision-making units – particularly tricky with gift products, eg at whom do you target the design, the giver or the receiver?
- Reason for design (eg pressure from retailers' own labels).

- Brand factors and personality, key design elements.
- Merchandising display opportunities.

Objectives

What packaging functions are prioritized (protection, convenience or communication)? If communication, state the objectives specifically; repositioning from what to what? Or is the new pack design primarily aimed at shouting louder or creating a stronger shelf presence, etc?

Strategy

How does the pack fit in with the rest of the communications mix (the communications objectives and mix)? The brief may also state whether the pack design is a low-risk design project (new unit load, new material, temporary sales promotion, secondary panel changes, new ingredients, etc) or a high-risk design project (new name, new colour, new image, new logo, new shape, etc).

Tactics

Details are not always required here.

Men/women

These are the contact names for technical discussions (eg the production manager) and for marketing discussions. Clarify who makes the key decisions (who signs off or approves artwork, etc) and who can provide answers to miscellaneous questions. Provide the names of any other agencies that may be working on other marketing communications aspects, such as advertising and sales promotion.

Money

Money means the design fee, rejection fee (some designers charge a rejection fee for presenting ideas or concepts, even during a pitch), changeover costs (this may incur capital expenditure if a change of shape requires a new machine tool) and, ideally, an indication of the maximum unit cost of the new pack (the designer will need to know the size of production runs, etc).

FIGURE 20.5   How design attention shifts between content and presentation as a product progresses through its life cycle

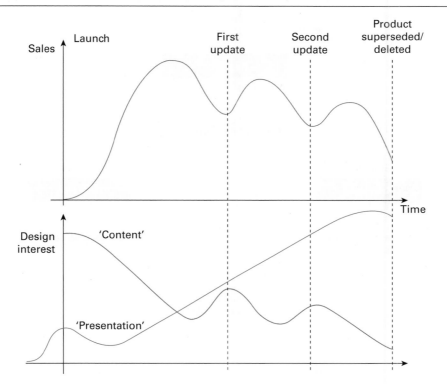

Minutes

This is the timescale. What are the launch deadlines? When must concepts be presented, agreed, researched, refined and approved? When must the final artwork be delivered? How long has been allowed for tooling (which can take up to 50 per cent of the total design time, eg three months)?

Measurement

What kind of research will be carried out to monitor the effectiveness of the new pack design?

Miscellaneous

Consider design constraints, eg size, shapes, colours, images or materials to be used or avoided because of technical, legislative and corporate restrictions on materials, warnings or warranties, and logos respectively.

The packaging design process

The brief may emerge after an initial review of the pack design. The designers (whether in-house or an external consultancy) often take the brief away, interpret it and rewrite it. Then they present this to the marketing team to ensure that everyone agrees with each other before embarking on any further creative work or research. This may be followed by further research, and eventually a range of concepts (two-dimensional labels and three-dimensional pack shapes, sizes and mechanisms) is developed for further research. This guides the selection of a concept for ultimate development into the new pack. Figure 20.6 shows the standard stages of a design project.

FIGURE 20.6   The packaging design process

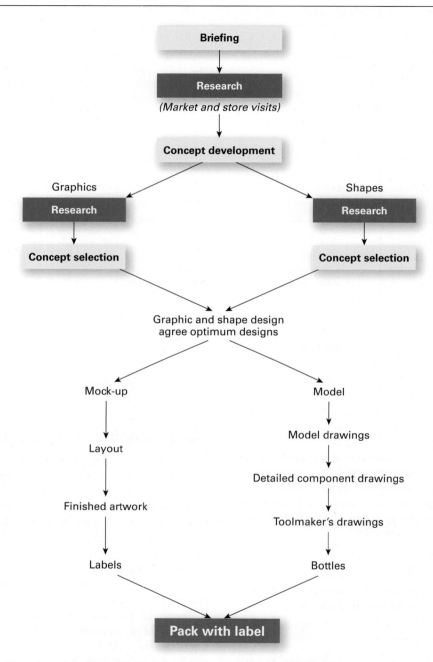

SOURCE: Adapted from the pack design management video *From Dream to Reality* (Smith, 1991)

CASE STUDY 20.1   Brand range development in India

Situation

The background

During the winter months in northern and eastern India evening temperatures can drop down as low as five degrees. This causes dry skin conditions ranging from general dehydrated, chapped skin to more serious cracked skin. The market is flooded with manufacturers advertising skincare products that promise to 'keep skin healthy'.

In 1929 GD Pharmaceuticals based in Calcutta identified the need for an antiseptic ointment to combat dry skin problems. Boroline was launched. It was effectively the first brand in the antiseptic cream category. The consumer offer was a perfumed multi-purpose skin cream for cuts, burns, chapped skin, etc. The trusted Boroline brand achieved strong penetration in eastern Indian markets. Although Boroline had firmly established itself within the market, it had not capitalized on the huge potential opportunity of national penetration into India's giant marketplace of a population of one billion.

Boro Plus Antiseptic Cream was launched in 1982 to revolutionize the antiseptic cream market, and differentiate Boro Plus from Boroline through product formulation and branding. The name Boro Plus was created, as it was seen to convey a sense of added value. The herbal formulation combined with the Ayurvedic concept (an ancient Indian healthcare system that means 'the science of life') was marketed as a preventative, curative and healing ointment. Leading Ayurvedic authorities endorsed the brand.

- *Competition.* During the 1980s an established Indian manufacturer of beauty and healthcare products, Emami, saw the bigger market opportunity to introduce a low-end product into the mass market to directly compete with Boroline. The low-end segment had cold creams (for night use) and vanishing creams (for day use). The antiseptic cream category offered a multi-purpose product in a massive market – if positioned and marketed correctly.

- *Packaging.* Boroline packaging was perceived to be dull and old-fashioned: an earthy green pack that had not changed since its 1929 launch and was not seen as attractive. It lacked 'Pick me up' appeal. The new 1980s Boro Plus pack colours were purple and white and delivered brighter, fresher contemporary colours. These colours were also attention grabbing.

- *Advertising.* An advertising campaign created the category for a more youthful and aspirational quality by bringing in Bollywood celebrities to endorse the brand.

The challenge

Although Boro Plus had performed consistently since its successful 1980s launch, it was meeting increased competition, in particular from international brands entering the massive Indian domestic market. Over 20 years after Boro Plus's launch, Emami needed to do something because, firstly, being recognized as an antiseptic cream with a multi-purpose benefit restricted new product extensions and, secondly, there was an opportunity to create a range of skin care products for both domestic and export markets. Emami recruited a London design agency, Evolve Creative, to work on the new branding and packaging because of its track record of working with international beauty and healthcare companies. They work closely together today developing and tweaking designs to meet the continually changing market opportunities.

Market research conducted by Emami among retail outlets and users revealed one factor that went against Boroline; the oiliness of the product on the skin, which meant that during warmer months the use of the cream was uncomfortable on the skin due to the heat, and therefore larger purchases were seasonal, ie during the winter. This, in turn, restricted the multi-purpose proposition, so Emami decided to reposition the brand from a traditional medical product to an aspirational beauty product.

Objectives

- To create a new brand (identity and packaging design) for both Indian and export markets.
- To strengthen the brand's credibility as a skin care expert by simultaneously expanding the product range to meet new needs.
- To help boost sales by a minimum of 30 per cent.

Strategy

Reposition the conservative multi-purpose pharmaceutical product to an aspirational skincare brand bridging skin health and beauty, and expand the product range to fill identified needs.

Brand development

The brand repositioning was achieved by highlighting the product's natural herbal formulation and creating a softer and more distinctive logotype. The design also linked the product more directly with the media personality used for a testimonial in the launch TV and cinema campaign. The result was highly successful, and the year-on-year sales increased by 32 per cent.

New product extensions

Immediately following the approval of the relaunch pack design, work began on a series of product range extensions for both the domestic and the international market, which were test marketed and launched in India. These successfully positioned Boro Plus as a substantial and serious contender in the broader skin care market with the consumer promise of a full, natural skin care regime. Emami now work closely with Evolve design agency extending the range further. Market research has revealed that there was also a need for a low-unit product (LUP) in the antiseptic category. It showed a large number of women wanted to carry a tube of Boro Plus in their handbags, but couldn't because of its size. With this in mind, Emami launched the 8-gram variant priced at five rupees. The affordable price point has triggered impulse purchasing, which allows customers to trade up as they move up the ladder of loyalty.

Results

Boro Plus now successfully dominates the market with a 70 per cent market share. It continues to expand the range to fill identified gaps as they emerge from ongoing market research. The brand's now extensive range is being established in international markets, including Russia and Africa.

Men/women

The team consisted of three people (two designers and an account handler).

Money/budget

The budget for branding was £6,500, and for packaging £7,000.

Minutes/timescales

The lead time required to create, develop, test, refine and roll out the brand and the pack was three months for the brand and five months for the pack.

FIGURE 20.7   Repositioning from a traditional medical product to an aspirational beauty product

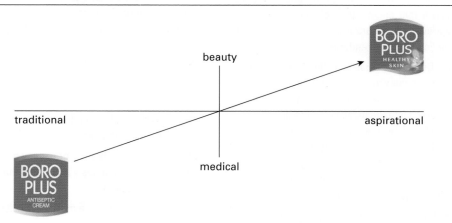

FIGURE 20.8
Original logotype vs
new identity

FIGURE 20.9
Boro Plus antiseptic
cream packaging

FIGURE 20.10
Boro Plus healthy skin
packaging

Advantages and disadvantages

Here are some of the advantages and disadvantages to consider when deciding whether to increase or reduce this communications tool.

Advantages

Packaging is the silent salesperson, catching customers' eyes, drawing them in and selling the finer detail as they digest the information. Like merchandising, it is often the last chance to communicate before the customer makes a decision. Packaging provides a platform where the exact message is controlled by the marketer (unlike PR and social media). It also carries the brand into the customers' homes or workplaces, so it keeps on working long after the sale. Great packaging stands out from the clutter and adds perceived value to a product. Within the retail environment, packaging can create or reinforce awareness as well as help to close the sale.

Disadvantages

Packaging requires long lead times and is expensive to change. The audience is obviously limited to retail traffic looking at the category. Wasteful packaging is not only an irritant for customers but also deemed to be un-environmental (in some markets this is a legal issue). If the pack is too trimmed or too light the product can get damaged.

Key points from Chapter 20

- Packaging has three functions: to protect, offer convenience and communicate.
- Packaging design presents an opportunity to create competitive advantage.
- The designer's six tools are shape, size, colour, graphics, materials and smell.
- All marketing is a series of processes, and packaging development is no different: there is a sequential method for managing the design process.

References and further reading

Bayley, S (1986) *Coke! Coca-Cola 1886–1986: Designing a megabrand*, Conran Foundation Boilerhouse Project, London

Dichter, E (1964) *Handbook of Consumer Motivations: The psychology of the world of objects*, McGraw-Hill, New York

Lewis, M (1996) In *Understanding Brands*, ed D Cowley, Kogan Page, London

Milton, H (1991) *Packaging Design*, Design Council, London

Nicholas, R (1991) Come home to a real beer, *Marketing Week*, 15 February

Opie, R (2001) *The Art of the Label*, Chartwell, London

Pilditch, J (1973) *The Silent Salesman*, 2nd edn, Business Books, London

Raeburn, O (2003) Design choice, *Marketing*, 8 May

Ronay, A (2005) Paint your brand, *The Marketer*, 15 September

Smith, PR (1991) *From Dream to Reality* (video), Media Services, London Metropolitan University, London

Southgate, P (1994) *Total Branding by Design*, Kogan Page, London

Topalian, A (1984) *Management of Design Projects*, Alto Design, London

Warden, J (1990) White paper gives shade to trademarks, *Marketing*, 27 September

Williams, T G (1982) *Consumer Behavior*, Research report, West Publishing, St Paul, MN

Further information

Chartered Society of Designers (CSD)
1 Cedar Court
Royal Oak Yard
Bermondsey Street
London SE1 3GA
Tel: +44 (0)20 7357 8088
www.csd.org.uk

Design Business Association
35–39 Old Street
London EC1V 9HX
Tel: +44 (0)20 7251 9229
Fax: +44 (0)20 7251 9221
www.dba.org.uk

The Packaging Society
A division of the Institute of Materials, Minerals
and Mining
297 Euston Road
London NW1 3AQ
Tel: +44 (0)20 7451 7300
Fax: +44 (0)20 7839 1702
www.iom3.org/packaging

The Museum of Brands
111–117 Lancaster Road
London
W11 1QT
44 (0)20 7908 0888
www.museumofbrands.com

Design Museum
28 Shad Thames
London
SE1 2YD
Tel: + 44 (0) 20 7403 6933
www.designmuseum.org

21
Owned media – websites and social media

LEARNING OBJECTIVES

By the end of this chapter you will be able to:

- Understand what makes websites succeed
- Understand what makes social media successful
- Ensure that the four key satisfaction factors are applied to your website
- Understand what increases the quality of the content on a website
- Understand what increases navigation's ease of use
- Convert visitors to customers and customers to lifetime customers
- Avoid the 10 common mistakes of social media

Owned media   534
Paid/owned/earned confluence and converged
    media   534

Successful websites   534
How to get visitors (SEO)   534
How to satisfy website visitors   536
Factor 1: high-quality relevant content   537
Personalized websites can build
    relationships   540
Factor 2: navigation   541
Convert visitors to customers   542
Convert customers into lifetime customers   546

Successful social media   547
10 steps to integrate social media into the
    business   547

Social media optimization – SMO is the
    new SEO   549
10 common social media mistakes   550
Excellent integrated social media –
    New York Giants   551

Advantages and disadvantages of permanent
    media   562
Advantages   562
Disadvantages   562

Conclusion   562

Key points from Chapter 21   563

References and further reading   563

Further information   564

Owned media

Owned media (your own website, social media platforms and apps), earned media (word of mouth, shares, likes, comments) and paid media (paid-for posts, tweets and advertisements) are referred to throughout this book. You have other owned media too including e-mail newsletters. Your content marketing is technically owned media and arguably your offices/buildings are permanent owned media because you can control and post your own messages, posters, images and ads (in the case of buildings – at least inside the building and sometimes outside too). However, 'owned' generally refers to your website, your apps and your online social media platforms such as Twitter, YouTube, Instagram, Pinterest, Facebook and LinkedIn. Owned media usually targets your brand's existing community/followers and/or current customers. We are going to concentrate on websites (first half of this chapter) and social media (second half) and finish the chapter (and the book) with some intriguing case studies including the most incredible Brazilian case of creating 'immortal fans' via owned media – all done by a football club that mobilizes its community primarily via social media.

Paid/owned/earned confluence and converged media

> According to the Altimeter Group, converged media utilizes two or more channels of paid, earned, and owned media. It is characterized by a consistent storyline, look, and feel. All channels work in concert, enabling brands to reach customers exactly where, how, and when they want, regardless of channel, medium, or device, online or offline. With the customer journey between devices, channels, and media becoming increasingly complex, and new forms of technology only making it more so, this strategy of paid/owned/earned confluence makes marketers impervious to the disruption caused by emerging technologies.
>
> Brito (2013)

Successful websites

Great websites are useless if they have no traffic. So before looking at what makes a great site, let us ensure we get the right traffic (or visitors). It is worth noting that many websites are built on social media engines like Wordpress, which also offers responsive design options/templates, ensuring the website is mobile friendly. In fact, it ensures it renders/displays differently ie it rearranges the website display (and apparent structure) to suit the device being used. Therefore many websites are effectively blogs (social media) although they may not look like a simple blog. However, we will separate 'websites' from the main public social media platforms like YouTube, LinkedIn and Instagram, Pinterest and Facebook.

> ### Why do you have a website?
>
> Do you remember the single most important reason discussed in Chapter 1, page 4?

How to get visitors (SEO)

A great website fails if it has no traffic or if it has poor quality traffic that does not convert into followers, enquirers or customers. Search Engine Optimization (SEO) can boost traffic as can all of the 10 tactical tools (advertising, PR, sponsorship, sales team/affiliates, sales promotions/content marketing, packaging, point-of-sale, events/exhibitions/conferences, social media, direct mail). Let us focus briefly on SEO.

SOSTAC® can be applied to each tactic (as demonstrated by the cases at the end of each chapter in the second half of this book). Here is SOSTAC® applied to SEO:

- Situation Analysis: see what works, what gets ranked highly and why (NB ask customers and prospects what would wow them).
- Objectives: set growth objectives; engagement levels (shares/likes/comments) and followers.
- Strategy: Think long term. Build an authoritative website with great content frequently posted using all media. Attract authoritative inbound links.
- Tactics: draw up a content calendar (see Chapter 16) and start creating great content

FIGURE 21.1

Here is an interesting approach to SEO

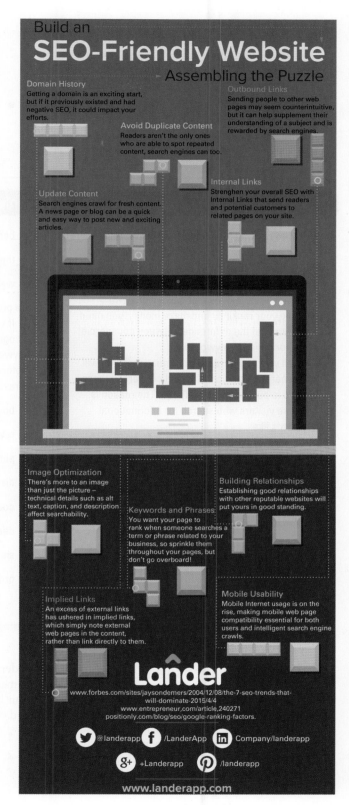

Courtesy of Landerapp.com

(avoid duplicate content); nurture relations with opinion formers/influencers/bloggers commenting, sharing, liking their content, offering to fill any dead links or any gaps in their content – get high-quality inbound links.

- Action: Optimize. Design and write for humans; insert key phrases and related phrases particularly in headings, headlines, bold text, initial paragraphs and tags. Make content and related content easy to find (internal links); nice design and layout, fast page load.

- Control: Measure and compare visitors/reach and engagement against (a) past performance and (b) competitor performance.

SEO: commercial phrases vs informational phrases

Keyword ranking for commercial keywords:
According to Brian Dean, *the #1 keyword research mistake is not spending enough time on commercial keywords.* That's because commercial keywords are the ones that make money. To improve your rankings and make money, you need to understand the difference between commercial and informational keywords.

If all your keywords are informational, you will still generate organic traffic, but converting those visitors to buyers may be difficult. The reason is because visitors who search for informational keywords like:

- how to clear acne with home products;
- how to install Wordpress;
- make money online for free;
- free ebook download;
- top 10 free article spinners

are not in a buying mood. They want you to speak their language – the language of free. In contrast, people who use keywords like:

- best acne products;
- top 10 web hosting providers;
- web designers in NY

are probably searching for a solution they can buy.

If you're in the e-commerce industry, you will recognize commercial keywords tend to convert well. Keywords that have the words below as a prefix (before) or suffix (after) to the rest of the keyword phrase tend to do well:

- buy;
- review;
- purchase;
- discount;
- coupon;
- deal;
- shipping;
- order.

Patel (2014)

How to satisfy website visitors

The quality of the customer's experience, both online and offline, directly affects brand image (see Chapter 2). Poor product quality and sloppy service destroy brands more quickly than any large advertising budget can build them. Sloppy websites not only kill sales, but they can destroy a brand. Whether it's broken links, long registration forms or confusing order forms, error-laden websites all do serious damage. Web usability expert Jacob Nielsen identifies four basic website factors that keep visitors satisfied and coming back again and again:

1 high-quality content;
2 easy navigation;
3 quick downloading;
4 updated information.

The last two factors are self-explanatory: sites that are slow to download (particularly on mobile handsets) will lose popularity, and sites that have out-of-date content will turn away visitors. This chapter concentrates on two of these factors: high-quality content and easy navigation. Marketers need to be familiar with various techniques to ensure they know how to use these factors properly. The chapter also explores 'sizzle' (exciting added-value content), customer engagement and customer conversion (from prospect to customer to lifetime customer), as well as the constant search for website improvement. The chapter then explores how to ensure social media actually win.

> In just a few seconds, sloppy websites destroy brands that took years to build.

Factor 1: high-quality relevant content

In addition to the usual offline and online market research (see Chapter 6), which reveals what the target market wants to see on a website, marketers can also ensure that their site is even more relevant by using:

- scenario planning;
- personas;
- sizzle;
- customer engagement.

Scenario planning

It's all about relevance. Once a brand stops being relevant to a customer, the relationship declines. One tried-and-tested technique for ensuring relevance is scenario planning. Marketers take each target customer type and consider, in detail, the customers' situation, how they might use the product or service and the steps they would take when buying. A chocolate company might have some customers who want to buy a gift for a loved one, some customers who want chocolates for a dinner party, and other customers who are looking for chocolates for a wedding. By exploring what would be helpful to

customers for each of these scenarios, marketers build sites that cater for each scenario, eg the wedding section might have ideas on wedding table layouts or love messages on chocolates, and the dinner party section might list ideas for dinner party games. **Scenario planning adds sizzle; because it is so relevant, customers love it.** A plumbing company might identify customers with emergencies (they need a big panel saying 'Emergency – call now 24/7' with a telephone number), while it should also have a section offering help and ideas for those who want to change a bathroom and those who want to redecorate a complete house. The ultimate example of scenario planning overleaf is so powerful that it delivered astonishing growth and created sustainable competitive advantage. This is National Semiconductor. Read on.

Personas

Personas also help decide what kind of content customers want. Essentially personas are 'thumbnail' descriptions of types of visitor. Advertising agencies used them for planning ads for many years, and now web designers find them helpful too.

Here is how Dulux use personas to create relevant and helpful websites. This case is adapted from Agency.com, which was available through the IAB (**www.iabuk.net**) and listed in Chaffey and Smith (2012).

The objectives of this project were to position Dulux.co.uk as 'the online destination for colour scheming and visualisation to help you achieve your individual style from the comfort of your home'. The objectives were to increase the number of unique visitors from 1 million to 3.5 million per annum and to drive 12 per cent of visitors to a desired outcome, eg ordering swatches.

The target audience profile:

- adventurous 25–44 women, online;
- lack of confidence;
- gap between inspiration (TV, magazines, advertising) and lived experience (sheds, nervous discomfort);
- no guidance or reassurance is available currently on their journey;
- colours and colour combining are key;
- online is a well-used channel for help and guidance on other topics;

Scenario planning that delivered massive success – National Semiconductor

National Semiconductor (NSC) supplies analogue and digital microchips that process sounds and images for mobiles and DVDs. Target decision makers are design engineers and corporate purchasing agents (they don't buy but they do specify what components they recommend at the beginning of new product development). This influences which components get bought later. The old website gave information about products.

The CEO one day challenged everyone and asked a great question: 'How can the website help engineers?' So a team launched a project to develop a deep understanding of engineers, including how they work (what their scenarios were). This helped them learn how engineers actually design components, leading them to consider creating online tools (on the website) to help engineers to do a better job (and save time).

They discovered that design engineers were under time pressure and realized that NSC could create easy-to-use tools that could speed the design process and save time, so they put a multifunctional team together (including marketing, application designers, web designers and engineers). They identified the design engineer's work process as follows:

1   create a part;

2   create a design;

3   analyse the design (simulations);

4   build a prototype.

NSC then created a web-based tool called 'web-bench', which helped engineers to complete the whole design process without special software. When engineers log on, they are prompted to specify overall parameters and key components. The web-bench auto-generates possible designs and complete technical specs, part lists, prices and cost-benefit analysis. The engineer then refines the design. Next, the design engineer can run a real-time simulation (using sophisticated software that NSC had licensed).

An engineer can then easily alter the design many times and save iterations in 'My portfolio', with an e-mail link to colleagues so they can run and save simulations. Once the engineer agrees the final design, the system generates a bill of materials for the prototype, complete with NSC's components and all requirements from other manufacturers, with links to distributors and prices.

The result is that an engineer can do in two hours what previously took months. Not surprisingly, design engineers loved it. More than 20,000 power supplies were designed in this way in the first year of operation.

What next? The team went on to ask engineers about other activities with which they had difficulty. This revealed thermal simulations and circuitry, so new scenarios and applications were built for engineers who design wireless devices. By the end of the year NSC had 31,000 visitors on-site, generating approximately 3,000 orders or referrals every day. One particular order, from Nokia, was for an integrated socket for 40 million units. National Semiconductor are now a part of Texas Instruments, but the web-bench facility lives on on the TI website.

Adapted from Seybold (2001)

- 12-month decorating cycle;
- propensity to socialize;
- quality, technical innovation and scientific proficiency of Dulux is a given.

Personas developed:

- first-time buyer Penny Edwards, age 27, partner: Ben, location: North London, occupation: sales assistant;

- part-time mum Jane Lawrence, age 37, husband: Joe, location: Manchester, occupation: part-time PR consultant;
- single mum Rachel Wilson, age 40, location: Reading, occupation: business analyst.

So personas help to tighten the content to match customer needs and ultimately help ensure high quality. Assuming your content is now relevant, how would you summarize your site? What is your overall theme or 'what is your one thing?'

Guidelines for using personas and scenarios to improve website design

'These are some guidelines and ideas on what can be included when developing a persona. Start or end with giving your persona a name. The detailed stages are:

1   Build personal attributes into personas:

   – demographic: age, gender, education, occupation and, for B2B, company size and position in buying unit;

   – psychographic: goals, tasks and motivation;

   – webographics: web experience (months), usage location (home or work), usage platform (dial-up, broadband), usage frequency and favourite sites.

2   Remember that personas are only models of characteristics and the environment:

   – design targets;

   – stereotypes;

   – three or four usually enough to improve general usability, but more are needed for specific behaviours;

   – choose one primary persona who, if satisfied, means others are likely to be satisfied.

3   Different scenarios can be developed for each persona as explained further below. Write three or four, for example:

   – information-seeking scenario (leads to site registration);

   – purchase scenario: new customer (leads to sale);

   – purchase scenario: existing customer (leads to sale).

After developing specific personas, a primary (most common) persona and a secondary persona can be identified. Other personas (complementary personas), although less common, may, if catered for on the site, generate extra revenues and can sometimes help marketers to think 'outside the box'.

Each persona may have a different way of deciding on which paint to buy (and ultimately interacting with the brand). Penny summarized her situation: 'I've got loads of ideas and enthusiasm. I just don't know where to start.' Customer journeys are worked out for different scenarios and personas, and the final website design reflects this by helping different types of customers through their buying journey.'

Wodtke (2002)

What is your 'One Thing'?

'Assuming your website content is relevant to your customers, what is your "One Thing"?

Jay Baer and Amber Naslund, authors of *The Now Revolution* (2011) explain the importance of defining your theme. Since you've identified your audience, the next step is to ask yourself what you want them to do. What's your theme? It's usually one of three things: awareness; sales; loyalty.

Loyalty and awareness can both lead to sales, of course – but stick to just one overarching goal for your strategy. Consistency and simplicity are key here.

Now it's time to get really specific. This might be the hardest piece in the assessment process, and yet it's critical to your success. Ask yourself, what does my business actually do? What do my fans say when they're happy? What is at the core?

Talk it out with your team. Together you can hone in on what Jay Baer calls your "One Thing" – the heart and soul of your brand. Your "One Thing" will affect every content and posting decision you make.

To borrow Jay's examples, if Disney = magic and Apple = innovation, what do *you* equal?

Your "One Thing" is the voice of your strategy across every network.'

Porterfield (2012)

Personalized websites can build relationships

How do you feel when a website addresses you by your name, and starts to show content that you particularly like? Personalized sites have been around for a decade, but soon it will be expected as visitors demand relevant content. 'Websites that lack the ability to change and respond to users will become ever less successful, predicts Sitecore marketing director, Shawn Cabral.

> The next page of content you show your website visitor should always be in response to your collective knowledge of them, and it should move the dialogue on to building a relationship with that visitor. Use implicit, situational data, such as a web visitor's location, device type, incoming search term or the website they were previously on. If you make it easier for visitors to find what they need, and make sure you display content that is suited to their device, they will stay on your site for longer and engage more.
>
> Hilpern (2013)

It is a simple as that.

Sizzle

The internet offers new opportunities to invigorate and add excitement to the brand, add some sizzle, add extra value (or 'added value'), extend the experience and enhance the image. Ask yourself, 'What experience could a website deliver that would be truly unique and representative of the brand?' Ask also 'How can my website help my customers [or other stakeholders – see 'Scenario planning' above]?' or 'How can my website add value that is so exciting that the site sizzles?'

Here are some creative ideas for sizzle. London's millennium wheel could offer a special virtual version of the tourist experience to those who have taken the actual tour. BBC TV shows could add a webcam into the green room where their celebrities congregate. Football clubs could add a webcam to their training ground or dressing rooms on certain days. A camera company could help users to learn how to take a great photograph by simulating taking photographs with different settings and allowing the user to compare and contrast the results (and also give tips on how to maintain the camera and invite users to send their best photos in to a

competition). A travel company could give customers a 'virtual friend' that advises on 'things you might like to do' in each city (determined by the customers' interests).

Drinks brand Bacardi sizzles online by maintaining the club scene atmosphere with its online value proposition including a pulsating beat, BAT radio (the logo contains a bat), video clips and cocktail recipes. Food websites offer printable recipes, video demonstrations and discussion forums, as well as 'Ask the expert' sessions. Chocolate companies generate ideas for using the chocolates creatively in desserts, dinner party games and designs for table layouts. One site that gives excellent service online is the UK Patent Office's trademark division, which allows visitors to search by name, design and date for similar or the same trademarks. Its integrated system ensures Patent Office staff are available to talk customers through any of the processes. It also gives visitors access to their own archived applications – all with the click of a button. A complicated and sometimes dull process has been made surprisingly user-friendly.

A more exciting brand perhaps is Harley-Davidson. Its motorcycle website offers web visitors a virtual ride and lets them actually see the same view a Harley driver enjoys, cruising through the countryside. This extra sizzle can enhance the brand in a way that can only be done online. Some sizzle is very simple but adds excitement and positive experiences to the brand. Now consider, arguably, another type of sizzle – customer engagement.

Customer engagement

Scenario planning, personas and sizzle should ensure reasonably high-quality content that customers are interested in. If the site content reflects the customers' interests, then the magic marketing formula is activated (identify needs, reflect them and satisfy them). This will bring visitors back to the site and boost results. Another approach is customer engagement, which means getting the visitor interacting, or engaging, with the site. The ultimate engagement is where customers create user-generated content (UGC). This collaborative co-creation is discussed fully in Chapter 1, 'The ladder of engagement'.

Some forms of customer engagement are so absorbing that they sizzle. One classic piece of engagement, discussed in Chapter 1, is threadless.com, where users send in their designs for T-shirts and all users vote for the best designs, which are then printed and sold online. This is UGC selling back to itself. These customers are highly engaged, as they are heavily involved with the brand – even creating some of its products. All brands have opportunities to extend the brand experience online by layering in new and exciting ways of engaging customers.

As customers move from giving a rating to a review to a discussion to collaborative co-creation, whether co-creating an ad, product or service, their level of engagement increases. UGC is a form of sizzle if it gets customers pouring their creative energies into a brand's website. This is collaborative co-creation, and it produces content. Some content will be better than other content, so a voting mechanism and/or a judging mechanism can be used to ensure that high-quality content receives prominence.

In summary, customer engagement, creating sizzle, developing personas and scenario planning combine to ensure a website contains high-quality content that is very relevant to customers, thereby exploiting the magic marketing formula (identify, reflect and deliver).

Now consider the second satisfaction factor – easy navigation.

Removing web content – difficult to do: why review and remove are such critical web skills

'There is often a fear of removal. Review and removal of old and out-of-date content is crucial for the successful management of large websites. And yet, these critical processes are lacking in most organizations.'

McGovern (2012)

Factor 2: navigation

Good websites are also carefully designed in terms of both form and function. Form means the way a site looks, ie the aesthetics, which includes layout, graphics, colour and typography. Function is interaction, integration, navigation and structure. Navigation and even the layout of each page require

expert advice and careful attention. Navigation is a critical aspect, as it determines how users can move around a site using menus, hyperlinks and signposts or panels.

Different visitors search in different ways. They use different keywords, headings and links. Placing an order should never be more than three clicks away. Remember, some people are ready to buy right now, others want to try it first and others again want more information. Telephone numbers and contact details should always be readily accessible. Site structure should be simple, consistent and well signposted in order to create flow.

Can customers easily find and use key pages?

What three things do you want visitors to get from your website?

Are they completing these tasks (eg viewing a page; registering; requesting a quote etc.)?

Is it easy to complete these tasks? Are there any barriers? And how do you know?

Navigation rules

The overall navigation structure should clearly demonstrate how content is grouped and how different pages relate to others. Without a planned structure, a site can soon end up as a 'spaghetti site'. At worst, this leaves visitors angry and frustrated. At best, it leaves them dazed, disorientated, confused and frustrated. If there is no natural flow, visitors may leave for ever.

Navigation requires careful consideration and eventual usability testing. This can be done on paper with mock-up screen grabs rather than on a fully developed site. Many navigation issues can be spotted before the site gets fully developed. Here are three navigation rules from *eMarketing eXcellence* (Chaffey and Smith, 2008):

1   *Keep it simple.* Do not have too many buttons. Psychologists who have analysed the behaviour of computer users in labs say the magic number is seven (or fewer). Any more than seven and the user will find it difficult

to choose. You can use nesting or pop-up menus to avoid the need for too many menus or too many menu items. Simplicity is necessary to avoid confusing the user.

2 *Be consistent*. Consistency is helpful, since you want to avoid users seeing different menus and page layouts as they move around the site. For example, the menu structures for customer support should be similar to those for browsing product information.

3 *Signposts*. There should be signposts to help visitors by telling them where they are within the website and what else they might like to see.

Cater for customers at different stages of the buying process. Some want to see more information, some want to try a sample, and some want to buy right now. So 'See', 'Try' and 'Buy' options can help (see below). These can be presented in different formats, particularly when catering for customers who prefer to receive information in different formats, eg video (demonstration), text (often a PDF article) or actually speaking to a human (call-back technology). Clearly label the different folders or directories on the site so they act as a reference point for describing particular types of content on the site (Chaffey and Smith, 2008).

Top tasks

Another aspect of navigation is identifying the main tasks that visitors want to do when on a website. The website design is consequently driven by these kinds of tasks. Although identifying the top tasks is important, it is ignored by many sites, particularly when different departments want to get some prominence on the home page. This is another form of scope creep (see Chapter 3, 'Beware of scope creep'). Here is Gerry McGovern (2010b) explaining how identifying top tasks can reveal insights that directly affect customer conversion rates, enquiries and, ultimately, sales:

> Another legal and medical publisher spent a long time trying to figure out what its customers' top tasks were. One area in which they publish is family law. After much discussion it dawned on them that there are really only two tasks that matter: getting married and getting divorced. If you went to their current website these tasks would have been very hard to find amidst all the clutter.

Have you heard of website creep? The new website launches and the top tasks are fairly visible. But there is an immediate and relentless pressure from the tiny tasks within the organization.

They all want to be on the homepage. They all want to be a news item or an ad. They want more links. And they will press and press the web team to give them these things. Little by little the tiny tasks clutter the homepage, the other major pages, the navigation and the search. And of course once these tiny tasks are published there is absolutely no incentive to review or remove them. Thus as the website gets old it gets worse. What is the classic solution? A redesign.

Raving alcoholics and web redesign

'A classic web redesign is like taking a raving alcoholic and sending them to rehab for a month. (Giving a website to a marketer or communicator is like giving a pub to an alcoholic.) They come out looking clean and redesigned. However, the underlying problems have not been addressed so six months later you're back in the same mess.'

McGovern (2010b)

Convert visitors to customers

In the offline world, many salespeople avoid asking for the sale or 'closing the sale', perhaps because of an unconscious fear of failure or possibly poor training. Whatever the reason, all the hard work of finding a prospect, getting an appointment, preparing, presenting, and handling objections is wasted if the salesperson does not ask for the business. The same applies online. Getting traffic to a website is one thing. The probability of a visitor actually buying increases if you:

1 apply the four basic satisfiers: relevance, navigation, fresh content and download speed;

2 develop credibility and reduce customer anxiety;

3 clear online value proposition (OVP);

4 have tailored landing pages with OVP tailored to a need (or a key phrase);

5   test multiple tailored landing pages;

6   have calls to action (many types of CTAs – consider adding a relevant incentive);

7   include 'See', 'Try' and 'Buy' options;

8   price lining;

9   simplify processes (remove barriers);

10   develop a contact strategy (potentially driven by digital body language).

We will now discuss each of these points in more detail.

1. Apply the four basic satisfiers

We have discussed these already. The four factors which satisfy customers and bring them back to a website are relevance, navigation, fresh content and download speed.

2. Develop credibility and reduce customer anxiety

Customers are nervous about giving their personal data and their money to someone they don't know, often thousands of miles away. They are also nervous about clicking a link that might take them somewhere irrelevant or aggravating, thereby wasting their third key resource – time. A typo-free professionally designed site is essential. An uncluttered design gives a reassuring sense of order amidst a chaotic world. Test the site regularly (so many sites do not do 'usability testing'). Customer endorsements, reviews and ratings and a list of high-profile customers reassure people, as do trusted internet infrastructure services like VeriSign, membership of professional bodies, and awards won. The 'About us' section should show photographs of real staff, contact details and, ideally, a photograph of a real building with a full address. Finally, at both 'Add to shopping basket' and the checkout it is worth reminding customers about money-back guarantees, whether the item is in stock and any express shipping options. Let customers know how quickly it can be received and what the next steps are. Buyer anxiety must be dispelled at every opportunity.

3. Clear online value proposition

You have got a couple of seconds (maximum) to communicate to a visitor why they should stay on your site. What is in it for them? What is the value proposition? Sometimes this is called the OVP (online value proposition). Is it clear exactly what benefits this site delivers? What's different, or better, about this site than all of the others? Ask six different members of staff to summarize what they think your home page offers (the OVP). Then repeat the exercise with many more customers. Use their feedback, along with your competitive advantage to improve your OVP to keep more visitors on your site longer, so that more will convert.

4. Tailored landing pages

When prospects click on a PPC adword or a hyperlink, they expect to land on a page that contains relevant information. They do not expect to land on a home page and have to start drilling down to find the relevant information, so make sure the visitors get to the relevant page with just one click. The more relevant the page the more closely it reflects the user's needs, ergo the more likely the visitor is to buy. Some sites serve personalized web pages that effectively remember the customer's preferences and therefore serve even more relevant content. Another approach is to create a microsite of tailored content to match a sales promotion or an ad campaign. Yet another approach is to create many variations of the same page, some with different offers, some with different images and some with different words, to see which page is the most relevant to customers by monitoring which test page converts the most prospects into customers. This is not as expensive as it sounds, as in the second case the marketing team can create and test these page variations themselves. First, see how some brands build tailor-made microsites dedicated to a relevant theme.

5. Test multiple tailored landing pages

Landing pages can be tested by splitting traffic so that equal amounts of visitors land on say, three variations of the OVPs for each relevant landing page. See the American Greeting ecards case at the end of this chapter for full details. Basically, three different landing pages are tested for each key phrase. The one that converts more visitors is retained and the other two are deleted. This optimizes your tailored landing pages.

6. Calls to action

Whether it is 'Register now' for an e-newsletter or 'Buy now', the call to action can be enhanced by adding an incentive to act now. Effective incentives include gifts, free products, reduced prices or anything that might nudge a prospect into taking action immediately as opposed to delaying a decision. A limited number of gifts or products may also act as an incentive to 'decide now'. (See Chapter 16 for more on sales promotions.) Well-targeted incentives do not have to cost very much but do have to be of value to the target market. Often these knowledge assets are content that the organization has already created for some other purpose. It effectively costs nothing to give it away as an incentive. Whatever the incentive, the calls to action should be visible across the site, as visitors land on different pages. Note that some countries do not allow free gifts and incentives. If targeting certain export countries, check first with UK Trade & Investment or the equivalent export bodies to see what is permissible. Finally, ensure customers are reassured by all the credibility factors, including money-back guarantees, customer ratings, reviews and endorsements, privacy policy, reassurance about security and full contact details including postal address and customer services (ideally via phone, e-mail and text or chat).

7. 'See', 'Try' and 'Buy' options

In the same way that an offline retail clothes store tries to let customers see its best clothes and then encourages customers to try them on in the hope of making a sale, websites can also accommodate the three stages of 'See it', 'Try it' and 'Buy it'. It can happen all in one go if online customers can try it there online immediately or try it for a period of time, followed by prompts to buy it (contact strategy). In the offline clothes retailing world, companies all know that getting customers to engage and try the clothes increases the chance of making a sale. The same applies online, although it may take a little longer. A key point to remember here is that some visitors have found exactly what they want and are ready to buy right now, while other visitors want to trial it, and others again are interested but want to see more about the product first. The site should accommodate all three types of visitor by offering all three options.

8. Price lining

Price lining effectively means having a range of prices so that anyone with any budget can always buy something, even if it is a sample unit or a small version. A range of sizes allows for a range of price points, which guarantees that anyone with any money can at least be in a position to buy something. Not having enough money or budget is no longer a barrier. A variation of this theme of having something for every budget is rental or leasing; some organizations partner with leasing companies that effectively give the customer a choice of paying a large capital sum or paying a smaller weekly or monthly amount.

9. Simplify processes/usability

All interactions should be easy, particularly form filling. Some marketers get greedy for data and think that, if customers are prepared to register for a newsletter or white paper or even buy a product, the marketers can collect a lot of data from the them (and maybe eventually do some really useful customer profiling or analyses). This is a mistake. Generally, visitors do not like having to register for anything, so if they do have to register make it easy for them by having only a few questions initially. More information can be collected later. If one of the top customer tasks is to download a white paper or register for a newsletter, make it easy for the busy visitor. Make the form short. Do not create barriers with forms.

Here is Gerry McGovern (2010a) with some stunning results that demonstrate how form filling can affect sales directly and indirectly.

Keep it simple. Keep it short. Visitors are under time pressure. Having seen the huge success of keeping things simple, HSBC wanted to see where else it could apply these insights. It decided to tackle travel insurance. Two per cent of travel insurance applications were coming through the web channel; it wanted to double that, so it improved the application form. It took only two weeks to redesign the website application form into a single one-page form. As McGovern (2010a) says: 'It took four months to get the compliance and legal department to sign off on the change, because they didn't like the simple approach – it lacked the detail they were used to. So how did that go? HSBC now receives more than 75 per cent of its applications for travel insurance online.'

Big forms kill customers

Some years ago, HSBC Hong Kong had what they thought was a reasonably straightforward mortgage inquiry form. It had 17 fields requesting:

- property information (address, price);
- applicant information (name, occupation);
- loan information (amount, repayment period, etc.).

They were getting two enquiries a week through the form. They felt that they could do better. They turned to Brett King, a well-known innovator in the industry (see his book *Bank 2.0*). Brett and his team convinced them to radically simplify the form.

They reduced the number of fields from 17 to 3: Name, E-mail and Phone number. The simplification process met some resistance. People said that the old form gathered data that integrated well into the internal system. People felt that the new form would encourage frivolous enquiries from the likes of Donald Duck and Arnold Schwarzenegger.

They finally launched the new form. There was no publicity or special promotion, so the basic number of visitors to the mortgage pages remained the same. However, enquiries jumped from two per week to 180 per week. And yes, they did indeed get mortgage requests from Arnie. Despite such frivolous enquiries, new mortgage business directly connected with the new, simpler online form reached $20 million in the first quarter after its release. With the old form they were doing less than $1 million a quarter.'

McGovern (2010a)

Tesco's usability tests focus on tiny details, integrating offline and online

'"Little tiny things make a big difference to the customer experience, and Tesco is unbelievably good at creating that differentiation", says Catriona Campbell, director at Foviance. When Tesco was developing Tesco Direct, Foviance was tasked with getting real customers to test the site.

"We used eye-tracking, so we literally tracked where their eyes were going on the catalogue and on the web, and we could see that some of the creative in the catalogue wasn't transferring to the web", she says. The usability innovations that came out of the research were not huge, but they made a big difference.

"It was things like putting the catalogue page number into the website, so you could search for something you had seen in the catalogue. Customers also wanted to see the Tesco Value 'stickers' throughout the website and the catalogue as well, the way they do in store. It doesn't make it easier to read, but they just wanted to see that big red splodge."

The point, says Campbell, is that true usability depends less on creative ideas that spring from nowhere than it does on asking the audience. "A lot of the things that came out of the research you couldn't have come up with in isolation", she says. "The creative had to go hand in hand with research into real-life situations, and the beauty is in combining the skills of researchers with those of the designers to get that creative idea out that really makes a difference.

"Little tiny things make a big difference to the customer experience, and Tesco is unbelievably good at creating that differentiation."' Woods (2007)

The ultimate way to check to see if the website is easy to use is to carry out usability testing. Here, customers matching the target market profile are given sets of tasks to complete.

10. Contact strategy

Visitors can be converted to customers even after they have left the website if, firstly, the organization has captured the prospect's e-mail address and name and, secondly, the organization follows up with a structured contact strategy. Each contact (e-mail, letter or phone call) usually contains an incentivized call to action. See Tesco's simple e-mail contact strategies for customers at different stages in the buying process in Chapter 3. There is usually a different sequence of contacts depending on whether customers registered for an e-mail newsletter, made an enquiry, took a trial or actually made a purchase. Making a purchase is just the start of what it is hoped is a lifetime relationship.

Advanced marketers watch website visitors' behaviour (or digital body language) to determine what, if any, contact is most helpful. This could be a pop-up message on a website, an offer of a phone call or a visit from a sales rep. A series of three visits online could trigger an alert to a sales rep (with the relevant prospect data) followed by a courtesy sales call. An alternative contact strategy would be where each prospect who engages with the brand through search, advertising, webinars or white papers is subsequently entered into a 'nurturing campaign' that combines direct mail and e-mail to strengthen the brand's proposition. Three visits trigger an attractive incentive-based offer to meet with a consultant.

> Excellent contact strategies vary according to the prospects' preferences in media type, frequency and style

Some prospects want information via RSS feeds into their RSS readers; others prefer e-mail, direct mail, podcasts, trade shows or industry analyst reports. Some want quarterly, monthly or weekly contact. The more engaged customers tend to be more comfortable with increased frequency of contact. The prospects' progression through the sales cycle can be identified by profiling both the communication frequency and any responses.

If open rates start dropping, prospects are either under time pressure or losing interest and therefore it may be worth reconsidering the contact strategy for them. Again all this can be managed by a set of rules that trigger various contact strategies and particular propositions and offers. Some prospects prefer rich graphical communication, while others just want the basic information in a text or e-mail.

Digital body language

B2B buyers today can do a lot of their procurement online without ever seeing a sales representative. They can compile a list of potential suppliers, brief them and subsequently analyse the best solution – all without a salesperson's visit, effectively squeezing the sales rep out of the equation. As mentioned in Chapter 1, many professional buyers meet fewer salespeople today, as they can complete a lot of the procurement process online. So, despite not being able to watch buyers' body language during a sales pitch, top marketers still know how to read (and use) their prospect buyers' digital body language. Marketers watch website visitors and know which prospects are at what stages, and almost what their thought processes are as they move through those stages. Marketers can give relevant information at the right time and ultimately help prospects to buy (either online or offline with a salesperson) without ever seeing the buyer physically. It combines digital body language with joined-up marketing.

Visitors can be scored according to their digital body language – how many visits to a particular section, how long spent on various pages, and what was downloaded – as these activities give an indication of how interested a visitor is in a product or service. Equally if several visitors from the same organization start spending time on a site, it may be an indicator that a prospect is warming up.

Expert marketers define what level of interest (or online activity) identifies a quality lead, where in the buying cycle the prospect is and when to bring a salesperson into a deal and when not to. Sales and marketing managers get to know which buyers are actively engaged in a buying process and which are not. Subtle digital buying signals are recognized. If digital body language is objectively scored and suddenly changes, this can indicate that the prospect has moved to a different phase in the buying process. It is the classic prospect entering the sales funnel and being helped through the sales process with highly relevant information and offers.

Convert customers into lifetime customers

The second visit to a website is the beginning of a relationship. Today marketers ask themselves whether they are giving customers enough reasons to come back and visit the site for a second time. It is a great question. Honest answers will improve the website. On the assumption that the site works and customers have bought once, how do marketers convert those same customers into lifetime customers?

How do marketers keep the relationship alive? Answer: the same way anyone keeps a relationship alive and well – by listening to them, understanding their needs, speaking to them regularly, always giving them good value (never breaking the promise) and occasionally giving them a nice surprise. What does that mean? It means marketers must deliver the quality the brand promises, have a contact strategy, respond to the customers – their questions, queries, worries, complaints or suggestions – and reward them occasionally. Part of the contact strategy includes acknowledging the order, confirming delivery dates, and following up with a satisfaction survey. Ongoing tailored special offers and reminders should help to keep the relationship alive.

Now that successful websites have been explored, consider successful social media: the key factors and the errors to avoid.

Successful social media

As mentioned in Chapter 1, social media is 'the biggest change since the industrial revolution'. Both Chapter 1 and all the other chapters refer to social media and how to integrate it into a wide range of campaigns. Chapter 16 specifically includes several social media campaigns that involve collaborative co-creation of digital art and music. This is exciting UGC and is at the top level of the ladder of engagement (Chapter 1). Chapter 13 discusses **UGC campaigns** that generate long-form ads, some of which have been broadcast as movies. As businesses scramble to jump on the social media bandwagon, it is now worth exploring how to integrate social media into business systems, how **social media optimization (SMO) is the new search engine optimization (SEO)**, and how to avoid the 10 most common social media mistakes.

10 steps to integrate social media into the business

Here are 10 steps towards integrating social media into business processes so that it becomes a normal process required to run a business (Brian Solis, 2010):

1 *Listen*. Staff members are allocated certain groups and communities. They search for the

---

Aren't lifetime relationships expensive?

'This is the age of customer engagement, experience, relationships and loyalty. There is an impression that these things matter when, in fact, they don't. Loyalty for most organizations is a one-way street. The customer is expected to be loyal to the brand. The idea of loyalty to the customer is not even considered... 66 per cent of marketers surveyed believed that loyalty programmes are for consumers to show loyalty to brands... relationships take time and effort... loyalty and caring are powerful human emotions but brands seem to want to get them on the cheap... Technology has been used to replace expensive human-to-human, face-to-face relationships...

- customer call to a US call centre costs $7.50;

- customer call to an overseas agent costs $2.35;

- automating the call/interactive voice response system costs $0.32.

"Our analysis suggests that migrating customers from channels they prefer to use to channels they don't, may lower their engagement with their bank" (Gallup 2013 study of banking customers).

A 2013 study by Accenture estimated "that the 'Switching Economy' puts up to $5.9 trillion of revenue up for grabs for companies globally."

So, organizations are saving on their relationship costs with customers but in the process are making customers less loyal and more likely to switch.'

McGovern (2015)

---

use of certain brands, people and key phrases and use listening tools such as Google Alerts, Twitter Search, Radian6, and PR Newswire's Social Media Metrics in addition to monitoring their own allocated communities. Log hot topics (generate a lot of comments) as well as the number of positive and negative mentions (sentiment). Listen for heated topics packed with emotion that could go viral.

2 *Create a presence*. Create a presence on the usual social networks, including Twitter and possibly Facebook (the fan pages), YouTube and Flickr. This is not strategic engagement, just experimental at this stage, 'resembling chatter or traditional broadcasting of messages'.

3 *Join the conversation*. Take the plunge, join some relevant conversations, and announce activities, events and competitions on your own pages or tweets. If in another community's discussion, add these announcements to the conversation only if they are relevant and useful. Keep a watch on the number or amount of friends, fans, followers, conversations, sentiment, mentions, traffic and reach.

4 *Identify communities, burning issues and opinion formers*. Moving beyond just listening to observing where the really significant conversations are, the types of responses and the language that is used can reveal burning issues, pain points, new ideas and a lot more valuable intelligence. Businesses do not have to be everywhere to create a presence, just where relevant conversations are occurring with significant audiences or influencers.

5 *Content strategy*. As the needs of relevant communities and opinion formers emerge, an organization can begin to define what kind of content, questions, challenges and collaborative co-creation it would be good to feed into these communities. This is the shift from ad hoc communications to a more carefully planned communications agenda. It means strategically defining the topics, questions, issues, worries and anxieties that a relevant community has that can be answered by the organization and its teams of experts. It is driven partly by the overall positioning the brand wants to achieve and partly by the market itself.

6 *Social media guidelines*. These guidelines are issued to everyone in the organization and particularly to those who blog, tweet or participate in discussions, or create videos, graphics or anything else that may be posted to social communities. The guidelines spell out the desired positioning of the brand, key phrases with which the brand wants to be

associated, typical hot issues in which the organization has expertise, and possible links to some of the brand's own popular pages, specific landing pages, articles, PowerPoint slide shows or videos. The guidelines can also include other brand guidelines covering tone of voice, use of logos and straplines, etc.

7 *Grow the community*. A community does not grow simply by establishing a blog, a Facebook fan page, a group or 'any old online profile'. A presence on these social media platforms is not enough. High-quality content that encourages members to share and engage with each other is required. Community members are also required, as are opinion formers. At this stage the brand must reach out and invite ideal participants and potential advocates to join the community. It is a significant task inviting and encouraging members to join a new social media community. This takes time and is part of an ongoing process.

8 *Socialization of the team*. The organization's own team has to believe in the power of social media, and needs to research and explore various social media platforms in search of useful information, whether for their personal hobbies or ultimately the business. Staff have got to get used to the sharing and collaborating potential of social media. The listening and conversing stages are only as effective as their ability to inspire transformation. Interdepartmental cooperation (sharing) is required. All staff are brand ambassadors and members of the social team. Social marketing integrates with CRM systems, as questions may need to be answered by the team. In fact any external-facing department will have to be socially mobilized. Internal social champions must be identified and encouraged to collaborate.

9 *Socialization of business processes and workflow*. Monitoring discussions, discovering great resources, participating in conversations, blogging and encouraging UGC all require staff time and also processes that ensure conversations are fulfilled and intelligence is collected, shared and used to make better decisions and ultimately run a better organization. New workflows require

the reorganization of teams and processes. Organizations will have to manage the social workflow. The ability to learn and adapt determines organizations' future survival. See Chapter 12 on Selling and Sales for specific examples of social media conversations converting to sales on page xx.

10 *Measure and report.* So that marketing can stop being referred to as the 'colouring department' (see Chapter 1), marketers must be able to evaluate the value of social media marketing (as well as all aspects of marketing) and present this to the board. For each social media tool, it is possible to quantify and compare ROI, cost per thousand, cost per enquiry, cost per order and cost per customer acquired across all other marketing communications tools, online and offline, inbound and outbound. The difficult bit is measuring the impact of social media on the brand value, which can now be included as an asset on the balance sheet.

Using Instagram photos to boost B2B sales

See Chapter 18, 'Exhibitions, conferences and events', page 488 for an Instagram checklist that boosts visitors, engagement, conversion and eventually sales, using simple photographs shot on a smartphone.

Social media optimization – SMO is the new SEO

Search engine optimization means optimizing a website so that it gets found by search engines and appears high up in the search engine results page (SERPs). A lot of effort goes into SEO but, as more and more searches being carried out start within social media platforms, it follows that social media platforms or, more specifically, the social media content needs to be optimized also. Social media content, otherwise known as social media objects, includes videos, photographs, blog posts, articles, white papers and even comments, status updates and wall posts. SMO boosts the findability and, consequently, the visibility of content created for social media.

When searching the combined universe of traditional websites and the new social media platforms, the same principles apply to SMO as SEO, and that is to use keywords and key phrases, titles, descriptions, tags and links:

- *Keywords and key phrases.* Use keywords or key phrases: the headlines, tags and descriptions. The first step here is building a key phrase list or inventory of words and phrases that the target market would use when searching for an organization's product or service. This requires marketers' empathy – the ability to think like their customers and list the words and phrases customers would use. Marketers also look at their own web analytics to see which words bring them the most traffic. They watch competitor sites to see what words and phrases they use. Their sales teams ask customers what phrases they use when searching. And the marketers use tools to generate keywords and compare popular ones with the same phrases used on other websites. Once equipped with key phrases for different products or services, marketers can then add them into the content as well as the headlines, tags and descriptions.

- *Titles.* These should include key phrases to attract searchers. It is worth trying to squeeze a keyword or phrase into a headline, rather than using sophisticated alliteration or intriguing wording.

- *Descriptions.* The same applies here. Key phrases should be included. In fact at least three can be inserted, but be careful to weave them in so that they sound sensible and not like contrived keyword manipulation.

- *Tags.* These are keywords that help to further categorize social media objects. Tags should include keywords that are relevant to the social media object.

- *Links.* As with SEO, links have the most impact on findability and visibility. Links drive traffic directly, as a link posted on Twitter or on a wall can boost traffic directly. They also tell a search engine that this object has some authority (as links equate to authority, particularly if the link is from a venerable institute or a popular site). This pushes it up the rankings, and it consequently appears higher in search results.

10 common social media mistakes

Here are 10 common social media mistakes highlighted by *Econsultancy*'s Patricia Robles (2010).

Many businesses are increasingly comfortable with social media, and many more have decided that social media is far too important not to experiment with. But the growing level of maturity in the world of social media doesn't mean that mistakes are uncommon. To the contrary: many businesses make the same mistakes over and over again. Here are 10 of the most common:

1 *Overfollowing*. Social media is called 'social' media for a reason, but there's nothing 'social' about following an ungodly number of users, especially in a short amount of time. Success with social media is just like marketing, sales and PR: results are achieved one victory at a time.

2 *Using every tool available*. Getting social media 'right' is harder than it looks. One of the things that's required: focus. But it's hard to focus when you try to build a presence on every popular social media website. Which is why companies should resist the urge to get involved with all the new and shiny toys and instead focus on the social media platforms that are most likely to be a good fit.

3 *Falling off the wagon*. A social media effort is easy to start, but it can be a challenge to keep going. In short, social media is a journey, not a destination. Businesses that aren't prepared for the long haul are far more likely to give up. That's not a good thing because social media is a party and the other partygoers (your customers, competitors, etc.) are likely to notice if you pass out.

4 *Not training employees*. Social media may look easy, but it really isn't. How your employees behave can have a big impact on your company's social media reputation. For companies that are actively involved with social media, setting expectations and creating policies for employees is the best way to ensure that they help your reputation, not hurt it.

5 *Letting the new kid or a low-level employee manage your profiles*. Who should be in charge of your social media endeavours? The young employee who joined Facebook back in 2004 and who has 5,000 followers on Twitter might seem like a good choice, but chances are he or she isn't. Your social media presence is far too valuable to leave in the hands of somebody who is new, inexperienced, lacks detailed knowledge about the company or isn't heavily invested in the company's success. Putting it in the hands of anyone else can quickly lead to disaster.

6 *Pretending that social media is free*. Signing up for a Twitter account and Facebook Page, for instance, may not cost any money, but managing them (and managing them well) doesn't magically happen without an investment that can be quantified in dollars and cents. Social media will always require somebody's time and may require that certain corporate resources be allocated differently. Businesses can't ignore these costs when planning their social media strategies and evaluating what they're delivering.

7 *Publishing first, thinking later*. In the world of social media, everything you say can and will be held against you. Unfortunately, the real-time nature of many social media websites encourages a 'publish first, think later' dynamic. Companies have far too much to lose, however, and need to ensure that what's being published is accurate, honest and in line with the company's values. Sometimes, it's better not to publish.

8 *Ignoring metrics*. When it comes to social media, companies need to be comfortable experimenting. But experimentation doesn't mean that companies shouldn't define the metrics by which progress and success can be measured. Measurement is just as important with social media as it is with any other business effort.

9 *Assuming ROI isn't possible to calculate*. The three letters R-O-I often make social media proponents cringe and social media sceptics grin. Many companies buy into the notion that social media is really, really important, but a lot of them also buy into

the notion that its value can't reasonably be calculated in terms of ROI. That's a mistake because for all of social media's virtues, any effort made by a business eventually has to produce tangible value that can be correlated to the bottom line.

CEO's cynicism of social media – mash me up?

'What's it going to be tomorrow – scan my body into a mash-up simulator to create a hologram so I can telepresence myself into sales calls in Madrid via FourSquare using Flickr? All I know is that I've spent a *lot* of time and money on a series of disjointed initiatives and campaigns and so far *none* have performed as advertised... so far nobody in my organization has stepped forward with a cerebral, strategic, multi-generational, integrated, systematic, and sustainable methodology and roadmap for synergistically capitalizing on this medium over the long haul.'

Byron, Kievman and Schrum (2010)

---

10 *Expecting the world.* Social media can do many great things for businesses, but it has its limitations. For instance, it isn't necessarily going to drive sales, increase brand loyalty or create buzz – especially overnight. Getting the most out of social media requires healthy, not unrealistic, expectations.

So these are the classic social media errors to avoid. CEOs are right to be cautious and right to demand more systematic and measured approaches to social media. However, the benefits of social media must not be ignored in deepening brand relationships, listening to stakeholders, and spreading awareness and presence, as well as generating enquiries, leads and sales.

Excellent integrated social media – New York Giants

American football team, the New York Giants use social media to 'give fans every opportunity to feel as if they are "part" of the team' ie they use social media to add value to the fan experience. Here's how:

FIGURE 21.2   The New York Giants integrate social media

May	August
FAN TICKET CONTEST	**TWITTER FEEDS IN BROADCAST/IN-STADIUM**
Ask fans to state why they were the biggest Giants fan. All stories narrowed down to 20 finalists. Giants then let the fans decide (vote) what they considered the best story. 10 winners were each featured on this year's game tickets. Total views of Facebook Tab: 238k. Total shares within Tab: 161k.	NYG integrate live tweets in the broadcast commentary during Giants preseason games. First team in professional sports to submit tweets using #NYGBCA which appeared on all of our stadium distribution channels. Giants fans loved the fact that NYG allowed fans to share with NYG how much the people they loved also loved the Giants.
September	**October**
9/11 ONLINE TRIBUTE MOSAIC	**ROOKIE HALLOWEEN COSTUME CONTEST**
By adding their own Facebook and Twitter profile photos, fans helped to complete a mosaic. Fans could also post a message in the mosaic. The hashtag #NYGneverforget allowed fans on Twitter to append themselves to the mosaic.	In partnership with Party City, fans vote via FB/Twitter for which Halloween costumes rookies would wear when do their hospital visits. Giants veteran players picked out the initial choice of costumes.

Continues over

FIGURE 21.2   *Continued*

ALL SEASON

Man Of The Match Extra Effort Player of the Game

Fans voted for their Man Of The Match (Extra Player Of The Game from a choice of three players for each game). Each player was given a unique hashtag, eg to vote for Eli Manning fans tweeted #Manning10.

PRE- SUPER BOWL

Social Media Night – #NYGsocial

On the Thursday before the Super Bowl whomever answers questions submitted to them via Twitter. Each player is given a hashtag which allows fans to submit their questions. The hour=long LIVE webcast was broadcasted from the Giants team hotel on Giants.com.

SUPERBOWL

Twibbon (Ribbon/Badge)

NFC East Champions/Super Bowl Champions Get Twibbon.

A Twibbon Campaign is your own microsite where users can support your *cause, brand* or *organization* in a variety of ways. Saves time.

Fans add a custom badge to their Facebook or Twitter profile by clicking one button.

Super Bowl Social Media Initiatives – Follow 30 Players Via One Microsite

Fans could follow the Giants players all the way to Indianapolis.

NYG launched a microsite that allowed our fans to follow all Giants players who had Twitter accounts.

Website: **http://www.giants.com/assets/standalone/connect/default.html**

Behind The Scenes Web Cam

Give fans access to behind the scenes video footage each day if 10,000 'likes' were given on NYG Facebook page. Each day, fresh footage was captured of training, eating and general behind the scenes.

What made this campaign a success? Unique, relevant content. This footage was genuine, behind-the-scenes material that no blog, website or TV network could get. So in this example, the social media actually helps to create a lot of relevant content, engage customers and add value to the overall brand experience. Four case studies follow that show creative social media in action. Social media can generate an ongoing systematic dialogue with stakeholders (rather than a one-off campaign). These social media campaigns are a starting point to create dialogue, interaction and UGC, which boost engagement and embed key messages.

CASE STUDY 21.1   Brazilian football club creates immortal fans via social media

Situation

Organ donation was taboo in Brazil for many people. Yet people are dying every day because they cannot find a suitable donated organ. Hospitals have waiting lists of desperately sick patients on stand-by waiting, hoping and praying that someone somewhere has been kind enough to have committed to donating an organ. Brazil's Sport Club Recife is known for having some of the most passionate football fans in Brazil. 'First God. Second Sport Club Recife. Third Family. Fourth work' says one fan. 'Nothing else matters... Sport Club Recife is everything' says another fan. They are passionate about life (and death too). Perhaps this passionate community can help each other by committing to become organ donors? The club has owned media which includes a Facebook page, website, match day programmes and signage (around the stadium).

Objective

The board agreed to mobilize the fans and get as many of them as they could to sign up and become organ donors. This supports the club's community goals and its corporate social responsibility goals of helping their community.

Strategy

Create the first football club organ donor card by mobilizing the passion, harnessing the club's community energy and creating 'Immortal Fans' whose organs keep on living (in other people's bodies), long after the donor has died. At minimal cost since it leverages the club's owned media, which includes its website, Facebook page, YouTube channel, match day programme and some posters around the stadium.

Sport Club Recife fans want to be fans forever. Now they can. The first organ donor card for a football team.

The club has created a new kind of fan – the immortal fan! Their hearts, eyes, lungs... could keep cheering for Sport Club Recife even after death. And the fans responded. Fifty thousand of them are committed to helping others after they die. Organ donation was taboo in Brazil for many people. Sport Club Recife are changing that. They have helped to **reduce the waiting list** for heart transplant and cornea transplant to zero.

Tactics

YouTube and Facebook were the main tactical tools used to drive this unique and highly successful campaign. The extraordinary YouTube video shows passionate fans that care – some that need an organ, some who have received an organ and some who want to donate. Adriano Dos Santos (was waiting for an eye transplant) says: 'I promise your eyes will keep on watching Sport Club Recife.' Luiz Antonio (who was waiting for a lung transplant) says: 'Your lungs will keep on breathing for Sport Club Recife.' Marleade Dos Santos (who was waiting for a heart transplant) says: 'I promise your heart will always beat for Sport Club Recife.'

One lady who received a heart transplant says: 'My new heart comes from a Sport Club Recife fan and it will keep on beating for Sport Club Recife. C'mon Sport Club Recife fans, let's donate! Let's form this chain and never stop donating.'

You can see this extraordinary YouTube video that helped to create the world's first organ donor football club on **www.GreatSportsmanship.org** (to find it, search for 'Brazil' or scroll back to Nov 2014).

FIGURE 21.3   The flowing banner says: Everything for Sport Recife. Even after death

Action

Fans get their organ donor card through their preferred channel:

- at the stadium;
- through a Facebook app; or
- receive it at home by mail.

The greatest difficulty that exists in the organ donation process, is the family authorization. So this barrier was removed by ensuring the donor cards communicate with the donor's family. The organ donor card also informs the family of the fan's donation wishes.

Control (measurement/results)

Fifty-one thousand Recife fans have signed up to donate their organs after they die (more than the stadium capacity).

Men/women

The agency Ogilvy shaped and executed the idea.

Money

This is a zero budget campaign, with time and effort donated by volunteers.

Minutes

In less than a season this campaign recruited 51,000 donors.

Note: This case was first posted on The Great Sportsmanship Programme blog (2014) 11 May. See **www. GreatSportsmanship.org**

FIGURE 21.4   The Great Sportsmanship Programme Blog was founded by PR Smith and is a NFP edutainment programme designed to inspire young people and boost their literacy, self-esteem and interest in sport via true two-minute stories about sportsmanship

CASE STUDY 21.2   *The Damned United*, Brian Clough microsite

Situation analysis

Digital agency Moonshine Media was asked by *Times Online* to create an engaging showcase to celebrate the colourful life and times of Brian Clough, one of England's most controversial and outspoken football managers.

Objectives

The ultimate objective for the website was to help promote *The Damned United* film, an adaption of David Peace's bestselling novel of the same name about Clough's stormy 44-day tenure as manager of Leeds United.

Strategy

The website was designed to focus on Clough's career as opposed to his personal life, which was why the inspiration for the website layout was derived from an interest in card collecting, as well as showing a clean and text-minimalist look.

Tactics

The site provided links to an archive of information including video, images and articles, and ultimately displayed an interactive timeline, 'Clough in the rough', and aggregated video as well as images. The *Sunday Times* archive content highlighted the key events in Clough's career, enabling readers to explore and navigate through the most memorable moments in Old Big 'Ead's life.

Action

The Action section is all about excellent execution of the tactics. This can include internal marketing (training, motivation and internal communications), mini project plans, action plans (see Figure 21.5), checklists and processes.

Control/results

Feedback from *Times Online* praised the website for having a 'slick and exciting design which showed off our content in a fresh and dynamic manner'. The project was completed with *Times Online* feeling 'confident' that the application would engage and entertain its readers.

Men/women

A research team involving five individuals from *Times Online* worked for a month before the project started in order to collect all the information with which to populate the site. They went through archives from newspapers, looked through interviews, and bought very limited film footage. Moonshine Media was given the content and populated the site with everything that was supplied.

Money

Times Online had a budget of £13,000 for the microsite (no retainer, pay by results).

Minutes

From start to finish took 30 days.

Do not forget internal communications – 10 per cent of the budget

Flawless execution of marketing campaigns and simple tools like websites is not as common as it should be. In fact some years ago a US book by Bossidy and Charan (2002) claimed that execution was the last bastion of competitive advantage, ie being able to execute plans better than your competitors created competitive advantage. One aspect that is critical to flawless execution of marketing communications is internal marketing, which means communicating to your team, colleagues, staff and other departments within your organization. Figures vary, but many well-run organizations allocate a minimum of 10 per cent of their resources to communicating internally.

FIGURE 21.5 *Times Online* microsite timetable

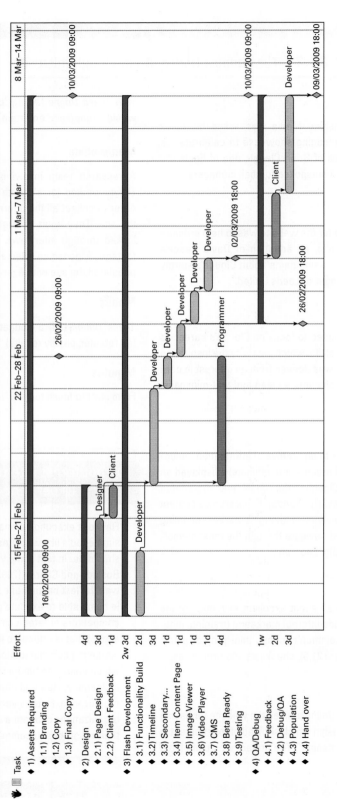

CASE STUDY 21.3   American Greetings e-cards optimized landing pages

Situation analysis

American Greetings has the largest collection of electronic greetings on the web, including cards available at AmericanGreetings.com through AG Interactive, Inc, the company's online division. AG Interactive funnelled online traffic to the **www.americangreetings.com** home page, or a single multivariate testing (MVT)-optimized landing page. The marketing team decided they needed to launch an aggressive landing page testing in order to lift visitor conversion rates from an average of 1.47 per cent to 2.01 per cent.

Objectives

The goal was to convert traffic using online registration for a free trial subscription (which later converted to a paid subscription on AmericanGreetings.com); however, one landing page was not converting enough of the total traffic. Implementing testing on one landing page was slow, with a multi-month feedback loop to the marketing team. Experimentation with alternative design and content was even slower.

Strategy

To lift conversions, the marketing team decided to create and test several different context-specific landing pages for each keyword: e-cards, free e-cards, birthday, create and print, and international. They determined they needed to experiment broadly with content and layout, test results and view analysis in real time to find which landing pages worked best. Their new strategy was based around a system (Ion's LiveBall) where the marketers could change the offers, propositions and even pictures directly without needing developers and designers to code and create new pages for them.

Tactics

American Greetings adopted LiveBall in order to increase agility, speed to market, specificity and ultimately to improve conversion performance to lower cost per customer acquisition. Ion worked closely with the AG Interactive marketing manager to launch and test alternative landing experiences that were specific to marketing segments and traffic sources.

Action

Within the first three months of testing with LiveBall, American Greetings moved from a single, optimized landing page to over 40 unique landing pages, each context-specific to its source of traffic. Three entirely different design formats were tested with 12 different price points across 200 different audience segments. By speaking to each segment, American Greetings was able to increase conversions despite an economic fallout that actually reduced the flow of traffic.

Customers looking for e-cards search using different phrases. Tests revealed which landing page performed best for each key phrase. Once these 'champion' landing pages were identified, all traffic from a particular ad word was directed to that champion page. Consider three search phrases: 'e-cards', 'birthdays' and 'create and print' (your own card). Each phrase is linked to a specific landing page that reflects the phrase. Each landing page has several versions tested before the marketing team selects the 'optimum' landing page for each key phrase. This is the magic marketing formula at work.

The key phrase 'e-cards' was tested against many different landing pages before choosing the landing page called 'Browse with Flash' (on the right hand side). This was the champion page (which made the most sales).

The key phrase 'birthdays' was tested against many different landing pages to see which page converted the most visitors into customers. The landing page called 'Browse with Flash' (in the middle) was the champion (ie it sold the most cards).

Many different landing pages were tested for the key phrase 'create and print'. The 'general' landing page (on the left hand side) converted higher than the other family-focused themes.

Control

Each unique landing page format was customized and matched with the PPC ad that was sending it traffic. The testing resulted in an almost immediate 30 per cent increase in conversion and a subsequent 20 per cent decrease in cost per acquisition (which is a net benefit that included the added expenses associated with Ion's LiveBall platform and conversion optimization services). E-cards run 13 or 14 tests simultaneously at any one time and get quick, actionable learning.

Over the first five months using LiveBall, the American Greetings online marketing team created over 700 unique landing pages, which were tested across hundreds of

FIGURE 21.6

The key phrase 'e-cards' was tested against many different landing pages before choosing the landing page called 'Browse with Flash' (on the right hand side). This was the champion page (which made the most sales).

The key phrase 'birthdays' was tested against many different landing pages to see which page converted the most visitors into customers. The landing page called 'Browse with Flash' (in the middle) was the champion (ie it sold the most cards).

Many different landing pages were tested for the key phrase 'Create and Print'.
The 'general' landing page (on the left hand side) converted higher than the other family focused themes.

unique traffic sources. The real-time testing and analytics in LiveBall ensured that traffic arrived at the best-performing landing page for each traffic source. As soon as American Greetings got statistical significance on a test, they drove traffic immediately to the champion landing page in real time. On Mother's Day alone this resulted in $45,000 in incremental revenue. That's revenue that would have been lost without LiveBall's actionable, real-time approach.

New tests are always in the works at American Greetings. The conversion goal was over 40 per cent higher than the previous year, and another 33 per cent lift was targeted for the next two years. American Greetings uses Ion's LiveBall platform to drive real business ROI at scale. Smaller-percentage improvements on the top-line sales figures have a big impact on the bottom-line profit figures. LiveBall gives fast speed to market and learning. It's a visual tool that lets marketers focus on what's working to improve results.

World-class marketers constantly try to optimize and improve their marketing performances, and American Greetings is a good example. Testing multiple landing pages is one of many ways to boost the conversion of visitors to customers.

Marketing professionals now need to convert existing customers to lifetime, repeat-purchasing customers. Here's how.

CASE STUDY 21.4   Social media helps stop smoking: using social media (and UGC movies) to help 11- to 15-year-olds to stop smoking

Situation

Although the proportion of young people aged 11–15 who smoke had fallen over the previous 10 years, it was reported that by age 15 the proportion who reported smoking at least once a week had approximately risen to one in seven (14 per cent). Smoking is the main cause of preventable morbidity and premature death in England. The Deborah Hutton Campaign is working in harmony with existing government and charitable initiatives to reduce the prevalence of smoking among young people.

Objectives

Change agency ICE has worked with the Deborah Hutton Campaign on a pilot, Cut Films, a film-making competition which took place across 10 schools and a youth club nationwide. The challenge was to develop a creative concept that would positively resonate with and inspire young people, so the campaign grew through genuine enthusiasm, supported by schools and young people across the country. Ultimately, the project aimed to engender 1,000 films, generating a change in the attitudes of young people

towards smoking and a reduction in the number of young people smoking.

Strategy

Cut Films used the creative film-making process, combined with the use of social media, to influence 11- to 15-year-olds. It attracted young people and encouraged them to share their own personal messages and creative work by using the relational nature of social media. This enabled users to forward films and messages, in order to create a snowball campaign that aimed to influence the cultural attitudes of young people towards smoking. The power of the campaign lay in the use of social media as part of a peer-to-peer approach engaging young people through the creative attraction of film and new media technologies.

Tactics

The campaign set up a presence for Cut Films on a range of social media sites. Films were uploaded to YouTube and then 'pinged' across to pages on Facebook and Twitter.

FIGURE 21.7   Cut Films – 'film page' containing multiscreen grabs

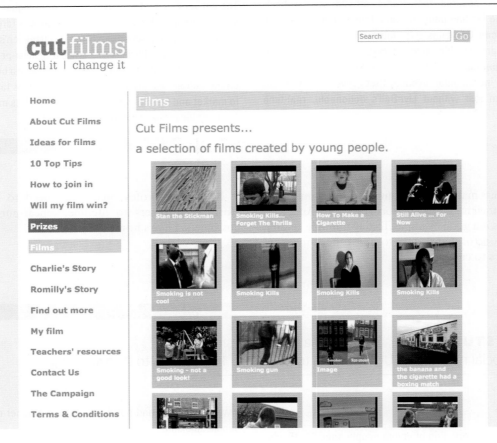

The campaign also promoted its presence among key stakeholders.

Action

The Cut Films competition was managed by the campaign director, who supported schools and youth clubs throughout the process. However, the main way of managing the results was through the 'My film' document that young people used to help them plan, reflect on and evaluate the process of producing a film, and reflect on the content they discovered throughout the process.

All films were submitted to the Cut Films website, moderated and uploaded to YouTube. There is an ongoing effort to introduce the campaign to schools, as well as constant communication with key stakeholders, including:

- the Department of Health;
- the head of features, ITV;
- key academic health promotion specialists;
- the head of public health sciences at the University of Edinburgh;
- schools and youth clubs;
- regional and local tobacco leads within local NHS services.

Control

Cut Films fed into health and citizenship issues within the PSHE curriculum, and this was underpinned with social marketing or social change principles from the National Social Marketing Centre. This provided rigorous evaluation and evidence for the campaign's long-term impact.

Underpinning every aspect of the project, ICE's social marketing division provided key insight focusing on realigning concepts of normal behaviour and identifying film topics that would inspire as well as nudge young people

FIGURE 21.8   'Smoking is not cool' on YouTube

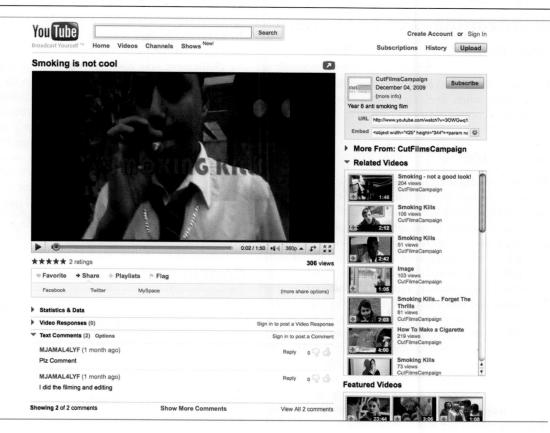

and their communities towards a move in behaviour. They also created an evaluation framework and focus groups to inform the roll-out and evaluation of the campaign nationally.

Men/women

The campaign director is the only full-time member of staff. She is supported at board level and is also working alongside social marketing company ICE, which as part of the pilot has provided free access to expertise in web development, design, social marketing and PR.

Money

ICE provided its expertise for the pilot free of charge, as a contribution to this charitable initiative.

Minutes

- Cut Films' pilot: June to March.
- Website and resources designed: August to September.
- Film deadline: December.
- Awards ceremony: March.
- National roll-out of campaign: September onwards.
- See the Deborah Hutton Campaign website (**www.deborahhuttoncampaign.org**) and the Cut Films website (**www.cutfilms.org**).

Advantages and disadvantages of permanent media

Here are some of the advantages and disadvantages to consider when deciding whether to increase or reduce this communications tool.

Advantages

Websites can help to establish the credibility of a brand, engage customers in a unique way and convert them into lifetime customers and brand advocates. Combine this with social media platforms, and the combination can be used to move customers up the ladder of engagement and spread the word. The website is owned media and therefore it is a controlled environment (assuming it is moderated). New ideas that add value to the customer experience can be given to the site continually. An infinite amount of new added value opportunities are emerging, particularly as technology develops. Deeply engaging, relevant experiences can be delivered. This is a form of competitive advantage. Social media can help to create awareness and engage customers all the way through a purchase cycle. It can also help to nurture influencer relationships and advocates who will spread your brand. While the website is generally not a tool for building awareness, it is a tool for nurturing awareness into relationships. Social media, on the other hand, can create awareness, change attitudes and help to convert prospects to customers and customers into lifetime customers.

Disadvantages

Websites are totally dependent on traffic. No traffic makes a website useless. Investment is required for, first, traffic-building campaigns and, second, maintenance of the site with fresh content. Equally, social media requires a continued feed of fresh content (as well as resources to respond to discussions).

This can be resource hungry (SMO is the new SEO), and as yet there are few models to indicate the optimum resource allocation here. The usual issues of servers crashing, security hackers, scams and spammers jeopardizing the control of the message are challenges, and constant vigilance is required. Equally, conversations across the full social media spectrum need to be monitored and tracked continually. Conversations also require moderation and response. Scope creep can mess up a website either at the development stages, or ongoing requests for website changes/improvements can eventually create a patchwork quilt that loses the site's cohesiveness and its 'thing', as can poor content management, eg out-of-date content left online. Maintenance is essential.

Conclusion

Owned media includes websites, social media platforms, apps and other tools like e-mail newsletters. There are four key websites satisfaction factors that bring visitors back to a website again and again: high-quality content; easy navigation; fast downloads; and updated content. High-quality content is more likely to be created if driven by some scenario planning, persona development, creative sizzle and customer engagement. The second factor, navigation, requires careful planning, including navigation rules and identifying the top tasks. Then comes the challenge of customer conversion (from prospect or visitor to customer). The probability of success increases with: a strong call to action; 'See', 'Try' and 'Buy'; price lining; simplified processes; reduced customer anxiety; a contact strategy and digital body language; and relevant landing pages. The chapter also focuses on successful social media, which require high-quality content, suitably optimized and spread across various social networks. The chapter explores how to integrate social media into business systems, optimize social media and, finally, avoid the 10 most common social media mistakes (the biggest one being a lack of usability testing).

Key points from Chapter 21

- There are four key satisfaction factors for websites: high-quality content, easy navigation, fast downloads and updated content.
- High-quality content is more likely with some scenario planning, persona development, creative sizzle and customer engagement.
- Navigation requires careful planning, including navigation rules and identifying the top tasks.
- Customer conversion increases with: a strong call to action; 'See', 'Try' and 'Buy'; price lining; simplified processes; reduced customer anxiety;

- a contact strategy and digital body language; and relevant landing pages.
- Successful social media requires high-quality content, suitably optimized and spread across various social networks.
- Social media must be integrated into business systems and databases.
- SMO is the new SEO – social media must be optimized.
- The 10 most common social media mistakes can be avoided with common sense.

References and further reading

Baer, J and Naslund, A (2011) *The Now Revolution*, Wiley

Bossidy, L and Charan, R (2002) *Execution: The discipline of getting things done*, Soundview Executive Books, Concordville, PA

Brito, M (2013) Your content strategy: Defining paid, owned and earned media, Hootsuite

Byron, D, Kievman, N and Schrum, R (2010) Why executives hate social media: An executive's guide to social media, Deming Hill

Chaffey, D and Smith, PR (2008) *eMarketing eXcellence*, Butterworth-Heinemann, Oxford

Gallup (2013) How customers interact with their banks, *Gallup Business Journal*, 7 May

Hilpern, K (2013) How to personalise your customers experience, *The Marketer* March/April

King, B (2010) *Bank 2.0*, Marshall Cavendish

McGovern, G (2010a) The customer is a stranger, *New Thinking*, 7 June

McGovern, G (2010b) Web manager: Top tasks versus tiny tasks, *New Thinking*, 28 June

McGovern, G (2012) Why review and remove are such critical web skills, *Gerry McGovern // New Thinking*, 8 July

McGovern, G (2015) Relationships are expensive, *Gerry McGovern // New Thinking*, 21 June

Patel, N (2014) The step-by-step guide on improving your Google rankings without getting penalized, *Neil Patel.com*, December 2

Porterfield, A (2012) 3 Steps to an effective social media strategy, *Social Examiner*, 1 March

Robles, P (2010) 10 common social media mistakes, *Econsultancy*, 31 March

Sexton, J (2010) Dispelling buyer anxiety and replacing it with buyer confidence, *Web Marketing Today*, 3 August

Seybold, P (2001) Get inside the lives of your customers, *Harvard Business Review*, May

Solis, B (2010) The 10 stages of social media integration in business, *BrianSolis.com*, 22 January

Surowiecki, J (2005) *The Wisdom of Crowds*, Anchor Books, New York

Woods, A (2007) The Revolution usability report: Creativity – looks aren't everything, *Revolution magazine.com*, 4 December

Woods, S (2009) *Digital Body Language*, New Year Publishing, Danville, CA

Wodtke, C (2002) *Information Architecture: Blueprints for the web*, New Riders, Indianapolis, IN

Further information

Advertising Standards Authority Limited (ASA)
Mid City Place
71 High Holborn
London
WC1V 6QT
Tel: +44(0) 20 7492 2222
www.asa.org.uk

Business Link (now part of Gov.uk)
Tel: 0845 600 9006
www.gov.uk

Wordtracker LLP
1 Euston Square
40 Melton Street
London NW1 2FD
United Kingdom
Tel: +44 0333 200 4555
www.wordtracker.com

Cloudmark Europe Ltd (anti-spam software)
Davidson House
Forbury Square
Reading, RG1 3EU
UK
www.cloudmark.com

Committee of Advertising Practice (CAP)
Mid City Place
71 High Holborn
London WC1V 6QT
Tel: +44 (0)20 7492 2100
www.cap.org.uk

Google Business Solutions
www.google.co.uk/services/

Information Commissioner's Office
Wycliffe House
Water Lane
Wilmslow
Cheshire SK9 5AF
Tel: +44 (0)30 3123 1113
Fax: +44 (0)1625 524510
www.ico.org.uk

Rivergold Associates Ltd (t/a Wordtracker)
Unit 11–12 Apollo Studios
Charlton King's Road
London NW5 2SB
Tel: +44 (0)33 3200 4555
Fax: +44 (0)20 7424 8844
www.wordtracker.com

INDEX

Note: The index is filed in alphabetical, word-by-word order. Numbers within main headings and 'Mc' are filed as spelt out. Acronyms are filed as presented. Page locators in *italics* denote information contained within a Figure or Table.

A/B testing 112, 186, 465
Abbott, David 230
Abbott Mead Vickers 230, 238
ABC 211, 215, 485
ABM (Allen, Brady & Marsh) 225, 230, 238, 308
Absolut Vodka 349
account
    executives 221–22, 223, 403
    management 221, 223, 320, 321–22
accounting rules 41
    see also finance
ACORN 82, 180, 340, 460, 461
acquisitions *see* customer acquisitions; mergers and acquisitions
Acronis 473–78
action (SOSTAC®) 6, 268, 284–85
    advertising 362, 367–69, 371, 372–73
    content marketing 446–47
    control systems 287
    direct mail 468–69, 472, 474
    exhibitions 483, 487, 494
    market research *171*
    merchandising 509
    owned media 536
    promotions 441–42, 449–50, 453, 455
    public relations 400, 401, 402–03
    social media 533–34, 560
    sponsorship 414–15, 421, 423
    websites 556, 557
    see also action plans; calls to action
action plans 268, 284, *286*, 488
added value 24–27, 82, 96, 200, 282, 310, 359, 446, 540
Adidas 231, 408, 418
adoption model 155–56
adult consumers 193–94, 195, *196*, 197, *203*, 305, 307, 519
advanced web communications model *154*
advertising 7, 71, 115, 127, *134*, 155, 192, 195, 258–62, 335–75
    agencies 172, 218–241, 262–64
    cars 51–52
    Coca-Cola 35, 128, 129, 408
    Colgate 107
    frequency 212
    Guinness 150
    patterns 213
    position 213
    regulations 295–302
    research *176*, 177, 183–84, 211
    Shell 276
    space 207, 209
    spend 222–23
    tracking 186–87
    see also Advertising Standards Authority; banner adverts;
        brand development; Code of Advertising Practice (CAP);
        contextual advertising; cooperative advertising; digital
        advertising; direct response advertising; geo-targeting

advertising; location-based advertising; Oxo ads;
        packaging; programmatic advertising; semiotics;
        TV advertising
Advertising Standards Authority (ASA) 303, 316
advocates (advocacy) 17, 26, 64, 71, 76, 147–48, 149
affiliate
    marketing 155, 331–32
    network programmes 331, 332
affordability 270
AGB *175*, 415
ageing population 306–07, 308
agencies 172, 218–41, 262–64, 441
    see also consultancies
agreements, sponsorship 414–15
AIDA communication model *119*, 208, 277, 323, 354
airline (air travel) industry 48, *54–55*, 57, 148, 275–76
Al Jazeera *45*, 244
Alamo Car Hire 431
Alibaba *5*, 41, 245
Allen, Brady & Marsh (ABM) 225, 230, 238, 308
Amazon *5*, 10, 18, 35, *37*, *42*, 46, 55, 60
    affiliate marketing 331, 332
    customer retention 270
ambassadors 13, 17, 18, 27, 149, 333, 548
ambient media 105, 203
ambush marketing 298, 418–19
American Express 89–90, 410, 411, 415
American Greetings 435, 557–58
analysis 21–22, 85, 88, 171, 276, 289, 327, 491
    LBA 180, 341
    sales *176*, 287, 328
    see also PEST analysis; situation analysis; SWOT analysis
analytics 6, 8, 21–22, 29, 111–12, 134–35, 160, 188, 285
    and advertising 180, 336, 338–39, 348
    see also data analytics; Google Analytics; predictive analytics;
        video analytics; web analytics
anti-brands 63
AOL Time Warner 41, 298
Apple 20, 36, *37*, *42*, 46–47, 97, 199, 282, 346, 501
    see also iPad; iPhone; iPod
apps 10, 26, 103, 148, 200–01, 346–47, 348, 499, 500
    Apple 20, 105
    Kelly HR 446
    Topline 449
AR (augmented reality) 16, 312, 314, 453, 483
Archaos fish diet 389
aromas 128, 504
    see also odours; scents; smells
Art of War, The (Sun Tzu) 4, 21, 271
artists (musicians) 166, 180, 200, 409, 455
arts sponsorship 409, 410, 411, 416
ASA (Advertising Standards Authority) 303, 316
aspirations 35, 110, 515–16, 521
assisted conversions reports 111

AT&T 58
Atlas particle detector 19–20
attention spans 125–26, 137, 305–06
attitudes 132–33
audience, target 204–07, 412, 434, 445, 449, 485, 493, 537–38
Audit Bureau of Circulation 211, 215, 485
audits *175*, 177, 179, 186
augmented reality (AR) 16, 312, 314, 453, 483
automation 7, 29, 159–60, 275, 309–10, *311*, 323, 468–69
   Acronis 473–78
   CRM 71, 72, 79, 81–82, *86*, 90
   see also programmatic advertising
avatars 16, *17*, 312, 384, 488
Avon 73
awareness
   questionnaires *187*
   trial reinforcement (ATR) model 115, *117*, 338
   see also brand awareness

Baidu 41, 251
banking sector *9*, 37–40, 56, 66, 72, 87, 89, 306, 307
   see also HSBC Bank International; Lloyd's Bank; NatWest Bank;
      TD Bank
banner adverts 89, 113, 118, *208*, 287, *288*, 331, 332, 343
bar codes *45*, 105, 177, 506, 522
BARB 211, 215
Bartle Bogle Hegarty (BBH) 226, 231, 236, 238
baseball sponsorship 410, 411
bastion brands 62
BBC Radio Northern Ireland 20
BCAP 302, 303
beacons 27, 199, 300, 346
behavioural
   change (Five Levers for Change) 139
   insights 179–80
      see also customer insights; group behaviour
   mapping 344
   targeting 343
Ben & Jerry's 169
Benefit 422–24
benefit-based brand names 53
benefit segmentation 132
Best West Hotels 411
beta culture 29, 126, 280
bias, interviewer 173
Big Data 8, *86*, 165–66, 309, *311*, 338–39
big idea, the 222, 224, 336
Bing 251, 252
black-box model 118, 119–20, 121–22
black swan events 306
blame storming 78
BlisMedia 179, 340, 341, 342, 363, *364*, 366
bloatware 108
blogger outreach programmes 148
blogs 12, 19, 44, 71, 112, 125, 146, 223, 282, *288*, 392
Blu-e-cig 279
Blue Band 259
Bluetooth Low Energy (BLE) 199
BMP 238, 355, *357*
body
   gestures 252
   language 145, 487
      digital 72, *86*, 104, 275, 281, 309, 312, 323–24, *546*
Boeing 19
Bond, James (fictional character) 153, 482

Boots 46, 177, 260
Boro Plus 527–29
Boston Matrix 62
bots 138
Bovis construction 55
BP 381, 395, 396, 412, 518
BRAD (British Rate and Data) 211, 215, 224
brain science 6, 109–10
brand
   activation 233, 410, 428, 429, 438
   Agency Leader Model (P&G) 220
   ambassadors 13, 17, 18, 27, 149, 333, 548
   assets 28, 73
   awareness 109, 132, 187, 289, 331, 367, 418
   consistency 56, *57–58*
   development 9–10, 48–62, 66
   entertainment 337
   experience 46, 47, 48, 60, 392, 482
   extension 61–62
   identity 47, *57–58*, 59–60
   logos 53, *54–58*, 59–60, 122–23, 128, 298
   names 19, 53–54
   personality 47, 52, 53, 78, 413
   promise 47, 52, 53
   value 36–41, 65–66
   values 48, 52, 53, 91
branding 9–10, 33–68, 213, 279, 280, 518, 528–29
   see also brand activation; Brand Agency Leadership Model
      (P&G); brand ambassadors; brand assets; brand
      awareness; brand entertainment; brand experience;
      brand logos; brand names; brand personality; brand values;
      corporate brands
Bribery Act (2010) 296
briefs 49, *50*, *52–53*, 91–94, 171, 228–30, *354–55*, *357*
British Airways 81, 230, 231
British Audience Research Bureau 211, 215
British Rate and Data (BRAD) 211, 215, 224
broadcast sponsorship 412, 418
Bruno Magli 393, 395
B2B 19, 87, 104, 106, 108, 136, 151, 153, 274–76, 428
   legislation 296
   media costs 207
   selling 320, 321, 324, 325, 327, 333
B2C 19, 77, 106, 153, 156, 207, 270, 274, 297, 463
budgets 269–71, 342, 416–17, 469–71, 517, 555
Budweiser 129, 338, 352
Burkitt Weinreich Bryant 230–31
burst strategy 213
Business Protection Regulations (2008) 295–96
'buy' option 544
buyer (buying) behaviour 87, 101–42, 305
   see also programmatic buying; real-time bidding (buying)

Cadbury 46, 237, 350, 380, 430, 432, 436
call
   centres 75, 78, 89–90, 96, 547
   tracking 362
calls to action 200, 250, 324
   direct mail 464, *478*
   EU laws 297
   and mobile 112, 192
   owned media 543, 544, 562
Campbell's Soup 6, 148, 419, 507–08, 516
Canon 412, 416
category-less competitors 10, 63, 294

cell phones *see* mobile phones
central advertising strategy 259–61, 263–64
change 9–10, 11, 29, 139, 293–316
chat rooms 181
checklists, exhibition 484–85, 490–91
children 193–94, 306
China 129, 136, 244, 247, 252, 253, 256–57, 338, 521
   communication 122–23, 145, 236, 250–51
choice 102–03
Chrysler 19
churn 77, 82, 83
cinema 144, 178, *196*, 202–03, 204, *205*, 206, 207, 208, 211
Cisco 53–54
Citröen 220, 337, *422–24*
classic brand names 53
classical conditioning 127–28, 429
clearance 208, 302, 303, *356*, 362, 441
Clearcast 208, 302, 303, *356*
click behaviour *see* digital body language
client approval *356, 358, 361*
closure 126
cloud technology 166, 310
co-branded e-mails 463, 465
co-creation 13, 18–20, 44, 149, 281, 423, 541
   see also collaboration; partnerships
Coca-Cola (Coke) 105, 106, 129, 173, 239, 255, 256, 258–59, 338
   branding 35, 36, *37, 42*, 46, 52, 54, 66, 337
   packaging 519, 520, 522
   promotions 430, 431, 436, 437
   sponsorship 58, 408, 416, 418
Cocker, Jarvis 385, *386*
Code of Advertising Practice (CAP) 302–04
cognitive
   dissonance 56, 57, 122, 373
   learning 129
cold e-mail campaigns 463, 465
Colgate 107
collaboration 22, 77, 78, 322
   see also co-creation; partnerships
collage boards 182, *183, 185*
colour 54, 55, 57, 126, 145, 245, 251–52, 520–21
   blocking 504
commission 224–25, 331, 332
Commission Junction 332
communications
   models 150–60
   plans 267–91
   theory 143–62
community sponsorship 411
company
   branding benefits 35–41
   reports 304
competition (competitive advantage) 9–11, 35–36, 63, 166–70, *176*, 255, 294–95, 340, 502
   hyper-competition 27, 78
   see also sustainable competitive advantage
competitive parity 270
complex buyer behaviour model 118–19, 121–22
concept
   development (generation) 49, *50*, 53–56, 355, 358
   testing (research) 174, *176*, 183–84, *185*
conferences 482–83
conflicts of interest 236
connectionist learning theories 127–29
connector panels 157, 184, 186

connectors 147
conscious reasoning 109
consensus of subjectivity 34
consistency, brand 56, 57–58
consultancies 218, 219, 220
   see also agencies
consultative selling 321
Consumer Contracts Regulations (2013) 296
consumer franchise 29
Consumer Protection from Unfair Trading Regulations (2008) 296
consumption, conspicuous 131
   see also media consumption
contact
   strategy process 80–82, 545–46
   workflow strategy *478*
content
   calendar 444
   marketing (design) 24–26, 90, 146, 281, 295, 309, *311*, 348, 428, 442–48
   pathways 444
   pyramid 443
   shock 444
   strategy 548
   see also user-generated content (UGC)
context 157
contextual advertising 343
contingency planning 441
continuous patterns, advertising 213
control (SOSTAC®) 268, 285–90
   advertising 362, 369, 371, 373
   briefs 228
   CRM 95–96
   of data 95–96
   direct mail 469–71, 472, 474
   exhibitions 489–92, 494
   merchandising 508, 509
   owned media 536, 553, 555, 557–59, 560–61
   PR 393–97, 400, 401–02, 403
   promotions 442, 447, 450–52, 454, 455
   sales 328
   sponsorship 416–17, 421, 423–24
Control of Misleading Advertisements Regulations (1988) 296
conversations 15, 21, 324–25
   see also discussions
cookies 84, 89, 180, 299, 365
cooling off periods 296, 297
cooperative advertising 333, 504
corporate
   brands 57, 58, 306, 518
   identity 518
   PR 379
   social responsibility 307, 380–82
Costco 282
costs 254, 287
   CRM 72, 74, 95–97
   exhibition 491, 494
   merchandising 509
   packaging 524
   per click (CPC) 225, 368, 371, 391–92, 402
   per customer acquisition 285, *288*
   per enquiry 285, 491
   per order 285, *288*, 462–63, 491
   per thousand (CPT/CPM) 207, *210*, 212, 330
   post 297
   see also advertising spend; fees; production costs

Cover My Cab 370–71
coverage 212, 392–96
CPM (CPT) *see* cost per thousand
creative
    departments *221*, 222
    destruction 11
creativity 6, 22–25, 238, 351, 354–55, *357*, 432–33
credentials pitch 227–28
credibility 91, *92*, 145–46, 254, 301–02, 373, 543
    PR 382, 392–93, 399
Credit Suisse 41
crisis management 396–97
critical paths 285
cross-cultural consumer characteristics 244, 264
cross-selling 87
crowdsourcing 18, 19, 20
CSR *see* corporate social responsibility
CTA *see* calls to action
culture 15, 90, 91, 145, 244, 245–46, 252–53, 258, 264
customer
    acquisitions 270, 287, *288*, 465–66
    centricity 5, 70, 91, 97, 245, 261
    conversions 542–47
    data 85–87, 92–93
    defection reduction 82
    engagement 17, 61, 540–41
    experience 5–6, 24, 26, 60–61, 78, 90, 281–82, 294–95, 310–11
        divide 64
    experience management *see* customer relationship
        management (CRM)
    feedback (complaints) 65, 79–80, 91
    insights 110
        see also behavioural insights
    managed relationships *see* customer relationship management (CRM)
    profiling 84–88, 89, 103–04, 460–61
        see also SUPER PROFILES
    relationship management (CRM) 7–8, 11, 69–99, *134*
        see also relationships
    research *175*
    retention 70, 71, 270, 465
    rewards 71
    satisfaction 73, 75, 80, 81, 96–97, 114
    service 8–9, 44, 73, 328–29
        see also personal service
    surveys 96, *175*, 177
    touchpoints 48, 70, 158
customers 34–35, 51, 75–76
    see also adult consumers; aspirations; children; customer
        acquisitions; customer centricity; customer conversions;
        customer data; customer defection reduction; customer
        engagement; customer experience; customer feedback;
        customer insights; customer profiling; customer
        relationship management; customer research; customer
        retention; customer rewards; customer satisfaction;
        customer service; customer surveys; customer touchpoints;
        long-term customers; relationships; target audience
customization 88–89
CX *see* customer experience

DAGMAR model 118, *119*, 186, 277, 354
Daily Mail 347
dark social 159
data 88, 93, 95–96, *171*, 299, 300, 309, 311, 340–48
    analytics 83, 87, 88
    integration 5–6, 8, 27
mining 83–84, 87, 88, 181
    see also Big Data; customer data; Data Protection Directive;
        databases; emotional data; explicit data; historical data;
        information; layered data; lifestyle data; maths men;
        predictive data
Data Protection Directive 298
databases 28, 45, 72, 73, 80, 82–88, 94–95, 461–62
decentralized strategy 259, 261–62
decision making 114, 165–66
    units 104–05, 273–74, 308
    see also purchase decision
decoding messages 150, 151
Deep Pan Pizza 436
defensive
    advertising 115
    strategies 257
deliverability, e-mail 466
Dell 18–19, 63, 270
Deloitte & Touche 22, 434
demographics 57, 180, 274, 308–09, *364*, 460, 517, 539
    see also adult consumers; ageing population; children
design 252, 485–86, 493, 524–26
desk research 174
development
    CRM 94
    message 354–58
    see also brand development; systems development
Diageo 151, 157
dialogue 13, 28, 77, 93, 218, 222, 413, 483
differentiation 35, 36, 53, 54, 78, 413
digital 21, 24, 26, *193*
    advertising 204, *205*, 338
    body language 72, *86*, 104, 275, 281, 309, 312, 323–24, 546
    press kits 384
Digital Economy Act (2010) 296
diluted brands (weak brands) 41, 62
direct
    mail campaigns 7, 88, *134*, *205*, 206, 207, *283*, 459–80
    response advertising 208, 329, 330, 428, 460, 462, 463
discussions 18, 21, 44, 180–81, 182–83, 324, 325, 548
    see also conversations
distributors *175*, 332–33, 501
DMUs 104–05, 273–74, 308
down-the-line interviews 385
drip strategy 127, 212, 213
Dulux 117, 498, 537, 538
dwell time 499, 501
dynamic positioning mode 233

e-mails 14, 112, *288*, 299, 463–67
e-newsletters 81, 160, *288*, 466
early
    adopters 147–48, 156, 157, 184, 186, 198
    majority 156, *157*
earned media 7, 201, 336, 339, 347, 435, 534
    see also word of mouth
easyJet 62
eBay 5, 10, *39*, 154, 245, 499
economics 304–05
Edison, Thomas 23–24
editorial coverage 392–96
electronic point-of-sale scanners (EPOS scanners) 506, 522
emotion 46, 48, 51–52, 109, 339, 358
emotional data 339
emotional-rational dichotomy 105–08

empathy 5, 11, 229, 501–02, 549
employees 27, 54, 56, 91, 327, 413, 420, 421, 550
    see also account executives; salesforce; staff
engagement 8, 12–13, 17–21, 28, 97, 106, 218
    customer 17, 61, 540–41
    employee 420, 421
enquirer profiling 84–85
Enterprise Act (2002) 296
environment 214, 304
EPOS scanners (electronic point-of-sale scanners) 506, 522
EPS (extensive problem solving) 111, 113, 114
equity, brand 46
essence, brand 46–47
ethics 63, 92, 95–96, 307, 379, 380, 381, 382
EU legislation 296, 297–98, 302
eureka moments 23, 25, 340
European, The 278
European advertising 261
evaluation 114, 117, 118, 155, 158, 393, 403, 421, 440, 489
execution see action
exhibitions 7, 134, 176, 283, 481–95
Experian 363, 364, 465
experience divide 64
    see also brand experience
experiential marketing 25, 48, 60, 66, 482
experimental
    curiosity 160
    non-attendance 492
explicit data 84
exposure 137
exposures data 86
extension see brand extension; product extension
extensive problem solving (EPS) 111, 113, 114
eye tracking 184, 545

Facebook 7, 10, 14, 15, 37, 111, 125, 274, 553
    advertising 343, 345, 346, 347, 348, 349, 350, 352
    global marketing 244, 262
    and market research 165, 166, 181
    and media buying 201, 208
    and PR 391, 392
    privacy 299–300
    promotions 435, 448, 449, 450, 452
familiarity 102–03, 111, 158
FAQs 25
FBI 165
fear 306
Federal Express 72
feedback 65, 79–80, 91
fees 225
FGF promotions 301
field marketing (fieldwork) 25, 171, 329–30, 504, 509
15 Second Film Festival 385
fighter brands 62
Film Audience Research and Evaluation (FAME) 211, 215
finance 65–66
    see also accounting rules
first moment of truth 115, 116
Five Levers for Change (Unilever) 139
5S's 28
flanker brands 62
Flickr 20, 385, 551
flighting advertising patterns 213
floating targets 150, 275
focus groups 174, 176, 177, 180, 181, 182–83, 188, 355, 372, 437

football 410, 411, 415, 416, 417–18, 553–54
Ford 255, 355
forecasting 168, 175, 218, 306, 328, 441
FRAC 85
fraud 173, 238, 430
friend get friend promotions 301
Friends of the Earth 385–86, 387–88, 389
Fujitsu 75
full-service agencies 218–19, 441
funnel communications model 158

Gaelic Athletic Association 419–22
GaggleAmp 443
gamification (gaming) 78, 88, 91, 180, 209, 432–35
Gap 1969 501
Gates, Bill 36
GE 22, 96, 321
General Motors (GM) 51–52, 255
Generation C (perpetuals) 104, 113
geo-targeting advertising 199, 341, 499
geodemographics 180, 274, 460
Germany 248, 249–50, 251, 253, 254–55, 302, 418, 431, 445, 523
Gestalt psychology 126–27
gestures 145, 252
GGT 237, 238
Ghostery 300
Gibson Guitars 26
Gillette 236, 362, 366
global
    advertising strategy 258–62
    brands 36–41, 42–43
    marketing strategy 257–58
    mercantilism 304
    niches 45
    segments 274
globalization 10, 244–65
GM (General Motors) 51–52, 255
golf sponsorship 410–11
Google 36, 37, 42, 43, 77, 97, 126, 208, 307
    AdWords 368, 370, 448
    Alerts 168, 289, 312, 397, 547
    Analytics 104, 111, 174, 179
    and British Airways 81
    DoubleClick Ad Planner 185
    Maps 200
    market share 251, 252
    and mobile 192
    News 312, 383
    privacy 299
    remarketing 345
    and research 166, 184
    Voice 148
    Wallet 342
graphics 55, 521–22
Grattan's 82
Great Moments of Sportsmanship 19
Great Sportsmanship Programme 282, 554
Greece 19, 246, 248
Greenwich, Royal Borough of 109
grocery shopping 115
group
    behaviour (influence) 14–15, 133–35, 153
    characterization 89
groups, tissue 231, 232
guidelines, brand 56, 58, 59

Guinness 107–08, 131, 156, 228, 299, 308, 353
    advertising 150, 361
    branding 45, 46, 61, 66
    packaging 521, 523
    promotions 432

Häagen-Daz 361
Halfords 365, 367–69
hall tests 50, 174, 176, 177
Hallmark 46–47
Harley-Davidson 45, 106, 540
head shots 389–90, 391
heat maps 123, 124, 184
Heineken 172–73, 355
Heinz 35, 54, 127, 179, 431, 438, 516, 517, 518
Help the Aged 389
heuristic planning 270
Hewlett-Packard (HP) 22, 349
high-involvement purchases 103, 114–15, 116
historical data 83
Hitwise 185
HMRC department 109
home audits 177, 186
Home Depot, The 18
Hong Kong 122–23, 252, 253, 545
Hoover 430, 431
hospitals 166, 184, 553
House of Fraser 499
house-buying apps 200
Hovis 66, 183, 355, 357, 358, 359, 360
Howard and Sheth's complex model 118, 121–22
Howell Henry Chaldecott 231
HP (Hewlett-Packard) 22, 349
HSBA 282
HSBC Bank International 89, 544, 545
hurdle rates 87
hyper-competition 9–11, 27, 78

IBM 20, 36, 37, 42, 53, 73, 153, 156, 219
    agency relations 237–38
    future vision 309
    pay 320
    and privacy 301
    promotions 257
    and publicity 395
ICO (Information Commissioner's Office) 301, 480
ideas see innovations; inventions; new ideas
Ideastorm (Dell) 18–19
identity see brand identity; corporate identity; national identity
IFRS 65–66
illegal competition 11
immature sponsorship 408–09
immovables 437
impacts 213
implicit data 84
Impulse 259
impulse buying 103
in-depth research (interviews) 175, 180, 181–82
in-house
    advertising 218, 219, 220, 224
    affiliate programmes 332
in-stream advertising see native advertising
inbound marketing 29
individualization 88–89

industrial
    buying 111, 114
    markets 148
    see also B2B
information 12, 164–70, 175–76
    processing 112, 137
    search 114
    see also data
Information Commissioner's Office (ICO) 301, 480
initial consideration sets 115, 116
InnoCentive 19
innovations 20, 22–23, 64, 79, 156–57, 173
    see also inventions; new ideas
inquisitiveness 25
Instagram 125, 488, 489, 549
integration 5–6, 8, 27, 281, 322–23, 348, 395–96, 446
    promotions 437
    reporting 379
    systems 462, 468–69
Intel 20, 48
intellectual assets 36
intelligent fridges 45, 105, 138, 276
international
    agencies 262–64
    marketing communications 243–65
International Financial Reporting Standard 65–66
internet 10, 12, 28, 45, 55, 89, 217, 312, 313
    consumption 194, 196, 199
    and globalization 244, 246, 247
Internet of Things (IoT) 159, 310
interruption marketing 12, 14, 113, 337
Interviewer Quality Control Service, The (IQCS) 172
interviews 173, 175, 180, 181–82, 384, 385, 392
inventions 24, 257
    see also innovations; new ideas
investment 58–59, 65, 233, 562
    see also return on investment
invisible badges 131
iPad 5, 499, 501
iPhone 5, 10, 20, 26, 105, 155, 200, 324, 346
iPod 10, 25, 26, 56, 107, 132, 159
IRD see magic marketing formula
ISO 10668 65–66
IT 78
    departments 29, 74, 75, 93
    skills 94

Jaguar Land Rover 482–83
Japan 144, 244, 245, 246, 251, 252, 255, 256, 304, 307
    buyer behaviour 107, 138
    product packaging 521
    sponsorship 410, 418
JCB 483
Jif Lemon 518, 519
John Lewis 115, 505
Johnson & Johnson 396, 515
joined-up marketing 29
joint promotions 432–33, 436, 439, 487
journalists 146, 148, 382, 383–84, 395, 404
JWT 229, 238

KangaROOS 153
Kellogg's 46, 48, 55, 66, 436
Kelly HR 444–48

Kern *398–401*
key
   account management (KAM) 320, 321–22
   frames 183, 355, 358, *359*
   performance indicators 91
   phrases (keywords) *368–69*, 536, 549
KFC 431
King, Don 54
Kingfisher *55*
Kiss FM Radio *229*
Klout 80, 81, 147, 149
Kodak 418
Kraft Foods 19, 26, 200, 346, 349, 431

ladder of engagement 8, 12–13, 17–21, 28, 97, 218
ladder of loyalty 76
laggards 156, *157*
landing pages 110, 112, 209, 252, 464, *478*, 488, 543, 557–59
   Halfords website 367, 368, 369
   Topline 449
   see also microsites
language 58, 249, 250, 487
   see also body language; nomenclature; straplines; word usage
late majority 156, *157*
law of the few 157
laws 254–55, 295–301
layered data 363
LBA *see* location-based advertising
LBM *see* location-based marketing
Lead Forensics 324
learning 127–29
left brain thinking 6
legislation 254–55, 295–301
LEGO 20, 436
lenticular displays 506
Lever 145
Levi Strauss 259
Liberty Insurance 419–22
life events 134–35
lifestyle data 178–79
lifetime customers 546–47
likeability, message 146
limited problem solving *see* LPS
linear additive models 120–21
LinkedIn 7, 10, 146, 208, 324, 325, 348, 446–47
Linux 20
listening 13, 14, 15, 21, 79–80
literacy 250, 255
living the brand 56, 57
Lloyd's Bank 56, 408
local
   agencies 262–63
   markets 45
location 103
location-based
   advertising (LBA) 340–43, 362–69, 373, 506
   analytics 180
   marketing (LBM) 26, 110, 199, 340–41, 362–65
logos 53, 54–58, 59–60, 122–23, 128, 298
London Fire Brigade 88
long-form ads 349
long-term
   brand building 64–65
   customers 50–51

'long tail' 44
low-involvement purchase model 115
Lowe Howard-Spink 237
loyal susceptibles 437
loyalty 71, *76*, 78, 110, *116*, 429
LPS 111, 113, *114*
Lucozade 57, 272, 280
Lunn Poly 128

M&C Saatchi 231, 236
McCann Erickson 229
McDonald's 54, 103, 128, 129, 252, 261, 395, 418, 431
Macy's 431
MAD 464
magic marketing formula 35, 110, 339–40, *557*
Mainstream Renewable Power 381
mall walking 498
management 20
   see also account management; crisis management; key account management; performance management; project management
Manchester United Football Club 45, 244, 408
Maritz Corporation 327, 435
marketing
   department 8, 28–29, 65–66, 94
   intelligence and information systems 167–68, 294
   objectives 277, 354
   research 23, 49–52, 163–90, 322, 330
markets, local 45
Marks & Spencer 177, 415
Marlboro 47, 54, *56*, 126
Marriott Hotels 331
Mars 255, 257–58
mashable web 160
Maslow's hierarchy of needs 102, 130–32, 327
mass
   communication 150–51
      see also newspaper advertising; TV advertising
   customization 89
materials 522–23
maths men 222, 336, 345, 348–59, 364–65
Mattel 396
mature sponsorship 409–10
measurement 83, 397–98, 416, 444, 472, 485, 506, 549, 550
   see also key performance indicators
media 192, 254
   buying (planning) 191–216, 359, *361*
   consumption 192–201
   departments *221*, 222–23
   mashing 192, 197–98
   multitasking 197, *198*
   relations 382–83, 397–98
   research bureaux 211
   schedules 361
   selection 204–09, 359–61
   stacking 197, *198*
   tie-ups 212
   see also advertising; ambient media; direct mail campaigns; earned media; movies; news releases; newsletters; newspapers; paid media; social media; websites
men and women (3Ms) 29, 228, 269, 454, 494, 509
   direct mail 473, 474
   owned media 554, 555, 561
   packaging 524, 528
   PR 401, 402, 403
   sponsorship 421, 424

Mercedes-Benz 76, 184, 337
merchandising 7, 498–511
mergers and acquisitions 28, 59, 236, 238
message models *see* response hierarchy models
messages 145–46, 150, 151, 354–58, 359, 389–90, 466–67
Metcalf network 14
Mexican wave 14–15
microsites 209, 453, 472–73, 543, 552, 555–56
    see also landing pages
Microsoft 36, 42, 147, 153, 157, 184, 186, 256–57
MIIS 167–68, 294
Miller Beer 350
mindshare 332–33, 504
Mini 51, 344
minutes (3Ms) 269
    direct mail 474
    exhibitions 494
    merchandising 509
    owned media 554, 555, 561
    packaging 525, 528
    promotions 454
    publicity campaigns 401, 402, *403*
    sponsorship 422, 424
MMOG 16, 19
mobile
    marketing 198–99, 311, 499
    phones (cell phones) 103, 105, 112, 113, 192, *194, 202*, 253, *313*
        messaging 466–67
    wallets 342
modelling 269
models 103, 113–22, 127-129, 150–60
    see also AIDA communication model; DAGMAR model
modified rebuy 111
moments, brand 48, 52, 57
money (3Ms) 269, 454, 474, 494
    owned media 554, 555, 561
    packaging 524, 528
    publicity 401, 402, 403
    sponsorship 422, 424
    see also budgets; costs; finance; payments
monitoring
    media relations 397
    social media 289
    sponsorship 415
mood boards *see* collage boards
Moore's Law 138, 312
Morrisons 411
Mortascreen 389
Morton's Steakhouse 80
MOSAIC 88, 180, 460, *511*
motivation 56–57, 74, 102, 106, 107–08, 129–32, 251, 327–28
movies 385, 454–55, 559–61
MTV 19, 182
multi-level marketing 330–31
multi-step
    linear communications models 151–53
    non-linear communications models 154–55
multichannel campaigns 310, *311*
multiplayer online games (MMOG) 16, 19
multivariate testing 181, 186, 464, 465, 479, 557
music 128
    see also artists (musicians)
Muzu 454–55
MyFootballClub.co.uk 20
MySpace 7, 455

names 71, 87, 88, 127, 255
    see also brand names
national identity 253
National Lottery 136
National Readership Survey 178, 211, 291
National Semiconductor 29, 97, 537, 538
National Union of Teachers *60*
Nationwide 299
native advertising 347–48
NatWest Bank 432
navigation 541–42
NCH Action for Children 489
negotiations 164–65, 192, 210, 226, 254, 322
neighbour get neighbour promotions 301
Nelson's Column 386, *388*
Nestlé 64, 239, 518
net promoter score 96–97, 281, 285, 289
NetBase 41
Netflix 52
network selling *see* multi-level marketing
networks 14–15
    see also affiliate network programmes
neuromarketing 184
new
    ideas 172–73
        see also innovations; inventions
    task buying 111, 114
New York Giants 551–52
news releases 384–85, 392, 393, *394*
newsletters 90, *288*, 460, 466, 487, 534, 544
newspapers 211, 343
NGN promotions 301
niche channels 209
Nielsen 174, *175, 176*, 177
Nike 90, 299, 303, 380, 435
    advertising 337, 349
    branding *42*, 46, 48, 53, 54, 56
    Nike+ 26, 433
    sponsorship 408, 409, 414, 415, 416, 418
Nokia 29, 149, 538
nomenclature 248
    see also language
non-scientific profiling 87–88
non-symbolic (non-verbal) communications 144–45
norms, group 133
North America 261, 262
Nortycams 299
NRS 178, 211, 291
nudge theory 109–10
nurturing brands 60
NUT 60

Oasis 118
Obama, Barack, (presidential campaign) 125, 126, 443
objectives (SOSTAC®) 228, 268, 269, 276–78, 280
    advertising 354, 367, 371, 372
    direct mail 467, 472, 473
    exhibitions 483, 493
    merchandising 500, 507, 509
    owned media 534, 553, 555, 557, 559
    packaging 524, 527
    promotions 437–39, *440*, 448, 453, 454
    publicity 398, 401, 402
    SMART 277, 354
    sponsorship 412–13, 419–20, 422–23

odours 504, 523
    see also aromas; scents; smells
O'Driscoll, Brian 123
Ofcom 142, 193, 302, 303–04
offensive strategies 257
Ogilvy, David 144, 203, 351
Ogilvy & Mather 109, 238, 353
Ogilvy PR 398–401, 554
old marketing mix 7, 8, *21*, 26, 271
omnibus surveys *175*, 177
On the Air (FlickrPix) 20
online
    newsrooms 383–84
    pitches 232
    research 180–81
open innovation 20
    see also crowdsourcing
operant conditioning 127, 128, 428
opinion
    formers 146–48, 151, *152*, 453
    forming panels 184–85
    leaders 146–48, 151, *152*, 153, 156
opportunities to see (OTS) 212
opting-in 297, 302, 463
opting-out 77
organizational
    culture 15, 90, 91
    structures 90
outbound marketing *see* interruption marketing
outdoor posters 203
outsourcing 78, 222
over-packaging 516–17
over-personalization 89–90
overload, information 168–69
overview reports 111
own brands 64
owned media 7, 201, 339, 347, 534–64
    see also social media
Oxo ads 308

P&G *see* Procter & Gamble (P&G)
packaging 7, 129, *134*, *176*, 226, *283*, 513–31
Paddy Power 351
PAGES 105
paid media 7, 201, 339, 347, 534
    see also advertising
Pareto 80/20 rule 149
partnerships 25, 280
    see also co-creation; collaboration; Transatlantic Trade
        Investment Partnership
path length reports 111
Pavlov's classical conditioning 102, 127–28
pay-by-results (PBR) 225–26
pay-per-click (PPC) 250, *288*, 331, 365, *367–71*, 373–74
payback periods 270
payments 252, 253
    see also pay-by-results (PBR); pay-per-click (PPC);
        payback periods; remuneration
PayPal 252, 346, 471–73
PCs 195, 253, *313*
Pedro, Dom 385, *386*
people brands 64
Pepsi 129, 246–47, 260, 312, 414, 418, 430–31, 436
percentage of sales 270, 491
perception 121, 122–27, 137

perceptual maps 272
performance
    feedback 65
    management 91
permission-based marketing 76–77, 155, 302
perpetuals (Generation C) 104, 113
Perrier 47, 518
Persil *58*, 97, 123, 308, 436
personal service 77, 502
personal-variable models 118, 120–21
personality 130
    see also brand personality
personalization 88–90, 199, 262, *311*, 540–42
personas 537–39
PEST analysis 272, 294
Peugeot 19
Philips 256
phones *see* mobile phones
photography 385–86, 389–90, *391*
Pierre Cardin 145
pilot schemes 415
Pimms 389
PINPOINT 180
Pinterest 112, 125
pitches 227–28, 228–32
Pizza Hut 410, 411
Plan UK 385, *387*
planning 237, 270, 441, 537, 538, 539
    departments 221–22
plans *see* action plans; communications plans; research plans;
        SOSTAC® plan
point of sale (POS) displays *134*, 158, 260, *283*, 498, 504, 507–08
politics 295–304
pool lists 227
positioning, brand 47, 53, 213, 279, 280, 528–29
positive reinforcement 129
post (mail) *194*, 297
post-digital advertising 336
Post-It notes 185
post-purchase dissonance 114, 115
post-show evaluation 489–92
posters 203
postmodern ads 350
power 157, 164–65
PPC (pay-per-click) 250, *288*, 331, 365, *367–71*, 373–74
PR *see* public relations (PR)
pre-digital advertising 336
pre-show promotions 486–87
predictive
    analytics 87, 88
    data 83
presentee-ism 134
press 201, *205*, 207, 362, 492
    conferences 384
previews 13, 118, 157, 453
price
    lining 544
    promotions 429
primacy 358
primary research data 173, 187
Prince's Trust, The 118, 468
prioritization, information 169
privacy 95–96, 112–13, 252, 299–301
problem
    definition 170, *171*, 173
    recognition 114

processes 74, 79–82, 280, 281, 548–49
Procter & Gamble (P&G) 19, 20, 153, 157, 290, 305, 381
    and agencies 220, 236, 239
    branding 58, 64
    market research 184, 186
product
    deletion 62
    extension 528
    failures 256–57
    function (brand names) 53
    interrogation 352–53
    placement 153
    portfolio 62
    PR 379
    quality 128–29, 146
    research 176
    reviews 17, 18
    switching 64
production 362
    costs 207
    departments 221, 223
profiling 84–88, 89, 103–04, 460–61
    see also SUPER PROFILES
profits 36, 72–73, 269–70, 310
programmatic
    advertising 210, 212, 345–46, 363
    buying 210–11
progressive profiling 85, 96
project
    management 74, 160, 322
    managers (leaders) 93, 95
    plans 285, 286
promotions see joint promotions; pre-show promotions;
        sales promotions
prototyping 94, 153, 538
Prudential 55, 482
psychic income 327–28, 435
psychological variables 122–35
public relations (PR) 7, 134, 377–405, 508
Publicis 229
publicity 283, 386–90
publishers 363
pulsing 213
purchase
    decision 115, 116
    model 115
purchasing cycles 87
push-based ads 343
pyramid selling see multi-level marketing

qualitative research 102, 130, 174, 175, 180, 181–85, 188,
        210, 211, 419
quality (product) 128–29, 146
quantitative
    research 174–80, 184, 186, 188
    sales measures 328
questionnaires 181, 184, 187
questions 165, 168, 173, 487
Quizmania 184

radio 10, 23, 202, 206, 207, 208, 213
    consumption 192, 193, 196, 204, 205
    interviews 385, 392
    and merchandising 508

sponsorship 413
    see also BBC Radio Northern Ireland; British Rate and
        Data (BRAD); Kiss FM Radio; Radio Advertising
        Clearance Centre (RACC); Radio Joint Audience
        Research (RAJAR)
Radio Advertising Clearance Centre (RACC) 302
Radio Joint Audience Research (RAJAR) 211, 216
rational
    brand benefits 46
    thinking 109
rational-emotional dichotomy 105–08
Ratners 393
reach 212
real-time
    bidding (buying) 345–46
    conversation prospecting 324–25
    personalization 89
rebating, commission 224–25
recency 358
recessions 305
Recife 553–54
recommendation scores 289
recruitment 326
Red Bull 40, 46, 48, 299, 455
Rediffusion 87
Reebok 410, 506
Reed network 14
reevoo.com (Reevoo) 7, 79, 146
regulations 295–302
    see also Code of Advertising Practice (CAP)
relationships 36, 70–71, 84, 97, 198, 322
    see also customer relationship management (CRM)
relevance 21, 53, 148, 158, 262, 273, 337, 537–39
    content marketing 24–26
    CRM 77, 82
    information 164–66
relief purchases 117
remarketing (retargeting) 199–200, 344–45
reminders 80–81
remuneration 224–26, 240
    see also payments
Renault 81, 259, 355
renderability 466, 467
repeat purchasing 103
reports (reporting) 111, 171, 304, 379
repositioning, brand 528–29
research
    logo development 55
    plans (strategy) 170–72
    see also marketing research; media research bureaux;
        secondary research
resonance 148
resources 466–67
response
    hierarchy models 118–19
    rates 208–09, 471
retail
    audits 175, 177
    networking see multi-level marketing
    strategy 502–04
retailer empathy 501–02
retention 137
return on investment 270, 289–90, 491–92, 550–51
reverse forensics (IP Look-Up prospecting) 324

reviews 17, 18, 59–60, 61, 114, 146, 353–54
reward purchases 117
RF 324
RFM analysis 85
right brain thinking 6
risk reduction 164
ROI 270, 289–90, 491–92, 550–51
roles, and behaviour 133–34, 153
roll out/delivery
    advertising 362, 373
    branding 56–57
    CRM 94
    sponsorship 415
Rothmans 72, 438
roughs 355, 358
routinized response behaviour (RRB) 103, 111, 115
Royal Borough of Greenwich 109
RTB 345–46
rumours 155
Russia 183, 251, 252, 253, 254, 429, 528
Ryanair 48

Saatchi & Saatchi 218, 229, 231
Safeway 84
Sale of Goods Act (1979) 295
sales 36, 64–65, 72, 270, 319–34
    analysis 176, 287
    promotions 7, 134, 174, 283, 428–42, 504, 508
    targets 327
    see also salesforce (salespeople)
salesforce (salespeople) 7, 167, 322–23, 325–33, 433–34
Samsung 78
Sarbanes-Oxley legislation 304
Sarnoff network 14
satisfaction scores 289
Saudi Arabia 256
Saudi Arabian Airlines 54–55
SCA see sustainable competitive advantage
scamps see roughs
scenario planning 537, 538, 539
scents 504, 523
    see also aromas; odours; smells
Schlitz 515
scientific planning 270
scope creep 93–94
search
    engine optimization 534–36
    terms 249–50, 251
Sears 132, 380
second
    moment of truth 115, 116
    screen 338
Second Life 16
secondary research 174, 187–88
security 90
Sedgwick 493–94
'see' option 544
seeding 391–92
segmentation 132, 170, 272–76
selection
    agency 172, 226–36
    media 204–09, 359–61
selective attention 125
self-regulation 301–02

self-service 83
selling see sales
semantic web 158–60, 313
semiotics 145
sensory branding 48
sentiment analysis 289
SEO 534–36
sequences (stages) 280–81
session maps 123, 124, 184
7P selling approach 326–27
Shanks & McEwan 55
shape, packaging 518–19
share of wallet 10
sharing 12, 15
    economy 11
Shazam 200
shelf stocking 503–04
Shell 55, 59, 276, 380, 381
shop windows 499
shopping malls 26
short-form ads 350
short-term sales 64–65
showboating 499
showrooming 115, 117, 499
simple web communications model 154
simplification 113, 544
simulated market tests 176
Singapore Airlines 48
single-step communications model 150–51
Sistine Chapel 24
situation analysis (SOSTAC®) 6, 21, 228, 271–76
    advertising 352–54, 367, 372
    direct mail 467, 471–72, 473
    exhibitions 483, 493
    merchandising 500, 509
    owned media 534, 553, 555, 557, 559
    packaging 524, 527
    PR 398–401, 402
    promotions 437, 445, 448, 453, 454
    sponsorship 412, 419, 422
size, packaging 519–20
sizzle 28, 29, 60, 537, 540, 541
skills development 74, 90, 94, 160, 322, 326–27
Skinner box 128
SlideShare 25, 447
SMART objectives 277, 354
smartphones see mobile phones
smells 46, 48, 128, 486, 504, 523
    see also aromas; odours; scents
SMO 547, 549–50
smoking campaign 559–61
social
    butlers 488
    capital 148
    change 305–09
    conversion scores 289
    CRM (customer relationship management) 7–8, 70
    forecasting 175
    media 7, 8, 11–15, 26, 28–29, 134, 251, 283, 311, 547–61
        and advertising 224, 338, 353
        analytics 165
        audits 179
        and branding 64
        budgets 271

social *con'd*
  media *con'd*
    and buying behaviour analysis 106
    and exhibitions 488–89
    monitoring 289
    optimization 547, 549–50
    and PR 379, 392
    and promotions 432, 435, 436–37, 448–52
    and sales 323–24
    see also dark social; Facebook; Flickr; LinkedIn;
      MySpace; Pinterest; Twitter; Web 2.0
  networks 14, 44
  responsibility 46, 63
  web prospecting 324–25
Solaris operating system 20
Sony 11, 180, 418
SOSTAC® Plan 6–7, 53, 268–69
  see also action; control; objectives; situation analysis;
    strategy; tactics
sounds 504
soup purchasing 103
  see also Campbell's Soup
source credibility 145–46
South Korea 248
specialist service agencies 218, *219*
speeches 25
speeding campaign 340, 372–73
split testing 465
sponsored TV advertising 351–52
sponsorship 7, *134*, *283*, 407–25
Stack da Police (E4) 391–92
staff 27, 56–57, 90, 168, 415, 443, 548
  see also account executives; employees; salesforce
stages 280–81
Starbuck's 45, 129, 149
statements, positioning 47
Stella Artois 416
Step2 435
Stew Leonard's 80
stickiness factor 157
stimulus-response models 103, 127–29
store design (layout) 498, 499, 502–03
storyboards 355, *358*
straight rebuying 111
straplines 255–56
strategy (SOSTAC®) 93, 278–82
  advertising 258–64, 354–61, 367, 371, 372
  brand 61–62
  briefs 228
  contact strategy process 80–82, 545–46
  contact workflow *478*
  content 548
  decentralized 259, 261–62
  defensive 257
  direct mail 467, 472, 473
  drip 127, 212, 213
  exhibitions 483–86, 493
  merchandising 500, 507, 509
  offensive 257
  owned media 534, 553, 555, 557, 559
  packaging 527
  PR 398–99, 401, 402
  promotions 438–41, 448, 453, 454
  retail 502–04
  sponsorship 413–14, 420, 423

style leaders 147
sub-brands 58
subcontracting 171, 218–19, 220
suggestion boxes 80
Sun Microsystem 20
Sunday Sport 432
SUPER PROFILES 180
supermarkets 10, 165
  see also Target; Tesco
surveys 96, *175*, 177, 187
sustainable competitive advantage (SCA) 9, 11, 17–18, 27, 28, 29,
  35, 537
SWOT analysis 168, 272, 294
symbolic communications 145
syndicated radio interviews 385
Systematics Association 411
systems
  CRM 72, 77–90, *86*
  development 94
  intelligence and information (MIIS) 167–68, 294
  thinking 160

tablets 197, 202, 311
tactics (SOSTAC®) 281, 282–84, 287
  advertising 354–61, 367, 371, 372
  direct mail 467–68, 472, 473–74
  exhibitions 486–87, 493
  merchandising 500, 504–06, 509
  owned media 534, 553, 555, 559–60
  PR 399–400, 401, 402
  promotions 441, 446, 448–49, 453, 455
  sponsorship 414, 420–21, 423
Tactics Matrix 282, *284*
Target 91, 135, 434
target audience 204–07, 412, 434, 445, 449, 485, 493,
  537–38
Target Group Index (TGI) 174, 177–79, 273
target markets (marketing) 272–76, 280, 362–63, 437, 445, 464
  see also floating targets
TD Bank 71
technology 43, 105, 138, 166, 193, 308–14, 460–61
  see also IT; mobile phones; PCs; tablets
Telecommunications Regulations (1999) 296
telemarketing 330
telephone
  networks 14
  surveys 187
telesales 462–63
television 247
  see also TV
television advertisements 254, 295, 303–04
  see also TV advertising
Telstra 415
Terry, John 396
Tesco 10, 64, 81–82, 110, 508, 545
test marketing 174, *176*, 185–87
testing 362, 471, 543
  see also A/B testing; concept testing; hall tests; multivariate testing;
    test marketing; three second test
Texas 48, 538
theory 143–62
3rd-party databased data *86*
third party e-newsletters 466
Thomson Holidays (Tours) *366*, 509
Threadless.com 19

3M 79
3Ms 269
    see also men and women; minutes; money
three second test 107, 485
Thresher 411
threshold models 121
Tia Maria 247
time
    lag reports 111
    pressures 112–13, 145, 182
    see also dwell time
Times, The 109
timing 173, 464, 469
Tipping Point, The (Gladwell) 146–47, 157
tissue groups 231–32
tone 250–51
top path reports 111
Topline 448–52
TOPPP SITE 278–79
touchpoints, brand 48, 52, 58
tracking 184, 186–87, 300, 362, 545
Trade Descriptions Act (1968) 295
Trade Marks Act (1994) 296
trade-off models 121
Trading Schemes Regulations (1997) 331
traffic departments 221, 223
training 56–57, 74, 326–27, 487
transaction data 86
transactional banners 343
Transatlantic Trade Investment Partnership (TTIP) 296–97
Transavia Airlines 275–76
Transcom 299
translation 249
travel apps 200
trends 50–51, 353
trialogues 13, 77, 93
trigger packs 516
triggers 115, 116
trust 34, 35, 36, 91, 92, 112–13, 146
'try' option 544
TSB mortgages 341
TV 10, 14, 150, 205, 313
    advertising 8, 12, 19, 204, 206, 207–08, 302, 303–04, 351–62
        and direct mail 463
        Persil 123
        speeding campaign 372–73
        see also television advertisements
    and apps 200–01
    consumption 193, 194, 195, 196, 197, 198–99, 201–02, 203
    debates 125
    rating points (TVRs) 212–13
    and sponsorship 408, 410
    see also Al Jazeera; broadcast sponsorship; media research
            bureaux; MTV; Quizmania; television; X Factor
tweets 240
Twitter 52, 56, 80, 106, 112, 125, 148, 166, 239
    see also New York Giants; Topline; tweets;
            Victoria & Albert Museum (V&A)
two screen audiences 338
two-step linear communications model 151, 152
Typhoo Tea 430

UGC (user-generated content) 18, 19–20, 44, 349, 508
UGD (user-generated discontent) 19
UK 193–94, 252

umbrella brands 58
unconferencing 483
unconscious
    messages 389–90
    reasoning 109, 110, 129–30, 182
Unilever 26, 109, 123, 153, 157, 201, 254, 269, 326
    and agencies 236, 239
    branding 58, 59, 62, 64
    and CRM 97
    Five Levers for Change 136, 139
unique device identifier (UDID) 365
United Airlines 148
United States 19, 150, 184, 194, 231–32, 254, 307, 312, 467
    communication 250, 252, 256
    legislation 304
    promotions 429, 433, 435
    and sponsorship 411
University of Tokyo 16
unreal similarities 247
up-selling 87
usability testing 20, 123, 544–45
user-generated
    ads 349
    content (UGC) 18, 19–20, 44, 349, 508
    discontent (UGD) 19

V&A (Victoria and Albert Museum) 432, 453–54
value
    chains 10–11, 28
    creation 74, 75, 321
    proposition 543
    restoration 74, 75
    see also added value; brand value
values, brand 48, 52, 53, 91
Victor Chandler 88
Victoria and Albert Museum (V&A) 432, 453–54
Vidal Sassoon 431
video 311, 336, 384–85
    analytics 165–66
Vine 125
viral marketing 390–92, 398–401
Virgin 20, 47, 48, 53, 58, 62, 149, 270, 346
Virgin Mobile 402–03
virtual
    events 483
    friends 61
    interactive POS 505–06
    press conferences 384
    promotions 435–36
    reality 16–17, 312, 314
vision, brand 48
visual language 58
VNR 384–85
Vodafone 20, 43, 465
Volkswagen 53, 355
Volvo 53, 255, 355, 415

Waitrose 349
weak
    brands (diluted brands) 41, 62
    theory of advertising 337–38
web
    analytics 285
    3.0 159, 311
        see also semantic web

web *con'd*
  2.0 44, 311
    see also social media
  see also mashable web; social web prospecting;
      websites
websites 4, 28, 84, 123–24, *134*, 207, *283*, 534–47, 562
  and branding 60–61, 63
  Campbell's Soup 508
  design 9, 137, 144–45, 192, 542
  eye tracking 184
  and mobile 112, 113
  and research 181
  Sistine Chapel 24
  see also landing pages; microsites; widgets
welcome programmes 81
whispering windows (John Lewis) *505*
White, Don 230
widgets 346

Wolters Kluwer UK 87
women *see* men and women
Woolworths group 55
word of mouth 7, 26, 154, 157, *283*
  see also earned media
word usage 126
WPP 106, 218, 222, 236, 238

X Factor 13, 19, 164

Yahoo 224, 251, 252, 289, 379, 383
Yandex 251
YouTube 19, 27, 125, 148, 195, 254, 553, *561*
  advertising 339, 349, 373

zero moment of truth (ZMOT) 115, *116*
02 97, 499
Zippo 200, 346